*Folens Dictionary and Thesaurus* is the fourth of the Folens dictionary series.

**Dictionary Features:**

- 8,000 headword entries
- Hundreds of useful examples to put words in context
- Entries in colour
- Definitions using carefully controlled examples
- Etymology of words
- Alphabet line to help children find the words
- Second letter colour change for quick scanning
- 'Dictionary fun' at the end of each letter section – puzzles, riddles and interesting information to entertain and educate.

**Thesaurus Features:**

- 2,500 headword entries
- Example sentences to put words into correct context
- Antonyms to build vocabulary
- Related words to help children find the right word
- All thesaurus words are included in the dictionary for cross-referencing.

# DICTIONARY

## Contents

**Flip the dictionary over to use the thesaurus.**

# The English language

The English language did not originate in England. It was brought to Britain by the Anglo-Saxons, who came from what we now call Germany in about AD 450. The ancient Britons or Celts, who lived in Britain before the Anglo-Saxons came, spoke a language related to Gaelic, Irish and Welsh, but very few words of it have survived. By about AD 700 the newcomers ruled most of the country and nearly everyone spoke their language, which we now call Old English or Anglo-Saxon. We still use many Old English words today, although it is hard to recognise some of them. For example, **heaven** was *heofonum*, **play** was *plega* and **head** was *heafod*. But some Old English words have hardly changed at all. **Bread**, **man** and **under** are the same, **drink** was *drinc*, **fish** was *fisc* and **sing** was *singan*. Over the years we have added words from many other languages, so that more than half the words we use today did not exist in Old English.

In the ninth and tenth centuries the Vikings came from Norway and Denmark. At first they attacked places around the coast, stole anything they could and sailed away, but later they settled in northern and eastern England and in parts of Scotland, Ireland and Wales. They spoke a language that we now call Old Norse, which was related to Old English and was quite like it. For example, the Old English word *scyrte* (ancestor of **shirt**) meant a kind of long tunic; the Old Norse word for this was *skyrta* (ancestor of **skirt**). Many common words, such as **same**, **take**, **sky** and **call**, come from Old Norse.

In 1066 the Normans, who lived in northern France, conquered England. After this the rulers of England all spoke a kind of French, although ordinary people still spoke English. Gradually the language changed so that French speakers and English speakers could understand each other, and many French words were adopted into English. Many of them were words to do with the law or with running the country, like **government**, **justice**, **lease** and **rule.** We call the language that was spoken at that time Middle English. It was much more like modern English than Old English, but is still quite difficult for us to understand today.

During all these centuries all church services were in Latin, the language spoken by the Romans, and educated people all over the world spoke Latin. Scholars would speak their own language at home, but when they wanted to talk or write about what they were studying they would use Latin so that scholars in other countries could understand them. In the 14th to the

16th centuries people throughout Europe became interested in the ancient civilisations of Rome and Greece, and over the years many Greek and Latin words found their way into English. A few Latin words were adopted into Old English and many more Latin and Greek words were added to Middle English and modern English. Most scientific and medical words, and many names of substances, animals and plants, come from Latin or Greek. As Latin had already adopted many Greek words, and as Latin is the ancestor of the French language, some Latin and Greek words came into English via French. Even today, if we want a new word, we sometimes make one from a Latin word. For example, **computer** comes from Latin *computare*, which means 'to calculate'.

From about the 16th century onwards the English language changed enormously, growing into the language we speak today. At this time people from Britain and other European countries were beginning to explore other parts of the world. The explorers brought back new plants and animals, and new words for them, usually taken from the language spoken by the people where they were found. **Chocolate**, **banana**, **bungalow** and **wallaby** all come from languages spoken outside Europe. In this way words from many other places, such as India, Africa and North and South America, came into English, sometimes through other European languages such as Portuguese, Spanish and Dutch.

At the same time, British explorers and settlers took the English language to other parts of the world, so that today people in North America, Australia and New Zealand have English as their native language. Many people in India, Pakistan and parts of Africa also speak English, although they may speak a different language at home. Children all over the world learn English at school. English has replaced Latin as the international language of educated people, so that people in other countries who want to study something often have to learn English first.

As you can see, the English language has been changing ever since it came to Britain, and it always will. We will always need new words for new things, and we will stop using words that we don't need any more. For example if your great-grandmother was British she would never have heard of **Diwali**, **kiwi fruit** or the **Internet**. But she would have used words like *warming-pan* and *hackney cab*, which her great-grandmother didn't know and which you probably don't know either, because we don't use those things today. You might find those words in an adult dictionary. Her great-grandmother would have used words like *distaff* and *shippon* – and you will need a very big dictionary to find out about those.

# Introduction to your dictionary

## How to find words in your dictionary

**Alphabetical order**

Your dictionary is in alphabetical order. To look up a word, start with the first letter. Words beginning with '**b**' will be near the beginning of the dictionary, words beginning with '**m**' will be in the middle and words beginning with '**w**' will be near the end.

Put these letters in alphabetical order.

s   m   b   z   r   a   g   j   n   e   o

Now find where they are in the dictionary.

Once you have found the first letter of the word you are looking up, you need to look at the next letter, then the third and fourth letters, because words are arranged in alphabetical order according to all the letters in the word. So *baby* comes before *bread* and *sun* comes before *swim*.

To help you find second letters quickly we have changed the colour of the first and second letters from red to black each time there is a change in the second letter. For example, the '**co**' in *coach*, the '**cr**' in *crab* and the '**cu**' in *cub* are all in black, because *coach* is the first word that begins with **co-**, *crab* is the first word that begins with **cr-** and *cub* is the first word that begins with **cu-**.

Put these words beginning with '**c**' in alphabetical order.

clever   circus   chimpanzee   cook   cloud   counter

Now find where they are in the dictionary.

Along the bottom of each double page you will see an **alphabet line**. You can use this to check whether the letter you are looking for comes before or after the letter you have on the page.

| | |
|---|---|
| **Guide words** | At the top of each page **guide words** appear. These show you the first and last words on the pages you have turned to. If the word you are looking for comes between these two words alphabetically then you will find it on these pages. If it comes before the first guide word then you will need to turn backward, if it comes after the last guide word then you need to turn forward. |
| **Headwords** | Use the guide words to find the correct page and then scan down the columns to find the word you need. It will be printed in red and to the left of the column. This is known as a **headword**. |

## What you can find out from your dictionary

**Meanings**

In your dictionary you will find the meanings of hundreds of words. The meaning of the word is called the **definition**.

**amphibian** *noun* **amphibians**
An **amphibian** is an animal that lives on land when it is an adult but hatches in water and returns there to breed.

Sometimes the dictionary will give you an example of how a word is used, especially a difficult word.

**account** *verb* **accounts, accounting, accounted**
If you **account for** something, you explain it: *Can you account for your absence yesterday?*

Some words have more than one meaning. Each meaning has its own number and definition.

**border** *noun* **borders**
1 A **border** is the line that divides two countries or regions.
2 A **border** is a line or decorated strip around the edge of something.

If two words have the same spelling but are pronounced differently or have different origins, each one is followed by a number above the line.

**bat**¹ *noun* **bats**
A **bat** is a piece of wood that you use for hitting the ball in a game such as cricket or baseball.

**bat¹** *verb* **bats, batting, batted**
When you **bat**, you have a turn at trying to hit the ball in a game.

**bat²** *noun* **bats**
A **bat** is a small animal that looks like a mouse with wings. Most **bats** fly at night.

Although these words look the same, they are different words. For example, **bat¹** comes from an Anglo-Saxon word, but **bat²** comes from a Scandinavian language that was brought to Britain by the Vikings.

**Related words**

Words that are related are shown after the main word and its definition. These words do not need a definition of their own because you can work out the meaning from the main word.

**helpless** *adjective*
If you are **helpless**, you are weak and cannot do anything without the help of other people. **helplessly** *adverb*. **helplessness** *noun*.

**Part of speech**

Your dictionary will tell you the part of speech of a word, such as whether it is a noun, adjective or verb.

**heartless** *adjective*
A person who is **heartless** shows no kind feelings or pity for other people.

**Plurals**

If the word has a plural form, the dictionary tells you what it is and how to spell it.

**city** *noun* **cities**
A **city** is a large town.

Some nouns have no plural form.

**milk** *noun*
**Milk** is a white liquid that female mammals feed their babies with.

Some nouns are always plural.

**clothes** *plural noun*
**Clothes** are things that you wear to cover your body or to keep warm.

A few nouns are nearly always used in the plural, so the plural form is shown first.

**dice** *plural noun* **die** *singular*
> **Dice** are small cubes used in games with a different number of spots on each face: *roll the dice*.

## Forms of a verb

The dictionary will also tell you about the different forms of a verb and how to spell them. The first form after *verb* is the one you use with he, she or it in the present tense: *he, she, it claps*. The form that ends with *-ing* is the present participle: *I am clapping, s/he is clapping, they are clapping.* The last form is the one used to make past tenses (past tense and past participle): *I clapped, I have clapped; s/he clapped, s/he has clapped; they clapped, they have clapped.*

**clap** *verb* **claps, clapping, clapped**
> To **clap** means to make a noise by hitting your hands together, usually to show you have enjoyed something.

If there are four forms of the verb, the past tense and past participle are different: *I go or s/he goes, I am going, I went, I have gone.*

**go** *verb* **goes, going, went, gone**
> **1** To **go** means to move from one place to another.

## Comparative and superlative

The dictionary will tell you the comparative and superlative forms of an adjective or adverb.

**rusty** *adjective* **rustier, rustiest**
> If metal is **rusty**, it has rust on it.

You use the form ending in *-er* to say that something is more rusty than something else, and the form ending in *-est* to say that something is the most rusty of three or more things. Occasionaly the word changes altogether.

**bad** *adjective* **worse, worst**

Some adjectives have no other forms. You use **more** or **most** with these.

**glamorous** *adjective*
> Something or someone that is **glamorous** seems very exciting and attractive.

The comparative of **glamorous is more glamorous**, and

the superlative is **most glamorous**.

At the back of the dictionary section, you can find some useful lists, such as prefixes and suffixes, collective nouns and countries of the world.

The dictionary will tell you where word comes from. The origin of a word is called its *etymology*. You will find the etymology after the definition or definitions, in square brackets, like this:

[**Cold** comes from Old English.]

If no etymology is given, this is because the word is the same as the one above, but has a different part of speech (for example, **cold** *noun* and **cold** *adjective*), because the word comes from another word nearby and you can easily see that the two are related (for example, because the definitions are very similar), or because the word is made up of two words that are both in the dictionary and you can easily see what those two words are (for example, **senior citizen**).

Some words come from Old English, which is a much older form of the language we speak today.

**bake** *verb* **bakes, baking, baked**
If you **bake** something, you cook it in the oven.
[**Bake** comes from Old English.]

Some words have been taken from other languages, although they have usually been changed in English.

**factory** *noun* **factories**
A **factory** is a building where large numbers or amounts of things are made by people who operate machines: *a car factory*.
[**Factory** comes from Latin *factorium* 'a place where things are made'. ]

Some words come from the name of a person or place.

**leotard** *noun* **leotards**
A **leotard** is a piece of clothing worn by dancers and gymnasts. It looks like a swimming costume with sleeves.
[The **leotard** is named after a French acrobat, Jules *Léotard*, who designed it.]

Some words are an imitation of a sound.

**cackle** *verb* **cackles, cackling, cackled**
> To **cackle** means to make the sound that a hen makes.
> [The word **cackle** is an imitation of the sound.]

Very often the dictionary will say that the word comes *via* a language.

**gastric** *adjective*
> **Gastric** means to do with the stomach and the digestion of food.
> [**Gastric** comes via Latin from Greek *gaster* 'stomach'.]

This means that the word came into English from Latin, but that the Latin word came from Greek.

The section on page 2 tells you more about the English language and how words have come into it from other languages. See how many languages you can find!

The dictionary cannot tell you everything about the origin of a word because there is not enough space. If you want to find out more about where words have come from, you can look them up in an adult dictionary.

**Dictionary words in the thesaurus**

After some words you will see (th). This tells you that this word also appears in the thesaurus section of this book.

**Appendices**

At the back of the dictonary section, you will find the appendices, which will help you with your spelling and your knowledge of words.

## Dictionary Fun

At the end of each letter section, you will find 'Dictionary Fun'. These are activities designed to help you get more from your dictionary – learn some interesting facts of etymology, see if you can solve a puzzle or a riddle and much more. If you're stuck, you can find the answers at the end of the dictionary section.

Remember there are more than 900,000 words in the English language and this dictionary contains a small proportion of them. If you cannot find a word in this dictionary, use an adult dictionary from your library.

# Aa

**abandon** *verb* **abandons, abandoning, abandoned** (th)
If you **abandon** a person or place, you leave and you do not go back.
[**Abandon** comes from French.]

**abattoir** *noun* **abattoirs**
An **abattoir** is a place where animals are killed so that they can be made into edible meat. [**Abattoir** comes from French.]

**abbey** *noun* **abbeys**
An **abbey** is a church with buildings where monks or nuns live, or used to live. [**Abbey** comes from Aramaic (a language once spoken in the Middle East) via Latin and Greek.]

**abbreviation** *noun* **abbreviations**
An **abbreviation** is a short way of writing or saying a word: *Dr is an abbreviation of Doctor.*
[**Abbreviation** comes from Latin *brevis* 'short' (the ancestor of **brief**).]

**abdicate** *verb* **abdicates, abdicating, abdicated**
To **abdicate** means to give up your job as king or queen of a country.
[**Abdicate** comes from Latin.]

**abdomen** *noun* **abdomens**
Your **abdomen** is the part of your body between your chest and your hips, where your stomach and intestines are.
[**Abdomen** comes from Latin.]

**abduct** *verb* **abducts, abducting, abducted**
If someone **abducts** a person, s/he kidnaps him/her.
[**Abduct** comes from Latin.]

**ability** *noun* **abilities**
If you have the **ability** to do something, you have the power or skill to do it.
[**Ability** comes from the same Latin word as **able**.]

**able** *adjective* (th)
1 If you are **able** to do something, you can do it.
2 An **able** person is skilful or clever and can do things well. **ably** *adverb*.
[**Able** comes from Latin.]

**abnormal** *adjective* (th)
Something that is **abnormal** is strange or different.
[**Abnormal** comes from Latin *ab* 'away from' and **normal**.]

**aboard** *adverb*
If you **go aboard**, you go onto a ship, aircraft, train or other vehicle.
[**Aboard** comes from **board**, which in an old sense meant 'the side of a ship'.]

**aboard** *preposition*
on a ship, aircraft, train, or other vehicle: *Is everybody safely aboard?*

**abolish** *verb* **abolishes, abolishing, abolished**
If you **abolish** something, you put a stop to it or get rid of it.
[**Abolish** comes from Latin.]

**abolition** *noun*
The **abolition** of something is the ending of it: *the abolition of slavery.*
[**Abolition** comes from the same Latin word as **abolish**.]

**Aboriginal** *adjective*
Something that is **Aboriginal** belongs to or comes from Aborigines: *an exhibition of Aboriginal paintings.*

**Aborigine** *noun* **Aborigines**
An **Aborigine** is one of the people who lived in Australia before Europeans went there, or someone who is descended from these people.
[**Aborigine** comes from Latin *ab origine* 'from the beginning'.]

**abort** *verb* **aborts, aborting, aborted**
If you **abort** something, you stop it.
[**Abort** comes from Latin.]

**abortion** *noun* **abortions**
If a woman has an **abortion**, a doctor takes a foetus out of her womb and it does not grow into a baby.
[**Abortion** comes from **abort**.]

**about** *preposition* (th)
1 on a particular subject: *We talked about the weather; a book about football.*
2 If you **do something about** a problem, you do something that you think may solve it: *I've got a terrible headache and I don't know what to do about it.*
[**About** comes from Old English.]

**about** *adverb* (th)
**1** in or around a place: *lying about by the pool; Is your brother about?*
**2** approximately; more or less: *add about a teaspoon of sugar; he's about 40.*
**3** If you are **about** or **just about to do** something, you are just going to do it: *I am just about to leave.*

**above** *adverb* (th)
in a higher place, or to a higher place: *The bird flew up to the branch above.*
[**Above** comes from Old English.]

**above** *preposition* (th)
**1** higher than: *flying above the rooftops; Put your arms above your head.*
**2** more than: *Did you get above five in the test?*

**abroad** *adverb*
**1** If you **go abroad**, you go to a foreign country.
**2** If you live **abroad**, you live in a foreign country.
[**Abroad** comes from **broad**.]

**abrupt** *adjective* (th)
**1** If you are **abrupt**, you are rude and unfriendly: *The waitress was very abrupt.*
**2** If something is **abrupt**, it is quick or sudden: *The bus came to an abrupt stop.*
**abruptly** *adverb*. **abruptness** *noun*.
[**Abrupt** comes from Latin.]

**absence** *noun* **absences**
The **absence** of someone or something is the fact that s/he or it is not there.
[**Absence** comes from the same Latin word as **absent**.]

**absent** *adjective* (th)
If you are not in a place where you are supposed to be, you are **absent** from it.
[**Absent** comes from Latin.]

**absolute** *adjective*
total or complete: *We had to work in absolute silence.* **absolutely** *adverb*.
[**Absolute** comes from Latin.]

**absorb** *verb* **absorbs, absorbing, absorbed**
**1** If something **absorbs** liquid, it soaks it up.
**2** If you are **absorbed**, you are giving something all your attention.
[**Absorb** comes from Latin *sorbere* 'to suck in'.]

**abundant** *adjective* (th)
If something is **abundant,** there is plenty of it. **abundantly** *adverb*. **abundance** *noun*.
[**Abundant** comes from Latin *abundare* 'to overflow'.]

**abuse** *noun* **abuses** (th)
**1 Abuse** is using something in a bad way: *drug abuse.*
**2 Abuse** is swearing or words shouted rudely at someone.
[**Abuse** comes from Latin *ab* 'away from' and **use**.]

**abuse** *verb* **abuses, abusing, abused** (th)
To **abuse** a person means to treat him or her badly by being violent or by saying rude and unkind things.

**accelerate** *verb* **accelerates, accelerating, accelerated**
To **accelerate** means to go faster.
[**Accelerate** comes from Latin *celer* 'swift, fast'.]

**accent** *noun* **accents**
Your **accent** is the way that you speak: *She has a Scottish accent.*
[**Accent** comes from Latin.]

**accept** *verb* **accepts, accepting, accepted** (th)
If you **accept** something, you agree to it or take it: *She accepted our invitation; Don't accept lifts from strangers.*
[**Accept** comes from Latin *capere* 'to take'.]

**accident** *noun* **accidents** (th)
**1** An **accident** is something that happens by chance, especially something that causes damage or injury.
**2** If something happens **by accident**, it happens by chance.
[**Accident** comes from Latin *accidere* 'to happen'.]

**accompany** *verb* **accompanies, accompanying, accompanied**
**1** If you **accompany** someone, you go somewhere with him/her.
**2** If you **accompany** someone who is singing or playing an instrument, you play another instrument or sing at the same time.
[**Accompany** comes from French *compagnon* 'companion'.]

**accomplice** *noun* **accomplices**
An **accomplice** is a person who has

helped somebody to do something, especially something that is wrong or against the law.
[**Accomplice** comes via French from the same Latin word as **complex**.]

**accomplish** *verb* **accomplishes, accomplishing, accomplished** (th)
If you **accomplish** something, you manage to complete it.
[**Accomplish** comes via French from the same Latin word as **complete**.]

**account** *noun* **accounts**
**1** If you give an **account** of an event, you say or write what happened.
**2** If you have an **account** with a bank, the bank keeps some of your money and you take it out when you need it.
[**Account** comes via French from the same Latin word as **count** and **computer**.]

**account** *verb* **accounts, accounting, accounted**
If you **account for** something, you explain it: *Can you account for your absence yesterday?*

**accurate** *adjective* (th)
If a thing is **accurate**, it is exact or correct.
**accurately** *adverb*. **accuracy** *noun*.
[**Accurate** comes from Latin.]

**accuse** *verb* **accuses, accusing, accused**
To **accuse** a person means to say that s/he has done something wrong: *accused him of eating all the biscuits.*
[**Accuse** comes from the same Latin word as **cause**.]

**ace** *noun* **aces**
**1** An **ace** is a playing card with only one symbol of the suit on it: *the ace of hearts.*
**2** In tennis, if you serve an **ace**, the other person fails to hit the ball.
[**Ace** comes from Latin.]

**ache** *noun* **aches**
An **ache** is a dull pain that goes on for a long time.
[**Ache** comes from Old English.]

**ache** *verb* **aches, aching, ached**
If part of your body **aches**, you can feel a dull pain there.

**achieve** *verb* **achieves, achieving, achieved** (th)
If you **achieve** something, you manage to do it.

[**Achieve** comes from the same French word as **chief**.]

**acid** *noun* **acids**
An **acid** is a substance that can burn, tastes sour and makes a chemical salt when it is mixed with an alkali.
[**Acid** comes from Latin *acere* 'to be sour'.]

**acorn** *noun* **acorns**
An **acorn** is the seed of an oak tree.
[**Acorn** comes from Old English.]

**acquaintance** *noun* **acquaintances**
An **acquaintance** is a person you know, but who is not a close friend.
[**Acquaintance** comes via French from the same Latin word as **recognise**.]

**acquire** *verb* **acquires, acquiring, acquired** (th)
To **acquire** something means to get it.
[**Acquire** comes from Latin.]

**acrobat** *noun* **acrobats**
An **acrobat** is a person who is good at gymnastics and balancing, for example on a trapeze or a tightrope.
[**Acrobat** comes from Greek *akrobatos* 'walking on tiptoe'.]

**across** *preposition*
**1** from one side to the other: *She ran across the road.*
**2** on the opposite side: *She lives across the road from me.*
[**Across** comes via French from the same Latin word as **cross**.]

**act** *noun* **acts** (th)
**1** An **act** is something that someone does: *a foolish act; an act of aggression.*
**2** An **act** is one of the main parts of a play.
**3** An **act** is a short performance: *a comedy act.*
**4** An **Act/act** is a set of laws made by parliament. [**Act** comes from Latin.]

**act** *verb* **acts, acting, acted** (th)
**1** To **act** means to do something: *We must act quickly; You're acting like a baby.*
**2** If you **act** in a play or a film, you perform in it.

**action** *noun* **actions**
**1** An **action** is something that someone does.
**2** If you **take action**, you do something for a particular purpose: *The government is taking action to stamp out smuggling.*

**a** b c d e f g h i j k l m

[**Action** comes from the same Latin word as **act**.]

**active** *adjective*
An **active** person or animal has lots of energy and is always moving about or doing things. **actively** *adverb*.
[**Active** comes from the same Latin word as **act**.]

**activity** *noun* **activities**
1 An **activity** is something that you do for fun or because it is interesting.
2 If there is a lot of **activity** somewhere, there are many things going on.
[**Activity** comes from the same Latin word as **act**.]

**actor** *noun* **actors**
An **actor** is a person who acts in a play or a film, or on television.

**actress** *noun* **actresses**
An **actress** is a woman who acts in a play or a film, or on television. Many **actresses** prefer to be called actors.

**actual** *adjective*
real or true: *Is that the actual house where he died?*
[**Actual** comes via French from the same Latin word as **act**.]

**acute** *adjective* (th)
1 An **acute** pain is a sharp or very bad pain.
2 An **acute** angle is an angle that measures less than 90°.
3 An **acute** sense is a very good sense: *an acute sense of hearing.* **acutely** *adverb*.
[**Acute** comes from Latin *acus* 'needle'.]

**AD** *abbreviation*
You write AD after a date to show that it comes after the birth of Christ.
[AD is short for Latin *Anno Domini*, 'in the year of the Lord'.]

**adapt** *verb* **adapts, adapting, adapted** (th)
1 If you **adapt** something, you change it so that it is suitable for a particular purpose or situation: *The car has been adapted to take his wheelchair.*
2 When you **adapt**, you change to fit in with a new situation.
[**Adapt** comes from Latin *aptus* 'suitable'.]

**add** *verb* **adds, adding, added** (th)
1 When you **add** numbers, you put them together and make another number.
2 If you **add** something, you put it with something else: *Add the flour gradually.*
3 If you **add** something to what you have said, you say more: *"But don't do it here!"* *she added.* [**Add** comes from Latin.]

**adder** *noun* **adders**
An **adder** is a small poisonous snake. You can find **adders** in Britain.
[**Adder** comes from Old English.]

**addict** *noun* **addicts**
An **addict** is a person who cannot give up something that is harmful, such as taking drugs. [**Addict** comes from **addicted**.]

**addicted** *adjective*
If you are **addicted** to something, you want to keep doing it or keep having it.
[**Addicted** comes from Latin.]

**addition** *noun* **additions**
1 **Addition** is when you add numbers together.
2 An **addition** is something that is added: *a new addition to the class.*
[**Addition** comes via French from the same Latin word as **add**.]

**additive** *noun* **additives**
An **additive** is something that is added to a food or a drink, for example to give it flavour or to make it stay fresh longer.
[**Additive** comes from the same Latin word as **add**.]

**address** *noun* **addresses**
An **address** tells you where someone's home or a business is by naming its house number, street, town and postcode.
[**Address** comes from Latin via French.]

**address** *verb* **addresses, addressing, addressed**
1 To **address** a letter, card or parcel means to write the address on it.
2 If you **address** people, you speak to them formally, or you make a speech to them.

**adequate** *adjective* (th)
If something is **adequate**, it is good enough, or there is just enough of it. **adequately** *adverb*.
[**Adequate** comes from Latin.]

**adhesive** *noun* **adhesives**
An **adhesive** is a substance that you can use to stick things together, such as glue.

[**Adhesive** comes from Latin.]

**adjacent** *adjective* (th)
A thing that is **adjacent** to another thing is next to it.
[**Adjacent** comes from Latin *adjacere* 'to lie next to'.]

**adjective** *noun* **adjectives**
An **adjective** is a word that describes a person or a thing. 'Small' and 'greedy' are adjectives. [**Adjective** comes from Latin.]

**adjust** *verb* **adjusts, adjusting, adjusted** (th)
1 To **adjust** something means to change it or move it slightly.
2 If you **adjust**, you get used to a new situation.
[**Adjust** comes from Latin via French.]

**admiral** *noun* **admirals**
An **admiral** is a person who is in charge of a ship or a fleet of ships in the navy.
[**Admiral** comes via French and Latin from Arabic *amir* 'commander'.]

**admire** *verb* **admires, admiring, admired** (th)
1 If you **admire** a person, you respect and look up to him/her.
2 If you **admire** something, you think it is good or beautiful.
[**Admire** comes from Latin *mirari* 'to wonder at'.]

**admission** *noun*
1 **Admission** means permission to go into a place: *No admission without a ticket.*
2 If you **make an admission**, you agree that something is true.
[**Admission** comes from the same Latin word as **admit**.]

**admit** *verb* **admits, admitting, admitted** (th)
1 When you **admit** someone, you let him/her in.
2 If you **admit** that you have done something bad or wrong, you say that you have done it.
[**Admit** comes from Latin *admittere* 'to allow'.]

**adolescence** *noun*
**Adolescence** is the time when you are not a child but not quite an adult.
[**Adolescence** comes from Latin *adolescere* 'to grow up'.]

**adolescent** *noun* **adolescents**
An **adolescent** is a young person who is not yet an adult.

**adopt** *verb* **adopts, adopting, adopted**
To **adopt** a child means to take him/her into your family and become the child's new father or mother.
[**Adopt** comes from Latin *optare* 'to choose'.]

**adoption** *noun* **adoptions**
**Adoption** is when a child is taken into a family and becomes legally part of it.

**adorable** *adjective*
Something that is **adorable** is sweet and easy to love. **adorably** *adverb*.
[**Adorable** comes from Latin via French.]

**adult** *noun* **adults**
An **adult** is a person or an animal who is fully grown.
[**Adult** comes from Latin *adultus* 'grown up', the past participle of *adolescere* 'to grow up' (the ancestor of **adolescent**).]

**adult** *adjective* (th)
fully grown: *A cat is an adult kitten.*

**adultery** *noun*
If a person **commits adultery**, s/he has a sexual relationship with someone other than the person s/he is married to.
[**Adultery** comes from Latin *adulterare* 'to make something corrupt'.]

**adulthood** *noun*
**Adulthood** is the time when someone is an adult.

**advance** *noun* **advances** (th)
1 An **advance** is a movement that takes something forward: *the army's advance on Rome; recent advances in medicine.*
2 **In advance** means before something happens: *You can buy the tickets in advance.*
[**Advance** comes via French from Latin *abante* 'in front'.]

**advance** *verb* **advances, advancing, advanced** (th)
To **advance** means to go forward.

**advantage** *noun* **advantages**
1 If you have an **advantage**, you have something that many people do not have that makes it easier for you to do something or get something: *Being tall is an advantage if you play basketball.*

**2** If you **take advantage** of something, you use it to help you: *I took advantage of Mum being away to have a big party.*
**3** If you **take advantage** of someone, you use that person's kindness or innocence unfairly: *Just because he's fond of her she takes advantage of him and gets him to do all her school work.*
[**Advantage** comes via French from the same Latin word as **advance**.]

**adventure** *noun* **adventures**
An **adventure** is something exciting or dangerous that happens to someone.
[**Adventure** comes from Latin via French.]

**adventurous** *adjective* (th)
Someone who is **adventurous** is not afraid to do new things or to take risks.
**adventurously** *adverb*. **adventurousness** *noun*.

**adverb** *noun* **adverbs**
An **adverb** is a word that is added to a verb or adjective to describe it. 'Quickly', 'stupidly' and 'very' are adverbs.
[**Adverb** comes from Latin.]

**advertise** *verb* **advertises, advertising, advertised** (th)
To **advertise** something means to tell people about it because you hope that they will buy it.
[**Advertise** comes from Latin via French.]

**advertisement** *noun* **advertisements**
An **advertisement** is something such as a poster or a short film that tells you about something, especially something that is for sale.

**advice** *noun* (th)
**Advice** is someone's opinion about what you should do: *Ask your teacher for advice about what courses to take.*
[**Advice** comes from Latin.]

**advise** *verb* **advises, advising, advised** (th)
To **advise** someone means to suggest what s/he should do.
[**Advise** comes from the same Latin word as **advice**.]

**aerial** *noun* **aerials**
An **aerial** is the wire or rod that picks up or sends radio and television signals.
[**Aerial** comes from Greek *aer* 'air'.]

**aeroplane** *noun* **aeroplanes**
An **aeroplane** is a vehicle with wings that can carry people or cargo through the air.
[**Aeroplane** comes from *aero-* 'air' and **plane**[2].]

**aerosol** *noun* **aerosols**
An **aerosol** is a can with liquid in. It has a button on the top and when you press it the liquid comes out in a spray.
[**Aerosol** comes from *aero-* 'air' and **solution**.]

**affair** *noun* **affairs** (th)
**1** An **affair** is an occasion or something that happens: *The party was a grand affair.*
**2** Something that is your **affair** is your business.
[**Affair** comes from French *à faire* 'to do'.]

**affect** *verb* **affects, affecting, affected** (th)
Something that **affects** you makes a difference to you in some way.
[**Affect** comes from Latin *afficere* 'to work on'.]

**affection** *noun* (th)
If you feel **affection**, you like or care about a person or a thing.
[**Affection** comes via French from the same Latin word as **affect**.]

**affectionate** *adjective* (th)
If you do something in an **affectionate** way, you do it lovingly: *gave her an affectionate pat.* **affectionately** *adverb*.

**afford** *verb* **affords, affording, afforded**
If you can **afford** something, you have enough money to be able to buy it.
[**Afford** comes from Old English.]

**afraid** *adjective* (th)
**1** Someone who is **afraid** is frightened: *afraid of spiders.*
**2** If you are sorry about something, you say that you are **afraid**: *I'm afraid I forgot my book.*
[**Afraid** comes from an old French word.]

**after** *adverb* (th)
at a later time: *left a few minutes after.*
[**After** comes from Old English.]

**after** *preposition* (th)
**1** later than: *Mathematics is after lunch.*
**2** behind in order: *B comes after A.*
**3** following behind or trying to catch someone or something: *The dog ran after the stick; The burglar knew they were after him.*
**4** If you are named **after** someone, you are

n o p q r s t u v w x y z

given his/her name: *named after her grandmother.*

**afternoon** *noun* **afternoons**
The **afternoon** is the part of the day between midday and the evening.

**afterwards** *adverb*
Something that happens at a later time happens **afterwards**.

**again** *adverb*
Something that happens more than once happens **again**.
[**Again** comes from Old English *on geaen* 'back to the beginning'.]

**age** *noun* **ages**
1 Your **age** is how old you are.
2 An **age** is a period of time in history: *the Victorian age.*
[**Age** comes from Latin via French.]

**age** *verb* **ages, ageing, aged** *Also* **aging**
When you **age**, you grow older or start to look older.

**agency** *noun* **agencies**
An **agency** is a business that arranges things for its customers: *an employment agency.*
[**Agency** comes from the same Latin word as **agent**.]

**agent** *noun* **agents**
1 An **agent** is a person who arranges things for other people: *a travel agent.*
2 An **agent** is a person who gets work for people such as actors and musicians.
3 An **agent** is a spy: *an enemy agent.*
[**Agent** comes from Latin *agens* 'doing things'.]

**aggression** *noun*
**Aggression** is fierce or threatening behaviour.
[**Aggression** comes from Latin *aggredi* 'to attack'.]

**aggressive** *adjective* (th)
An **aggressive** person or animal likes fighting and often acts in an angry or violent way. **aggressively** *adverb*.
[**Aggressive** comes from the same Latin word as **aggression**.]

**agile** *adjective* (th)
If you are **agile**, you move around easily and quickly. **agilely** *adverb*. **agility** *noun*.
[**Agile** comes from Latin.]

**ago** *adverb*
in the past, before now: *five weeks ago.*
[**Ago** comes from an old word *agone* meaning 'gone by'.]

**agony** *noun* **agonies** (th)
**Agony** is great pain: *rolling around on the floor in agony.*
[**Agony** comes from Greek *agon* 'struggle'.]

**agree** *verb* **agrees, agreeing, agreed** (th)
1 To **agree** or **agree with** someone means to share the same views or opinions.
2 If you **agree to** something, you say that you will do it.
[**Agree** comes from an old French word.]

**agreement** *noun* **agreements** (th)
1 An **agreement** is an arrangement that you make with someone else, usually saying that you will do something for each other.
2 If you and another person are **in agreement**, you agree.

**agricultural** *adjective*
**Agricultural** means to do with farms or farming: *a factory making agricultural machines.*

**agriculture** *noun*
**Agriculture** is farming, growing crops and keeping animals for food.
[**Agriculture** comes from Latin *ager* 'field' and *cultura* 'growing'.]

**ahead** *adverb*
1 in front: *well ahead of the other runners.*
2 in the future: *planning ahead.*
[**Ahead** comes from **head**.]

**aid** *noun* **aids**
1 **Aid** means help: *Some older children came to her aid.*
2 If you give people **aid**, you give them money or other things that they need.
3 An **aid** is something that helps you: *He used armbands as a swimming aid.*
4 If something is **in aid of** a charity, it is to help raise money for it.
5 If you do something **with the aid of** something, you use it to help you: *reading with the aid of a lamp.*
[**Aid** comes from French.]

**aid** *verb* **aids, aiding, aided**
To **aid** someone means to help him or her in some way.

**a b c d e f g h i j k l m**

**AIDS** *noun*

AIDS is a disease that destroys your body's ability to fight infection. It is caused by a virus.
[**AIDS** comes from the initials of *acquired immune deficiency syndrome*, the scientific name of the disease.]

**aim** *verb* **aims, aiming, aimed** (th)

1 To **aim** something means to point it.
2 To **aim to do** something means to try to do it.
3 To **aim** at something means to try to hit it. [**Aim** comes from an old French word.]

**aim** *noun* **aims** (th)

An **aim** is something that you want to do.

**air** *noun*

1 **Air** is the mixture of gases around the earth.
2 If you travel **by air**, you go in a plane.
[**Air** comes from Greek via French and Latin.]

**aircraft** *noun* **aircraft**

An **aircraft** is a machine that can fly in the air, such as a plane or a helicopter.

**airport** *noun* **airports**

An **airport** is a place where planes take off and land.

**airtight** *adjective*

If something is **airtight**, it is sealed so that air cannot get in or out: *an airtight box.*

**airy** *adjective* **airier, airiest**

1 An **airy** place is full of fresh air.
2 If you do something in an **airy** way, you do it cheerfully or light-heartedly, not seriously.

**aisle** *noun* **aisles**

An **aisle** is the gap left between rows of seats for people to walk along, for example in a church.
[**Aisle** comes from Latin via French.]

**alarm** *noun* **alarms** (th)

1 An **alarm** is a warning sound or signal.
2 If you feel **alarm**, you feel frightened.
[**Alarm** comes from Italian *all' arme!* 'to arms!']

**alarm** *verb* **alarms, alarming, alarmed**

If you **alarm** someone, you frighten him/her.

**albatross** *noun* **albatrosses**

An **albatross** is a large white seabird that has long wings.
[**Albatross** comes via Spanish and Portuguese from Arabic.]

**albino** *noun* **albinos**

An **albino** is a person or an animal with no natural colouring. **Albinos** have pink eyes and very pale skin and hair.
[**Albino** comes from Latin *albus* 'white, blank'.]

**album** *noun* **albums**

1 An **album** is a blank book for sticking things in, such as photographs or stamps.
2 An **album** is a record or CD with several songs on it.
[**Album** comes from the same Latin word as **albino**.]

**alcohol** *noun*

**Alcohol** is a liquid that is in some kinds of drinks, such as beer or wine. It can make you drunk.
[**Alcohol** comes from Arabic.]

**alcoholic** *adjective*

Something that is **alcoholic** has alcohol in it: *an alcoholic drink.*

**alcoholic** *noun* **alcoholics**

An **alcoholic** is a person who drinks too much alcohol and who cannot give up drinking it.

**alcove** *noun* **alcoves**

An **alcove** is a place in a room where part of the wall goes back a bit further than the main part.
[**Alcove** comes from Arabic.]

**alert** *adjective* (th)

Someone who is **alert** is paying attention and watching what is happening.
[**Alert** comes from Italian *all' erta!* 'to the watchtower!']

**algae** *plural noun*

**Algae** are small plants without roots or leaves. They grow in water or in damp places. [**Algae** comes from Latin.]

**algebra** *noun*

**Algebra** is a kind of mathematics. It uses letters or other symbols to stand for numbers. [**Algebra** comes from Arabic.]

**alibi** *noun* **alibis**

If you have an **alibi**, you have proof that you were somewhere else when a crime took place.

[**Alibi** comes from Latin *alibi* 'at another place'.]

**alien** *noun* **aliens**
1 An **alien** is a creature from another planet: *a story about aliens from Mars.*
2 An **alien** is a person who is not a citizen of the country where s/he is living.
[**Alien** comes from Latin *alienus* 'belonging to another'.]

**alike** *adjective* (th)
Two things that are **alike** are the same or similar.
[**Alike** comes from Old English.]

**alike** *adverb* (th)
If you treat people **alike**, you treat them in the same way.

**alive** *adjective* (th)
If something is **alive**, it is living or full of life. [**Alive** comes from Old English.]

**alkali** *noun* **alkalis**
An **alkali** is a substance that makes a salt when you mix it with an acid, turns litmus paper blue and can often burn.
[**Alkali** comes from Arabic.]

**all** *noun*
**All** means the whole of something: *I ate all the chocolate.*
[**All** comes from Old English.]

**Allah** *noun*
**Allah** is the Muslim name for God.
[**Allah** comes from Arabic.]

**allergic** *adjective*
If you are **allergic** to something, you can become ill or get a rash when you touch, eat or breathe that particular thing: *allergic to seafood.* [**Allergic** comes from **allergy**.]

**allergy** *noun* **allergies**
If you have an **allergy**, your body is sensitive to a particular thing, and you have to be careful to keep away from it: *Hay fever is an allergy.*
[**Allergy** comes via German from Greek *allos* 'other, different'.]

**alley** *noun* **alleys**
An **alley** is a narrow lane between buildings.
[**Alley** comes from French *aller* 'to go'.]

**alligator** *noun* **alligators**
An **alligator** is a reptile of the crocodile family. Alligators live in hot parts of North and South America and China.
[**Alligator** comes from Spanish *el lagarto* 'the lizard'.]

**alliteration** *noun*
**Alliteration** is when words that follow each other or are close to each other begin with the same sound: *several slithery snakes; one white whale.*
[**Alliteration** comes from Latin *littera* 'letter'.]

**allow** *verb* **allows, allowing, allowed** (th)
1 If you **allow** something, you say that it can happen: *Running isn't allowed in school; She allowed me to go.*
2 If you **allow** time for something, you give yourself time for it: *Allow plenty of time to get there.*
[**Allow** comes from Latin via French.]

**alloy** *noun* **alloys**
An **alloy** is a metal made by mixing other metals together: *Brass is an alloy made by mixing copper and zinc.*
[**Alloy** comes via an old French word from the same Latin word as **ally**.]

**ally** *noun* **allies**
Someone who is your **ally** is on your side.
[**Ally** comes from Latin *alligare* 'to bind together'.]

**almond** *noun* **almonds**
An **almond** is a brown oval-shaped nut.
[**Almond** comes via French and Latin from Greek.]

**almost** *adverb* (th)
nearly: *He is almost two; We almost missed the bus.*
[**Almost** comes from Old English.]

**alms** *plural noun*
If you give **alms** to poor people, you give money, food or other gifts.
[**Alms** comes from Old English.]

**alone** *adjective, adverb* (th)
1 on your own: *She sang the chorus alone.*
2 by itself: *The house stood alone on the hill.*
[**Alone** comes from *all one*.]

**along** *adverb*
forward or onward: *Keep moving along; The play is coming along well.*
[**Along** comes from Old English.]

**along** *preposition*
from one end to the other: *walked along the road.*

**aloof** *adjective* (th)
Someone who is **aloof** does not join in with other people, and is not very friendly.
[**Aloof** comes from an old phrase *a luff*, meaning 'away, at a distance'.]

**aloud** *adverb*
If you say something **aloud**, you say it so that people can hear you.
[**Aloud** comes from **loud**.]

**alphabet** *noun* **alphabets**
An **alphabet** is the letters of a language arranged in order.
[**Alphabet** comes from *alpha* and *beta*, the first two letters of the Greek alphabet.]

**alphabetical** *adjective*
**Alphabetical** means in the same order as the alphabet. **alphabetically** *adverb*.

**already** *adverb*
by now or before now: *He had read the book already; I've already eaten.*
[**Already** comes from *all ready*.]

**also** *adverb* (th)
as well: *Bring your book, and you also need a pencil.* [**Also** comes from Old English.]

**altar** *noun* **altars**
An **altar** is a special table in a church or a temple. It is used in religious ceremonies.
[**Altar** comes via Old English from the same Latin word as **altitude**.]

**alter** *verb* **alters, altering, altered** (th)
**1** If you **alter** something, you change it: *We can alter the dress to fit.*
**2** If something **alters**, it changes: *You haven't altered at all!*
[**Alter** comes from Latin *alter* 'other'.]

**alternate** *adjective*
If you do something on **alternate** days, you do it on every other day, for example on Monday, Wednesday and Friday.
[**Alternate** comes from Latin *alternatus* 'done by turns '.]

**alternative** *noun* **alternatives**
**1** An **alternative** is a choice: *You can have ice cream as an alternative to cake.*
**2** If you give someone **no alternative**, you give him/her no choice.
[**Alternative** comes via French from the same Latin word as **alternate**.]

**alternative** *adjective*
**Alternative** means different, or instead of something else: *take an alternative route.*

**although** *conjunction*
**1** even though: *I like her although she's bossy.*
**2** but: *You can have more cake, although I don't think you should.*
[**Although** comes from *all though*.]

**altitude** *noun* **altitudes**
Something's **altitude** is how high it is in the air, usually how high it is above the level of the sea.
[**Altitude** comes from Latin *altus* 'high'.]

**altogether** *adverb* (th)
**1** in total: *I had 100 coins altogether.*
**2** completely: *Eventually my watch stopped altogether.*
[**Altogether** comes from *all together*.]

**always** *adverb* (th)
If something **always** happens, it happens all the time: *He's always late.*
[**Always** comes from Old English.]

**a.m.** *abbreviation*
You write **a.m.** after a time to show that it is before noon: *9 a.m.*
[**a.m.** is short for Latin *ante meridiem* 'before noon'.]

**amateur** *noun* **amateurs**
An **amateur** is someone who does something as a hobby, not because s/he is paid to do it: *an amateur photographer.*
[**Amateur** comes from Latin *amator* 'lover'.]

**amaze** *verb* **amazes, amazing, amazed** (th)
To **amaze** means to surprise.
[**Amaze** comes from Old English.]

**amazement** *noun*
**Amazement** is great surprise: *To her amazement, she won the race!*

**amazing** *adjective* (th)
Something **amazing** is hard to believe or very surprising. **amazingly** *adverb*.

**amber** *noun*
**1 Amber** is a hard yellowish-brown substance that can be made into jewellery. It comes from the sap of trees.
**2 Amber** is an orange colour, one of the colours in a traffic light.

[**Amber** comes from Arabic.]

**amber** *adjective*
1 made of amber: *an amber necklace.*
2 of the colour amber.

**ambiguous** *adjective*
If something that is said or written is **ambiguous**, it could have more than one meaning and you cannot tell which one is right. *Dancing teacher* is **ambiguous** because it might mean a person who teaches dancing, or a teacher who is dancing. **ambiguously** *adverb*. **ambiguity** *noun*.
[**Ambiguous** comes from Latin *ambiguus* 'doubtful'.]

**ambition** *noun* **ambitions** (th)
1 An **ambition** is something that you want to do or succeed at in the future.
2 If you have **ambition**, you are ambitious. **ambitiously** *adverb*.
[**Ambition** comes from Latin.]

**ambitious** *adjective* (th)
If you are **ambitious**, you have a strong desire to be successful.

**ambulance** *noun* **ambulances**
An **ambulance** is a vehicle for carrying sick or injured people.
[**Ambulance** comes from French *hôpital ambulant* 'mobile hospital'.]

**ambush** *verb* **ambushes, ambushing, ambushed**
If you **ambush** someone, you hide and then come out and attack him/her.
[**Ambush** comes from Latin via French.]

**ambush** *noun* **ambushes**
An **ambush** is a surprise attack.

**amethyst** *noun* **amethysts**
An **amethyst** is a purple precious stone.
[**Amethyst** comes from Greek *amethystos* 'not drunk', because people believed that if you put an amethyst in your drink, you would not get drunk.]

**amiable** *adjective* (th)
Someone who is **amiable** is friendly and kind. **amiably** *adverb*.
[**Amiable** comes from Latin *amicus* 'friend'.]

**amoeba** *noun* **amoebas**
An **amoeba** is a very tiny creature that is made of only one cell.

[**Amoeba** comes from Greek.]

**among** *preposition*
1 surrounded by or in the middle of: *a tree growing among the daffodils.*
2 between more than two people: *shared the treasure among the crew.*
[**Among** comes from Old English *ongemang* 'in a crowd'.]

**amount** *noun* **amounts**
The **amount** of something is how much of it there is. [**Amount** comes from Latin.]

**amount** *verb* **amounts, amounting, amounted**
If a sum **amounts** to a total, it adds up to that number.

**amphibian** *noun* **amphibians**
An **amphibian** is an animal that lives on land when it is an adult but hatches in water and returns there to breed.
[**Amphibian** comes from Greek.]

**amphitheatre** *noun* **amphitheatres**
An **amphitheatre** is a large open-air theatre with rows of seats rising high up in a circle around a central area.
[**Amphitheatre** comes via Latin from Greek *amphi* 'on all sides' and *theatron* 'theatre'.]

**ample** *adjective* (th)
more than enough: *There was an ample supply of food.*
[**Ample** comes from Latin *amplus* 'large, abundant']

**amplifier** *noun* **amplifiers**
An **amplifier** is a piece of electrical equipment that makes things sound louder.

**amplify** *verb* **amplifies, amplifying, amplified**
To **amplify** something means to make it sound louder.
[**Amplify** comes via French from the same Latin word as **ample**.]

**amputate** *verb* **amputates, amputating, amputated**
To **amputate** someone's arm, leg or another part of his/her body means to cut it off. [**Amputate** comes from Latin.]

**amuse** *verb* **amuses, amusing, amused** (th)
To **amuse** someone means to make him/

her laugh or smile.
[**Amuse** comes from French.]

**anaesthetic** *noun* **anaesthetics**
An **anaesthetic** is a drug that a doctor
gives you during an operation so that you
do not feel any pain.
[**Anaesthetic** comes from Greek *an*
'without' and *aisthesis* 'feeling'.]

**anagram** *noun* **anagrams**
An **anagram** is a word that is made using
the letters of another word: *Lemon is an
anagram of melon.*
[**Anagram** comes from Greek.]

**analgesic** *noun* **analgesics**
An **analgesic** is something that takes
away pain.
[**Analgesic** is from Greek *an* 'without' and
*algesis* 'pain'.]

**analyse** *verb* **analyses, analysing,
analysed**
If you **analyse** something, you look at it
or think about it carefully in order to
understand it.
[**Analyse** comes from Greek via Latin.]

**anatomy** *noun*
**1 Anatomy** is the structure of a person's
or an animal's body.
**2 Anatomy** is the study of the way parts
of a person's or an animal's body fit
together.
[**Anatomy** comes via Latin from Greek
*anatomia* 'cutting up'.]

**ancestor** *noun* **ancestors** (th)
An **ancestor** is a relative who lived a long
time ago.
[**Ancestor** is from Latin *antecessor*
'someone who goes before'.]

**anchor** *noun* **anchors**
An **anchor** is a heavy metal hook with a
long chain that sailors throw into the sea
to stop a ship from moving.
[**Anchor** comes from Greek via Latin.]

**ancient** *adjective*
Something that is **ancient** is very old.
[**Ancient** comes from an old French
word.]

**and** *conjunction*
**1** You use **and** to join two words or parts
of a sentence: *a cup and saucer; I looked at
my watch and saw that it was late.*
**2** You use **and** before the last item in a list:

*She's got a dog, a cat and a hamster.*
[**And** comes from Old English.]

**angel** *noun* **angels**
In some religions, an **angel** is a messenger
that is sent by God.
[**Angel** comes via Latin from Greek
*angelos* 'messenger'.]

**anger** *noun* (th)
**Anger** is a strong feeling that makes
people want to fight or shout.
[**Anger** comes from Old Norse.]

**angle** *noun* **angles**
An **angle** is the space between two lines
at the point where they meet.
[**Angle** comes from Latin *angulus*
'corner'.]

**angrily** *adverb*
If you do something **angrily**, you do it in
a way that shows you are angry.

**angry** *adjective* **angrier, angriest** (th)
If you are **angry**, you are very annoyed
because of what someone has done or
said. *He was angry when I broke his mug.*
[**Angry** comes from **anger**.]

**anguish** *noun* (th)
If someone feels **anguish**, they feel a lot of
sadness, worry and suffering.
[**Anguish** comes from Latin via French.]

**animal** *noun* **animals**
An **animal** is a living creature that can
breathe and move.
[**Animal** comes from Latin *anima* 'life'.]

**animated** *adjective*
**1** If pictures are **animated**, they are
moving, as in a cartoon film.
**2** If a person is **animated**, s/he is lively.
[**Animated** comes from the same Latin
word as **animal**.]

**ankle** *noun* **ankles**
Your **ankle** is the joint connecting your
leg and your foot.
[**Ankle** comes from Old English.]

**anniversary** *noun* **anniversaries**
An **anniversary** is a date which people
celebrate or remember every year because
of something important that happened on
that day in the past.
[**Anniversary** comes from Latin *annus*
'year' and *vertere* 'to turn'.]

**announce** *verb* **announces, announcing, announced**
To **announce** something means to tell it officially to many people.
[**Announce** comes from Latin *nuntius* 'messenger'.]

**announcement** *noun* **announcements**
If you **make an announcement**, you announce something.

**announcer** *noun* **announcers**
An **announcer** is someone on television or the radio who tells you about the programmes.

**annoy** *verb* **annoys, annoying, annoyed** (th)
To **annoy** someone means to make him or her cross.
[**Annoy** comes from Latin.]

**annual** *noun* **annuals**
1 An **annual** is a plant that lives for only one year or for only one season.
2 An **annual** is a book that is published every year.
[**Annual** comes from Latin *annus* 'year'.]

**annual** *adjective*
An **annual** event happens once every year.

**anonymous** *adjective*
If something is **anonymous**, you do not know who wrote it, gave it or did it.
[**Anonymous** comes from Greek *an* 'without' and *onyma* 'name'.]

**another** *adjective, pronoun*
1 one more of something: *Can I have another biscuit?*
2 a different one: *If you don't like that one, choose another one.*
[**Another** comes from *an other*.]

**answer** *noun* **answers** (th)
1 An **answer** is a reply to a question.
2 An **answer** is a solution to a problem: *There is no easy answer to the problem of global warming.*
[**Answer** comes from Old English.]

**answer** *verb* **answers, answering, answered** (th)
To **answer** means to reply to something, or to respond to something: *answer my question; answer the telephone; "No," she answered.*

**ant** *noun* **ants**
An **ant** is a small insect with no wings that lives in big groups.
[**Ant** comes from Old English.]

**Antarctic** *noun*
The **Antarctic** is the area of the world at the South Pole.
[**Antarctic** comes via Latin from Greek *anti* 'against, opposite' and *arktikos* 'Arctic'.]

**anteater** *noun* **anteaters**
An **anteater** is a South American animal with a long tongue that feeds on ants.

**antelope** *noun* **antelopes**
An **antelope** is a wild animal that is similar to a deer. **Antelopes** live in Africa and in parts of Asia.
[**Antelope** comes from Greek.]

**antenna** *noun* **antennae** *or* **antennas**
1 An **antenna** is a feeler on an insect's head.
2 An **antenna** is a piece of wire that receives television or radio signals.
[**Antenna** comes from Latin.]

**anthem** *noun* **anthems**
An **anthem** is a proud song that people sing together, for example about their country: *a national anthem.*
[**Anthem** comes from Latin via Old English.]

**anthology** *noun* **anthologies**
An **anthology** is a collection of stories, plays or poems that are published together in one book.
[**Anthology** comes from Greek.]

**antibiotic** *noun* **antibiotics**
An **antibiotic** is a drug that kills germs.
[**Antibiotic** comes from Greek *anti* 'against' and *bios* 'life' (the ancestor of **biology**).]

**anticipate** *verb* **anticipates, anticipating, anticipated**
If you **anticipate** something, you expect it to happen and you get ready for it.
[**Anticipate** comes from Latin.]

**anticlimax** *noun* **anticlimaxes**
If something is an **anticlimax**, it is not as exciting as you expected it to be so you are disappointed.
[**Anticlimax** comes from *anti-* 'opposite' and **climax**.]

**a** b c d e f g h i j k l m

**anticlockwise** *adjective, adverb*
When something moves **anticlockwise**, it goes in the opposite direction to the hands of a clock.
[**Anticlockwise** comes from Greek *anti* 'opposite' and **clockwise**.]

**antidote** *noun* **antidotes**
An **antidote** is something that stops a poison from working.
[**Antidote** comes from *anti-* 'opposite' and *dotos* 'given'.]

**antiquated** *adjective*
Something such as a machine that is **antiquated** is very old-fashioned and usually does not work very well.
[**Antiquated** comes from the same Latin word as **antique**.]

**antique** *noun* **antiques**
An **antique** is an object that is very old and can be valuable.
[**Antique** comes from Latin *antiquus* 'ancient'.]

**antiseptic** *noun* **antiseptics**
An **antiseptic** is a substance that destroys germs or stops them spreading.
[**Antiseptic** comes from Greek *anti* 'opposite, against' and *septikos* 'infected, rotten'.]

**antisocial** *adjective*
1 Someone who is **antisocial** does not like being with other people.
2 Behaviour that is **antisocial** is unpleasant and upsetting for other people.
[**Antisocial** comes from *anti-* 'opposite, against' and **social**.]

**antler** *noun* **antlers**
An **antler** is a horn that looks like a branch growing from a stag's head.
[**Antler** comes from an old French word.]

**antonym** *noun* **antonyms**
The **antonym** of a word is its opposite. 'Start' is the antonym of 'finish'.
[**Antonym** comes from Greek *anti* 'opposite' and *onyma* 'name'.]

**anus** *noun* **anuses**
An **anus** is the ring of muscle through which solid waste material comes out of the body.
[**Anus** comes from Latin.]

**anxiety** *noun* **anxieties** (th)
1 **Anxiety** is a feeling of fear and worry.
2 An **anxiety** is something you worry about a lot.
[**Anxiety** comes from the same Latin word as **anxious**.]

**anxious** *adjective* (th)
Someone who is **anxious** is worried.
**anxiously** *adverb*.
[**Anxious** comes from Latin.]

**any** *pronoun*
1 one out of several: *Take any cake you like.*
2 some: *Is there any milk?; I haven't got any money.*
[**Any** comes from Old English.]

**anybody** *pronoun*
**Anybody** is any person: *It's nothing, anybody could do it; Is anybody there?*

**anyhow** *adverb*
in any case: *I don't want to go to the party anyhow.*

**anyone** *pronoun*
**Anyone** is another word for **anybody**.

**anything** *pronoun*
**Anything** is a thing of any kind: *If you want anything, just ask; My dog will eat anything.*

**anywhere** *adverb*
in or to any place: *You can sit anywhere in the cinema; Are you going anywhere now?*

**apart** *adverb*
If things or people are **apart**, they are separated or not near each other.
[**Apart** comes from French *à parte* 'to the side'.]

**apathy** *noun* (th)
**Apathy** is a feeling of not being interested in anything and not wanting to do anything.
[**Apathy** comes from Greek *a* 'without' and *pathos* 'feeling' (ancestor of **pathetic**).]

**ape** *noun* **apes**
An **ape** is an animal like a monkey with long arms and no tail, such as a chimpanzee or a gorilla.
[**Ape** comes from Old English.]

**apex** *noun* **apexes**
An **apex** is the highest point of something.
[**Apex** comes from Latin.]

**aphid** *noun* **aphids**
An **aphid** is a small insect that feeds on plants. [**Aphid** comes from Latin.]

**aplomb** *noun*
**Aplomb** is the ability someone has to be confident in a difficult situation. [**Aplomb** comes from French.]

**apologise** *verb* **apologises, apologising, apologised** *Also* **apologize**
To **apologise** means to say you are sorry. [**Apologise** comes from Greek.]

**apology** *noun* **apologies**
An **apology** is what you say or write to someone to show that you are sorry.
**apologetic** *adjective*. **apologetically** *adverb*.

**apostle** *noun* **apostles**
An **apostle** is one of the twelve men who were followers of Christ.
[**Apostle** comes from Greek.]

**apostrophe** *noun* **apostrophes**
An **apostrophe** is a small sign like a comma above the line that you use to show that a letter is missing in a word, or that something belongs to someone: *That's not fair!*; *Jack's bike.*
[**Apostrophe** comes from Greek.]

**appal** *verb* **appals, appalling, appalled** (th)
If something **appals** you, it shocks you because it is so horrible.
[**Appal** comes from old French *apalir* 'to go pale'.]

**appalling** *adjective* (th)
Something that is **appalling** is horrible or shocking.

**apparatus** *noun*
**Apparatus** is equipment used in science or in gymnastics.
[**Apparatus** comes from Latin *apparare* 'to get ready'.]

**appear** *verb* **appears, appearing, appeared** (th)
1 To **appear** means to come into sight: *A ship appeared in the distance.*
2 To **appear** means to be seen in a public place, such as on a stage or in a court of law.
3 To **appear** means to seem: *She doesn't appear to understand.*
[**Appear** comes from Latin.]

**appearance** *noun* **appearances**
1 An **appearance** is when someone or something comes into sight: *The appearance of the teacher put a stop to the fight.*
2 Your **appearance** is the way you look or seem.

**appendicitis** *noun*
**Appendicitis** is a painful infection of the appendix.

**appendix** *noun* **appendices** *or* **appendixes**
1 Your **appendix** is a small tube in the bottom of your intestines.
2 An **appendix** is a section that is added to the back of a book.
[**Appendix** comes from Latin *appendere* 'to hang or add on'.]

**appetising** *adjective*
Something that is **appetising** looks and smells nice to eat.
[**Appetising** comes from the same French word as **appetite**.]

**appetite** *noun* **appetites**
An **appetite** is a desire for something, especially food.
[**Appetite** comes from Latin via French.]

**applaud** *verb* **applauds, applauding, applauded**
To **applaud** means to clap or cheer to show that you have enjoyed something.
[**Applaud** comes from Latin *plaudere* 'to clap your hands'.]

**applause** *noun*
**Applause** is when a lot of people clap and cheer to show that they have enjoyed something.

**apple** *noun* **apples**
An **apple** is a hard round fruit.
[**Apple** comes from Old English.]

**appliance** *noun* **appliances**
An **appliance** is a piece of equipment that you use for a special purpose: *kitchen appliances.* [**Appliance** comes from **apply**.]

**apply** *verb* **applies, applying, applied**
1 To **apply** for something means to write to ask for it.
2 To **apply** means to be important to someone or to be about someone or something: *These rules apply to children under 16.* [**Apply** comes from Latin.]

**a** b c d e f g h i j k l m

**appoint** *verb* **appoints, appointing, appointed**
To **appoint** someone means to choose him/her for a job.
[**Appoint** comes from French.]

**appointment** *noun* **appointments** (th)
An **appointment** is an arrangement to see someone at a particular time.
[**Appointment** comes from the same French word as **appoint**.]

**appreciate** *verb* **appreciates, appreciating, appreciated**
To **appreciate** something means to be pleased and grateful about it: *I appreciate your help.*
[**Appreciate** comes from Latin *appreciare* 'to value or set a price for something'.]

**apprehensive** *adjective* (th)
If you are **apprehensive**, you are worried and a bit frightened about something that is going to happen: *Most children are apprehensive about starting a new school.*
**apprehensively** *adverb.*
[**Apprehensive** comes from Latin via French.]

**apprentice** *noun* **apprentices**
An **apprentice** is someone who is learning the skills needed to work in a particular trade.
[**Apprentice** comes from French *apprendre* 'to learn'.]

**approach** *verb* **approaches, approaching, approached** (th)
To **approach** someone or something means to move towards that person or thing.
[**Approach** comes from Latin via French.]

**appropriate** *adjective* (th)
Something that is **appropriate** is suitable or right for the time or place it is being used: *Jeans are not appropriate to wear at a wedding.* **appropriately** *adverb.*
[**Appropriate** comes from Latin.]

**approve** *verb* **approves, approving, approved** (th)
**1** To **approve** a plan or idea means to agree with it and allow it to happen.
**2** To **approve of** something means you accept it and think it is good.
[**Approve** comes from Latin via French.]

**approximate** *adjective* (th)
Something that is **approximate** is nearly correct but is not exact.
**approximately** *adverb.*
[**Approximate** comes from Latin *proximus* 'very near'.]

**apricot** *noun* **apricots**
An **apricot** is a soft orange-coloured fruit with a stone in it.
[**Apricot** comes from Arabic via Portuguese or Spanish.]

**apron** *noun* **aprons**
An **apron** is a piece of clothing you wear over the front of your clothes to keep them clean. [**Apron** comes from French.]

**aptitude** *noun*
**Aptitude** is someone's natural ability or talent for something.
[**Aptitude** comes from Latin via French.]

**aquarium** *noun* **aquariums** *or* **aquaria**
**1** An **aquarium** is a glass tank for keeping fish in.
**2** An **aquarium** is a building containing several tanks of fish.
[**Aquarium** comes from the same Latin word as **aquatic**.]

**aquatic** *adjective*
**1** An **aquatic** animal or plant lives in water.
**2** An **aquatic** sport is one that is played in or on water.
[**Aquatic** comes from Latin *aqua* 'water'.]

**aqueduct** *noun* **aqueducts**
An **aqueduct** is a bridge that carries water across a valley.
[**Aqueduct** comes from Latin *aqua* 'water' and *ducere* 'to lead'.]

**arable** *adjective*
**Arable** land is used for growing crops.
[**Arable** comes from Latin *arare* 'to plough'.]

**arc** *noun* **arcs**
An **arc** is part of the edge of a circle.
[**Arc** comes from Latin *arcus* 'a bow or curve'.]

**arcade** *noun* **arcades**
**1** An **arcade** is a covered area with shops on both sides.
**2** An **arcade** is a building where there are machines and video games that you pay to play on.

[**Arcade** comes via French or Italian from the same Latin word as **arc**.]

**arch** *noun* **arches**
An **arch** is the curved shape seen in bridges and buildings.
[**Arch** comes via French from the same Latin word as **arc**.]

**arch** *verb* **arches, arching, arched**
To **arch** means to make a curved shape: *The cat arched its back.*

**archaeology** *noun*
**Archaeology** is the study of old things that are found in the ground, in order to find out about life long ago.
[**Archaeology** comes from Greek *arkhaios* 'ancient'.]

**archaic** *adjective*
Something that is **archaic** is old-fashioned and not used very often.
[**Archaic** comes via French from the same Greek word as **archaeology**.]

**archbishop** *noun* **archbishops**
An **archbishop** is a head bishop in the Christian church.
[**Archbishop** comes from Greek *arkhos* 'chief' and **bishop**.]

**archipelago** *noun* **archipelagos** *or* **archipelagoes**
An **archipelago** is a group of islands in the sea.
[**Archipelago** comes from Greek via Italian.]

**architect** *noun* **architects**
An **architect** is a person who plans and designs buildings.
[**Architect** comes from Greek *arkhos* 'chief' and *tekton* 'builder'.]

**architecture** *noun*
**Architecture** is the planning and designing of buildings.

**Arctic** *noun*
The **Arctic** is the area of the world at the North Pole.
[**Arctic** comes from Greek.]

**arctic** *adjective*
**1** living in the Arctic: *the arctic fox.*
**2** like or to do with the Arctic: *arctic weather.*

**arduous** *adjective* (th)
Something that is **arduous** needs a lot of effort and is very difficult.
[**Arduous** comes from Latin *arduus* 'steep'.]

**area** *noun* **areas** (th)
**1** An **area** is a part of a town or a country: *the area near the school.*
**2** An **area** is a measurement of the amount of space in a flat shape: *calculate the area of the circle.*
**3** An **area** is a space that is used for something in particular: *a play area.*
[**Area** comes from Latin *area* 'empty piece of ground'.]

**arena** *noun* **arenas** (th)
An **arena** is a place where you can watch sports or entertainment.
[**Arena** comes from Latin.]

**argue** *verb* **argues, arguing, argued** (th)
To **argue** means to talk about something, often in an angry way, with someone because you do not agree with each other.
[**Argue** comes from Latin via French.]

**aria** *noun* **arias**
An **aria** is a song sung by someone in an opera. [**Aria** comes from Italian.]

**arid** *adjective*
Land that is **arid** is very dry and gets hardly any rain. [**Arid** comes from Latin.]

**aristocrat** *noun* **aristocrats**
An **aristocrat** is a person who comes from a family that has a very high social position. **aristocratic** *adjective*.
[**Aristocrat** comes from Greek *aristos* 'best'.]

**arithmetic** *noun*
**Arithmetic** is the study or use of numbers.
[**Arithmetic** comes via French from Greek *arithmos* 'number'.]

**arm¹** *noun* **arms**
**1** Your **arm** is the part of your body from your shoulder to your hand.
**2** An **arm** is anything that is shaped like an arm: *the arm of a coat; an arm of the sea.*
[**Arm¹** is from Old English.]

**arm²** *verb* **arms, arming, armed**
To **arm** someone means to give him/her a weapon for fighting.
[**Arm²** comes from the same Latin word as **armour**.]

**a** b c d e f g h i j k l m

**armed** *adjective*
1 A person who is **armed** is carrying a weapon, usually a gun.
2 If you are **armed** with something useful, such as information or a skill, you have it and are ready to use it: *I went into the exam armed with all the facts and figures.*

**armour** *noun*
**Armour** is the metal covering that soldiers wore in the past to protect themselves.
[**Armour** comes from Latin *arma* 'weapon'.]

**armpit** *noun* **armpits**
Your **armpit** is the place under your arm where it joins the shoulder.

**arms** *plural noun*
**Arms** are weapons.
[**Arms** comes from the same Latin word as **armour**.]

**army** *noun* **armies**
An **army** is a large group of people trained to fight on land.
[**Army** comes from the same Latin word as **armour**.]

**aroma** *noun* **aromas** (th)
An **aroma** is a very pleasant smell.
[**Aroma** comes from Greek *aroma* 'spice'.]

**aromatic** *adjective*
Something that is **aromatic** smells very pleasant.

**around** *adverb*
1 in many different parts of a place: *He drove around looking for somewhere to park.*
2 approximately, more or less: *Around 40 people came to the meeting.*
3 in or at a place: *I called out but there was no one around to hear me.*
[**Around** comes from **round**.]

**around** *preposition*
on all sides or in a circle: *Trees grew around the lake; We walked around the park.*

**arrange** *verb* **arranges, arranging, arranged** (th)
1 To **arrange** things means to put them in their proper place or order.
2 To **arrange** something means to make plans for it.
[**Arrange** comes via French from the same Latin word as **range**.]

**arrangement** *noun* **arrangements** (th)
1 An **arrangement** is an agreement with someone to do something: *We made an arrangement to meet here every Tuesday.*
2 The **arrangements** are the plans and preparations for something: *travel arrangements.*
3 An **arrangement** is a group of things placed in a particular order: *a flower arrangement.*

**arrest** *verb* **arrests, arresting, arrested** (th)
If the police **arrest** someone, they take him/her prisoner in order to ask questions about a crime.
[**Arrest** comes via French from Latin *restare* 'to stop' (ancestor of **rest**).]

**arrive** *verb* **arrives, arriving, arrived** (th)
To **arrive** means to come to the end of a journey.
[**Arrive** comes from Latin via French.]

**arrogant** *adjective* (th)
Someone who is **arrogant** thinks s/he is better and more important than other people.
**arrogantly** *adverb.* **arrogance** *noun.*
[**Arrogant** comes from Latin.]

**arrow** *noun* **arrows**
1 An **arrow** is a pointed stick that is shot from a bow.
2 An **arrow** is a sign in the shape of an arrow that points to something or points the way. [**Arrow** comes from Old Norse.]

**arson** *noun*
**Arson** is the crime of deliberately setting fire to a place.
[**Arson** comes from Latin *ardere* 'to burn'.]

**art** *noun* **arts**
1 **Art** is the making of drawings, paintings, sculptures or carvings, or the things that are made: *He studied art at college; an exhibition of Indian art.*
2 The **arts** are painting, sculpture, carving, literature, music and theatre.
3 An **art** is a skill: *the art of letter-writing.*
[**Art** comes from Latin via French.]

**artery** *noun* **arteries**
An **artery** is a tube that carries blood from the heart all around the body.
[**Artery** comes from Greek via Latin.]

**arthritis** *noun*
Arthritis is a disease that makes the joints in the body swollen, stiff and painful. [**Arthritis** comes from Greek *arthron* 'joint'.]

**article** *noun* **articles** (th)
1 An **article** is an object or a thing, especially one of a group: *an article of clothing; Several valuable articles are missing.*
2 An **article** is a piece of writing, other than a story, in a magazine or newspaper. [**Article** comes via French from Latin *articulus* 'small connecting part'.]

**articulate** *adjective*
Someone who is **articulate** is able to say what they mean very clearly. [**Articulate** comes from the same Latin word as **article**.]

**artificial** *adjective* (th)
Something that is **artificial** is made by people and does not exist in nature. [**Artificial** comes from Latin via French.]

**artillery** *noun* **artilleries**
1 Artillery is the big guns in an army.
2 The **artillery** is the part of the army that uses big guns. [**Artillery** comes from an old French word.]

**artist** *noun* **artists**
An **artist** is a person who produces art. [**Artist** comes via French and Italian from the same Latin word as art.]

**ascend** *verb* **ascends, ascending, ascended** (th)
To **ascend** means to go up or climb up. [**Ascend** comes from Latin *ascendere* 'to climb up'.]

**ash**[1] *noun* **ashes**
Ash is the grey powder that is left after something has been burned: *cigarette ash.* [**Ash**[1] comes from Old English *aesce.*]

**ash**[2] *noun* **ash** *Also* **ash tree**
An **ash** is a kind of tree with smooth grey bark and winged seeds. [**Ash**[2] comes from Old English *aesc.*]

**ashamed** *adjective* (th)
If someone is **ashamed**, s/he feels very sorry, guilty or embarrassed about something: *You should be ashamed of hitting your little brother; She was ashamed of her shabby clothes.*

[**Ashamed** comes from the same Old English word as **shame**.]

**ashore** *adverb*
If you go **ashore**, you go onto the land from a boat. [**Ashore** comes from **shore**.]

**ask** *verb* **asks, asking, asked** (th)
1 To **ask** means to speak in order to find out or request something: *He asked what time the train was due.*
2 To **ask** someone means to invite them: *They've asked us to lunch on Sunday.* [**Ask** comes from Old English.]

**asleep** *adjective*
Someone who is sleeping is **asleep**. [**Asleep** comes from **sleep**.]

**asparagus** *noun*
Asparagus is a plant with long green stems that you can cook and eat. [**Asparagus** comes from Greek via Latin.]

**aspect** *noun* **aspects**
An **aspect** of something is one part of its character or nature: *Crime is one of the most worrying aspects of life in the city.* [**Aspect** comes from Latin.]

**ass** *noun* **asses**
An **ass** is a donkey. [**Ass** comes from Old English.]

**assassinate** *verb* **assassinates, assassinating, assassinated**
To **assassinate** an important person, such as a politician, means to kill him/her. [**Assassinate** comes from Arabic via French or Latin.]

**assault** *verb* **assaults, assaulting, assaulted**
To **assault** someone is to attack and hurt him/her. [**Assault** comes from Latin.]

**assemble** *verb* **assembles, assembling, assembled** (th)
1 To **assemble** somewhere means to gather together in a group in that place.
2 To **assemble** something means to fit all the pieces of it together. [**Assemble** comes from an old French word.]

**assembly** *noun* **assemblies**
An **assembly** is a large gathering of people, especially of schoolchildren at the beginning of the day.

a b c d e f g h i j k l m

**assert** *verb* **asserts, asserting, asserted**
1 If you **assert** something, you state it firmly: *She asserted her belief in his innocence.*
2 If you **assert yourself**, you behave in a firm and determined way so that people take notice of you.
[**Assert** comes from Latin.]

**assess** *verb* **assesses, assessing, assessed** (th)
To **assess** something means to work out how good it is: *The teacher assessed our work at the end of term.*
[**Assess** comes from an old French word.]

**assist** *verb* **assists, assisting, assisted** (th)
To **assist** someone means to help him/her to do something.
[**Assist** comes from Latin via French.]

**assistance** *noun*
**Assistance** is help: *There's a lot to do and we need some assistance.*

**assistant** *noun* **assistants**
An **assistant** is a person whose job is to help someone: *a shop assistant.*

**associate** *verb* **associates, associating, associated** (th)
1 To **associate** with someone means to spend time with that person.
2 To **associate** two things means to make a connection between them in your mind: *I always associate summer with the beach.*
[**Associate** comes from Latin *associare* 'to unite'.]

**association** *noun* **associations**
An **association** is a club, group or organisation for people with the same interests or jobs.
[**Association** comes from the same Latin word as **associate**.]

**assortment** *noun* **assortments**
An **assortment** is a mixture of different kinds of something: *an assortment of fruits.*
[**Assortment** comes via French from the same Latin word as **sort**.]

**assume** *verb* **assumes, assuming, assumed**
If you **assume** something, you suppose it is true but you do not know for sure because you have not checked.
[**Assume** comes from Latin.]

**assure** *verb* **assures, assuring, assured** (th)
To **assure** someone means to promise him/her that something is true.
[**Assure** comes from the same Latin word as **secure** and **sure**.]

**asterisk** *noun* **asterisks**
An **asterisk** is the sign *. It is used in printing and writing, for example to mark something as important.
[**Asterisk** comes from Greek *asteriskos* 'little star'.]

**asteroid** *noun* **asteroids**
An **asteroid** is a very small planet.
[**Asteroid** comes from the same Greek word as **astral**.]

**asthma** *noun*
**Asthma** is a disease that makes it difficult to breathe. **asthmatic** *adjective*.
[**Asthma** comes from Greek via Latin.]

**astonish** *verb* **astonishes, astonishing, astonished**
If something **astonishes** you, it surprises you very much.
[**Astonish** comes from an old word *astone*, from the same old French word as **stun**.]

**astound** *verb* **astounds, astounding, astounded**
If something **astounds** you, it shocks and amazes you.
[**Astound** comes from *astoned*, past participle of *astone* (ancestor of **astonish**).]

**astral** *adjective*
**Astral** means to do with stars.
[**Astral** comes from Greek *astron* 'star'.]

**astride** *preposition*
If you sit **astride** something such as a bicycle or a horse, you put one leg on either side of it.
[**Astride** comes from **stride**.]

**astrologer** *noun* **astrologers**
An **astrologer** is a person who studies and understands astrology.

**astrology** *noun*
**Astrology** is the study of how the stars and planets move, in the belief that these movements can influence people's lives.
[**Astrology** comes from Greek *astrologia* 'study of the stars'.]

**astronaut** *noun* **astronauts**
An **astronaut** is a person who travels in space.
[**Astronaut** comes from Greek *astron* 'star' and *nautes* 'sailor' (ancestor of **nautical**).]

**astronomer** *noun* **astronomers**
An **astronomer** is a person who studies the stars and planets in a scientific way.

**astronomy** *noun*
**Astronomy** is the science of studying the stars and planets.
[**Astronomy** comes from Greek *astronomia* 'arrangement of the stars'.]

**astute** *adjective*
Someone who is **astute** understands things very quickly.
[**Astute** comes from Latin *astus* 'cleverness, cunning'.]

**asylum** *noun* **asylums**
1 If a country gives **asylum** to someone who is escaping from danger, it gives him/her protection.
2 An **asylum** is an old-fashioned word for a hospital for people who are mentally ill.
[**Asylum** comes via Latin from Greek *asylon* 'refuge'.]

**ate** *verb*
**Ate** is the past tense of **eat**.

**atheist** *noun* **atheists**
An **atheist** is a person who does not believe that there is a God.
[**Atheist** comes from Greek *a* 'without' and *theos* 'god'.]

**athlete** *noun* **athletes**
An **athlete** is a person who takes part in sports like running, jumping and throwing.
[**Athlete** comes via Latin from Greek *athlein* 'to compete for a prize'.]

**athletics** *noun*
**Athletics** is sport like running, jumping and throwing, especially in competitions.

**atlas** *noun* **atlases**
An **atlas** is a book of maps.
[**Atlas** comes from Atlas, a giant in Greek mythology who carried the earth on his shoulders.]

**atmosphere** *noun*
1 The **atmosphere** is the air around the earth that we breathe.

2 An **atmosphere** is the feeling a place has.
[**Atmosphere** comes from Greek *atmos* 'vapour' and **sphere**.]

**atom** *noun* **atoms**
An **atom** is the smallest part of a chemical or substance. Everything is made up of **atoms**.
[**Atom** comes from Greek *atomos* 'impossible to divide'.]

**atrocity** *noun* **atrocities**
An **atrocity** is a very cruel and wicked act.
**atrocious** *adjective*. **atrociously** *adverb*.
[**Atrocity** comes from Latin *atrox* 'cruel'.]

**attach** *verb* **attaches, attaching, attached**
If you **attach** one thing to another, you fasten or join the two things together.
[**Attach** comes from an old French word.]

**attack** *noun* **attacks** (th)
1 An **attack** is when someone suddenly tries to hurt someone.
2 An **attack** is when soldiers try to take over a place or defeat their enemy.
3 An **attack** is a sudden illness or pain: *an attack of flu*.
[**Attack** comes from French via Italian.]

**attack** *verb* **attacks, attacking, attacked** (th)
1 To **attack** means to start fighting in order to hurt someone.
2 If soldiers **attack** a place, they try to take it over, or defeat their enemy.

**attempt** *verb* **attempts, attempting, attempted** (th)
To **attempt** to do something means to try to do it.
[**Attempt** comes from Latin *temptare* 'to try' (ancestor of **tempt**).]

**attend** *verb* **attends, attending, attended**
1 To **attend** something means to go to or be at the place where it is happening: *Hundreds of people attended the conference.*
2 To **attend** means to pay attention.
3 If you **attend to** something, you deal with it.
[**Attend** comes from Latin via French.]

**attendant** *noun* **attendants**
An **attendant** is a person whose job is to look after a person or place.

a b c d e f g h i j k l m

[**Attendant** comes from French *attendant* 'attending'.]

**attention** *noun*
1 **Attention** is the careful thought you give to something.
2 If you pay **attention**, you listen carefully and think about what you hear.
[**Attention** comes from the same Latin word as **attend**.]

**attic** *noun* **attics**
An **attic** is a room in the roof of a house.
[**Attic** comes from Greek via French.]

**attitude** *noun* **attitudes** (th)
An **attitude** is a way of thinking about something.
[**Attitude** comes from Latin via Italian and French.]

**attract** *verb* **attracts, attracting, attracted**
1 If something **attracts** you, you are interested in it.
2 If someone **attracts** you, you like that person and you would like to know him/ her better.
3 To **attract** something means to pull it nearer: *Magnets attract metals.*
[**Attract** comes from Latin *attractum* 'pulled towards'.]

**attractive** *adjective*
Someone or something that is **attractive** is beautiful or interesting to look at.

**aubergine** *noun* **aubergines**
An **aubergine** is a shiny purple vegetable.
[**Aubergine** comes via French and Arabic from Sanskrit (a very old Indian language).]

**auburn** *adjective*
If your hair is **auburn**, it is a reddish-brown colour.
[**Auburn** comes from an old French word.]

**auction** *noun* **auctions**
An **auction** is a sale where each thing is sold to the person who offers the most money for it.
[**Auction** comes from a Latin word meaning 'to increase'.]

**audible** *adjective*
If something is **audible**, it is loud enough for you to hear it. **audibly** *adverb*.
[**Audible** comes from Latin *audire* 'to hear'.]

**audience** *noun* **audiences**
An **audience** is the group of people who have come to look at or hear something, such as a concert.
[**Audience** comes from the same Latin word as **audible**.]

**audio** *adjective*
**Audio** means to do with recording and listening to sound: *audio tape*.
[**Audio** comes from the same Latin word as **audible**.]

**audition** *noun* **auditions**
An **audition** is a short performance by an actor or singer to find out if s/he is good enough for a part in a play or show.
[**Audition** comes from the same Latin word as **audible**.]

**auditorium** *noun* **auditoriums** *or* **auditoria**
An **auditorium** is the part of a theatre or concert hall where people sit.
[**Auditorium** comes from the same Latin word as **audible**.]

**aunt** *noun* **aunts**
Your **aunt** is the sister of your mother or father, or the wife of your uncle.
[**Aunt** comes from Latin via French.]

**au pair** *noun* **au pairs**
An **au pair** is a young person from a foreign country who lives with a family so that s/he can learn their language, in return for doing housework and perhaps looking after children.
[**Au pair** is a French phrase meaning 'as an equal'.]

**aural** *adjective*
**Aural** means to do with listening and hearing. **aurally** *adverb*.
[**Aural** comes from Latin *auris* 'ear'.]

**austere** *adjective*
Something that is **austere** is very plain and simple with nothing unnecessary added.
[**Austere** comes via French and Latin from Greek *austeros* 'severe'.]

**authentic** *adjective* (th)
If something is **authentic**, you know it is real and not a copy.
[**Authentic** comes via French and Latin from Greek *authentikos* 'genuine'.]

**author** *noun* **authors**
An **author** is a person who writes stories or books.
[**Author** comes from Latin *auctor* 'someone who originates something'.]

**authoress** *noun* **authoresses**
An **authoress** is a woman who writes stories or books. Many **authoresses** prefer to be called authors.

**authority** *noun* **authorities**
1 **Authority** is the right or power that someone has to give orders: *The police have the authority to stop cars.*
2 An **authority** is a group of people who have the right or power to give orders.
[**Authority** comes from the same Latin word as **author**.]

**autobiography** *noun* **autobiographies**
An **autobiography** is a book written by someone about his/her life.
[**Autobiography** comes from *autos-* 'self' and **biography**.]

**automatic** *adjective*
1 A machine or piece of equipment that is **automatic** works by itself without a person controlling it.
2 If something is **automatic**, you do it without thinking. **automatically** *adverb*.
[**Automatic** comes from Greek *automatos* 'self-operating'.]

**autumn** *noun*
**Autumn** is the season after summer and before winter. **autumnal** *adjective*.
[**Autumn** comes from Latin.]

**available** *adjective*
1 If something is **available**, it is ready for you to get, use or buy.
2 If a person is **available**, s/he is free to see you or talk to you.
[**Available** comes from Latin.]

**avalanche** *noun* **avalanches**
An **avalanche** is a sudden mass of snow falling down a mountain.
[**Avalanche** comes from French.]

**avenue** *noun* **avenues**
An **avenue** is a road or driveway usually with trees along each side of it.
[**Avenue** comes from French *avenir* 'to come towards'.]

**average** *noun* **averages**
You find the **average** of two or more numbers by adding them together and dividing the total by the number of numbers you started with: *The average of 2, 9 and 10 is 7.*
[**Average** comes from Arabic.]

**average** *adjective*
Something that is **average** is usual or ordinary: *Her weight is about average for her height; The average family has two children.*

**aversion** *noun* **aversions** (th)
An **aversion** is an extremely strong dislike of something.
[**Aversion** comes from a Latin word meaning 'turning away'.]

**aviary** *noun* **aviaries**
An **aviary** is a place for keeping a lot of birds.
[**Aviary** comes from Latin *avis* 'bird'.]

**aviation** *noun*
**Aviation** is the science and practice of flying aircraft.
[**Aviation** comes from the same Latin word as **aviary**.]

**avid** *adjective*
**Avid** means keen and very interested: *She is an avid reader.* **avidly** *adverb*.
[**Avid** comes from Latin *avere* 'to long for'.]

**avoid** *verb* **avoids, avoiding, avoided** (th)
1 To **avoid** someone or something means to try hard to keep away from that person or thing: *The driver managed to avoid the bike.*
2 To **avoid** doing something or **avoid** something means to try not to do it or not to let it happen: *I avoid travelling by boat because I get seasick.*
[**Avoid** comes from an old French word meaning 'to get rid of'.]

**awake** *adjective*
Someone who is not asleep is **awake**.
[**Awake** comes from Old English.]

**award** *noun* **awards**
An **award** is a prize or money that someone receives, for example for doing something very well.
[**Award** comes from an old French word.]

**award** *verb* **awards, awarding, awarded**
To **award** something to someone means to give that person an award.

**aware** *adjective*
If you are **aware** of something, you know about it or know it is there.
[**Aware** comes from Old English.]

**away** *adverb*
**1** from a place: *The dog ran away; Go away!*
**2** at a certain distance: *He is ten miles away.*
**3** Someone who is not at home is **away**.
[**Away** comes from Old English.]

**awful** *adjective* (th)
Something that is very bad or dreadful is **awful**. **awfully** *adverb*.
[**Awful** comes from Old English.]

**awkward** *adjective* (th)
**1** Someone who is **awkward** is clumsy.
**2** Someone who is **awkward** is difficult to please.
**3** Something that is **awkward** is not easy to do, use or carry.
[**Awkward** comes from Old Norse *ofugr* 'round the wrong way'.]

**awning** *noun* **awnings**
An **awning** is a covering made of cloth in front of a shop, doorway or window.
[No one knows where **awning** comes from.]

**axe** *noun* **axes**
An **axe** is a tool used for chopping wood.
[**Axe** comes from Old English.]

**axis** *noun* **axes**
An **axis** is an imaginary line that goes through the centre of an object and that the object turns around on: *The earth spins on its axis.*
[**Axis** comes from Latin *axis* 'axle'.]

**axle** *noun* **axles**
An **axle** is a rod in the centre of a wheel that the wheel turns around on.
[**Axle** comes from Old Norse.]

**azure** *noun*
**Azure** is a sky-blue colour.
[**Azure** comes via old French from Persian (the language spoken in Iran).]

**azure** *adjective*
Something that is **azure** is sky-blue.

---

# Dictionary Fun

**Etymology**
1. Which '**a**' word comes from Greek *atomos* 'impossible to divide'?
2. Which word is derived from the French *à faire* 'to do'.

**What do these idioms mean?**
1. To keep someone at arm's length
2. To cost an arm and a leg
3. To welcome something/someone with open arms

**Complete the proverbs**
1. A _____ speak louder than words.
2. An a _____ a day keeps the doctor away.

**Riddle**
Which animal can jump higher than a house?

**Did you know?**
◆ In America they call an **aubergine** an *eggplant* and they call **autumn** *fall*.
◆ The word **amethyst** comes from the Greek word *amethystos*, which means 'not drunken' – the stone was supposed to stop people from becoming drunk!

**Work it out**
Which was the largest island before Australia was discovered?

---

# Bb

**babble** *verb* **babbles, babbling, babbled** (th)
1 To **babble** means to make the sound of water flowing over stones.
2 To **babble** means to talk like a baby or talk in an unclear way.
[The word **babble** is an imitation of the sound.]

**baboon** *noun* **baboons**
A **baboon** is a large monkey with a short tail. **Baboons** live in parts of Africa.
[**Baboon** comes from French.]

**baby** *noun* **babies**
A **baby** is a very young child.
[The word **baby** is probably an imitation of the sounds a baby makes before it can talk.]

**bachelor** *noun* **bachelors**
A **bachelor** is a man who is not married.
[**Bachelor** comes from an old French word.]

**back** *noun* **backs**
1 Your **back** is the part of your body between your shoulders and your bottom.
2 The **back** is the side opposite the front.
[**Back** comes from Old English.]

**back** *adjective*
opposite the front: *the back door.*

**back** *verb* **backs, backing, backed**
To **back** something somewhere means to move it backwards: *Back the lorry into the yard.*

**back** *adverb*
1 done in reply or in return: *I gave the money back.*
2 in or to an earlier place or time: *It started to rain and we turned back.*

**backbone** *noun* **backbones**
A **backbone** is the line of bones that runs down a person's or animal's back.

**backfire** *verb* **backfires, backfiring, backfired**
1 If a car **backfires**, there is a small explosion in the exhaust pipe.
2 If a plan **backfires**, it goes wrong.

**background** *noun* **backgrounds**
1 The **background** of a picture is the part behind the main person or thing in it.
2 The **background** of a story or event is everything that happened first or the facts that help explain it.
[**Background** comes from **back** *adjective* and **ground**[1].]

**backlog** *noun* **backlogs**
A **backlog** of work is a lot of work that is waiting to be done.
[A **backlog** was originally a log placed at the back of a fire that burned very slowly and lasted a long time.]

**backstroke** *noun*
**Backstroke** is a way of swimming lying on your back.

**backwards** *adverb*
1 If you do something **backwards**, you do it in a way that is opposite to the usual way: *Say the alphabet backwards.*
2 If you move **backwards**, you move towards a place behind you.

**bacon** *noun*
**Bacon** is meat, that has been salted or smoked, from the back or sides of a pig.
[**Bacon** comes from an old French word.]

**bacteria** *plural noun* **bacterium** *singular*
**Bacteria** are tiny living things that you cannot see. Some **bacteria** are harmful and cause illnesses.
[**Bacteria** comes from Greek.]

**bad** *adjective* **worse, worst** (th)
1 Something that is not good is **bad**.
2 Something that is serious or severe is **bad**: *a bad illness; a bad mistake.*
3 If food is **bad**, it is not fit to eat.
[**Bad** probably comes from Old English.]

**badge** *noun* **badges**
A **badge** is something you pin onto your clothes, often with a picture or your name on it.
[No one knows where **badge** comes from.]

**badger** *noun* **badgers**
A **badger** is an animal with a grey body and white stripes on its head. **Badgers** live underground and come out at night.
[No one knows where **badger** comes from.]

**badly** *adverb*
1 If you do something **badly**, you do not do it very well.

**2** If you want something **badly**, you want it very much.

**badminton** *noun*
Badminton is a game played on a court in which you use a racket to hit a small light object, called a shuttlecock, over a net. [**Badminton** is named after a big house in south-west England where the game was first played.]

**bag** *noun* **bags**
A **bag** is a container for carrying things in. [**Bag** comes from Old Norse.]

**baggage** *noun* (th)
**Baggage** is the bags and cases that people have with them when they travel. [**Baggage** comes from an old French word.]

**baggy** *adjective* **baggier, baggiest**
If a piece of clothing is **baggy**, it hangs loosely.

**bagpipes** *plural noun*
**Bagpipes** are a musical instrument that you play by blowing air into a bag, and then squeezing the air out through the pipes. **Bagpipes** are mainly played in Scotland and Ireland.

**bail** *noun*
**Bail** is money that someone pays to set a prisoner free until his/her trial in court. [**Bail** comes from an old French word.]

**bail** *verb* **bails, bailing, bailed**
**Bail** is another way to spell the verb **bale**.

**bait** *noun*
**Bait** is the food put on a hook to catch fish or in a trap to catch animals. [**Bait** comes from Old Norse.]

**bake** *verb* **bakes, baking, baked**
If you **bake** something, you cook it in the oven. [**Bake** comes from Old English.]

**baker** *noun* **bakers**
A **baker** is a person whose work is to make bread, cakes and pies.

**balance** *noun* **balances**
**1** Your **balance** is your ability to keep steady and not fall to one side or the other: *He lost his balance and fell off the bike.*
**2** **Balance** is when two things are of equal weight or equal importance: *You have to find a balance between spoiling a child and being too strict.*

**3** A **balance** is a pair of scales for weighing things.
**4** The **balance** is what you have left when you take one amount away from another. [**Balance** comes from Latin via French.]

**balance** *verb* **balances, balancing, balanced**
**1** To **balance** means to make or keep something steady or still.
**2** If two things **balance**, they are of equal weight or equal importance.

**balcony** *noun* **balconies**
**1** A **balcony** is a platform with railings round it, outside an upstairs window.
**2** A **balcony** is the area of upstairs seats in a theatre or cinema. [**Balcony** comes from Italian.]

**bald** *adjective*
Someone who has no hair is **bald**. [No one knows where **bald** comes from.]

**bale** *noun* **bales**
A **bale** is a large bundle of something: *a bale of hay.* [**Bale** probably comes from Dutch.]

**bale** *verb* **bales, baling, baled** *Also* **bail**
**1** To **bale** water or to **bale** water **out** means to empty water out of a boat with a container.
**2** To **bale out** of an aircraft means to jump out of it because you think it is going to crash. [**Bale** comes from French *baille* 'bucket'.]

**ball**[1] *noun* **balls**
A **ball** is a round object used in games such as football or tennis. [**Ball**[1] comes from Old Norse.]

**ball**[2] *noun* **balls**
A **ball** is a large formal party with dancing. [**Ball**[2] comes via French from Latin *ballare* 'to dance'.]

**ballad** *noun* **ballads**
A **ballad** is a poem or song that tells a story. [**Ballad** comes from the same Latin word as **ball**[2].]

**ballast** *noun*
**Ballast** is heavy material that is put in a ship to keep it steady. [**Ballast** probably comes from a Scandinavian language.]

**ballerina** *noun* **ballerinas**
A **ballerina** is a female ballet dancer.
[**Ballerina** comes via Italian from the
same Latin word as **ball**².]

**ballet** *noun* **ballets**
1 **Ballet** is a style of dancing with special,
very difficult, movements.
2 A **ballet** is a performance of a story that
is acted out by dancing to music.
[**Ballet** comes via French and Italian from
the same Latin word as **ball**².]

**balloon** *noun* **balloons**
1 A **balloon** is a small, rubber bag that can
be filled with air.
2 A **balloon** is a huge bag filled with hot
air or gas that floats in the sky and
sometimes carries passengers in a basket
underneath.
[**Balloon** comes from French *ballon* or
Italian *ballone*, both meaning 'large ball'.]

**ballot** *noun* **ballots**
A **ballot** is when people vote. Each person
writes his/her vote on a piece of paper
and puts it in a box without showing
anyone else.
[**Ballot** comes from Italian *ballotta* 'small
ball', because people sometimes vote by
putting a white ball into a box if they
agree with something, and a black ball if
they are against it.]

**ballpoint** *noun* **ballpoints**
A **ballpoint** is a pen that has a small ball
at the end that makes the ink come out
when you write.

**balm** *noun*
**Balm** is a soothing cream that helps get
rid of pain.
[**Balm** comes from Greek via French and
Latin.]

**balmy** *adjective*
If the weather is **balmy**, it is warm and
calm. [**Balmy** comes from **balm**.]

**bamboo** *noun*
A **bamboo** is a tall plant with hollow
stems or canes.
[**Bamboo** comes via Dutch from Malay (a
language spoken in Malaysia).]

**ban** *verb* **bans, banning, banned** (th)
If you **ban** something, you say that it is
not allowed.
[**Ban** comes from Old English.]

**banana** *noun* **bananas**
A **banana** is a long, curved fruit with a
thick yellow skin.
[**Banana** comes via Spanish and
Portuguese from a West African
language.]

**band**¹ *noun* **bands** (th)
A **band** is a strip of material shaped in a
loop. [**Band**¹ comes from Old Norse.]

**band**² *noun* **bands** (th)
A **band** is a group of people who play
musical instruments together.
[**Band**² comes from an old French word.]

**bandage** *noun* **bandages**
A **bandage** is a strip of material for
wrapping round a wound.
[**Bandage** comes from French.]

**bandit** *noun* **bandits** (th)
A **bandit** is a robber. **Bandits** usually
work in gangs.
[**Bandit** comes from Latin.]

**bang** *verb* **bangs, banging, banged**
If you **bang** something, you hit it or hit it
on something else: *bang the drum; banged
her knee on the table.*
[The word **bang** is an imitation of the
sound.]

**bang** *noun* **bangs**
A **bang** is a sudden loud noise: *The
window shut with a bang.*

**bangle** *noun* **bangles**
A **bangle** is a kind of bracelet made in the
shape of a ring.
[**Bangle** comes from Hindi (a language
spoken in India).]

**banish** *verb* **banishes, banishing,
banished** (th)
To **banish** someone means to send
him/her away from a place: *The king
banished the giant from the kingdom.*
[**Banish** comes from an old French word.]

**banister** *noun* **banisters** Also **bannister**
A **banister** is a long rail that is part of a
staircase. You hold onto it when you go
up or down.
[**Banister** comes from Greek via French,
Italian and Latin.]

**banjo** *noun* **banjos**
A **banjo** is a musical instrument like a
guitar. It has a small round body and a

a **b** c d e f g h i j k l m

long neck.
[The word **banjo** was invented by Black people in America.]

**bank¹** *noun* **banks**
A **bank** is a place that looks after people's money.
[**Bank¹** comes from Latin via French and Italian.]

**bank²** *noun* **banks**
A **bank** is a sloping piece of ground, often on the edge of a pond or river.
[**Bank²** comes from Old Norse.]

**bankrupt** *adjective*
If you are **bankrupt**, you have no money and you cannot pay people the money that you owe them.
[**Bankrupt** comes from *banca* Italian ancestor of **bank¹** and Latin *ruptus* 'broken'.]

**banner** *noun* **banners**
A **banner** is a big piece of material with writing on it: *The marchers carried banners saying 'Save Our Jobs'.*
[**Banner** comes from an old French word.]

**banquet** *noun* **banquets**
A **banquet** is a feast or a special meal with many courses.
[**Banquet** comes from French.]

**baptise** *verb* **baptises, baptising, baptised** *Also* **baptize**
If you are **baptised**, water is sprinkled on you, or you go into a pool of water, as a sign that you are a Christian.
[**Baptise** comes via French and Latin from Greek *baptizein* 'to dip'.]

**baptism** *noun* **baptisms**
A **baptism** is when a person is baptised.

**bar** *noun* **bars**
1 A **bar** is a long piece of hard material such as metal or chocolate.
2 A **bar** is a place where people can buy drinks.
3 In music, the notes are divided into equal groups, called **bars**.
[**Bar** comes from an old French word.]

**barbaric** *adjective* (th)
Something that is **barbaric** is very cruel.
[**Barbaric** comes from Greek via French or Latin.]

**barbecue** *noun* **barbecues**
1 A **barbecue** is a grill that you can cook food on outdoors.
2 If you have a **barbecue**, you invite people to come and eat food cooked outside.
[**Barbecue** comes via Spanish from Arawak (a South American Indian language).]

**barbed wire** *noun*
**Barbed wire** is wire that has very sharp knots of wire along it. Fences are made from it.
[**Barbed** comes from *barb* 'a spike', which comes from Latin *barba* 'a pointed beard'.]

**barber** *noun* **barbers**
A **barber** is a men's hairdresser.
[**Barber** comes from Latin *barba* 'a pointed beard'.]

**bar code** *noun* **bar codes**
A **bar code** is a rectangle made up of thick and thin black lines. It contains information that a computer can read.

**bard** *noun* **bards**
**Bard** is an old word for a poet.
[**Bard** comes from a Celtic word.]

**bare** *adjective* **barer, barest** (th)
1 If you are **bare**, you have no clothes on.
2 If a room or a cupboard is **bare**, it is empty, or nearly empty.
[**Bare** comes from Old English.]

**bare** *verb* **bares, baring, bared** (th)
If you **bare** something, you show something that is usually hidden: *The dog bared its teeth.*

**barely** *adverb* (th)
**Barely** means only just: *She could barely reach.* [**Barely** comes from **bare**.]

**bargain** *noun* **bargains** (th)
1 A **bargain** is an object that is much cheaper than it usually costs.
2 If you make a **bargain**, you make a promise or an agreement.
[**Bargain** comes from an old French word.]

**barge** *noun* **barges**
A **barge** is a long boat used on a canal or river for carrying goods.
[**Barge** comes from Latin *barca* 'boat'.]

**bark¹** *noun* **barks**
A **bark** is the sound a dog makes.
[**Bark¹** comes from Old English *beorc*, imitating the sound of a dog's bark.]

**bark¹** *verb* **barks, barking, barked**
To **bark** means to make the sound that a dog makes.

**bark²** *noun*
**Bark** is the outer covering on a tree trunk.
[**Bark²** comes from Old Norse.]

**barley** *noun*
**Barley** is a kind of cereal plant.
[**Barley** comes from Old English.]

**barn** *noun* **barns**
A **barn** is a large building on a farm for storing things and for keeping animals in.
[**Barn** comes from Old English.]

**barrel** *noun* **barrels**
1 A **barrel** is a large container with curved sides and flat ends.
2 A **barrel** is the narrow tube at the front of a gun.
[**Barrel** comes from Latin.]

**barren** *adjective*
**Barren** land is land that nothing can grow on.
[**Barren** comes from an old French word.]

**barrier** *noun* **barriers** (th)
A **barrier** is something like a fence or a wall that stops something getting through.
[**Barrier** comes from an old French word.]

**base** *noun* **bases** (th)
1 A **base** is the lowest part of something or the part on which something stands: *the base of the tree; a statue on a tall base.*
2 A **base** is a place that you run to in the games of rounders and baseball.
3 A **base** is a place where soldiers or sailors live, or where the main building of a company is.
[**Base** comes from Greek via French and Latin.]

**base** *verb* **bases, basing, based**
If you **base** a story on something, you start with that and then add ideas of your own: *a film based on the book.*

**baseball** *noun*
**Baseball** is a game that you play with a bat and ball on a field marked out in a diamond shape.
[**Baseball** comes from **base**, from the places on the field, called bases, that the batter has to reach before the ball can be thrown there.]

**bashful** *adjective* (th)
If you are **bashful**, you are shy.
**bashfully** *adverb.* **bashfulness** *noun.*
[**Bashful** comes from an old French word.]

**basic** *adjective* (th)
If something is **basic**, it is simple and important. [**Basic** comes from **base**.]

**basil** *noun*
**Basil** is a herb. People often eat it with pasta or tomatoes.
[**Basil** comes from Greek via French and Latin.]

**basin** *noun* **basins**
1 A **basin** is a bowl: *a pudding basin.*
2 A **basin** is a small sink for washing your hands in.
[**Basin** comes from Latin via French.]

**bask** *verb* **basks, basking, basked**
To **bask** means to sit or lie in the sun and enjoy being warm.
[No one knows where **bask** comes from.]

**basket** *noun* **baskets**
A **basket** is a container, usually with handles and often made of cane or wire.
[**Basket** comes from an old French word.]

**basketball** *noun*
**Basketball** is a game that you play on a court, using a big ball. You score by getting the ball into a high round net.

**bassoon** *noun* **bassoons**
A **bassoon** is a musical instrument of the woodwind family.
[**Bassoon** comes from Italian *basso* 'low', because of the low sound it makes.]

**bat¹** *noun* **bats**
A **bat** is a piece of wood that you use for hitting the ball in a game such as cricket or baseball.
[**Bat¹** comes from Old English.]

**bat¹** *verb* **bats, batting, batted**
When you **bat**, you have a turn at trying to hit the ball in a game.

**bat²** *noun* **bats**
A **bat** is a small animal that looks like a

a **b** c d e f g h i j k l m

mouse with wings. Most **bats** fly at night.
[**Bat²** comes from a Scandinavian language.]

**bath** *noun* **baths**
1 A **bath** is a large container that is filled with water, which you sit in to wash yourself.
2 If you **have a bath** or **take a bath**, you sit in the bath and wash yourself.
[**Bath** comes from Old English.]

**bath** *verb* **baths, bathing, bathed**
To **bath** someone means to give him/her a bath: *Can I help you bath the baby?*

**bathe** *verb* **bathes, bathing, bathed** (th)
1 To **bathe** means to swim in the sea, or in a lake or a river.
2 To **bathe** something means to wash it carefully: *bathe the cut with warm salt water.*
[**Bathe** comes from Old English.]

**bathroom** *noun* **bathrooms**
A **bathroom** is a room in a house. It usually has a bath, a toilet and a sink in it.

**baton** *noun* **batons**
A **baton** is a short light stick. Orchestra conductors use a **baton**.
[**Baton** comes from Latin via French.]

**batter** *noun* **batters**
**Batter** is a mixture of flour, milk and eggs. You can make pancakes with it or fry food in it.
[**Batter** comes via French from Latin *battuere* 'to beat'.]

**batter** *verb* **batters, battering, battered** (th)
To **batter** something means to hit it many times.

**battered** *adjective*
Something that is **battered** is old and out of shape: *a battered old suitcase.*

**battery** *noun* **batteries**
A **battery** is a container that stores electricity and is used to make things work.
[**Battery** comes from Latin via French.]

**battle** *noun* **battles** (th)
1 A **battle** is a fight between two armies.
2 A **battle** is a struggle to get something or to stop something: *her battle against cancer.*
[**Battle** comes via French from the same

Latin word as **batter**.]

**battle** *verb* **battles, battling, battled**
If you **battle** to do or get something, you try very hard to do or get it.

**battleship** *noun* **battleships**
A **battleship** is a large ship used in a war. It has guns and other weapons on it.

**bay¹** *noun* **bays**
A **bay** is a place where the coast curves inwards: *a sandy bay.*
[**Bay¹** comes from Spanish via French.]

**bay²** *noun* **bays**
A **bay** is a type of tree. You can use **bay** leaves to add flavour to food.
[**Bay²** comes from Latin.]

**bazaar** *noun* **bazaars**
A **bazaar** is a market, especially one in the street in India or in a Middle Eastern country.
[**Bazaar** comes from Persian (the language spoken in Iran).]

**BC** *abbreviation*
You write **BC** after a date to show that it comes before the birth of Christ. **BC** is short for 'Before Christ'.

**beach** *noun* **beaches** (th)
A **beach** is the land at the edge of the sea, which is usually covered in sand or pebbles.
[**Beach** probably comes from Old English.]

**bead** *noun* **beads**
1 A **bead** is a small object, usually round, with a hole through it. **Beads** are often threaded on a string to make a necklace.
2 A **bead** of liquid is a small drop: *beads of sweat.*
[**Bead** comes from Old English.]

**beak** *noun* **beaks**
A **beak** is the hard part of a bird's mouth.
[**Beak** comes via French and Latin from a Celtic language.]

**beaker** *noun* **beakers**
1 A **beaker** is a kind of cup, often a plastic one without handles.
2 A **beaker** is a small jar made of glass or plastic that you can use when you are doing a scientific experiment.
[**Beaker** comes from Old Norse.]

**beam** *noun* **beams** (th)
1 A **beam** of light is a line of light coming from a torch, the sun or a lamp.
2 A **beam** is a big smile.
3 A **beam** is a long piece of wood, metal or concrete. **Beams** are used to hold up roofs. [**Beam** comes from Old English.]

**beam** *verb* **beams, beaming, beamed**
To **beam** means to give a big smile because you are happy.

**bean** *noun* **beans**
1 A **bean** is a plant that has long pods with seeds in. You can eat **beans** as a vegetable.
2 A **bean** is the seed of some plants: *coffee beans*. [**Bean** comes from Old English.]

**bear¹** *noun* **bears**
A **bear** is a large furry animal with large teeth and claws.
[**Bear** comes from Old English *bera*.]

**bear²** *verb* **bears, bearing, bore, borne** (th)
1 If you cannot **bear** something, you do not like it at all.
2 If a tree **bears** fruit, it has fruit on it.
3 To **bear** a child means to give birth to a child.
[**Bear** comes from Old English *beran*.]

**beard** *noun* **beards**
A **beard** is the hair that grows on a man's chin. [**Beard** comes from Old English.]

**beast** *noun* **beasts**
A **beast** is an animal.
[**Beast** comes from Latin.]

**beat** *verb* **beats, beating, beat, beaten** (th)
1 To **beat** means to hit someone or something several times.
2 You **beat** something such as cream or a cake mixture by stirring it hard with a fork or a whisk.
3 If you **beat** someone, you do better than him/her in a game or a contest.
[**Beat** comes from Old English.]

**beat** *noun* **beats**
A **beat** is a rhythm: *clap in time to the beat.*

**beautiful** *adjective* (th)
Something that is **beautiful** is very nice to look at or very pleasant: *a beautiful woman; a beautiful day.* **beautifully** *adverb.*

**beauty** *noun* (th)
The **beauty** of something is how beautiful or lovely it is: *she was famous for her beauty.* [**Beauty** comes from an old French word.]

**beaver** *noun* **beavers**
A **beaver** is an animal that has a large flat tail. **Beavers** live on land and in water. [**Beaver** comes from Old English.]

**because** *conjunction*
You use **because** when you are giving the reason for something: *I felt very full because I had eaten too much.*
[**Because** comes from **by** and **cause**.]

**beckon** *verb* **beckons, beckoning, beckoned**
To **beckon** to someone means to make a sign with your hand telling him/her to come. [**Beckon** comes from Old English.]

**become** *verb* **becomes, becoming, became, become** (th)
To **become** something means to start to be that thing: *She's becoming tired.*
[**Become** comes from Old English.]

**bed** *noun* **beds** (th)
1 A **bed** is a piece of furniture that you sleep on.
2 A **bed** is a part of the garden where you plant flowers or shrubs.
3 The **bed** of the ocean or a river is the bottom of it.
[**Bed** comes from Old English.]

**bedroom** *noun* **bedrooms**
A **bedroom** is a room for sleeping in.

**bee** *noun* **bees**
A **bee** is an insect that can fly and sting and that makes honey.
[**Bee** comes from Old English.]

**beech** *noun* **beeches**
A **beech** is a large tree that has a smooth grey trunk.
[**Beech** comes from Old English.]

**beef** *noun*
**Beef** is the meat from a cow, bull or ox. [**Beef** comes from Latin via old French *boef* 'ox'.]

**beehive** *noun* **beehives**
A **beehive** is a kind of box for bees to live in.

**beer** *noun*
**Beer** is an alcoholic drink made from malt

a **b** c d e f g h i j k l m

and hops. [**Beer** comes from Old English.]

**beetle** *noun* **beetles**
A **beetle** is an insect with hard cases over its wings.
[**Beetle** comes from Old English.]

**beetroot** *noun* **beetroots**
**Beetroot** is a dark red, round root. You cook it and usually eat it cold.
[**Beetroot** comes from Old English *bete* and **root**.]

**before** *preposition* (th)
**1** at an earlier time: *Don't open it before your birthday.*
**2** in front of: *Three comes before four; The plains stretched before us into the distance.*
[**Before** comes from Old English.]

**before** *adverb* (th)
If you have done something **before**, you have already done it: *Have you eaten here before?*

**beg** *verb* **begs**, **begging**, **begged** (th)
**1** If you **beg** for something, you ask for something that you want very much.
**2** To **beg** in the streets means to ask people for money or food.
[**Beg** probably comes from Old English.]

**beggar** *noun* **beggars**
A **beggar** is someone who is very poor and who has to ask people for food or money.

**begin** *verb* **begins**, **beginning**, **began**, **begun** (th)
To **begin** means to start.
[**Begin** comes from Old English.]

**beginner** *noun* **beginners** (th)
A **beginner** is someone who is learning to do something: *a guitar class for beginners.*

**behave** *verb* **behaves**, **behaving**, **behaved**
**1** The way that you **behave** means the way that you act: *You're behaving like animals!*
**2** To **behave** means to be polite and sensible, and not to be silly or noisy.
[**Behave** comes from **have** which in an old sense meant 'to show how you feel by the way you act'.]

**behaviour** *noun*
**Behaviour** is the way that someone behaves: *The teacher was impressed with your behaviour.*

**behind** *preposition*
**1** at the back of, or on the other side of: *the road behind the school; The sun went behind a cloud.*
**2** following: *She walked behind us.*
[**Behind** comes from Old English.]

**behind** *adverb*
**1** If you **leave** something **behind**, you do not take it with you.
**2** If you **stay behind**, you stay somewhere after other people have gone.

**beige** *noun*
**Beige** is a light brown colour.
[**Beige** comes from French.]

**beige** *adjective*
of a light brown colour. **Beige** is mainly used to describe clothes: *dressed in a beige coat and carrying a beige handbag.*

**belief** *noun* **beliefs** (th)
A **belief** is something that you think is true or right, especially about religion.
[**Belief** comes from Old English.]

**believe** *verb* **believes**, **believing**, **believed** (th)
**1** If you **believe** something, or **believe in** something, you think that it is true or right.
**2** If you **believe** someone, you think that s/he is telling the truth.
[**Believe** comes from Old English.]

**bell** *noun* **bells**
A **bell** is a metal instrument that makes a ringing sound.
[**Bell** comes from Old English.]

**bellow** *noun* **bellows**
A **bellow** is a loud shout or roar: *The animal gave a bellow of pain.*
[The word **bellow** is probably an imitation of the sound.]

**bellow** *verb* **bellow**, **bellowing**, **bellowed**
**1** If you **bellow**, you shout loudly.
**2** If an animal **bellows**, it gives a loud deep cry.

**bellows** *noun*
A **bellows** is a device for pumping air onto or into something.
[**Bellows** comes from Old English.]

**belly** *noun* **bellies**
Your **belly** is your stomach, or the part of your body below your chest.

[**Belly** comes from Old English.]

**belong** verb **belongs, belonging, belonged** (th)
1 If something **belongs** to you, you own it.
2 To **belong** to something, such as a group or a club, means to be part of it.
3 If something **belongs** somewhere, that is where it should be.
[**Belong** comes from Old English.]

**belongings** plural noun (th)
Your **belongings** are the things that belong to you: *Take your belongings home.*

**below** adverb
in a lower position: *We looked down from the mountain to the valley below; They live on the 10th floor and I live on the floor below.*
[**Below** comes from **by** and **low**.]

**below** preposition
in a lower position than something else: *The sun sank below the horizon; children below the age of five.*

**belt** noun **belts**
A **belt** is a strip of material, usually leather, that you wear around your waist.
[**Belt** comes from Latin.]

**bench** noun **benches**
A **bench** is a long hard seat for more than one person to sit on.
[**Bench** comes from Old English.]

**bend** noun **bends** (th)
A **bend** is a curve: *a bend in the road.*
[**Bend** comes from Old English.]

**bend** verb **bends, bending, bent** (th)
1 If you **bend** something, you press it or push it so that it becomes crooked or curved.
2 When something **bends**, it turns or curves so that it is not straight.
3 If you **bend down** or **bend over**, you lean forward so that your head and shoulders are lower.

**beneath** preposition
under: *The ground was slippery beneath my feet.* [**Beneath** comes from Old English.]

**benefit** noun **benefits**
1 A **benefit** is something that helps you or makes your life better: *the benefits of modern medicine.*
2 **Benefit** is money that some people who

cannot earn enough money to live on can claim from the government.

**benefit** verb **benefits, benefiting, benefited**
If you **benefit** from something, or if something **benefits** you, it helps you or makes your life better.
[**Benefit** comes via French from Latin *bene facere* 'to do good to someone'.]

**benign** adjective
Something that is **benign** is harmless.
[**Benign** comes from Latin *benignus* 'kind-hearted'.]

**bent** verb
**Bent** is the past participle of **bend**.

**berry** noun **berries**
A **berry** is a small round fruit with seeds in it. [**Berry** comes from Old English.]

**berserk** adjective (th)
If you go **berserk**, you go mad or become extremely angry, and you might hurt someone.
[**Berserk** comes from Icelandic *berserkr* 'wild warrior'.]

**beside** preposition
next to: *She sat beside me on the way home.*
[**Beside** comes from Old English *be sidan* 'by the side'.]

**best** adjective **best** is the superlative of **good** (th)
better than everything else or everyone else: *the best score; their best song.*
[**Best** comes from Old English.]

**best** adverb **best** is the superlative of **well**
better than other things or other people: *I like chocolate ice cream best.*

**bet** verb **bets, betting, bet** or **betted**
1 If you **bet** someone that s/he cannot do something, you say that you do not think s/he can do it: *I bet you won't ask her out.*
2 If you **bet** on a race, you pay some money and say who you think will win. If you are wrong you lose your money, but if you are right you win more money.
[No one knows where **bet** comes from.]

**bet** noun **bets**
1 If you **make a bet** or **put a bet on**, you bet.
2 A **bet** is the amount of money you bet.
3 If you say that something is someone's

**best bet**, you mean that it is probably the best thing for him/her to do.

**betray** *verb* **betrays, betraying, betrayed** (th)
1 If you hurt or make trouble for a person who trusts you, you **betray** him/her.
2 You **betray** a secret when you tell it to another person.
[**Betray** comes from Latin.]

**better** *adjective* **better** is the comparative of **good** (th)
1 If something is **better**, it is more satisfactory: *Our new car is better than our old one; Fruit is better for you than chocolate; I'm better at history than I am at science.*
2 If you are **better**, you are no longer ill.
3 If someone is **better off**, s/he is richer or in a better situation.
[**Better** comes from Old English.]

**better** *adverb* **better** is the comparative of **well**
1 If someone can do something **better**, s/he can do it more skilfully: *I can swim better than my sister; Some people can sew better than others.*
2 If you like something **better**, you like it more: *I like chocolate better than fruit; I like him better now I've got to know him.*

**between** *preposition*
1 **Between** two things means having one of them on each side: *He stood between his two children.*
2 **Between** two times means at a time that is after the first time and before the second time: *We met between 4:00 and 4:30.*
3 To choose **between** things means to choose one of them.
[**Between** comes from Old English.]

**beware** *verb* (th)
To **beware** of something means to be careful because it may harm you.
[**Beware** comes from an old phrase *beware* 'be wary'.]

**bewitch** *verb* **bewitches, bewitching, bewitched**
If you **bewitch** someone, you put a spell on him/her. The word **bewitch** is mainly used in stories.
[**Bewitch** comes from an old verb *witch* 'to put a spell on someone', which came from the same Old English word as the noun **witch**.]

**beyond** *preposition*
on the far side of something: *Beyond the church was a stream.*
[**Beyond** comes from Old English.]

**bib** *noun* **bibs**
A **bib** is a piece of cloth or plastic that you tie around a baby's neck to stop food getting onto his/her clothes.
[**Bib** probably comes from Latin *bibere* 'to drink'.]

**Bible** *noun* **Bibles**
The **Bible** is a holy book for Christians. It has two parts, the Old Testament and the New Testament.
[The word **Bible** comes via French and Latin from Greek *biblia* 'books'.]

**biblical** *adjective*
**Biblical** means to do with the Bible.

**bicycle** *noun* **bicycles**
A **bicycle** is a vehicle with two wheels. You sit on the saddle and turn its pedals to make it go.
[**Bicycle** comes from *bi-* 'two' and the same Greek word as **cycle**.]

**big** *adjective* **bigger, biggest** (th)
1 Something that is **big** is of great size, or of greater size than normal.
2 Something that is **big** is important: *a big day; a big decision.*
[No one knows where **big** comes from.]

**bike** *noun* **bikes**
A **bike** is a bicycle or a motorcycle.
[**Bike** is an abbreviation of **bicycle**.]

**bikini** *noun* **bikinis**
A **bikini** is a swimming costume for women that has a top and a bottom piece.
[The **bikini** was named after the island of *Bikini* in the Pacific Ocean, where an atom bomb was exploded in 1946. The **bikini** was said to be as 'explosive' as the bomb.]

**bilingual** *adjective*
Someone who is **bilingual** can speak two languages very well.
[**Bilingual** comes from Latin *bis* 'having two' and *lingua* 'tongue, language'.]

**bill**[1] *noun* **bills**
1 A **bill** is a piece of paper showing you how much money to pay in a shop or a restaurant.
2 A **bill/Bill** is a plan for a new law which is going to be discussed in parliament.

[**Bill**[1] comes from Latin *bulla* 'a sealed letter'.]

**bill**[2] *noun* **bills**
A **bill** is a bird's beak.
[**Bill**[2] comes from Old English.]

**bind** *verb* **binds, binding, bound** (th)
1 To **bind** means to tie someone or something up: *Bind the wound with a bandage; He was bound to a chair.*
2 To **bind** a book means to fasten the pages together and put a cover on them.
[**Bind** comes from Old English.]

**binoculars** *plural noun*
You use **binoculars** to see things that are far away more clearly. **Binoculars** have two tubes with lenses in, which you hold in front of your eyes.
[**Binoculars** comes from Latin *bini* 'two together' and *oculus* 'eye'.]

**biography** *noun* **biographies**
A **biography** is the story of a person's life, told by someone else.
[**Biography** comes from Greek *bios* 'life' and *graphein* 'to write'.]

**biology** *noun*
If you study **biology**, you learn about living things.
[**Biology** comes from Greek *bios* 'life' and *-logia* 'study'.]

**birch** *noun* **birches**
A **birch** is a tall, slender tree with thin branches.
[**Birch** comes from Old English.]

**bird** *noun* **birds**
A **bird** is a creature with wings and feathers. Female **birds** lay eggs.
[**Bird** comes from Old English.]

**bird of prey** *noun* **birds of prey**
A **bird of prey** is a bird that lives by hunting and killing other birds or animals. Hawks, owls and eagles are **birds of prey**.

**birth** *noun* **births**
1 A baby's **birth** is when it comes out of its mother's body and starts to breathe on its own.
2 When a female **gives birth**, her baby comes out of her body.
[**Birth** comes from Old Norse.]

**birthday** *noun* **birthdays**
Your **birthday** is the day each year that is the same date as the day you were born.

**biscuit** *noun* **biscuits**
A **biscuit** is a small, flat, crisp cake made of dough and then baked.
[**Biscuit** comes via French from Latin *bis coctus* 'twice cooked', because biscuits used to be baked and then dried in a cool oven so that they would keep longer.]

**bishop** *noun* **bishops**
1 A **bishop** is an important priest who is in charge of the churches for a whole area.
2 A **bishop** is a piece in the game of chess. **Bishops** move diagonally across the board.
[**Bishop** comes from Latin via Old English.]

**bit**[1] *noun* **bits** (th)
1 A **bit** is a small piece of something.
2 On a drill, the **bit** is the long metal part that does the cutting.
3 A **bit** is a piece of metal that goes in a horse's mouth and is attached to the reins. [**Bit**[1] comes from Old English.]

**bit**[2] *noun* **bits**
A **bit** is the smallest piece of information that a computer uses.
[**Bit**[2] is short for *binary digit*, part of a kind of code that a computer stores information in.]

**bitch** *noun* **bitches**
A **bitch** is an adult female dog.
[**Bitch** comes from Old English.]

**bite** *verb* **bites, biting, bit, bitten** (th)
1 To **bite** something means to cut into it with your teeth.
2 If a snake or an insect **bites** you, it pierces your skin and can force poison into your body.
[**Bite** comes from Old English.]

**bitter** *adjective* **bitterest** (th)
1 A **bitter** taste is an unpleasant sharp taste.
2 A **bitter** wind is a very cold wind.
3 You feel **bitter** when you are angry about the way you have been treated.
**bitterly** *adverb.* **bitterness** *noun.*
[**Bitter** comes from Old English.]

**black** *noun*
**Black** is the darkest colour, the colour of

a **b** c d e f g h i j k l m

coal. [**Black** comes from Old English.]

**black** *adjective* **blacker, blackest**
1 of the colour of coal.
2 **Black** coffee or tea is coffee or tea made without any milk.

**blackberry** *noun* **blackberries**
A **blackberry** is a small, dark purple fruit. Blackberries grow on bramble bushes.

**bladder** *noun* **bladders**
Your **bladder** is a kind of bag below your kidneys where urine is stored.
[**Bladder** comes from Old English.]

**blade** *noun* **blades**
1 A **blade** is the flat, sharp part of a knife.
2 A **blade** is something that is shaped like the blade of a knife: *a blade of grass*.
[**Blade** comes from Old English.]

**blame** *verb* **blames, blaming, blamed**
If you **blame** someone, you say that something is that person's fault.
[**Blame** comes from Greek via French and Latin.]

**blame** *noun*
If you get the **blame** for something bad that happens, people say that it was your fault.

**blancmange** *noun* **blancmanges**
**Blancmange** is a kind of cold pudding made with milk, usually flavoured with fruit.
[**Blancmange** comes from old French *blanc mangier* 'white food'.]

**blank** *adjective* **blanker, blankest** (th)
1 A **blank** page is a page with no writing on it.
2 A **blank** tape is one that has not been used to record on.
3 If you **look blank**, your face does not show what you are thinking.
[**Blank** comes from French *blanc* 'white'.]

**blanket** *noun* **blankets**
A **blanket** is a thick cover used on a bed.
[**Blanket** comes from French *blanc* 'white', because blankets were originally made of wool that had not been dyed.]

**blast** *noun* **blasts**
1 A **blast** is a sudden loud noise or an explosion: *a blast on a whistle*.
2 A **blast** of air is a strong gust.
[**Blast** comes from Old English.]

**blaze** *noun* **blazes**
1 A **blaze** is a big fire that is burning strongly.
2 A **blaze** of light is a very bright light.
[**Blaze** comes from Old English.]

**blaze** *verb* **blazes, blazing, blazed**
To **blaze** means to burn brightly.

**bleat** *verb* **bleats, bleating, bleated**
To **bleat** means to make the noise that a sheep makes.
[The word **bleat** is an imitation of the sound.]

**bleed** *verb* **bleeds, bleeding, bled**
When a part of your body **bleeds**, blood comes out of it.
[**Bleed** comes from Old English.]

**blend** *verb* **blends, blending, blended**
1 If you **blend** things, you mix them thoroughly.
2 If things **blend**, they go together very well: *Their voices blended harmoniously.*
3 If something **blends into** something else, it seems to become part of it: *The tiger's stripes help it to blend into its surroundings.*
[**Blend** probably comes from a Scandinavian word.]

**blew** *verb*
**Blew** is the past tense of **blow.**

**blind** *adjective*
A person who is **blind** is unable to see.
**blindly** *adverb.* **blindness** *noun.*
[**Blind** comes from Old English.]

**blind** *noun* **blinds**
A **blind** is a screen that you can pull or roll down to cover a window.

**blindfold** *noun* **blindfolds**
A **blindfold** is something such as a piece of cloth that is put over your eyes so that you cannot see.
[**Blindfold** comes from Old English *blindfeld* 'made blind'.]

**blindfold** *verb* **blindfolds, blindfolding, blindfolded**
When someone **blindfolds** you, s/he puts a blindfold over your eyes.

**blink** *verb* **blinks, blinking, blinked**
You **blink** when you open and shut your eyes quickly.
[**Blink** comes from Old English.]

**blister** *noun* **blisters**
A **blister** is a sore place on your skin like a bubble. You get a **blister** if something rubs or burns your skin.
[No one knows where **blister** comes from.]

**blizzard** *noun* **blizzards**
A **blizzard** is a very windy snowstorm.
[No one knows where **blizzard** comes from.]

**block** *noun* **blocks** (th)
A **block** is a thick, solid lump of something such as wood or stone.
[**Block** comes from Dutch via French.]

**block** *verb* **blocks, blocking, blocked** (th)
To **block** something means to stop it getting through.

**blond** *adjective* **blonder, blondest** Also **blonde**
**Blond** hair is fair hair. You use **blond** for boys and men, and **blonde** for girls and women.
[**Blond** comes from Latin *blondus* 'yellow'.]

**blood** *noun*
**Blood** is a red liquid that flows round your body.
[**Blood** comes from Old English.]

**bloodthirsty** *adjective* **bloodthirstier, bloodthirstiest** (th)
Someone who is **bloodthirsty** likes killing and violence.

**blossom** *noun* **blossoms**
A **blossom** is a flower, especially the small flowers that grow on a tree before the fruit.
[**Blossom** comes from Old English.]

**blossom** *verb* **blossoms, blossoming, blossomed**
1 When a tree **blossoms**, flowers appear on it.
2 When a person **blossoms**, s/he begins to do well: *She's really blossoming in her new school.*

**blot** *noun* **blots**
A **blot** is a spot of ink that has been spilt.
[**Blot** probably comes from a Scandinavian language.]

**blouse** *noun* **blouses**
A **blouse** is a shirt worn by women and girls. [**Blouse** comes from French.]

**blow** *verb* **blows, blowing, blew, blown**
1 To **blow** means to move in the wind.
2 If you **blow**, you make air come out of your mouth.
3 If something **blows up**, it explodes.
4 If you **blow** something **up**, you make it explode.
[**Blow** comes from Old English.]

**blue** *noun*
1 **Blue** is the colour of the sky on a sunny day.
2 If something comes **out of the blue**, it comes suddenly and with no warning.
[**Blue** comes from French.]

**blue** *adjective* **bluer, bluest**
1 of the colour of the sky on a sunny day.
2 If you feel **blue**, you feel miserable.

**blunt** *adjective*
Something that is **blunt** is not sharp.
[**Blunt** probably comes from a Scandinavian language.]

**blur** *noun* **blurs**
A **blur** is something that is not clear, because you cannot see it clearly or you cannot remember it clearly: *We drove so fast that the scenery was just a blur.*
[No one knows where **blur** comes from.]

**blur** *verb* **blurs, blurring, blurred** (th)
To **blur** something means to make it smudged or unclear: *old blurred photographs; The book blurs the line between fact and fiction.*

**blurt** *verb* **blurts, blurting, blurted** (th)
If you **blurt** something, or **blurt** something **out**, you say it suddenly, usually without thinking.
[No one knows where **blurt** comes from.]

**blush** *verb* **blushes, blushing, blushed**
If you **blush**, your cheeks go red because you feel embarrassed or silly.
[**Blush** comes from Old English.]

**boa constrictor** *noun* **boa constrictors**
A **boa constrictor** is a large South American snake that kills animals for food by winding its body round them and crushing them.
[**Boa constrictor** comes from Latin.]

**boar** *noun* **boars**
1 A **boar** is an adult male pig.

**a b c d e f g h i j k l m**

2 A **boar** is a wild pig.
[**Boar** comes from Old English.]

**board** noun **boards**
A **board** is a long, flat piece of wood or other material.
[**Board** comes from Old English.]

**board** verb **boards, boarding, boarded**
To **board** a bus, train, ship or aircraft means to get on it.

**boarding school** noun **boarding schools**
A **boarding school** is a school where children live except during the holidays.

**boast** verb **boasts, boasting, boasted** (th)
To **boast** means to show off by talking very proudly about what you can do or what you own.
[No one knows where **boast** comes from.]

**boat** noun **boats**
A **boat** is something made to float on water that can carry people or objects.
[**Boat** comes from Old English.]

**bob** verb **bobs, bobbing, bobbed**
To **bob** means to move quickly up and down, especially on water: *boats bobbing.*
[No one knows where **bob** comes from.]

**body** noun **bodies**
1 A **body** is all the parts that a person or animal is made up of.
2 A **body** is the body of a dead person.
3 A **body** is all of a person or animal except the head, arms and legs.
[**Body** comes from Old English.]

**bog** noun **bogs** (th)
A **bog** is an area of soft wet land.
[**Bog** comes from Gaelic *bog* 'soft'.]

**bogus** adjective (th)
Something that is **bogus** is false or fake.
[No one knows where **bogus** comes from.]

**boil¹** noun **boils**
A **boil** is a big spot full of infected liquid on the skin.
[**Boil¹** comes from Old English.]

**boil²** verb **boils, boiling, boiled**
1 To **boil** means to heat a liquid until it bubbles and gives off steam.
2 If a liquid, or something containing a liquid, **boils**, the liquid begins to bubble and give off steam because it is very hot: *Water boils at 100°C; Kettle's boiling!*

[**Boil²** comes via French from Latin *bulla* 'bubble' (ancestor of **bowl²**).]

**boiling point** noun
The **boiling point** of a liquid is the temperature at which it boils.

**boisterous** adjective (th)
A **boisterous** person or activity is noisy and rough.
[No one knows where **boisterous** comes from.]

**bold** adjective **bolder, boldest** (th)
1 A **bold** person is confident and brave.
2 **Bold** colours or images stand out clearly. **boldly** adverb. **boldness** noun.
[**Bold** comes from Old English.]

**bollard** noun **bollards**
A **bollard** is a post in the road that stops traffic getting into the road or going in the wrong direction.
[**Bollard** probably comes from Old Norse *bolr* 'tree trunk'.]

**bolt** noun **bolts**
A **bolt** is a sliding metal bar that locks a door or gate.
[**Bolt** comes from Old English.]

**bolt** verb **bolts, bolting, bolted**
1 To **bolt** means to lock a door or gate with a bolt.
2 To **bolt** means to run away quickly: *The horse bolted.*

**bomb** noun **bombs**
A **bomb** is a container filled with a substance that explodes and blows things up.
[**Bomb** comes via French, Italian and Latin from Greek *bombos* 'booming'.]

**bomb** verb **bombs, bombing, bombed**
To **bomb** a place means to attack it with a bomb or bombs.

**bombard** verb **bombards, bombarding, bombarded**
1 To **bombard** a place means to attack it with heavy guns.
2 If you **bombard** someone with questions, you ask him/her a lot of questions in a short time.
[**Bombard** comes from the same Greek word as **bomb**.]

**bombshell** noun **bombshell**
A **bombshell** is something that happens,

or that you are told, which makes you very surprised and upset: *Her poor results were an absolute bombshell to her parents.*

**bond** *noun* **bonds** (th)
1 A **bond** is a strong feeling that joins two people.
2 **Bonds** are ropes that tie someone up.
[**Bond** is a different spelling of **band¹**.]

**bone** *noun* **bones**
A **bone** is one of the hard parts of the body that make up the skeleton.
[**Bone** comes from Old English.]

**bonfire** *noun* **bonfires**
A **bonfire** is a large fire that you make in the open air.
[**Bonfire** comes from *bone fire*, a fire on which animal bones were burnt.]

**bonnet** *noun* **bonnets**
1 A **bonnet** is a baby's or woman's hat that is tied under the chin.
2 The **bonnet** of a car is the cover for the engine.
[**Bonnet** comes via French from Latin *abonnis* 'hat'.]

**bonsai** *noun*
A **bonsai** is a miniature tree or bush that is grown in a pot.
[**Bonsai** comes from Japanese.]

**bonus** *noun* **bonuses**
A **bonus** is an extra payment or an extra reward: *a Christmas bonus.*
[**Bonus** comes from Latin *bonus* 'good'.]

**booby prize** *noun* **booby prizes**
A **booby prize** is a prize that is given to the loser in a game or competition.
[**Booby** comes from Spanish *bobo* 'a fool'.]

**booby trap** *noun* **booby traps**
A **booby trap** is a hidden trap that is set to trick someone.

**book** *noun* **books**
A **book** is a set of sheets of paper fixed together inside a cover.
[**Book** comes from Old English.]

**book** *verb* **books, booking, booked** (th)
To **book** means to arrange in advance for something to be kept for you: *We've booked our seats on the train; It's a good idea to book in advance because the hotel gets very busy.*

**bookcase** *noun* **bookcases**
A **bookcase** is a piece of furniture made to hold books.

**bookkeeping** *noun*
**Bookkeeping** is the job of keeping records for a business of how much money is spent.

**booklet** *noun* **booklets**
A **booklet** is a small book with paper covers that gives you information about something.

**bookworm** *noun* **bookworms**
A **bookworm** is someone who spends a lot of time reading books.
[**Bookworm** originally meant a small maggot that fed on books.]

**boom¹** *noun* **booms**
1 A **boom** is a very loud deep sound, such as an explosion or the sound of a large drum.
2 A **boom** is a rapid increase in something: *a boom in world trade.*
[The word **boom¹** is an imitation of the sound.]

**boom¹** *verb* **booms, booming, boomed**
1 To **boom** means to make a very loud deep sound or bang.
2 To **boom** means to speak in a loud deep voice.
3 To **boom** means to increase suddenly and quickly: *Business is booming.*

**boom²** *noun* **booms**
A **boom** is the long wooden post along the bottom edge of the sail in a boat.
[**Boom²** comes from Old Norse.]

**boomerang** *noun* **boomerangs**
A **boomerang** is a curved piece of wood that is thrown through the air and can return to the person who threw it. **Boomerangs** were used as weapons by the Australian Aborigines.
[**Boomerang** comes from an Australian Aboriginal word.]

**boost** *verb* **boosts, boosting, boosted** (th)
To **boost** something means to increase its amount or its power.
[No one knows where **boost** comes from.]

**boot** *noun* **boots**
1 A **boot** is a kind of strong shoe that also covers the ankle or part of the leg.
2 A **boot** is a place at the back of a car where you can put luggage.
[**Boot** comes from French via Old Norse.]

**boot** *verb* **boots, booting, booted**
1 If you **boot** something, you kick it hard.
2 To **boot up** a computer means to get it ready to work.

**border** *noun* **borders** (th)
1 A **border** is the line that divides two countries or regions.
2 A **border** is a line or decorated strip around the edge of something.
[**Border** comes from an old French word.]

**bore¹** *verb* **bores, boring, bored**
If something **bores** you, you do not find it interesting.
[**Bore¹** comes from Old English.]

**bore²** *verb* **bores, boring, bored**
To **bore** means to drill a deep hole into something such as rock.
[No one knows where **bore²** comes from.]

**bore³** *verb*
**Bore** is the past tense of **bear**.

**born** *adjective*
1 When a child is **born**, it comes out of its mother's body: *the house where I was born; My sister was born deaf.*
2 very good at something, as though you have always been able to do it: *a born cook.*
[**Born** comes from Old English.]

**borne** *verb*
**Borne** is the past participle of **bear**: *Paul's disappointment was borne well.*

**borough** *noun* **boroughs**
A **borough** is a town that has its own local government.
[**Borough** comes from Old English.]

**borrow** *verb* **borrows, borrowing, borrowed**
To **borrow** something means to use something that belongs to someone else and then give it back.
[**Borrow** comes from Old English.]

**boss** *noun* **bosses**
A **boss** is someone in charge of people at work.
[**Boss** comes from Dutch *baas* 'master'.]

**boss** *verb* **bosses, bossing, bossed**
To **boss** someone or **boss** someone **about** means to tell him/her what to do.

**botany** *noun*
**Botany** is the study of plants and flowers.
[**Botany** comes via French and Latin from

Greek *botane* 'a plant'.]

**both** *adjective*
**Both** means the two, not just one: *We both like swimming.*
[**Both** comes from Old Norse.]

**bother** *verb* **bothers, bothering, bothered** (th)
1 If you **bother** to do something, you remember and make an effort to do it.
2 If something **bothers** you, it annoys you and is a nuisance.
[**Bother** probably comes from Irish *bodhraim* 'to deafen or annoy'.]

**bottle** *noun* **bottles**
A **bottle** is a glass container for liquids that is usually narrower at the top.
[**Bottle** comes via French from the same Latin word as **butt²**.]

**bottom** *noun* **bottoms** (th)
1 Your **bottom** is the part of your body that you sit on.
2 The **bottom** is the lowest part of something: *the bottom of the sea.*
[**Bottom** comes from Old English.]

**bough** *noun* **boughs**
A **bough** is a large thick branch of a tree.
[**Bough** comes from Old English.]

**bought** *verb*
**Bought** is the past tense and past participle of **buy**.

**boulder** *noun* **boulders**
A **boulder** is a large rock.
[**Boulder** comes from a Scandinavian language.]

**bounce** *verb* **bounces, bouncing, bounced** (th)
1 To **bounce** means to spring back.
2 To **bounce** means to jump up and down.
[No one knows where **bounce** comes from.]

**bound¹** *verb* **bounds, bounding, bounded** (th)
To **bound** means to move forward with big jumps.
[**Bound¹** comes from Latin via French.]

**bound²** *verb*
**Bound²** is the past tense and past participle of **bind**.

**bound²** *adjective*
If something is **bound** to happen, it is

certain to happen.

**boundary** *noun* **boundaries** (th)
A **boundary** is a line or fence that separates one place from another.
[**Boundary** comes from **bounds**.]

**bounds** *noun*
1 The **bounds** of something are the limits of it.
2 If a place is **out of bounds**, you are not allowed to go there.
[**Bound** comes from Latin via French.]

**bouquet** *noun* **bouquets**
A **bouquet** is a bunch of flowers that you give someone as a present.
[**Bouquet** comes from French.]

**bout** *noun* **bouts** (th)
1 A **bout** is a match in a sport.
2 A **bout** is a period of time when someone is ill: *a bout of flu.*
[**Bout** probably comes from a German word.]

**bow¹** *noun* **bows**
1 A **bow** is a bent piece of wood with a string joining the two ends, used for shooting arrows.
2 A **bow** is a wooden rod with hair stretched tightly along it. It is used to play some kinds of musical string instruments, such as a violin.
3 A **bow** is a kind of knot with loops.
[**Bow¹** comes from Old English *boga*.]

**bow²** *verb* **bows, bowing, bowed**
To **bow** means to bend forwards politely when meeting someone.
[**Bow²** comes from Old English *bugan*.]

**bowel** *noun* **bowels**
Your **bowels** are the tubes in the lower part of your body where waste products from your food are turned into faeces.
[**Bowel** comes via French from Latin *botellus* 'little sausage'.]

**bowl¹** *noun* **bowls**
A **bowl** is a round open container.
[**Bowl¹** comes from Old English.]

**bowl²** *verb* **bowls, bowling, bowled**
To **bowl** means to throw the ball towards the person batting, especially in cricket.
[**Bowl²** comes via old French *boule* 'ball' from the same Latin word as **boil²**.]

**bowler** *noun* **bowlers**
A **bowler** is the player in cricket who bowls the ball.

**box¹** *noun* **boxes** (th)
A **box** is a container, usually with four flat sides and a lid.
[**Box¹** comes from Greek via Latin.]

**box²** *verb* **boxes, boxing, boxed**
To **box** means to fight or punch with the fists as a sport.
[No one knows where **box²** comes from.]

**Boxing Day** *noun*
In some countries, the day after Christmas Day is called **Boxing Day**.
[On **Boxing Day** people used to give small gifts, called *Christmas boxes*, to people like the milkman and the postman who brought things to their houses.]

**box office** *noun* **box offices**
The **box office** in a theatre or cinema is the place where you can buy tickets.
[The **box office** was originally just for reserving a *box*, a private area with seats for a small group of people.]

**boy** *noun* **boys** (th)
A **boy** is a male child.
[No one knows where **boy** comes from.]

**brace** *noun* **braces**
1 A **brace** is something that holds or supports something in the correct position.
2 A **brace** or **braces** is a special wire that someone wears over the teeth to straighten them.
3 **Braces** are elastic straps that you wear over your shoulders to hold up your trousers.
[**Brace** comes from Latin *bracchia*, plural of *bracchium* 'arm'.]

**bracelet** *noun* **bracelets**
A **bracelet** is a decorated ring worn round the wrist or arm.
[**Bracelet** comes via French from the same Latin word as **brace**.]

**bracken** *noun*
**Bracken** is a plant like a fern that grows mostly on hills and in woods.
[**Bracken** comes from Old Norse.]

**bracket** *noun* **brackets**
1 A **bracket** is a piece of metal or wood fixed to the wall to support something.

**a b c d e f g h i j k l m**

**2** A **bracket** is one of a pair of marks like these ( ) that you use to separate some words from the main part of a sentence or paragraph. [**Bracket** comes from Latin.]

**brag** *verb* **brags, bragging, bragged** (th)
To **brag** means to show off by talking proudly about something you can do or have done.
[No one knows where **brag** comes from.]

**braille, Braille** *noun*
**Braille** is an alphabet for blind people. It uses raised dots that you can read by touching them with your fingers.
[**Braille** is named after Louis *Braille*, a blind teacher who invented it.]

**brain** *noun* **brains** (th)
**1** Your **brain** is an organ inside your head that controls your body and allows you to think.
**2** Your **brain** is your ability to think clearly and to learn: *He's got a good brain.*
[**Brain** comes from Old English.]

**brake** *noun* **brakes**
A **brake** is the part of a vehicle that makes it slow down or stop.
[No one knows where **brake** comes from.]

**bramble** *noun* **brambles**
A **bramble** is a prickly bush that blackberries grow on.
[**Bramble** comes from Old English.]

**bran** *noun*
**Bran** is the outer covering of grains like wheat. **Bran** is often separated from the rest of the grain and used to make breakfast cereals.
[**Bran** comes from an old French word.]

**branch** *noun* **branches** (th)
**1** A **branch** is a part that sticks out from the main part, especially on a tree.
**2** A **branch** of a group of shops or banks is one of its shops or banks in a particular place. [**Branch** comes from Latin.]

**branch** *verb* **branches, branching, branched**
To **branch** means to split and go in two different directions: *The river branches into two.*

**brand** *noun* **brands**
A **brand** is a product that is made by a particular company: *a new brand of soap.*
[**Brand** comes from Old English. It used

to mean a mark put on an animal to show who it belonged to.]

**brandish** *verb* **brandishes, brandishing, brandished**
To **brandish** something means to wave it about in a dangerous way.
[**Brandish** comes from an old French word.]

**brash** *adjective*
Someone who is **brash** is confident in a loud unpleasant way.
[No one knows where **brash** comes from.]

**brass** *noun*
**Brass** is a yellow metal made from copper and zinc. [**Brass** comes from Old English.]

**brass** *adjective*
**1** made of brass: *a brass candlestick.*
**2** A **brass** musical instrument is one made of brass that you blow into, such as a trumpet or horn.

**bravado** *noun*
**Bravado** is when someone pretends to be braver and more confident than s/he really is.
[**Bravado** comes via Spanish from the same Latin word as **brave** and **barbaric**.]

**brave** *adjective* **braver, bravest** (th)
Someone who is **brave** can face danger or pain without showing fear.
**bravely** *adverb*. **bravery** *noun*.
[**Brave** comes from the same Latin word as **barbaric**.]

**brawl** *noun* **brawls** (th)
A **brawl** is a noisy fight between a lot of people.
[No one knows where **brawl** comes from.]

**bray** *verb* **brays, braying, brayed**
To **bray** means to make the noise of a donkey.
[**Bray** comes from an old French word meaning 'to cry'.]

**brazier** *noun* **braziers**
A **brazier** is a metal container that you can make a fire in for cooking or keeping people warm outside.
[**Brazier** comes from old French *braise* 'burning pieces of coal'.]

**bread** *noun*
**Bread** is a food made by baking flour, yeast and water.

n o p q r s t u v w x y z

[**Bread** comes from Old English.]

**break** *noun* **breaks**
A **break** is a short rest from work.
[**Break** comes from Old English.]

**break** *verb* **breaks, breaking, broke, broken** (th)
1 To **break** something means to crack or smash it.
2 If you **break** a law, a rule or a promise, you do not do what it says.
3 If a car or other vehicle **breaks down**, it stops moving because there is something wrong with it.

**breakdown** *noun* **breakdowns**
1 If you have a **breakdown**, the car or vehicle you are travelling in stops moving because there is something wrong with it.
2 If you have a **breakdown**, you become ill because you are very worried or depressed.

**breaker** *noun* **breakers**
A **breaker** is a large wave in the ocean that breaks into a line of foam.

**breakfast** *noun* **breakfasts**
Breakfast is the first meal of the day.
[**Breakfast** comes from **break** and **fast**[1].]

**breakneck** *adjective*
If something moves at **breakneck** speed, it is too fast and very dangerous.

**breakthrough** *noun* **breakthroughs** (th)
A **breakthrough** is an important discovery or new development: *a breakthrough in medicine.*

**breakwater** *noun* **breakwaters**
A **breakwater** is a wall or barrier built in the sea to protect the land from strong waves.

**breast** *noun* **breasts**
1 A woman's **breasts** are the two round parts on her chest that can produce milk to feed a baby.
2 A person's or animal's **breast** is the chest: *The bird has a red breast.*
[**Breast** comes from Old English.]

**breaststroke** *noun*
Breaststroke is a way of swimming on your front in which you move your arms out from your chest and kick your legs out and backwards.

**breath** *noun* **breaths**
A **breath** is the air that someone breathes in and out.
[**Breath** comes from Old English.]

**breathe** *verb* **breathes, breathing, breathed**
To **breathe** means to take air into the lungs through the nose or mouth and let it out again. [**Breathe** comes from **breath**.]

**breather** *noun*
A **breather** is a short rest from what you are doing.
[**Breather** comes from **breathe**.]

**breathtaking** *adjective*
Something that is **breathtaking** is amazing and beautiful to look at.

**breed** *noun* **breeds** (th)
A **breed** of an animal is a particular type of that animal: *What breed is your dog?*
[**Breed** comes from Old English.]

**breed** *verb* **breeds, breeding, bred**
1 When animals **breed**, they produce babies.
2 Someone who **breeds** animals keeps them in order to produce more of them.

**breeze** *noun* **breezes**
A **breeze** is a gentle wind.
[**Breeze** probably comes from a Spanish or Portuguese word for the north-east wind.]

**brew** *verb* **brews, brewing, brewed**
1 To **brew** beer means to make it.
2 To **brew** tea means to make a cup of tea.
3 If a storm or trouble is **brewing**, it is going to start soon.
[**Brew** comes from Old English.]

**brewery** *noun* **breweries**
A **brewery** is a place where beer is made or is a company that makes beer.

**bribe** *noun* **bribes**
A **bribe** is a present, especially of money, that someone offers another person in order to persuade him/her to do something.
[**Bribe** comes from an old French word.]

**bribe** *verb* **bribes, bribing, bribed**
To **bribe** someone means to offer him/her a present, especially of money, in order to persuade him/her to do something.

**bribery** *noun*
Bribery is when someone offers another person a bribe.

**brick** *noun* **bricks**
A **brick** is a block of baked clay used to build walls.
[**Brick** comes from an old German or Dutch word.]

**bride** *noun* **brides**
A **bride** is a woman on her wedding day.
[**Bride** comes from Old English.]

**bridegroom** *noun* **bridegrooms**
A **bridegroom** is a man on his wedding day.
[**Bridegroom** comes from Old English *brydguma* 'bride's man'.]

**bridesmaid** *noun* **bridesmaids**
A **bridesmaid** is a girl or unmarried woman who helps a bride on her wedding day.

**bridge** *noun* **bridges**
A **bridge** is something built over a railway, river or road so that you can get across it.
[**Bridge** comes from Old English.]

**bridle** *noun* **bridles**
A **bridle** is the set of straps that fit around a horse's head so that you can control it.
[**Bridle** comes from Old English.]

**brief** *adjective* **briefer, briefest** (th)
Something that is **brief** is short: *a brief visit; a brief account of her travels.*
[**Brief** comes from Latin **brevis** 'short'.]

**briefcase** *noun* **briefcases**
A **briefcase** is a small, flat case for carrying papers.
[A **briefcase** was originally a case in which a lawyer carried a *brief* (a short account of the main facts) to use in court.]

**brigade** *noun* **brigades**
1 A **brigade** is a section in the army.
2 A **brigade** is a team of workers: *the fire brigade.*
[**Brigade** comes via French from Italian *brigata* 'a troop'.]

**bright** *adjective* **brighter, brightest** (th)
1 Something that is **bright** is shining.
2 Someone who is **bright** is clever.
3 Someone who is **bright** is cheerful.
[**Bright** comes from Old English.]

**brilliant** *adjective* (th)
1 Something that is **brilliant** shines very brightly.
2 Someone who is **brilliant** is extremely clever or good at something.
3 Something that is **brilliant** is extremely good: *a brilliant story.*
[**Brilliant** comes via French from Italian *brillare* 'to shine'.]

**brim** *noun* **brims**
1 The **brim** of a container is the top edge of it: *full to the brim.*
2 The **brim** of a hat is the part that sticks out all round it.
[No one knows where **brim** comes from.]

**brine** *noun*
**Brine** is salty water.
[**Brine** comes from Old English.]

**bring** *verb* **brings, bringing, brought**
To **bring** means to carry or to take something with you.
[**Bring** comes from Old English.]

**brink** *noun*
1 The **brink** of something is the edge of it: *the brink of the cliff.*
2 If you are on the **brink** of something, you are going to do it very soon: *He was on the brink of bursting into tears.*
[**Brink** comes from Old Norse.]

**brisk** *adjective* **brisker, briskest**
Something that is **brisk** is quick and full of energy: *We had a brisk walk.*
[**Brisk** comes from Italian via French.]

**bristle** *noun* **bristles**
A **bristle** is a short hair that stands up stiffly. [**Bristle** comes from Old English.]

**bristle** *verb* **bristles, bristling, bristled**
1 To **bristle** means to show you are annoyed about something: *He bristled at the suggestion.*
2 If something or somewhere is **bristling** with something, it is full of that thing: *The harbour was bristling with ships.*

**brittle** *adjective*
Something that is **brittle** is hard but can easily break or snap.
[**Brittle** comes from Old English.]

**broad** *adjective* **broader, broadest** (th)
Something that is **broad** is wide.
[**Broad** comes from Old English.]

**broadcast** *noun* **broadcasts**
A **broadcast** is a radio or television programme.
[**Broadcast** comes from **broad** and **cast** 'to throw', and originally meant 'to scatter

widely'.]

**broadcast** *verb* **broadcasts,
broadcasting, broadcasted**
To **broadcast** means to send out a radio or
television programme.

**broadminded** *adjective* (th)
A **broadminded** person accepts the
different ideas and views of other people.

**broccoli** *noun*
Broccoli is a green or purple vegetable
that has round heads like a cauliflower on
thick stalks. [**Broccoli** comes from Italian.]

**brochure** *noun* **brochures**
A **brochure** is a magazine or booklet that
gives you pictures and information: *a
holiday brochure.*
[**Brochure** comes from French *brochure*
'stitching', because the pages used to be
stitched together.]

**broke** *verb*
Broke is the past tense of **break**.

**broken** *verb*
Broken is the past participle of **break**.

**broken** *adjective*
1 If something is **broken**, it is cracked,
smashed or in lots of pieces.
2 If something is **broken**, you cannot use
it because it has something wrong with it.

**bronchitis** *noun*
Bronchitis is an illness of the lungs and
chest that makes you cough a lot.
[**Bronchitis** comes from Greek *bronchos*
'windpipe'.]

**bronze** *noun*
Bronze is a reddish-brown metal made
from copper and tin.
[**Bronze** probably comes from Persian (the
language spoken in Iran).]

**brooch** *noun* **brooches**
A **brooch** is a piece of jewellery that you
can pin to your clothes.
[**Brooch** comes from Latin via French.]

**brood** *noun* **broods**
A **brood** is a family of young birds that
are hatched at the same time.
[**Brood** comes from Old English.]

**brood** *verb* **broods, brooding, brooded**
(th)
1 To **brood** means to think and worry
about something a lot.

2 When a bird **broods**, it sits on its eggs to
hatch them.

**brook** *noun* **brooks** (th)
A **brook** is a small stream.
[**Brook** comes from Old English.]

**broom** *noun* **brooms**
A **broom** is a brush with a long handle for
sweeping the floor.
[**Broom** comes from Old English.]

**broth** *noun*
Broth is thin soup.
[**Broth** comes from Old English.]

**brother** *noun* **brothers**
Your **brother** is a male child of your
parents.
[**Brother** comes from Old English.]

**brother-in-law** *noun* **brothers-in-law**
Your **brother-in-law** is the brother of your
husband or wife, or the husband of your
sister.

**brought** *verb*
Brought is the past tense and past
participle of **bring**.

**brow** *noun* **brows**
1 The **brow** on your face is your forehead.
2 The **brow** of a hill or other high place is
the top of it.
[**Brow** comes from Old English.]

**brown** *noun* **browns**
Brown is the colour of earth, wood or
chocolate.
[**Brown** comes from Old English.]

**brown** *adjective*
of the colour of earth, wood or chocolate.

**browse** *verb* **browses, browsing,
browsed**
To **browse** means to look through
something or look around a shop in a
casual way.
[**Browse** comes from an old French word.]

**bruise** *noun* **bruises**
A **bruise** is a coloured mark on the skin
caused by a hard knock.
[**Bruise** comes from Old English.]

**brunette** *adjective*
If your hair is **brunette**, it is a dark brown
colour.
[**Brunette** comes from French *brun*
'brown'.]

**brush** *noun* **brushes**
A **brush** is a tool with bristles and, usually, a short handle, used for sweeping, painting, or brushing hair.
[**Brush** comes from an old French word.]

**brush** *verb* **brushes, brushing, brushed**
1 To **brush** something means to clean it or make it tidy by using a brush.
2 To **brush** means to touch lightly: *He brushed past me.*

**Brussels sprout** *noun* **Brussels sprouts**
A **Brussels sprout** is a vegetable like a very small green cabbage.
[**Brussels sprouts** are named after *Brussels,* the capital of Belgium.]

**brute** *noun* **brutes** (th)
A **brute** is a cruel rough person.
[**Brute** comes via French from Latin *brutus* 'stupid'.]

**bubble** *noun* **bubbles**
A **bubble** is a small ball of liquid filled with air.

**bubble** *verb* **bubbles, bubbling, bubbled** (th)
To **bubble** means to make bubbles.
[The word **bubble** is an imitation of the sound.]

**buccaneer** *noun* **buccaneers**
**Buccaneer** is an old-fashioned word for a pirate.
[**Buccaneer** comes via French from Tupi (a South American Indian language).]

**buck** *noun* **bucks**
A **buck** is a male of some animals such as deer, goats or rabbits.

**buck** *verb* **bucks, bucking, bucked**
If a horse **bucks**, it jumps or kicks wildly.
[**Buck** comes from Old English.]

**bucket** *noun* **buckets**
A **bucket** is a container with a handle for carrying liquids.
[**Bucket** comes from an old French word which may have come from Old English.]

**buckle**[1] *noun* **buckles**
A **buckle** is a fastener on a belt or strap.
[**Buckle**[1] comes from Latin *buccula* 'cheek strap or a helmet'.]

**buckle**[1] *verb* **buckles, buckling, buckled** (th)
To **buckle** means to fasten with a buckle: *She buckled her belt.*

**buckle**[2] *verb* **buckles, buckling, buckled**
To **buckle** means to bend or crumple: *Her legs buckled and she fell to the ground.*
[**Buckle**[2] comes from French *boucler* 'to bulge'.]

**bud** *noun* **buds**
A **bud** is a flower or leaf before it has opened fully.
[No one knows where **bud** come from.]

**Buddhism** *noun*
**Buddhism** is a religion from Asia. It is based on the teachings of Gautama Bhudda, who lived in the 6th century BC in India.
[*Buddha* means 'the wise one' in Sanskrit (a very old Indian language).]

**Buddhist** *noun* **Buddhists**
A **Buddhist** is a person who follows the teachings of Buddhism.

**budge** *verb* **budges, budging, budged**
To **budge** is to move from a position in which someone or something is stuck: *The piano is too heavy, it won't budge.*
[**Budge** comes from French.]

**budgerigar** *noun* **budgerigars**
A **budgerigar** is a brightly coloured Australian bird that is often kept as a pet.
[**Budgerigar** comes from Australian Aboriginal *budgeri gar* 'good cockatoo'.]

**budget** *noun* **budgets**
1 A **budget** is a plan for how a person or organisation is going to spend money.
2 The **budget** for something is the amount of money that you can spend on it.
[**Budget** comes from old French *bougette* 'purse'.]

**buffalo** *noun* **buffaloes**
A **buffalo** is a kind of large ox with big horns.
[**Buffalo** comes from Greek via Portuguese and Latin.]

**buffet**[1] *noun* **buffets**
1 A **buffet** is a meal in which there are a lot of different dishes laid out on a table and people can help themselves.
2 A **buffet** is a small café, usually at a railway station.
[**Buffet**[1] comes from French.]

**buffet**[2] *verb* **buffets, buffeting, buffeted**
To **buffet** something means to hit it very hard: *Waves buffeted the shore.*
[**Buffet**[2] comes from old French *bufe* 'a

blow'.]

**bug** *noun* **bugs**
1 A **bug** is any kind of small insect.
2 A **bug** is an illness that is usually not very serious: *a stomach bug.*
3 A **bug** is a fault in something, such as a computer program, that stops it working properly.
4 A **bug** is a small hidden microphone used to record people's conversations secretly.
[No one knows where **bug** comes from.]

**bug** *verb* **bugs, bugging, bugged**
1 To **bug** someone means to annoy him/her.
2 To **bug** a place means to hide a microphone there so that people's conversations can be secretly recorded.

**bugle** *noun* **bugles**
A **bugle** is a musical instrument like a small trumpet that is often used in the army by soldiers.
[No one knows where **bugle** comes from.]

**build** *verb* **builds, building, built** (th)
To **build** means to make something by putting parts together.
[**Build** comes from Old English.]

**building** *noun* **buildings**
A **building** is something that has been built, such as a house, factory or shop.

**bulb** *noun* **bulbs**
1 A **bulb** is the root of some flowers and plants. It is shaped like an onion.
2 A **bulb** is the glass part of an electric light or torch that lights up when you switch it on.
[**Bulb** comes via Latin from Greek *bolbos* 'onion'.]

**bulge** *verb* **bulges, bulging, bulged**
To **bulge** means to swell or stick out in a round shape: *Her pocket bulged with sweets.*
[**Bulge** comes via French from Latin *bulga* 'bag'.]

**bulk** *noun*
If you buy something in **bulk**, you buy a lot of it at the same time.
[**Bulk** comes from Old English.]

**bulky** *adjective* **bulkier, bulkiest** (th)
If something is **bulky**, it is large or awkward to carry.

**bull** *noun* **bulls**
A **bull** is the adult male of animals such as a cow, seal, elephant or whale.
[**Bull** comes from Old English.]

**bulldozer** *noun* **bulldozers**
A **bulldozer** is a powerful tractor used for moving earth or flattening the ground.
[No one knows where **bulldozer** comes from.]

**bullet** *noun* **bullets**
A **bullet** is a small ball of metal that is shot from a gun.
[**Bullet** comes via French *boulet* 'small ball' from the same Latin word as **bowl**².]

**bulletin** *noun* **bulletins**
A **bulletin** is a short report of the news on the radio or television.
[**Bulletin** comes via French and Italian from the same Latin word as **bill**¹.]

**bullion** *noun*
**Bullion** is bars of gold or silver.
[**Bullion** comes from Latin via French.]

**bullock** *noun* **bullocks**
A **bullock** is a castrated bull.
[**Bullock** comes from Old English.]

**bullseye** *noun* **bullseyes**
A **bullseye** is the small circle at the centre of a target.

**bully** *noun* **bullies**
A **bully** is someone who tries to hurt or frighten a smaller or weaker person.
[**Bully** probably comes from a Dutch word.]

**bully** *verb* **bullies, bullying, bullied** (th)
To **bully** means to try to hurt or frighten a smaller or weaker person.

**bulrush** *noun* **bulrushes**
**Bulrushes** are plants like tall thick reeds that grow beside a river or wet ground.
[**Bulrush** probably comes from **bull** (suggesting something large, like a bull), and **rush**².]

**bump** *noun* **bumps**
A **bump** is a lump or swelling.
[**Bump** probably comes from a Scandinavian word that imitated the sound of things bumping into each other.]

**bump** *verb* **bumps, bumping, bumped**
To **bump** means to knock into or against something by accident.

**bumper** *noun* **bumpers**
A **bumper** is a bar at the front and back of a car that can take some of the shock if it

a **b** c d e f g h i j k l m

hits something.

**bumpy** *adjective* **bumpier, bumpiest**
Something that is **bumpy** has a lot of bumps.

**bun** *noun* **buns**
1 A **bun** is a small soft cake or bread roll.
2 If you wear your hair in a **bun**, you wind it into a tight round shape and fasten it at the back or top of your head.
[No one knows where **bun** comes from.]

**bunch** *noun* **bunches** (th)
A **bunch** is a group of things held or tied together: *a bunch of flowers*.
[No one knows where **bunch** comes from.]

**bundle** *noun* **bundles** (th)
A **bundle** is a group of things tied or wrapped together.
[**Bundle** probably comes from an old German or Dutch word.]

**bundle** *verb* **bundles, bundling, bundled**
1 To **bundle** things **up** means to tie or wrap them up together quickly or untidily: *She bundled up her clothes and thrust them into a bag.*
2 If you **bundle** a person into or out of a place, you push him/her there quickly or roughly: *The police bundled him into the car.*

**bungalow** *noun* **bungalows**
A **bungalow** is a house with only a ground floor and no upstairs rooms.
[**Bungalow** comes from Hindi (a language spoken in India).]

**bungee jumping** *noun*
**Bungee jumping** is a sport in which you jump from a high place and bounce up and down on a long thick elastic cord tied to your legs.
[No one knows where **bungee** comes from.]

**bunk** *noun* **bunks**
1 A **bunk** is a bed in a ship or train.
2 **Bunks** or **bunk beds** are beds built one above the other.
[No one knows where **bunk** comes from.]

**bunker** *noun* **bunkers**
A **bunker** is a place underground where people can shelter from bomb attacks.
[No one knows where **bunker** comes from.]

**buoy** *noun* **buoys**
A **buoy** is a round object that floats in the sea and marks something dangerous, or shows where it is safe to go.
[**Buoy** probably comes from an old Dutch word.]

**buoyant** *adjective*
If something is **buoyant**, it is able to float easily.
[**Buoyant** probably comes via Spanish from the same old Dutch word as **buoy**.]

**burden** *noun* **burdens** (th)
1 A **burden** is a heavy load that someone has to carry.
2 A **burden** is a problem or responsibility that causes a lot of work or worry.
[**Burden** comes from Old English.]

**burger** *noun* **burgers**
A **burger** is a small, flat cake of meat which is usually served in a bread roll.
[**Burger** is short for **hamburger**.]

**burglar** *noun* **burglars**
A **burglar** is someone who breaks into people's houses and steals things.
[**Burglar** comes from French.]

**burgle** *verb* **burgles, burgling, burgled**
To **burgle** means to break into people's houses and steal things.
[**Burgle** comes from **burglar**.]

**burly** *adjective* **burlier, burliest** (th)
A **burly** person is large and strong: *a burly firefighter*.
[**Burly** comes from Old English.]

**burn** *verb* **burns, burning, burned** *or* **burnt** (th)
1 To **burn** means to hurt or damage someone or something by fire, heat or acid.
2 To **burn** something means to set fire to it so that you can use the heat or energy the fire produces.
3 To **burn** means to be on fire.
[**Burn** comes from Old English.]

**burrow** *noun* **burrows**
A **burrow** is a hole in the ground made by an animal for it to live in.
[**Burrow** comes from Old English.]

**burst** *verb* **bursts, bursting, burst**
To **burst** means to explode or break open.
[**Burst** comes from Old English.]

**bury** *verb* **buries, burying, buried**
To **bury** means to put something in a hole in the ground and cover it.

[**Bury** comes from the same Old English word as **burrow**.]

**bus** noun **buses**
A **bus** is a large road vehicle that people travel in.
[**Bus** comes from Latin *omnibus* 'for all' (because anyone can travel on one).]

**bush** noun **bushes**
1 A **bush** is a shrub or plant like a small tree.
2 The **bush** is an area of wild land in Australia or Africa.
[**Bush** comes from an old French word.]

**bushy** adjective **bushier, bushiest**
Something that is **bushy** grows thickly: *a bushy beard.*

**business** noun **businesses** (th)
1 A **business** is the type of work someone does to earn a living: *She's in the hotel business.*
2 A **business** is a shop, industry or firm.
3 **Business** is buying and selling goods and services: *Our firm does a lot of business with Eastern Europe.*
4 Something that is your **business** is nothing to do with anyone else.
[**Business** comes from Old English *bisignis* 'busyness'.]

**busker** noun **buskers**
A **busker** is someone who sings or plays music in the street in order to get money from people passing by.
[**Busker** comes from an old word *busk* 'to sell things in the street', which comes from Italian or Spanish via French.]

**bust** noun **busts**
1 A woman's **bust** is her chest or breasts.
2 A **bust** is a statue of someone's head and shoulders.
[**Bust** comes from Latin via French.]

**bustle** noun
A **bustle** is great activity: *There was a bustle to get the festival organised.*
[**Bustle** probably comes from Old Norse.]

**busy** adjective **busier, busiest** (th)
1 Someone who is **busy** has a lot to do.
2 A place that is **busy** has a lot going on: *a busy market.*
[**Busy** comes from Old English.]

**but** conjunction
1 You use **but** when you are about to say something that is different or opposite to something you have just said: *It was hard work, but it was worth it.*
2 You use **but** when you are about to talk about a different subject: *Later we'll have a report on the Health Service. But first, the news headlines.*
3 You use **but** after expressions such as *I'm sorry* or *Excuse me: I'm sorry, but I can't come today; Excuse me, but aren't you Linda's father?*
4 You say **but** at the start of your reply to something that has surprised you and pleased you or shocked you: *"She thinks you don't like her." "But that's ridiculous!"*
[**But** comes from Old English.]

**but** preposition
1 except: *Everyone had gone but John; All but three of the children had colds.*
2 **But for** means except for the efforts of a particular person or the effect of a particular thing: *But for him, we would have been stranded.*

**butcher** noun **butchers**
A **butcher** is someone who prepares and sells meat.
[**Butcher** comes from an old French word.]

**butt¹** noun **butts**
A **butt** is the thick end of something: *a rifle butt.* [**Butt¹** comes from Dutch.]

**butt²** noun **butts**
A **butt** is a large barrel for collecting or storing water. [**Butt²** comes from Latin.]

**butt³** verb **butts, butting, butted**
To **butt** means to hit using the head or horns.
[**Butt³** comes from an old French word.]

**butter** noun
**Butter** is a food made from cream that you can spread on bread or use in cooking.
[**Butter** comes from Old English.]

**buttercup** noun **buttercups**
A **buttercup** is a small yellow wild flower.

**butterfly** noun **butterflies**
A **butterfly** is an insect with large coloured wings.
[**Butterfly** may come from an old belief that the insects stole butter.]

**buttocks** noun
Your **buttocks** are the two fleshy parts of the body that you sit on.
[**Buttocks** comes from Old English.]

**button** *noun* **buttons**
1 A **button** is a small round object sewn to clothes to fasten them.
2 A **button** is a small object on a machine that you press to make it start or stop.
[**Button** comes from an old French word.]

**buy** *verb* **buys, buying, bought**
To **buy** something means to get it by giving money for it.
[**Buy** comes from Old English.]

**buzz** *noun* **buzzes**
A **buzz** is the noise that bees make.

**buzz** *verb* **buzzes, buzzing, buzzed**
To **buzz** means to make the noise of a bee.
[The word **buzz** is an imitation of the sound.]

**by** *adverb*
1 past: *She walked by without looking at him.*
2 saved for later: *We've put some money by for our holidays.*
[**By** comes from Old English.]

**by** *preposition*
1 near or next to: *the house by the bridge; Sit here by me.*
2 using: *Travel by train; They got in by the back door; Pick it up by the handle.*
3 past: *I go by her house every day.*
4 before or not later than: *I need it by Tuesday.*
5 during: *We hid by day and travelled by night.*
6 You use **by** to show who or what does something or causes something: *She was stung by a bee; The car was destroyed by fire.*
7 You use **by** when you are talking about multiplying or dividing numbers: *20 divided by 4 is 5.*

**bypass** *noun* **bypasses**
A **bypass** is a road that goes around a town instead of through the centre.

**byte** *noun* **bytes**
A **byte** is a unit of information in a computer's memory.
[**Byte** is a made-up word based on **bit**² and **bite**.]

---

# Dictionary Fun

### Complete the proverbs
1. B_____ is only skin deep.
2. B_____ of a feather flock together.

### What do these idioms mean?
1. On the ball
2. To beat about the bush
3. To have a bee in one's bonnet

### Homographs
Which '**b**' words are homographs? (Clue: You might do one of these in front of an audience.)

### Complete the similes
1. As busy as a b_____.
2. As blind as a b _____.
   Make up your own '**b**' similes.

### Etymology
1. Which '**b**' word meaning a small tree comes from the Japanese language?
2. How are the words **bicycle** and **bilingual** related?

### Work it out
Which word towards the end of the '**b**' list is onomatopoeic?

### Did you know?
◆ The **bikini** was named after a small coral island where an atom bomb was exploded in 1946, and was so named because of its 'explosive' effect.
◆ The word **bonfire** is derived from *bone fire* – bones used to be the main material used.

---

n o p q r s t u v w x y z

# Cc

**cab** *noun* **cabs**
    1 A **cab** is a taxi.
    2 A **cab** is the compartment for the driver in a truck, train or other large vehicle.
    [**Cab** is short for *cabriolet*, a light carriage pulled by one horse, which comes from French.]

**cabbage** *noun* **cabbages**
    A **cabbage** is a round vegetable with a lot of green or purple leaves.
    [**Cabbage** comes from an old French word.]

**cabin** *noun* **cabins** (th)
    1 A **cabin** is a hut.
    2 A **cabin** is a room in a ship or plane.
    [**Cabin** comes from Latin via French.]

**cabinet** *noun* **cabinets**
    1 A **cabinet** is a cupboard with shelves or drawers and doors.
    2 A **cabinet** is a group of important ministers in a government.
    [**Cabinet** comes from **cabin**.]

**cable** *noun* **cables**
    1 A **cable** is a thick strong wire or rope.
    2 A **cable** is a group of wires protected in a plastic tube that carry or send electricity.
    [**Cable** comes from Latin via French.]

**cackle** *verb* **cackles, cackling, cackled**
    To **cackle** means to make the sound that a hen makes.
    [The word **cackle** is an imitation of the sound.]

**cacophony** *noun* **cacophonies** (th)
    A **cacophony** is a loud, unpleasant sound, especially when a lot of things or people are making a noise at the same time.
    [**Cacophony** comes via French from Greek *kakaphonia* 'a bad sound'.]

**cactus** *noun* **cacti** *or* **cactuses**
    A **cactus** is a prickly plant found in the desert.
    [**Cactus** comes from Greek via Latin.]

**cadet** *noun* **cadets**
    A **cadet** is a young person who is training to serve in the army, navy, air force or police. [**Cadet** comes from French.]

**café** *noun* **cafés**
    A **café** is a place that sells drinks, snacks and meals.
    [**Café** is a French word meaning 'coffee' or 'coffee house'.]

**cafeteria** *noun* **cafeterias**
    A **cafeteria** is a restaurant or café where you serve yourself from a counter and then take your food to a table.
    [**Cafeteria** comes from American Spanish *cafetería* 'coffee shop'.]

**caffeine** *noun*
    **Caffeine** is a substance in coffee and tea that makes you more active.
    [**Caffeine** comes from French *café* 'coffee'.]

**cage** *noun* **cages**
    A **cage** is a box or room with bars across it for keeping animals and birds in.
    [**Cage** comes from Latin via French.]

**cake** *noun* **cakes** (th)
    1 A **cake** is a mixture of flour, butter, eggs and sugar that is baked.
    2 A **cake** of something is a small flat lump of it: *a cake of soap*.
    [**Cake** comes from a Scandinavian language.]

**cake** *verb* **cakes, caking, caked**
    If you are **caked** in something like mud, you are covered in it.

**calamity** *noun* **calamities** (th)
    A **calamity** is something terrible that has happened.
    [**Calamity** comes from Latin via French.]

**calcium** *noun*
    **Calcium** is a chemical element that is found in bones and teeth, and some kinds of rock. [**Calcium** comes from Latin.]

**calculate** *verb* **calculates, calculating, calculated** (th)
    To **calculate** a sum means to work out the answer. [**Calculate** comes from Latin.]

**calculator** *noun* **calculators**
    A **calculator** is a small electronic machine that can do sums.

**calendar** *noun* **calendars**
    A **calendar** is a chart showing the months and days of the year.
    [**Calendar** comes via French from Latin *kalendae* 'the first day of the month'.]

**calf**[1] *noun* **calves**
    A **calf** is the young of some animals such as cows, elephants, whales or seals.

[**Calf¹** comes from Old English.]

**calf² noun calves**
Your **calf** is the back part of your leg between your knee and your ankle.
[**Calf²** comes from Old Norse.]

**calico noun**
**Calico** is a rough cotton material.
[**Calico** is named after *Calicut*, a town in India from which the material was sent abroad.]

**call noun calls**
1 A **call** is a shout.
2 A **call** is a conversation on the telephone.
3 A bird's or animal's **call** is the sound it makes. [**Call** comes from Old Norse.]

**call verb calls, calling, called** (th)
1 To **call** means to shout something out, especially to shout out someone's name to make him/her come to you.
2 To **call** means to give someone or something a name: *We're going to call the baby Stephen; a black cat called Sooty.*
3 To **call** someone something means to say that s/he is that thing: *She called me a liar.*
4 To **call** someone means to telephone him/her: *I'll call you on Sunday.*

**calligraphy noun**
**Calligraphy** is the art of writing beautifully with a special pen or brush.
[**Calligraphy** comes from Greek *kalos* 'beauty' and *graphein* 'to write'.]

**callous adjective** (th)
Someone who is **callous** is cruel and does not care about hurting people.
[**Callous** comes from Latin *callus* 'hard skin'.]

**calm adjective calmer, calmest** (th)
1 Something that is **calm** is quiet or still.
2 Something or someone who is **calm** is not excited or anxious.
[**Calm** comes from Greek *kauma* 'the hot time of the day', when people rested.]

**calorie noun calories**
1 A **calorie** is a unit for measuring the energy that is in food.
2 A **calorie** is a unit for measuring heat.
[**Calorie** comes from Latin *calor* 'heat'.]

**calypso noun calypsos**
A **calypso** is a Caribbean song or dance with a strong rhythm.
[No one knows where the word **calypso** comes from.]

**camcorder noun camcorders**
A **camcorder** is a video camera that you can carry with you to record pictures and sound.
[**Camcorder** comes from **camera** and **record**.]

**came verb**
**Came** is the past tense of **come**.

**camel noun camels**
A **camel** is a large animal with one or two humps on its back that lives in hot countries or deserts. A *dromedary* has one hump, and a *bactrian camel* has two.
[**Camel** comes from Greek via Latin.]

**cameo noun cameos**
A **cameo** is a plain-coloured brooch or piece of stone with a picture of someone carved on it in a different colour.
[**Cameo** comes from an old French word.]

**camera noun cameras**
A **camera** is a piece of equipment for taking photographs, films or videos.
[**Camera** comes from Latin.]

**camouflage verb camouflages, camouflaging, camouflaged**
To **camouflage** something means to cover it or colour it so that it blends into the background.
[**Camouflage** comes from French *camoufler* 'to disguise'.]

**camouflage noun**
**Camouflage** is colours or patterns that make something, such as an animal, harder to see.

**camp noun camps**
A **camp** is a group of tents or huts where people live, usually for a short time.
[**Camp** comes via French and Italian from Latin *campus* 'field, level ground'.]

**camp verb camps, camping, camped**
To **camp** means to stay in a tent.

**campaign noun campaigns**
A **campaign** is a series of things that you do to try to win something or to change something.
[**Campaign** comes from the same Latin word as **camp**.]

**can¹** *noun* **cans**
A **can** is a metal container, usually for food or drink.
[**Can¹** comes from Old English *canne* 'container for liquids'.]

**can²** *verb* **can, could**
**1** If you **can** do something, you are able to do it: *I can speak German*; *Can you reach the ceiling?*
**2** If you **can** do something, you are allowed to do it: *Can I come to your party?*
[**Can²** comes from Old English *cunnan* 'to know how to'.]

**canal** *noun* **canals**
A **canal** is a long narrow waterway that has been made by people.
[**Canal** comes from Latin *canalis*.]

**canary** *noun* **canaries**
A **canary** is a small yellow bird. **Canaries** are often kept as pets.
[**Canaries** originally came from the *Canary Islands*, near the north-west coast of Africa.]

**cancel** *verb* **cancels, cancelling, cancelled** (th)
To **cancel** something means to say that it is not going to happen any more: *They cancelled the school disco.*
[**Cancel** comes from Latin *cancellare* 'to scratch out'.]

**cancer** *noun* **cancers**
**Cancer** is a serious disease. It makes the cells in your body grow in a bad way.
[**Cancer** comes from Latin.]

**candle** *noun* **candles**
A **candle** is a stick of wax with a string, called a wick, through the centre. When you light the wick, the **candle** burns and gives light.
[**Candle** comes via Old English from Latin *candere* 'to shine'.]

**cane** *noun* **canes**
**1** A **cane** is a stick, such as a walking stick.
**2** The hollow stem of bamboo or a similar plant is called a **cane**.
[**Cane** comes from Greek via French and Latin.]

**canine** *noun* **canines**
A **canine** or **canine tooth** is a pointed tooth. Human adults have four **canines**.

[**Canine** comes from Latin *canis* 'dog', because dogs and other carnivores have large canines.]

**canine** *adjective*
**Canine** means to do with dogs.

**cannon** *noun* **cannons**
A **cannon** is a large heavy gun that fires heavy metal balls.
[**Cannon** comes via French from Italian *cannone* 'big tube'.]

**canoe** *noun* **canoes**
A **canoe** is a light narrow boat with pointed ends. You make a **canoe** move with paddles.
[**Canoe** comes via Spanish from Carib (a South American Indian language).]

**canopy** *noun* **canopies**
A **canopy** is a cover or a shelter, often made from cloth.
[**Canopy** comes from Greek *konopeion* 'a bed with a net to keep off mosquitoes'.]

**canteen** *noun* **canteens**
A **canteen** is a big dining-room in a school or a factory.
[**Canteen** comes from Italian via French.]

**canter** *verb* **canters, cantering, cantered**
When a horse **canters**, it gallops slowly.
[**Canter** is short for *Canterbury gallop*, the pace used by pilgrims riding to the city of *Canterbury* in Kent.]

**canvas** *noun* **canvases**
**1** **Canvas** is a kind of strong material. Tents are made from **canvas**.
**2** A **canvas** is a piece of this material that an artist uses for painting on.
[**Canvas** comes from Latin.]

**canyon** *noun* **canyons**
A **canyon** is a deep river valley with steep sides.
[**Canyon** comes from Spanish *cañón* 'tube'.]

**cap** *noun* **caps**
**1** A **cap** is a soft hat with a peak: *a baseball cap*; *a tweed cap*.
**2** A **cap** is a lid or a top for something: *a bottle cap*; *a pen cap*.
[**Cap** comes from Latin *cappa* 'hood'.]

**capable** *adjective* (th)
**1** If you are **capable** of doing something,

you have the power or skill to do it: *I think you're capable of reading that book.*
**2** If you are **capable**, you are good at something, or can do it well: *a capable cook.*
[**Capable** comes from Latin via French.]

## capacity *noun* capacities
The **capacity** of a container is the amount that it can hold.
[**Capacity** comes via French from Latin *capere* 'to take or hold' (ancestor of **captive** and **catch**).]

## cape¹ *noun* capes
A **cape** is a short cloak.
[**Cape**¹ comes from the same Latin word as **cap**.]

## cape² *noun* capes
A **cape** is an area of land that sticks out into the sea.
[**Cape**² comes from the same Latin word as **capital**.]

## caper¹ *noun* capers
**Capers** are small buds from a plant. They are pickled and used in cooking.
[**Caper**¹ comes from Greek via French or Latin.]

## caper² *verb* capers, capering, capered (th)
To **caper** means to dance or run about.
[**Caper**² comes from Latin *caper* 'goat'.]

## capital *noun* capitals
**1** The **capital** of a country is the most important city in it, usually where the government is based.
**2** A **capital** is a large letter, such as A, B, C, used at the beginning of names and sentences.
[**Capital** comes via French from Latin *caput* 'head'.]

## capsize *verb* capsizes, capsizing, capsized
If a boat **capsizes**, it turns upside down in the water.
[No one knows where **capsize** comes from.]

## capsule *noun* capsules
**1** A **capsule** is a small case with medicine in that you swallow.
**2** A **capsule** is the part of a spacecraft in which people travel.
[**Capsule** comes from Latin *capsa* 'box'.]

## captain *noun* captains
**1** A **captain** is a leader in charge of a team.
**2** A **captain** is an officer in the army, navy or air force.
[**Captain** comes via French from the same Latin word as **capital**.]

## captive *noun* captives (th)
A **captive** is someone who has been caught and put in a prison.
[**Captive** comes from Latin *capere* 'to take' (ancestor of **capacity** and **catch**).]

## captive *adjective* (th)
If you are **captive**, you have been caught and you cannot escape.

## capture *verb* captures, capturing, captured (th)
**1** To **capture** someone means to take him or her prisoner.
**2** To **capture** a place means to take it by using force.
[**Capture** comes via French from the same Latin word as **captive**.]

## car *noun* cars
A **car** is a vehicle with four wheels that goes on roads.
[**Car** comes via French from Latin *carrus* 'vehicle with wheels'.]

## caravan *noun* caravans
A **caravan** is a vehicle that you can live in and that can be pulled by a car or a horse.
[**Caravan** comes via French from Persian (the language spoken in Iran).]

## carbohydrate *noun* carbohydrates
**Carbohydrates** are in food such as pasta and bread. Your body needs **carbohydrates** for energy.
[**Carbohydrate** comes from **carbon** and Greek *hydor* 'water'.]

## carbon *noun*
**Carbon** is an element that is found in diamonds, coal and petrol. All living things contain **carbon**.
[**Carbon** comes from Latin *carbo* 'coal'.]

## carbon dioxide *noun*
**Carbon dioxide** is a gas that you cannot see or smell. Humans and animals breathe out **carbon dioxide**.
[**Dioxide** comes from Greek *di-* 'two' and English *oxide* 'a substance containing oxygen' (because carbon dioxide contains two atoms of oxygen).]

**carcass** *noun* **carcasses** *Also* **carcase**
A **carcass** is the body of a dead animal, especially one that is to be used for food. [**Carcass** comes from French.]

**card** *noun* **cards**
1 **Card** is stiff paper.
2 A **card** is a piece of card or plastic with writing or pictures on it, such as a Christmas card or a credit card.
3 A **card** is a small rectangular piece of card that is part of a pack. You can play games such as rummy or snap with **cards**. [**Card** comes from Latin *charta* 'papyrus leaf, paper' (ancestor of **cartoon** and **chart**).]

**cardboard** *noun*
**Cardboard** is thick card or very thick strong paper: *a cardboard box.*

**cardigan** *noun* **cardigans**
A **cardigan** is a knitted sweater or jacket with buttons down the front. [The **cardigan** is named after Lord *Cardigan*, a general in the Crimean war, in which soldiers wore knitted jackets.]

**cardinal number** *noun* **cardinal numbers**
A **cardinal number** is a number that tells you how many things or people there are. *One, two* and *ten* are all **cardinal numbers**. [**Cardinal** comes from Latin.]

**care** *noun* **cares** (th)
1 If you do something with **care**, you take time and trouble over it.
2 To **take care** means to be careful.
3 If you **take care of** someone, you look after that person. [**Care** comes from Old English.]

**care** *verb* **cares, caring, cared** (th)
1 To **care** or **care about** something means to mind about it: *people who care about animal rights.*
2 To **care for** someone means to like him/her a lot.
3 To **care for** someone means to look after him/her.

**career** *noun* **careers**
A **career** is a series of jobs that someone does in their working lives, especially when each job is more important than the one before. [**Career** comes from Latin via French.]

**careful** *adjective* (th)
Someone who is **careful** does things safely, well or with care. **carefully** *adverb*.

**careless** *adjective* (th)
Someone who is **careless** does not take care or trouble about what s/he is doing. **carelessly** *adverb*. **carelessness** *noun*.

**caress** *verb* **caresses, caressing, caressed** (th)
To **caress** someone means to touch him/her gently and lovingly. [**Caress** comes via French and Italian from Latin *carus* 'dear'.]

**cargo** *noun* **cargoes**
A ship's or a plane's **cargo** is the load that it is carrying. [**Cargo** comes via Spanish from the same Latin word as **car**.]

**carnation** *noun* **carnations**
A **carnation** is a flower. **Carnations** can be pink, red or white. [**Carnation** probably comes from Greek via Arabic.]

**carnival** *noun* **carnivals**
A **carnival** is a festival, usually with a procession of people in fancy dress. [**Carnival** comes from Latin *carnis* 'to do with meat', because carnivals were held before Lent, when people gave up eating meat until Easter.]

**carnivore** *noun* **carnivores**
A **carnivore** is an animal that eats meat. [**Carnivore** comes from Latin *carnis* 'to do with meat' and *vorare* 'to devour'.]

**carnivorous** *adjective*
A **carnivorous** animal is one that eats meat.

**carol** *noun* **carols**
A **carol** is a special Christmas song. [**Carol** comes from an old French word.]

**carpenter** *noun* **carpenters**
A **carpenter** is someone who works with wood, especially someone who makes the wooden parts of a building. [**Carpenter** comes from Latin.]

**carpet** *noun* **carpets**
A **carpet** is a thick, soft cover for the floor. [**Carpet** comes from Latin via French and Italian.]

**carriage** *noun* **carriages**
1 A **carriage** is a vehicle pulled by a horse or horses.
2 A **carriage** is one of the parts that make up a train.
[**Carriage** comes from the same old French word as **carry**.]

**carrot** *noun* **carrots**
A **carrot** is a long orange vegetable.
[**Carrot** comes from Greek via French and Latin.]

**carry** *verb* **carries, carrying, carried** (th)
1 To **carry** means to lift and move someone or something from one place to another: *He carried the child on his shoulders*.
2 To **carry on** doing something is to keep doing it: *She ignored him and carried on reading*.
3 To **carry out** something, such as a plan, is to do it.
[**Carry** comes via old French *carier* from the same Latin word as **car**.]

**cart** *noun* **carts**
A **cart** is a small vehicle for goods that is pulled by a person or a horse.
[**Cart** comes via Old Norse from the same Latin word as **car**.]

**carton** *noun* **cartons**
A **carton** is a cardboard or plastic box.
[**Carton** comes via French from the same Italian word as **cartoon**.]

**cartoon** *noun* **cartoons**
1 A **cartoon** is a film made from drawings.
2 A **cartoon** is a funny drawing or a series of funny drawings.
[**Cartoon** comes via Italian from Latin *carta* 'papyrus leaf, paper' (ancestor of **card** and **chart**).]

**cartwheel** *noun* **cartwheels**
If you do a **cartwheel**, you throw yourself onto your hands and then round so that you are on your feet again.

**carve** *verb* **carves, carving, carved** (th)
To **carve** something means to cut it, or to cut slices from it.
[**Carve** comes from Old English.]

**cascade** *verb* **cascades, cascading, cascaded**
To **cascade** means to fall or flow down like a waterfall.

[**Cascade** comes via French from Italian *cascare* 'to fall', from the same Latin word as **casual**.]

**case** *noun* **cases**
A **case** is a bag or container for carrying or keeping things in: *a suitcase; a packing case; a pillowcase*.
[**Case** comes via French from the same Latin word as **capsule** and **cash**.]

**cash** *noun*
**Cash** is coins or paper money.
[**Cash** originally meant a money box, and comes via French or Italian from Latin *capsa* 'box' (ancestor of **capsule**).]

**cashew** *noun* **cashews**
A **cashew** is a small curved nut.
[**Cashew** comes via Portuguese from Tupi (a South American Indian language).]

**cashier** *noun* **cashiers**
A **cashier** is a person in a bank or a shop who takes or gives out money.

**cashpoint** *noun* **cashpoints**
A **cashpoint** is a machine, usually on the wall outside a bank. You use a special card to take money out of your bank account.

**cash register** *noun* **cash registers**
A **cash register** is a machine, used in a shop, that records how much money is put in it.

**casket** *noun* **caskets**
A **casket** is a box, especially one for jewellery.
[**Casket** comes via French from the same Latin word as **capsule** and **cash**.]

**casserole** *noun* **casseroles**
1 A **casserole** is a stew of meat and vegetables.
2 A **casserole** or a **casserole dish** is a pot with a lid used for cooking.
[**Casserole** comes from Greek via French and Latin.]

**cassette** *noun* **cassettes**
A **cassette** is a plastic case with a tape inside it for playing or recording music.
[**Cassette** comes from the same French word as **casket**.]

**cassette recorder** *noun* **cassette recorders**
A **cassette recorder** is a machine that you

can use if you want to listen to tapes or record something onto a tape.

**cast** *noun* **casts**
1 The **cast** of a play is all the people who are acting in it.
2 A **cast** is a hard covering of plaster put on a broken arm or leg while it heals.
[**Cast** comes from Old Norse.]

**cast** *verb* **casts, casting, cast**
1 To **cast** something means to throw it or scatter it.
2 To **cast** something means to make it by shaping it while it is wet or molten and leaving it to set.
3 To **cast** a play means to choose who is to play all the different parts.

**castaway** *noun* **castaways**
A **castaway** is someone who has been shipwrecked.

**caster sugar** *noun Also* **castor sugar**
Caster sugar is very fine white sugar.
[**Caster** comes from **cast** (because caster sugar was sprinkled or scattered on food).]

**castle** *noun* **castles** (th)
1 A **castle** is a large strong building with thick stone walls to keep enemies out.
2 A **castle** is a piece in the game of chess that can move in any direction except diagonally. It is also called a **rook**.
[**Castle** comes via French from Latin *castrum* 'fort'.]

**castrate** *verb* **castrates, castrating, castrated**
If someone **castrates** a male animal, s/he cuts off its testicles so that it cannot breed.
[**Castrate** comes from Latin.]

**casual** *adjective* (th)
1 **Casual** clothes are clothes that you wear when you do not want to dress smartly.
2 **Casual** means relaxed or not particularly interested in something.
3 **Casual** means happening by chance.
**casually** *adverb*.
[**Casual** comes via French from Latin *casus* 'to happen' or 'to fall'.]

**casualty** *noun* **casualties**
A **casualty** is someone who is hurt or killed in an accident or in a war.
[**Casualty** comes from the same Latin word as **casual**.]

**cat** *noun* **cats**
1 A **cat** is a small furry animal often kept as a pet.
2 A **cat** is a larger animal that is a member of the cat family. Lions and tigers are **cats**.
[**Cat** comes from Old English.]

**catalogue** *noun* **catalogues** (th)
A **catalogue** is a list of things that are in a particular place, or a list of things that you can buy.
[**Catalogue** comes from a Greek word meaning 'to choose'.]

**catapult** *noun* **catapults**
A **catapult** is a weapon for shooting stones. It is a Y-shaped stick with elastic tied to the top.
[**Catapult** comes from a Greek word meaning 'to throw'.]

**catastrophe** *noun* **catastrophes** (th)
A **catastrophe** is something very bad that happens, for example an earthquake.
[**Catastrophe** comes from a Greek word meaning 'turning over or down'.]

**catch** *verb* **catches, catching, caught** (th)
1 To **catch** a person or an animal means to capture them by finding, chasing or trapping them.
2 If you **catch** something like a ball, you get hold of it and stop it from falling.
3 If you **catch** an illness, you get it from someone else: *She caught my cold.*
4 If you find someone doing something wrong, you **catch** him/her doing it: *I caught her stealing my sandwich.*
5 If you manage to get on a bus or a train, you **catch** it.
6 If something **catches** on a hook or something sharp, it gets held or pulled by it.
7 If you **catch up** with someone, you reach that person by moving faster than him/her.
[**Catch** comes via French from Latin *capere* 'to take' (ancestor of **capacity**, **captive** and **chase**).]

**catchy** *adjective* **catchier, catchiest**
If a song or a tune is **catchy**, it is easy to remember.

**category** *noun* **categories** (th)
A **category** is a group of things that are the same in some way: *The books in the library are divided into categories.*

**a b c d e f g h i j k l m**

[Category comes from Greek.]

**caterpillar** noun **caterpillars**
A **caterpillar** is a long, thin, creeping creature. **Caterpillars** turn into butterflies or moths.
[**Caterpillar** comes from an old French word.]

**cathedral** noun **cathedrals**
A **cathedral** is a large important church.
[**Cathedral** comes from Greek.]

**cattle** plural noun
**Cattle** are cows and bulls.
[**Cattle** comes from Latin via French.]

**caught** verb
**Caught** is the past tense and past participle of **catch.**

**cauldron** noun **cauldrons**
A **cauldron** is a large cooking pot used on a fire. **Cauldrons** are often used by witches in stories.
[**Cauldron** comes from *caldarium* 'a hot bath'.]

**cauliflower** noun **cauliflowers**
A **cauliflower** is a vegetable with a hard white flower that you eat.
[**Cauliflower** comes from French *chou fleuri* 'flowered cabbage'.]

**cause** noun **causes** (th)
**1** The **cause** of something is what makes it happen: *Poor hygiene is a major cause of disease.*
**2** A **cause** is something that you believe in and that you will work or fight for.
[**Cause** comes from Latin via French.]

**cause** verb **causes, causing, caused** (th)
To **cause** something means to be the reason why it happens: *Her illness caused her to give up work.*

**cautious** adjective (th)
To be **cautious** means to be careful, especially so that you do not get hurt.
**cautiously** adverb.
[**Cautious** comes from Latin.]

**cave** noun **caves**
A **cave** is a big hole under the ground or in a mountain or cliff.
[**Cave** comes from Latin *cavus* 'hollow'.]

**cavern** noun **caverns**
A **cavern** is a big cave.
[**Cavern** comes via French from the same Latin word as **cave.**]

**cavity** noun **cavities**
A **cavity** is a small hole, especially a hole in your tooth.
[**Cavity** comes via French from the same Latin word as **cave.**]

**CD** noun **CDs**
CD is short for **compact disc** or **compact disk.**

**CD-ROM** noun **CD-ROMs**
A **CD-ROM** is a compact disk that you use on a computer. The disk has programs and information, in the form of words, pictures or sounds, stored on it.
[**CD-ROM** stands for *Compact Disk-Read Only Memory* (because you can only read the information on the disk, not change it).]

**cease** verb **ceases, ceasing, ceased**
If something **ceases**, it stops.
[**Cease** comes from Latin via French.]

**cease-fire** noun **cease-fires**
A **cease-fire** is a time when people who are fighting agree to stop fighting for a while.

**ceiling** noun **ceilings**
A **ceiling** is the top surface or roof of a room.
[No one knows where **ceiling** comes from.]

**celebrate** verb **celebrates, celebrating, celebrated** (th)
To **celebrate** means to do something special and enjoyable, for example because it is your birthday or a holiday.
[**Celebrate** comes from Latin.]

**celebration** noun **celebrations**
A **celebration** is a special occasion such as a party.
[**Celebration** comes from the same Latin word as **celebrate.**]

**celebrity** noun **celebrities**
A **celebrity** is a famous person.
[**Celebrity** comes via French from the same Latin word as **celebrate.**]

**celery** noun
**Celery** is a vegetable with long, pale green stems. It is crunchy if you eat it raw.
[**Celery** comes from Greek via French and Italian.]

## cell noun cells
1 A **cell** is a very small part of an animal or a plant. Your body is made up of millions of **cells**.
2 A **cell** is a room in a prison.
[**Cell** comes from Latin *cella* 'storeroom'.]

## cellar noun cellars
A **cellar** is a room underneath a building, usually used for storing things.
[**Cellar** comes via French from the same Latin word as **cell**.]

## cello noun cellos
A **cello** is a stringed instrument like a large violin.
[**Cello** is short for *violoncello*, which comes from Italian *violone* 'large viola']

## cement noun
**Cement** is a grey powder used to make concrete and mortar for building.
[**Cement** comes from Latin via French.]

## cemetery noun cemeteries
A **cemetery** is a place where dead people are buried.
[**Cemetery** comes via Latin from Greek *koimeterion* 'a place where people sleep'.]

## census noun censuses
A **census** is a count of all the people who live in a country.
[**Census** comes from Latin *censere* 'to estimate or judge'.]

## centaur noun centaurs
A **centaur** is a mythical creature that is made up of the top half of a man and the bottom half of a horse.
[**Centaur** comes via Latin from the Greek name for a tribe of expert horsemen.]

## centimetre noun centimetres
A **centimetre** is a unit of length. There are 100 **centimetres** in one metre.
[**Centimetre** comes from Latin *centum* 'a hundred' and **metre**.]

## centipede noun centipedes
A **centipede** is a small, long, creeping creature with many tiny legs.
[**Centipede** comes from Latin *centum* 'a hundred' and *pedes* 'feet'.]

## central adjective (th)
1 Something that is **central** is in the middle: *Make sure that the picture is central.*
2 A **central** person or thing is important: *a central character in the story.*

[**Central** comes via French from the same Latin word as **centre**.]

## centre noun centres (th)
1 The **centre** of something is the middle of it: *the town centre.*
2 A **centre** is a place where people go to get help or to take part in a particular activity: *a health centre; a sports centre.*
[**Centre** comes via French and Latin from Greek *kentron* 'point of a compass'.]

## centurion noun centurions
A **centurion** in the Roman army was in charge of a hundred soldiers.
[**Centurion** comes from the same Latin word as **century**.]

## century noun centuries
A **century** is a period of 100 years.
[**Century** comes from Latin *centum* 'a hundred'.]

## ceramic adjective
**Ceramic** means made from clay: *ceramic tiles.*
[**Ceramic** comes from Greek *keramos* 'pottery'.]

## cereal noun cereals
1 A **cereal** is a grain that farmers grow to be used as food. Wheat is a **cereal**.
2 A **cereal** is a food made from grain. People often eat **cereals** with milk for breakfast.
[**Cereal** comes from *Ceres*, the name of the Roman goddess of agriculture.]

## ceremony noun ceremonies
A **ceremony** is an important occasion, often with special words and music.
[**Ceremony** comes from Latin *caerimonia* 'ritual'.]

## certain adjective (th)
1 If you are **certain**, you are sure.
2 **Certain** means some or particular: *We were told to stay out of certain rooms.*
**certainly** adverb.
[**Certain** comes from Latin *certus*.]

## certificate noun certificates
A **certificate** is a piece of paper that shows you have achieved something: *a swimming certificate.*
[**Certificate** comes from Latin *certificare* 'to make something certain'.]

## chain noun chains
A **chain** is a row of metal rings linked

a b **c** d e f g h i j k l m

together.
[**Chain** comes from Latin via French.]

**chair** *noun* **chairs**
A **chair** is a seat with a back for one person to sit on.
[**Chair** comes from Greek via French and Latin.]

**chalk** *noun* **chalks**
1 **Chalk** is a soft white rock.
2 A **chalk** is a stick of chalk used for writing and drawing on a board.
[**Chalk** comes from Old English.]

**challenge** *noun* **challenges**
A **challenge** is something that is new and difficult.
[**Challenge** comes from Latin via French.]

**challenge** *verb* **challenges, challenging, challenged** (th)
If you **challenge** someone, you try to make that person fight you or compete with you.

**challenging** *adjective* (th)
Something that is **challenging** is hard for you: *a challenging book.*

**chamber** *noun* **chambers**
A **chamber** is a large room.
[**Chamber** comes from Greek via French and Latin.]

**chameleon** *noun* **chameleons**
A **chameleon** is a kind of lizard that can change colour to match its background.
[**Chameleon** comes from Greek via Latin.]

**champagne** *noun*
**Champagne** is a fizzy white wine. People drink **champagne** on special occasions.
[**Champagne** is named after the *Champagne* region of France, where it is made.]

**champion** *noun* **champions**
A **champion** is someone or something that wins a competition or a sport.
[**Champion** comes via French from Latin *campionis* 'a fighter'.]

**championship** *noun* **championships**
A **championship** is a competition among a lot of people or teams to see who is the best at a sport or game.

**chance** *noun* **chances** (th)
1 A **chance** is an opportunity to do something: *We had a chance to go camping.*

2 A **chance** is a possibility: *There's a slight chance that it will rain.*
3 Something that happens **by chance** doesn't happen on purpose.
[**Chance** comes from an old French word.]

**change** *noun* **changes** (th)
1 A **change** is something different from usual or from what something was like before: *a change in the weather.*
2 If you pay too much money for something in a shop, the shop assistant gives you some money back which is your **change**.
3 **Change** is coins, not banknotes: *I need some change for the bus.*
[**Change** comes from Latin via French.]

**change** *verb* **changes, changing, changed** (th)
1 If something **changes**, it is different from how it used to be: *The town has changed a lot.*
2 If you **change** something, you make it different: *She changed her name.*

**channel** *noun* **channels**
1 A **channel** is a narrow stretch of sea between two areas of land.
2 A **channel** is a trench that holds water.
3 A **channel** is a television or radio station.
[**Channel** comes via French from Latin *canalis* (ancestor of **canal**).]

**Chanukkah** *noun*
**Chanukkah** is another way of spelling **Hanukkah**.

**chaos** *noun* (th)
If there is **chaos**, everyone is confused and everything is in a mess.
[**Chaos** comes from Greek via French and Latin.]

**chapel** *noun* **chapels**
A **chapel** is a small church.
[**Chapel** comes from Latin via French.]

**chapter** *noun* **chapters**
A **chapter** is a part of a book.
[**Chapter** comes from Latin via French.]

**character** *noun* **characters** (th)
1 A **character** is a person in a story or a play.
2 Your **character** is your nature or your personality.
[**Character** comes from Greek via French

and Latin.]

**charcoal** noun
Charcoal is wood that has been burned. You can draw with **charcoal** or use it to make a fire.
[No one knows where **charcoal** comes from.]

**charge** noun **charges**
1 The **charge** for something is the amount that it costs.
2 If you are **in charge** of something, or you **take charge** of something, you are in control of it or looking after it: *I'm in charge of organising the school trip.*
[**Charge** comes from Latin via French.]

**charge** verb **charges, charging, charged** (th)
1 To **charge** a price for something means to ask people to pay that price.
2 To **charge** means to rush forward or to attack.

**chariot** noun **chariots**
A **chariot** is a vehicle with two wheels that is pulled by a horse or horses. **Chariots** were used in the past in battles and in races.
[**Chariot** comes via French from Latin *carrus* (ancestor of **car**).]

**charity** noun **charities**
A **charity** is an organisation that collects money to help people who need it.
[**Charity** comes via French from Latin *caritas* 'love'.]

**charm** noun **charms** (th)
A **charm** is a small object that is supposed to be lucky.
[**Charm** comes via French from Latin *carmen* 'magic spell'.]

**charming** adjective (th)
1 Someone who is **charming** is friendly and pleasant.
2 A **charming** place or thing is attractive and pleasant. **charmingly** adverb.

**chart** noun **charts**
1 A **chart** is a large sheet of paper with information such as a table or diagram on it.
2 A **chart** is a map used by sailors.
[**Chart** comes via French from Latin *charta* 'papyrus leaf, paper' (ancestor of **card** and **cartoon**).]

**chase** verb **chases, chasing, chased** (th)
To **chase** means to run after and try to catch someone or something.
[**Chase** comes via French from Latin *capere* 'to take' (ancestor of **capacity**, **captive** and **catch**).]

**chase** noun **chases**
A **chase** is when someone is trying to catch someone or something: *The film had an exciting car chase in it.*

**chat** verb **chats, chatting, chatted** (th)
To **chat** means to talk, usually about things that aren't very important.
[**Chat** comes from **chatter**.]

**chat** noun **chats**
A **chat** is a friendly talk.

**chatter** verb **chatters, chattering, chattered** (th)
1 If you **chatter**, you talk very quickly, usually about things that are not very important.
2 If your teeth **chatter**, they repeatedly click together because you are cold.
[The word **chatter** is an imitation of the sound.]

**cheap** adjective **cheaper, cheapest** (th)
Something that is **cheap** does not cost very much or costs less than usual.
**cheaply** adverb. **cheapness** noun.
[**Cheap** comes from Old English *ceap* 'a bargain'.]

**cheat** verb **cheats, cheating, cheated** (th)
To **cheat** means to break the rules in order to do better in a game or a test.
[**Cheat** comes from an old French word.]

**cheat** noun **cheats**
A **cheat** is someone who breaks the rules so that s/he can win.

**check**[1] noun **checks**
A **check** is a pattern of coloured squares.
[**Check**[1] comes from *exchequer*, a place where money was counted, originally on a check tablecloth. *Exchequer* meant a chessboard.]

**check**[2] verb **checks, checking, checked** (th)
1 To **check** something means to make sure that it is working properly or is correct.
2 To **check** means to stop someone or something from moving, doing

something, or growing: *measures to check the rise in crime; She began to laugh, but checked herself when she saw his face.*
[**Check**² comes from French *eschequier* 'to put the king in check', which comes via Latin and Arabic from Persian *sah* 'king' (Persian is the language spoken in Iran). In chess, when the king is in check, none of the pieces can move except to get the king out of check.]

**checkout** *noun* **checkouts**
A **checkout** is the counter in a shop where you pay for what you want to buy.

**checkup** *noun* **checkups**
A dentist or a doctor gives you a **checkup** to make sure that nothing is wrong with you.

**cheek** *noun* **cheeks**
1 Your **cheek** is the side of your face below your eye.
2 **Cheek** is rude behaviour.
[**Cheek** comes from Old English.]

**cheeky** *adjective* **cheekier**, **cheekiest** (th)
Someone who is **cheeky** is rude, sometimes in a way that makes people laugh. **cheekily** *adverb*.

**cheer** *noun* **cheers**
A **cheer** is a shout to show that you are pleased, or that you want someone to do well.
[**Cheer** comes from an old French word.]

**cheer** *verb* **cheers**, **cheering**, **cheered**
1 To **cheer** means to shout for someone to do well, or to show that you think something was good.
2 If you **cheer up**, you stop feeling sad.

**cheerful** *adjective* (th)
Someone who is **cheerful** is happy.
**cheerfully** *adverb*. **cheerfulness** *noun*.

**cheese** *noun* **cheeses**
**Cheese** is a white or yellow food made from milk. Edam and Cheddar are kinds of cheese.
[**Cheese** comes from Old English.]

**cheetah** *noun* **cheetahs**
A **cheetah** is a wild cat with a spotted coat. **Cheetahs** live in Africa and can run very fast.
[**Cheetah** comes from Hindi (a language spoken in India).]

**chef** *noun* **chefs**
A **chef** is a professional cook, usually in a restaurant or hotel.
[**Chef** comes from old French *ch(i)ef* 'chief'.]

**chemical** *noun* **chemicals**
A **chemical** is a substance, such as a liquid, that is made using chemistry: *Keep harmful chemicals safely locked away.*
[**Chemical** comes from Latin.]

**chemical** *adjective*
**Chemical** means to do with substances that are made using chemistry.

**chemist** *noun* **chemists**
1 A **chemist** is someone who makes up drugs and medicines.
2 A **chemist** or a **chemist's** is a shop where you can buy medicines, as well as things such as make-up and toothpaste.
[**Chemist** comes from the same Latin word as **chemical**.]

**chemistry** *noun*
If you study **chemistry**, you learn about substances and about what happens to substances when you put them together.
[**Chemistry** comes from the same Latin word as **chemical**.]

**cheque** *noun* **cheques**
A **cheque** is a piece of paper that you can use when you pay for something. You write on the **cheque** to tell your bank how much money to pay to the other person.
[**Cheque** is a different spelling of **check**².]

**cherry** *noun* **cherries**
A **cherry** is a small red or black fruit with a stone in it.
[**Cherry** comes from Greek via French and Latin.]

**chess** *noun*
**Chess** is a game for two people. You play **chess** on a board of black and white squares.
[**Chess** comes from the same French word as **check**².]

**chest** *noun* **chests**
1 A **chest** is a large strong box with a lid.
2 Your **chest** is the front part of your body between your neck and your waist.
[**Chest** comes from Old English.]

**chestnut** *noun* **chestnuts**
1 A **chestnut** is a brown nut that grows

inside a prickly green case.
**2** A **chestnut** is a tree that these nuts grow on.
**3 Chestnut** is a reddish-brown colour.
[**Chestnut** comes from Greek.]

**chestnut** *adjective*
of a reddish-brown colour: *a chestnut horse; chestnut hair.*

**chew** *verb* **chews, chewing, chewed** (th)
To **chew** means to bite food into tiny pieces with your teeth.
[**Chew** comes from Old English.]

**chick** *noun* **chicks**
A **chick** is a baby bird.
[**Chick** is short for **chicken**.]

**chicken** *noun* **chickens**
**1** A **chicken** is a kind of bird that is kept for its meat and eggs.
**2 Chicken** is the meat that comes from a chicken.
[**Chicken** comes from Old English.]

**chickenpox** *noun*
**Chickenpox** is a disease that you can catch. When you have **chickenpox** you have a high temperature and spots all over your body.
[**Chickenpox** comes from **chicken** and an old word *pox* 'a disease that gives you spots', probably because chickenpox is milder than other diseases, just as a chicken is smaller than other farmyard animals.]

**chief** *noun* **chiefs** (th)
A **chief** is the leader of a group of people.
[**Chief** comes from the same old French word as **chef**.]

**chief** *adjective* (th)
The **chief** thing is the most important thing or the main thing: *That was the chief reason why she left.*

**chieftain** *noun* **chieftains**
A **chieftain** is a leader of a group of people, especially a clan or a tribe.

**child** *noun* **children** (th)
**1** A **child** is a young girl or boy.
**2** Your **child** is your son or daughter.
[**Child** comes from Old English.]

**childhood** *noun* **childhoods**
Your **childhood** is the time when you are a child: *She had a happy childhood.*

**childish** *adjective* (th)
**Childish** means silly or stupid.
**childishly** *adverb*. **childishness** *noun*.

**chill** *verb* **chills, chilling, chilled**
To **chill** something means to make it cold.
[**Chill** comes from Old English.]

**chill** *noun* **chills**
**1** A **chill** is a feeling of coldness: *There was a chill in the air.*
**2** A **chill** is a cold: *I caught a chill.*

**chilly** *adjective* **chillier, chilliest**
**Chilly** means rather cold: *It's a bit chilly in here.*

**chime** *verb* **chimes, chiming, chimed**
To **chime** means to ring: *The clock chimed half past three.*
[No one knows where **chime** comes from.]

**chimes** *plural noun*
**Chimes** are bells or small objects that ring when the wind blows them.

**chimney** *noun* **chimneys**
A **chimney** is a tall pipe through the wall and roof of a building to take away the smoke from a fire.
[**Chimney** comes from French.]

**chimpanzee** *noun* **chimpanzees**
A **chimpanzee** is an African ape.
**Chimpanzees** are our closest animal relatives.
[**Chimpanzee** comes via French from Kikongo (an African language).]

**chin** *noun* **chins**
Your **chin** is the part of your face below your mouth.
[**Chin** comes from Old English.]

**china** *noun*
**China** is thin baked clay made into cups, plates and dishes.
[**China** comes from Persian *Chini* 'from China' (Persian is the language spoken in Iran).]

**chip** *noun* **chips**
**1** A **chip** is a small piece of potato that is fried.
**2** A **chip** is a microchip.
**3** A **chip** is a very small piece that has broken off something.
**4** A **chip** is the place where a very small piece has broken off something.

[**Chip** comes from Old English.]

**chip** *verb* **chips, chipping, chipped**
To **chip** something means to knock it so that a small piece breaks off.

**chisel** *noun* **chisels**
A **chisel** is a metal tool with a sharp flat end used for cutting or shaping wood.
[**Chisel** comes via French from the same Latin word as **scissors**.]

**chivalry** *noun*
**Chivalry** is the brave and polite way that knights in the past were supposed to behave.
[**Chivalry** is from an old French word.]

**chlorine** *noun*
**Chlorine** is a greenish-yellow gas with a strong smell that is used to kill harmful germs in water.
[**Chlorine** comes from Greek *chloros* 'green'.]

**chloroform** *noun*
**Chloroform** is a liquid with a strong smell that was used in the past to make people unconscious.
[**Chloroform** comes from **chlorine**.]

**chlorophyll** *noun*
**Chlorophyll** is the substance in plants that makes them green and allows them to take energy from the sun.
[**Chlorophyll** comes from Greek *chloros* 'green' and *phyllon* 'leaf'.]

**chocolate** *noun* **chocolates**
**Chocolate** is a sweet food or a drink made from cocoa powder.
[**Chocolate** comes via Spanish from Nahuatl (a South American Indian language).]

**choice** *noun* **choices**
**1** If you have a **choice**, you can choose from several different things: *There's a choice of skating, football or swimming after school.*
**2** Your **choice** is what you have chosen: *My parents didn't approve of my choice of career.*
[**Choice** comes from an old French word.]

**choir** *noun* **choirs**
A **choir** is a group of people who sing together.
[**Choir** comes from the same Latin word as **chorus**.]

**choke** *verb* **chokes, choking, choked**
If you **choke** or you **choke on** something, you have trouble breathing because something is blocking your throat.
[**Choke** comes from Old English.]

**cholesterol** *noun*
**Cholesterol** is a fatty substance that is found in food such as eggs and some meat. Too much **cholesterol** is bad for you because it can block up your arteries.
[**Cholesterol** comes from Greek.]

**choose** *verb* **chooses, choosing, chose, chosen** (th)
To **choose** something from a group of things means to pick it because it is the one you want or prefer.
[**Choose** comes from Old English.]

**chop** *noun* **chops**
A **chop** is a thick slice of meat with a bone along one side.
[No one knows where **chop** comes from.]

**chop** *verb* **chops, chopping, chopped** (th)
To **chop** something means to cut it using an axe or a sharp knife.

**chopstick** *noun* **chopsticks**
**Chopsticks** are narrow sticks used for eating food in China, Japan and other Far Eastern countries.
[**Chopsticks** comes from pidgin English *chop* 'quick' and **stick**.]

**chord**[1] *noun* **chords**
A **chord** is several musical notes played together.
[**Chord**[1] comes from *accord* 'agreement'.]

**chord**[2] *noun* **chords**
A **chord** is a straight line that joins two points on the edge of a circle.
[**Chord**[2] is a different spelling of *cord* 'thick string'.]

**chore** *noun* **chores**
A **chore** is a job of housework that has to be done every day or quite often.
[**Chore** comes from an Old English word meaning 'to do some work'.]

**choreography** *noun*
**Choreography** is the work of making up and arranging the steps and movements in dance, especially ballet.
[**Choreography** comes from Greek *choreia* 'dance'.]

**chorus** *noun* **choruses**
1 A **chorus** is the part of a song that is repeated in between the verses.
2 A **chorus** is a large group of people speaking or singing together.
[**Chorus** comes from Greek via Latin.]

**chose** *verb*
Chose is the past tense of **choose**.

**chosen** *verb*
Chosen is the past participle of **choose**.

**christen** *verb* **christens, christening, christened**
To **christen** someone means to accept someone, especially a young child, into the Christian Church and give him/her a name.
[**Christen** comes from Old English.]

**Christian** *noun* **Christians**
A **Christian** is someone who follows the teachings of Jesus Christ and the rules and beliefs of Christianity.

**Christianity** *noun*
**Christianity** is a religion based on the teachings of Jesus Christ and the belief that he was the son of God.

**Christmas** *noun*
**Christmas** is the day when Christians celebrate the birth of Jesus Christ. Most Christian churches celebrate **Christmas** on 25 December.
[**Christmas** comes from Old English *Cristes maesse* 'Christ's feast day'.]

**chromosome** *noun* **chromosomes**
A **chromosome** is the tiny part of a living cell in the body that carries genes. Genes give each living thing its special characteristics.
[**Chromosome** comes from Greek *chroma* 'colour' and *soma* 'body'.]

**chronic** *adjective*
A **chronic** illness is one that does not get better for a long time.
[**Chronic** comes from Greek *chronos* 'time'.]

**chronological** *adjective*
If things are arranged in **chronological** order, they are in the order in which they happened, from the first to the most recent.
[**Chronological** comes from the same

Greek word as **chronic**.]

**chrysalis** *noun* **chrysalises**
A **chrysalis** is the stage of the life of an insect such as a butterfly or moth when it is changing from a caterpillar into its adult form and it is wrapped in a kind of hard shell. [**Chrysalis** comes from Greek.]

**chuckle** *verb* **chuckles, chuckling, chuckled**
To **chuckle** means to laugh quietly.
[The word **chuckle** is an imitation of the sound.]

**chunk** *noun* **chunks**
A **chunk** is a thick piece of something.
[**Chunk** comes from an old French word.]

**church** *noun* **churches**
1 A **church** is a building where Christians meet to worship God.
2 A **church/Church** is an organised group of Christians who worship in the same way: *the Roman Catholic Church.*
[**Church** comes via Old English from Greek *kyriakon* 'the Lord's house'.]

**churn** *verb* **churns, churning, churned**
1 To **churn** cream means to shake and beat it until it becomes butter.
2 To **churn** something or **churn** something **up** means to turn or move it around with a lot of force: *The motor boat churned up the water.*
3 If your stomach **churns**, you feel as if it is turning over, usually because you are nervous or scared.
[**Churn** comes from Old English.]

**cider** *noun*
**Cider** is an alcoholic drink made from apples.
[**Cider** comes via French and Latin from ancient Hebrew (the language once spoken in Israel).]

**cigarette** *noun* **cigarettes**
A **cigarette** is a thin tube of tobacco wrapped in paper, which some people smoke.
[**Cigarette** comes via French and Spanish from Mayan *sik'ar* 'smoking' (Mayan is a South American Indian language).]

**cinder** *noun* **cinders**
A **cinder** is a small piece of coal or wood after it has been burned.
[**Cinder** comes from Old English.]

**cinema** *noun* **cinemas**
A **cinema** is a place where people go to watch films.
[**Cinema** comes via French from Greek *kinema* 'movement'.]

**cinnamon** *noun*
**Cinnamon** is a sweet spice used in cooking that comes from the bark of a tropical tree.
[**Cinnamon** comes from Greek.]

**circle** *noun* **circles**
A **circle** is a round flat shape like a wheel.
[**Circle** comes via French from the same Latin word as **circus**.]

**circuit** *noun* **circuits** (th)
1 A **circuit** is the path that a current of electricity flows around.
2 A **circuit** is a route or track that finishes where it started: *a motor-racing circuit*.
[**Circuit** comes via French from Latin *circum* 'around'.]

**circular** *adjective*
Something that is **circular** is shaped like a circle or goes round in a circle: *a circular pond; a circular route*.
[**Circular** comes via French from the same Latin word as **circus**.]

**circulation** *noun*
**Circulation** is the movement of blood around the body.
[**Circulation** comes via French from Latin *circulare* 'to go round in a circle'.]

**circumference** *noun*
The **circumference** of a circle is the complete distance around its edge.
[**Circumference** comes from Latin *circum* 'around' and *ferre* 'to go'.]

**circumstance** *noun* **circumstances**
1 The **circumstances** of an event are the facts about how and why it happened: *He died in mysterious circumstances.*
2 If you say you will do something **in the circumstances** or **under the circumstances**, you mean that you will do it because of a particular situation: *My grandparents are not very well, and in the circumstances I think we should visit them.*
[**Circumstances** comes from Latin *circum* 'around' and *stans* 'standing'.]

**circus** *noun* **circuses**
A **circus** is a show, usually in a large tent,

with acrobats, clowns and, sometimes, performing animals.
[**Circus** comes from Latin *circus* 'a ring'.]

**cistern** *noun* **cisterns**
A **cistern** is a tank for storing water, especially one connected to a toilet.
[**Cistern** comes from Latin.]

**citizen** *noun* **citizens**
A **citizen** of a country is a person who was born there or who has a right to live there: *a British citizen*.
[**Citizen** comes via French from Latin *civis*.]

**citrus fruit** *noun* **citrus fruits**
A **citrus fruit** is a fruit with a sharp taste, such as a lemon or an orange, that grows in hot countries.
[**Citrus** comes from Latin.]

**city** *noun* **cities**
A **city** is a large town.
[**City** comes via French from the same Latin word as **citizen**.]

**civilisation** *noun* **civilisations** *Also* **civilization**
1 A **civilisation** is a very well organised and developed way of life in a country: *ancient Greek civilisation*.
2 **Civilisation** is when a society has reached an advanced stage of development in its organisation and in art and science: *The Romans brought civilisation to most of Europe*.
[**Civilisation** comes from the same Latin word as **citizen**.]

**claim** *verb* **claims, claiming, claimed**(th)
1 To **claim** something means to ask for it because you have a right to it.
2 To **claim** something means to say that it is true.
[**Claim** comes from Latin *clamare* 'to call out'.]

**clam** *noun* **clams**
A **clam** is a large shellfish with two shells that close tightly.
[**Clam** comes from Old English.]

**clamber** *verb* **clambers, clambering, clambered** (th)
To **clamber** means to climb over or up something with difficulty.
[**Clamber** comes from *clamb*, the old past tense of **climb**.]

**clammy** *adjective*
Something that is **clammy** is damp and sticky in an unpleasant way.
[**Clammy** comes from Old English.]

**clamp** *noun* **clamps**
A **clamp** is a tool for holding something firmly.
[**Clamp** probably comes from a Dutch or old German word.]

**clamp** *verb* **clamps, clamping, clamped**
To **clamp** something means to hold it firmly using a clamp.

**clan** *noun* **clans**
A **clan** is a very large family or group of families, especially in Scotland.
[**Clan** comes from Gaelic.]

**clandestine** *adjective*
An activity that is **clandestine** is done in secret, especially because other people do not agree with it.
[**Clandestine** comes from Latin.]

**clang** *noun*
A **clang** is the ringing sound of two metal objects hitting each other.
[The word **clang** is an imitation of the sound.]

**clap** *verb* **claps, clapping, clapped**
To **clap** means to make a noise by hitting your hands together, usually to show you have enjoyed something.
[**Clap** comes from Old English.]

**clarify** *verb* **clarifies, clarifying, clarified**
To **clarify** something means to make it clear so that it can be understood more easily.
[**Clarify** comes via French from Latin *clarus* 'clear'.]

**clarinet** *noun* **clarinets**
A **clarinet** is a musical instrument of the woodwind family. It has metal keys that you press and a mouthpiece that you blow into. [**Clarinet** comes from French.]

**clash** *verb* **clashes, clashing, clashed**
1 To **clash** means to make a loud crashing sound.
2 If two people or groups **clash**, they argue or fight because they disagree seriously about something.
3 If things such as colours **clash**, they look ugly or unpleasant together.
[The word **clash** is an imitation of the sound.]

**class** *noun* **classes** (th)
1 A **class** is a number of pupils or students who are taught together as a group.
2 A **class** is a group of animals, plants or objects that are similar: *a class of insects*.
3 A **class** is a group of people in society: *the middle class*.
[**Class** comes from Latin.]

**classic** *adjective* (th)
1 Something that is a **classic** example is a typical example: *a classic example of a spoilt child*.
2 Something that people believe is very good and that is popular for a long time is **classic**: *a classic car*.
[**Classic** comes from Latin *classicus* 'of the highest class'.]

**classify** *verb* **classifies, classifying, classified** (th)
To **classify** things means to put them into groups with other similar things.
[**Classify** comes via French from the same Latin word as **class**.]

**classroom** *noun* **classrooms**
A **classroom** is a room in a school where a group of pupils or students learn together.

**clatter** *verb* **clatters, clattering, clattered**
To **clatter** means to bang or rattle things together noisily.
[The word **clatter** is an imitation of the sound.]

**claw** *noun* **claws**
A **claw** is a sharp pointed nail on the feet of some animals and birds.
[**Claw** comes from Old English.]

**clay** *noun*
**Clay** is a sticky kind of earth that becomes very hard when dry and is used for making pottery and bricks.
[**Clay** comes from Old English.]

**clean** *verb* **cleans, cleaning, cleaned** (th)
To **clean** means to remove dirt from something.
[**Clean** comes from Old English.]

**clean** *adjective* **cleaner, cleanest** (th)
Something that is **clean** is not dirty.

**clear** *verb* **clears, clearing, cleared** (th)
**1** To **clear** means to move things out of the way: *clear a space; clear the table.*
**2** To **clear** something means to jump over it without touching it.
**3** If you **clear** someone, you prove that s/he is not guilty of a crime.
[**Clear** comes via French from the same Latin word as **clarify**.]

**clear** *adjective* **clearer, clearest** (th)
**1** Something that is easy to see, hear or understand is **clear**.
**2** Something that is easy to see through is **clear**.
**3** Something that has nothing on it or nothing in the way is **clear**: *The road is clear.* **clearly** *adverb.*

**clearing** *noun* **clearings**
A **clearing** is an area in a wood or forest where trees have been cut down.

**clearly** *adverb*
**1** If you speak **clearly**, you speak in a way that is easy to hear and understand.
**2** If you see, hear, or understand something **clearly**, you do so easily and without any mistake.

**clergy** *noun*
The **clergy** are the priests in the Christian religion.
[**Clergy** comes via French from the same Latin word as **clerical**.]

**clerical** *adjective*
**1 Clerical** work is work that is done in an office involving sorting out letters and papers.
**2 Clerical** means to do with the clergy: *The vicar wore a clerical collar.*
[**Clerical** comes via Latin from Greek *klerikos* 'to do with the Christian Church'.]

**clerk** *noun* **clerks**
A **clerk** is someone whose job is sorting out letters and papers in an office.
[**Clerk** comes from the same Latin word as **clerical** and **clergy** (because in the old days only the clergy could read and write).]

**clever** *adjective* **cleverer, cleverest** (th)
**1** Someone who is **clever** can learn things very easily or do things skilfully.
**2** Something that is **clever** is carefully thought out and will probably work:

*What a clever idea!*
[No one knows where **clever** comes from.]

**click** *verb* **clicks, clicking, clicked**
To **click** means to make a short sharp sound.
[The word **click** is an imitation of the sound.]

**cliff** *noun* **cliffs** (th)
A **cliff** is a very steep rock-face, usually at the edge of the sea.
[**Cliff** comes from Old English.]

**climate** *noun* **climates**
The **climate** of a place is the normal kind of weather it has.
[**Climate** comes from Greek.]

**climax** *noun* **climaxes**
The **climax** of something is the most important or most exciting part of it.
[**Climax** comes from Greek.]

**climb** *verb* **climbs, climbing, climbed**
To **climb** means to go up something such as a ladder or a hill.
[**Climb** comes from Old English.]

**cling** *verb* **clings, clinging, clung**
To **cling** means to hold on tightly to someone or something.
[**Cling** comes from Old English.]

**clinic** *noun* **clinics**
A **clinic** is a place like a hospital where people go if they are ill or if they need advice from a doctor: *the ear, nose and throat clinic.* [**Clinic** comes from Greek.]

**clip**[1] *noun* **clips**
A **clip** is a fastener for holding things together, such as papers or hair.
[**Clip**[1] comes from Old English.]

**clip**[1] *verb* **clips, clipping, clipped**
To **clip** things means to fasten them together with a clip.

**clip**[2] *verb* **clips, clipping, clipped**
To **clip** means to cut something short with scissors or shears.
[**Clip**[2] comes from Old Norse.]

**clipper** *noun* **clippers**
**1** You use **clippers** to cut something short: *nail clippers.*
**2** A **clipper** was a fast sailing ship in the past.
[**Clipper** comes from **clip**[2].]

### cloak *noun* **cloaks**

A **cloak** is a loose coat with no sleeves that hangs from the shoulders.
[**Cloak** comes via French from Latin *clocca* 'bell', because of the shape of someone wearing a cloak.]

### clock *noun* **clocks**

A **clock** is a machine for measuring and showing the time.
[**Clock** comes from the same Latin word as **cloak**.]

### clockwise *adjective, adverb*

If something moves **clockwise**, it moves round in the same direction as the hands of a clock.
[**Clockwise** comes from **clock** and Old English *wise* 'a manner or way of doing something.']

### clockwork *adjective, adverb*

**1** Something that is **clockwork** has a key that you wind up to make it move: *clockwork toys*.
**2** If something happens **like clockwork**, it happens exactly on time and without any problems.

### clog *noun* **clogs**

A **clog** is a heavy wooden shoe.
[No one knows where **clog** comes from.]

### clone *noun* **clones**

A **clone** is a plant or animal that is grown from a cell of one parent and is an exact copy of the parent.
[**Clone** comes from Greek.]

### close *verb* **closes, closing, closed**

If something **closes**, or if you **close** something, it shuts: *Close the door!; The pool closes at four.*
[**Close** comes from Latin via French.]

### close *adjective* **closer, closest** (th)

**1** Something that is very near is **close**: *Our house is close to the sea; close relatives such as your parents, brothers and sisters; The exams are getting close.*
**2** If you have a **close** look at something, you look at it very carefully or thoroughly.
**3** If the result of a contest is **close**, there is very little difference between the contestants: *a close finish.*
**4** People that know each other very well and like each other very much are **close**: *a close family; my closest friend.*

### clot *noun* **clots**

A **clot** of blood is a lump that is formed when the blood dries and becomes thicker. [**Clot** comes from Old English.]

### cloth *noun* **cloths** (th)

**1 Cloth** is material used for making things like clothes or bedding.
**2** A **cloth** is a piece of cloth used to cover things or clean things.
[**Cloth** comes from Old English.]

### clothes *plural noun*

**Clothes** are things that you wear to cover your body or to keep warm.
[**Clothes** comes from the old plural of **cloth**.]

### cloud *noun* **clouds**

**1** A **cloud** is a white or grey mass of tiny drops of water that floats in the sky.
**2** A **cloud** is a mass of smoke or dust.
[**Cloud** comes from Old English.]

### clove *noun* **cloves**

A **clove** is a spice used in cooking that comes from the dried flower of a tropical bush. [**Clove** comes from Old English.]

### clover *noun*

**Clover** is a small plant with pink or white flowers that is often eaten by animals. It usually has three small leaves, but a four-leafed clover is believed to be lucky.
[**Clover** comes from Old English.]

### clown *noun* **clowns**

A **clown** is someone in a circus who wears funny clothes and does tricks to make people laugh.
[No one knows where **clown** comes from.]

### club *noun* **clubs** (th)

**1** A **club** is a group of people with the same interest who meet together.
**2** A **club** is a heavy stick used as a weapon or in some games.
**3 Clubs** is one of the suits in a pack of playing cards: *the four of clubs.*
[**Club** comes from Old Norse.]

### cluck *verb* **clucks, clucking, clucked**

To **cluck** means to make the noise of a hen.
[The word **cluck** is an imitation of the sound.]

### clue *noun* **clues**

A **clue** is something that helps you to find

a b **c** d e f g h i j k l m

the answer to something or solve a
puzzle.
[**Clue** comes from Old English *cliw* 'ball of
thread'. A man called Theseus in a Greek
myth had to go into a maze. As he went
in he unwound a ball of thread, and he
found his way out by winding it up
again.]

**clump** *noun* **clumps**
A **clump** of trees or plants is a group of
them growing together.
[**Clump** comes from a Dutch or old
German word.]

**clumsy** *adjective* **clumsier, clumsiest** (th)
Someone who often drops things or
knocks things over is **clumsy**.
[**Clumsy** probably comes from a
Scandinavian language.]

**clung** *verb*
**Clung** is the past tense and past participle
of **cling**.

**clutch** *verb* **clutches, clutching,
clutched** (th)
To **clutch** something means to hold it very
tightly. [**Clutch** comes from Old English.]

**clutter** *noun*
**Clutter** is an untidy mess in a room.
[**Clutter** comes from an old word *clotter*
'to clot'.]

**coach** *noun* **coaches**
1 A **coach** is a bus used for long journeys
or special trips.
2 A **coach** is a person whose job is
training people for a particular sport or
competition.
[**Coach** is named after the *Kocs*, a town in
Hungary where large carts were made.
Sense 2 comes from the idea that you
travelled faster if you went by coach, so
your coach was someone who helped you
get on.]

**coach** *verb* **coaches, coaching, coached**
To **coach** means to train people for a
particular sport or competition.

**coal** *noun* **coals**
**Coal** is a hard black substance that can be
burned on a fire.
[**Coal** comes from Old English.]

**coarse** *adjective*
Something that is **coarse** is rough to
touch.

[No one knows where **coarse** comes
from.]

**coast** *noun* **coasts** (th)
The **coast** is the land next to the sea.
[**Coast** comes from Latin *costa* 'side'.]

**coastguard** *noun* **coastguards**
A **coastguard** is a person whose job is to
watch the sea and get help for boats or
people in danger.

**coax** *verb* **coaxes, coaxing, coaxed** (th)
To **coax** means to gently persuade
someone to do something.
[**Coax** comes from an old word *cokes* 'a
fool', from the idea that you made a fool
of someone by coaxing him or her to do
something s/he didn't want to.]

**cobble** *noun* **cobbles**
**Cobbles** are the round stones that form
the surface of very old streets.
[**Cob** comes from an old word *cob*
'round'.]

**cobra** *noun* **cobras**
A **cobra** is a poisonous snake from Africa
and Asia. It has a hood of skin over its
neck.
[**Cobra** comes from Portuguese *cobra de
capello* 'snake with a hood'.]

**cobweb** *noun* **cobwebs**
A **cobweb** is a fine sticky net spun by a
spider to catch insects for food.
[**Cobweb** comes from Old English *coppe*
'spider' and **web**.]

**cock** *noun* **cocks**
A **cock** is an adult male bird, especially a
chicken. [**Cock** comes from Old English.]

**cockatoo** *noun* **cockatoos**
A **cockatoo** is a kind of parrot with a crest
on its head. **Cockatoos** are found in
Australia and Papua New Guinea.
[**Cockatoo** comes via Dutch from Malay
(a language spoken in Malaysia).]

**cockerel** *noun* **cockerels**
A **cockerel** is a young male bird,
especially a chicken.
[**Cockerel** comes from **cock**.]

**cockpit** *noun* **cockpits**
The **cockpit** of a plane is the area at the
front where the pilot sits to fly it.
[**Cockpit** used to mean a pit where cocks
were made to fight.]

**cockroach** *noun* **cockroaches**
A **cockroach** is a large brown insect that lives in warm places.
[**Cockroach** comes from Spanish.]

**cocoa** *noun*
1 **Cocoa** is a brown powder made from the beans of the cacao tree, which grows in hot countries. It is used to make chocolate.
2 **Cocoa** is a hot drink made with cocoa, milk and sugar.
[**Cocoa** comes via Spanish from Nahuatl (a South American Indian language).]

**coconut** *noun* **coconuts**
A **coconut** is a large brown nut that grows on a palm tree and has sweet white flesh and milky juice inside it.
[**Coconut** comes from Spanish or Portuguese *coco* 'grinning face', because the base of the nut looks something like a face.]

**cocoon** *noun* **cocoons**
A **cocoon** is a covering that some insects spin to protect themselves or their eggs.
[**Cocoon** comes from French.]

**cod** *noun* **cod**
A **cod** is a large fish with white flesh that is often eaten.
[No one knows where **cod** comes from.]

**code** *noun* **codes**
1 A **code** is a set of rules: *the Highway Code.*
2 A **code** is a set of signs or letters for sending secret messages.
[**Code** comes from Latin.]

**coffee** *noun*
1 **Coffee** is a brown powder made from the roasted beans of the coffee plant, which grows in hot countries.
2 **Coffee** is a hot drink made from the roasted and ground beans of the coffee plant. [**Coffee** comes from Arabic.]

**coffin** *noun* **coffins**
A **coffin** is a box that a dead person is buried or cremated in.
[**Coffin** comes from Greek via French and Latin.]

**cog** *noun* **cogs**
A **cog** is a tooth on a wheel that turns a machine.
[No one knows where **cog** comes from.]

**coin** *noun* **coins**
A **coin** is a piece of metal with a design on it, used as money.
[**Coin** comes from Latin via French.]

**coincide** *verb* **coincides, coinciding, coincided**
If two things **coincide**, they both happen at the same time or place.
[**Coincide** comes from Latin *co-* 'together' and *incidere* 'to happen'.]

**cold** *noun* **colds**
A **cold** is an illness that makes a person cough and sneeze.
[**Cold** comes from Old English.]

**cold** *adjective* **colder, coldest** (th)
Someone or something that is **cold** is not warm or has not been heated: *It's cold in here; Do you feel cold?; a cold meal.*

**cold-blooded** *adjective*
1 Animals such as reptiles and fish are **cold-blooded**. The temperature of their bodies changes with the temperature around them, and they have to be warm before they can move about.
2 A person who is **cold-blooded** does not show any feeling for others: *a cold-blooded murderer.*

**collapse** *verb* **collapses, collapsing, collapsed** (th)
1 To **collapse** means to fall down or faint suddenly because you are ill or weak: *The actor collapsed on stage.*
2 To **collapse** means to fall, break or crash to the ground: *The shed collapsed in the storm.* [**Collapse** comes from Latin.]

**collar** *noun* **collars**
1 A **collar** is the part of a shirt, dress or jumper that goes round the neck.
2 A **collar** is a band or strap that goes round the neck of an animal.
[**Collar** comes via French from Latin *collum* 'neck'.]

**collect** *verb* **collects, collecting, collected** (th)
1 To **collect** means to gather things together in one place.
2 To **collect** means to go and fetch someone or something.
[**Collect** comes from Latin via French.]

**collection** *noun* **collections** (th)
A **collection** is a group of things that have

a b **c** d e f g h i j k l m

been collected.
[**Collection** comes via French from the same Latin word as **collect**.]

## college *noun* colleges

A **college** is a place like a school where people who have finished school go to learn more.
[**College** comes from Latin via French.]

## collide *verb* collides, colliding, collided (th)

To **collide** means to bump into someone or something: *The lorry collided with the bus; John and I collided in the corridor*.
[**Collide** comes from Latin.]

## colloquial *adjective*

Language that is **colloquial** is spoken every day and is not written or formal.
[**Colloquial** comes from Latin.]

## colon *noun* colons

A **colon** is a punctuation mark like this : . It is used to introduce an explanation of something you have just mentioned or a list of things such as you have just mentioned.
[**Colon** comes from Greek via Latin.]

## colonel *noun* colonels

A **colonel** is a senior officer in the army in charge of a regiment of soldiers.
[**Colonel** comes from Italian via French.]

## colony *noun* colonies

**1** A **colony** is a country that is lived in and governed by settlers from another country. Some European countries had many colonies in the past.
**2** A **colony** is a place where a lot of birds, insects or animals of the same type live together: *a colony of ants*.
[**Colony** comes from Latin *colonia* 'farm, settlement'.]

## colour *noun* colours (th)

The **colour** of something is whether it is blue, red, yellow, black or white, etc.
[**Colour** comes from Latin via French.]

## column *noun* columns (th)

**1** A **column** is a tall round pillar that holds up part of a building or a statue.
**2** A **column** is something that has a long, narrow shape: *a column of figures; a column of smoke; a column of ants*.
**3** A **column** in a newspaper is a piece of writing by the same person or on the same subject that appears regularly: *a sports column*.
[**Column** comes from Latin via French.]

## coma *noun* comas

A **coma** is when someone is unconscious for a long time because of an illness or injury and they cannot wake up.
[**Coma** comes from Greek *koma* 'deep sleep'.]

## comb *noun* comb

A **comb** is a piece of metal or plastic with a row of teeth along it that you use to keep your hair tidy or to get tangles out of it. [**Comb** comes from Old English.]

## comb *verb* combs, combing, combed

**1** To **comb** your hair means to tidy it or untangle it with a comb.
**2** To **comb** a place means to search it carefully for something.

## combine *verb* combines, combining, combined (th)

To **combine** two or more things means to mix or join them together.
[**Combine** comes from Latin.]

## combustible *adjective*

Something that is **combustible** will catch fire or burn very easily.
[**Combustible** comes from Latin via French.]

## come *verb* comes, coming, came, come (th)

**1** If someone **comes** somewhere, s/he moves there with you or moves to where you are: *Will you come to the park with me?*
**2** If something **comes**, it arrives or gets nearer: *The bus is coming; Christmas is coming*. [**Come** comes from Old English.]

## comedian *noun* comedians

A **comedian** is someone whose job is to tell jokes and make people laugh.
[**Comedian** comes via French from the same Latin word as **comedy**.]

## comedy *noun* comedies

A **comedy** is a funny film or play.
[**Comedy** comes via French and Latin from Greek *komos* 'having fun' and *oide* 'song' (ancestor of **ode**).]

## comet *noun* comets

A **comet** is a bright object in space that travels across the sky leaving a tail of light.

[**Comet** comes via Latin from Greek *kometes* 'long-haired star'.]

**comfort** *verb* **comforts, comforting, comforted** (th)
To **comfort** someone means to make him/her feel better when s/he is worried, upset or unhappy.
[**Comfort** comes from Latin *confortare* 'to strengthen'.]

**comfortable** *adjective* (th)
**1** Something that is **comfortable** is pleasant to use or to be in: *comfortable slippers; a comfortable room.*
**2** If you are **comfortable**, you are relaxed: *I never feel comfortable with new people.*
**comfortably** *adverb.*
[**Comfortable** comes via French from the same Latin word as **comfort**.]

**comic** *noun* **comics**
A **comic** is a paper with stories told mainly in pictures or cartoons.
[**Comic** comes from Greek *komos* 'having fun' (ancestor of **comedy**).]

**comic** *adjective* (th)
Something or someone that is **comic** is funny.

**comma** *noun* **commas**
A **comma** is a punctuation mark like this ,. It is used between words or parts of a sentence to show a pause, and between items in a list.
[**Comma** comes from Greek.]

**command** *verb* **commands, commanding, commanded** (th)
**1** To **command** someone to do something means to order him/her to do it: *"Come here!" she commanded.*
**2** To **command** a ship or army means to have control over it.
[**Command** comes from Latin via French.]

**commit** *verb* **commits, committing, committed**
**1** To **commit** a crime means to do it.
**2** To **commit** yourself to something means to promise to do it.
[**Commit** comes from Latin.]

**common** *noun* **commons**
A **common** is an open piece of land for anyone to use.
[**Common** comes from Latin.]

**common** *adjective* **commoner, commonest**
Something that is ordinary or that you often see is **common**.

**communicate** *verb* **communicates, communicating, communicated**
If you **communicate** with someone, or you **communicate** with each other, you pass on or share what you know, think or feel by speaking or writing, or by the way you look or move: *Ships communicate by radio; I can't really communicate with my parents; Her frown communicated her anger.*
[**Communicate** comes from the same Latin word as **common**.]

**Communion** *noun* Also **Holy Communion**
In Christianity, **Communion** is a service in which people share bread and wine which has been consecrated.
[**Communion** comes from Latin.]

**community** *noun* **communities**
**1** A **community** is the people living in an area: *The Health Centre serves the whole community.*
**2** A **community** is a group of people who live or work together, or are united because they are alike in some way: *the business community; the Asian community.*
[**Community** comes via French from the same Latin word as **common**.]

**compact** *adjective*
Something that is **compact** is designed so that it does not take up very much space.
[**Compact** comes from Latin *compactum* 'put closely together.]

**compact disc** *noun* **compact discs** Also **compact disk**
A **compact disc** is a shiny circular object with music or information stored on it.

**comparative** *adjective*
**1** You use **comparative** to say that you are comparing something with something else, or with what is normal or expected. For example, if you say *They worked in comparative silence*, you mean that they were quieter than usual.
**2** You use the **comparative** form of an adjective or adverb to show that the noun or verb it describes is more or greater in some way than something else, or than it used to be. **Comparative** forms usually

end in *-er*; if the adjective or adverb has no comparative form you use *more* in front of it.
[**Comparative** comes from Latin *comparare* 'to pair up or match'.]

**compare** *verb* **compares, comparing, compared**

If you **compare** two or more things or people, you see how similar they are, and whether one is better than the others: *The magazine article compared three types of small car; Compared to his brother, he's a genius!*
[**Compare** comes via French from the same Latin word as **comparative**.]

**compass** *noun* **compasses**

A **compass** is an instrument with a needle that always points north.
[**Compass** comes from an old French word.]

**compete** *verb* **competes, competing, competed** (th)

To **compete** means to try to win against other people in a game or sport.
[**Compete** comes from Latin.]

**competition** *noun* **competitions**

A **competition** is a game or contest, usually with a prize for the winner.
[**Competition** comes from the same Latin word as **compete**.]

**competitor** *noun* **competitors** (th)

A **competitor** is someone who competes with other people in a sport or competition.
[**Competitor** comes from **compete**.]

**complain** *verb* **complains, complaining, complained** (th)

To **complain** means to say that something is not right and that you are not happy about it.
[**Complain** comes from Latin via French.]

**complete** *verb* **completes, completing, completed** (th)

1 To **complete** something means to finish doing it: *Work on the new road will be completed in the autumn.*
2 If you **complete** something, you add what is needed to make it perfect or complete: *This stamp completes my collection; He completed his outfit with a tie.*
[**Complete** comes from Latin *completum* 'full up'.]

**complete** *adjective* (th)

1 Something that is **complete** is finished or has all its parts: *a complete set of Shakespeare's plays.*
2 You use **complete** before a noun to show that something is as great as it can be: *I need a complete change; You're a complete idiot.* **completely** *adverb.*

**complex** *adjective*

Something that is **complex** has many different parts and is often difficult to understand: *a complex network of roads; a complex problem.*
[**Complex** comes from Latin *complexum* 'plaited or folded together'.]

**complexion** *noun* **complexion**

Your **complexion** is the natural colour and appearance of the skin on your face.
[**Complexion** comes from an old French word.]

**complicated** *adjective* (th)

Something that is **complicated** has so many parts or aspects that it is difficult to understand.
[**Complicated** comes from Latin *complicare* 'to fold things together'.]

**compose** *verb* **composes, composing, composed**

1 To **compose** a piece of music means to write or create it.
2 To **compose** a letter or poem means to write it.
[**Compose** comes via French from Latin *compositus* 'put together'.]

**compost** *noun*

**Compost** is a mixture of plant and vegetable material that rots and turns back into soil.
[**Compost** comes from the same Latin word as **compose**.]

**compound** *noun* **compounds**

A **compound** is a mixture of two or more substances or chemicals.
[**Compound** comes from Latin *componere* 'to put things together'.]

**comprehension** *noun*

Your **comprehension** of a subject or a piece of writing is your understanding of it.
[**Comprehension** comes from Latin *prehendere* 'to take in' or 'to seize'.]

**compulsory** *adjective*
If something is **compulsory**, there is a rule or law that says you must do it.
[**Compulsory** comes from Latin.]

**computer** *noun* **computers**
A **computer** is an electronic machine that can store a lot of information and do calculations and other tasks very quickly.
[**Computer** comes from Latin *computare* 'to calculate' (ancestor of **count**).]

**concave** *adjective*
Something that is **concave** curves inwards, like the inside of a bowl.
[**Concave** comes from Latin *cavus* 'hollow'.]

**conceal** *verb* **conceals, concealing, concealed**
To **conceal** something means to hide it.
[**Conceal** comes from Latin via French.]

**conceive** *verb* **conceives, conceiving, conceived**
1 If you **conceive** an idea, you form it or think it up.
2 If a woman **conceives**, she becomes pregnant.
[**Conceive** comes from Latin via French.]

**concentrate** *verb* **concentrates, concentrating, concentrated**
To **concentrate** on what you are doing or what is happening means to think very hard about it.
[**Concentrate** comes from Latin via French.]

**concern** *noun* **concerns**
1 **Concern** is worry about something: *concern about standards in education.*
2 If something is your **concern**, it is your business and you should take care of it.
3 A **concern** is a company or business.
[**Concern** comes from Latin.]

**concern** *verb* **concerns, concerning, concerned**
1 If something **concerns** you, or if you are **concerned** about something, you care about it or worry about it: *I'm very concerned about my mother's health.*
2 If something **concerns** you, it affects you: *This problem concerns all of us.*

**concert** *noun* **concerts**
A **concert** is a performance where music is played.

[**Concert** comes via French from Italian *concertare* 'to play in harmony'.]

**concrete** *noun*
**Concrete** is a mixture of cement and sand that sets very hard and is used for building.
[**Concrete** comes from Latin *concretus* 'hard or stiff'.]

**condemn** *verb* **condemns, condemning, condemned** (th)
1 To **condemn** something means to say very strongly that it is wrong and you do not approve of it.
2 To **condemn** someone means to say that s/he must be punished in a particular way: *The pirates were condemned to death.*
[**Condemn** comes from Latin via French.]

**condense** *verb* **condenses, condensing, condensed**
1 If a gas **condenses**, it gets cooler and turns to liquid.
2 If you **condense** something, you make it smaller or shorter: *condensed soup; a condensed account of the events.*
[**Condense** comes from Latin *condensus* 'very thick'.]

**condom** *noun* **condoms**
A **condom** is a tube made of very thin rubber with one end closed that a man puts over his penis when he is about to have sexual intercourse. It is used as a contraceptive and also to avoid spreading disease.
[No one knows where **condom** comes from.]

**conductor** *noun* **conductors**
1 A **conductor** is a person whose job is to direct an orchestra.
2 A **conductor** is something that lets heat, electricity or sound travel through it.
[**Conductor** comes via French from Latin *conducere* 'to bring or lead along together'.]

**cone** *noun* **cones**
1 A **cone** is a solid shape with a round base and a pointed top, like an ice-cream cone.
2 A **cone** is a case in which the seeds of an evergreen tree grow.
[**Cone** comes from Greek via French and Latin.]

**confess** verb **confesses, confessing, confessed** (th)
If you **confess**, you admit that you did something wrong.
[**Confess** comes from Latin.]

**confidence** noun
1 If you have **confidence**, you believe that you can do something.
2 If you tell someone something **in confidence**, you expect that person not to tell anyone else.
[**Confidence** comes from Latin *confidere* 'to trust completely'.]

**confidential** adjective
Something that is **confidential** is secret or private.
[**Confidential** comes from the same Latin word as **confidence**.]

**confine** verb **confines, confining, confined** (th)
To **confine** a person or animal to a place means to force them to stay there: *It's cruel to confine a tiger in a cage.*
[**Confine** comes via French from Latin *finis* 'end, limit' (ancestor of **finish**).]

**confirm** verb **confirms, confirming, confirmed**
1 To **confirm** something means to make sure that it is true or going to happen.
2 To **confirm** something means to reassure someone that it is true or that it is going to happen.
[**Confirm** comes via French from Latin *firmus* 'firm' (ancestor of **firm**).]

**conflict** noun **conflicts**
1 If there is a serious disagreement between two sides or between different ideas or beliefs, there is a **conflict** between them or they are **in conflict**: *The conflict between religion and science.*
2 **Conflict** is fighting between countries or groups of people.
[**Conflict** comes from Latin.]

**conflict** verb **conflicts, conflicting, conflicted**
If things **conflict**, they cannot both exist, or they cannot both be true: *Your story conflicts with hers.*

**confuse** verb **confuses, confusing, confused** (th)
1 If you are **confused** by something, you do not understand it or know what to do.
2 To **confuse** two or more things means to mistake them or mix them up: *I often confuse the twins.* **confusion** noun.
[**Confuse** comes from Latin via French.]

**congratulate** verb **congratulates, congratulating, congratulated**
To **congratulate** someone means to tell that person you are very pleased because of something good that has happened to him/her, or something good or clever that s/he has done.
[**Congratulate** comes from Latin *congratulari* 'to be happy with someone'.]

**conical** adjective
Something that is **conical** is shaped like a cone.
[**Conical** comes from the same Greek word as **cone**.]

**conifer** noun **conifers**
A **conifer** is an evergreen tree that cones grow on.
[**Conifer** comes from the same word as cone.]

**conjunction** noun **conjunctions**
A **conjunction** is a word that joins together other words or parts of a sentence. *And, but, although* and *because* are all **conjunctions**.
[**Conjunction** comes from Latin *conjunctum* 'fixed together'.]

**connect** verb **connects, connecting, connected** (th)
1 To **connect** things means to join them together: *The computer is connected to a telephone line.*
2 To **connect** things or people means to put them together in your mind: *I knew about both events, but I didn't connect them.*
[**Connect** comes from Latin *connectere* 'to bind together'.]

**conquer** verb **conquers, conquering, conquered** (th)
To **conquer** an enemy army or country means to defeat it and take control of it.
[**Conquer** comes from Latin via French.]

**conquest** noun **conquests**
A **conquest** is when one army or country has defeated and taken control of another.
[**Conquest** comes from the same Latin word as **conquer**.]

**conscience** *noun* **consciences**
Your **conscience** is your knowledge about what is right and wrong.
[**Conscience** comes from Latin *conscientia* 'knowledge'.]

**conscious** *adjective*
1 If you are **conscious**, you are awake and not asleep.
2 If you are **conscious** of something, you realise it is there.
[**Conscious** comes from Latin *conscius* 'knowing'.]

**consecrate** *verb* **consecrates, consecrating, consecrated**
To **consecrate** something is to make it holy. [**Consecrate** comes from Latin.]

**consent** *verb* **consents, consenting, consented**
If you **consent** to something, you agree to it: *He consented to marry her.*
[Consent comes from Latin via French.]

**consequence** *noun* **consequences** (th)
The **consequence** of something that you do is the result of it.
[**Consequence** comes from Latin *consequi* 'to follow closely'.]

**conservation** *noun*
**Conservation** is protecting wildlife and other important things and keeping them safe for the future.
[**Conservation** comes from the same Latin word as **conserve**.]

**conserve** *verb* **conserves, conserving, conserved**
To **conserve** something means to keep it and not use too much: *We should conserve water during the summer.*
[**Conserve** comes from Latin.]

**consider** *verb* **considers, considering, considered** (th)
To **consider** something means to think carefully about it.
[**Consider** comes from Latin via French.]

**consist** *verb* **consists, consisting, consisted**
To **consist** of certain things means to be made up of them: *The United Kingdom consists of England, Wales, Scotland and Northern Ireland.*
[**Consist** comes from Latin.]

**consonant** *noun* **consonants**
A **consonant** is any letter of the alphabet except the five vowels (a, e, i, o, u).
[**Consonant** comes from Latin.]

**constellation** *noun* **constellations**
A **constellation** is a group of stars.
[**Constellation** comes from Latin *con* 'together' and *stella* 'star'.]

**construct** *verb* **constructs, constructing, constructed** (th)
To **construct** something means to build it.
[**Construct** comes from Latin.]

**consult** *verb* **consults, consulting, consulted** (th)
1 To **consult** someone means to ask that person for information or advice: *You should consult a doctor.*
2 To **consult** a book or map means to look in it for information.
[**Consult** comes from Latin *consulere* 'to take advice'.]

**consumer** *noun* **consumers**
A **consumer** is someone who buys things.
[**Consumer** comes from *consume* 'to eat, drink, or use up', which comes from Latin.]

**contact** *verb* **contacts, contacting, contacted** (th)
To **contact** someone means to write or telephone that person.
[**Contact** comes from Latin *con* 'together' and *tactum* 'touched'.]

**contact lens** *noun* **contact lenses**
A **contact lens** is a thin plastic disc that you can put onto the surface of your eye to help you see better. You can wear **contact lenses** instead of glasses.

**contagious** *adjective*
A **contagious** disease is one that can easily be passed from one person to another by touching the person who has the disease or by touching something that s/he has touched.
[**Contagious** comes from Latin *con* 'together' and *tangere* 'to touch'.]

**contain** *verb* **contains, containing, contained** (th)
To **contain** something means to have or to hold it inside: *a box containing books and toys; chemical compounds containing iron.*
[**Contain** comes via French from the same

Latin word as **continue**.]

**container** noun **containers**
A **container** is something that can hold things inside it.

**contaminate** verb **contaminates, contaminating, contaminated** (th)
To **contaminate** something means to make it dirty or polluted.
[**Contaminate** comes from Latin.]

**contemporary** adjective
Something that is **contemporary** exists now and is not from the past.
[**Contemporary** comes from Latin con 'together' and tempus 'time'.]

**contempt** noun (th)
If you feel **contempt** for someone, you dislike that person and have no respect for him or her.
[**Contempt** comes from Latin.]

**content** noun **contents**
The **contents**, of something are what is inside it: *He opened the case and examined the contents.*
[**Contents** comes from Latin contenta 'the things contained'.]

**content** adjective
If you are **content**, you feel happy and do not want anything more than you have.
[**Content** comes from Latin.]

**contest** noun **contests**
A **contest** is a game or competition.
[**Contest** comes from Latin.]

**context** noun **contexts**
The **context** of something is the information around it that helps you to understand it.
[**Context** comes from Latin con 'together' and textum 'woven'.]

**continent** noun **continents**
A **continent** is one of the seven very large areas of land in the world: *the continent of Europe.*
[**Continent** comes from Latin terra continens 'continuous land'.]

**continual** adjective
Something that is **continual** keeps happening again and again.
**continually** adverb.
[**Continual** comes via French from the same Latin word as **continue**.]

**continue** verb **continues, continuing, continued** (th)
To **continue** means to go on, or to go on doing something: *The noise continued for three hours; I want to continue my education.*
[**Continue** comes via French from Latin continere 'to hold or keep together' (ancestor of **contain**).]

**continuous** adjective
Something that is **continuous** does not stop and is not interrupted: *a continuous line; a continuous supply.*
**continuously** adverb.
[**Continuous** comes from the same Latin word as **continue**.]

**contour** noun **contours**
1 A **contour** is an outline of something.
2 A **contour** on a map is a line that joins places of the same height.
[**Contour** comes via French from Italian contornare 'to draw in outline'.]

**contraceptive** noun **contraceptives**
A **contraceptive** is something that people use or a drug that people take so that when they have sexual intercourse, the woman does not get pregnant.
[**Contraceptive** comes from Latin contra 'against' and English conception 'conceiving'.]

**contradict** verb **contradicts, contradicting, contradicted**
To **contradict** someone means to say the opposite of what s/he has said.
[**Contradict** comes from Latin contra 'against' and dicere 'to say'.]

**contrast** noun **contrasts**
A **contrast** is a great difference between things when you compare them: *the contrast between light and dark.*
[**Contrast** comes from Latin contra 'against' and stare 'to stand'.]

**contrast** verb **contrasts, contrasting, contrasted**
1 To **contrast** means to be very different from something else: *His expensive new trainers contrasted with his patched old jeans.*
2 To **contrast** one thing with another means to look at the differences between them: *The book contrasts classical and popular music.*

**contribute** *verb* **contributes, contributing, contributed**
To **contribute** means to pay some money or give help towards something.
[**Contribute** comes from Latin.]

**contribution** *noun* **contributions** (th)
A **contribution** is what you pay or give towards something.

**control** *verb* **controls, controlling, controlled**
To **control** means to make someone or something do what you want.
[**Control** comes from Latin via French.]

**convenient** *adjective* (th)
Something that is **convenient** is useful or suitable for a particular purpose: *Would it be convenient if I came tomorrow?*
[**Convenient** comes from Latin *convenire* 'to go together'.]

**convent** *noun* **convents**
A **convent** is a place where nuns live and work together.
[**Convent** comes from the same Latin word as **convenient**.]

**conversation** *noun* **conversations** (th)
A **conversation** is when two or more people talk and listen to each other.
[**Conversation** comes from Latin *conversare* 'to mix with people'.]

**convert** *verb* **converts, converting, converted**
**1** To **convert** something means to change it into something else: *Your body converts food into energy.*
**2** To **convert** something is to change it to make it suitable for a different purpose: *Their house was converted from an old barn.*
**3** If you **convert,** or if someone **converts** you, you change your religion or the way you think: *I used to hate pop music, but my son converted me.*
[**Convert** comes via French from Latin *convertere* 'to turn around'.]

**convex** *adjective*
Something that is **convex** curves outwards, like the outside of a ball or circle.
[**Convex** comes from Latin *convexus* 'arched'.]

**convict** *noun* **convicts**
A **convict** is someone who is in prison for committing a crime.
[**Convict** comes from the same Latin word as **convince**.]

**convict** *verb* **convicts, convicting, convicted**
To **convict** someone means to find that person guilty of a crime.

**convince** *verb* **convinces, convincing, convinced** (th)
To **convince** someone means to persuade that person to believe something.
[**Convince** comes from Latin *convincere* 'to overcome'.]

**cook** *noun* **cooks**
A **cook** is someone whose job is to cook food.
[**Cook** comes from Latin via Old English.]

**cook** *verb* **cooks, cooking, cooked** (th)
To **cook** means to prepare food for eating by heating it in different ways.

**cooker** *noun* **cookers**
A **cooker** is an oven used for cooking food.

**cool** *adjective* **cooler, coolest** (th)
**1** Something that is **cool** is fairly cold, but in a pleasant way: *a cool drink; It's cooler in the shade.*
**2** Someone who is **cool** is calm and not agitated or excited: *Keep cool!*
[**Cool** comes from Old English.]

**cooperate** *verb* **cooperates, cooperating, cooperated** (th)
To **cooperate** means to be willing to help and work with other people.
[**Cooperate** comes from Latin *co* 'together' and *operari* 'to work' (ancestor of **operate**).]

**cooperation** *noun* (th)
**Cooperation** is when people work together and help each other.

**copper** *noun*
**Copper** is a reddish-brown metal used to make coins and water pipes.
[**Copper** comes via Old English from Latin *cyprium* 'metal from Cyprus'.]

**copy** *noun* **copies**
A **copy** is something that is exactly the same as something else.
[**Copy** comes from Latin via French.]

a b **c** d e f g h i j k l m

**copy** *verb* **copies, copying, copied** (th)
**1** To **copy** something means to write or draw exactly what has already been written or drawn.
**2** To **copy** someone means to do exactly the same as someone else: *He always copies my ideas.*

**coral** *noun*
**Coral** is a living thing found under the sea that is made up of the skeletons of tiny sea creatures. It looks like coloured rock of different shapes and can be either soft or hard.
[**Coral** comes from Greek via French and Latin.]

**core** *noun* **cores**
The **core** of something is the central or most important part of it: *an apple core; the core of the problem.*
[No one knows where **core** comes from.]

**cork** *noun* **corks**
**1 Cork** is the bark of a special kind of tree.
**2** A **cork** is a piece of cork used to close a bottle.
[**Cork** comes from Latin via Dutch and Spanish.]

**corn** *noun*
**Corn** is grain such as wheat, barley or oats. [**Corn** comes from Old English.]

**cornea** *noun* **corneas**
The **cornea** is the clear layer that covers the front of your eyeball.
[**Cornea** comes from Latin.]

**corner** *noun* **corners**
A **corner** is the point where two roads, walls or lines meet.
[**Corner** comes from Latin.]

**corner** *verb* **corners, cornering, cornered**
**1** If you **corner** someone, you trap that person in a corner or a similar place that s/he cannot get out of.
**2** When a vehicle **corners**, it goes round a corner: *The car corners well.*

**cornet** *noun* **cornets**
**1** A **cornet** is a musical instrument like a small trumpet.
**2** A **cornet** is a conical wafer to hold ice cream.
[**Cornet** comes from French *cornet* 'small horn'.]

**coronation** *noun* **coronations**
A **coronation** is the ceremony when a king or queen is crowned.
[**Coronation** comes from Latin *corona* 'a crown'.]

**corpse** *noun* **corpses**
A **corpse** is a dead body.
[**Corpse** comes from Latin *corpus* 'body'.]

**correct** *verb* **corrects, correcting, corrected** (th)
**1** To **correct** something means to make it right.
**2** To **correct** someone means to tell that person that s/he has done something or said something that is not right.
[**Correct** comes from Latin *corrigere* 'to put straight'.]

**correct** *adjective* (th)
**1** Something that has no mistakes or is completely right is **correct**.
**2 Correct** behaviour is what is right or polite. **correctly** *adverb.*

**corridor** *noun* **corridors**
A **corridor** is a narrow passage with doors leading to different rooms or compartments along it.
[**Corridor** comes from Italian via French.]

**corrode** *verb* **corrodes, corroding, corroded**
If a chemical or natural substance **corrodes** metal, it gradually destroys it.
[**Corrode** comes from Latin *rodere* 'to gnaw' (ancestor of **rodent**).]

**corrugated** *adjective*
Something that is **corrugated** has the shape of wavy ridges: *corrugated iron.*
[**Corrugated** comes from Latin *corrugare* 'to wrinkle'.]

**corrupt** *adjective*
**1** If a person is **corrupt**, s/he is not honest.
**2** If information on a computer is **corrupt**, it is no longer correct or able to be used.
[**Corrupt** comes from Latin.]

**cosmetics** *plural noun*
**Cosmetics** are make-up and creams that you can put on your skin to make you look better.
[**Cosmetics** comes via French from Greek *kosmein* 'to decorate'.]

## cosmic *adjective*

**Cosmic** means to do with the whole universe.
[**Cosmic** comes from **cosmos**.]

## cosmos *noun*

The **cosmos** is the whole universe.
[**Cosmos** comes from Greek *kosmos* 'arrangement, organisation'.]

## cost *noun* **costs**

The **cost** of something is its price.
[**Cost** comes from an old French word.]

## costume *noun* **costumes**

1 A **costume** is the clothes worn by an actor in a play.
2 A **costume** is a set of clothes like those worn a long time ago.
[**Costume** comes via Italian *costume* 'fashion, habit' from the same Latin word as **custom**.]

## cot *noun* **cots**

A **cot** is a bed for a baby. It has high sides so that the baby cannot fall out.
[**Cot** comes from Hindi (a language spoken in India).]

## cottage *noun* **cottages**

A **cottage** is a small house.
[**Cottage** comes from Old English.]

## cotton *noun*

**Cotton** is thread or cloth made from the cotton plant.
[**Cotton** comes from Arabic via French.]

## couch *noun* **couches**

A **couch** is a long seat like a sofa.
[**Couch** comes from French *coucher* 'to lay something down'.]

## cougar *noun* **cougars**

**Cougar** is another word for a puma.
[**Cougar** comes via French from Guarani (a South American Indian language).]

## cough *noun* **coughs**

A **cough** is a sudden loud noise that you make when you are trying to get rid of something in your throat or stop a tickling feeling in your throat.
[The word **cough** is an imitation of the sound.]

## could *verb*

1 **Could** is the past tense of **can**.
2 **Could** means that someone was able or may be able to do something: *I couldn't sleep; Could you come tomorrow?*
3 **Could** means that something may happen or might have happened: *We could have been killed!*

## council *noun* **councils**

A **council** is a group of people who are chosen to make decisions about the town or area they live in.
[**Council** comes from Latin *concilium* 'an assembly'.]

## count *verb* **counts, counting, counted** (th)

1 To **count** means to say the numbers in order: *Count up to twenty.*
2 To **count** things is to find out how many there are: *She counted all the cars in the car park; He sat counting his money.*
3 To **count** is to be important: *Every vote will count; Your opinions don't count.*
[**Count** comes via French from Latin *computare* 'to calculate' (ancestor of **computer**).]

## counter *noun* **counters**

1 A **counter** is a long narrow table where people are served in a shop, bank or café.
2 A **counter** is a small disc used to keep the score in some games.
[**Counter** comes from the same French word as **count**.]

## couple *noun* **couples** (th)

1 A **couple** is two of something: *a couple of weeks.*
2 Two people who are in love are a **couple**: *a married couple.*
[**Couple** comes via French from Latin *copulare* 'to fix together'.]

## course *noun* **courses**

1 A **course** is a group of lessons that lasts for a certain amount of time: *a four-week German course.*
2 A **course** is an area of land where some sports are played: *a golf course.*
3 If you are given a **course** of medicine, you have to take a certain amount of it for a certain length of time: *a five-day course of penicillin.*
4 A **course** is the food you eat as the beginning, middle or end of a meal: *The last course was pudding.*
5 A **course** is the direction that something moves in: *The submarine steered a course towards the Arctic.*
[**Course** comes via French from Latin

*cursus* 'running'.]

**course** *verb* **courses, coursing, coursed**
When a liquid **courses**, it flows quickly. The word **course** is mainly used in stories: *Tears coursed down her cheeks.*

**cousin** *noun* **cousins**
Your **cousin** is the child of your uncle or aunt.
[**Cousin** comes from an old French word.]

**cover** *noun* **covers** (th)
1 A **cover** is something that is put over something else to protect it, hide it or keep it warm: *Put a cover over the computer to protect it from dust.*
2 The **covers** are the sheets and blankets on a bed: *hide under the covers.*
3 The **cover** is the front or back page of a newspaper, book or magazine. *The title of the book is on the cover.*
[**Cover** comes from Latin via French.]

**cover** *verb* **covers, covering, covered** (th)
1 To **cover** something is to put something on top of something or someone: *Cover the baby with blankets to keep her warm; Cover the cake with icing.*
2 If you **cover** a certain distance, you travel that far: *We covered 700km in two weeks.*
3 If you **cover** a subject you learn about it or give information about it: *Class 3 haven't covered the Tudors yet; Our reporter is in Atlanta to cover the Olympics.*

**cow** *noun* **cows**
1 A **cow** is an adult female animal that produces milk and can be eaten.
2 A **cow** is an adult female of some animals, such as a whale, elephant or seal. [**Cow** comes from Old English.]

**crab** *noun* **crabs**
A **crab** is a creature with a hard shell, eight legs and two pincers. It lives in the sea and it moves sideways.
[**Crab** comes from Old English.]

**crack** *noun* **cracks** (th)
1 A **crack** is a narrow line in something where it has broken but not fallen apart.
2 A **crack** is a small gap between two things: *a crack in the curtains.*
3 A **crack** is a sudden loud noise: *the crack of a gun; a thunder crack.*
[**Crack** comes from Old English.]

**crack** *verb* **cracks, cracking, cracked**
1 When something **cracks**, it splits or breaks: *The glass cracked in the bowl of hot water.*
2 If you **crack** something, you split it or make a crack in it: *crack an egg.*
3 When something **cracks**, it makes a sharp loud noise: *Did you hear my knee crack?*
4 When you find the solution to something difficult, you **crack** it: *crack the code.*

**cracker** *noun* **crackers**
1 A **cracker** is a paper-covered tube that bangs when you pull it apart. It usually contains a paper hat, a toy and a joke: *a Christmas cracker.*
2 A **cracker** is a thin dry biscuit that is not sweet and is often eaten with cheese.
[**Cracker** comes from **crack**.]

**cradle** *noun* **cradles**
A **cradle** is a baby's bed, especially one that rocks.

**cradle** *verb* **cradles, cradling, cradled**
If you **cradle** something, you hold it carefully in your arms.
[**Cradle** comes from Old English.]

**craft** *noun* **crafts**
1 A **craft** is work or a hobby such as weaving, woodwork or pottery where you make things skilfully with your hands.
2 A **craft** is a vehicle that travels through water, air or space, such as a boat, an aircraft or a spacecraft: *pleasure craft.* The plural is **craft**: *The bay was full of craft.*
[**Craft** comes from Old English.]

**crafty** *adjective* **craftier, craftiest** (th)
A **crafty** person gets what s/he wants in a clever way, usually by tricking other people.
[**Crafty** comes from **craft**, and originally meant 'skilful'.]

**crane** *noun* **cranes**
1 A **crane** is a tall narrow machine that moves very heavy objects and is often used on building sites.
2 A **crane** is a large bird with long legs and a long neck that lives by lakes and rivers. [**Crane** comes from Old English.]

**crane** *verb* **cranes, craning, craned**
When you **crane** your neck, you stretch it

it so that you can see or hear something better.

## crash noun crashes

**1** A **crash** is a loud noise like drums or thunder: *The bottle hit the floor with a crash.*
**2** A **crash** is an accident that happens when something that is moving fast hits something else: *a plane crash; a car crash.*
[The word **crash** is an imitation of the sound.]

## crash verb crashes, crashing, crashed

**1** To **crash** means to hit something very hard while moving: *The car crashed into a tree; The two trains crashed head-on.*
**2** When a plane **crashes**, it hits the ground.
**3** When a computer or a computer program **crashes**, it stops working because of a problem.

## crate noun crates

A **crate** is a large wooden or plastic box that is used for carrying bottles and fruit: *a crate of beer.*
[No one knows where **crate** comes from.]

## crater noun craters

**1** A **crater** is the round opening at the top of a volcano.
**2** A **crater** is a large hole in the ground that is caused by a bomb exploding or a meteorite hitting the ground: *a bomb crater; The moon is full of craters.*
[**Crater** comes via Latin from Greek *krater* 'bowl'.]

## crave verb craves, craving, craved

When you **crave** something, you want it desperately: *crave love and attention.*
[**Crave** comes from Old English.]

## craving noun cravings

A **craving** is a strong desire for something, especially a certain food or drink: *a craving for chocolate.*

## crawl noun

A **crawl** is a swimming stroke: *the front crawl.*
[No one knows where **crawl** comes from.]

## crawl verb crawls, crawling, crawled

**1** When you **crawl**, you move on your hands and knees: *The baby crawled across the floor.*
**2** When something **crawls**, it moves very slowly: *The traffic crawled along in the jam.*

## crayon noun crayons

A **crayon** is a coloured pencil or stick of wax that is used for drawing and colouring: *an orange crayon.*
[**Crayon** comes from French *craie* 'chalk'.]

## craze noun crazes (th)

A **craze** is something that quickly becomes very popular but only stays popular for a short time.
[**Craze** probably comes from Old Norse.]

## crazy adjective crazier, craziest (th)

**1** Someone or something that is **crazy** is mad, silly or very strange: *You're crazy to spend £300 on a jacket; Eating soup with a fork is crazy.*
**2** If you are **crazy about** someone or something, you like that person very much or you are very enthusiastic about something: *She's crazy about him; He's crazy about football.*
**crazily** adverb. **craziness** noun.
[**Crazy** comes from **craze**.]

## creak verb creaks, creaking, creaked

When something **creaks**, it makes a squeaky noise; *The floorboards creak when you walk on them.*
[The word **creak** is an imitation of the sound.]

## cream noun creams

**1** **Cream** is thick milk that contains a lot of fat: *strawberries and cream.*
**2** **Cream** is a substance that you rub into your skin, especially if it is dry: *hand cream.*
**3** **Cream** is a yellowish-white colour: *The walls are painted cream.*
**4** The **cream** of something is the very best of something: *This vegetable soup is made from the cream of the crop.*
[**Cream** comes from an old French word.]

## cream adjective creamier, creamiest

Of the colour of cream: *a cream skirt.*

## cream verb creams, creaming, creamed

**1** When you **cream** ingredients, you stir them together until they look thick and pale: *Cream the butter and the sugar.*
**2** If you **cream off** part of something, you take the best part: *The best footballers in the school were creamed off by the local team.*

**crease** *noun* **creases**
1 A **crease** is a line or wrinkle in paper or clothes.
2 A **crease** is a line in a part of your body, especially where your arms and legs bend. [**Crease** is an old spelling of **crest**.]

**crease** *verb* **creases, creasing, creased**
To **crease** means to make a line or wrinkles in clothes or paper: *Crease the paper by folding it down the middle; Silk and linen crease very easily.*

**create** *verb* **creates, creating, created** (th)
To **create** something is to make or design something: *Tourism creates jobs; a dress created by a top designer.*
[**Create** comes from Latin.]

**creation** *noun* **creations** (th)
1 The **creation** of something is the act of making it: *The creation of life is amazing.*
2 Someone's **creation** is something special that s/he has made: *This recipe is my own creation.*
3 In the Bible, the **Creation** is when God made the earth, the universe and everything in it: *The Creation took six days.*
4 **Creation** is the whole universe and everything in it. The word **creation** with this meaning is usually used in stories: *He was the biggest, fiercest giant in creation.*
[**Creation** comes via French from the same Latin word as **create**.]

**creator** *noun* **creators** (th)
1 The **creator** of something is the person who made or invented it: *Sir Arthur Conan Doyle is the creator of Sherlock Holmes.*
2 The **Creator** is another word for God.
[**Creator** comes via French from the same Latin word as **create**.]

**creature** *noun* **creatures**
A **creature** is any real or imaginary animal, bird, fish or insect: *sea creatures; a creature from Mars.*
[**Creature** comes via French from the same Latin word as **create**.]

**crèche** *noun* **crèches**
A **crèche** is a place like a nursery where babies and small children are looked after while their parents do something else: *a workplace crèche.*
[**Crèche** is a French word.]

**credible** *adjective* (th)
You trust or believe something or someone that is **credible**: *He looks like a credible salesman but he's really a thief; a credible excuse.* **credibly** *adverb*.
[**Credible** comes from the same Latin word as **credit**.]

**credit** *noun*
1 If you buy something on **credit**, you pay for it later.
2 If your bank account is in **credit**, there is money in it.
3 If you get **credit** for something, people praise you because you have done something well: *You should get the credit for making the party such a success.*
[**Credit** comes via French from Latin *credere* 'to trust or believe'.]

**creek** *noun* **creeks**
A **creek** is a narrow area of water near the coast or a narrow stream or river.
[**Creek** probably comes from Old Norse.]

**creep** *verb* **creeps, creeping, crept**
1 To **creep** is to move in a careful way without making any noise: *We have to creep around the house when Dad's asleep.*
2 When something **creeps**, it moves slowly: *The caterpillar crept up the stalk; Mist crept over the fields.*
[**Creep** comes from Old English.]

**creep** *noun* **creeps**
1 If something or someone **gives you the creeps**, you feel nervous or frightened: *Graveyards give me the creeps.*
2 You call someone a **creep** when they want to make friends by saying nice things that they do not mean.

**creepy** *adjective* **creepier, creepiest**
Something or someone that is **creepy** makes you feel nervous or frightened: *a creepy film; The woods are creepy at night.*

**cremate** *verb* **cremates, cremating, cremated**
When dead people are **cremated**, their bodies are burned at their funerals.
[**Cremate** comes from Latin *cremare* 'to burn'.]

**crematorium** *noun* **crematoriums** *or* **crematoria**
A **crematorium** is the building where the bodies of dead people are burnt at their funerals.

n o p q r s t u v w x y z

**crept** *verb*

**Crept** is the past tense and past participle of **creep**.

**crescendo** *noun* **crescendos**

A **crescendo** is when a noise or a piece of music gets louder and louder: *The cheering reached a crescendo when the striker scored.*
[**Crescendo** comes from Italian *crescendo* 'increasing'.]

**crescent** *noun* **crescents**

1 A **crescent** is a curved shape like the shape of a new moon.
2 A **crescent** is a row of houses built in a curve.
[**Crescent** comes from Latin *crescens* 'growing'.]

**cress** *noun*

**Cress** is a green plant with tiny leaves that you eat in salads or sandwiches.
[**Cress** comes via French from Old English.]

**crest** *noun* **crests**

1 The **crest** of a hill or a wave is the top of it: *a surfer on the crest of a wave.*
2 A bird's **crest** is the tuft of feathers on top of its head.
3 A **crest** is a design that is the symbol of a noble family, a town or an organisation: *The family crest is on our coat of arms.*
[**Crest** comes via French from Latin *crista* 'tuft'.]

**crevasse** *noun* **crevasses**

A **crevasse** is a deep crack in thick rock or ice, especially a glacier.
[**Crevasse** comes from old French *crevace* 'a split'.]

**crevice** *noun* **crevices**

A **crevice** is a narrow crack, especially in a rock.
[**Crevice** comes from the same old French word as **crevasse**.]

**crew** *noun* **crews**

1 A **crew** of a ship, aircraft or spacecraft is the people who work on it or sail or fly it.
2 A **crew** is a group of people with special skills who work together to do a certain job: *a film crew; an ambulance crew.*
[**Crew** comes from an old French word.]

**crew** *verb* **crews, crewing, crewed**

The people who **crew** a boat or ship are the people who row or sail it: *Twelve*

people are crewing the boat in the race.

**crib** *noun* **cribs**

A **crib** is a baby's cot.
[**Crib** comes from Old English.]

**cricket**[1] *noun*

**Cricket** is an outdoor game played by two teams of eleven players with a ball, bats and wickets.
[No one knows where **cricket**[1] comes from.]

**cricket**[2] *noun* **crickets**

A **cricket** is an insect like a grasshopper that makes a noise by rubbing its back legs together.
[**Cricket**[2] comes from French *criquet*, an imitation of the sound.]

**crime** *noun* **crimes**

A **crime** is something that someone does that is against the law: *Stealing is a crime.*
[**Crime** comes via French from Latin *crimen* 'an offence'.]

**criminal** *noun* **criminals** (th)

A **criminal** is someone who has broken the law: *The criminal was sent to prison.*
[**Criminal** comes from the same Latin word as **crime**.]

**crimson** *noun*

**Crimson** is a dark red colour.
[**Crimson** comes from Arabic.]

**crimson** *adjective*

of a dark red colour.

**cripple** *verb* **cripples, crippling, crippled** (th)

1 If someone is **crippled**, they are so badly injured that they will never walk again: *She was crippled after a car accident.*
2 If something is **crippled**, it is badly damaged and does not work properly: *cut the phone lines and cripple communication.*
[**Cripple** comes from Old English.]

**crisis** *noun* **crises** (th)

A **crisis** is a situation where there are serious problems or difficulties: *Divorce causes a crisis in the family.*
[**Crisis** comes via Latin from Greek *krisis* 'decision'.]

**crisp** *adjective* **crisper, crispest**

1 Food that is **crisp** is hard and crunchy: *crisp bacon.*
2 Something that is **crisp** is dry, fresh and

cool: *a crisp winter morning; crisp sheets.*
[**Crisp** comes from Latin.]

### crisp *noun* **crisps**

A **crisp** is a thin slice of potato that is fried to make it crunchy: *cheese and onion crisps.*

### crispy *adjective* **crispier, crispiest**

**Crispy** food is crunchy: *crispy stir-fried vegetables.*

### critic *noun* **critics**

1 A **critic** is someone whose job is to talk or write about what is good and bad about books, television programmes, films and plays: *The film had good reviews from the critics.*
2 A **critic** is someone who finds fault with someone or something: *Critics of the government say that it has lost touch with ordinary people.*
[**Critic** comes via Latin from Greek *krites* 'a judge'.]

### critical *adjective* (th)

1 If you are **critical** of people or things, you notice and talk about their faults: *Nothing pleases him – he's so critical of everything.*
2 If a situation is **critical**, it is dangerous or uncertain: *There might be a war: the situation is critical right now.*
3 If someone is in a **critical** condition, s/he is very ill and you do not know if s/he will live or die.
[**Critical** comes via Latin from the same Greek word as **critic**.]

### criticise *verb* **criticises, criticising, criticised** *Also* **criticize** (th)

1 If you **criticise** things or people, you say what you think is wrong with them.
2 To **criticise** a book, play, film or television programme is to say what is good and bad about it.
[**Criticise** comes from **critic**.]

### croak *verb* **croaks, croaking, croaked**

1 When a frog **croaks**, it makes a deep throaty sound.
2 When a person **croaks**, s/he speaks with a deep hoarse voice: *"I've got a terrible cold," she croaked.*
[The word **croak** is an imitation of the sound.]

### crockery *noun*

**Crockery** is all the china and pottery cups, plates and bowls that people use for drinks and meals.
[**Crockery** comes from Old English *croc* 'a piece of crockery'.]

### crocodile *noun* **crocodiles**

1 A **crocodile** is a long large reptile with sharp teeth and strong jaws.
2 A **crocodile** is a line of children walking along in twos.
3 If you say someone is crying **crocodile tears**, you mean that s/he is only pretending to be sad about something.
[**Crocodile** comes from Greek via Latin.]

### crocus *noun* **crocuses**

A **crocus** is a white, purple or yellow spring flower that grows from a bulb.
[**Crocus** comes from Greek via Latin.]

### crook *noun* **crooks**

1 A **crook** is a criminal or a dishonest person.
2 A shepherd's **crook** is a long stick with a hook at the end.
3 The **crook** of your arm is the place inside your elbow where it bends.
[**Crook** comes from Old Norse.]

### crooked *adjective* (th)

1 If something is **crooked**, it is uneven, bent or twisted: *crooked teeth.*
2 If something is **crooked**, it is dishonest or illegal: *a crooked scheme to sell land on the moon.*
3 Someone who is **crooked** is dishonest or a criminal: *a crooked car dealer.*

### crop *noun* **crops**

A **crop** is a plant grown in large quantities for food: *a potato crop.*
[**Crop** comes from Old English.]

### crop *verb* **crops, cropping, cropped**

If you **crop** something such as hair or grass, you cut it very short: *Grazing sheep crop the grass.*

### cross *noun* **crosses**

1 A **cross** is a mark or a shape like this + or this x.
2 A **cross** is a large wooden object in the shape of a **cross** that was used in the past for crucifying criminals.
[**Cross** comes via Old Norse and Irish from Latin *crux* (ancestor of **crucify**).]

### cross *adjective*

Someone who is **cross** is angry.
**crossly** *adverb.*

**cross** verb **crosses, crossing, crossed**
**1** To **cross** something is to move from one side of it to the other: *cross the ocean.*
**2** If you **cross** two things, or if two things **cross**, one goes across the other: *cross your fingers; where the road and the railway cross.*

**crossing** noun **crossings**
**1** A **crossing** is a journey on a boat or ship across the sea: *The ferry crossing was rough.*
**2** A **crossing** is a place where you can cross a road or railway: *a pedestrian crossing; a level crossing.*

**crouch** verb **crouches, crouching, crouched** (th)
To **crouch** is to get close to the ground by bending your legs underneath you: *I crouched in the bushes so she wouldn't see me.*
[**Crouch** probably comes from an old French word.]

**crowd** noun **crowds** (th)
A **crowd** is a large group of people gathered together in one place: *crowds of people in the January sales.*
[**Crowd** comes from Old English.]

**crowd** verb **crowds, crowding, crowded**
When people **crowd** a place, a lot of people are packed into it: *Football fans crowded into the stadium.*

**crown** noun **crowns**
A **crown** is a headdress made of gold and jewels that is worn by a king or queen.
[**Crown** comes from Latin *corona* (ancestor of **coronation**).]

**crown** verb **crowns, crowning, crowned**
When someone is **crowned**, s/he becomes the queen or king: *Queen Elizabeth was crowned in 1953.*

**crucifixion** noun
**Crucifixion** is when someone is crucified: *Christ's crucifixion.*

**crucify** verb **crucifies, crucifying, crucified**
If someone is **crucified**, s/he is fastened to a cross and left to die.
[**Crucify** comes via French from Latin *crux* 'a cross'.]

**cruel** adjective (th)
**1** A **cruel** person is very unkind to people or animals, or does not mind seeing them suffer.
**2** Something that is **cruel** is unkind and causes suffering: *a cruel remark.*
**cruelly** adverb. **cruelty** noun.
[**Cruel** comes from Latin via French.]

**crumb** noun **crumbs**
A **crumb** is a tiny piece of bread, cake or biscuit: *There are toast crumbs in the bed.*
[**Crumb** comes from Old English.]

**crunchy** adjective **crunchier, crunchiest**
**Crunchy** food is hard and makes a noise when you eat it.
[The word **crunchy** is an imitation of the sound.]

**crush** verb **crushes, crushing, crushed** (th)
**1** If you **crush** something, you break it or make it lose its shape by pressing it very hard: *Grain is crushed to make flour; People were crushed in the rush for the door.*
**2** If an army or an organisation is **crushed**, it is defeated and destroyed: *The revolt was crushed by the government.*
[**Crush** comes from an old French word.]

**crust** noun **crusts**
**1** A **crust** is the hard outer covering of a loaf of bread or a pie: *cut the crusts off the sandwiches.*
**2** The earth's **crust** is the thin layer of rock on its surface.
[**Crust** comes from Latin *crusta* 'rind or shell'.]

**cry** verb **cries, crying, cried** (th)
**1** When you **cry**, tears fall from your eyes because you are happy, sad or in pain: *I cried when I broke my arm.*
**2** To **cry** means to shout something out: *"Fire!" she cried.*
[**Cry** comes from Latin via French.]

**crystal** noun **crystals**
A **crystal** is a piece of hard glassy rock.
[**Crystal** comes from Greek.]

**crystallise** verb **crystallises, crystallising, crystallised** Also **crystallize**
When a substance **crystallises**, it forms into crystals.

**cub** noun **cubs**
A **cub** is the young of some animals such as lions, wolves, bears or foxes.
[No one knows where **cub** comes from.]

**cube** noun **cubes**
A **cube** is a solid shape with six square sides.
[**Cube** comes from Greek via French or Latin.]

**cube** verb **cubes, cubing, cubed**
**1** To **cube** something means to cut it into cubes.
**2** To **cube** a number means to multiply it

by itself twice. The sign for a number that has been **cubed** is ³. 10³ means 10 **cubed**, or 10 x 10 x 10.

**cubic** *adjective*
Something that is **cubic** is shaped like a cube.

**cuckoo** *noun* **cuckoos**
A **cuckoo** is a bird that lays its eggs in another bird's nest.
[The word **cuckoo** is an imitation of its call.]

**cucumber** *noun* **cucumbers**
A **cucumber** is a long green vegetable eaten in salads and sandwiches.
[**Cucumber** comes from Latin via French.]

**cuff** *noun* **cuffs**
A **cuff** is the part of a sleeve that goes around the wrist.
[No one knows where **cuff** comes from.]

**culprit** *noun* **culprits**
A **culprit** is someone who has committed a crime or done something wrong: *We have to find the culprit.*
[**Culprit** comes from an old French word.]

**cup** *noun* **cups**
1 A **cup** is a small bowl with a handle that you drink from: *a cup and saucer.*
2 A **cup** is a gold or silver trophy given as a sports prize.
[**Cup** comes from Latin via Old English.]

**cupboard** *noun* **cupboards**
A **cupboard** is a piece of furniture with doors or a small room that is used for storing things in: *a built-in cupboard.*
[**Cupboard** originally meant a sideboard on which cups and other crockery were kept.]

**cure** *verb* **cures, curing, cured** (th)
To **cure** someone is to make that person better when s/he is ill.
[**Cure** comes from Latin *curare* 'to care for'.]

**cure** *noun* **cures** (th)
A **cure** for an injury or illness is the medicine or treatment that makes it better: *The best cure for a headache is rest.*

**curious** *adjective* (th)
1 If you are **curious** about something you are interested in it and want to find out more about it.
2 Something that is unusual or strange is **curious**: *That's a curious tool – what's it for?*
[**Curious** comes via French from Latin *curiosus* 'careful'.]

**curl** *noun* **curls**
A **curl** is a lock of hair that twists into a curve or spiral. **curly** *adjective.*
[**Curl** comes from an old Dutch word.]

**curl** *verb* **curls, curling, curled**
To **curl** means to bend into the shape of a spiral or curve: *He curled up in the chair; My hair curls naturally.*

**currant** *noun* **currants**
A **currant** is a dried grape.
[**Currant** comes from an old French word.]

**currency** *noun* **currencies**
A country's **currency** is the kind of money that it uses: *The currency of Australia is the dollar; Do you change foreign currency?*
[**Currency** comes from **current**.]

**current** *noun* **currents**
A **current** is a stream or flow of air, water or electricity.

**current** *adjective*
Something that is **current** is happening or existing now: *There are three German marks to the pound at the current rate.*
[**Current** comes via French from Latin *currens* 'running'.]

**curriculum** *noun* **curriculums** *or* **curricula**
A **curriculum** is all the different subjects that are taught in a school or college: *French isn't on the curriculum this year.*
[**Curriculum** comes from Latin *curriculum* 'a course'.]

**curtain** *noun* **curtains**
A **curtain** is a piece of cloth that is pulled across a window or across the front of a stage. [**Curtain** comes from Latin via French.]

**curve** *noun* **curves** (th)
A **curve** is a smooth bend with no sharp corners. [**Curve** comes from Latin.]

**curve** *verb* **curves, curving, curved**
To **curve** is to bend or turn smoothly: *The road curves to the right; The plane curved towards the runway.*

**cushion** *noun* **cushions**
A **cushion** is a type of pillow for chairs, sofas or the floor.
[**Cushion** comes from an old French word.]

**custom** *noun* **customs** (th)
1 A **custom** is something that the people of a society usually do or have done for a long time: *It's the custom to send people*

cards at Christmas.

**2 Customs** is the place at the border of a country where officers check that nothing illegal is being brought into the country: *I'll meet you once I've been through Customs.* [**Custom** comes via French from Latin *consuetus* 'used to'.]

**cut** *noun* **cuts**
A **cut** is a wound in the skin made by something sharp: *put a plaster on the cut.* [**Cut** is probably from Old English.]

**cut** *verb* **cuts**, **cutting**, **cut** (th)
**1** If you **cut** something with a knife or scissors, you separate it into two or more pieces: *Cut the cake into equal slices.*
**2** To **cut** someone or something means to hurt or damage that person or thing with a sharp object.

**cutlery** *noun*
**Cutlery** is the knives, forks and spoons that you eat your food with.

[**Cutlery** comes via French from Latin *culter* 'knife'.]

**cycle** *noun* **cycles**
**1** A **cycle** is a series of events, or a series of movements, that is repeated many times: *the cycle of the seasons; Wash the sheets on the hot cycle.*
**2** A **cycle** is a bicycle, tricycle or motorcycle.
[**Cycle** comes via French and Latin from Greek *kuklos* 'circle'.]

**cycle** *verb* **cycles**, **cycling**, **cycled**
To **cycle** means to ride a bicycle: *Do you cycle to school?*

**cylinder** *noun* **cylinders**
A **cylinder** is a shape with circular ends and straight sides.
[**Cylinder** comes via Latin from Greek *kulindros* 'roller'.]

## Dictionary Fun

### Complete the proverbs
1. Cut your c_____ according to your cloth.
2. Don't c_____ your c_____ before they're hatched.
3. Every c_____ has a silver lining.
4. Too many c____ spoil the broth.

### What do these idioms mean?
1. To go like hot cakes
2. To carry the can
3. To put the cart before the horse

### Etymology
1. Which 'c' word comes from a French word meaning 'coffee' or 'coffee house'?
2. How are the words **centipede** and **centimetre** related?

3. Which 'c' word comes from the Greek word *koimeterion*, which means 'sleeping room'?

### Riddle
The person that made it never used it. The person that used it, never saw it. Which 'c' word is it?

### Did you know?
◆ The word **coconut** comes from the Spanish and Portuguese *coco* 'grimace' + *nut* because the base of the shell looks like a face.
◆ The word **cardigan** is named after the Earl of Cardigan, whose army first wore them in the Crimean War.

a b **c** d e f g h i j k l m

# Dd

**dab** *verb* **dabs, dabbing, dabbed**
If you **dab** a surface, you touch it or press it with quick, light strokes: *He dabbed his face with a towel; She dabbed disinfectant on the cut.*
[The word **dab** is an imitation of the sound of dabbing something wet.]

**dabble** *verb* **dabbles, dabbling, dabbled**
If you **dabble** in something, you take part in it or study it, but not very seriously.
[**Dabble** comes from **dab**.]

**daffodil** *noun* **daffodils**
A **daffodil** is a yellow flower that grows from a bulb in the spring.
[**Daffodil** comes from *asphodel*, the name of another plant with yellow flowers.]

**daily** *adjective, adverb*
produced or happening every day: *a daily paper; The bus goes twice daily.*
[**Daily** comes from **day**.]

**dairy** *noun* **dairies**
A **dairy** is a building where cows are milked or where milk is made into butter, cheese and yoghurt.
[**Dairy** comes from Old English.]

**daisy** *noun* **daisies**
A **daisy** is a flower with a yellow centre surrounded by white petals. **Daisies** open their petals when the sun shines and close them when it goes down.
[**Daisy** comes from *day's eye.*]

**dam** *noun* **dams**
A **dam** is a strong barrier built across a river or lake to hold the water back.
[**Dam** comes from Old English.]

**damage** *noun* (th)
**Damage** is harm that is done to something: *The fire did a lot of damage; the damage to the school's reputation.*
[**Damage** comes from Latin *damnum* 'loss'.]

**damage** *verb* **damages, damaging, damaged** (th)
To **damage** something is to break or spoil it: *Too much sugar damages your teeth.*

**damp** *adjective* **damper, dampest**
Something that is **damp** is slightly wet.
[**Damp** probably comes from an old Dutch or German word.]

**dance** *verb* **dances, dancing, danced**
When people **dance**, they move their bodies to the rhythm of music: *Megan danced with Tony.*
[**Dance** comes from an old French word.]

**dancer** *noun* **dancers**
A **dancer** is a person who dances, often as a job: *a good dancer; a ballet dancer.*

**danger** *noun* **dangers** (th)
**1** A **danger** is something or someone that is not safe or could hurt you: *Electric sockets are a danger to babies; a criminal who is a danger to the public.*
**2** If someone is **in danger**, s/he could be hurt or killed.
[**Danger** comes from an old French word.]

**dangerous** *adjective* (th)
Someone or something that is **dangerous** could hurt or kill someone: *Fire is dangerous; dangerous sports.*
**dangerously** *adverb.*

**dark** *adjective* **darker, darkest** (th)
not light: *dark blue; It's dark during the night.* **darkness** *noun.*
[**Dark** comes from Old English.]

**Dark Ages** *noun*
The time in history between about AD 450 and AD 1000 is called the **Dark Ages**.
[The **Dark Ages** were so called because people did not know very much about them.]

**dart** *noun* **darts**
A **dart** is a short arrow that you throw at a dartboard in the game of **darts**.
[**Dart** comes from an old French word.]

**dart** *verb* **darts, darting, darted**
To **dart** is to move suddenly and quickly: *Fish darted around the pond.*

**data** *plural noun* **datum** *singular*
**Data** is information, especially information stored on a computer: *The data is stored on the hard disk.*
[**Data** comes from Latin.]

**date¹** *noun* **dates**
A **date** is a certain day, month and year: *The date on the letter is 28 July 1999; What date do you go on holiday?*
[**Date¹** comes from Latin.]

**date² noun dates**
A **date** is a soft, brown, sweet fruit that grows on a palm tree.
[**Date²** comes from Greek via French and Latin.]

**daughter noun daughters**
Your **daughter** is your female child.
[**Daughter** comes from Old English.]

**daughter-in-law noun daughters-in-law**
Your **daughter-in-law** is your son's wife.

**dawn noun dawns (th)**
**1** **Dawn** is when it gets light early in the morning: *the crack of dawn.*
**2** The **dawn** of something is the beginning of something new: *The Industrial Revolution was the dawn of a new age.*
[**Dawn** comes from Old English.]

**day noun days**
**1** A **day** is a 24-hour period from midnight to midnight.
**2** The **day** is the time between sunrise and sunset when it is light.
[**Day** comes from Old English.]

**dazzle verb dazzles, dazzling, dazzled**
**1** If someone is **dazzled** by a bright light, it shines into their eyes and blinds them for a few moments: *The fox was dazzled by the car's headlights.*
**2** If people are **dazzled** by something someone does, they are amazed and impressed: *The magician dazzled the audience with her tricks.*
[**Dazzle** comes from Old Norse.]

**dead adjective (th)**
**1** Something or someone that is **dead** is no longer alive.
**2** If a place is **dead**, it is very quiet because no people are there: *The streets are dead at this time of night.*
[**Dead** comes from Old English.]

**deadline noun deadlines**
A **deadline** is a time when something must be done by: *The deadline for entering the competition is 5 o'clock on Tuesday.*
[**Deadline** originally meant a line round an American prison. Prisoners could be shot if they went beyond it.]

**deadly adjective deadlier, deadliest (th)**
Something that is **deadly** is so dangerous that it could kill you: *a deadly poison; Ice on roads is deadly.*

**deaf adjective deafer, deafest**
Someone who is **deaf** cannot hear properly. **deafness** *noun.*
[**Deaf** comes from Old English.]

**deal noun deals (th)**
A **deal** is an agreement, especially in business: *We made a deal with the farmer for him to supply vegetables to our shop.*
[**Deal** comes from Old English.]

**deal verb deals, dealing, dealt (th)**
**1** When you **deal** with someone, you do business with them: *deal with companies all over the world.*
**2** When you **deal** with something, you sort it out: *deal with a problem.*
**3** When you **deal** cards, you give some to each player in the game.

**dear adjective dearer, dearest (th)**
**1** A **dear** person is someone you like very much or love: *my dear daughter.*
**2** You write **Dear** before someone's name at the beginning of a letter: *Dear Mum; Dear Sir.*
**3** Something that costs a lot is **dear**: *Caviar is very dear.*
[**Dear** comes from Old English.]

**death noun deaths**
Someone's **death** is the end of that person's life: *The fire caused the death of three people; She bled to death.*
[**Death** comes from Old English.]

**debate noun debates**
A **debate** is a serious discussion between two groups of people with different opinions: *a political debate.*
[**Debate** comes from Latin via French.]

**debate verb debates, debating, debated (th)**
To **debate** something is to discuss it with someone who has a different opinion: *The government debated whether to change the law; They are debating whether to go out or stay in and watch television.*

**debt noun debts**
**1** A **debt** is money that you owe someone.
**2** If you are **in debt**, you owe someone money.
[**Debt** comes from Latin *debitum* 'what is owed'.]

**debtor noun debtors**
A **debtor** is a person or a company that

owes money: *The company's debtors owe them millions.*

## debug *verb* **debugs, debugging, debugged**

To **debug** a computer program is to remove the faults in it: *The software was debugged during testing.*
[**Debug** comes from *de-* 'undoing, taking away' and **bug**.]

## debut *noun* **debuts** *Also* **début**

When someone makes their **debut**, they appear in public for the first time: *The band made their stage debut in 1997.*
[**Debut** comes from French *débuter* 'to begin'.]

## decade *noun* **decades**

A **decade** is a period of ten years.
[**Decade** comes via French and Latin from Greek *deka* 'ten'.]

## decapitate *verb* **decapitates, decapitating, decapitated**

To **decapitate** someone is to cut off his/her head: *Henry VIII had two of his wives decapitated.*
[**Decapitate** comes from Latin *de-* 'taking away' and *caput* 'head'.]

## decay *verb* **decays, decaying, decayed** (th)

If something **decays**, it rots: *the smell of decaying meat; Sugar decays your teeth.*
[**Decay** comes from Latin via French.]

## deceit *noun*

**Deceit** is telling someone something that is not true: *I'm fed up with all his lies and deceit.* **deceitful** *adjective*.
[**Deceit** comes via French from the same Latin word as **deceive**.]

## deceive *verb* **deceives, deceiving, deceived** (th)

When you **deceive** someone, you tell them something that is not true because you want to trick them: *He deceived me in order to steal my money.*
[**Deceive** comes from Latin via French.]

## deceptive *adjective*

If something is **deceptive**, it makes you think that something is not what it really is: *Appearances are deceptive; His mild manner is deceptive – he has a really bad temper.* **deceptively** *adverb*.
[**Deceptive** comes from the same Latin word as **deceive**.]

## decibel *noun* **decibels**

A **decibel** is a unit for measuring how loud a sound is.
[**Decibel** comes from Latin *decimus* 'a tenth' and *bel*, a unit for measuring sound which was named after Alexander Graham *Bell*, who invented the telephone. A **decibel** is one-tenth of a bel.]

## decide *verb* **decides, deciding, decided** (th)

To **decide** is to make up your mind about something: *Have you decided what you want to do this weekend?*
[**Decide** comes from Latin via French.]

## decided *adjective* (th)

If you are **decided** about something, you are very certain of it: *Now I'm decided about buying a car, I won't change my mind.*

## deciduous *adjective*

**Deciduous** trees lose their leaves every year before winter: *Is this tree deciduous or evergreen?*
[**Deciduous** comes from Latin *decidere* 'to fall off'.]

## decimal *noun* **decimals**

1 In a **decimal** system, you count in units of ten: *decimal currency.*
2 A **decimal** is a fraction that is written as a dot followed by one or more figures. The first figure after the dot stands for so many tenths, the second figure for so many hundredths, and so on: *7.3 equals 7 and 3 tenths.*
[**Decimal** comes from Latin *decimus* 'a tenth'.]

## decipher *verb* **deciphers, deciphering, deciphered**

To **decipher** something is to work out something that is written in code or is very difficult to understand: *I can't decipher his handwriting.*
[**Decipher** comes from *de-* 'undoing' and *cipher* 'a code'.]

## decision *noun* **decisions**

If you **make a decision** about something, you make up your mind about it.
[**Decision** comes from the same Latin word as **decide**.]

## decisive *adjective* (th)

1 A **decisive** person can make up his/her

mind quickly.

**2** If something is **decisive**, it decides something or makes sure of a certain result: *a decisive battle*.
**decisively** *adverb*. **decisiveness** *noun*.
[**Decisive** comes via French from the same Latin word as **decide**.]

**deck** *noun* **decks**
A **deck** is a floor in a ship or bus: *the top deck; Restaurants are on deck B*.
[**Deck** comes from an old Dutch word.]

**decline** *verb* **declines, declining, declined** (th)
**1** If something **declines**, it becomes worse or less: *His health has declined recently; Her interest in her work has declined*.
**2** If you **decline** something, or **decline to do** something, you refuse politely to take it or to do it: *He declined the invitation; We asked her to tell us what happened, but she declined*.
[**Decline** comes via French from Latin *decliner* 'to bend down'.]

**decorate** *verb* **decorates, decorating, decorated** (th)
**1** If you **decorate** a room, you paint it or wallpaper it.
**2** If you **decorate** something, you put pretty things on or in it to make it look nice: *decorate the Christmas tree; a hat decorated with flowers*.
[**Decorate** comes from Latin *decor* 'beauty'.]

**decrease** *verb* **decreases, decreasing, decreased** (th)
To **decrease** is to make or become less or smaller: *After twenty minutes, decrease the temperature to 150°; Unemployment has decreased in the past year*.
[**Decrease** comes via French from Latin *de-* 'down' and *crescere* 'to grow' (ancestor of **increase**).]

**decrease** *noun* **decreases** (th)
A **decrease** is the amount by which something becomes less: *a decrease from 6% to 4%*.

**decree** *noun* **decrees**
A **decree** is an official order that must be obeyed. [**Decree** comes from Latin.]

**decree** *verb* **decrees, decreeing, decreed**
To **decree** something is to give an official order that must be obeyed: *The court decreed that he had to return to his own country*.

**decrepit** *adjective* (th)
Something or someone that is **decrepit** is old and weak or in bad condition.
[**Decrepit** comes from Latin.]

**dedicate** *verb* **dedicates, dedicating, dedicated** (th)
**1** If you **dedicate** yourself to something, you spend a lot of time and energy doing it: *Mother Teresa dedicated her life to helping the poor*.
**2** An author **dedicates** a book to someone by putting that person's name at the front as a way of showing love or saying thanks: *This book is dedicated to my dear parents*. [**Dedicate** comes from Latin.]

**deed** *noun* **deeds**
**1** A **deed** is something that someone has done: *a good deed*.
**2** The **deed** of a house is a legal document that shows who owns it.
[**Deed** comes from Old English.]

**deep** *adjective* **deeper, deepest**
Something that is **deep** goes a long way down from the top to the bottom: *the deep end of the swimming pool; The crater is 12 metres deep*.
[**Deep** comes from Old English.]

**deer** *noun* **deer**
A **deer** is a wild animal that lives in forests. Some deer have antlers.
[**Deer** comes from Old English.]

**deface** *verb* **defaces, defacing, defaced** (th)
To **deface** something is to spoil the way it looks, especially by writing on it: *The statue was defaced when vandals sprayed paint on it*.
[**Deface** comes from old French *desfacier* 'to spoil the face of'.]

**defeat** *verb* **defeats, defeating, defeated** (th)
To **defeat** someone means to beat someone in a competition or battle: *Napoleon was defeated at the battle of Waterloo*.

[**Defeat** comes from Latin via French.]

**defect** *noun* **defects**
A **defect** is a fault in something or someone: *His main defect is that he is so untidy.*
[**Defect** comes via French from Latin *deficere* 'to abandon' or 'to fail to do'.]

**defect** *verb* **defects, defecting, defected**
To **defect** is to move to another country or political party for political reasons: *The Russian spy defected to the USA in 1956.*

**defective** *adjective* (th)
If something is **defective**, it has something wrong with it so that it does not work properly: *The car crashed because its brakes were defective.*

**defend** *verb* **defends, defending, defended**
1 To **defend** means to protect something or someone from harm.
2 A lawyer **defends** someone in court by trying to show that s/he is not guilty of committing a crime.
3 If you **defend** the goal in games such as football or hockey, you try to stop the other team from scoring.
[**Defend** comes from Latin *fendere* 'to hit' (ancestor of **offend**).]

**defendant** *noun* **defendants**
A **defendant** is a person in court who has been accused of committing a crime.

**defer** *verb* **defers, deferring, deferred** (th)
If you **defer** something, you put it off until later: *She deferred her entry to university for a year.*
[**Defer** comes from Latin via French.]

**defiant** *adjective*
If you are **defiant**, you disobey rules that you do not agree with: *Defiant students refused to attend extra lessons.*
[**Defiant** comes from old French *desfier* 'to challenge'.]

**define** *verb* **defines, defining, defined**
If you **define** something, you say exactly what it is or what it means.
[**Define** comes via French from Latin *finis* 'end, limit' (ancestor of **finish**).]

**definite** *adjective*
1 If something is **definite**, it is firm and clear and is not likely to change: *He has very definite opinions; We had a definite arrangement to meet here tonight.*
2 If someone is **definite**, s/he is quite sure and firm about something.
**definitely** *adverb*.
[**Definite** comes from the same French word as **define**.]

**definition** *noun* **definitions**
The **definition** of a word is an explanation of what it means.

**degree** *noun* **degrees**
1 A **degree** is a measurement used for temperatures and angles. The symbol for a degree is °: *20° Celsius; a 45-degree angle.*
2 A **degree** is a qualification that students study for at university: *a degree in Chemistry.*
[**Degree** comes via French from Latin *gradus* 'a step' (ancestor of **grade**).]

**dehydrated** *adjective*
1 If a person is **dehydrated** they do not have enough water in their body: *I felt very dehydrated after the flu.*
2 If something such as a food is **dehydrated**, the water has been taken out of it so that it will keep better, and you add water before you use it.
[**Dehydrated** comes from Lati *de-* 'taking away' and Greek *hydor* 'water'.]

**deity** *noun* **deities**
A **deity** is a god or goddess.
[**Deity** comes from Latin *deus* 'god'.]

**dejected** *adjective* (th)
A **dejected** person feels disappointed and depressed, usually because they have failed at something: *I felt very dejected when I failed my driving test.*
[**Dejected** comes from Latin *dejectum* 'thrown down'.]

**delay** *verb* **delays, delaying, delayed** (th)
1 To **delay** something is to put it off until later: *I'll delay my holiday for a few months because I've got too much work to do.*
2 If someone or something is **delayed**, something makes him/her or it late: *The flight was delayed for a few hours.*
[**Delay** comes from French.]

**delay** *noun* **delays**
1 A **delay** is the amount of time that something is late by: *There was a 15-minute delay before the film started.*
2 A **delay** on the road is the extra time it

takes to travel somewhere because of an accident or roadworks: *Delays on the High Street are likely for the next two months.*

**delegate** *verb* **delegates, delegating, delegated**
When you **delegate**, you give some of your work to other people: *I delegate work to my assistants.*
[**Delegate** comes from Latin *delegatus* 'sent to do something'.]

**delegate** *noun* **delegates**
A **delegate** is a person who represents others at a meeting or conference.

**delete** *verb* **deletes, deleting, deleted**
To **delete** something is to remove words from a piece of writing or to wipe something off a computer: *delete the first paragraph; delete old e-mails.*
[**Delete** comes from Latin.]

**deliberate** *adjective* (th)
If something is **deliberate,** someone has planned it: *Was that deliberate or was it an accident?* **deliberately** *adverb.*
[**Deliberate** comes from Latin *deliberatus* 'weighed carefully'.]

**deliberate** *verb* **deliberates, deliberating, deliberated** (th)
If you **deliberate,** you think very carefully about something: *We're deliberating whether to go on holiday or save our money.*

**delicacy** *noun* **delicacies**
A **delicacy** is food that is special because it is rare and usually expensive.
[**Delicacy** comes from **delicate.**]

**delicate** *adjective* (th)
If something is **delicate,** it is carefully made or very pretty but often easily damaged: *the delicate wings of a butterfly.*
[**Delicate** comes from Latin via French.]

**delicatessen** *noun* **delicatessens**
A **delicatessen** is a shop that sells cooked meats, cheeses and unusual or foreign food.
[**Delicatessen** comes via Dutch or German from the same French word as **delicate.**]

**delicious** *adjective* (th)
Food that tastes or smells good is **delicious.**
[**Delicious** comes via French from the same Latin word as **delight.**]

**delight** *noun* **delights** (th)
**Delight** is a feeling of great happiness: *She shrieked with delight when she saw him.*
[**Delight** comes from Latin.]

**delight** *verb* **delights, delighting, delighted**
Something that **delights** you makes you feel very happy: *The puppet show delighted the children; We'd be delighted if you would join us for dinner.*

**delinquent** *noun* **delinquents**
A **delinquent** is a young person who is often in trouble with the police.
[**Delinquent** comes from Latin *deliquere* 'to offend'.]

**delirious** *adjective*
1 If you are **delirious** you are confused and you talk a lot because you are ill.
2 Someone who is **delirious** is wildly happy or excited: *I'll be delirious if she wants to go out with me.* **deliriously** *adverb.*
[**Delirious** comes from Latin.]

**deliver** *verb* **delivers, delivering, delivered**
1 To **deliver** something is to take it to wherever it has to go: *Rick delivers newspapers.*
2 When a baby is **delivered**, it is born: *The baby was delivered at home.*
[**Deliver** comes from Latin via French.]

**delivery** *noun* **deliveries**
1 A **delivery** is the arrival of something that someone has sent: *I'm expecting a delivery from the postman this morning.*
2 A **delivery** is the birth of a baby: *She stayed in hospital after a difficult delivery.*

**delta** *noun* **deltas**
A **delta** is an area of land where a river slows down and splits into smaller rivers and deposits its sediment before it enters the sea.
[**Delta** is the name of the fourth letter of the Greek alphabet and looks like this: Δ, something like the shape of a delta.]

**delude** *verb* **deludes, deluding, deluded**
If you **delude** people, you make them believe something that is not true.
[**Delude** comes from Latin *deludere* 'to make fun of'.]

**deluge** *noun* **deluges**
1 A **deluge** is heavy rain or floods of

**a b c d e f g h i j k l m**

water: *Houses are under water after this morning's deluge.*
**2** A **deluge** of telephone calls, letters or questions is too many of them to cope with.
[**Deluge** comes via French from a Latin word meaning 'to wash away'.]

**deluge** *verb* **deluges, deluging, deluged**
If you are **deluged** with telephone calls, letters or questions, you receive too many to cope with: *The television station was deluged with phone calls of complaint.*

**delusion** *noun* **delusions** (th)
A **delusion** is a false belief about something: *She's under the delusion that she's the most popular girl in the school; He's mentally ill and suffers from delusions.*
[**Delusion** comes from the same Latin word as **delude**.]

**demand** *noun* **demands**
If there is a **demand** for something, or it is **in demand**, a lot of people want it: *Computer games are in great demand this Christmas.*
[**Demand** comes from Latin via French.]

**demand** *verb* **demands, demanding, demanded** (th)
If you **demand** something, you ask for it firmly: *demand the truth.*

**demanding** *adjective*
Something or someone that is **demanding** requires a lot of energy and attention: *a demanding job; Babies are very demanding.*

**demeanour** *noun*
Someone's **demeanour** is the way they look and behave that gives you an idea of what they are like.
[**Demeanour** comes from an old French word.]

**demise** *noun*
The **demise** of something is the end of its existence: *the demise of the corner shop.*
[**Demise** comes from French.]

**democracy** *noun* **democracies**
**1 Democracy** is a way of governing a country where people are allowed to vote freely for the leader they want: *Most people think democracy is better than dictatorship.*
**2** A **democracy** is a country where people are allowed to vote freely for the leader

they want.
[**Democracy** comes via French and Latin from Greek *demos* 'the people' and *kratia* 'power'.]

**demolish** *verb* **demolishes, demolishing, demolished** (th)
**1** To **demolish** something is to destroy it completely: *The bomb demolished the building.*
**2** To **demolish** food is to eat it very quickly: *He demolished the meal in two minutes.*
[**Demolish** comes via French from Latin *de-* 'undoing' and *moliri* 'to build'.]

**demonstrate** *verb* **demonstrates, demonstrating, demonstrated** (th)
**1** If you **demonstrate** something, you show people how it works: *Rachel demonstrated the vacuum cleaner.*
**2** If people **demonstrate** about something, they gather together to protest about it: *The crowd is demonstrating against nuclear weapons.*
[**Demonstrate** comes from Latin *demonstrare* 'to point out'.]

**demonstration** *noun* **demonstrations**
**1** When someone gives you a **demonstration** of something, s/he shows you how it works.
**2** A **demonstration** is a group of people who are gathered together to protest about something: *Police broke up a demonstration outside the factory.*

**demote** *verb* **demotes, demoting, demoted**
A person who is **demoted** is given a less important job: *He was demoted from manager to assistant manager.*
[**Demote** comes from *de-* 'undoing' and **promote**.]

**denominator** *noun* **denominators**
The **denominator** in a fraction is the number at the bottom that shows how many equal parts the whole number is divided into: *In the fraction ¾, 4 is the denominator.*
[**Denominator** comes from Latin *nominare* 'to name'.]

**denounce** *verb* **denounces, denouncing, denounced**
If you **denounce** someone, you say in public that they have done something

wrong: *She was denounced as a traitor.*
[**Denounce** comes from Latin via French.]

## dense *adjective* **denser, densest**
1 If something is **dense**, it is made up of a lot of people or things in a small area: *a dense crowd; dense traffic.*
2 **Dense** fog or smoke is thick and difficult to see through.
[**Dense** comes from Latin.]

## dent *noun* **dents**
A **dent** is a hollow in the surface of something caused by something hitting it.
[**Dent** comes from Old English.]

## dent *verb* **dents, denting, dented**
To **dent** something is to hit it and make a hollow in it: *The car's door was dented in the accident.*

## dentist *noun* **dentists**
A **dentist** is someone whose job is to look after people's teeth.
[**Dentist** comes from French *dent* 'tooth'.]

## deny *verb* **denies, denying, denied**
1 If you **deny** something, you say that it is not true.
2 If you **deny** something, you refuse to give it or allow it.
[**Deny** comes via French from Latin *denegare* 'to say no'.]

## deodorant *noun* **deodorants**
**Deodorant** is a liquid that you put on your body so that you do not smell when you sweat.
[**Deodorant** comes from *de-* 'taking away' and Latin *odor* 'smell' (ancestor of **odour**).]

## depart *verb* **departs, departing, departed**
To **depart** means to leave a place: *The train will depart in five minutes.*
[**Depart** comes from an old French word.]

## deposit *noun* **deposits**
1 A **deposit** is part of the price of something that you pay to make sure you get it: *put down a deposit on a house.*
2 A **deposit** is an amount of money that you pay when you rent or hire something. This money is given back to you when you finish renting or hiring it, unless you have damaged it.
3 A **deposit** of something like rock or oil develops in the earth over millions of

years: *Oil deposits have been found under the ocean.*
[**Deposit** comes from Latin *depositum* 'something put down'.]

## deposit *verb* **deposits, depositing, deposited**
If you **deposit** something, you put it somewhere, especially in order to keep it safe: *deposit the money in a bank account.*

## depress *verb* **depresses, depressing, depressed**
1 If you **depress** someone, you make them feel sad: *I don't want to depress you, but it's raining again.*
2 If you push something down, you **depress** it.
[**Depress** comes from Latin via French.]

## depression *noun* **depressions**
1 If someone is suffering from **depression**, they are feeling very sad.
2 A **depression** is a time when a country's economy is not doing very well.
3 A **depression** is an area of low air pressure which sometimes leads to rain.

## depth *noun* **depths**
The **depth** of something is a measure of how deep it is either from the top to the bottom or the front to the back: *The depth of the pool at the shallow end is one metre; The sides of a cube are the same height, width and depth.* [**Depth** comes from **deep.**]

## deputy *noun* **deputies**
A **deputy** is an assistant who does the boss's job when the boss is away.
[**Deputy** comes via French from Latin *deputare* 'to consider someone to be something'.]

## descend *verb* **descends, descending, descended** (th)
1 To **descend** is to go down to a lower level from a higher level: *The parachute descended to the ground.*
2 If you are **descended** from someone, you are related to someone who lived in the past: *Queen Elizabeth II is descended from Henry VIII.*
[**Descend** comes from Latin *descendere* 'to climb down'.]

## descent *noun* **descents**
1 The **descent** is the way down from somewhere: *the steep descent into the canyon.*

**2** If you are of French **descent**, for example, you are related to people who lived in France in the past.

**describe** *verb* **describes, describing, described**
To **describe** is to explain what someone or something is like: *Describe your new bike.* [**Describe** comes from Latin *describere* 'to write down'.]

**description** *noun* **descriptions**
A **description** is the words that explain what someone or something is like: *I gave the police a description of the man who stole my bag.* [**Description** comes via French from the same Latin word as **describe**.]

**desert** *noun* **deserts**
A **desert** is a large, dry area of land where not much grows because there is very little rain. [**Desert** comes from Latin *desertus* 'abandoned'.]

**desert** *verb* **deserts, deserting, deserted** (th)
**1** If you **desert** someone, you abandon that person: *He deserted his wife and family.* **2** A soldier who **deserts** runs away from the army.

**deserve** *verb* **deserves, deserving, deserved** (th)
If you **deserve** something, you have earned it because of the way you have behaved: *He deserves to be unhappy after the trouble he caused.* [**Deserve** comes from Latin *deservire* 'to serve someone right'.]

**dessert** *noun* **desserts**
**Dessert** is sweet food that you eat as the last course of a meal. [**Dessert** comes from French *desservir* 'to clear the table'.]

**dessertspoon** *noun* **dessertspoons**
A **dessertspoon** is a spoon that is bigger than a teaspoon but not as big as a tablespoon.

**destroy** *verb* **destroys, destroying, destroyed** (th)
To **destroy** something is to damage it so badly that it cannot be repaired: *Fire destroyed the house.* [**Destroy** comes via French from Latin *de-*

'undoing' and *struere* 'to build'.]

**deteriorate** *verb* **deteriorates, deteriorating, deteriorated** (th)
To **deteriorate** is to get worse: *He deteriorated during the night and died this morning; The weather will deteriorate, with snow forecast for the weekend.* [**Deteriorate** comes from Latin *deterior* 'worse'.]

**develop** *verb* **develops, developing, developed**
**1** If someone **develops** something, or if something **develops**, it becomes bigger, better, or more important: *He exercises to develop his muscles; The company developed until it was the largest in the country.* **2** If someone **develops** something, or if something **develops**, it begins gradually: *She's developed some very bad habits; Storms are developing in the south.* **3** If you **develop** land, you build houses, shops or factories on it. **4** To **develop** a photographic film means to treat it with chemicals so that you can see the pictures on it. [**Develop** comes from French.]

**devour** *verb* **devours, devouring, devoured** (th)
To **devour** something is to eat it quickly and greedily: *The lion devoured its prey.* [**Devour** comes via French from Latin *vorare* 'to swallow'.]

**dew** *noun*
**Dew** is tiny drops of water that form overnight on surfaces, especially on plants outside. [**Dew** comes from Old English.]

**diagonal** *noun* **diagonals**
A **diagonal** is a straight line that goes from one corner of a square or rectangle to the opposite corner. [**Diagonal** comes via Latin from Greek *diagonios* 'from angle to angle'.]

**diagram** *noun* **diagrams**
A **diagram** is a picture or plan that explains something. [**Diagram** comes via Latin from Greek *diagraphein* 'to mark out with lines'.]

**dial** *noun* **dials**
A **dial** is the round face of a clock, watch or any instrument that is used for measuring. [**Dial** comes from Latin.]

**dialogue** noun **dialogues**
1 A **dialogue** is a conversation between two people.
2 The **dialogue** in a book, play or film is the conversations between the characters.
[**Dialogue** comes from Greek via French and Latin.]

**diamond** noun **diamonds**
1 A **diamond** is a hard, sparkling, precious stone that is clear like glass: *a diamond ring.*
2 A **diamond** is a shape with four equal sides like a square that stands on one of its points.
3 **Diamonds** is one of the suits in a pack of playing cards: *the four of diamonds.*
[**Diamond** comes via French and Latin from a Greek word meaning a very hard stone.]

**diaphragm** noun **diaphragms**
Your **diaphragm** is the strong muscle between your lungs and your stomach that helps you to breathe.
[**Diaphragm** comes from Greek via Latin.]

**diarrhoea** noun
If you have **diarrhoea**, your faeces become thin and watery and you have to keep going to the toilet.
[**Diarrhoea** comes via Latin from Greek *diarrhoia* 'flowing through'.]

**diary** noun **diaries**
A **diary** is a book with dates that people write things down in: *I'll look in my diary to see if I'm free next Thursday.*
[**Diary** comes from Latin *dies* 'day'.]

**dice** plural noun **die** singular
**Dice** are small cubes used in games with a different number of spots on each face: *roll the dice.*
[**Dice** comes from an old French word.]

**dictionary** noun **dictionaries**
A **dictionary** is a book that contains words and their meanings.
[**Dictionary** comes from Latin *dictio* 'word'.]

**die** verb **dies, dying, died**
1 If someone **dies**, they stop living: *My grandmother died last year.*
2 If something **dies** or **dies out**, it disappears: *Many different species of bird have died out because of pollution.*
[**Die** comes from Old Norse.]

**diet** noun **diets**
1 Someone's **diet** is the food they eat: *an unhealthy diet of chips and chocolate.*
2 If you are **on a diet**, you are eating less food, or only special food, because you want to lose weight.
[**Diet** comes via French and Latin from Greek *diaita* 'a way of life'.]

**difference** noun **differences**
1 A **difference** is the way in which one thing is not like another.
2 If people **have** their **differences**, they have disagreements about things: *My parents and I have our differences.*
[**Difference** comes via French from the same Latin word as **different**.]

**different** adjective (th)
A thing or a person that is **different** is not like something or someone else, or is not the same as before: *She's so different from her sister; You look very different with that hairstyle.* **differently** adverb.
[**Different** comes via French from Latin *differe* 'to carry away' or 'to separate'.]

**difficult** adjective (th)
1 Something that is **difficult** is not easy.
2 A person who is **difficult** is hard to please and does not try to get on with other people.
[**Difficult** comes from **difficulty**.]

**difficulty** noun **difficulties** (th)
1 A **difficulty** is a problem that stops you from doing something easily: *The main difficulty has been lack of money; We should have finished yesterday but we ran into difficulties.*
2 If you **have difficulty** doing something, or do something **with difficulty**, you do not find it easy: *She has difficulty walking; He speaks German with difficulty.*
[**Difficulty** comes from Latin.]

**dig** verb **digs, digging, dug**
To **dig** means to break up the soil and make a hole in it, usually with a spade.

**digest** verb **digests, digesting, digested**
When you **digest** food, it turns into substances that your body can use.
[**Digest** comes from Latin.]

**digit** noun **digits**
1 A **digit** is a finger or toe.
2 A **digit** is a symbol for any of the numbers from 0 to 9: *20 is a two-digit*

number. [**Digit** comes from Latin.]

**digital** *adjective*
1 **Digital** means to do with or using numbers, especially showing information as a series of numbers.
2 A **digital** watch or clock shows the time in figures, instead of by the hands pointing to numbers on the face as a traditional watch or clock does.

**dilemma** *noun* **dilemmas**
A **dilemma** is a difficult situation where you have to choose between two or more possible actions, although each of them may be difficult and you do not really want to do any of them.
[**Dilemma** comes from Greek via Latin.]

**dim** *adjective* **dimmer, dimmest**
Something that is **dim** is not bright: *a dim light.* **dimly** *adverb*.
[**Dim** comes from Old English.]

**dimension** *noun* **dimensions**
1 A **dimension** is a measurement such as length, width or height.
2 The **dimension** or **dimensions** of something is how big or important it is: *a problem of enormous dimensions.*
[**Dimension** comes from Latin *dimensio* 'measuring out'.]

**dine** *verb* **dines, dining, dined**
When you **dine**, you eat your meal: *Tonight we are dining at a pizza parlour.*
[**Dine** comes from an old French word.]

**dingy** *adjective* **dingier, dingiest** (th)
A **dingy** house or room is dark, dirty and in a bad condition.
[**Dingy** probably comes from the same Old English word as **dung**.]

**dinner** *noun* **dinners**
**Dinner** is the main meal of the day and is eaten at midday or in the evening.
[**Dinner** comes from the same old French word as **dine**.]

**dinosaur** *noun* **dinosaurs**
A **dinosaur** is a prehistoric reptile. **Dinosaurs** died out about 65 million years ago. There were many different kinds.
[**Dinosaur** comes from Greek *deinos* 'terrible' and *sauros* 'lizard'.]

**diplomat** *noun* **diplomats**
**Diplomats** represent their country's government in a foreign country.
[**Diplomat** comes from Latin *diploma*, meaning an official document like a passport that travellers used to carry.]

**diplomatic** *adjective* (th)
1 If you are **diplomatic**, you are able to say difficult things to people without upsetting them: *Shop assistants have to be very diplomatic with difficult customers.*
2 Something that is **diplomatic** is connected with diplomats: *the diplomatic service.*

**dire** *adjective* **direr, direst** (th)
1 Something that is **dire** is very serious or very bad: *I'm in dire trouble; That food was dire.*
2 If someone is in **dire straits**, they are in a very bad or serious situation.
[**Dire** comes from Latin *dirus* 'frightening'.]

**direction** *noun* **directions**
1 A **direction** is the way that something or someone is moving or pointing: *He was walking in the direction of the park; What direction should the aerial point in?*
2 **Directions** are instructions on how to get somewhere: *Can you give me directions to the bank?*
[**Direction** comes from Latin *directio* 'putting straight'.]

**dirt** *noun* (th)
1 **Dirt** is something such as mud or dust that makes things dirty: *The floor was covered in dirt.*
2 **Dirt** is loose soil or earth: *chickens scratching in the dirt.*
[**Dirt** comes from Old Norse.]

**dirty** *adjective* **dirtier, dirtiest** (th)
If something is **dirty**, it has dirt on it and needs cleaning.

**disabled** *adjective*
A **disabled** person is not able to use every part of his/her body: *Some disabled people use wheelchairs.*
[**Disabled** comes from *dis-* 'not' and **able**.]

**disagree** *verb* **disagrees, disagreeing, disagreed**
If you **disagree** with someone, you have a different opinion from that person: *You think this is a good story, but I disagree.*
[**Disagree** comes from *dis-* 'not' and **agree**.]

**disappear** *verb* **disappears,
disappearing, disappeared**
If something **disappears**, you cannot see
it or find it: *The magician made the rabbit
disappear.*
[**Disappear** comes from *dis-* 'undoing'
and **appear**.]

**disappoint** *verb* **disappoints,
disappointing, disappointed**
If you **disappoint** someone, you let that
person down because you do not do what
s/he expected you to do.
[**Disappoint** comes from an old French
word.]

**disappointed** *adjective*
If you are **disappointed**, you feel sad
because something that you wanted to
happen did not happen: *He didn't get a
new bike for Christmas so he's very
disappointed.*

**disaster** *noun* **disasters** (th)
**1** A **disaster** is a serious accident that
happens suddenly: *The sinking of the
Titanic was a disaster.*
**2** If something is a **disaster**, it is very, or it
goes completely, wrong: *Our holiday was a
disaster – it rained every day.*
[**Disaster** comes from Italian.]

**disc** *noun* **discs** *Also* **disk** (if you are talking
about computers)
**1** A **disc** is a flat, circular object like a
plate.
**2** A **disc** is a piece of plastic used to record
music or information: *a compact disc; the
computer's hard disk.*
[**Disc** comes from Latin.]

**discount** *noun* **discounts**
A **discount** is a price cut: *There's a 10%
discount on every holiday booked before April.*
[**Discount** comes from Latin via French or
Italian.]

**discourage** *verb* **discourages,
discouraging, discouraged**
If you **discourage** someone, or **discourage**
someone from doing something, you try
to persuade him/her not to do it: *If he
wants to go to university, you shouldn't
discourage him.*
[**Discourage** comes from an old French
word meaning 'to destroy someone's
courage'.]

**discover** *verb* **discovers, discovering,
discovered** (th)
To **discover** something means to find it or
to find out about it: *I never discovered what
was bothering her.*
[**Discover** comes via French from a Latin
word meaning 'to uncover'.]

**discuss** *verb* **discusses, discussing,
discussed** (th)
To **discuss** something is to talk about it
with other people: *Let's discuss what we
want to do at the weekend.*
[**Discuss** comes from Latin.]

**disease** *noun* **diseases**
**1** A **disease** is an illness that happens in
particular circumstances, has particular
symptoms, or which affects a certain part
of your body: *Measles is a childhood disease;
She suffers from heart disease.*
**2 Disease** is illness in humans, animals or
plants: *Many cattle died of disease.*
[**Disease** comes from an old French
word.]

**disembark** *verb* **disembarks,
disembarking, disembarked**
When you **disembark** from a ship or a
plane, you get off it.
[**Disembark** comes from Latin *dis-*
'undoing' and the same French word as
**embark**.]

**disgrace** *noun*
**1 Disgrace** is when people disapprove of
someone or do not respect him/her
because of something s/he has done:
*You've brought disgrace on the family; She
was sent home in disgrace.*
**2** A **disgrace** is something that you should
be ashamed of: *Your room's a disgrace!*
[**Disgrace** comes via French and Italian
from Latin *dis-* 'not' and *gratus* 'pleasing'.]

**disguise** *noun* **disguises**
A **disguise** is something that you wear or
a change you make in your appearance so
that no one recognises you: *He wore a false
beard as a disguise; You'd better go in
disguise.*
[**Disguise** comes from an old French
word.]

**disguise** *verb* **disguises, disguising,
disguised**
**1** If you **disguise** yourself, you change
your appearance so that people will think

# divide

you are someone else: *He disguised himself with a wig and glasses.*

**2** If you **disguise** something, you hide it or change it so that no one will recognise it: *She tried to disguise her voice.*

**dish** *noun* **dishes**

**1** A **dish** is a shallow bowl for food: *a serving dish.*

**2** A **dish** is a kind of aerial for receiving television broadcasts: *a satellite dish.*

**3** If you **wash the dishes** or **do the dishes**, you wash all the crockery and cutlery used at a meal.

[**Dish** comes via Old English from the same Latin word as **disc**.]

**dishonest** *adjective* (th)

Someone who is **dishonest** does not tell the truth or does something illegal. **dishonestly** *adverb.*

[**Dishonest** comes via French from Latin *dis-* 'not' and *honestus* 'honest' (ancestor of **honest**).]

**dishwasher** *noun* **dishwashers**

A **dishwasher** is a machine for washing dishes.

**disk** *noun* **disks**

**Disk** is another way of spelling **disc**. You use **disk** if you are talking about computers.

**dislike** *verb* **dislikes, disliking, disliked** (th)

If you **dislike** something or someone, you do not like that thing or person: *I really dislike her new hairstyle.*

[**Dislike** comes from *dis-* 'not' and **like**¹.]

**disobey** *verb* **disobeys, disobeying, disobeyed** (th)

If you **disobey** a rule, or someone in authority, you do something you are not allowed to do: *He was given a detention for disobeying school rules.*

[**Disobey** comes from an old French word.]

**display** *noun* **displays**

**1** A **display** is something attractive that is designed for people to look at: *a firework display; a wall display.*

**2** If something is **on display**, it is put in a place for people to look at: *Many new pictures are on display in the gallery.*

[**Display** comes from Latin via French.]

**display** *verb* **displays, displaying, displayed** (th)

If you **display** something, you put it in a public show or exhibition: *The designer displayed his latest collection at the fashion show.*

**distance** *noun* **distances**

**1** The **distance** between two places is the amount of space between them: *The distance between our houses is 15km.*

**2** If something is **in the distance**, it is far away from you: *They could just see a light in the distance.*

[**Distance** comes from Latin *distantia* 'standing apart'.]

**distress** *noun* (th)

**1** **Distress** is when you feel very worried or upset: *The argument caused a lot of distress.*

**2** If a boat or a plane is **in distress**, it is in a very dangerous situation: *The oil tanker was in distress in stormy seas.*

[**Distress** comes from an old French word.]

**disturb** *verb* **disturbs, disturbing, disturbed** (th)

**1** To **disturb** someone is to interrupt that person when they are busy: *Please don't disturb me when I'm working.*

**2** To **disturb** someone is to worry that person: *My son's strange behaviour really disturbs me.*

**3** To **disturb** something is to move it or fiddle with it: *Don't disturb the nest.*

[**Disturb** comes from the same Latin word as **turbulent**.]

**ditch** *noun* **ditches**

A **ditch** is a long, narrow trench that drains water away.

[**Ditch** comes from Old English.]

**Divali** *noun*

**Divali** is another way to spell **Diwali**.

**dive** *verb* **dives, diving, dived** (th)

To **dive** means to go down steeply and suddenly: *He dived off the side of the pool.*

[**Dive** comes from Old English.]

**divide** *verb* **divides, dividing, divided** (th)

**1** To **divide** something means to separate it into smaller parts: *Divide the cake mixture evenly between two tins.*

**2** To **divide** something means to share it out: *Divide the cards between all the players.*

**3** If you **divide** one number by another number, you work out how many times the second number will go into the first number. The symbol for dividing one number by another is ÷: *16÷8=2; Twenty divided by five is four.* **division** *noun.*
[**Divide** comes from Latin.]

**Diwali** *noun Also* **Divali**
**Diwali** is a Hindu festival held in October or November to celebrate the new year. During **Diwali**, people visit each other, give each other presents, and light lamps in their houses to invite in Lakshmi, the goddess of good luck.
[**Diwali** comes from Sanskrit *dipavali* 'row of lights'. Sanskrit is a very old Indian language.]

**doctor** *noun* **doctors**
A **doctor** is a person whose job is to try to make sick people better.
[**Doctor** comes from Latin *doctor* 'teacher'.]

**document** *noun* **documents**
A **document** is a sheet or sheets of paper with writing or printing, giving information about something or acting as a record of something.
[**Document** comes from Latin *documentum* 'official paper'.]

**doe** *noun* **does**
A **doe** is a female of some animals, such as deer or rabbits.
[**Doe** comes from Old English.]

**dog** *noun* **dogs**
A **dog** is an animal that is often kept as a pet. Some **dogs** can be trained to do jobs such as guarding buildings, guiding blind people and herding sheep.
[**Dog** comes from Old English.]

**doll** *noun* **dolls**
A **doll** is a toy in the shape of a baby or person.
[**Doll** is short for the name *Dorothy*.]

**dollar** *noun* **dollars**
A **dollar** is the name given to money used in the USA, Canada, Australia and some other countries.
[**Dollar** comes from German *Thaler*, meaning a silver coin once used in parts of North and South America.]

**dolphin** *noun* **dolphins**
A **dolphin** is an animal like a small whale that lives in the sea.
[**Dolphin** comes from Greek via French and Latin.]

**dome** *noun* **domes**
A **dome** is a rounded shape, like the top half of a ball. Buildings sometimes have a **dome** on the top.
[**Dome** comes from Latin via French and Italian.]

**domestic** *adjective*
**1 Domestic** animals are animals that are kept as pets or on a farm.
**2 Domestic** means to do with homes and families: *domestic science.*
[**Domestic** comes via French from Latin *domus* 'house'.]

**dominate** *verb* **dominates, dominating, dominated** (th)
To **dominate** means to be very powerful and to take control of someone or something.
[**Dominate** comes from Latin *dominus* 'master'.]

**domino** *noun* **dominoes**
A **domino** is a small oblong piece of wood or plastic marked with a pattern of dots. You use them to play a game called **dominoes.**
[**Domino** comes from French.]

**donate** *verb* **donates, donating, donated** (th)
If you **donate** something, you give it: *donating money to charity.*
[**Donate** comes from Latin *donum* 'gift'.]

**donation** *noun* **donations** (th)
A **donation** is something such as a sum of money that someone has given: *Put your donation in this envelope.*
[**Donation** comes via French from the same Latin word as **donate**.]

**donkey** *noun* **donkeys**
A **donkey** is an animal like a small horse with long ears.
[No one knows where **donkey** comes from.]

**donor** *noun* **donors**
A **donor** is a person who gives something: *a blood donor.*
[**Donor** comes via French from the same

Latin word as **donate**.]

**doodle** verb **doodles, doodling, doodled**
If you **doodle**, you draw or scribble,
usually while you are thinking about
something else: *She always doodles while
she's on the phone.*
[**Doodle** comes from an old German word
for a fool.]

**doom** noun (th)
**Doom** is something terrible that is going
to happen. **Doom** is mainly used in
stories: *The witch lured the knight to his
doom.*
[**Doom** comes from Old English.]

**doomed** adjective (th)
**1** If something is **doomed**, it is certain to
turn out badly.
**2** If you are **doomed** to something, that is
what is going to happen to you.

**door** noun **doors**
A **door** is something that opens and closes
to allow people to get into or out of a
building, room or cupboard.
[**Door** comes from Old English.]

**doorstep** noun **doorsteps**
A **doorstep** is a step outside a door.

**doorway** noun **doorways**
A **doorway** is the place in a wall where
there is an opening for a door.

**dormant** adjective
**1** When an animal goes to sleep for the
winter, it is **dormant** and does not move.
**2** A volcano is **dormant** when it is not
erupting but it might erupt again in the
future.
**3** A seed or a plant is **dormant** when it is
alive but is not growing.
[**Dormant** comes from French *dormant*
'sleeping'.]

**dormitory** noun **dormitories**
A **dormitory** is a large room with beds for
many people.
[**Dormitory** comes from Latin *dormire* 'to
sleep'.]

**dormouse** noun **dormice**
A **dormouse** is an animal like a mouse
that has a furry tail. In the winter,
**dormice** sleep so deeply that they do not
need any food.
[**Dormouse** may be from French *dormir* 'to
sleep' and **mouse**, or from French

*dormeuse* 'sleeper'.]

**dose** noun **doses**
A **dose** is an amount of medicine that you
take at one time.
[**Dose** comes from Greek *dosis* 'something
given'.]

**dot** noun **dots**
A **dot** is a very small round mark: *Put a
dot on the letter i.*
[**Dot** comes from Old English.]

**double** adjective
**1** twice as big: *She asked for a double helping
of pudding.*
**2** for two people or things: *a double garage;
a double bed.*
[**Double** comes via French from the same
Latin word as **duplicate**.]

**double** verb **doubles, doubling, doubled**
**1** If something **doubles**, it becomes twice
as big: *The number of pupils in the school has
doubled.*
**2** If you **double** a number, you multiply it
by two.
**3** If you **double back**, you go back the
way you have come.

**double agent** noun **double agents**
A **double agent** is a spy who works for
the enemy as well as for his/her own
country.

**double bass** noun **double basses**
A **double bass** is the largest musical
instrument in the violin family.
[**Bass** comes via French from Latin *bassus*
'low'; the double bass has a very low
sound.]

**doubt** verb **doubts, doubting, doubted**
(th)
To **doubt** means to be unsure about
something.
[**Doubt** comes via French from Latin
*dubitare* 'to hesitate'.]

**doubt** noun **doubts**
A **doubt** is a feeling that you are not sure
about something.

**doubtful** adjective (th)
**1** If it is **doubtful** that something will
happen, it is unlikely to happen.
**2** If you feel **doubtful** about something,
you do not feel sure or happy about it.
**doubtfully** adverb.

**doubtless** adverb (th)
**Doubtless** means probably or almost certainly: *Doubtless we will be having PE outside today.*

**dough** noun
**Dough** is a mixture of flour and water used for making bread and cakes. [**Dough** comes from Old English.]

**doughnut** noun **doughnuts**
A **doughnut** is a small round sugary cake made from dough. Some **doughnuts** are ring-shaped and others have jam in the middle.

**dove** noun **doves**
A **dove** is a bird like a small pigeon, often white. [**Dove** comes from Old Norse.]

**down¹** preposition
from a higher to a lower place: *She fell down the stairs.*
[**Down¹** comes from Old English.]

**down¹** adverb
**1** towards the ground: *Bend down.*
**2** onto a surface: *Put your cup down.*

**down²** noun
**Down** is the soft, fluffy feathers on birds. [**Down²** comes from Old Norse.]

**downhearted** adjective (th)
If you are **downhearted**, you feel sad and want to give up.

**downhill** adverb
going down a slope: *It was easier riding downhill.*

**downpour** noun **downpours**
A **downpour** is a heavy shower of rain.

**downstairs** adverb
on or to the ground floor or a lower floor: *She ran downstairs to answer the phone; He's downstairs having breakfast.*

**downstairs** adjective
on the ground floor or a lower floor: *a downstairs toilet.*

**dowry** noun **dowries**
In some countries when a woman gets married, she has to give money or presents to her husband or his family. This is called her **dowry**.
[**Dowry** comes from Latin via French.]

**doze** noun
A **doze** is a short or light sleep.

[No one knows where **doze** comes from.]

**doze** verb **dozes, dozing, dozed**
**1** If you **doze**, you have a short sleep.
**2** If you **doze off**, you fall asleep.

**dozen** noun **dozens**
A **dozen** is a set or group of twelve things.
[**Dozen** comes via French from Latin *duodecim* 'twelve'.]

**draft** noun **drafts**
A **draft** is a first written form of something such as a speech, a letter or a book, which will probably be changed later.
[**Draft** is a different spelling of **draught**.]

**drag** verb **drags, dragging, dragged** (th)
If you **drag** something, you pull it along.
[**Drag** comes from Old English or Old Norse.]

**dragon** noun **dragons**
A **dragon** is a fire-breathing monster in stories.
[**Dragon** comes via French and Latin from Greek *drakon* 'snake'.]

**dragonfly** noun **dragonflies**
A **dragonfly** is a brightly coloured insect with a thin body and two pairs of wings.

**drain** noun **drains**
**1** A **drain** is a pipe for taking away water or sewage.
**2** A **drain** in a road is a metal grid that water flows through.
[**Drain** comes from Old English.]

**drain** verb **drains, draining, drained**
**1** If you **drain** something, you take the liquid away from it: *drain the peas.*
**2** If something **drains**, the liquid flows away from it: *plates draining on a rack; The water had drained away.*

**drama** noun **dramas**
**1** If you do **drama** at school, you act something out or perform a play.
**2** A **drama** is a play.
**3** Something exciting that happens in real life can be called a **drama**.
[**Drama** comes from Greek via Latin.]

**dramatic** adjective (th)
**1** Something that is **dramatic** is very big, noticeable or exciting: *a dramatic change in the weather; He made a dramatic entrance.*

**2** If you do something in a **dramatic** way, you make a big fuss about it so that people notice you.
[**Dramatic** comes via Latin from Greek *dramatikos* 'to do with drama'.]

**drank** *verb*
**Drank** is the past tense of **drink**.

**drastic** *adjective* (th)
If you do something **drastic**, you do something that makes a big difference.
**drastically** *adverb*.
[**Drastic** comes from Greek.]

**draught** *noun* **draughts**
**1** A **draught** is cold air that blows indoors: *Don't sit in the draught*.
**2 Draughts** is a game for two people. You play it with round flat pieces on a board marked out into squares.
[**Draught** comes from Old Norse via French.]

**draughty** *adjective* **draughtier, draughtiest**
If a room or a place is **draughty**, you can feel air blowing through it.

**draw** *verb* **draws, drawing, drew, drawn**
**1** To **draw** means to make a picture or diagram with a pen or pencils: *draw a picture; draw a cat*.
**2** To **draw** means to pull or attract someone or something: *The donkey drew the cart; The event drew a large crowd*.
**3** To **draw** in a game means to finish the game with each side scoring the same.
**4** To **draw** the curtains means to shut them or to open them.
[**Draw** comes from Old English.]

**draw** *noun* **draws**
A **draw** is when both sides finish a game with the same score.

**drawback** *noun* **drawbacks** (th)
A **drawback** is a problem that makes something not so good: *His plan didn't seem to have any drawbacks*.

**drawbridge** *noun* **drawbridges**
A **drawbridge** is a bridge over a moat round a castle that used to be pulled up to stop people attacking the castle.

**drawer** *noun* **drawers**
A **drawer** is a tray or box that slides into a piece of furniture.
[**Drawer** comes from **draw**.]

**drawing** *noun* **drawings**
A **drawing** is a picture or diagram drawn with pens or pencils.

**drawing pin** *noun* **drawing pins**
A **drawing pin** is a sharp pin with a round, flat end, used for displaying pieces of paper on a board.

**drawn** *verb*
**Drawn** is the past participle of **draw**.

**dread** *noun* (th)
**Dread** is the feeling that you have when you are very worried or scared about something that might happen or will happen.
[**Dread** comes from Old English.]

**dread** *verb* **dreads, dreading, dreaded** (th)
When you are very worried about something that might happen or will happen, you **dread** it.

**dreadful** *adjective* (th)
Something that is very bad is **dreadful**.
**dreadfully** *adverb*.

**dreadlocks** *plural noun*
If you have **dreadlocks**, you wear your hair long and tightly twisted.
[**Dreadlocks** comes from **dread** and **lock**[2], because the style was taken from pictures of Ethiopian warriors, who looked very frightening.]

**dream** *noun* **dreams** (th)
**1** A **dream** is the things that happen in your mind when you are asleep: *I had a strange dream last night*.
**2** Your **dream** is something that you want very much to do or to have, although you are not likely to do it or have it: *my dream of winning the Olympics*.
[**Dream** probably comes from Old English.]

**dream** *verb* **dreams, dreaming, dreamed**
**1** When you **dream**, you see and hear things when you are asleep.
**2** If you **dream of** something, you have a dream about it.

**dreary** *adjective* **drearier, dreariest** (th)
Something that is **dreary** makes you feel bored or depressed: *dreary music*.
[**Dreary** comes from Old English.]

**dregs** *plural noun*
The tiny bits at the bottom of a container of liquid are the **dregs**.
[**Dregs** comes from a Scandinavian language.]

**drench** *verb* **drenches, drenching, drenched** (th)
If something **drenches** you, it makes you soaking wet.
[**Drench** comes from Old English.]

**dress** *verb* **dresses, dressing, dressed**
To **dress** means to put clothes on.
[**Dress** comes from French *dresser* 'to get ready'.]

**dress** *noun* **dresses**
1 A **dress** is a piece of clothing that has a top joined to a skirt.
2 **Dress** is the kind of clothes that someone wears: *evening dress; casual dress.*

**dresser** *noun* **dressers**
A **dresser** is a tall piece of furniture with cupboards at the bottom and shelves at the top.
[**Dresser** comes from the same French word as **dress**: a **dresser** was originally a table for preparing food.]

**dressing** *noun* **dressings**
A **dressing** is a sauce that you can put on salad to give it extra taste.
[**Dressing** comes from **dress**.]

**dressing gown** *noun* **dressing gowns**
A **dressing gown** is like a coat that you wear indoors, over your night-clothes.

**dress rehearsal** *noun* **dress rehearsals**
A **dress rehearsal** is the last practice before a play, when the actors wear their costumes.

**drew** *verb*
**Drew** is the past tense of **draw**.

**dribble** *verb* **dribbles, dribbling, dribbled**
1 If you **dribble**, saliva comes slowly out of your mouth: *Babies often dribble.*
2 If liquid **dribbles** out, it comes out slowly.
3 If you **dribble** a ball, you tap it lightly so that you keep it close to you as you run.
[**Dribble** comes from *drib*, an old spelling of **drip**.]

**drier** *noun* **driers**
A **drier** is a machine in which washing is dried.

**drift** *verb* **drifts, drifting, drifted**
To **drift** means to be carried along gently by a current of air or water.
[**Drift** comes from Old Norse.]

**driftwood** *noun*
**Driftwood** is wood floating on the sea or on a river. You sometimes find **driftwood** on a beach.

**drill** *noun* **drills**
1 A **drill** is a tool for making holes.
2 A **drill** is a way of practising or training to do something: *We had a fire drill at school today.*
[**Drill** comes from an old Dutch word.]

**drill** *verb* **drills, drilling, drilled**
If you **drill** something, you make a hole in it with a drill.

**drink** *noun* **drinks** (th)
A **drink** is some liquid that you can drink: *Do you want a drink?; a drink of orange juice.*
[**Drink** comes from Old English.]

**drink** *verb* **drinks, drinking, drank, drunk** (th)
To **drink** means to swallow any kind of liquid.

**drip** *verb* **drips, dripping, dripped** (th)
To **drip** means to fall in drops of liquid.
[**Drip** comes from Old English.]

**drip** *noun* **drips**
A **drip** is a drop of liquid.

**drive** *noun* **drives**
1 A **drive** is a road that leads up to a house.
2 If you **go for a drive**, you go for a ride in a car.
[**Drive** comes from Old English.]

**drive** *verb* **drives, driving, drove, driven**
1 If you **drive** a car or another vehicle, you make it move and control where it goes.
2 If you **drive** animals, you make them go somewhere: *The farmer drove the cows to market.*

**driver** *noun* **drivers**
A **driver** is the person who drives a vehicle: *She's a careful driver.*

**dromedary** *noun* **dromedaries**
A **dromedary** is a camel with one hump.
[**Dromedary** comes from Greek.]

**drop** *noun* **drops** (th)
A **drop** is a very small amount of liquid.
[**Drop** comes from Old English.]

**drop** *verb* **drops**, **dropping**, **dropped** (th)
**1** If you **drop** something, you let it fall.
**2** If something **drops**, it falls.

**droppings** *plural noun*
**Droppings** are the faeces left by birds or small animals: *They found mouse droppings under the sink.*

**drought** *noun* **droughts**
When it does not rain for a long time, there is a **drought**.
[**Drought** comes from Old English.]

**drove** *verb*
**Drove** is the past tense of **drive**.

**drown** *verb* **drowns**, **drowning**, **drowned**
**1** To **drown** means to die because you are under water and cannot breathe.
**2** You **drown** or **drown out** a sound by making a noise that is louder: *The music drowned the noise coming from upstairs.*
[**Drown** comes from Old Norse.]

**drowsy** *adjective* **drowsier**, **drowsiest** (th)
If you feel **drowsy**, you feel very sleepy.
[**Drowsy** comes from Old English.]

**drug** *noun* **drugs**
**1** A **drug** is a medicine or pill that a doctor gives you to make you better: *a new drug to treat hay fever.*
**2** A **drug** is something that people take to make themselves feel good, but these drugs can be dangerous. Tobacco, cannabis and heroin are types of **drugs**.
[**Drug** probably comes from an old French word.]

**drum** *noun* **drums**
A **drum** is a musical instrument that you bang with a stick.
[**Drum** comes from an old German or Dutch word that was an imitation of the sound.]

**drummer** *noun* **drummers**
A **drummer** is a person who plays a drum.

**drumstick** *noun* **drumsticks**
**1** A **drumstick** is a stick that you use when you play a drum.
**2** A **drumstick** is the thin part of a cooked chicken's leg.

**drunk** *verb*
**Drunk** is the past participle of **drink**.

**drunk** *adjective* (th)
If you are **drunk**, you have had too much beer, wine or other alcoholic drink, and you cannot think properly.

**dry** *adjective* **drier**, **driest** (th)
Something that is not wet is **dry**.
[**Dry** comes from Old English.]

**dry** *verb* **dries**, **drying**, **dried**
You **dry** something by taking liquid away from it: *Dry your hair with a towel; Leave your painting here to dry.*

**duchess** *noun* **duchesses**
A **duchess** is a noblewoman who is not quite as important as a princess, or a woman who is married to a duke.
[**Duchess** comes via French from Latin *ducissa*, the feminine of *dux* 'leader' (ancestor of **duke**).]

**duck¹** *noun* **ducks**
A **duck** is a bird that lives near water and makes a quacking noise.
[**Duck¹** comes from Old English.]

**duck²** *verb* **ducks**, **ducking**, **ducked**
To **duck** means to bend down quickly so that you do not get hit by something.
[**Duck²** may be from an Old English word meaning 'to dive'.]

**duckling** *noun* **ducklings**
A **duckling** is a young duck.

**due** *adjective* (th)
If something is **due** at a particular time, it should happen or arrive at that time.
[**Due** comes from French *dû* 'what is owed'.]

**due** *preposition*
**Due to** means caused by: *The success of the play was due to your hard work.*

**duel** *noun* **duels**
A **duel** is a fight between two people, especially when they use guns or swords.
[**Duel** comes from Latin.]

**duet** *noun* **duets**
A **duet** is a piece of music for two people to play or sing.
[**Duet** comes via Italian from Latin *duo* 'two'.]

**duffel coat** *noun* **duffel coats**
A **duffel coat** is a thick coat with a hood. It has toggles instead of buttons.

[**Duffel** is named after the Belgian town of *Duffel*, where the cloth for duffel coats was made.]

**dug** *verb*
**Dug** is the past tense and past participle of **dig**.

**duke** *noun* **dukes**
A **duke** is a nobleman who is not quite as important as a prince.
[**Duke** comes via French from Latin *dux* 'leader'.]

**dull** *adjective* **duller, dullest** (th)
1 Something that is **dull** is not interesting.
2 A colour that is **dull** is not bright.
3 A day that is **dull** is cloudy.
4 A blade that is **dull** is not sharp.
[**Dull** comes from Old English.]

**dumb** *adjective* **dumber, dumbest**
Someone who is unable to speak is **dumb**: *She was born deaf and dumb.*
[**Dumb** comes from Old English.]

**dumbfounded** *adjective*
If you are **dumbfounded**, you are amazed or shocked.
[**Dumbfound** comes from **dumb** and *confound* 'to amaze or puzzle someone'.]

**dummy** *noun* **dummies**
1 A **dummy** is a model of something, for example a model of a person in a shop window.
2 A **dummy** is a specially shaped piece of plastic or rubber for a baby to suck.
[**Dummy** comes from **dumb**.]

**dump** *noun* **dumps**
A **dump** is a place where people leave rubbish.
[**Dump** comes from a Scandinavian language.]

**dump** *verb* **dumps, dumping, dumped**
If you **dump** something, you throw it down or leave it somewhere.

**dumpling** *noun* **dumplings**
A **dumpling** is a round piece of dough, usually cooked in a stew.
[**Dumpling** comes from an old word *dump* 'a short, fat person'.]

**dune** *noun* **dunes**
A **dune** is a hill of sand near the sea or in a desert.
[**Dune** comes from Dutch via French.]

**dung** *noun*
**Dung** is manure from the faeces of cows or horses.
[**Dung** comes from Old English.]

**dungarees** *plural noun*
**Dungarees** are trousers with a square part above the waist at the front and straps that go over your shoulders.
[**Dungarees** comes from Hindi *dungri*, the name of the cloth they were originally made from. Hindi is an Indian language.]

**dungeon** *noun* **dungeons**
A **dungeon** is an underground prison.
[**Dungeon** comes from an old French word.]

**duplicate** *verb* **duplicates, duplicating, duplicated**
If you **duplicate** something, you make an exact copy of it.
[**Duplicate** comes from Latin *duplicare* 'to double'.]

**duplicate** *noun* **duplicates**
A **duplicate** is something that is an exact copy of something else.

**during** *preposition*
while something else is happening: *Please don't talk during the programme.*
[**During** comes from Latin *durans* 'lasting'.]

**dusk** *noun* (th)
**Dusk** is the time when it starts to get dark in the evening.
[**Dusk** comes from Old English.]

**dust** *noun*
**Dust** is powdery, dry dirt.
[**Dust** comes from Old English.]

**dust** *verb* **dusts, dusting, dusted**
To **dust** means to clean away dust.

**duster** *noun* **dusters**
A **duster** is a cloth used for cleaning away dust.

**dusty** *adjective* **dustier, dustiest**
Something that is **dusty** is covered with dust.

**duty** *noun* **duties**
1 Your **duty** is something that you have to do or that you should do.
2 Someone who is **on duty** is at work.
3 Someone who is **off duty** is not at work.
[**Duty** comes from the same French word as **due**.]

**duvet** noun **duvets**
A **duvet** is a thick warm cover that you use on a bed.
[**Duvet** comes from French *duvet* 'feathers, down'.]

**dwarf** noun **dwarfs**
A **dwarf** is a very small person or animal.
[**Dwarf** comes from Old English.]

**dwelling** noun **dwellings** (th)
A **dwelling** is a place where someone lives.
[**Dwelling** comes from *dwell* 'to live at a place', which comes from Old English.]

**dwindle** verb **dwindles, dwindling, dwindled** (th)
If something **dwindles**, it gets smaller or weaker: *Their supply of food dwindled until they had none left.*
[**Dwindle** comes from Old English.]

**dye** noun **dyes**
**Dye** is something that you can use to colour material or hair.
[**Dye** comes from Old English.]

**dye** verb **dyes, dying, dyed**
If you **dye** material or hair, you colour it or change its colour by soaking it in dye: *Can you believe she dyed her hair orange!*

**dyke** noun **dykes**
A **dyke** is a thick wall that stops water from the sea or a river flooding the land.
[**Dyke** comes from Old Norse.]

**dynamite** noun
**Dynamite** is a mixture of several chemicals that is used to blow things up.
[**Dynamite** comes from Greek *dynamis* 'power'.]

**dyslexic** adjective
If you are **dyslexic**, you have a particular problem with reading and spelling.
[**Dyslexic** comes from Greek.]

---

# Dictionary Fun

**What do these idioms mean?**
1. To be dead to the world
2. To go to the dogs
3. To be down in the mouth

**Etymology**
1. How are the words **decibel** and **decimal** related?
2. Which word comes from old French *desfier* 'to challenge'?
3. Which word comes from Greek *dosis* 'something given'?

**Complete the proverbs**
1. Better the d_____ you know than the d_____ you don't.
2. Who d_____, wins.

**Riddle**
When is a door not a door?

**Did you know?**
♦ Originally the word **doodle** meant a foolish person.
♦ The word **dinosaur** comes from Greek *deinos* 'terrible' + *sauros* 'lizard'.
♦ The first recorded **dam** was built about 4000 BC to divert the Nile in Egypt to provide a site for the city of Memphis.

**Brainteaser**
A boy and his father are in a serious accident. They are rushed to different hospitals. The boy is taken straight to surgery but the surgeon in the theatre says, "I can't operate on him, he's my son." How is this possible?

n o p q r s t u v w x y z

# Ee

**each** *adjective*
every one or every thing: *He gave an apple to each child.*
[**Each** comes from Old English.]

**each** *pronoun*
every one or every thing: *The houses were the same and each had a large garden.*

**eager** *adjective* (th)
Someone who is **eager** wants to do something very much.
**eagerly** *adverb.* **eagerness** *noun.*
[**Eager** comes from Latin via French.]

**eagle** *noun* **eagles**
An **eagle** is a very large bird that lives by eating small animals.
[**Eagle** comes from Latin via French.]

**ear** *noun* **ears**
Your **ears** are the parts of your body that you use for hearing.
[**Ear** comes from Old English.]

**eardrum** *noun* **eardrums**
Your **eardrum** is a piece of skin inside your ear that vibrates when sound hits it.

**earl** *noun* **earls**
An **earl** is a British nobleman.
[**Earl** comes from Old English.]

**earlobe** *noun* **earlobes**
Your **earlobe** is the soft part at the bottom of your ear.
[**Earlobe** comes from **ear** and *lobe* 'a round part', which comes from Greek *lobos* 'pod'.]

**early** *adjective* **earlier, earliest**
The **early** part of something is the part that comes first: *They lived in the early part of this century.*
[**Early** comes from Old English.]

**early** *adverb* (th)
Something that happens **early** happens before the proper time: *He went to bed early; The train was early.*

**earn** *verb* **earns, earning, earned** (th)
1 Money that you **earn** is money that you are paid when you have done some work.
2 If you **earn** praise, you get it because you have done something well.
[**Earn** comes from Old English.]

**earnings** *plural noun*
**Earnings** are money that you get by working: *She saved half of her earnings.*

**earphones** *plural noun*
**Earphones** are small speakers that you put next to your ears so that you can listen to discs, tapes or a radio by yourself.
[**Earphones** comes from **ear** and **phone** 'something for receiving or sending sound', which comes from Greek *phone* 'sound'.]

**earring** *noun* **earrings**
An **earring** is a piece of jewellery that you wear on your ear.

**earth** *noun* Also **Earth**
1 The **earth** is the planet we live on.
2 **Earth** is soil.
[**Earth** comes from Old English.]

**earthquake** *noun* **earthquakes**
When there is an **earthquake**, the ground suddenly shakes and can split open.
[**Earthquake** comes from **earth** and *quake* 'to shake', which comes from Old English.]

**earthworm** *noun* **earthworms**
An **earthworm** is a common worm that you can find in the soil in a garden.

**earwig** *noun* **earwigs**
An **earwig** is a thin brown insect that has pincers at the end of its body.
[**Earwig** comes from Old English.]

**easel** *noun* **easels**
An **easel** is a stand for holding a picture or blackboard. [**Easel** comes from Dutch.]

**easily** *adverb* (th)
If you can do something **easily**, it is not hard for you to do it: *I can easily make it.*
[**Easily** comes from **easy**.]

**east** *noun*
**East** is one of the points of the compass and is the direction from which the sun rises. [**East** comes from Old English.]

**Easter** *noun*
**Easter** is the day on which Christians believe that Jesus Christ rose from the dead.
[**Easter** was named after *Eastre*, the Anglo-Saxon goddess of the spring.]

**easterly** *adjective*
1 to the east or towards the east: *The road ran in an easterly direction.*
2 An **easterly** wind blows from the east.

**eastern** *adjective*
in the east or from the east: *eastern England.*

**easy** *adjective* **easier, easiest** (th)
1 If something is **easy**, you don't have to work hard or be clever to do it.
2 An **easy** chair is a comfortable chair.
3 Someone who has an **easy** life has no problems or worries.
[**Easy** comes from an old French word.]

**eat** *verb* **eats, eating, ate, eaten**
1 To **eat** means to put food into your mouth, bite it and swallow it: *Eat your dinner; We'll eat later.*
2 To **eat** something **away** means to destroy it slowly: *a bike being eaten away by rust.* [**Eat** comes from Old English.]

**ebb** *verb* **ebbs, ebbing, ebbed** (th)
1 When the tide **ebbs**, it flows out.
2 If something **ebbs**, or **ebbs away**, it gradually gets weaker and weaker: *Her life is ebbing away.*
[**Ebb** comes from Old English.]

**ebony** *noun*
**Ebony** is a very hard, dark-coloured wood.
[**Ebony** comes from Greek via French and Latin.]

**eccentric** *adjective* (th)
An **eccentric** person has opinions or habits that seem strange to other people: *My eccentric Aunt Susan never washed and believed that cats came from Mars.*
[**Eccentric** comes via Latin from Greek *ekkentros* 'away from the middle'.]

**echo** *noun* **echoes**
An **echo** is a sound that you hear again because it bounces back off a surface such as the wall of a cave.
[**Echo** comes via French and Latin from Greek *ekhe* 'a sound'.]

**echo** *verb* **echoes, echoing, echoed**
A sound that **echoes** bounces back off a surface and you hear it again.

**eclipse** *noun* **eclipses**
An **eclipse** is the time when the moon is between the earth and the sun and blocks out the sun's light, or when the sun is between the earth and the moon and blocks out the moon's light.
[**Eclipse** comes via French and Latin from Greek *ekleipsis* 'failure to appear'.]

**ecology** *noun*
If you study **ecology**, you learn about plants and animals and the environment.
[**Ecology** comes from Greek.]

**economical** *adjective*
If something is **economical**, it is quite cheap to buy or to use and doesn't waste anything: *Small cars are more economical than big ones.*
[**Economical** comes via French and Latin from the same Greek word as **economy**.]

**economise** *verb* **economises, economising, economised** Also **economize** (th)
When you **economise**, you spend your money carefully and try not to waste it: *We can economise by walking instead of going on the bus.*
[**Economise** comes from the same Greek word as **economy**.]

**economy** *noun* **economies**
A country's **economy** is its wealth and resources: *Switzerland has a strong economy.*
[**Economy** comes via French and Latin from Greek *oikos* 'house' and *nomia* 'management'.]

**eczema** *noun*
**Eczema** is a disease that makes your skin itchy and sore.
[**Eczema** comes from Greek via Latin.]

**edge** *noun* **edges** (th)
The **edge** of something is its end or side: *The house stood at the edge of the forest; She sat on the edge of her chair.*
[**Edge** comes from Old English.]

**edgy** *adjective* **edgier, edgiest** (th)
If you are **edgy**, you are nervous or worried about something.
[**Edgy** comes from **edge**.]

**edible** *adjective*
Food that is **edible** is safe to eat.
[**Edible** comes from Latin *edere* 'to eat'.]

**edit** *verb* **edits, editing, edited**
1 When you **edit** a piece of writing, you check that there are no mistakes in it and make it better if you can.

2 When someone **edits** a book, s/he checks it and gets it ready to be printed. [**Edit** comes from **editor**.]

**edition** noun **editions**
An **edition** of a book or a magazine is all the copies that are printed at a particular time: *The first edition of 'Alice in Wonderland'*.
[**Edition** comes via French from the same Latin word as **editor**.]

**editor** noun **editors**
The **editor** of a newspaper is the person in charge who decides what will be in it. [**Editor** comes from Latin *edere* 'to produce'.]

**educate** verb **educates, educating, educated** (th)
To **educate** someone means to teach him/her: *He was educated at a local school.* [**Educate** comes from Latin *educare* 'to lead out'.]

**education** noun (th)
**Education** is the teaching and learning that takes place in a school or college: *the importance of education; a good education.* [**Education** comes from the same Latin word as **educate**.]

**educational** adjective (th)
Something that is **educational** teaches you something: *They watched an educational programme on whales.* [**Educational** comes from **education**.]

**eel** noun **eels**
An **eel** is a long thin fish that looks like a snake. [**Eel** comes from Old English.]

**eerie** adjective **eerier, eeriest** (th)
Something that is **eerie** is strange and frightening: *an eerie silence.* [**Eerie** comes from Old English.]

**effect** noun **effects** (th)
1 An **effect** is the result of something: *The effects of the illness include tingling in the hands and feet; His father's death had a lasting effect on him.*
2 If something has **no effect**, nothing happens.
[**Effect** comes from Latin *efficere* 'to succeed in doing'.]

**effective** adjective (th)
If someone or something is **effective**, s/he or it works well: *an effective remedy* for the common cold; *He's been a very effective teacher.* **effectively** adverb.
[**Effective** comes from the same Latin word as **effect**.]

**effort** noun **efforts** (th)
An **effort** is the hard work someone is doing or trying to do.
[**Effort** comes via French from Latin *fortis* 'strong' (ancestor of **force** and **fort**).]

**e.g.** abbreviation
You use **e.g.** when you want to give an example of something: *Too much junk food, e.g. burgers, is bad for you.*
[**E.g.** is short for Latin *exempli gratia*, which means 'for example'.]

**egg** noun **eggs**
1 An **egg** is an oval or round object that a bird, fish, insect or reptile lays. The young animal starts to grow in the egg and hatches when it is ready.
2 A human baby grows when an **egg** in a woman's body meets sperm from a man's body.
3 The **eggs** we eat as food are usually laid by hens. [**Egg** comes from Old Norse.]

**eiderdown** noun **eiderdowns**
An **eiderdown** is a warm quilt or cover for a bed.
[**Eiderdown** comes from *eider*, a kind of duck, and **down²**. Eiders have thick, warm down that was used to stuff eiderdowns.]

**either** conjunction
**Either** of two things means one thing or the other thing: *You can come either on Wednesday or on Thursday.*
[**Either** comes from Old English.]

**either** adverb
**Either** means also: *I didn't see him and she didn't either.*

**elastic** noun
**Elastic** is a material that can stretch and then go back to its original size: *trousers with elastic in the waist.*
[**Elastic** comes from Greek via Latin.]

**elated** adjective (th)
Someone who is **elated** feels extremely happy: *I was elated when I passed the exam.* [**Elated** comes from Latin via French.]

**elbow** noun **elbows**
Your **elbow** is the joint that bends in the

a b c d **e** f g h i j k l m

middle of your arm.
[**Elbow** comes from Old English.]

**elderly** *adjective*
An **elderly** person is old.
[**Elderly** comes from Old English.]

**electric** *adjective*
Something that works by using electricity
is **electric**: *an electric toothbrush.*
[**Electric** comes from Greek via Latin.]

**electrician** *noun* **electricians**
An **electrician** is a person who works
with and repairs electrical equipment.

**electricity** *noun*
**Electricity** is energy that is used for
lighting, heating and making machines
work: *The electricity went off because there
was a power cut.*

**electrocute** *verb* **electrocutes,
electrocuting, electrocuted**
If someone is **electrocuted**, s/he gets a
powerful electric shock that kills him/her.

**element** *noun* **elements** (th)
**1** An **element** is a substance that cannot
be split into simpler substances.
**2** The **elements** of a subject are the basic
parts of it: *You should learn the elements of
cooking before you grow up.*
**3** An **element** of something is a part of it:
*Keeping order is one of the elements of
teaching.*
**4** The **element** of an electrical appliance
such as a kettle or a toaster is the metal
part that heats up when electricity passes
through it.
[**Element** comes from Latin via French.]

**elementary** *adjective* (th)
Something that is **elementary** is simple or
basic: *elementary mathematics.*
[**Elementary** comes from the same Latin
word as **element**.]

**elephant** *noun* **elephants**
An **elephant** is a very large, grey animal
with tusks and a long trunk. **Elephants**
live in Africa and parts of Asia.
[**Elephant** comes via French and Latin
from Greek *elephas* 'ivory'.]

**elevate** *verb* **elevates, elevating,
elevated**
If you **elevate** something, you lift it up.

**elf** *noun* **elves**
An **elf** is a small mischievous person in
legends and fairy stories.
[**Elf** comes from Old English.]

**eligible** *adjective* (th)
**1** People who are **eligible** for something
can have something or do something
because they have the right qualifications
or because they are the right age: *People
over 65 are eligible for free bus travel.*
**2** An **eligible** man or woman is someone
who people think it would be good to
marry: *an eligible bachelor.*
[**Eligible** comes via French from Latin
*eligere* 'to choose'.]

**eliminate** *verb* **eliminates, eliminating,
eliminated** (th)
To **eliminate** something or someone is to
get rid of them completely: *Polio has been
eliminated from parts of the world.*
[**Eliminate** comes from Latin *eliminare* 'to
turn out of doors'.]

**elite** *noun* **elites** *Also* **élite**
An **elite** is a group of people who have
special advantages because they are very
rich, very intelligent or very talented:
*Only the elite go to expensive restaurants.*
[**Elite** comes from French *élite* 'chosen',
which comes from the same Latin word
as **eligible**.]

**ellipse** *noun* **ellipses**
An **ellipse** is an oval shape.
[**Ellipse** comes from Greek via French and
Latin.]

**elope** *verb* **elopes, eloping, eloped**
When a man and a woman **elope**, they
run away together to get married.
[**Elope** comes from an old French word.]

**e-mail** *noun* **e-mails** *Also* **email**
An **e-mail** is a message that is sent from
one computer to another computer over
the Internet: *I've just had an e-mail from my
brother in Greece.*
[**E-mail** is short for *electronic mail.*]

**e-mail** *verb* **e-mails, e-mailing, e-mailed**
*Also* **email**
To **e-mail** someone is to send that person
a message over the Internet from your
computer to his/her computer.

**embalm** *verb* **embalms, embalming, embalmed**
When a dead person is **embalmed**, his/her body is treated with special chemicals to stop it decaying.
[**Embalm** comes from an old French word.]

**embark** *verb* **embarks, embarking, embarked** (th)
**1** Passengers who **embark** get on board a ship or plane: *Passengers can start to embark at 10 o'clock.*
**2** If you **embark** on something, you start something new that will take a lot of time and energy. [**Embark** comes from French.]

**embarrassed** *adjective* (th)
If you feel **embarrassed**, you feel ashamed and think that everyone is looking at you because of something you have done: *I was so embarrassed when I spilled cola over their carpet.*
[**Embarrassed** comes from Spanish via French.]

**embassy** *noun* **embassies**
An **embassy** is the official building of a government in a foreign country: *the French embassy in London.*
[**Embassy** comes from an old French word.]

**embezzle** *verb* **embezzles, embezzling, embezzled**
A person who **embezzles** steals money from the place where they work.
[**Embezzle** comes from an old French word.]

**emblem** *noun* **emblems**
An **emblem** is the sign or the symbol of a country or an organisation: *The emblem of the Miami Dolphins is a dolphin.*
[**Emblem** comes from Greek via Latin.]

**embrace** *verb* **embraces, embracing, embraced**
If you **embrace** someone, you give that person a hug; if two people **embrace**, they give each other a hug: *They embraced when they met at the airport.*
[**Embrace** comes via French from Latin *bracchium* 'arm'.]

**embryo** *noun* **embryos**
An **embryo** is an animal or a human that has not yet been born and has just begun to develop inside its mother.
[**Embryo** comes via Latin from Greek *bryein* 'to grow'.]

**emerald** *noun* **emeralds**
An **emerald** is a shiny green precious stone: *emerald earrings.*
[**Emerald** comes from an old French word.]

**emergency** *noun* **emergencies** (th)
An **emergency** is a dangerous situation that has to be dealt with very quickly.
[**Emergency** comes from Latin.]

**emigrate** *verb* **emigrates, emigrating, emigrated**
When someone **emigrates**, s/he leaves his/her country to go and live permanently in another country: *Many Irish people emigrated to the USA in the nineteenth century.*
[**Emigrate** comes from Latin *e-* 'out' and *migrare* 'to migrate' (ancestor of **migrate**).]

**emit** *verb* **emits, emitting, emitted** (th)
To **emit** something such as heat, light, or a gas means to give it out: *Fire emits light and heat; Waste gases are emitted through the exhaust pipe.*
[**Emit** comes from Latin *e-* 'out' and *mittere* 'to send'.]

**emotion** *noun* **emotions**
An **emotion** is a strong feeling such as love, anger or happiness.
[**Emotion** comes from an old French word.]

**emotional** *adjective* (th)
Someone who is **emotional** is showing his/her feelings, especially by crying: *She got very emotional at her daughter's wedding.*

**emphasise** *verb* **emphasises, emphasising, emphasised** *Also* **emphasize** (th)
When you **emphasise** something, you make it stand out clearly because it is very important: *Teachers always emphasise the importance of doing homework.*
[**Emphasise** comes from Greek via Latin.]

**employ** *verb* **employs, employing, employed**
When you **employ** someone, you give him/her a job: *The new company will employ 150 people.*
[**Employ** comes from French.]

a b c d **e** f g h i j k l m

**employee** *noun* **employees**
An **employee** is someone who is paid to do a job: *The company has 25 employees.*

**employer** *noun* **employers**
An **employer** is a person or company that pays people to do a job: *I worked for my last employer for 20 years.*

**empty** *adjective* **emptier, emptiest**
If something is **empty**, there is nothing inside it.
[**Empty** comes from Old English.]

**empty** *verb* **empties, emptying, emptied**
If you **empty** something, you take everything out of it: *empty your pockets.*

**emu** *noun* **emus**
An **emu** is a large Australian bird that runs fast but cannot fly.
[**Emu** comes from Portuguese.]

**encourage** *verb* **encourages, encouraging, encouraged**
1 If you **encourage** someone, or **encourage** someone to do something, you try to give that person confidence by showing that you approve of him/her or what s/he is doing.
2 To **encourage** something means to make it more likely that it will come or happen: *Leaving food uncovered encourages flies; encouraging good relations between teachers, parents and pupils.*
[**Encourage** comes from French *en-* 'in' and *courage* 'courage'.]

**encyclopaedia** *noun* **encyclopaedias**
Also **encyclopedia**
An **encyclopaedia** is a book, a set of books, or a CD-ROM, which contains facts about many different subjects, usually arranged in alphabetical order.
[**Encyclopaedia** comes via Latin from Greek *enkyklios paideia* 'general education'.]

**end** *noun* **ends** (th)
1 An **end** is the finish or the last part of something: *My job comes to an end in April; They live at the end of the road.*
2 The **end** of something is the part furthest from the middle: *a pencil sharpened at both ends.*
[**End** comes from Old English.]

**end** *verb* **ends, ending, ended** (th)
To **end** is to finish or stop: *School ends in December for the Christmas holidays; The performance ended with a song.*

**endanger** *verb* **endangers, endangering, endangered** (th)
To **endanger** something is to put it in danger: *Smoking endangers your health.*
[**Endanger** comes from *en-* 'in' and **danger.**]

**endangered** *adjective*
If a plant or animal species is **endangered**, there are very few left and it may die out altogether: *The giant panda is an endangered species.*

**endeavour** *verb* **endeavours, endeavouring, endeavoured** (th)
If you **endeavour** to do something, you try very hard to do it: *I'll endeavour to help.*
[**Endeavour** comes from French *devoir* 'duty'.]

**endure** *verb* **endures, enduring, endured** (th)
If you **endure** something horrible or painful, you put up with it.
[**Endure** comes from Latin *durus* 'hard'.]

**enemy** *noun* **enemies** (th)
1 Your **enemy** is someone who hates you and wants to harm you.
2 The **enemy** is the army or the country you are fighting a war against.
[**Enemy** comes via French from Latin *in-* 'not' and *amicus* 'friend'.]

**energetic** *adjective* (th)
Someone who is **energetic** has lots of energy and can do things without getting too tired.

**energy** *noun* **energies** (th)
1 **Energy** is the strength to be very active without getting too tired: *You use lots of energy when you swim.*
2 **Energy** is the power from coal, gas and oil that is used to run machines and provide heat and light: *Coal is one of the world's energy resources.*
[**Energy** comes from Greek *ergon* 'work'.]

**engine** *noun* **engines**
An **engine** is a machine that changes power from fuel such as petrol or electricity into movement: *This car has a very powerful engine.*

[**Engine** comes from Latin via French.]

**engineer** *noun* **engineers**
An **engineer** is a person whose job is to design machines, vehicles, roads and bridges: *A civil engineer designs bridges and roads.*
[**Engineer** comes via French from the same Latin word as **engine**.]

**engineering** *noun*
**Engineering** is designing the way roads, vehicles, bridges and machines are built.

**English** *adjective*
Someone or something from England is **English**.
[**English** comes from Old English.]

**English** *noun*
**English** is the main language spoken in the British Isles, the United States of America, Canada and Australia. **English** is also spoken by some people in many other countries.

**engrave** *verb* **engraves, engraving, engraved**
To **engrave** a glass, metal or stone item means to cut words or a pattern into it. *His name is engraved on his gold pen.*
[**Engrave** comes from en- 'in' and Old English *grafan* 'to carve'.]

**engrossed** *adjective* (th)
If you are **engrossed** in something such as a book, a television programme or a conversation, you are so interested in it that you do not notice anything else.
[**Engrossed** comes from French.]

**engulfed** *verb* **engulfs, engulfing, engulfed**
When something **engulfs** something else, it completely covers it or swallows it up: *The explosion engulfed the building in flames.*
[**Engulf** comes from en- 'in' and **gulf**.]

**enigma** *noun* **enigmas** (th)
Something or someone that is an **enigma** is mysterious or puzzling: *I never know what she's thinking en- she's a real enigma.*
[**Enigma** comes from Greek via Latin.]

**enjoy** *verb* **enjoys, enjoying, enjoyed** (th)
If you **enjoy** something, you like it very much: *I really enjoy listening to music.*
[**Enjoy** comes from French.]

**enlarge** *verb* **enlarges, enlarging, enlarged**
To **enlarge** means to get bigger or to make something bigger.
[**Enlarge** comes from the same French word as **large**.]

**enlist** *verb* **enlists, enlisting, enlisted**
1 To **enlist** is to join the army, navy or airforce.
2 If you **enlist** someone's help, you get that person to help you: *We can enlist the help of parents for the school party.*
[**Enlist** comes from en- 'in' and **list**.]

**enormous** *adjective* (th)
Something that is **enormous** is very big.
[**Enormous** comes from Latin e- 'out' and *norma* 'standard' (ancestor of **normal**).]

**enough** *adjective, adverb, pronoun* (th)
If you have **enough** of something, you have as much as you need: *Are three bottles of lemonade enough?*
[**Enough** comes from Old English.]

**enquire** *verb* **enquires, enquiring, enquired** (th)
If you **enquire** about something, you ask for information about it: *I'll phone to enquire about the price of the tickets.*
[**Enquire** comes via French from Latin in- 'into' and *quaerere* 'to seek' (ancestor of **query**).]

**enquiry** *noun* **enquiries**
An **enquiry** is a question you ask in order to get information about something: *We've had lots of enquiries about our house, which is for sale.*

**enrol** *verb* **enrols, enrolling, enrolled**
If you **enrol** at a school or on a course, for example, you join it or you put your name on a list so that you can join it later.
[**Enrol** comes from old French en- 'in' and *rolle* 'a roll'; originally people's names were written on a roll of parchment.]

**ensure** *verb* **ensures, ensuring, ensured** (th)
To **ensure** something is to make certain that it happens: *Please ensure all lights are switched off at the end of the day.*
[**Ensure** comes from an old French word.]

**enter** *verb* **enters, entering, entered** (th)
1 If you **enter** a place, you go into it.
2 If you **enter** a race, a competition or an

examination, you take part in it.
[**Enter** comes via French from Latin *intra* 'inside'.]

**entertain** *verb* **entertains, entertaining, entertained** (th)
1 To **entertain** people is to amuse them: *The computer keeps her entertained for hours.*
2 To **entertain** is to invite friends to your house for a meal: *I've got a lot of cooking to do because we're entertaining tonight.*
[**Entertain** comes from an old French word.]

**entertainment** *noun* **entertainments** (th)
**Entertainment** is something that people watch or take part in for pleasure: *The hotel has comedy acts every night for your entertainment; games, films and other entertainments.*

**entire** *adjective* (th)
**Entire** means whole: *He covered the entire wall with posters; I've never been so frightened in my entire life.*
[**Entire** comes from an old French word.]

**entrance¹** *noun* **entrances** (th)
An **entrance** is a way in: *I'll meet you at the entrance to the cinema.*
[**Entrance¹** comes from the same French word as **enter**.]

**entrance²** *verb* **entrances, entrancing, entranced** (th)
Someone who is **entranced** by something or someone thinks that thing or person is wonderful and amazing: *She was entranced by the music.*
[**Entrance²** comes from *en-* 'in' and *trance*.]

**entrepreneur** *noun* **entrepreneurs**
An **entrepreneur** is someone who is good at finding new ways to make money by starting businesses.
[**Entrepreneur** comes from French.]

**envelop** *verb* **envelops, enveloping, enveloped** (th)
When something **envelops** something, it surrounds and covers it: *The fields were enveloped in early morning mist.*
[**Envelop** comes from French.]

**envelope** *noun* **envelopes**
You put a letter or a card into an **envelope** before you post it: *write the address on the envelope.*
[**Envelope** comes from the same French word as **envelop**.]

**environment** *noun*
1 The **environment** is the air, sea and land in the natural world: *Cars pollute the environment.*
2 An **environment** is everything that affects your life, such as where you live, your family situation and things that happen to you: *The inner city can be an exciting environment for children.*
[**Environment** comes from French *environs* 'surroundings'.]

**envy** *verb* **envies, envying, envied**
If you **envy** someone, you wish that you had something that s/he has: *I really envy people with lots of money.*
[**Envy** comes via French from Latin *invidere* 'to look at spitefully'.]

**epidemic** *noun* **epidemics**
There is an **epidemic** when an infectious disease spreads very quickly to many people: *a cholera epidemic.*
[**Epidemic** comes via Latin from Greek *epi-* 'upon' and *demos* 'the people'.]

**epilepsy** *noun*
**Epilepsy** is an illness of the brain that causes people to have fits.
[**Epilepsy** comes from Greek via Latin or French.]

**epilogue** *noun* **epilogues**
An **epilogue** is a short speech or piece of writing at the end of a play or book.
[**Epilogue** comes via French and Latin from Greek *epilogos* 'a speech added on'.]

**episode** *noun* **episodes** (th)
An **episode** is one programme in a series of radio or television programmes that tells a story: *The fifth episode of the serial starts at 7 o'clock.*
[**Episode** comes from Greek.]

**epitaph** *noun* **epitaphs**
An **epitaph** is the words written on someone's gravestone.
[**Epitaph** comes from Greek *epi-* 'upon' and *taphos* 'tomb'.]

**equal** *noun* **equals**
If someone is your **equal**, that person is as intelligent and as important and capable as you: *Men and women should be treated as*

*equals.* [**Equal** comes from Latin.]

**equal** *adjective* (th)
Something that is **equal** to something else is the same in size, amount or value: *A litre is equal to one-and-three-quarter pints.*

**equal** *verb* **equals, equalling, equalled**
To **equal** a score or an achievement is to match it: *She equalled the world record of just under 11 minutes in this race.*

**equator** *noun* **equators**
The **equator** is an imaginary line round the middle of the earth.
[**Equator** comes from Latin *circulus aequator diei et noctis* 'circle making day and night equal', because at the equator the day and night each last twelve hours.]

**equip** *verb* **equips, equipping, equipped** (th)
**1** To **equip** someone or something is to provide the equipment that is necessary: *Firefighters are equipped with breathing gear; equip the kitchen with appliances.*
**2** If you are **equipped** for something, you have the equipment and training you need to do something: *Ambulance crews are equipped to deal with emergencies.*
[**Equip** comes from a French word which may in turn come from Old Norse.]

**equipment** *noun* (th)
**Equipment** is the tools and machines that you need to do a particular job: *Divers need breathing equipment.*

**era** *noun* **eras**
An **era** is a period of time in history: *the Victorian era.* [**Era** comes from Latin.]

**eradicate** *verb* **eradicates, eradicating, eradicated**
To **eradicate** something is to get rid of it completely: *bleach eradicates germs.*
[**Eradicate** comes from Latin *eradicare* 'to pull something up by the roots'.]

**erase** *verb* **erases, erasing, erased**
**1** When you **erase** a tape or computer disk, you remove the sound or data stored on it.
**2** If you **erase** the sound or data stored on a tape or computer disk, you remove it.
**3** If you **erase** writing or a drawing, you rub it out.
[**Erase** comes from Latin *erasum* 'scraped off'.]

**errand** *noun* **errands**
An **errand** is a short journey to deliver or collect something or to give someone a message: *I have a few errands to run.*
[**Errand** comes from Old English.]

**erratic** *adjective*
Something that is **erratic** does not follow any pattern: *erratic driving.*
**erratically** *adverb.*
[**Erratic** comes from Latin *errare* 'to wander'.]

**error** *noun* **errors** (th)
An **error** is a mistake.
[**Error** comes from the same Latin word as **erratic**.]

**erupt** *verb* **erupts, erupting, erupted**
**1** When a volcano **erupts**, it throws out smoke, ashes and lava: *Vesuvius might erupt again soon.*
**2** If something such as fighting or violence **erupts**, it happens suddenly: *Suddenly the march erupted into violence.*
**3** When someone **erupts**, s/he suddenly gets very angry.
[**Erupt** comes from Latin *erumpere* 'to burst out'.]

**escapade** *noun* **escapades**
An **escapade** is an adventure that is exciting and slightly dangerous.
[**Escapade** comes from Latin via French and Spanish.]

**escape** *verb* **escapes, escaping, escaped** (th)
**1** To **escape** is to get away from a place where you have been forced to stay or where you do not want to be: *Three prisoners have escaped; I escaped to my room after lunch with the family.*
**2** If you **escape**, you get away from something dangerous: *Three passengers escaped uninjured from the burning bus; Most people couldn't escape the war.*
[**Escape** comes from the same French word as **escapade**.]

**especially** *adverb*
**1** You use the word **especially** to show an important example of what you are talking about: *It gets very hot in school, especially in the afternoon.*
**2** **Especially** means more than usual: *It's especially cold this morning.*
**3** If a certain thing is **especially** for

something or someone in particular, it is meant for them: *This hospital is especially for children; I made this especially for you.*
[**Especially** comes via French from Latin *specialis* 'special' (ancestor of **special**).]

**espionage** *noun*
**Espionage** is spying: *a double agent involved in espionage.*
[**Espionage** comes from French *espion* 'a spy'.]

**essay** *noun* **essay**
An **essay** is a short piece of writing about a particular subject: *For homework, I want you to write an essay on the subject of Napoleon.*
[**Essay** comes from French *essayer* 'to try'.]

**estate** *noun* **estates**
1 An **estate** is an area of houses, offices or factories that were all built at about the same time: *an industrial estate; a housing estate.*
2 An **estate** is an area of land with a very large house on it that belongs to a rich person: *Lord Cranborne's estate.*
3 Someone's **estate** is all that person's money and everything that person owns that is left when s/he dies: *She left her whole estate to charity.*
[**Estate** comes from French.]

**estimate** *verb* **estimates, estimating, estimated** (th)
When you **estimate** something, you work it out roughly: *We estimated our holiday would cost about a month's wages.*
[**Estimate** comes from Latin *aestimare* 'to decide the value of something'.]

**estimate** *noun* **estimates**
An **estimate** is a rough guess of how much something will cost or how much time it will take: *The estimate for the cost of the repairs is reasonable.*

**estuary** *noun* **estuaries**
The **estuary** of a river is the wide part of it before it meets the sea.
[**Estuary** comes from Latin *aestuarium* 'tidal part of a river'.]

**etc** *abbreviation*
You write **etc** at the end of a list of things to show that there are more things of a similar kind that you are not going to mention: *Many children have pets, such as dogs, cats, hamsters, etc.*

[**Etc** is short for for Latin *et cetera*, which means 'and the other things'.]

**eternal** *adjective* (th)
Something that is **eternal** lasts for ever, or seems to last for ever: *the promise of eternal life; I'm fed up with their eternal squabbling.*
**eternally** *adverb*.
[**Eternal** comes from Latin via French.]

**etymology** *noun* **etymologies**
The **etymology** of a word is an account of its origin and history.
[**Etymology** comes via French and Latin from Greek *etymon* 'something that is true'.]

**even** *adjective*
1 An **even** number can be divided by two, with nothing left over. Ten is an even number.
2 Something that is equal is **even**: *The score is even at two goals each; Cut the cake into six even slices.*
3 A level or flat surface is **even**: *Lay the carpet on an even floor.*
[**Even** comes from Old English.]

**evening** *noun* **evenings**
**Evening** is the time of day between afternoon and night: *I'll see you this evening at about six o'clock.*
[**Evening** comes from Old English.]

**event** *noun* **events** (th)
1 An **event** is something important, interesting or exciting that happens: *The wedding was a great event.*
2 An **event** is a sports competition: *The next event is the 100 metre sprint.*
[**Event** comes from Latin *evenire* 'to happen'.]

**eventually** *adverb* (th)
If something happens **eventually**, it happens after a long time, often because there have been problems or delays: *We eventually arrived after a long delay.*
[**Eventually** comes from the same Latin word as **event**.]

**ever** *adverb* (th)
1 **Ever** means at any time: *Have you ever eaten frogs' legs?; Can you ever forgive me?*
2 **For ever** means always: *I will love you for ever.*
3 If something is **ever-growing** or **ever-increasing**, it is always growing or increasing: *The ever-increasing use of cars.*

n o p q r s t u v w x y z

[**Ever** comes from Old English.]

**every** *adjective*
You use the word **every** to show you are talking about all the people in a group or all the parts of something, not just some of them: *They decorated every room in the house.* [**Every** comes from Old English.]

**everybody** *pronoun*
**Everybody** is every person: *Is everybody here?*

**everyone** *pronoun*
**Everyone** is every person: *Please be quiet everyone!*

**everything** *pronoun*
**Everything** is all things: *Everything is ready for the party.*

**everywhere** *adverb*
**Everywhere** is all places: *I've looked everywhere for my keys.*

**evidence** *noun*
1 **Evidence** is information or facts that make you believe something exists or is true: *Is there any evidence of life on Mars?*
2 **Evidence** that is given in a law court is information and facts about the court case: *The evidence proves she's not guilty.* [**Evidence** comes from the same Latin word as **evident**.]

**evident** *adjective* (th)
If something is **evident**, it is clear and obvious: *She was so pale and thin it was evident that she had been ill.*
**evidently** *adverb*.
[**Evident** comes from Latin.]

**evil** *adjective* (th)
Something or someone that is **evil** is wicked and cruel: *an evil dictator.* [**Evil** comes from Old English.]

**exactly** *adverb* (th)
You use the word **exactly** before a time or an amount, for example, to show that it is no more or no less than you say it is: *It's exactly half past five.* [**Exactly** comes from Latin.]

**exam** *noun* **exams**
An **exam** is an important test: *She takes her final exams next year.* [**Exam** is short for **examination**.]

**examination** *noun* **examinations**
1 An **examination** is an important test:

*Candidates must not be late for examinations.*
2 An **examination** by a doctor is when s/he checks you to find out whether you are healthy or to find out more about a problem: *He had a medical examination.* [**Examination** comes via French from the same Latin word as **examine**.]

**examine** *verb* **examines, examining, examined** (th)
1 If you are **examined** on something, your knowledge is tested in an examination: *You'll only be examined on the three topics.*
2 To **examine** something is to look at it very carefully: *The police examined the car for fingerprints.*
3 When a doctor **examines** you, s/he looks carefully at your body to find out whether you are healthy or to find out more about a problem: *The doctor examined my bad knee.*
[**Examine** comes from Latin *examinare* 'to weigh or test'.]

**example** *noun* **examples** (th)
1 An **example** of something represents other similar things: *An oak is an example of a tree.*
2 You give an **example** of something to show people what you mean. You can use **for example** when you give an **example**: *people without much money, for example the elderly and the unemployed; I'd like to do something exciting – bungee jumping, for example.*
3 If someone is an **example** to you, that person has done something very good and you should copy it: *She works very hard and is an example to us all.*
4 If you **make an example of** someone, you punish that person so that other people will not do what s/he has done. [**Example** comes via French from Latin *exemplum* 'something taken out' (ancestor of **sample**).]

**excellent** *adjective* (th)
Something that is very good is **excellent**: *an excellent exam result.* [**Excellent** comes from Latin.]

**except** *preposition* (th)
You use the word **except** to show that what you have just said is not true for a certain thing or person in a group: *She works every day except Sundays; Everyone except our teacher is here.*

a b c d **e** f g h i j k l m

[**Except** comes from Latin.]

**excite** *verb* **excites, exciting, excited** (th)
To **excite** someone is to make that person feel happy, interested or hopeful: *The thought of a holiday in America really excites me.* **excitement** *noun.*
[**Excite** comes from Latin via French.]

**exclaim** *verb* **exclaims, exclaiming, exclaimed**
If you **exclaim**, you shout or cry out suddenly. [**Exclaim** comes from Latin.]

**exclamation mark** *noun* **exclamation marks**
An **exclamation mark** is a punctuation mark like this !. It is used to show surprise, anger and other strong emotions.

**excuse** *verb* **excuses, excusing, excused** (th)
1 If you **excuse** someone, you forgive them: *I'll excuse you for being late this time, but don't do it again.*
2 If you **excuse** someone, you give them permission not to do something: *He was excused from games because he had a bad cold.*
3 You say **excuse me** to get someone's attention, to ask them to move out of your way, or to say sorry for something you have done: *Excuse me, can you help me?; Excuse me, can I get past?*
[**Excuse** comes via French from Latin *excusare* 'to free from blame'.]

**excuse** *noun* **excuses**
1 An **excuse** is a lie you tell to get yourself out of a difficult situation: *The party was so boring that I made an excuse and left.*
2 An **excuse** is the reason you give to explain why you have or haven't done something: *His excuse for not doing the work was that he had been ill; There's no excuse for being so late.*

**exempt** *adjective*
If you are **exempt** from something, you don't have to do it: *Children are exempt from paying tax.*
[**Exempt** comes from Latin *exemptus* 'let out, freed'.]

**exercise** *verb* **exercises, exercising, exercised** (th)
If you **exercise**, you do physical activity in order to keep fit.
[**Exercise** comes via French from Latin *execere* 'to practise or keep busy'.]

**exercise** *noun* **exercises**
1 **Exercise** is physical activity that keeps you fit: *She does a lot of exercise in the gym; You should take more exercise.*
2 An **exercise** is a piece of work that you do as part of your studies: *Do exercise 3 on page 76.*

**exhale** *verb* **exhales, exhaling, exhaled**
When you **exhale**, you breathe out: *Breathe in slowly and then exhale.*
[**Exhale** comes from Latin *ex-* 'out' and *halare* 'to breathe'.]

**exhaust** *verb* **exhausts, exhausting, exhausted** (th)
1 If something **exhausts** you, it makes you extremely tired: *He was so ill it exhausted him to walk across the room.*
2 If you use something up, you have **exhausted** your supply of that thing: *When will we exhaust the world's oil supplies?*
[**Exhaust** comes from Latin *ex-* 'out' and *haustum* 'drained'.]

**exhaust** *noun* **exhausts**
The **exhaust** or **exhaust pipe** of a vehicle is the pipe at the back where used gases from the engine escape: *Fumes belched from the lorry's exhaust pipe.*

**exhausted** *adjective* (th)
If you are **exhausted**, you are extremely tired and have no energy: *I'm too exhausted to go out tonight.*

**exhibition** *noun* **exhibitions**
1 An **exhibition** is a public show where people look at things on display: *an exhibition of dresses from the nineteenth century.*
2 If you make an **exhibition** of yourself, you behave in a silly or embarrassing way so that everyone looks at you.
[**Exhibition** comes via French from Latin *exhibere* 'to hold out'.]

**exit** *noun* **exits**
1 An **exit** is a way out of a place: *a fire exit.*
2 An **exit** on a motorway or roundabout is a road that takes you off it: *Take the exit to Heathrow off the M25.*
[**Exit** comes from Latin *exit* 's/he goes out'.]

**exodus** *noun* **exoduses**
An **exodus** is when a lot of people leave a place at the same time: *the exodus of Jews from Germany before the war.*

[**Exodus** comes via Latin from Greek *exodos* 'a way out'.]

**exotic** *adjective* (th)
Something that is **exotic** is unusual and exciting, usually because it is from a foreign country: *exotic Malayan food.*
[**Exotic** comes via Latin from Greek *exoticus* 'foreign'.]

**expand** *verb* **expands, expanding, expanded** (th)
When something **expands**, it gets bigger.
[**Expand** comes from Latin *expandere* 'to spread out'.]

**expanse** *noun* **expanses**
An **expanse** is a very large area: *a great expanse of water.*
[**Expanse** comes from the same Latin word as **expand**.]

**expect** *verb* **expects, expecting, expected** (th)
**1** If you **expect** something to happen, you think it will happen: *I expect the taxi will be here soon.*
**2** If you **expect** someone to do something, you think that person should do it: *I expect you to keep your room tidy.*
**3** If you **expect** someone or something, you think that s/he or it will come soon: *I can't go out, I'm expecting my mother.*
**4** If a woman is **expecting**, she is pregnant: *She's expecting – the baby's due in the summer.*
[**Expect** comes from Latin *exspectare* 'to look out for'.]

**expensive** *adjective* (th)
Something that is **expensive** costs a lot of money: *five-star hotels are expensive.*
**expensively** *adverb.*
[**Expensive** comes via French from Latin *expendus* 'to pay out'.]

**expert** *noun* **experts**
An **expert** is someone with a special skill or a lot of knowledge about something: *a computer expert; an expert on 18th-century china.* [**Expert** comes from Latin.]

**expertise** *noun*
**Expertise** is a special skill or a lot of knowledge of a certain subject.
[**Expertise** comes via French from the same Latin word as **expert**.]

**expire** *verb* **expires, expiring, expired**
**1** If something such as an official

document **expires**, the time when it can be used has ended: *Passports expire after ten years.*
[**Expire** comes from Latin via French.]

**explain** *verb* **explains, explaining, explained** (th)
**1** To **explain** something is to make it clear and easy to understand: *She explained it in a way that everyone could understand.*
**2** To **explain** something is to give the reason for it: *I can explain why I'm late.*
[**Explain** comes from Latin *explanare* 'to make plain'.]

**explanation** *noun* **explanations** (th)
**1** An **explanation** is a statement that is meant to help you understand something.
**2** An **explanation** is a reason why something happened.
[**Explanation** comes from the same Latin word as **explain**.]

**explode** *verb* **explodes, exploding, exploded** (th)
To **explode** is to blow apart with a loud noise: *Bombs exploded all around us.*
[**Explode** comes from Latin.]

**explore** *verb* **explores, exploring, explored**
To **explore** an area is to look or travel round it to discover what it is like: *We explored the old part of the city.*
[**Explore** comes via French from Latin *explorare* 'to search out'.]

**explorer** *noun* **explorers**
An **explorer** is a person who goes to an area where not many people have been before.

**explosive** *adjective*
Something that is **explosive** is likely to explode.

**export** *verb* **exports, exporting, exported**
To **export** is to sell goods to people in other countries.
[**Export** comes from Latin *exportare* 'to take out'.]

**export** *noun* **exports**
**Exports** are goods sent abroad to be sold.

**express** *verb* **expresses, expressing, expressed** (th)
To **express** an idea or feeling is to show it especially by talking or writing about it:

a b c d e f g h i j k l m

*This poem expresses feelings of sadness; She expressed her happiness with a big smile.*
[**Express** comes via French from the same Latin word as **expression**.]

**expression** *noun* **expressions**
1 An **expression** is the look on someone's face: *a sad expression.*
2 An **expression** is a phrase with a certain meaning: *The expression 'Take the bull by the horns' means 'face danger'.*
[**Expression** comes from Latin.]

**extinct** *adjective*
1 When a volcano will never erupt again, it is **extinct**.
2 When a plant or animal species has died out, it is **extinct**: *The dodo is extinct.*
[**Extinct** comes from Latin *exstinguere* 'to quench'.]

**extra** *adjective* (th)
Something **extra** is more of it, or more than usual: *Take some extra money, in case you need it.*

[**Extra** comes from Latin *extra* 'outside'.]

**extra** *adverb* (th)
more or more than usual: *They charge extra for a double room; You'll have to work extra hard.*

**eye** *noun* **eyes**
**Eyes** are the two parts of the body that people and animals use to see.
[**Eye** comes from Old English.]

**eyebrow** *noun* **eyebrows**
Your **eyebrow** is the curved line of hair above your eye.

**eyelash** *noun* **eyelashes**
An **eyelash** is one of the short hairs that grows on the edge of your eyelid.

**eyelid** *noun* **eyelids**
An **eyelid** is one of the pieces of skin that covers your eye when it is closed.

**eyesight** *noun*
Your **eyesight** is your ability to see: *People with poor eyesight need glasses.*

# Dictionary Fun

**Work it out**
What is strange about this passage? Clue: it's related to this section!

Ivor always thought going to a circus was thrilling. His family had paid a visit to Mario's Circus in January but for Ivor's birthday Dad said an additional trip was okay. Ivor was so happy that it was difficult to wait until his big day on Friday. His mind was full of clowns, lions and flying acrobats. Ivor just could not wait!

Can you write a similar passage?

**What do these idioms mean?**
1. To have egg on your face

2. To eat your words
3. To make both ends meet

**Complete the proverbs**
1. E_____ vessels make the most noise.
2. Don't put all your e_____ in one basket.
3. The e_____ bird catches the worm.

**Did you know?**
◆ The word **electric** comes from the Greek word *elektron*, meaning 'amber', because early experiments involved rubbing amber to create static electricity.
◆ 'e' is the most commonly used letter in the English language.

# Ff

**fable** *noun* **fables**
A **fable** is a traditional story that teaches you a lesson about how to behave. Animals are usually the main characters in **fables**: *the fable of the hare and the tortoise.*
[**Fable** comes from Latin *fabula* 'story'.]

**fabric** *noun* **fabrics** (th)
**Fabric** is cloth or material that is used to make clothes and curtains: *Cotton is a natural fabric.*
[**Fabric** comes from Latin via French.]

**face** *noun* **faces**
1 Your **face** is the front part of your head from the chin to the forehead.
2 A mountain **face** is its steep sloping surface: *the north face of the Eiger.*
[**Face** comes from Latin via French.]

**face** *verb* **faces, facing, faced** (th)
1 If something **faces** a certain direction, it points in that direction.
2 If you **face** a problem, you admit that the problem exists and that you will have to deal with it.

**fact** *noun* **facts** (th)
A **fact** is anything that is true: *It's a fact that London is the capital of England.*
[**Fact** comes from Latin *factum* 'something done'.]

**factory** *noun* **factories** (th)
A **factory** is a building where large numbers or amounts of things are made by people who operate machines: *a car factory.*
[**Factory** comes from Latin *factorium* 'a place where things are made'.]

**fade** *verb* **fades, fading, faded** (th)
1 To **fade** is to become paler in colour: *Bright colours fade after many washes.*
2 To **fade** is to become weaker or to slowly disappear: *He's very ill and fading fast; Hope of finding survivors is fading.*
[**Fade** comes from old French *fade* 'dull'.]

**faeces** *plural noun* Also **feces**
**Faeces** are solid waste that comes out of the bowels: *dog faeces on the grass.*
[**Faeces** comes from Latin *faeces* 'dregs'.]

**fail** *verb* **fails, failing, failed** (th)
1 If you **fail**, you are not able to do something you wanted to do: *I failed to get tickets because they had sold out.*
2 To **fail** is to not do something that is important or necessary: *You failed to mention how much you will pay me.*
3 If you **fail** a test or an examination, you do not pass it: *He failed his driving test.*
[**Fail** comes from Latin via French.]

**failing** *noun* **failings** (th)
A **failing** is a fault or a weakness in a thing or a person: *His main failing is his bossiness.*

**faint** *adjective* **fainter, faintest** (th)
1 Something that is **faint** is difficult to see, hear or smell: *There's a faint smell of gas in here.* **faintly** *adverb.*
2 If you feel **faint** you feel dizzy or weak because you are ill or hungry: *I feel faint from hunger.*
[**Faint** comes from an old French word.]

**faint** *verb* **faints, fainting, fainted**
To **faint** is to lose consciousness: *Many screaming fans fainted when the band came onto the stage.*

**fair**[1] *noun* **fairs**
1 A **fair** is an outside entertainment with rides, games, displays and stalls: *Did you go on the big wheel at the fair?*
2 A **fair** is a place where companies set up stands to advertise the work they do: *a trade fair; a book fair.*
[**Fair**[1] comes from Latin *feriae* 'holy days', on which fairs were often held.]

**fair**[2] *adjective* **fairer, fairest** (th)
1 Something that is **fair** is reasonable and acceptable: *Is that a fair wage for the job?*
2 A system or a person that is **fair** treats everyone properly and equally: *Sometimes life just isn't fair.*
3 Hair or skin that is **fair** is light in colour: *He's got fair hair and blue eyes.*
[**Fair**[2] comes from Old English.]

**fairy** *noun* **fairies**
A **fairy** is an imaginary small person with magical powers: *The good fairy said Cinderella could go to the ball.*
[**Fairy** comes from Latin.]

**fairy story** *noun* **fairy stories** Also **fairy tale**
A **fairy story** is a story about magic, fairies and sometimes witches and elves, which is told to young children.

**faith** *noun* (th)
**1** If you have **faith** in a thing or person, you trust them and know they will not let you down: *I have faith in the doctors because I know they're well trained.*
**2 Faith** is a religion or religious beliefs: *the Jewish faith; Have faith in God.*
[**Faith** comes from Latin via French.]

**faithful** *adjective* (th)
If you are **faithful** to a person or an organisation, you are loyal to them and support them: *She's given the company 20 years of faithful service.*

**faithfully** *adverb*
**1** in a loyal or faithful way: *He served the family faithfully for many years.*
**2** exactly or accurately: *She copied the drawings faithfully.*
**3** You end a letter with *Yours faithfully* when you begin with *Dear Sir* or *Dear Madam.*

**fake** *noun* **fakes**
A **fake** is an exact copy of something valuable that is made in order to trick people into believing it is the real thing: *The painting was found to be a fake.*
[No one knows where **fake** comes from.]

**fake** *adjective* (th)
Something that is **fake** is made to look like the real thing, usually in order to deceive people: *a fake passport; fake fur.*

**fake** *verb* **fakes, faking, faked** (th)
To **fake** something is to pretend something is real in order to trick people: *She faked a headache to get out of helping with the housework.*

**falcon** *noun* **falcons**
A **falcon** is a bird of prey that can be trained to hunt birds and small animals.
[**Falcon** comes from Latin via French.]

**fall** *verb* **falls, falling, fell, fallen** (th)
**1** To **fall** is to come down from somewhere high to somewhere lower: *Snow is falling; The temperature fell to below freezing.*
**2** To **fall** is to hit the ground, especially by accident: *She slipped and fell on the ice.*
**3** If you **fall out** with someone, you are no longer friends with that person because you have had an argument.
**4** If an arrangement **falls through**, it does not happen: *We were going to Spain, but*

*that fell through.*
[**Fall** comes from Old English.]

**fallacy** *noun* **fallacies** (th)
A **fallacy** is a false idea or belief that a lot of people think is true: *It's a fallacy that girls cannot play football.*
[**Fallacy** comes from the same Latin word as **false**.]

**false** *adjective* (th)
**1** Something that is not true or not real is **false**: *Montreal is the capital of France – true or false?; The criminal used a false name.*
**2** A **false** eye or leg, for example, is a replacement for a missing part of the body: *He's got false teeth.*
[**False** comes from Latin *fallere* 'to deceive'.]

**family** *noun* **families** (th)
**1** A **family** is a group of people who are related to each other: *We've got uncles, aunts and lots of other family in Australia.*
**2** A **family** is a group of related animals or plants: *Lions are part of the cat family.*
[**Family** comes from Latin.]

**famine** *noun* **famines**
A **famine** is a serious shortage of food that causes people to die of hunger.
[**Famine** comes from Latin *fames* 'hunger'.]

**famished** *adjective* (th)
If you are **famished**, you are extremely hungry: *I'm famished – I haven't eaten anything since breakfast.*
[**Famished** comes via French from the same Latin word as **famine**.]

**famous** *adjective* (th)
Someone or something that is **famous** is very well known: *a famous actor.*
[**Famous** comes from Latin via French.]

**fan**[1] *noun* **fans**
A **fan** is someone who really likes something such as a football team or a pop group: *a football fan.*
[**Fan**[1] is short for **fanatic**.]

**fan**[2] *noun* **fans**
A **fan** is something that moves air around to cool people or machines.
[**Fan**[2] comes from Old English.]

**fanatic** *noun* **fanatics** (th)
A **fanatic** is someone with very strong religious beliefs or political views who

some people think is dangerous: *religious fanatics who commit acts of terrorism.*
[**Fanatic** comes from Latin.]

**fancy** *verb* **fancies, fancying, fancied** (th)
1 If you **fancy** something, you want it or you want to do it: *Fancy a drink?; I fancy going swimming this weekend.*
2 If you **fancy** someone, you are attracted to that person: *He's good-looking and all the girls fancy him like mad.*
[**Fancy** is short for **fantasy**.]

**fancy** *adjective* **fancier, fanciest**
A **fancy** place such as a restaurant is high-quality and expensive: *They stayed in a fancy five-star hotel.*

**fang** *noun* **fangs**
A **fang** is a long, sharp tooth: *The snake sank its fangs into its prey.*
[**Fang** comes from Old English.]

**fantastic** *adjective* (th)
Something that is **fantastic** is really good or wonderful: *That was a fantastic film; You got the job? That's fantastic!*
[**Fantastic** comes via French and Latin from the same Greek word as **fantasy**.]

**fantasy** *noun* **fantasies**
A **fantasy** is something that you imagine, especially something that is not likely to be true or to happen: *She says she's going to be an actress, but that's pure fantasy.*
[**Fantasy** comes from Greek *phantazein* 'to make something visible'.]

**far** *adjective, adverb* **farther, farthest** *Also* **further, furthest** (th)
1 If something or someone is **far** from something else or someone else, there is a big distance between them: *We can't walk to the shops from here, it's much too far.*
2 If you ask how **far** one place is from another place, you want to know the distance between them: *How far is your house from the station?*
[**Far** comes from Old English.]

**fare** *noun* **fares**
1 A **fare** is the money you pay to travel in a taxi or on a bus, train or plane.
2 **Fare** is an old-fashioned word for food and drink: *traditional fare.*
[**Fare** comes from Old English.]

**farm** *noun* **farms**
A **farm** is an area of land where animals

are kept and crops are grown for food: *a sheep farm.*
[**Farm** comes from Latin via French.]

**farmer** *noun* **farmers**
A **farmer** is someone who has a farm.

**fascinate** *verb* **fascinates, fascinating, fascinated** (th)
If something or someone **fascinates** you, you find that thing or person extremely interesting: *He's fascinated by anything to do with trains.*
[**Fascinate** comes from Latin *fascinum* 'a magic spell'.]

**fashion** *noun* **fashions** (th)
1 A **fashion** is a way of dressing or behaving that is popular at a particular time: *the latest Paris fashions; Fashions have changed since I was young.*
2 A **fashion** is a way of doing something: *She greeted us in a friendly fashion.*
3 If something is **in fashion**, it is popular at a particular time. If it is **out of fashion**, it is not popular.
[**Fashion** comes via French from Latin *factio* 'making or doing'.]

**fashion** *verb* **fashions, fashioning, fashioned**
To **fashion** something means to make it, often from unusual materials or in an unusual way: *They fashioned a tent out of a sheet slung over a rope.*

**fashionable** *adjective* (th)
If something is **fashionable**, it is in fashion.

**fast**[1] *noun* **fasts**
A **fast** is a time when people do not eat anything, especially for religious reasons.
[**Fast**[1] comes from Old English *faesten*.]

**fast**[1] *verb* **fasts, fasting, fasted**
To **fast** is to give up eating food for a certain amount of time, especially for religious reasons.

**fast**[2] *adjective* **faster, fastest** (th)
1 Something or someone that is **fast** moves or does something quickly: *a fast car; a fast worker.*
2 If a clock or a watch is **fast**, it is ahead of the right time: *It can't be 12 o'clock already – my watch must be fast.*
[**Fast**[2] comes from Old English *faest*.]

**fast²** *adverb* **faster, fastest** (th)
1 quickly: *The car went faster and faster.*
2 firmly: *stuck fast in the mud.*

**fasten** *verb* **fastens, fastening, fastened** (th)
To **fasten** something is to join one part of it to the other part: *fasten your seat belt.*
[**Fasten** comes from Old English.]

**fat** *noun* **fats**
1 **Fat** is the substance under the skin of people and animals that helps keeps them warm: *Seals are covered in a thick layer of fat called blubber.*
2 **Fat** is an oily substance found in some foods and used in cooking: *Skimmed milk contains hardly any fat.*
[**Fat** comes from Old English.]

**fat** *adjective* **fatter, fattest** (th)
1 A **fat** person weighs too much: *If you eat too much, you get fat.*
2 Something that is **fat** is very thick: *a fat book.*

**fatal** *adjective* (th)
1 Something that is **fatal** causes someone to die: *a fatal illness; a fatal accident.*
2 Something that is **fatal** is disastrous: *Once she starts playing computer games it's fatal because she never gets any work done.*
**fatally** *adverb.*
[**Fatal** comes from the same Latin word as **fate**.]

**fate** *noun* **fates** (th)
1 **Fate** is a force that some people believe controls what happens to us: *Maybe I'll win or maybe I won't – it's all down to fate.*
2 Your **fate** is what happens to you: *The fate of the planet is uncertain; His was a terrible fate.*
[**Fate** comes from Latin *fatum* 'what has been spoken'.]

**father** *noun* **fathers**
Your **father** is your male parent.
[**Father** comes from Old English.]

**father-in-law** *noun* **fathers-in-law**
Your **father-in-law** is the father of your husband or wife.

**fathom** *noun* **fathoms**
A **fathom** is a unit of measurement of the depth of water. One **fathom** is 18 metres.
[**Fathom** comes from Old English.]

**fathom** *verb* **fathoms, fathoming, fathomed**
To **fathom** something **out** is to understand it after thinking carefully about it: *It took me ages to fathom out these instructions.*

**fatigue** *noun* (th)
**Fatigue** is great tiredness.
[**Fatigue** comes from Latin via French.]

**fault** *noun* **faults** (th)
1 If something is somebody's **fault**, that person is to blame for it: *It's your fault we're late!*
2 A **fault** is a weakness in someone's character.
3 If there is a **fault** in something, part of it does not work properly: *an electrical fault.*
4 A **fault** is a crack in the earth's surface that can cause an earthquake.
5 If you **find fault with** someone or something, you are always complaining and you only look for bad things.
[**Fault** comes via French from the same Latin word as **fail**.]

**fault** *verb* **faults, faulting, faulted**
To **fault** something is to find mistakes in it.

**faulty** *adjective* (th)
If something is **faulty**, it has a fault and does not work properly.

**fauna** *noun* **faunas**
The **fauna** of an area is all the animals that live there.
[**Fauna** comes from *Fauna*, the name of an ancient Roman goddess of the countryside.]

**favourite** *adjective* (th)
Your **favourite** thing or person is the one you like most: *My favourite food is strawberry ice cream; her favourite niece.*
[**Favourite** comes from Latin via French and Italian.]

**favourite** *noun* **favourites**
The **favourite** in a race is the person, team or animal that is expected to win.

**fawn** *noun* **fawns**
A **fawn** is a young deer.
[**Fawn** comes via French from the same Latin word as **foetus**.]

**fax** *noun* **faxes**
A **fax** is a letter or document that is sent from a fax machine or a computer to

another fax machine or computer over the telephone lines: *a three-page fax.*
[**Fax** is short for *facsimile* 'an exact copy', which comes from Latin.]

**fax** *verb* **faxes, faxing, faxed**
To **fax** is to send a letter or document from a fax machine or a computer to another fax machine or computer over the telephone lines: *fax the order through.*

**fear** *noun* **fears** (th)
**Fear** is a feeling of worry or fright: *Being in a plane crash is my worst fear.*
[**Fear** comes from Old English.]

**fear** *verb* **fears, fearing, feared** (th)
If you **fear** a thing or a person, you are frightened of them.

**feast** *noun* **feasts** (th)
A **feast** is a large meal for many people to celebrate something: *a wedding feast.*
[**Feast** comes from French.]

**feat** *noun* **feats** (th)
1 A **feat** is something that someone does which needs a lot of strength or skill: *Climbing Everest was a remarkable feat.*
2 If something is **no mean feat** it is not easy to do: *Getting top grades in all your exams was no mean feat!*
[**Feat** comes via French from the same Latin word as **fact**.]

**feather** *noun* **feathers**
A **feather** is one of the light soft things that cover a bird's body to keep it warm and help it to fly.
[**Feather** comes from Old English.]

**feces** *noun*
**Feces** is another way to spell **faeces**.

**feeble** *adjective* **feebler, feeblest** (th)
Someone or something that is **feeble** is weak: *He's old and feeble; What a feeble excuse!* [**Feeble** comes from Latin.]

**feed** *verb* **feeds, feeding, fed** (th)
1 To **feed** someone or something is to give them food: *Don't forget to feed the cat; feed and water the plants.*
2 To **feed** is to eat food: *The baby feeds every three hours.*
[**Feed** comes from Old English.]

**feel** *verb* **feels, feeling, felt** (th)
1 To **feel** something is to have a feeling, an emotion or an opinion: *I feel sick; I've never felt so happy.*

2 If you **feel** something, you touch it: *Feel how soft this is.*
3 If you **feel** something, you know that it is touching you: *I can feel a spider crawling up my leg.* [**Feel** comes from Old English.]

**feeling** *noun* **feelings** (th)
1 A **feeling** is something that your body is aware of: *a feeling of hunger.*
2 A **feeling** is an emotion: *a feeling of happiness.*
3 If you **have a feeling** about something, you think something about it although you do not know for sure: *I've got a feeling John's coming today.*
4 If you **hurt** someone's **feelings**, you upset him/her.

**feet** *noun*
**Feet** is the plural of **foot**.

**feign** *verb* **feigns, feigning, feigned** (th)
To **feign** is to pretend that you feel something: *He feigned illness to get time off.*
[**Feign** comes from Latin via French.]

**feline** *adjective* **felines**
**Feline** means to do with cats or the cat family.
[**Feline** comes from Latin *feles* 'cat'.]

**fell** *verb*
**Fell** is the past tense of **fall**.

**felt** *verb*
**Felt** is the past tense and past participle of **feel**.

**female** *noun* **females**
A **female** is a woman or a girl, or a female animal or plant.
[**Female** comes via French from Latin *femelle* 'small woman'.]

**female** *adjective*
A **female** animal can have babies and a **female** plant or flower produces seeds and fruit.

**feminine** *adjective*
1 Something that is **feminine** is considered typical of women or suitable for women: *Looking after children is traditionally a feminine occupation.*
2 In some languages, a **feminine** word belongs to a class of words that includes the words to do with women: *In French, the word for table is feminine.*
[**Feminine** comes from Latin *femina* 'woman'.]

**fence** *noun* **fences**
A **fence** is a row of posts with wood or wire between them: *a garden fence; There's a high fence around the prison.*
[**Fence** is short for *defence* 'something that defends'.]

**ferment** *verb* **ferments, fermenting, fermented**
When fruit, beer or wine **ferments**, the sugar in it turns into alcohol.
[**Ferment** comes from Latin *fermentum* 'yeast', which makes things ferment.]

**ferocious** *adjective* (th)
A **ferocious** animal is fierce and dangerous.
[**Ferocious** comes from Latin *ferox* 'fierce'.]

**ferry** *noun* **ferries**
A **ferry** is a boat that carries people, lorries and cars across a stretch of water.
[**Ferry** comes from Old Norse.]

**fertilise** *verb* **fertilises, fertilising, fertilised** *Also* **fertilize**
**1** To **fertilise** land means to spread manure or chemicals on it so that plants will grow well on it.
**2** To **fertilise** an animal or plant means to put sperm into the egg of a female animal so that a young animal begins to grow, or to put pollen into a plant so that seeds form. [**Fertilise** comes from Latin.]

**fertiliser** *noun* *Also* **fertilizer**
**Fertiliser** is manure or chemicals used to fertilise the land.

**festival** *noun* **festivals** (th)
**1** A **festival** is an occasion when people can watch performances of films, plays or music: *the Cannes film festival.*
**2** A **festival** is a celebration, especially a religious celebration: *the festival of Diwali.*
[**Festival** comes via old French from Latin *festum* 'feast'.]

**fetch** *verb* **fetches, fetching, fetched** (th)
To **fetch** is to go to a place where someone or something is and bring that person or thing back: *I fetch the children from school at three o'clock.*
[**Fetch** comes from Old English.]

**fête** *noun* **fêtes**
A **fête** is an outdoor event where there are competitions and things to buy that is

organised to raise money for a good cause: *a school fête.*
[**Fête** is a French word meaning 'feast', from Latin *festum* (ancestor of **festival**).]

**fetus** *noun* **fetuses**
**Fetus** is another way to spell **foetus**.

**feud** *noun* **feuds** (th)
A **feud** is an angry quarrel between people that lasts for a long time.
[**Feud** comes from an old French word.]

**feudalism** *noun*
**Feudalism** was a system in the Middle Ages under which people received land and protection from a lord, in return for working and fighting for him.
[**Feudalism** comes from Latin.]

**fever** *noun* **fevers**
A **fever** is a high temperature that is caused by an illness.
[**Fever** comes from Latin.]

**few** *adjective, noun* (th)
A **few** is some but not many: *There are a few biscuits in the tin; Few people visit this part of Scotland.*
[**Few** comes from Old English.]

**fiancé** *noun* **fiancés**
A **fiancé** is a man who is engaged to be married.
[**Fiancé** is a French word meaning 'someone who has promised'.]

**fiancée** *noun* **fiancées**
A **fiancée** is a woman who is engaged to be married.
[**Fiancée** is the feminine of French *fiancé*.]

**fiasco** *noun* **fiascos** (th)
A **fiasco** is a complete failure or disaster: *The party was a fiasco – no one came.*
[**Fiasco** comes from Italian.]

**fibre** *noun* **fibres**
**1** A **fibre** is a very thin thread of cloth or a type of cloth: *wool fibres; Nylon is a synthetic fibre.*
**2** **Fibre** is the part of food that you cannot digest but which helps food move through your system. Fibre is sometimes called roughage: *Brown bread is rich in fibre.* [**Fibre** comes from Latin via French.]

**fiction** *noun* (th)
**Fiction** is made-up stories about people and events.

[**Fiction** comes via French from Latin *fictio* 'something made up'.]

**fiddle** *verb* **fiddles, fiddling, fiddled** (th)
**1** To **fiddle** means to keep touching something or moving something, especially when you are nervous or bored: *I always fiddle with my hair when I'm bored.*
**2** If you **fiddle about** or **fiddle around**, you do little things that are not important: *She's fiddling around with the television; Stop fiddling about and do some work!*
**3** To **fiddle** means to get money in a dishonest way: *fiddle the accounts; They fiddled me out of a fortune.*
[**Fiddle** comes from Old English.]

**fidget** *verb* **fidgets, fidgeting, fidgeted** (th)
To **fidget** is to keep making little movements in a way that shows you are bored or nervous.
[No one knows where **fidget** comes from.]

**field** *noun* **fields** (th)
**1** A **field** is a piece of land with a fence or hedge round it that is used for growing crops or playing sports: *a field of wheat; a football field.*
**2** A **field** is an area of interest, work or study: *He's an expert in the field of biology.*
**3** In a race, the **field** is all the competitors.
[**Field** comes from Old English.]

**fiend** *noun* **fiends** (th)
A **fiend** is a wicked or cruel person or an evil spirit.
[**Fiend** comes from Old English.]

**fierce** *adjective* **fiercer, fiercest** (th)
**1** A **fierce** animal is angry and ready to attack.
**2** A **fierce** person is not very friendly and quite frightening.
**3** Something that is **fierce** is energetic or violent: *fierce fighting; Fierce fires are blazing.* **fiercely** *adverb.*
[**Fierce** comes from Latin via French.]

**fig** *noun* **figs**
A **fig** is a small, soft fruit.
[**Fig** comes from Latin via French.]

**fight** *noun* **fights** (th)
**1** A **fight** is when people argue, or push and hit each other: *Those two are always getting into fights.*
**2** If someone has got a lot of **fight** in them, they are very determined to do something: *I'm not beaten yet – I've still got a lot of fight left in me.*
[**Fight** comes from Old English.]

**fight** *verb* **fights, fighting, fought** (th)
**1** When people **fight**, they push and hit each other, or shout and argue: *My parents are always fighting about something.*
**2** When countries **fight**, they go to war against each other: *Britain fought America in The War of Independence.*

**figure** *noun* **figures**
**1** A **figure** is a number that is written as 0, 1, 2, 3, 4, 5, 6, 7, 8, 9, not as a word.
**2** A **figure** is an amount of money: *a six-figure salary.*
**3** A **figure** is a painting or a model of a person: *a carved wooden figure.*
**4** Your **figure** is the shape of your body: *She has a lovely figure; a slim figure.*
**5** A **figure** is a person who is important in some way: *Nelson Mandela is an important figure in history.*
[**Figure** comes from Latin via French.]

**file¹** *noun* **files**
**1** A **file** is a box or folder for storing documents: *The letter is in the file marked 'letters'.*
**2** A computer **file** is a collection of data that is stored under a certain name.
[**File¹** comes from Latin *filium* 'string', which used to be threaded through papers to keep them in order.]

**file¹** *verb* **files, filing, filed**
**1** When you **file** a document, you store it so that it can easily be found: *File these forms in alphabetical order.*
**2** When people **file past** something, they walk past it slowly in a line: *Mourners filed past Mother Teresa's coffin.*

**file²** *noun* **files**
A **file** is a tool that is used for smoothing rough surfaces: *a nail file.*
[**File²** comes from Old English.]

**file²** *verb* **files, filing, filed**
When you **file** something rough, you smooth its surface with a special tool: *She's filing her nails.*

**fill** *verb* **fills, filling, filled**
To **fill** is to make something full or to become full: *Fill the bath with water; The*

*hall was filling with people.*
[**Fill** comes from Old English.]

**fillet** *noun* **fillets**
A **fillet** is a piece of meat or fish with no bones in it: *a fillet of cod.*
[**Fillet** comes from French.]

**film** *noun* **films**
**1** A **film** is the roll of plastic used in a camera to take photographs.
**2** A **film** is a series of moving pictures, usually with sound.
**3** A **film** is a very thin layer of something that covers the surface of something else: *There's a film of oil covering the puddle.*
[**Film** comes from Old English *filmen* 'thin skin'.]

**film** *verb* **films, filming, filmed**
To **film** something means to record it using a camera, or to make a movie: *The latest Bond movie is being filmed in Berlin.*

**filthy** *adjective* **filthier, filthiest** (th)
Something that is **filthy** is very dirty or rude: *Take those boots off before you come in – they're filthy!*
[**Filthy** comes from Old English.]

**fin** *noun* **fins**
A **fin** is a flap on the body of a fish that it moves to help it to swim: *a dorsal fin.*
[**Fin** comes from Old English.]

**final** *adjective* (th)
**1** Something that is **final** comes last or is at the end: *the final episode of the series.*
**2** You say **that's final** to show that you are not going to discuss what you have just said: *You'll do your homework or you won't go out – and that's final!*
[**Final** comes from the same Latin word as **finish**.]

**finally** *adverb* (th)
Something that happens **finally** happens after a long time or happens last in a series of events: *It took me ages, but finally I found the book I wanted.*

**find** *verb* **finds, finding, found** (th)
**1** To **find** something is to come across something that you have been searching for: *I found my keys in the fridge!*
**2** If you **find** something interesting or terrifying, for example, you have that opinion or feeling about it: *I find reading really relaxing.*

[**Find** comes from Old English.]

**fine** *noun* **fines**
A **fine** is money someone has to pay for doing something wrong: *a parking fine.*
[**Fine** comes from the same Latin word as **finish**.]

**fine** *verb* **fines, fining, fined**
When someone is **fined**, that person has to pay money as a punishment for doing something wrong.

**fine** *adjective* **finer, finest** (th)
**1** If you feel **fine**, you feel well and happy: *I'm fine thanks, and you?*
**2** **Fine** weather is dry and bright.
**3** **Fine** food, wine and clothes, for example, are high-quality and expensive.
**4** **Fine** materials are thin and delicate: *fine china; fine lace; a fine thread.*

**finger** *noun* **fingers**
Your **finger** is one of the four long movable parts at the end of your hand.
[**Finger** comes from Old English.]

**finger** *verb* **fingers, fingering, fingered**
To **finger** something is to touch it carefully.

**finish** *noun* **finish** (th)
**1** The **finish** of something is the end or last part of it: *the finish of the race.*
**2** The **finish** of a surface is the way it looks and feels: *The work surface comes in two finishes: wood or marble.*
[**Finish** comes from Latin *finis* 'end'.]

**finish** *verb* **finishes, finishing, finished** (th)
**1** To **finish** something is to complete it: *I've finished my homework.*
**2** To **finish** something is to come to the end of an activity or period of time: *I finish school when I'm 18.*
**3** To **finish** is to stop: *What time does the film finish?*

**finite** *adjective*
Something that is **finite** has an end or will not last for ever: *Oil supplies are finite.*
[**Finite** comes from Latin *finitus* 'finished'.]

**fire** *noun* **fires**
**1** **Fire** is the flames and heat that are produced when something burns: *Don't play with fire – it's dangerous!*
**2** A **fire** is when something is burning out

of control: *A fire in the kitchen destroyed the whole building.*

**3** A **fire** is something you light or turn on to keep you warm: *a coal fire; a gas fire.*

**4 Fire** is shots from enemy weapons: *The soldiers were under heavy fire.*
[**Fire** comes from Old English.]

**fire** *verb* **fires, firing, fired**
To **fire** means to shoot a bullet from a gun or other weapon: *Ready, aim, fire!*

**fireplace** *noun* **fireplaces**
A **fireplace** is the part of a room where the fire is.

**firework** *noun* **fireworks**
A **firework** is a tube full of powder that explodes with bright lights and loud noises when you set light to it: *a firework display.*

**firm** *noun* **firms**
A **firm** is a small company: *a family firm.*
[**Firm** comes from Latin.]

**firm** *adjective* **firmer, firmest** (th)
**1** Something that is **firm** is fixed into a position so that it cannot move: *This shelf feels firm.*
**2** Something that is **firm** is quite hard: *a firm mattress.*
**3** Someone who is **firm** behaves or speaks in a way that shows they are in control: *a firm teacher.*

**first person** *noun*
To find **first person**, look under **person**.

**fish** *noun* **fish** *or* **fishes**
A **fish** is a cold-blooded animal with scales that lives in water.
[**Fish** comes from Old English.]

**fish** *verb* **fishes, fishing, fished**
To **fish** is to try to catch fish: *The trawler fishes for cod.*

**fist** *noun* **fists**
You make a **fist** when you close your fingers into your palm: *He hit me with his fist.* [**Fist** comes from Old English.]

**fit¹** *noun* **fits**
**1** A **fit** is a sudden attack of something: *a fit of anger; fits of laughter; a coughing fit.*
**2** If someone has a **fit**, s/he loses consciousness and his/her body makes uncontrollable movements.
[**Fit¹** comes from Old English.]

**fit²** *verb* **fits, fitting, fitted** (th)
**1** Something that **fits** is the right size or shape for a thing or a person: *Does this chair fit here, or is it too big?*
**2** If you **fit** something, you put it in place and fix it there: *He fitted the carpet.*
[No one knows where **fit²** comes from.]

**fit²** *adjective* **fitter, fittest** (th)
**1** Someone who is **fit** is healthy: *Exercise keeps you fit.*
**2** Something that is suitable for a thing or person is **fit** for it: *This food is not fit for a dog!*

**fix** *verb* **fixes, fixing, fixed** (th)
**1** If you **fix** something, you mend it: *I'll need a screwdriver to fix this machine.*
**2** To **fix** something means to join it firmly onto something else: *fix shelves onto the walls.* [**Fix** comes from Latin.]

**flag** *noun* **flags** (th)
A **flag** is a piece of cloth with a coloured design on it that represents a country or an organisation: *The flag of the Red Cross is a red cross on a white background.*
[No one knows where **flag** comes from.]

**flame** *noun* **flames**
A **flame** is the fire that comes from something that is burning.
[**Flame** comes from Latin via French.]

**flamingo** *noun* **flamingos**
A **flamingo** is a large, long-legged bird with pink feathers.
[**Flamingo** comes from Spanish.]

**flannel** *noun* **flannels**
A **flannel** is a small piece of soft cloth that is used for washing the body: *a face flannel.* [**Flannel** comes from Welsh.]

**flap** *noun* **flaps**
A **flap** is a piece of material or paper that hangs from one edge of something to cover an opening: *seal down the flap on the envelope.*
[The word **flap** is an imitation of the sound of something flapping in the wind.]

**flap** *verb* **flaps, flapping, flapped** (th)
**1** When a bird **flaps** its wings, it moves them up and down when it is flying.
**2** When something **flaps** in the wind, for example, it moves around: *The washing on the line flapped in the breeze.*

**3** When someone **flaps**, they behave in a nervous or excited way: *Calm down and stop flapping!*

**flare** *noun* **flares**
A **flare** is something that produces a very bright light that acts as a signal.
[No one knows where **flare** comes from.]

**flash** *noun* **flashes**
A **flash** is a light that is very bright for a few moments: *a flash of lightning.*
[No one knows where **flash** comes from.]

**flash** *verb* **flashes, flashing, flashed** (th)
**1** If a light **flashes**, it becomes very bright for a few moments: *Lightning flashed across the sky; Did the camera flash?*
**2** Something that **flashes** moves very quickly: *An idea flashed through my mind.*

**flask** *noun* **flasks**
**1** A **flask** is a container for liquid.
**2** A **flask** is a vacuum flask: *a flask of coffee.*
[**Flask** comes from Latin via Old English.]

**flat** *adjective* (th)
Something that is level or smooth with no bumps is **flat**.
[**Flat** comes from Old Norse.]

**flat** *noun* **flats**
A **flat** is a home on one floor of a larger building.

**flavour** *noun* **flavours**
A **flavour** is the taste of a food: *There are two flavours – vanilla and strawberry.*
[**Flavour** comes from an old French word.]

**flavour** *verb* **flavours, flavouring, flavoured**
If you **flavour** food, you put something in it to give it a particular taste: *tea flavoured with lemon.*

**fleet** *noun* **fleets**
A **fleet** is a group of ships, aircraft or vehicles controlled by the same person or company. [**Fleet** comes from Old English.]

**flesh** *noun*
Flesh is the meat on the bones of a person or an animal: *horse flesh.*
[**Flesh** comes from Old English.]

**flew** *verb*
Flew is the past tense of **fly**.

**flexible** *adjective* (th)
**1** Something that is **flexible** is easy to bend or stretch.
**2** Something that is **flexible** can easily be changed or adapted.
**3** Someone who is **flexible** is willing to change or adapt.
[**Flexible** comes from Latin.]

**flight** *noun* **flights**
**1** A **flight** is a journey made through the air or into space: *the first flight to the moon.*
**2** A **flight** is a set of stairs: *My office is up four flights of stairs.*
**3** A **flight** is an escape from a dangerous situation.
[**Flight** comes from Old English.]

**flipper** *noun* **flippers**
**1** A **flipper** is a thick fin on the bodies of dolphins and seals that helps them swim and move around.
**2** A **flipper** is a flat rubber shoe worn by swimmers to help them move through water faster.
[**Flipper** comes from *flip* 'to move or move something with a quick, light movement', but no one knows where *flip* comes from.]

**float** *verb* **floats, floating, floated**
**1** To **float** is to rest on the surface of a liquid: *Oil floats on water.*
**2** Something that **floats** in air stays up in the air and moves slowly along: *petals floating on the breeze.*
[**Float** comes from Old English.]

**flock** *noun* **flocks**
A **flock** is a group of sheep, goats or birds. [**Flock** comes from Old English.]

**flock** *verb* **flocks, flocking, flocked**
If people **flock** to a place, crowds of them go there.

**flood** *noun* **floods**
A **flood** is a large amount of water that covers an area that is usually dry.
[**Flood** comes from Old English.]

**floor** *noun* **floors**
**1** A **floor** is the flat surface you walk on indoors: *She slipped on the wet floor.*
**2** A **floor** is a level of a building: *a third-floor room.* [**Floor** comes from Old English.]

**floppy disk** *noun* **floppy disks**
A **floppy disk** is a computer disk. You can take a **floppy disk** out of one computer

and put it into another to transfer the data on it.
[**Floppy** means 'soft and bendy' and comes from *flop* 'to move or hang loosely or clumsily' (which is a different spelling of **flap**), because a floppy disk is flexible compared to a **hard disk**.]

**flora** *noun*
The **flora** of an area is all the plants that grow there: *the flora of tropical rainforests.*
[**Flora** comes from *Flora*, the name of the ancient Roman goddess of flowers; her name comes from the same Latin word as **flower**.]

**floral** *adjective*
Something that is **floral** has a flowery pattern on it: *floral cushions.*
[**Floral** comes from the same Latin word as **flower**.]

**flounder** *verb* **flounders, floundering, floundered** (th)
1 To **flounder** is to struggle through water, mud or snow: *The soldiers floundered through the mud in the trenches.*
2 To **flounder** is to have a lot of problems with something: *He's floundering because the job is too difficult for him.*
3 If something **flounders**, it is unsuccessful and comes to an end: *The business floundered after just a few months.*
[No one knows where **flounder** comes from.]

**flour** *noun*
**Flour** is crushed grain, usually wheat, that is used for making bread and cakes.
[**Flour** is an old spelling of **flower**, which was used to mean 'the best part' of the grain.]

**flout** *verb* **flouts, flouting, flouted** (th)
If you **flout** the law or a rule, you deliberately disobey it: *Children who flout school rules will be punished.*
[**Flout** probably comes from Dutch *fluiten* 'to whistle or hiss at'.]

**flow** *verb* **flows, flowing, flowed** (th)
1 When liquid **flows**, it moves along smoothly: *Blood flows through your veins.*
2 If people or things **flow**, they move continuously from one place to another: *Refugees flowed across the border.*
[**Flow** comes from Old English.]

**flower** *noun* **flowers** (th)
1 A **flower** is the part of a plant that has white or coloured petals.
2 A **flower** is a plant that is grown for its flowers.
3 When a plant is **in flower**, it has flowers on it.
[**Flower** comes via French from Latin *floris.*]

**flower** *verb* **flowers, flowering, flowered**
When a plant **flowers**, its flowers appear and open: *Snowdrops flower in the spring.*

**flown** *verb*
**Flown** is the past participle of **fly**.

**flu** *noun*
**Flu** is an illness that gives you a high temperature, aches in your joints and a headache: *He's gone down with the flu.*
[**Flu** is short for **influenza**, which comes from Italian.]

**fluctuate** *verb* **fluctuates, fluctuating, fluctuated** (th)
If something **fluctuates**, it changes all the time: *The price of fruit fluctuates according to the time of year.*
[**Fluctuate** comes from Latin *fluctus* 'a wave'.]

**fluent** *adjective*
Someone who is **fluent** in a language speaks it very well: *She's Spanish but she speaks fluent English.* **fluently** *adjective.*
[**Fluent** comes from Latin *fluens* 'flowing'.]

**fluid** *noun* **fluids**
A **fluid** is something that flows, especially a liquid: *Drink plenty of fluids.*
[**Fluid** comes from Latin *fluere* 'to flow'.]

**fluke** *noun* **flukes**
A **fluke** is something lucky that happens by chance.
[No one knows where **fluke** comes from.]

**fluoride** *noun*
**Fluoride** is a chemical that is put in water and toothpaste to help prevent tooth decay. [**Fluoride** comes from Latin.]

**fly**[1] *noun* **flies**
A **fly** is an insect with wings: *a housefly.*
[**Fly**[1] comes from Old English *flycge.*]

**fly**[2] *verb* **flies, flying, flew, flown** (th)
1 To **fly** is to travel through the air: *fly*

*from Seattle to New York.*
**2** To **fly** is to move fast: *Time flies when you're having fun; She flew upstairs.*
[**Fly**[2] comes from Old English *fleogan*.]

**foal** *noun* **foals**
A **foal** is a young horse.
[**Foal** comes from Old English.]

**focus** *noun* **focuses** or **foci** (th)
**1** The **focus** is the point at which rays of light or heat meet.
**2** The **focus** of someone's interest or attention is the centre of it.
**3** If something is **in focus**, it appears clear and sharp. If it is **out of focus**, it appears blurred.
[**Focus** comes from Latin *focus* 'fireplace', the part of the house where everyone met.]

**focus** *verb* **focuses, focusing, focused**
**1** If you **focus** your eyes or an instrument such as a telescope or a camera, you adjust them or it so that what you are looking at appears clear and sharp.
**2** If you **focus** on something, you give it most of your attention.
**3** If you **focus** a beam of light, you make it narrower and point it towards something.

**foetus** *noun* **foetuses** *Also* **fetus**
A **foetus** is an animal or a human that is developing inside its mother and will soon be ready to be born.
[**Foetus** comes from Latin *fetus* 'pregnancy, offspring'.]

**fog** *noun* **fogs**
**Fog** is a thick mist that it is difficult to see through: *Fog on the road causes accidents.*
[No one knows where the word **fog** comes from.]

**foil**[1] *noun*
**Foil** is a very thin sheet of metal, especially aluminium, that is used for wrapping food: *kitchen foil; Foil-wrapped tea stays fresher.*
[**Foil**[1] comes from Latin *folium* 'leaf'.]

**foil**[2] *noun* **foils**
A **foil** is the sword used in fencing.
[No one knows where **foil**[2] comes from.]

**foil**[3] *verb* **foils, foiling, foiled**
To **foil** a plan is to stop it being carried out: *Police foiled the bank robbers' plans.*
[**Foil**[3] probably comes from old French *fouler* 'to trample'.]

**fold** *noun* **folds**
A **fold** is a line in something made by bending it back over itself: *A birthday card has a fold down the middle.*
[**Fold** comes from Old English.]

**fold** *verb* **folds, folding, folded** (th)
**1** To **fold** something is to bend it back over itself: *fold the paper in half.*
**2** If a business **folds**, it closes because of problems: *The restaurant folded because it had too many debts.*

**folk** *noun* **folks**
**1** **Folk** or **folks** are a group of people: *A lot of old folk live around here; Hello, folks, welcome to the show!*
**2** Your **folks** are your parents: *His folks come from New York.*
[**Folk** comes from Old English.]

**folk** *adjective*
**Folk** stories and music, for example, are traditional stories and music of ordinary people from a certain place: *traditional Russian folk music.*

**folklore** *noun*
**Folklore** is the traditional stories, customs and beliefs of ordinary people from a certain place.
[**Folklore** comes from **folk** and *lore* 'traditional beliefs', which comes from Old English.]

**follow** *verb* **follows, following, followed** (th)
**1** To **follow** something or someone is to go behind them: *Is that car following us?*
**2** If something **follows** something else, it comes after it: *Ice cream followed the turkey.*
**3** If you **follow** someone's orders or advice, for example, you do what s/he told you to do: *Soldiers must follow orders.*
**4** If you **follow** something, you understand it: *I couldn't follow what she was saying.* [**Follow** comes from Old English.]

**folly** *noun* **follies** (th)
**1** **Folly** is silliness or a silly act.
**2** A **folly** is a building, such as a tower, that was built just for decoration and was not meant to be used.
[**Folly** comes from French *folie* 'madness'.]

**font**[1] *noun* **fonts**
A **font** is a large bowl in a church. It holds the water for baptisms.
[**Font**[1] comes from the same Latin word as

fountain.]

**font² noun font**
A **font** is a style of printed letters.
[**Font²** comes from French.]

**food noun**
**Food** is something that people and animals eat in order to live and grow: *Fish and chips is my favourite food; a can of dog food.* [**Food** comes from Old English.]

**fool noun fools**
A **fool** is someone who is very silly.
[**Fool** comes from Latin via French.]

**fool verb fools, fooling, fooled** (th)
To **fool** someone is to trick that person, especially as a joke.

**foolish adjective** (th)
Someone or something that is **foolish** is very silly: *It was foolish to go for a walk in the rain.* **foolishly** *adverb.* **foolishness** *noun.*

**foot noun feet**
1 Your **foot** is the part of your body at the end of your leg.
2 A **foot** is a measurement in the imperial system of length equal to about 30 centimetres.
[**Foot** comes from Old English.]

**football noun footballs**
1 **Football** is an outdoor game played by two teams who try to get a ball into the goal without using their hands.
2 A **football** is the ball used in the game of football.

**footprint noun footprints**
A **footprint** is the mark left by a foot or shoe on the ground: *footprints in the mud.*

**footstep noun footsteps**
A **footstep** is the sound of someone walking: *She heard footsteps in the hall.*

**for preposition**
1 You use **for** to say what the purpose of something is: *a box for the rubbish; What's this box for?*
2 You use **for** to say who is to have or use something: *a present for my sister; a school for blind children; Can you hold this for me?*
3 You use **for** when you are talking about distance or time: *We walked for five kilometres; We've been waiting for hours.*
4 You use **for** to say how much something costs or what you might get in exchange:

*He swapped his bike for a guitar.*
5 You use **for** to say why something happened or why something was done: *She was fined for speeding; I got a CD player for my birthday.*
6 You use **for** when you are talking about people or things that are similar and could be confused: *I mistook him for his brother; Do you take me for a fool?*
[**For** comes from Old English.]

**for conjunction**
because: *She lay down, for she was very tired.* **For** is mainly used in stories.

**forage verb forages, foraging, foraged**
To **forage** for something, especially food, is to search for it.
[**Forage** comes from an old French word.]

**foray noun forays**
1 A **foray** is an attempt at doing something new, especially a job: *her foray into politics.*
2 A **foray** is a sudden attack by a group of soldiers: *a foray behind enemy lines.*
[**Foray** comes from the same old French word as **forage**.]

**forbid verb forbids, forbidding, forbade, forbidden** (th)
To **forbid** something is to say that it must not happen: *I forbid you to see him again!*
[**Forbid** comes from Old English.]

**forbidden adjective**
If something is **forbidden**, it is not allowed: *Smoking in school is forbidden.*

**forbidding adjective** (th)
A **forbidding** place or person is frightening or unfriendly: *Exam halls are forbidding places.*

**force noun forces** (th)
1 **Force** is physical strength that moves something: *apply force to the door to open it.*
2 A **force** is a group of people who are trained to do a certain job: *the police force.*
[**Force** comes from the same Latin word as **fort**.]

**force verb forces, forcing, forced** (th)
1 To **force** someone to do something is to make that person do something s/he doesn't want to do: *I forced him to get out of bed; Illness forced her to give up her job.*
2 To **force** something **open** or to **force** your way **through** something is to use a

a b c d e **f** g h i j k l m

lot of physical strength to do it. *The robbers forced the door open; The police forced their way through the rioters.*

**forecast** *noun* **forecasts** (th)

A **forecast** is when someone says what will probably happen in the future: *The weather forecast says snow at the weekend.*
[**Forecast** comes from *fore* 'in front, forward' (which comes from Old English) and **cast**.]

**forehead** *noun* **foreheads**

Your **forehead** is the top part of your face above your eyebrows and below your hair.
[**Forehead** comes from *fore* 'in front, forward' (which comes from Old English) and **head**.]

**foreign** *adjective* (th)

Something or someone that is **foreign** comes from another country: *Many foreign tourists come to Greece every year.*
[**Foreign** comes via French from Latin *foras* 'outside'.]

**foreigner** *noun* **foreigners** (th)

A **foreigner** is a person from another country.

**forest** *noun* **forests**

A **forest** is a large piece of land covered with trees.
[**Forest** comes from an old French word.]

**forever** *adverb* (th)

If someone is **forever** doing something, s/he keeps doing the same thing in a way that annoys you: *He's forever asking stupid questions.*

**forgave** *verb*

**Forgave** is the past tense of **forgive**.

**forge** *verb* **forges, forging, forged** (th)

To **forge** something is to make an illegal copy of it and use it as if it were the real thing: *She forged his signature on the cheque.*
[**Forge** comes from an old French word.]

**forgery** *noun* **forgeries**

A **forgery** is an illegal copy of something that is used as if it were the real thing: *The painting was a forgery.*

**forget** *verb* **forgets, forgetting, forgot, forgotten**

When you **forget** something, you don't remember it: *I forgot her birthday.*

[**Forget** comes from Old English.]

**forgetful** *adjective* (th)

If you are **forgetful**, you are always forgetting things. **forgetfulness** *noun*.

**forgive** *verb* **forgives, forgiving, forgave, forgiven** (th)

When you **forgive** someone, you stop being angry or annoyed with that person for doing something wrong: *Will you forgive me for shouting at you?*
[**Forgive** comes from Old English.]

**fork** *noun* **forks**

**1** A **fork** is an implement with prongs that you use with a knife for eating your food.
**2** A **fork** is a tool with prongs that you use in the garden for digging.
[**Fork** comes from Latin via Old English.]

**fork** *verb* **forks, forking, forked**

If a river or a road **forks**, it branches off into two or more different directions: *Where the road forks, keep to the left.*

**forlorn** *adjective* (th)

Someone who is **forlorn** feels sad and lonely: *She felt forlorn and homesick when she travelled to India.*
[**Forlorn** comes from Old English *forloren* 'lost'.]

**form** *noun* **forms** (th)

**1** A **form** of something is a kind of it: *Bikes are a form of transport.*
**2** The **form** of something is its shape or design: *a birthday cake in the form of a train.*
**3** A **form** is an official piece of paper that you have to write information on: *Fill in the form, starting with your name.*
[**Form** comes via French from Latin *forma* 'a mould'.]

**form** *verb* **forms, forming, formed** (th)

To **form** something is to make it: *How do you form the plural of bus? How are emeralds formed?*

**formal** *adjective*

**1 Formal** language or behaviour is very correct and serious, not relaxed or friendly: *a formal dinner; her tone was stiff and formal.*
**2** A **formal** statement or announcement is an official one. **formally** *adverb*.
[**Formal** comes from Latin *formalis* 'having a traditional shape or form'.]

**format** *noun* **format** (th)
1 The **format** of something is the way it is arranged and presented: *The format of the show is music mixed with interviews.*
2 The **format** of data on a computer disk is the way it has been stored on the disk, which means that the disk can only be used with compatible equipment.
[**Format** comes from Latin *formatus* 'formed or shaped'.]

**format** *verb* **formats, formatting, formatted**
When a computer **formats** a disk, it organises the space on that disk so data can be stored on it.

**formation** *noun* **formations**
1 The **formation** of something is the process by which it is made: *The formation of carbon into diamonds takes millions of years.*
2 The **formation** of something is the way it is arranged in a shape or pattern: *Planes at the airshow flew in formation.*
[**Formation** comes from Latin *formare* 'to mould or form'.]

**former** *adjective*
1 **Former** means what something or someone used to be: *Ronald Reagan is a former president of the United States; the former Soviet Union.*
2 If you talk about two things, the **former** is the first one you mention: *The second idea is all right, but I prefer the former one.*
[**Former** comes from Old English.]

**fort** *noun* **forts**
A **fort** is a strong building used by soldiers to protect a place.
[**Fort** comes from Latin *fortis* 'strong' (ancestor of **force**).]

**fortnight** *noun* **fortnights**
A **fortnight** is a period of two weeks.
[**Fortnight** comes from Old English *feowertiene niht* 'fourteen nights'.]

**fortunately** *adverb* (th)
**Fortunately** means luckily: *Fortunately no one was hurt in the accident.*
[**Fortunately** comes from Latin *fortunatus* 'to do with Fortuna' (see under **fortune**).]

**fortune** *noun* **fortunes**
1 A **fortune** is a lot of money: *They won a fortune on the lottery.*
2 **Good fortune** is good luck.

[**Fortune** comes from *Fortuna*, the name of the Roman goddess of luck or chance.]

**forward** *adjective, adverb* Also **forwards**
1 towards a place or position in front of you: *The cars moved slowly forward.*
2 towards a time in the future: *Forget the past and look forward to the future.*
[**Forward** comes from Old English.]

**fossil** *noun* **fossils**
A **fossil** is a plant or an animal that died millions of years ago and has hardened into rock.
[**Fossil** comes from Latin *fossilis* 'something dug up'.]

**fought** *verb*
**Fought** is the past tense and past participle of **fight**.

**foul** *noun* **fouls**
A **foul** in sport is unfair play, or play that is not allowed by the rules.
[**Foul** comes from Old English.]

**foul** *adjective* **fouler, foulest** (th)
1 Something that is **foul** is horrible or disgusting: *I can't eat this food – it's foul; I can't stand his foul language.*
2 A **foul** temper is a very bad temper.

**foul** *verb* **fouls, fouling, fouled** (th)
To **foul** something means to make it dirty with waste matter: *Dogs must not foul the park.*

**found** *verb*
**Found** is the past tense and past participle of **find**.

**fountain** *noun* **fountains**
A **fountain** is an ornament or a statue in a pool that has water pumped through it.
[**Fountain** comes from Latin via French.]

**fowl** *noun* **fowls or fowl**
A **fowl** is a bird, such as a hen or a goose, that is kept for its eggs and meat.
[**Fowl** comes from Old English.]

**fox** *noun* **foxes**
A **fox** is a wild animal like a small dog, with a reddish coat and a bushy tail.
[**Fox** comes from Old English.]

**fraction** *noun* **fractions**
1 A **fraction** is part of a whole number: ¾ is a fraction.
2 A **fraction** is a very small amount: *Move a fraction to the left.*

[**Fraction** comes via French from Latin *fractio* 'breaking'.]

**fragile** *adjective* (th)
1 Something that is **fragile** is delicate and easy to break: *a fragile china plate.*
2 If you are feeling **fragile**, you feel weak because you have been ill: *I'm over the flu but I still feel a bit fragile.*
[**Fragile** comes from Latin.]

**fragment** *noun* **fragments** (th)
A **fragment** is a small piece of something that has broken off something or is part of something larger: *Police found fragments of material at the crime scene; I only heard a fragment of their conversation.*
[**Fragment** comes from Latin.]

**frame** *noun* **frames** (th)
1 A **frame** is the solid edge round a picture, door or window: *She's painting the window frames.*
2 A person's **frame** is the structure formed by the bones in his/her body: *A petite person has a small frame.*
[**Frame** comes from Old English.]

**free** *adjective* **freer, freest** (th)
1 Something that is **free** does not cost anything: *Buy two and get the third one free.*
2 A person or an animal that is **free** can do what they like: *Now I don't have to work I'm free to travel the world; a free press.*
**freely** *adverb.*
[**Free** comes from Old English.]

**free** *verb* **frees, freeing, freed** (th)
To **free** someone is to let them leave prison: *Nelson Mandela was freed after nearly 30 years in prison.*

**freedom** *noun* (th)
**Freedom** is the right to do or say whatever you want.

**freeze** *verb* **freezes, freezing, froze, frozen**
1 If a liquid **freezes**, it turns solid because it has become very cold: *Clean water freezes at 0°C.*
2 To **freeze** something means to cool it until the liquid in it becomes solid: *Freeze water to make ice-cubes.*
3 If you **freeze**, you are unable to move because you are frightened: *She froze when she heard a strange noise in the kitchen.*
[**Freeze** comes from Old English.]

**freezer** *noun* **freezers**
A **freezer** is a piece of kitchen equipment like a chest or cupboard that keeps food frozen.

**freezing point** *noun*
The **freezing point** of a liquid is the temperature at which it will turn solid.

**frequently** *adverb* (th)
If something happens **frequently**, it happens very often: *It rains frequently in winter.* **frequent** *adjective.*
[**Frequently** comes from Latin.]

**fresh** *adjective* **fresher, freshest** (th)
1 Something that is **fresh** is new: *Journalists have no fresh information on the story.*
2 Food that is **fresh** is not stale, canned or frozen: *There's fresh tea in the pot; Fresh fruit is good for you.*
3 Something that is **fresh** is cool and clean: *There are fresh sheets on your bed; a fresh breeze.*
[**Fresh** comes from Old English.]

**friction** *noun*
1 When there is **friction** between two people they disagree a lot and are angry or unfriendly towards each other: *There was a lot of friction between my parents before they divorced.*
2 In science, **friction** is the force that slows objects down and produces heat when they rub against each other.
[**Friction** comes from Latin *frictio* 'rubbing'.]

**fridge** *noun* **fridges**
A **fridge** is a piece of kitchen equipment like a cupboard that keeps food cool.
[**Fridge** is short for **refrigerator**.]

**friend** *noun* **friends** (th)
1 A **friend** is someone who is not related to you who you like and enjoy spending time with: *I love going out with my friends.*
2 A **friend** is someone who cares for you and will help you: *Mum's been a real friend to me.* [**Friend** comes from Old English.]

**friendly** *adjective* **friendlier, friendliest**
1 Someone who likes other people and is kind and helpful is **friendly**.
2 Something that is **environment-friendly** or **environmentally friendly** is not harmful to the environment.
3 Something that is **user-friendly** is

designed to be easy to use.

**fright** *noun* (th)
A **fright** is a sudden feeling of fear: *You gave me such a fright when you fainted.*
[**Fright** comes from Old English.]

**frighten** *verb* **frightens, frightening, frightened** (th)
To **frighten** someone is to make them feel afraid: *Horror films frighten me; Are you frightened of spiders?*
[**Frighten** comes from **fright**.]

**frog** *noun* **frogs**
A **frog** is a small amphibian that develops from a tadpole and moves by jumping.
[**Frog** comes from Old English.]

**frogman** *noun* **frogmen**
A **frogman** swims underwater using diving equipment in order to investigate something: *Police frogmen searched the lake for the missing woman.*

**frolic** *verb* **frolics, frolicking, frolicked** (th)
To **frolic** is to play or jump around happily: *Kids frolicked in the water.*
[**Frolic** comes from Dutch *vrolijk* 'joyfully'.]

**front** *noun*
1 The **front** of something is the part that faces forward: *The driver sits at the front of the bus.*
2 A **front** in a war is a line where armies fight: *Troops were sent to the front.*
3 A weather **front** is the line on a weather map where cold air and warm air meet: *The cold front will bring snow.*
[**Front** comes from Latin via French.]

**frost** *noun* **frosts**
**Frost** is a white icy powder that covers things in freezing weather: *a hard frost.*
[**Frost** comes from Old English.]

**frown** *noun* **frowns**
A **frown** is an expression on your face that shows you are angry, unhappy or confused.
[**Frown** comes from an old French word.]

**froze** *verb*
**Froze** is the past tense of **freeze**.

**frozen** *verb*
**Frozen** is the past participle of **freeze**.

**frozen** *adjective*
1 Something that is **frozen** has been

cooled to 0°C or below: *frozen food.*
2 Something or someone that is **frozen** feels very cold: *Turn the heating up – I'm frozen.*

**fruit** *noun* **fruits**
The **fruit** of a plant or tree contains its seeds and is often eaten: *Strawberries are my favourite fruit.*
[**Fruit** comes via French from Latin *frui* 'to enjoy'.]

**fry** *verb* **fries, frying, fried**
When you **fry** food, you cook it in hot fat or oil.
[**Fry** comes from Latin via French.]

**fuel** *noun* **fuels**
**Fuel** is something such as oil or gas that is burned to provide energy for heat and light.
[**Fuel** comes via French from the same Latin word as **focus**.]

**full** *adjective* **fuller, fullest** (th)
1 Something that is **full** has no extra space inside it: *The car park is full.*
2 A **full** report or explanation contains every important detail: *We'll have a full report on the football match later in the programme.*
[**Full** comes from Old English.]

**full stop** *noun* **full stops**
A **full stop** is a punctuation mark, like this .. It is used in some abbreviations and to show a sentence has come to an end.

**fun** *noun, adjective*
1 Something that is **fun** is something interesting or amusing that you really enjoy: *ice skating is a lot of fun.*
2 If you **have fun**, you enjoy yourself by doing something interesting or amusing.
[No one knows where **fun** comes from.]

**fungus** *noun* **fungi** *Also* **funguses**
A **fungus** is a plant, such as a mould or mushroom, that has no leaves, flowers or roots, and grows quickly in shady, damp places. [**Fungus** comes from Latin.]

**funny** *adjective* **funnier, funniest** (th)
1 Something that is **funny** amuses you or makes you laugh: *Do you know any funny jokes?*
2 Something that is **funny** is odd or strange: *What's that funny smell?*
[**Funny** comes from **fun**.]

a b c d e **f** g h i j k l m

**fur** *noun* **furs**
Fur is the soft hair that covers the skin of some animals.
[**Fur** comes from an old French word.]

**furious** *adjective*
1 If you are **furious**, you are very angry indeed.
2 Something that is **furious** is wild or violent: *a furious hammering on the door.*
**furiously** *adverb.*
[**Furious** comes from the same Latin word as **fury**.]

**furnish** *verb* **furnishes, furnishing, furnished**
If you **furnish** a home, you put in the things such as furniture and kitchen equipment that you need to live in it comfortably.
[**Furnish** comes from an old French word.]

**furniture** *noun*
The **furniture** in a home is all the things such as beds, tables and chairs that you need to live comfortably.
[**Furniture** comes from the same old French word as **furnish**.]

**further** *adjective*
**Further** means more or extra: *Do you need any further help?*
[**Further** comes from Old English.]

**further** *adverb* (th)
1 **Further** means at a greater distance: *We live further from the sea than we used to.*
2 If something is **further on**, it is further in the direction in which you are going: *There's a shop a bit further on; The chapter you want is further on in the book.*

**fury** *noun* (th)
**Fury** is violent anger.
**furious** *adjective.* **furiously** *adverb.*
[**Fury** comes from Latin via French.]

**future** *noun*
1 The **future** is the time still to come: *Will people live on the moon in the future?*
2 **In future** means from now on: *In future, all homework must be handed in the next day.*

---

# Dictionary Fun

## Complete the proverbs
1. F_____ is a good servant but a bad master.
2. A f_____ and his money are soon parted.
3. A f_____ in need is a friend indeed.

## What do these idioms mean?
1. To face the music
2. To have a feather in your cap
3. To sit on the fence

## Etymology
1. Which word comes from Latin *fascinum* 'a magic spell'?
2. Which word comes from Latin *fallere* 'to deceive'?

## Work it out
1. Which '**f**' word was Aesop famous for writing?
2. Which '**f**' word featured in the stories of 'Cinderella', 'Sleeping Beauty' and 'Peter Pan'?

## Think about it
What is the difference between 'fish-eating cats' and 'fish eating cats'?

## Did you know?
◆ **Fireworks** were invented in China in about the 6th century but they weren't generally used for displays until the 17th century.
◆ Children in some parts of the world are still forced to work in **factories.**

# Gg

**gable** *noun* **gables**
A **gable** is a triangular part of a wall between the two slopes of a roof.
[**Gable** comes from Old Norse.]

**gadget** *noun* **gadgets**
A **gadget** is a small useful tool, especially a modern one.
[No one knows where **gadget** comes from.]

**gaggle** *noun* **gaggles**
A **gaggle** is a large group of geese.
[The word **gaggle** is an imitation of the sound of a group of geese.]

**gain** *verb* **gains, gaining, gained** (th)
1 To **gain** something means to get something that you did not have before.
2 If you **gain on** someone you are chasing, you gradually catch that person up.
[**Gain** comes from an old French word.]

**gait** *noun* **gaits**
Your **gait** is the way you walk or run.
[**Gait** comes from Old Norse.]

**gala** *noun* **galas**
A **gala** is special event for a lot of people to enjoy sport or entertainment: *a swimming gala.*
[**Gala** comes via Italian and Spanish from old French *gale* 'rejoicing'.]

**galaxy** *noun* **galaxies**
A **galaxy** is a very large group of stars.
[**Galaxy** comes from Greek.]

**gale** *noun* **gales** (th)
A **gale** is a very strong wind.
[No one knows where **gale** comes from.]

**galleon** *noun* **galleons**
A **galleon** was a Spanish sailing ship. **Galleons** were used from the 15th to the early 18th centuries.
[**Galleon** comes via Spanish or French from the same Latin word as **galley**.]

**gallery** *noun* **galleries**
1 A **gallery** is a room or building for showing paintings and sculptures.
2 A **gallery** is a raised balcony with seats in a building such as a church or theatre.
[**Gallery** comes from Italian.]

**galley** *noun* **galleys**
1 A **galley** is the kitchen on a ship.
2 A **galley** was a flat sailing boat rowed by many people, usually slaves or criminals, in the past.
[**Galley** comes from Greek via French and Latin.]

**gallon** *noun* **gallons**
A **gallon** is a unit of measurement in the imperial system for liquids, equal to 4.546 litres.
[**Gallon** comes via old French from Latin *galleta* 'bucket'.]

**gallop** *verb* **gallops, galloping, galloped**
When a horse **gallops**, it runs very quickly.
[**Gallop** comes from an old French word.]

**gallows** *noun*
A **gallows** is a wooden frame that was used in the past for hanging criminals.
[**Gallows** comes from Old English.]

**gamble** *verb* **gambles, gambling, gambled**
To **gamble** means to bet money on the result of a race or game. If you guess the winner, you win more money than you bet. [**Gamble** comes from Old English.]

**gambol** *verb* **gambols, gambolling, gambolled** (th)
To **gambol** means to jump about playfully.
[**Gambol** comes via French from Italian *gambata* 'to trip up'.]

**game** *noun* **games** (th)
1 A **game** is a sport or something that is played with rules: *a card game; a game of football.*
2 **Game** is wild animals and birds that are hunted and caught for sport and food.
[**Game** comes from Old English.]

**gander** *noun* **ganders**
A **gander** is a male goose.
[**Gander** comes from Old English.]

**gang** *noun* **gangs**
A **gang** is a group of people, especially criminals, who go around and do things together. [**Gang** comes from Old Norse.]

**gangplank** *noun* **gangplanks**
A **gangplank** is a movable bridge that is used to get on and off a ship.

a b c d e f **g** h i j k l m

[**Gangplank** comes from Old Norse *gangr* 'going' and **plank**.]

**gangrene** *noun*
**Gangrene** is when flesh goes bad and dies in a part of the body because the blood supply has been cut off.
[**Gangrene** comes from Greek via French and Latin.]

**gangster** *noun* **gangsters**
A **gangster** is a criminal who is part of a gang.

**gangway** *noun* **gangways**
A **gangway** is a passage between rows of seats for people to walk down.
[**Gangway** comes from Old Norse *gangr* 'going' and **way**.]

**gaol** *noun* **gaols**
**Gaol** is another way of spelling **jail**.

**gap** *noun* **gaps** (th)
A **gap** is an empty space or some free time between two things: *The dog got out through a gap in the fence; She went back to work after a gap of five years.*
[**Gap** comes from Old Norse.]

**gape** *verb* **gapes, gaping, gaped** (th)
1 To **gape** means to open your mouth and stare in surprise.
2 To **gape** means to be wide open or hang open. [**Gape** comes from Old Norse.]

**garage** *noun* **garages**
1 A **garage** is a building where vehicles are kept.
2 A **garage** is a place where vehicles are repaired and fuel is sold.
[**Garage** comes from French *garage* 'shelter'.]

**garbage** *noun* (th)
**Garbage** is rubbish.
[**Garbage** comes from an old French word.]

**garden** *noun* **gardens**
A **garden** is a piece of land where flowers and plants are grown.
[**Garden** comes from an old French word.]

**gargle** *verb* **gargles, gargling, gargled**
To **gargle** means to move liquid up and down your throat without swallowing it.
[**Gargle** comes from old French *gargouille* 'throat', which came from Greek.]

**gargoyle** *noun* **gargoyles**
A **gargoyle** is an ugly stone head carved on an old building that was used as a water spout.
[**Gargoyle** comes from the same old French word as **gargle**.]

**garish** *adjective* (th)
If something is **garish**, it is too brightly coloured or decorated to be attractive.
[No one knows where **garish** comes from.]

**garland** *noun* **garlands**
A **garland** is a ring of flowers that is worn round the neck or hung as a decoration.
[**Garland** comes from an old French word.]

**garlic** *noun*
**Garlic** is a plant like a small white onion. It has a strong taste and is used in cooking.
[**Garlic** comes from Old English.]

**garment** *noun* **garments**
A **garment** is a piece of clothing.
[**Garment** comes from old French *garnement* 'equipment'.]

**garnish** *verb* **garnishes, garnishing, garnished**
To **garnish** means to decorate food with herbs or small pieces of other food such as tomatoes.
[**Garnish** comes from old French *garnir* 'to equip or dress'.]

**garret** *noun* **garrets**
A **garret** is an attic.
[**Garret** comes from old French *garite* 'watchtower'.]

**gas** *noun* **gases**
1 **Gas** is a substance like air that can change its shape and expand to fill the space it is in. Some **gases** have a strong smell.
2 **Gas** is a kind of gas that can be burned and used as a fuel.
[**Gas** is a made-up word suggested by Greek *khaos* 'chaos', because gas has no shape.]

**gas** *verb* **gases, gassing, gassed**
To **gas** someone means to poison them by making them breathe a dangerous gas.

**gash** *noun* **gashes**
A **gash** is a deep cut in the skin.

[**Gash** comes from an old French word which may come from Greek.]

**gasoline** *noun*
Gasoline is another name for petrol.
[**Gasoline** comes from **gas** and Latin *oleum* 'oil' (ancestor of **oil**).]

**gasp** *noun* **gasps**
A **gasp** is a sound you make when you breathe in suddenly because you are surprised or in pain.
[**Gasp** comes from Old Norse.]

**gastric** *adjective*
**Gastric** means to do with the stomach and the digestion of food.
[**Gastric** comes via Latin from Greek *gaster* 'stomach'.]

**gate** *noun* **gates**
A **gate** is a kind of door across an opening in a wall, fence or hedge.
[**Gate** comes from Old English.]

**gather** *verb* **gathers, gathering, gathered** (th)
To **gather** people or things means to collect or bring them together.
[**Gather** comes from Old English.]

**gaudy** *adjective* **gaudier, gaudiest** (th)
Something that is **gaudy** is very brightly coloured in an unpleasant way.
[**Gaudy** comes from Latin.]

**gauge** *noun* **gauges**
1 A **gauge** is an instrument that is used for measuring the amount of something.
2 The **gauge** of a railway line is the distance between the two rails.
[**Gauge** comes from an old French word.]

**gaunt** *adjective* (th)
A person who is **gaunt** is too thin so that s/he looks unhealthy.
[No one knows where **gaunt** comes from.]

**gauntlet** *noun* **gauntlets**
A **gauntlet** is a long thick glove worn to protect your hands and arms.
[**Gauntlet** comes from French *gant* 'glove'.]

**gauze** *noun*
**Gauze** is a thin material, often used to cover wounds.
[**Gauze** is named after *Gaza*, a town in Palestine where it was first made.]

**gave** *verb*
Gave is the past tense of **give**.

**gay** *adjective*
1 If you say that a person is **gay**, you mean that s/he is homosexual.
2 Gay is an old-fashioned word meaning bright, lively or cheerful.
[**Gay** comes from French.]

**gaze** *verb* **gazes, gazing, gazed** (th)
To **gaze** means to look in a steady way without fixing your eyes on any particular thing: *We gazed at the stars.*
[No one knows where **gaze** comes from.]

**gazelle** *noun* **gazelles**
A **gazelle** is an animal like a small antelope from Africa or Asia that can run very fast.
[**Gazelle** comes from Arabic via French.]

**gazetteer** *noun* **gazetteers**
A **gazetteer** is an index of place names at the back of an atlas or map.
[**Gazetteer** originally meant a journalist, and the original list of places was published to help journalists.]

**gear** *noun* **gears**
1 A **gear** is a wheel with teeth that is used in a machine to change its movement or speed: *change down to third gear.*
2 Gear is equipment and clothing, especially for a sport: *camping gear.*
[**Gear** comes from Old Norse.]

**gelatine** *noun* Also **gelatin**
Gelatine is a clear substance made from animal bones that dissolves in water and is used to make jelly and other foods.
[**Gelatine** comes from Italian *gelata* 'jelly'.]

**gelignite** *noun*
Gelignite is an explosive substance similar to dynamite.
[**Gelignite** comes from *gel*, meaning a substance like jelly (short for **gelatine**), and Latin *lignis* 'wood', because gelignite contains wood pulp.]

**gem** *noun* **gems**
A **gem** is a precious stone such as a diamond or a ruby.
[**Gem** comes from Latin via Old English.]

**gender** *noun* **genders**
1 Your **gender** is whether you are male or female.
2 The **gender** of a noun in some

a b c d e f **g** h i j k l m

languages is whether it is a masculine, feminine or neuter word. There are rules about how to use words that have a particular **gender**.
[**Gender** comes from Latin *genus* 'a kind'.]

**gene** *noun* **genes**
A **gene** is the part of a cell of a living thing that contains information about the physical characteristics that are passed from parent to child. Your **genes** decide what you look like and what your body is like.
[**Gene** comes via German from Greek *genos* 'race, offspring'.]

**general** *adjective* (th)
**1** Something that is **general** relates to everyone or everything: *general knowledge.*
**2** Something that is **general** is connected with many different things, not one particular thing: *a general rule.*
[**General** comes from Latin.]

**general** *noun* **generals**
A **general** is a senior officer in the army.

**generation** *noun* **generations**
**1** A **generation** is the people in a society who are about the same age: *my parents' generation.*
**2** The **generation** of power such as electricity is the process of producing it.
[**Generation** comes from Latin *generare* 'to create' or 'to father'.]

**generator** *noun* **generators**
A **generator** is a machine that produces electricity.
[**Generator** comes from the same Latin word as **generation**.]

**generous** *adjective* (th)
**1** Someone who is **generous** is always willing to share what s/he has and to help others.
**2** Something that is **generous** is more than expected: *a generous donation; a generous helping.*
[**Generous** comes from Latin *generosus* 'noble'.]

**genetics** *noun*
**Genetics** is the study of genes and how they pass on physical characteristics from parents to children.
[**Genetics** comes from the same Greek word as **gene**.]

**genie** *noun* **genies**
A **genie** is a spirit who appears in some Middle Eastern stories.
[**Genie** comes via French from the same Latin word as **genius**.]

**genitals** *plural noun*
The **genitals** are the sexual organs on the outside of the body.
[**Genitals** comes from Latin via French.]

**genius** *noun* **geniuses**
Someone who is a **genius** has unusually high intelligence or extraordinary talent and ability.
[**Genius** comes from Latin *genius* 'spirit' or 'natural ability'.]

**genocide** *noun* **genocides**
**Genocide** is the murder of a whole race of people.
[**Genocide** comes from Greek *genos* 'race' and Latin *-cidium* 'killing'.]

**genre** *noun* **genres**
A **genre** is a kind of literature, art or music that has a particular style or subject. Detective stories, science fiction and romances are different **genres** of fiction writing.
[**Genre** comes via French from the same Latin word as **gender**.]

**gentle** *adjective* **gentler, gentlest** (th)
Someone who is **gentle** is kind and quiet. **gently** *adverb*.
[**Gentle** comes from Latin *gentilis* 'coming from a good family', which later meant 'polite'.]

**gentleman** *noun* **gentlemen**
A **gentleman** is a polite word for a man.

**genuine** *adjective* (th)
Something that is **genuine** is real and not fake or pretend. **genuinely** *adverb*.
[**Genuine** comes from Latin.]

**geography** *noun*
**Geography** is the study of the earth, its climate and how people live on it.
[**Geography** comes from Greek *geographia* 'writing about the earth'.]

**geology** *noun*
**Geology** is the study of rocks and the development of the earth's surface.
[**Geology** comes via Latin from Greek *ge* 'earth' and *logia* 'study'.]

**geometry** *noun*
Geometry is the part of mathematics that deals with shapes, lines and angles. [**Geometry** comes via Latin from Greek *geometrikos* 'to do with measuring the earth'.]

**gerbil** *noun* **gerbils**
A **gerbil** is a small brown animal with long back legs. **Gerbils** are sometimes kept as pets. [**Gerbil** comes from Latin.]

**germ** *noun* **germs**
A **germ** is a tiny living thing that sometimes makes people ill. [**Germ** comes from Latin *germen* 'seed or sprout'.]

**germinate** *verb* **germinates, germinating, germinated**
If a seed **germinates**, it starts to grow and put roots into the soil. [**Germinate** comes from the same Latin word as **germ**.]

**gesticulate** *verb* **gesticulates, gesticulating, gesticulated**
To **gesticulate** means to make movements with your hands while you are talking or in order to express something. [**Gesticulate** comes from Latin *gesticulari* 'to make gestures'.]

**gesture** *noun* **gestures**
1 A **gesture** is a movement that you make with your hand in order to express a feeling.
2 A **gesture** is something you do that shows a feeling: *a gesture of friendship.* [**Gesture** comes from Latin.]

**get** *verb* **gets, getting, got** (th)
1 To **get** means to be given, to buy, to win or to fetch something.
2 If you have **got** something, you have it or you own it: *Have you got a pencil?*
3 To **get** means to become: *I'm getting hungry.*
4 If you **get** to a place, you arrive there. [**Get** comes from Old English.]

**geyser** *noun* **geysers**
A **geyser** is a natural spring that throws out hot water and steam. [**Geyser** comes from *Geysir*, the name of a large geyser in Iceland.]

**ghastly** *adjective* **ghastlier, ghastliest** (th)
Something that is unpleasant and horrible is **ghastly**. [**Ghastly** comes from Old English.]

**ghee** *noun*
Ghee is butter or other fat that has been treated so that it can be made very hot without burning. **Ghee** is used in Indian cooking. [**Ghee** comes from Hindi (an Indian language).]

**gherkin** *noun* **gherkins**
A **gherkin** is a small pickled cucumber. [**Gherkin** comes from Dutch.]

**ghetto** *noun* **ghettos** *or* **ghettoes**
A **ghetto** is an area of a city where people of the same nationality or race live together, usually in poor conditions. [**Ghetto** probably comes from Italian; the first ghetto was in Venice.]

**ghost** *noun* **ghosts** (th)
Some people believe a **ghost** is the spirit of a dead person that can be seen. [**Ghost** comes from Old English.]

**ghoul** *noun* **ghouls**
A **ghoul** is an imaginary evil spirit. [**Ghoul** comes from Arabic.]

**giant** *noun* **giants**
A **giant** is a huge person from old stories such as fairy tales. [**Giant** comes from Greek via Latin and French.]

**gibbon** *noun* **gibbons**
A **gibbon** is a small South Asian ape with long arms. [**Gibbon** comes from French.]

**giblets** *plural noun*
Giblets are the parts, such as the heart and liver, that you remove from a chicken before cooking and eating it. [**Giblets** comes from an old French word.]

**gift** *noun* **gifts** (th)
1 A **gift** is a present.
2 If someone has a **gift** for doing something, s/he has a natural ability to do it well. [**Gift** comes from Old Norse.]

**gigabyte** *noun* **gigabytes**
A **gigabyte** is about 1,024 megabytes. **Gigabyte** is used to talk about how much memory a computer has. [**Gigabyte** comes from Greek *gigas* 'giant' and **byte**.]

a b c d e f **g** h i j k l m

**gigantic** adjective (th)
Something that is huge is **gigantic**.
[**Gigantic** comes via Latin from the same Greek word as **giant**.]

**giggle** verb **giggles**, **giggling**, **giggled**
To **giggle** means to laugh in a silly way, making high-pitched sounds.
[The word **giggle** is an imitation of the sound.]

**gill** noun **gills**
A **gill** is one of two organs on the side of a fish that it uses to breathe.
[**Gill** comes from Old Norse.]

**gilt** noun, adjective
**Gilt** is a thin layer of gold used to decorate or cover something.
[**Gilt** comes from Old English.]

**gin** noun
**Gin** is a strong, colourless alcoholic drink made from grain.
[**Gin** comes from *Geneva*, the name of a city in Switzerland.]

**ginger** noun, adjective
**Ginger** is the root of a tropical plant that is used as a spice.
[**Ginger** comes via Old English, Latin and Greek from Pali (a language of southern India).]

**gingham** noun
**Gingham** is a special cotton cloth with a checked or striped pattern.
[**Gingham** comes via Dutch from Malay (a language spoken in Malaysia).]

**gipsy** noun **gipsies**
**Gipsy** is another way of spelling **gypsy**.

**giraffe** noun **giraffes**
A **giraffe** is a large African animal with long legs and a very long neck.
[**Giraffe** comes from Arabic.]

**girder** noun **girders**
A **girder** is a strong iron or steel beam used in building.
[**Girder** comes from *gird* 'to prepare or strengthen', which comes from Old English.]

**girl** noun **girls**
A **girl** is a female child.
[No one knows where **girl** comes from.]

**gist** noun
The **gist** of a story or conversation is the main meaning of it.
[**Gist** comes from old French.]

**give** verb **gives**, **giving**, **gave**, **given** (th)
**1** To **give** means to let someone have something: *He gave money to charity; She gave her mother a hug.*
**2** If you **give in** or **give up**, you admit that you are defeated or that you cannot do something.
**3** If you **give** something **up**, you stop using it or doing it: *give up smoking.*
[**Give** comes from Old English.]

**glacier** noun **glaciers**
A **glacier** is a mass of ice that flows very slowly.
[**Glacier** comes from Latin *glacies* 'ice'.]

**glad** adjective **gladder**, **gladdest** (th)
Someone who is **glad** is pleased and happy. [**Glad** comes from Old English.]

**gladiator** noun **gladiators**
A **gladiator** was a fighter in Roman times. **Gladiators** fought each other or wild animals to entertain the public.
[**Gladiator** comes from Latin *gladius* 'sword'.]

**glamorous** adjective (th)
Something or someone that is **glamorous** seems very exciting and attractive.
[**Glamorous** comes from Greek via Latin.]

**glance** verb **glances**, **glancing**, **glanced**
To **glance** means to look at something for only a very short time.
[No one knows where **glance** comes from.]

**gland** noun **glands**
A **gland** is an organ in the body that produces natural chemical substances for the body to use or to get rid of.
[**Gland** comes from Latin via French.]

**glare** noun **glares**
**Glare** is bright light that gets in your eyes.
[**Glare** comes from an old German or Dutch word.]

**glare** verb **glares**, **glaring**, **glared** (th)
**1** If light **glares**, it shines very brightly and dazzles you.
**2** If you **glare** at someone, you look at him/her in a way that shows you are angry.

**glass** *noun* **glasses**
1 **Glass** is a hard clear substance used to make windows, mirrors and bowls.
2 A **glass** is a kind of cup without a handle, made of glass.
[**Glass** comes from Old English.]

**glasses** *plural noun*
**Glasses** are a pair of lenses in a frame that people wear to see better.

**glaze** *noun* **glazes**
A **glaze** is a thin layer of a liquid that makes something shiny when it is dry.
[**Glaze** comes from **glass**.]

**glaze** *verb* **glazes, glazing, glazed**
To **glaze** something means to cover it with a liquid that makes it shiny when it is dry.

**glazier** *noun* **glaziers**
A **glazier** is someone whose job is to fit glass into windows and doors.
[**Glazier** comes from **glaze**.]

**gleam** *verb* **gleams, gleaming, gleamed** (th)
If something **gleams**, it reflects light because it is clean and shiny.
[**Gleam** comes from Old English.]

**glean** *verb* **gleans, gleaning, gleaned**
1 To **glean** news or information means to collect it slowly, piece by piece.
2 To **glean** means to collect grain that is left in the field after the harvest.
[**Glean** comes via Latin from a Celtic language.]

**glen** *noun* **glens**
A **glen** is a valley among mountains, especially in Scotland and Ireland.
[**Glen** comes from Gaelic (an old language still sometimes spoken in Scotland).]

**glide** *verb* **glides, gliding, glided** (th)
To **glide** means to move smoothly.
[**Glide** comes from Old English.]

**glider** *noun* **gliders**
A **glider** is a kind of plane without an engine. [**Glider** comes from **glide**.]

**glimmer** *verb* **glimmers, glimmering, glimmered**
To **glimmer** means to shine with a faint unsteady light.
[**Glimmer** probably comes from a Scandinavian language.]

**glimpse** *verb* **glimpses, glimpsing, glimpsed**
To **glimpse** something means to see it for only a very short time.
[**Glimpse** probably comes from Old English.]

**glint** *verb* **glints, glinting, glinted**
To **glint** means to shine or flash with light for a moment.
[**Glint** probably comes from a Scandinavian language.]

**glisten** *verb* **glisten, glistening, glistened**
To **glisten** means to shine and sparkle.
[**Glisten** comes from Old English.]

**global** *adjective*
**Global** means to do with the whole world. **globally** *adverb*.
[**Global** comes from **globe**.]

**global warming** *noun*
**Global warming** is a gradual increase in the temperature of the earth caused by gases in the atmosphere that trap the sun's heat.

**globe** *noun* **globes**
1 A **globe** is a ball with the map of the earth on it.
2 The **globe** is the whole world.
[**Globe** comes from Latin.]

**gloom** *noun*
1 **Gloom** is when it is almost dark: *We could only just see them in the gloom.*
2 **Gloom** is a feeling of sadness and despair.
[No one knows where **gloom** comes from.]

**gloomy** *adjective* **gloomier, gloomiest**
1 A **gloomy** place is dark and unpleasant: *a gloomy prison.*
2 A **gloomy** day is cloudy and dark.
3 If a situation is **gloomy**, it makes you think that nothing good will happen: *a gloomy future.*
4 If you feel **gloomy**, you are sad and afraid that nothing good will happen.

**glorify** *verb* **glorifies, glorifying, glorified**
To **glorify** something means to praise it or make it seem good, especially giving more praise than the thing is worth: *The film glorifies war.*
[**Glorify** comes via French from the same

a b c d e f g h i j k l m

Latin word as **glory**.]

**glorious** *adjective*
Something that is **glorious** is very beautiful and impressive.
[**Glorious** comes from the same Latin word as **glory**.]

**glory** *noun* **glories** (th)
1 **Glory** is admiration and fame for doing something impressive: *the team's moment of glory*.
2 The **glory** of something is how beautiful and impressive it is.
[**Glory** comes from Latin via French.]

**gloss** *noun* **glosses**
1 **Gloss** is a bright shine on a surface.
2 **Gloss** paint is very shiny paint for wood and metal.
[No one knows where **gloss** comes from.]

**glossary** *noun* **glossaries**
A **glossary** is a list of words, with their meanings, that have been used in a book and that the writer thinks that the readers might not know.
[**Glossary** comes via Latin from Greek *glossa* 'tongue, language'.]

**glove** *noun* **gloves**
A **glove** is a covering for the hand and fingers. [**Glove** comes from Old English.]

**glow** *verb* **glows**, **glowing**, **glowed** (th)
If something **glows**, it gives out a steady light, especially because it is hot.
[**Glow** comes from Old English.]

**glow-worm** *noun* **glow-worms**
A **glow-worm** is a type of beetle with an organ in its body that gives out a green light in the dark.

**glucose** *noun*
**Glucose** is a type of sugar that gives you energy very quickly.
[**Glucose** comes from Greek via French.]

**glue** *noun*
**Glue** is a thick liquid that you use to stick things together.
[**Glue** comes from Latin via French.]

**gnarled** *adjective* (th)
Something that is **gnarled** is twisted and has bumps on it because it is old.
[**Gnarled** comes from an old German or Dutch word]

**gnat** *noun* **gnats**

A **gnat** is a small fly that bites.
[**Gnat** comes from Old English.]

**gnaw** *verb* **gnaws**, **gnawing**, **gnawed** (th)
To **gnaw** means to bite or chew something.
[**Gnaw** comes from Old English.]

**gnome** *noun* **gnomes**
A **gnome** is a little person from folk tales and fairy stories who guards treasure underground.
[**Gnome** comes from Latin via French.]

**gnu** *noun* **gnus**
A **gnu** is a large, dark grey African antelope. It is also called a wildebeest.
[**Gnu** comes from a southern African language.]

**go** *verb* **goes**, **going**, **went**, **gone** (th)
1 To **go** means to move from one place to another.
2 To **go** means to become: *My hair is going grey*.
3 If a vehicle or machine **goes**, it works properly.
4 To **go** means to belong: *Where do these go?; Does this blouse go with my skirt?*
[**Go** comes from Old English.]

**goal** *noun* **goals**
1 A **goal** is the two posts the ball must pass between to score a point in some games.
2 A **goal** is the point scored in some games.
3 Your **goal** is something that you aim to do or to achieve.
[No one knows where **goal** comes from.]

**goalkeeper** *noun* **goalkeepers**
A **goalkeeper** is the player in some games who guards the goal and tries to stop the other team from scoring.

**goat** *noun* **goats**
A **goat** is a farm animal with horns and a beard, kept for its milk and meat.
[**Goat** comes from Old English.]

**goblet** *noun* **goblets**
A **goblet** is a large glass or old-fashioned drinking cup with a long stem and a base but no handle.
[**Goblet** comes from French *gobelet* 'small cup'.]

**goblin** *noun* **goblins**
A **goblin** is a bad or cheeky fairy.
[**Goblin** comes from an old French word.]

**god** *noun* **gods** Also **God**
1 In the Christian, Jewish and Muslim religions **God** is the single creator and ruler of the universe.
2 In many religions a **god** is a male spirit or being that has power over a particular thing in nature.
[**God** comes from Old English.]

**goddess** *noun* **goddesses**
In many religions a **goddess** is a female spirit or being that has power over a particular thing in nature.

**godparent** *noun* **godparents**
In the Christian religion a **godparent** is a person who promises to help with a child's religious education.

**goggles** *plural noun*
**Goggles** are large glasses that you wear to protect your eyes.
[No one knows where **goggles** comes from.]

**gold** *noun*
1 **Gold** is a very valuable, yellow metal.
2 **Gold** is the bright yellow colour of gold.
[**Gold** comes from Old English.]

**gold** *adjective*
1 made of gold: *a gold necklace.*
2 of the colour of gold: *gold braid.*

**golden** *adjective*
1 of the colour of gold: *golden hair.*
2 made of gold: *a golden crown.*
**Golden** is mainly used in stories.

**golf** *noun*
**Golf** is a game in which you try to hit a ball into a series of holes. The winner is the person who uses the smallest number of strokes.
[**Golf** was originally a Scots word, which may be from Dutch.]

**gone** *verb*
**Gone** is the past participle of **go**.

**gong** *noun* **gongs**
A **gong** is a large metal disc that makes a deep ringing sound when it is hit with a soft hammer. It is used as a musical instrument or to announce that something is going to happen.
[**Gong** comes from Malay (a language spoken in Malaysia).]

**good** *adjective* **better, best** (th)
1 Something that you enjoy or think is done well is **good**.
2 Someone who is well behaved is **good**.
3 Someone who is kind is **good**.
[**Good** comes from Old English.]

**Good Friday** *noun*
**Good Friday** is the Friday before Easter that Christians remember as the day on which Jesus died.
[**Good** here means 'holy', an old sense of the word.]

**goods** *plural noun*
**Goods** are things that companies make to sell. [**Goods** comes from **good**.]

**goodwill** *noun*
**Goodwill** is when people have kind feelings towards each other.
[**Goodwill** comes from **good** and **will** in the sense 'a wish to do something'.]

**goose** *noun* **geese**
A **goose** is a large bird kept for its meat and eggs.
[**Goose** comes from Old English.]

**gooseberry** *noun* **gooseberries**
A **gooseberry** is a small green fruit that grows on a prickly bush. It is usually eaten cooked.
[**Gooseberry** comes from **goose** and **berry**, but no one knows why the fruit is named after the bird.]

**gorge** *noun* **gorges** (th)
A **gorge** is a narrow valley between very steep sides of rock, often with a river or stream running through it.
[**Gorge** comes from an old French word.]

**gorgeous** *adjective*
Something that is **gorgeous** is very good, very pleasant or very beautiful: *What a gorgeous day!; My girlfriend is gorgeous.*
[**Gorgeous** comes from an old French word.]

**gorilla** *noun* **gorillas**
A **gorilla** is a large ape that lives in the forests of central Africa.
[**Gorilla** comes via Latin from Greek *Gorillai*, the name of an African tribe who were said to be very hairy, which probably comes from an African word.]

**gosling** *noun* **goslings**
A **gosling** is a young or baby goose.

a b c d e f **g** h i j k l m

[**Gosling** comes from Old Norse.]

**gospel** *noun* **gospels**
 1 The **gospel** in the Christian religion is the teaching of Jesus.
 2 The **Gospels** are the four books of the Bible that describe Jesus' life and teaching.
 [**Gospel** comes from Old English *god spel* 'good news'.]

**got** *verb*
 **Got** is the past tense and past participle of **get**.

**govern** *verb* **governs, governing, governed** (th)
 1 To **govern** means to control a country by making laws and being in charge of its money.
 2 To **govern** something means to rule or control it.
 [**Govern** comes via French and Latin from Greek *kubernan* 'to steer'.]

**governess** *noun* **governesses**
 A **governess** is a woman who teaches children in their own home.
 [**Governess** comes from old French *governeresse* 'a female governor or ruler', which comes via Latin from the same Greek word as **govern**.]

**government** *noun* **governments**
 A **government** is the group of people who are in charge of a country or state.
 [**Government** comes from the same French word as **govern**.]

**governor** *noun* **governors**
 1 A **governor** is a person who is in charge of an institution: *a prison governor; the school governors.*
 2 A **governor** is the elected head of a state in the USA.
 [**Governor** comes via French and Latin from the same Greek word as **govern**.]

**gown** *noun* **gowns**
 1 A **gown** is a long dress worn especially in the past for formal occasions and parties: *a ball gown.*
 2 A **gown** is a long black robe worn on formal occasions by people such as judges and university teachers.
 [**Gown** comes from Latin via French.]

**grab** *verb* **grabs, grabbing, grabbed** (th)
 To **grab** means to take something in a forceful sudden way.
 [**Grab** comes from an old German or Dutch word.]

**grade** *noun* **grades**
 1 A **grade** is a mark given by a teacher for a piece of school work.
 2 The **grade** of something is the quality that it is judged to have.
 [**Grade** comes from Latin *gradus* 'a step' (ancestor of **degree**).]

**grade** *verb* **grades, grading, graded**
 To **grade** something means to give it a mark or judge its quality.

**gradient** *noun* **gradients**
 The **gradient** of a hill or slope is how steep it is.
 [**Gradient** comes from **grade**.]

**gradual** *adjective* (th)
 Something that happens slowly happens in a **gradual** way. **gradually** *adverb*.
 [**Gradual** comes from the same Latin word as **grade**.]

**graffiti** *noun*
 **Graffiti** is writing and drawing on a wall or in other public places.
 [**Graffiti** comes from Italian *graffio* 'a scratch'.]

**grain** *noun* **grains**
 1 **Grain** is the seed in a crop such as corn or wheat.
 2 A **grain** is a tiny hard piece of something such as sand or salt.
 3 The **grain** of wood is the natural pattern in it. [**Grain** comes from Latin.]

**gram** *noun* **grams**
 A **gram** is a small measure of weight. There are a thousand **grams** in a kilogram. [**Gram** comes from Latin.]

**grammar** *noun*
 **Grammar** is the system of rules for writing and speaking a language.
 [**Grammar** comes from Greek.]

**granary** *noun* **granaries**
 A **granary** is a building for storing grain.
 [**Granary** comes from the same Latin word as **grain**.]

**grand** *adjective* **grander, grandest** (th)
 Something that is **grand** is important or great. [**Grand** comes from Latin.]

**grandchild** *noun* **grandchildren**
Your **grandchild** is the child of your son or daughter.

**grandparent** *noun* **grandparents**
Your **grandparent** is the father or mother of one of your parents.

**granite** *noun*
Granite is a very hard type of rock used in building.
[**Granite** comes via Italian from the same Latin word as **grain**, because of the small specks you can see in the rock.]

**grant** *verb* **grants, granting, granted** (th)
To **grant** something means to allow it or give someone permission for it.
[**Grant** comes from an old French word.]

**grape** *noun* **grapes**
A **grape** is a small soft green or purple fruit that grows in bunches on vines.
[**Grape** comes from an old French word.]

**grapefruit** *noun* **grapefruits**
A **grapefruit** is a yellow fruit like a large orange.
[**Grapefruits** are so called because they grow in bunches like grapes.]

**graph** *noun* **graphs**
A **graph** is a chart or diagram showing changes in sets of numbers or measurements.
[**Graph** comes from Greek *graphe* 'writing or drawing'.]

**grass** *noun* **grasses**
Grass is a plant with narrow pointed leaves that grows in fields and lawns.
[**Grass**[1] comes from Old English.]

**grasshopper** *noun* **grasshoppers**
A **grasshopper** is an insect that makes a chirping sound and can jump a long way.

**grate**[1] *noun* **grates**
A **grate** is a frame of metal bars that holds the wood or coal in a fireplace.
[**Grate**[1] comes from Latin via French.]

**grate**[2] *verb* **grates, grating, grated**
1 To **grate** means to break cheese, carrots or other food into small thin pieces by rubbing it over a sharp metal tool.
2 If something **grates**, or **grates on** you, it makes you feel annoyed.
[**Grate**[2] comes from an old French word.]

**grateful** *adjective* (th)
Someone who is **grateful** is very thankful.
[**Grateful** comes from Latin *gratus* 'pleasing, thankful'.]

**gratitude** *noun*
Gratitude is when you feel thankful for something.
[**Gratitude** comes via French from the same Latin word as **grateful**.]

**grave**[1] *noun* **graves**
A **grave** is the place in the ground where a dead person is buried.
[**Grave**[1] comes from Old English.]

**grave**[2] *adjective* **graver, gravest** (th)
Something or someone that is **grave** is very serious. **gravely** *adverb*.
[**Grave**[2] comes via French from the same Latin word as **gravity**.]

**gravel** *noun*
Gravel is small loose pieces of stone used on paths.
[**Gravel** comes from an old French word.]

**gravity** *noun*
Gravity is the force that pulls everyone and everything towards the earth.
[**Gravity** comes from Latin *gravis* 'heavy' (ancestor of **grieve**).]

**gravy** *noun*
Gravy is a hot, brown sauce eaten with meat.
[**Gravy** probably comes from an old French word.]

**graze** *verb* **grazes, grazing, grazed**
1 To **graze** means to eat grass that is growing.
2 To **graze** means to scrape the skin on something hard or rough.
[**Graze** comes from the same Old English word as **grass**.]

**grease** *noun*
Grease is thick oil or soft, sticky fat.
[**Grease** comes via French from Latin *crassus* 'thick or fat'.]

**great** *adjective* **greater, greatest** (th)
1 Something that is **great** is very good.
2 Someone who is **great** is very important.
3 Something that is **great** is very large.
[**Great** comes from Old English.]

**greedy** *adjective* **greedier, greediest**
Someone who wants more food or money than s/he needs is **greedy**.
[**Greedy** comes from Old English.]

**green** *noun* **greens**
1 **Green** is the colour of grass and leaves, between yellow and blue.
2 A **green** is a flat area covered with short grass.
3 **Greens** are green vegetables, such as cabbage.
[**Green** comes from Old English.]

**green** *adjective* **greener, greenest**
1 of the colour green: *a green T-shirt.*
2 A fruit that is **green** is not ripe enough to eat.
3 If you feel **green**, you feel jealous: *He was green with envy when he saw my new bike.*
4 Someone who is **green** is interested in looking after the environment.

**greenhouse** *noun* **greenhouses**
A **greenhouse** is a small glass building in a garden for growing plants where they can be protected from bad weather.

**greenhouse effect** *noun*
The **greenhouse effect** is a problem caused by gases in the atmosphere which trap the sun's heat.

**greet** *verb* **greets, greeting, greeted**
To **greet** means to say or do something pleasant and friendly to welcome someone.
[**Greet** comes from Old English.]

**greeting** *noun* **greetings**
1 A **greeting** is something that you say or do to welcome someone.
2 **Greetings** are the friendly words you write as a message on something such as a postcard or a birthday card.

**gremlin** *noun* **gremlins**
A **gremlin** is a naughty imaginary creature that is blamed for a problem, especially a machine breaking down.
[No one knows where **gremlin** comes from.]

**grenade** *noun* **grenades**
A **grenade** is a small bomb that can be thrown by hand or fired from a weapon.
[**Grenade** comes from an old French word.]

**grew** *verb*
**Grew** is the past tense of **grow**.

**grey** *noun*
The colour that is between black and white is **grey**.
[**Grey** comes from Old English.]

**grey** *adjective* **greyer, greyest**
of the colour grey: *grey skies.*

**greyhound** *noun* **greyhounds**
A **greyhound** is a thin dog with short hair that can run very fast.
[**Greyhound** comes from Old English *grighound*, which may mean 'a female hound'.]

**grid** *noun* **grids**
1 A **grid** is a set of lines that form squares on a map. It helps you to find a particular place.
2 A **grid** is a system of wires that supply electricity to all parts of a town or country.
[**Grid** comes via French from the same Latin word as **grate**.]

**griddle** *noun* **griddles**
A **griddle** is a heavy flat pan for cooking food over a flame.
[**Griddle** comes from the same French word as **grid**.]

**grief** *noun* (th)
**Grief** is a very sad feeling.
[**Grief** comes from the same French word as **grieve**.]

**grieve** *verb* **grieves, grieving, grieved** (th)
To **grieve** means to feel very sad after someone has died.
[**Grieve** comes via French from Latin *gravis* 'heavy' (ancestor of **grave**[2] and **gravity**).]

**grill** *verb* **grills, grilling, grilled**
1 To **grill** food means to cook it under a strong source of heat.
2 To **grill** someone means to ask him/her a lot of questions.
[**Grill** comes from French.]

**grimace** *verb* **grimaces, grimacing, grimaced**
To **grimace** means to twist your face into an ugly expression because you do not like something or feel pain.
[**Grimace** comes from Spanish *grima* 'fright'.]

**grind** *verb* **grinds, grinding, ground** (th)
To **grind** something means to crush it into a powder.
[**Grind** comes from Old English.]

**grip** *verb* **grips, gripping, gripped** (th)
To **grip** something means to hold it very tightly. [**Grip** comes from Old English.]

**gristle** *noun*
**Gristle** is the tough tissue in meat.
[**Gristle** comes from Old English.]

**grizzly bear** *noun* **grizzly bears**
A **grizzly bear** is a large brown bear from North America.
[**Grizzly** comes from old French *grisel* 'grey', because the hairs of the bear's fur have grey tips.]

**grocer** *noun* **grocers**
A **grocer** is a person who has a shop selling food and other goods.
[**Grocer** comes from Latin *grossus* 'large', because the grocer buys large quantities of goods.]

**groin** *noun* **groins**
Your **groin** is the part of your body at the top of your legs, where they join the body.
[No one knows where **groin** comes from.]

**groom** *noun* **grooms**
1 A **groom** is a person whose job is to look after horses.
2 A **groom** is another word for a **bridegroom**.
[No one knows where **groom** comes from.]

**groove** *noun* **grooves**
A **groove** is a long channel cut into the surface of something.
[**Groove** comes from an old Dutch word.]

**grotto** *noun* **grottos** or **grottoes**
A **grotto** is a cave, especially one with interesting rocks in it.
[**Grotto** comes from Greek via Italian and Latin.]

**ground¹** *noun* **grounds** (th)
1 **Ground** is the earth or soil.
2 A **ground** is a piece of land used for a special purpose: *a sports ground.*
3 The **grounds** of a large building are the gardens or other land around it: *the grounds of the palace.*
[**Ground¹** comes from Old English.]

**ground²** *verb*
**Ground²** is the past tense and past participle of **grind**.

**group** *noun* **groups** (th)
A **group** is a number of people or things that belong together or do things together.
[**Group** comes from Italian via French.]

**grove** *noun* **groves**
A **grove** is a group of trees.
[**Grove** comes from Old English.]

**grow** *verb* **grows, growing, grew, grown** (th)
1 To **grow** means to get bigger or taller.
2 To **grow** something means to plant it in the ground and look after it.
[**Grow** comes from Old English.]

**growl** *verb* **growls, growling, growled**
To **growl** means to make a rough angry noise in the throat.
[The word **growl** is an imitation of the sound.]

**grown-up** *noun* **grown-ups** (th)
A **grown-up** is a fully grown person.

**grub** *noun* **grubs**
A **grub** is a tiny creature that will become an insect.
[No one knows where **grub** comes from.]

**grudge** *noun* **grudges**
If you **have**, **hold** or **bear a grudge** against someone, you dislike him/her because of something s/he has done to you in the past that you will not forgive.
[**Grudge** comes from old French *grouchier* 'to grumble'.]

**gruelling** *adjective* (th)
Something that is **gruelling** is very hard work and makes you tired.
[**Gruelling** comes from an old French word.]

**gruesome** *adjective* (th)
Something that is **gruesome** is horrible or shocking, especially because it is to do with death or injury.
[**Gruesome** comes from an old Scots word *grue* 'to shudder'.]

**grunt** *verb* **grunts, grunting, grunted**
To **grunt** means to make a sound like a pig. [**Grunt** comes from Old English.]

**guarantee** *noun* **guarantees**
A **guarantee** is a promise that if anything

a b c d e f **g** h i j k l m

goes wrong before a certain time with something you buy, the makers will give you a new one or repair it.
[**Guarantee** comes from Spanish.]

**guarantee** *verb* **guarantees, guaranteeing, guaranteed** (th)
To **guarantee** means to make a promise or give a guarantee: *The watch is guaranteed for one year.*

**guard** *verb* **guards, guarding, guarded** (th)
To **guard** means to keep someone or something safe or away from other people.
[**Guard** comes from an old French word.]

**guess** *verb* **guesses, guessing, guessed** (th)
To **guess** means to say what you think is right when you do not really know.
[**Guess** probably comes from an old German or Dutch word.]

**guest** *noun* **guests**
1 A **guest** is a person who you have invited to your house.
2 A **guest** is someone who is staying in a hotel. [**Guest** comes from Old Norse.]

**guide** *noun* **guides**
A **guide** is someone or something that shows people the way to go or how to do something.
[**Guide** comes from an old French word.]

**guillotine** *noun* **guillotines**
1 A **guillotine** is a tool with a sharp blade used for cutting paper.
2 A **guillotine** is a machine with a sharp blade that was used in the past, mainly in France, for cutting criminals' heads off.
[The **guillotine** is named after Dr *Guillotine*, who suggested its use.]

**guilt** *noun* (th)
**Guilt** is the feeling you have when you know or think that you have done something wrong.
[**Guilt** comes from Old English.]

**guilty** *adjective* **guiltier, guiltiest** (th)
Someone who feels **guilty** feels bad because s/he knows or thinks that s/he has done something wrong.

**guinea pig** *noun* **guinea pigs**
1 A **guinea pig** is a small furry animal

with a short tail. **Guinea pigs** are often kept as pets.
2 A **guinea pig** is a person who is used in an experiment.
[The **guinea pig** was named by mistake after *Guinea* in West Africa. It actually comes from Guiana in South America.]

**guitar** *noun* **guitars**
A **guitar** is a musical instrument that has strings across it which are plucked.
[**Guitar** comes via Spanish from Greek *kithara*, a kind of harp.]

**gulf** *noun* **gulfs**
1 A **gulf** is an area of sea in a large bay.
2 A **gulf** is a large or serious difference or disagreement between people.
[**Gulf** comes from Greece via French and Italian.]

**gull** *noun* **gulls** *Also* **seagull**
A **gull** is a grey and white bird that lives near the sea.
[**Gull** comes from a Celtic word.]

**gullet** *noun* **gullets**
Your **gullet** is the tube that carries food and drink from your throat to your stomach.
[**Gullet** comes via French from Latin *gula* 'throat'.]

**gully** *noun* **gullies**
A **gully** is a long or deep narrow valley.
[**Gully** comes from the same French word as **gullet**.]

**gum¹** *noun* **gums**
Your **gums** are the areas of firm pink flesh around your teeth.
[**Gum¹** comes from Old English.]

**gum²** *noun* **gums**
1 **Gum** is a sweet for chewing: *bubble gum, fruit gum.*
2 **Gum** is a type of glue.
[**Gum²** comes from Egyptian via French, Latin and Greek.]

**gun** *noun* **guns**
A **gun** is a weapon that fires bullets from a metal tube.
[**Gun** probably comes from Swedish *gunnr* 'war'.]

**gunpowder** *noun*
**Gunpowder** is a powder that explodes easily.

**guru** noun **gurus**
A **guru** is a religious teacher in some eastern religions.
[**Guru** comes from Sanskrit *guru* 'teacher'. Sanskrit is a very old Indian language.]

**gush** verb **gushes**, **gushing**, **gushed** (th)
If a liquid **gushes**, it flows out very quickly and in large amounts.
[The word **gush** is an imitation of the sound.]

**gust** noun **gusts**
A **gust** is a sudden burst of wind.
[**Gust** comes from Old Norse.]

**gut** noun **guts**
**1** Your **gut** is your stomach and intestines.
**2** **Gut** is a type of string that comes from the stomach of some animals.
**3** If you have **guts**, you are brave.
[**Gut** comes from Old English.]

**gutter** noun **gutters**
A **gutter** is a channel at the side of a road or on the edge of a roof to take rainwater away.
[**Gutter** comes from Latin via French.]

**gym** noun **gyms**
A **gym** is a hall with equipment for indoor sports.
[**Gym** is short for **gymnasium**, which comes via Latin from Greek.]

**gymnastics** noun
**Gymnastics** is a form of exercise that develops your strength, balance and physical control, often using equipment such as bars and ropes.
[**Gymnastics** comes from the same Greek word as **gym**.]

**gypsy** noun **gypsies** Also **gipsy**
A **gypsy** is someone from a race of people who travel from place to place especially in caravans.
[**Gypsy** is short for *Egyptian,* because people used to think that gypsies came from Egypt.]

# Dictionary Fun

## Complete the proverbs
1. Nothing ventured, nothing g_____.
2. People who live in g_____ houses shouldn't throw stones.

## Complete the idioms
1. Against the g_____ (*opposite to a person's natural feeling*)
2. To get in on the g_____ floor (*become a part of something at an early stage*)
3. To stick to your g_____ (*maintain a position*)

## Etymology
1. Which word comes via Italian and Spanish from old French *gale* 'rejoicing'?
2. Which word comes via French from Latin *crassus* 'thick or fat'?

## Complete the simile
As green as g_____ .

## Did you know?
◆ The word **gorilla** comes from the Greek word *Gorillai,* the Greek name for a tribe that were especially hairy.
◆ The word **gypsy** comes from the word *Egyptian,* as gypsies were thought to come from Egypt when they came to England in the early 16th century.

## Brainteaser
Which was the largest island before Australia was discovered?

a b c d e f **g** h i j k l m

# Hh

**habit** noun **habits** (th)
1 A **habit** is something that you do often without thinking about it, especially something that you find difficult to stop doing.
2 A **habit** is a long robe worn by monks or nuns.
[**Habit** comes from Latin via French.]

**habitat** noun **habitats**
A **habitat** is a place where an animal or plant usually lives.
[**Habitat** comes from Latin *habitat* 'it lives'.]

**hack** verb **hacks, hacking, hacked**
1 To **hack** means to chop in a careless way.
2 To **hack** means to find a way into a computer system without permission.
[**Hack** comes from Old English.]

**had** verb
**Had** is the past tense and past participle of **have**.

**haemorrhage** noun **haemorrhages**
A **haemorrhage** is when there is sudden bleeding, especially inside the body.
[**Haemorrhage** comes from Greek.]

**haggis** noun **haggises**
A **haggis** is a traditional food in Scotland, made from oatmeal, onions and offal cooked in the inner skin of a sheep's stomach.
[**Haggis** probably comes from Old Norse.]

**haggle** verb **haggles, haggling, haggled** (th)
To **haggle** means to argue about the price of something.
[**Haggle** comes from Old Norse.]

**haiku** noun **haiku**
A **haiku** is a type of Japanese poem that has three lines of five, seven and five syllables.
[**Haiku** comes from Japanese *haiku no ku* 'light verse'.]

**hail**[1] noun
1 **Hail** is large drops of frozen rain.
2 A **hail** of something is a shower of it: *a hail of bullets.*
[**Hail**[1] comes from Old English.]

**hail**[1] verb **hails, hailing, hailed**
If it **hails**, large drops of frozen rain fall.

**hail**[2] verb **hails, hailing, hailed**
To **hail** a bus or taxi means to put out your hand to show that you want it to stop.
[**Hail**[2] comes from Old Norse.]

**hair** noun **hairs**
**Hair** is the fine, soft covering that grows on the heads and bodies of people and some animals.
[**Hair** comes from Old English.]

**hairdresser** noun **hairdressers**
A **hairdresser** is a person whose job is to cut, wash and style people's hair.

**hairy** adjective **hairier, hairiest**
Someone or something that is **hairy** is covered in hair.

**halal** adjective
**Halal** meat is meat from animals that have been killed in a way allowed by the rules of Islam.
[**Halal** comes from Arabic *halal* 'according to religious law'.]

**half** noun **halves**
A **half** is one of the two equal parts into which something can be divided.
[**Half** comes from Old English.]

**half-brother** noun **half-brothers**
Your **half-brother** is the son of one of your parents but not of the other.

**half-sister** noun **half-sisters**
Your **half-sister** is the daughter of one of your parents but not of the other.

**half-mast** noun
If a flag is flying at **half-mast**, it is flying in the middle of the flagpole instead of at the top. It is a sign of mourning.

**hall** noun **halls**
1 A **hall** is a very large room where a lot of people can meet.
2 A **hall** is the area or passage inside the front door of a house.
[**Hall** comes from Old English.]

**Hallowe'en** noun
**Hallowe'en** is an ancient festival celebrated on the night of 31 October. People in the past believed that witches and ghosts were active on this night.
[**Hallowe'en** comes from *All Hallow*

*Evening*, the evening before the festival of *All Hallows* 'all the saints'.]

**halo** *noun* **halos** *or* **haloes**
A **halo** is a circle of light painted around an angel or a saint's head in religious paintings.
[**Halo** comes from Greek via Latin.]

**halve** *verb* **halves, halving, halved**
To **halve** something means to divide it in half. [**Halve** comes from **half**.]

**ham** *noun* **hams**
**Ham** is the meat from a pig's leg that is salted or smoked.
[**Ham** comes from Old English.]

**hamburger** *noun* **hamburgers**
A **hamburger** is a small, flat cake of meat that is usually served in a bread roll.
[**Hamburger** is named after *Hamburg*, a city in Germany.]

**hammer** *noun* **hammers**
A **hammer** is a tool used for hitting nails.
[**Hammer** comes from Old English.]

**hammock** *noun* **hammocks**
A **hammock** is a piece of cloth or net that can be hung between two supports and used as a bed.
[**Hammock** comes via Spanish from Taino (a South American Indian language).]

**hamper** *noun* **hampers**
A **hamper** is a large basket for carrying food, especially a picnic.
[**Hamper** comes from an old French word.]

**hamster** *noun* **hamsters**
A **hamster** is a small animal with smooth brown fur. They are often kept as pets.
[**Hamster** comes from German.]

**hand** *noun* **hands**
Your **hand** is the part of your body at the end of your arm.
[**Hand** comes from Old English.]

**handbag** *noun* **handbags**
A **handbag** is a small bag that is usually carried by a woman.

**handbook** *noun* **handbooks**
A **handbook** is a small book that gives you information or tells you how to do something.

**handcuffs** *plural noun*
**Handcuffs** are a pair of metal rings linked by a chain that are locked around a criminal's wrists.

**handful** *noun* **handfuls**
1 A **handful** is the amount of something that you can hold in your hand.
2 A **handful** is a small number of people or things.

**handicap** *noun* **handicaps** (th)
1 A **handicap** is something that makes it hard for you to do something.
2 A **handicap** is a disadvantage given to a competitor in a sport who is better than the others, to make the contest more even.
[**Handicap** comes from *hand in cap*, an old game in which money was put into a cap and then taken out by the winner.]

**handkerchief** *noun* **handkerchiefs**
A **handkerchief** is a square of cloth for blowing your nose.
[**Handkerchief** comes from **hand** and *kerchief* 'a cloth or scarf', which comes from French.]

**handle** *noun* **handles**
A **handle** of something is the part that you use to hold or carry it.
[**Handle** comes from the same Old English word as **hand**.]

**handle** *verb* **handles, handling, handled** (th)
To **handle** something means to touch, feel or hold it with your hands.

**handlebars** *plural noun*
**Handlebars** are the bars with handles on each end that you use to steer a bicycle.

**hang** *verb* **hangs, hanging, hung**
1 If something **hangs** or **hangs down**, the top of it is fixed to something and the bottom is free and not supported.
2 If you **hang** something or **hang** something **up**, you fix the top of it to something and leave the bottom free.
3 If you **hang** someone, you kill that person by tying a rope around his/her neck and taking the support from under his/her feet so that s/he is hanging by the rope. The past tense and past participle of this sense is **hanged**.
[**Hang** comes from Old English.]

**hangar** *noun* **hangars**
A **hangar** is a large shed where planes are kept. [**Hangar** comes from French.]

**hang-glider** *noun* **hang-gliders**
A **hang-glider** is a large kind of kite that a person can hang from and fly through the air.

**Hanukkah** *noun* *Also* **Chanukkah**
**Hanukkah** is a Jewish festival held in December that celebrates the purifying of the Temple at Jerusalem after it was recaptured from the Syrians in 164 BC. [**Hanukkah** comes from Hebrew *hanukkah* 'dedication to God'.]

**haphazard** *adjective*
Something that is **haphazard** is done without being planned, or is not arranged in any order. **haphazardly** *adverb*.
[**Haphazard** comes from an old word *hap* 'luck' (which comes from Old Norse) and **hazard**.]

**happen** *verb* **happens, happening, happened** (th)
1 To **happen** means to take place.
2 If you **happen** to do something, you do it by chance.
[**Happen** comes from the same old word *hap* as **haphazard**.]

**happy** *adjective* **happier, happiest** (th)
Someone who is **happy** is pleased, joyful or content.
**happily** *adverb*. **happiness** *noun*.
[**Happy** comes from the same old word *hap* as **haphazard**.]

**harass** *verb* **harasses, harassing, harassed** (th)
To **harass** someone means to keep doing things that upset or anger that person.
[**Harass** comes from French *harer* 'to set a dog on someone'.]

**harbour** *noun* **harbours** (th)
A **harbour** is a place where ships can shelter and unload.
[**Harbour** comes from Old English.]

**hard** *adjective* **harder, hardest** (th)
1 Something that is **hard** is firm and solid, not soft.
2 Something that is **hard** is not easy or needs a lot of effort.
3 Something that is **hard** is difficult and unpleasant.

4 A person who is **hard** is strict or unkind.
[**Hard** comes from Old English.]

**hard disk** *noun* **hard disks**
A **hard disk** is a disk inside a computer where information is stored.

**hardware** *noun*
1 **Hardware** is tools and equipment that you use in the home.
2 **Hardware** is all the mechanical and electrical parts of a computer. Programs that run on computers are called software.
[**Hardware** comes from **hard** and *ware* 'goods' (which comes from Old English).]

**hardy** *adjective* **hardier, hardiest** (th)
A **hardy** person, animal or plant is strong and able to survive in bad or cold conditions.
[**Hardy** comes from an old French word.]

**hare** *noun* **hares**
A **hare** is an animal like a large wild rabbit that lives in the countryside and can run very fast.
[**Hare** comes from Old English.]

**harm** *verb* **harms, harming, harmed** (th)
To **harm** means to hurt or damage someone or something.
[**Harm** comes from Old English.]

**harmonica** *noun* **harmonicas**
A **harmonica** is a small musical instrument that you play by moving it across your lips while blowing and sucking air through it.
[**Harmonica** comes from Latin *harmonicus* 'musical'.]

**harmony** *noun* **harmonies** (th)
1 A **harmony** is a pleasant combination of musical notes that is sung or played.
2 **Harmony** is when there is peace and agreement between people.
[**Harmony** comes via French from Latin *harmonia* 'agreement'.]

**harness** *noun* **harnesses**
1 A **harness** is the set of straps put on a horse's head and body to control it or to attach it to a cart.
2 A **harness** is a set of straps put around someone's body to keep him/her safe.
[**Harness** comes from Old Norse via French.]

**harness** *verb* **harnesses, harnessing, harnessed** (th)
**1** If you **harness** a horse, you put a harness on it, or attach it to a cart with a harness.
**2** If you **harness** something, you control it and use it: *harnessing nuclear energy to make electricity.*

**harp** *noun* **harps**
A **harp** is a large triangular musical instrument with long strings that you pluck. [**Harp** comes from Old English.]

**harpoon** *noun* **harpoons**
A **harpoon** is a spear for catching fish and sea animals.
[**Harpoon** comes from Greek via French and Latin.]

**harsh** *adjective* **harsher, harshest** (th)
**1** Someone who is **harsh** is cruel or very strict.
**2** Weather or a place that is **harsh** is very unpleasant and difficult to live in.
**3** Something that is **harsh** is rough or harmful: *the harsh glare of the sun.*
**harshly** *adverb.* **harshness** *noun.*
[**Harsh** comes from an old German word.]

**harvest** *noun* **harvests**
**1** **Harvest** is when farmers pick or gather in the crops they have grown.
**2** A **harvest** is the crops that are picked or gathered.
[**Harvest** comes from Old English.]

**harvest** *verb* **harvests, harvesting, harvested** (th)
To **harvest** crops is to pick or gather them in when they are ripe.

**hat** *noun* **hats**
A **hat** is a piece of clothing for covering the head. [**Hat** comes from Old English.]

**hatch** *verb* **hatches, hatching, hatched**
**1** When a baby bird **hatches**, it breaks out of its egg.
**2** To **hatch** means to think up a secret plan.
[**Hatch** probably comes from a Scandinavian language.]

**hate** *verb* **hates, hating, hated** (th)
To **hate** means to dislike someone or something very much.
[**Hate** comes from Old English.]

**haunt** *verb* **haunts, haunting, haunted**
A place that is **haunted** is said to have a ghost in it.
[**Haunt** comes from an old French word.]

**have** *verb* **has, having, had** (th)
**1** To **have** means to own: *Do you have a computer?*
**2** To **have** means to contain: *The house has six rooms.*
**3** If you **have to** do something, or **have** something **to do,** you must do it or you are responsible for it.
**4** If you **have** something **done,** you arrange for someone to do it for you.
**5** You use **have** with the past participle of a verb to show that the action happened in the past, or at an earlier time: *I've already seen her; He had just finished when she arrived.*
[**Have** comes from Old English.]

**hawk** *noun* **hawks**
A **hawk** is a large bird with sharp claws that eats small animals.
[**Hawk** comes from Old English.]

**hay** *noun*
**Hay** is dried grass used to feed animals.
[**Hay** comes from Old English.]

**hazard** *noun* **hazards**
A **hazard** is something that might be dangerous. **hazardous** *adjective.*
[**Hazard** comes via Spanish or Arabic from Persian or Turkish *zar* 'dice'.]

**hazel** *noun* **hazels**
**1** A **hazel** is a small tree that produces nuts that you can eat.
**2** A **hazel** or **hazelnut** is a light brown nut from a hazel tree.
[**Hazel** comes from Old English.]

**he** *pronoun*
**1** You use **he** when you are talking about a male person or animal that has already been mentioned and who is the subject of a verb: *I've invited John but I don't know if he will come.* [**He** comes from Old English.]

**head** *noun* **heads** (th)
**1** Your **head** is the part of your body where your face and brains are.
**2** The **head** of something is the person in charge of it: *the head of the government.*
**3** The **head** of something is the top or the front of it: *the head of the queue.*
[**Head** comes from Old English.]

**headache** *noun* **headaches**
A **headache** is a pain in your head.

**headlight** *noun* **headlights**
A **headlight** is one of two lights on the front of a vehicle.

**headline** *noun* **headlines**
1 A **headline** is a title in large letters above a piece of writing in a newspaper.
2 The **headlines** are the main stories in the news on the radio or television.

**headquarters** *plurals noun*
The **headquarters** of an organisation is its main or central offices.

**heal** *verb* **heals, healing, healed**
1 To **heal** means to make someone healthy again.
2 If a wound **heals**, it gets better.
[**Heal** comes from Old English.]

**health** *noun* (th)
1 **Health** is when your body is fit and you are not ill.
2 A person's **health** is the condition his/her body is in.
[**Health** comes from Old English.]

**healthy** *adjective* **healthier, healthiest** (th)
1 Someone who is **healthy** is fit and well.
2 Something that is **healthy** is good for you and helps to keep you fit.

**heap** *noun* **heaps** (th)
A **heap** is a pile of things, especially when it looks untidy.
[**Heap** comes from Old English.]

**hear** *verb* **hears, hearing, heard** (th)
To **hear** means to take in sounds through the ears. [**Hear** comes from Old English.]

**hearing** *noun*
**Hearing** is the ability to take in sounds through the ears.

**hearse** *noun* **hearses**
A **hearse** is a large car that carries the coffin to a funeral.
[**Hearse** comes from an old French word.]

**heart** *noun* **hearts**
1 Your **heart** is the part of your body that pumps the blood round it.
2 A **heart** is a shape like a heart, such as the red shape on a valentine card.
3 The **heart** of something is the centre of it.
4 **Hearts** is one of the suits of a pack of playing cards: *the six of hearts.*
[**Heart** comes from Old English.]

**heartless** *adjective* (th)
A person who is **heartless** shows no kind feelings or pity for other people.

**heat** *noun*
1 **Heat** is hot weather or a high temperature.
2 A **heat** is a stage in a competition. The winners of a **heat** continue towards the final. [**Heat** comes from Old English.]

**heat** *verb* **heats, heating, heated**
To **heat** something means to make it warm or hot.

**heath** *noun* **heaths**
A **heath** is an open wild area of land without many trees.
[**Heath** comes from Old English.]

**heaven** *noun* **heavens**
**Heaven** is the place where some people believe that God lives and that good people go to after they die.
[**Heaven** comes from Old English.]

**heavy** *adjective* **heavier, heaviest** (th)
Something that weighs a lot is **heavy**.
[**Heavy** comes from Old English.]

**hectare** *noun* **hectares**
A **hectare** is a measure of land that equals 10 000 square metres.
[**Hectare** comes from Greek *hekaton* 'a hundred' and French *are* 'a hundred square metres'.]

**hedge** *noun* **hedges**
A **hedge** is a row of bushes grown to form a boundary.
[**Hedge** comes from Old English.]

**hedgehog** *noun* **hedgehogs**
A **hedgehog** is a small nocturnal European animal covered in spikes.

**heel** *noun* **heels**
1 Your **heel** is the back part of your foot.
2 The **heel** of a shoe is the part that supports the back part of the foot.
[**Heel** comes from Old English.]

**Hegira** *noun*
**Hegira** is another way of spelling **Hijra**.

**height** *noun* **heights**
1 The **height** of something is the distance from the bottom of it to the top.

**2** The **height** of something is how far it is above the ground.
[**Height** comes from Old English.]

**heir** *noun* **heirs**
Someone's **heir** has the legal right to get that person's money, property or title when s/he dies.
[**Heir** comes from Latin via French.]

**heiress** *noun* **heiresses**
An **heiress** is a woman or girl who has the legal right to get someone's money, property or title when that person dies.

**Hejira** *noun*
Hejira is another way of spelling **Hijra**.

**held** *verb*
**Held** is the past tense and past participle of **hold**.

**helicopter** *noun* **helicopters**
A **helicopter** is a kind of aircraft with large blades on top that spin round.
[**Helicopter** comes from Greek *helix* 'a spiral' and *pteron* 'wing'.]

**helium** *noun*
**Helium** is a gas with no colour or smell that is lighter than air.
[**Helium** comes from Greek.]

**hell** *noun*
**1** Hell is a place where some people believe that wicked people go after they die to be punished for ever.
**2** Hell is a very unpleasant place or situation: *War is hell.*
[**Hell** comes from Old English.]

**helmet** *noun* **helmets**
A **helmet** is a strong hard covering to protect the head.
[**Helmet** comes from an old French word.]

**help** *verb* **helps, helping, helped** (th)
To **help** means to do something that makes another person's work easier.
[**Help** comes from Old English.]

**helpful** *adjective* (th)
**1** Someone who is **helpful** is willing to help.
**2** Something that is **helpful** makes it easier to do something: *You'll find this book very helpful.*
**helpfully** *adverb*. **helpfulness** *noun*.

**helping** *noun* **helpings** (th)
A **helping** of food is the amount that you get on your plate at one time: *Can I have another helping of mashed potatoes?*

**helpless** *adjective* (th)
If you are **helpless**, you are weak and cannot do anything without the help of other people.
**helplessly** *adverb*. **helplessness** *noun*.

**hem** *noun* **hems**
A **hem** is the border on a piece of cloth made by turning the edge under and sewing it down.
[**Hem** comes from Old English.]

**hemisphere** *noun* **hemispheres**
**1** A **hemisphere** is half of a sphere.
**2** The two halves of the earth north and south of the equator are called the **northern hemisphere** and the **southern hemisphere**.
[**Hemisphere** comes from Greek *hemi-* 'half' and *sphaira* 'sphere'.]

**hemp** *noun*
**Hemp** is a plant. The fibres from **hemp** are used to make ropes.
[**Hemp** comes from Old English.]

**hen** *noun* **hens**
**1** A **hen** is a chicken that is kept for its eggs.
**2** A **hen** is any female bird.
[**Hen** comes from Old English.]

**heptagon** *noun* **heptagons**
A **heptagon** is a flat shape that has seven straight sides and seven angles.
[**Heptagon** comes from Greek *hepta* 'seven' and *gonia* 'angle'.]

**her** *pronoun*
**1** You use **her** when you are talking about a female person or animal that has already been mentioned and who is the object of a verb: *The girl hit me so I pushed her.*
**2** belonging to a girl or a woman: *What colour is her hair?*; *That's her dog.*
[**Her** comes from Old English.]

**herb** *noun* **herbs**
A **herb** is a plant. The leaves or seeds of **herbs** can be used in cooking or to make medicines.
[**Herb** comes from Latin via French.]

**herbal** *adjective*
**Herbal** means made from herbs: *a herbal medicine*; *herbal tea.*

a b c d e f g **h** i j k l m

**herbivore** noun **herbivores**
A **herbivore** is an animal that eats plants and does not eat other animals.
[**Herbivore** comes from Latin *herba* 'herb' and *vorare* 'to devour'.]

**herbivorous** adjective
A **herbivorous** animal eats only plants.

**herd** noun **herds**
A **herd** is a group of animals of the same kind that stay together: *a herd of buffalo*.
[**Herd** comes from Old English.]

**here** adverb
in, at or to this place: *I've lived here for ten years; Come here!*
[**Here** comes from Old English.]

**hereditary** adjective
If something is **hereditary**, a parent can pass it on to a child through his/her genes: *a hereditary disease*.
[**Hereditary** comes from the same Latin word as **heir**.]

**heritage** noun (th)
Special buildings, traditions, or other things from the past that we want to keep and look after for the future are our **heritage**.
[**Heritage** comes via French from the same Latin word as **heir**.]

**hero** noun **heroes**
1 A **hero** is someone who has done something brave or good.
2 In a story, the **hero** is the main character.
[**Hero** comes from Greek via Latin.]

**heroic** adjective (th)
If you do something **heroic**, you do something very brave.
[**Heroic** comes via French and Latin from the same Greek word as **hero**.]

**heroin** noun
**Heroin** is a strong drug. People who take **heroin** often become addicted to it.
[**Heroin** comes from Latin via German.]

**heroine** noun **heroines**
1 A **heroine** is a girl or a woman who has done something brave or good.
2 In a story, the **heroine** is the main female character.
[**Heroine** comes via French and Latin from the same Greek word as **hero**.]

**heroism** noun (th)
**Heroism** means great bravery or courage.
[**Heroism** comes via French and Latin from the same Greek word as **hero**.]

**heron** noun **herons**
A **heron** is a bird that has long legs and a long beak. **Herons** live near water and eat frogs and fish.
[**Heron** comes from an old French word.]

**herring** noun **herring** or **herrings**
A **herring** is a small silvery sea fish that you can eat.
[**Herring** comes from Old English.]

**herself** pronoun
1 You use **herself** when you are talking about a female person or animal who is the object of a verb of which she is also the subject: *She saw herself in the mirror*.
2 If a girl or woman does something **herself** or **by herself**, she does it without help from anyone.
[**Herself** comes from Old English.]

**hesitate** verb **hesitates, hesitating, hesitated** (th)
If you **hesitate**, you wait for a short time before you do something.
[**Hesitate** comes from Latin *haesitare* 'to get stuck'.]

**hesitation** noun (th)
**Hesitation** is when someone waits for a short time before s/he does something, because s/he is not sure whether to do it or not.
[**Hesitation** comes from the same Latin word as **hesitate**.]

**heterosexual** adjective
A **heterosexual** person is attracted to people of the opposite sex.
[**Heterosexual** comes from Greek *heteros* 'other' and English *sexual* 'to do with sex'.]

**hexagon** noun **hexagons**
A **hexagon** is a flat shape that has six straight sides and six angles.
[**Hexagon** comes from Greek *hexa* 'six' and *gonia* 'angle'.]

**hibernate** verb **hibernates, hibernating, hibernated**
To **hibernate** means to go into a deep sleep for the winter. Tortoises and squirrels **hibernate**.

[**Hibernate** comes from Latin *hibernare* 'to spend the winter'.]

**hibernation** *noun*
**Hibernation** is when an animal goes to sleep so that it can survive the winter. During **hibernation** its breathing and heartbeat slow down, its temperature drops and it does not need food.

**hiccup** *verb* **hiccups, hiccuping, hiccuped** *Also* **hiccough**
When you **hiccup**, you make a sudden, short choking sound.
[The word **hiccup** is an imitation of the sound.]

**hiccup** *noun* **hiccups** *Also* **hiccough**
A **hiccup** is a short choking sound in your throat. You sometimes **get hiccups** if you eat or drink too quickly.

**hide¹** *verb* **hides, hiding, hid, hidden** (th)
1 When you **hide**, you go somewhere so that no one can see you.
2 If you **hide** something, you put it somewhere safe so that no one else can find it.
3 When you **hide** your feelings, you keep them secret and do no let them show.
[**Hide¹** comes from Old English *hydan*.]

**hide²** *noun* **hides**
An animal's **hide** is its skin.
[**Hide²** comes from Old English *hyd*.]

**hieroglyphics** *plural noun*
**Hieroglyphics** are pictures and symbols used as writing. People in ancient Egypt used **hieroglyphics**.
[**Hieroglyphics** comes from Greek *hieros* 'sacred' and *glyphe* 'carving'.]

**high** *adjective* **higher, highest** (th)
1 Something that is **high** is tall or a long way up: *a high mountain; high clouds*.
2 Something that is **high** is more than the usual amount: *a high temperature*.
3 A musical note at the top of the scale is **high**. [**High** comes from Old English.]

**high** *adverb*
a long way up: *He hit the ball high*.

**highlight** *noun* **highlights** (th)
The **highlight** of something is the best part or the most exciting part.

**highlight** *verb* **highlights, highlighting, highlighted** (th)
If you **highlight** something, you make people notice it: *The book highlighted the dangers of playing on railway lines*.

**hijack** *verb* **hijacks, hijacking, hijacked** (th)
When someone **hijacks** an aircraft or some other vehicle, s/he gets on board and takes control of it by force.
[No one knows where **hijack** comes from.]

**Hijra** *noun* *Also* **Hegira, Hejira**
**Hijra** was the escape of Muhammad from Mecca to Medina in the year AD 622 that marks the beginning of the Muslim era.
[**Hijra** comes via Latin from Arabic *hijra* 'departure'.]

**hike** *noun* **hikes** (th)
A **hike** is a long walk through the countryside.
[No one knows where **hike** comes from.]

**hike** *verb* **hikes, hiking, hiked**
If you **hike**, you take a long walk in the countryside.

**hiker** *noun* **hikers**
A **hiker** is someone who is going on a long walk for fun.

**hilarious** *adjective*
**Hilarious** means very funny.
[**Hilarious** comes via Latin from Greek *hilaros* 'cheerful'.]

**hill** *noun* **hills**
A **hill** is an area of land with sloping sides that is higher than the land around.
[**Hill** comes from Old English.]

**hilly** *adjective* **hillier, hilliest**
Land that is **hilly** has lots of hills.

**hilt** *noun* **hilts**
A **hilt** is the handle of a knife or a sword.
[**Hilt** comes from Old English.]

**him** *pronoun*
You say **him** when you are talking about a male person or animal that you have already mentioned and who is the object of a verb: *I've met the new teacher and I like him*. [**Him** comes from Old English.]

**himself** *pronoun*
1 You use **himself** when you are talking about a male person or animal who is the

object of a verb of which he is also the subject: *He got himself a book to read.*

**2** If a boy or man does something **himself** or **by himself**, he does it without help from anyone.

[**Himself** comes from Old English.]

**hind¹** *noun* **hinds**

A **hind** is a female deer.

[**Hind¹** comes from Old English.]

**hind²** *adjective*

An animal's **hind** legs are its back legs.

[**Hind²** comes from **behind**.]

**hinder** *verb* **hinders, hindering, hindered** (th)

To **hinder** means to get in the way or make things harder for someone: *The heavy suitcase hindered me.*

[**Hinder** comes from Old English.]

**Hindu** *noun* **Hindus**

A **Hindu** is a person who follows the religion of Hinduism. **Hindus** have many gods, and believe that when we die our soul comes back and we live again in a new body.

[**Hindu** comes via Urdu from Persian *Hind* 'India'. Urdu is a language spoken in India and Pakistan, and Persian is the language spoken in Iran.]

**Hinduism** *noun*

**Hinduism** is an Indian religion. **Hinduism** teaches people to respect all life and many Hindus are vegetarians.

**hinge** *noun* **hinges**

A **hinge** is a metal part that joins a window or a door to the frame, and lets it open and close.

[**Hinge** comes from an old word that is related to **hang**.]

**hint** *noun* **hints** (th)

**1** A **hint** is a clue: *Give me a hint about where we're going.*

**2** A **hint** is a piece of advice: *helpful hints.*

**3** A **hint** of something is a tiny amount of it: *I tasted a hint of ginger.*

[**Hint** comes from an old word *hent* 'to understand something'.]

**hint** *verb* **hints, hinting, hinted**

When you **hint**, you give someone a clue: *He hinted that it was time for us to go.*

**hip** *noun* **hips**

Your **hips** are the parts of your body at the top of your legs, between your thighs and your waist.

[**Hip** comes from Old English.]

**hippo** *noun* **hippos**

**Hippo** is short for **hippopotamus**.

**hippopotamus** *noun* **hippopotamuses** *or* **hippopotami**

A **hippopotamus** is a very large, thick-skinned, African animal that lives near water.

[**Hippopotamus** comes via Latin from Greek *hippos ho potaimos* 'horse of the river'.]

**hire** *verb* **hires, hiring, hired**

**1** When you **hire** something, you pay to use it for a while.

**2** If you **hire** a person, you pay him/her to do a job.

[**Hire** comes from Old English.]

**hire** *noun*

If something is **for hire**, you can pay to use it or borrow it.

**his** *pronoun*

belonging to a boy or a man: *What colour are his eyes?*; *It's his birthday today.*

[**His** comes from Old English.]

**hiss** *verb* **hisses, hissing, hissed**

To **hiss** means to make a noise like a snake.

[The word **hiss** is an imitation of the sound.]

**hiss** *noun* **hisses**

A **hiss** is a long 'ssss' sound.

**historic** *adjective*

If something that happens is **historic**, people in the future look back at it and think that it was important: *the historic moment when the Berlin Wall came down.*

[**Historic** comes via Latin from the same Greek word as **history**.]

**historical** *adjective*

Something that is **historical** happened in the past, or is about something in the past: *a historical novel about life in Roman times.* **historically** *adverb*.

[**Historical** comes via Latin from the same Greek word as **history**.]

**history** *noun*

If you study **history**, you learn about things that happened in the past.

[**History** comes from Greek *historia* 'finding out'.]

**hit** *verb* **hits, hitting, hit** (th)
1 To **hit** means to knock or hurt a thing or a person.
2 To **hit** a ball means to strike it hard with a bat or a racket so that it moves.
[**Hit** comes from Old Norse.]

**hit** *noun* **hits**
1 A **hit** is when you hit something: *She gave the ball a good hit.*
2 If something is a **hit**, it is a success and people like it: *a CD with all the latest hits.*

**hitch-hike** *verb* **hitch-hikes, hitch-hiking, hitch-hiked**
If you **hitch-hike**, you try to get somewhere by asking strangers for lifts in a vehicle.
[**Hitch-hike** comes from *hitch* 'to move with a jerk' and **hike**.]

**hitch-hiker** *noun* **hitch-hikers**
A **hitch-hiker** is a person who is travelling by getting lifts with strangers.

**hive** *noun* **hives**
A **hive** is a kind of box for bees to live in.
[**Hive** comes from Old English.]

**hoard** *noun* **hoards** (th)
A **hoard** is a pile or a store of things that you keep in a safe place.
[**Hoard** comes from Old English.]

**hoard** *verb* **hoards, hoarding, hoarded** (th)
If you **hoard** things, you collect them and keep them: *Squirrels hoard nuts.*

**hoarse** *adjective* **hoarser, hoarsest**
A **hoarse** voice sounds croaky and harsh.
**hoarsely** *adverb*. **hoarseness** *noun*.
[**Hoarse** comes from Old English.]

**hoax** *noun* **hoaxes** (th)
A **hoax** is a trick that someone plays on other people, usually by pretending that something is true when it is not: *When the fire engines arrived they found out that the call had been a hoax.*
[**Hoax** probably comes from *hocus pocus*, which was used as a magic word by magicians.]

**hob** *noun* **hobs**
A **hob** is the top part of a cooker where there are rings for heating saucepans.

[No one knows where **hob** comes from.]

**hobble** *verb* **hobbles, hobbling, hobbled**
To **hobble** means to walk unsteadily, or to limp, usually because you are injured.
[**Hobble** probably comes from an old German or Dutch word.]

**hobby** *noun* **hobbies**
A **hobby** is something interesting that you like to do in your spare time.
[**Hobby** comes from *hobbyhorse*, a stick with a horse's head used as a toy.]

**hockey** *noun*
**Hockey** is an outdoor game played by two teams using sticks with curved ends to hit a ball and try to score goals.
[No one knows where the word **hockey** comes from.]

**hoe** *noun* **hoes**
A **hoe** is a garden tool that you use to get weeds out of the soil.
[**Hoe** comes from an old French word.]

**hog** *noun* **hogs**
A **hog** is a male pig, especially a castrated one, kept for its meat.
[**Hog** comes from Old English.]

**hoist** *verb* **hoists, hoisting, hoisted** (th)
To **hoist** something heavy means to lift it, especially using a machine.
[**Hoist** probably comes from an old German or Dutch word.]

**hold¹** *verb* **holds, holding, held** (th)
1 To **hold** something means to have it in your hands.
2 To **hold** means to have room inside for something: *The hall holds 200 people.*
3 To **hold** something like a party means to organise it.
[**Hold¹** comes from Old English.]

**hold¹** *noun* **holds** (th)
A **hold** is a grasp or a grip: *She kept a firm hold on the toddler.*

**hold²** *noun* **holds**
A **hold** is the part of a ship below deck where the cargo is kept.
[**Hold²** comes from an old word *holl*, which comes from the same Old English word as **hole**.]

**hole** *noun* **holes** (th)
1 A **hole** in the surface of something is a hollow or a pit: *a hole in the road.*

a b c d e f g **h** i j k l m

**2** A **hole** is an opening or a gap: *a hole in the fence.* [**Hole** comes from Old English.]

**Holi** *noun*
Holi is a festival that Hindus hold in the spring in honour of the god Krishna. During **Holi** people play tricks such as throwing coloured water or powder at each other.
[**Holi** comes from Sanskrit (a very old Indian language).]

**holiday** *noun* **holidays**
**1** A **holiday** is a time when you do not have to go to school or work.
**2** A **holiday** is when you go to stay somewhere and do things that are fun or relaxing.
[**Holiday** comes from Old English *haligdaeg* 'holy day', because the Christian holy days used to be the only days when people did not work.]

**hollow** *noun* **hollows** (th)
A **hollow** is a hole or empty space.
[**Hollow** comes from Old English.]

**hollow** *adjective* (th)
**1** Something that is **hollow** is not solid but has an empty space inside it.
**2** A **hollow** sound is a dull sound that echoes.

**hollow** *verb* **hollows, hollowing, hollowed**
To **hollow** something **out** means to make a dip or a hole in it.

**holly** *noun* **hollies**
Holly is a prickly, dark green tree or bush that has red berries in the winter.
[**Holly** comes from Old English.]

**hologram** *noun* **holograms**
A **hologram** is a picture made with laser beams. **Holograms** look three-dimensional.
[**Hologram** comes from Greek *holos* 'whole' and *gramma* 'drawing'.]

**holster** *noun* **holsters**
A **holster** is a case for a gun, usually attached to a belt.
[**Holster** may come from Dutch.]

**holy** *adjective* **holier, holiest** (th)
**1** Something that is **holy** is very special and linked to religious belief.
**2** A **holy** person is someone who is very religious and good.

[**Holy** comes from Old English.]

**home** *noun* **homes** (th)
**1** Your **home** is the place where you live.
**2** Your **home** is the place where you feel you belong: *I live in London now, but Ottawa is my home.*
**3** A **home** is a place where people who cannot look after themselves, such as very old people or children without parents, can be cared for.
[**Home** comes from Old English.]

**homeless** *adjective*
Someone who is **homeless** has no home to live in. **Homeless** people have to live outside or in a special shelter.
**homelessness** *noun.*

**homesick** *adjective*
If you feel **homesick**, you feel very sad because you are away from your home and your family and you miss them.
**homesickness** *noun.*

**homework** *noun*
Homework is work that a teacher gives you to do at home.

**homograph** *noun* **homographs**
Words that are **homographs** are spelled the same but have different meanings. *Sow* (a female pig) and *sow* (to plant a seed) are **homographs** and are also pronounced differently.
[**Homograph** comes from Greek *homos* 'same' and *graphein* 'to write'.]

**homonym** *noun* **homonyms**
Words that are **homonyms** have the same spelling or pronunciation but have different meanings or origins. **Homonyms** may be homographs or homophones.
[**Homonym** comes from Greek *homonumon* 'having the same name'.]

**homophone** *noun* **homophones**
Words that are **homophones** sound the same but have different meanings. *So* and *sew* are **homophones**.
[**Homophone** comes from Greek *homos* 'same' and *phone* 'sound'.]

**homosexual** *adjective*
Someone who is **homosexual** is attracted to people of the same sex.
[**Homosexual** comes from Greek *homos* 'same' and English *sexual* 'to do with sex'.]

n o p q r s t u v w x y z

**honest** *adjective* (th)
If you are **honest**, you tell the truth and people can trust you not to steal or cheat. **honestly** *adverb*. **honesty** *noun*.
[**Honest** comes via French from the same Latin word as **honour**.]

**honey** *noun*
**Honey** is a golden, sweet, sticky food made by bees.
[**Honey** comes from Old English.]

**honeycomb** *noun* **honeycombs**
A **honeycomb** is made by bees to store their eggs and their honey. **Honeycombs** are made up of rows of wax cells that have six sides.
[**Honeycomb** comes from **honey** and **comb**, perhaps because the rows of open wax cells look like the teeth of a comb.]

**honeymoon** *noun* **honeymoons**
A **honeymoon** is a special holiday that a man and a woman go on just after their wedding.
[**Honeymoon** comes from **honey**, meaning something very sweet, and **moon**, because the first strong loving feelings gradually wane like the moon.]

**honk** *noun* **honks**
A **honk** is a loud, short sound that a goose or the horn on a car makes.
[The word **honk** is an imitation of the sound.]

**honk** *verb* **honks, honking, honked**
To **honk** means to make a loud, short sound like a goose.

**honour** *noun*
**1** You say that something is an **honour** if you are pleased and proud to do it.
**2** When you do something in a person's **honour**, you do it to show your respect and admiration for that person.
**3 Honour** is someone or something's good name: *We fought for our country's honour*.
[**Honour** comes from Latin via French.]

**hood** *noun* **hoods**
A **hood** is a covering for your head and neck, usually joined to a jacket.
[**Hood** comes from Old English.]

**hoof** *noun* **hoofs** or **hooves**
A **hoof** is the hard part of a horse's foot.
[**Hoof** comes from Old English.]

**hook** *noun* **hooks**
A **hook** is a bent piece of metal or other material for hanging or catching things on. [**Hook** comes from Old English.]

**hooligan** *noun* **hooligans** (th)
A **hooligan** is a violent person who likes to make trouble.
[**Hooligan** comes from the name of a family in a cartoon who were always fighting.]

**hoop** *noun* **hoops**
A **hoop** is a large ring.
[**Hoop** comes from Old English.]

**hoot** *verb* **hoots, hooting, hooted**
To **hoot** means to make an 'oo' sound like an owl.
[The word **hoot** is an imitation of the sound.]

**hoot** *noun*
A short loud sound from a car horn is a **hoot**.

**hop** *noun* **hops**
A **hop** is a jump on one leg.
[**Hop** comes from Old English.]

**hop** *verb* **hops, hopping, hopped**
**1** If a person **hops**, s/he moves by jumping on one leg.
**2** If an animal **hops**, it moves in small jumps, rather than walking or running.

**hope** *verb* **hopes, hoping, hoped**
To **hope** means to wish that something that you want will happen.
[**Hope** comes from Old English.]

**hope** *noun* **hopes** (th)
**1** A **hope** is a wish or a feeling that something good will happen.
**2** When you have **hope**, you feel that good things will probably happen.
**3** If something is your **only hope**, it is your only chance.

**hopeful** *adjective* (th)
To be **hopeful** means to think that good things will probably happen.
**hopefully** *adverb*.

**hopeless** *adjective* (th)
**1** When a situation is **hopeless**, there is no chance that it will work out well.
**2** When you feel **hopeless**, you feel sure that nothing good will happen.
**3** To say that you are **hopeless** at

something means that you are very bad at it. **hopelessly** *adverb.* **hopelessness** *noun.*

**horizon** *noun* **horizons**
A **horizon** is the line where the sky and the land or sea seem to meet.
[**Horizon** comes via French and Latin from Greek *horizon kuklos* 'limiting circle, boundary'.]

**horizontal** *adjective*
Something that is level like the horizon is **horizontal**. **horizontally** *adverb.*
[**Horizontal** comes via French from the same Latin word as **horizon**.]

**hormone** *noun* **hormones**
**Hormones** are chemicals made in your body that affect how your body works.
[**Hormone** comes from Greek *hormon* 'to get something going', because hormones start many of the processes that take place in the body.]

**horn** *noun* **horns**
1 A **horn** is a kind of pointed bone growing on the head of some animals such as cattle and goats.
2 A **horn** is a musical instrument made of brass. [**Horn** comes from Old English.]

**horoscope** *noun* **horoscopes**
1 A **horoscope** is a diagram that shows where stars and planets were when a person was born.
2 Your **horoscope** is an account of what some people believe will happen to you in the future because of where the stars and planets were when you were born and where they are now.
[**Horoscope** comes from Greek *hora* 'time, hour' (ancestor of **hour**) and *skopos* 'someone who watches'.]

**horrible** *adjective* (th)
Something that is **horrible** is disgusting or frightening. **horribly** *adverb.*
[**Horrible** comes via French from Latin *horrere* 'to shudder'.]

**horrid** *adjective* (th)
Something that is **horrid** is unpleasant or nasty. **horridly** *adverb.*
[**Horrid** comes from the same Latin word as **horrible**.]

**horrific** *adjective* (th)
Something that is **horrific** shocks or scares you. **horrifically** *adverb.*

[**Horrific** comes from the same Latin word as **horrible**.]

**horrified** *adjective* (th)
If you are **horrified**, you are shocked or disgusted.
[**Horrified** comes from *horrify* 'to shock or disgust', which comes from the same Latin word as **horrible**.]

**horrifying** *adjective* (th)
Something that is **horrifying** is alarming or shocking. **horrifyingly** *adverb.*
[**Horrifying** comes from *horrify* 'to shock or disgust', which comes from the same Latin word as **horrible**.]

**horror** *noun* **horrors** (th)
1 **Horror** is a feeling of very great fear or disgust: *I looked at the burning house in horror.*
2 If you have a **horror** of something, you are afraid of it or do not like it: *She has a horror of speaking in front of lots of people.*
[**Horror** comes via French from the same Latin word as **horrible**.]

**horse** *noun* **horses**
A **horse** is a large animal used for riding and pulling carts.
[**Horse** comes from Old English.]

**hose** *noun* **hoses**
A **hose** is a long pipe made of rubber or plastic. [**Hose** comes from Old English.]

**hospice** *noun* **hospices**
A **hospice** is a small hospital where people who are dying can be looked after.
[**Hospice** comes via French from the same Latin word as **hospitable**.]

**hospitable** *adjective* (th)
To be **hospitable** means to look after people in a friendly way that makes them feel welcome.
[**Hospitable** comes via French from Latin *hospitare* 'to look after a guest'.]

**hospital** *noun* **hospitals**
A **hospital** is a building in which people who are ill or hurt are looked after.
[**Hospital** comes via French from the same Latin word as **hospitable**.]

**host¹** *noun* **hosts**
1 The **host** at a party is the person whose party it is.
2 A **host** is a plant or animal that has a parasite living on it or in it.

[**Host**[1] comes via French from Latin *hospes* 'Lost, guest'.]

**host**[2] *noun* **hosts** (th)
A **host** of things is a large number of things: *They had a whole host of questions for me.*
[**Host**[2] comes via French from Latin *hostis* 'enemy' or 'army'.]

**hostage** *noun* **hostages**
**1** A **hostage** is a person who has been taken prisoner by someone who threatens to harm him/her unless certain things are done.
**2** If you **take** someone **hostage**, you capture him/her and s/he becomes a **hostage**.
[**Hostage** comes from Latin via French.]

**hostile** *adjective* (th)
A **hostile** person is unfriendly and seems to want to fight.
[**Hostile** comes from the same Latin word as **host**[2].]

**hot** *adjective* **hotter**, **hottest** (th)
**1** Something that is **hot** is very warm.
**2** A taste that has a burning flavour like pepper is **hot**.
[**Hot** comes from Old English.]

**hotel** *noun* **hotels**
A **hotel** is a building where people can pay to have meals and stay the night.
[**Hotel** comes via French from the same Latin word as **hospitable**.]

**hour** *noun* **hours**
An **hour** is a length of time lasting 60 minutes.
[**Hour** comes via French and Latin from Greek *hora* 'time, hour'.]

**hourly** *adverb*
Something that happens **hourly** happens every hour.

**house** *noun* **houses** (th)
A **house** is a building where people, usually from one family, live.
[**House** comes from Old English.]

**houseboat** *noun* **houseboats**
A **houseboat** is a boat that people live in, on a river or a canal.

**household** *noun* **households**
A **household** is a group made up of all the people who live in one house.

**housekeeper** *noun* **housekeepers**
A **housekeeper** is a person whose job is to look after someone's house and do all the housework.

**housework** *noun*
**Housework** is the jobs that have to be done in a home, such as cleaning, washing and ironing.

**hovel** *noun* **hovels** (th)
A **hovel** is a small, dirty or broken-down house.
[No one knows where **hovel** comes from.]

**hover** *verb* **hovers, hovering, hovered** (th)
**1** To **hover** means to stay in one place in the air.
**2** To **hover** means to hang around often because you are not sure what to do.
[No one knows where **hover** comes from.]

**hovercraft** *noun* **hovercraft**
A **hovercraft** is a large vehicle that travels just above the surface of land or water.

**how** *adverb*
**1** in what way: *How did you get to school?*; *I'd like to help him, but I don't know how.*
**2** You use **how** when you are asking about a number or amount: *How many people are coming?*; *How much money do you need?* [**How** comes from Old English.]

**however** *adverb*
**1** **However** means in spite of this: *She didn't want to come. However, I made her.*
**2** **However** means in whatever way: *However he combs his hair, it always sticks up.*

**howl** *verb* **howls, howling, howled**
To **howl** means to make a long, loud cry.
[The word **howl** is an imitation of the sound.]

**hug** *verb* **hugs, hugging, hugged** (th)
To **hug** means to hold someone in your arms in a loving way.
[**Hug** probably comes from a Scandinavian language.]

**hug** *noun* **hugs**
When you give someone a **hug**, you put your arms around him/her tightly in a loving way.

**huge** *adjective* (th)
Something that is **huge** is very big.
[**Huge** comes from an old French word.]

a b c d e f g **h** i j k l m

**hum** *verb* **hums, humming, hummed**
**1** When you **hum**, you sing with your mouth closed.
**2** When something **hums**, it makes a buzzing noise.
[The word **hum** is an imitation of the sound.]

**human being** *noun* **human beings**
A **human being** is a man, woman or child. [**Human** comes from Latin.]

**humane** *adjective*
Something that is done in a **humane** way is done kindly, without hurting anyone.
**humanely** *adverb*.
[**Humane** is an old spelling of **human**.]

**humble** *adjective* **humbler, humbest** (th)
You are **humble** if you are not too proud of yourself and you do not think that you are better than other people.
[**Humble** comes via French from Latin *humilis* 'low, near the ground'.]

**humid** *adjective* (th)
When the weather is **humid**, it is hot and damp.
[**Humid** comes from the same Latin word as **humour**.]

**humiliate** *verb* **humiliates, humiliating, humiliated** (th)
To **humiliate** someone means to make him/her feel stupid and embarrassed.
[**Humiliate** comes from the same Latin word as **humble**.]

**humorous** *adjective* (th)
**Humorous** means funny or amusing.
[**Humorous** comes from **humour**.]

**humour** *noun* (th)
**1** Something that has **humour** is funny or amusing.
**2** If you have a **sense of humour**, you realise when things are funny or you can be funny.
[**Humour** comes from Latin *humere* 'to be damp', because it used to mean one of the liquids in the body that people thought affected the way you felt and what mood you were in.]

**hump** *noun* **humps**
**1** A **hump** is a small hill or a rounded, raised part of a road: *speed humps*.
**2** A **hump** is the round lump on a camel's back.

[**Hump** probably comes from an old German or Dutch word.]

**hung** *verb*
**Hung** is the past tense and past participle of **hang**.

**hungrily** *adverb*
If you look at food **hungrily**, you look at it in a way that shows that you are **hungry**.

**hungry** *adjective* **hungrier, hungriest** (th)
When you are **hungry**, you feel as if you want to eat some food.
[**Hungry** comes from Old English.]

**hunt** *verb* **hunts, hunting, hunted** (th)
**1** To **hunt** means to chase after wild animals and try to kill them.
**2** To **hunt** means to look for something very carefully.
[**Hunt** comes from Old English.]

**hunt** *noun* **hunts**
A **hunt** is when people get together to chase wild animals.

**hurdle** *noun* **hurdles**
**1** A **hurdle** is a kind of frame that you jump over in a race: *the 400 metres hurdles*.
**2** A **hurdle** is a difficulty that you have to overcome.
[**Hurdle** comes from Old English.]

**hurricane** *noun* **hurricanes**
A **hurricane** is a storm with a very strong wind.
[**Hurricane** comes via Spanish and Portuguese from Taino (a South American Indian language).]

**hurry** *verb* **hurries, hurrying, hurried** (th)
To **hurry** means to move or do something quickly.
[No one knows where **hurry** comes from.]

**hurry** *noun*
When you are **in a hurry**, you are trying to do something or get somewhere quickly.

**hurt** *verb* **hurts, hurting, hurt** (th)
**1** If you **hurt** someone, you make that person feel pain or feel sad.
**2** If a part of your body **hurts**, you can feel pain in it.
[**Hurt** comes from an old French word.]

**husband** *noun* **husbands**
A woman's **husband** is the man she is

married to.
[**Husband** comes from Old Norse.]

**hut** *noun* **huts** (th)
A **hut** is a small simple house or shelter.
[**Hut** comes from German via French.]

**hydrogen** *noun*
**Hydrogen** is a gas that is lighter than air and has no colour or smell.
[**Hydrogen** comes from Greek.]

**hyena** *noun* **hyenas** *Also* **hyaena**
A **hyena** is an animal like a wolf. The cry of a **hyena** is like a laugh.
[**Hyena** comes from Greek via Latin.]

**hygienic** *adjective*
Something that is **hygienic** is clean and will not make people ill.
[**Hygienic** comes via French and Latin from Greek *hygies* 'healthy'.]

**hymn** *noun* **hymns**
A **hymn** is a song that people sing to praise God.
[**Hymn** comes from Greek via Latin.]

**hyphen** *noun* **hyphens**
A **hyphen** is a very short line that you use to join words, or to show that a word continues on the next line. The word *meat-eater* has a **hyphen** in it.
[**Hyphen** comes via Latin from Greek *hyphen* 'together'.]

**hypnotise** *verb* **hypnotises, hypnotising, hypnotised** *Also* **hypnotize**
If someone **hypnotises** you, you go into a trance so that you seem to be asleep but you can still hear what the person is saying.
[**Hypnotise** comes from Greek *hypnos* 'sleep'.]

**hypocrite** *noun* **hypocrites**
A **hypocrite** is a person who says s/he has certain beliefs and principles but who behaves in a way that shows that s/he doesn't really believe in them: *He's such a hypocrite – he says everyone should work for a living but he hasn't had a job for years.*
[**Hypocrite** comes via French and Latin from Greek *hypokrites* 'actor'.]

# Dictionary Fun

**Complete the proverbs**
1. Make h____ while the sun shines.
2. More h_____ , less speed.
3. H_____ a loaf is better than no bread.

**Complete the simile**
As old as the h_____.

**What do these idioms mean?**
1. To hit the nail on the head
2. To wear your heart on your sleeve
3. To have your hands full

**Work it out**
There are two birds in the 'h' section. Can you find them?

**Riddle**
What gets bigger, the more you take away from it?

**Did you know?**
◆ The word **humour** comes from Latin *humere* 'to be damp', because it used to mean one of the liquids in the body that people thought affected the way you felt and what mood you were in.
◆ The **helicopter** was probably first designed by Leonardo da Vinci, the artist, in about 1500. It was not until the 1930s that the first helicopter actually flew!

a b c d e f g h i j k l m

# Ii

**I** *pronoun*
I is a word that you use to talk about yourself. [**I** comes from Old English.]

**ice** *noun*
Ice is frozen water.
[**Ice** comes from Old English.]

**ice** *verb* **ices, icing, iced**
1 To **ice** a cake means to put icing on it.
2 An **iced** drink has ice in it.

**ice age** *noun* **ice ages**
An **ice age** is a long period of time when a lot of the earth is covered with ice.

**iceberg** *noun* **icebergs**
An **iceberg** is a mountain of ice floating in the sea.
[**Iceberg** comes from Dutch *ijs* 'ice' and *berg* 'hill, mountain'.]

**ice cream** *noun* **ice creams**
Ice cream is a sweet frozen food.

**ice-skate** *noun* **ice-skates**
Ice-skates are boots that have a blade along the bottom under the sole and heel. You use **ice-skates** to move around or dance on the ice.
[**Skate** comes from French via Dutch.]

**icicle** *noun* **icicles**
An **icicle** is a thin, pointed piece of ice hanging down from something.
[**Icicle** comes from Old English.]

**icing** *noun*
Icing is a sweet topping put on cakes.

**icon** *noun* **icons**
1 An **icon** is a painting or carving showing a religious figure, usually made in Russia.
2 An **icon** is a symbol on a computer screen that represents a certain feature of the program.
[**Icon** comes from Greek *eikon* 'image'.]

**idea** *noun* **ideas** (th)
An **idea** is a thought, a suggestion or a belief: *Good idea!; She's has strange ideas.*
[**Idea** comes via Latin from Greek *idea* 'pattern or model'.]

**ideal** *noun* **ideals** (th)
An **ideal** is a principle that you believe is right and that you try to live up to.

[**Ideal** comes from the same Latin word as **idea**.]

**ideal** *adjective* (th)
Something that is **ideal** is perfect for a particular purpose: *Shorts are ideal in hot weather.* **ideally** *adverb*.

**identical** *adjective* (th)
Two things that are **identical** are exactly the same: *identical twins.*
[**Identical** comes from Latin *idem* 'the same'.]

**identify** *verb* **identifies, identifying, identified**
If you **identify** someone or something, you recognise or say who or what that person or thing is: *He identified the criminal; How many trees can you identify?*
[**Identify** comes from Latin *identificare* 'to make the same'.]

**idle** *adjective* **idler, idlest** (th)
1 A machine that is not being used or a person who is not busy is **idle**: *The printer is idle; She hates being idle.*
2 Someone who is **idle** is lazy and does not want to work: *He's bone idle.*
[**Idle** comes from Old English.]

**idol** *noun* **idols**
1 An **idol** is a statue or a symbol that people worship as a god.
2 An **idol** is a famous person who people love and admire very much: *a pop idol.*
[**Idol** comes from Greek via French and Latin.]

**i.e.** *abbreviation*
You use **i.e.** when you want to explain exactly what you mean: *soft drinks, i.e. cola and lemonade.*
[**I.e.** is short for Latin *id est*, which means 'that is'.]

**ignite** *verb* **ignites, igniting, ignited** (th)
If something **ignites**, it starts burning.
[**Ignite** comes from Latin *ignis* 'fire'.]

**ignorant** *adjective* (th)
1 If you are **ignorant** of something, you do not know about it.
2 An **ignorant** person is uneducated and does not know very much.
[**Ignorant** comes from Latin via French.]

**iguana** *noun* **iguanas**
An **iguana** is a type of lizard that is mainly found in South America.

[**Iguana** comes via Spanish from Arawak (a South American Indian language).]

**ill** *adjective* **worse, worst** (th)
**1** Someone who is **ill** is not well: *She didn't go to school because she was ill; I felt really ill when I had flu.*
**2** If you **fall ill** or are **taken ill**, you become ill.
**3** Something that is **ill** is bad: *ill effects; ill fortune.* [**Ill** comes from Old Norse.]

**illegal** *adjective* (th)
Something that is **illegal** is against the law. **illegally** *adverb.*
[**Illegal** comes via French from Latin *il-* 'not' and *legalis* 'allowed by law' (ancestor of **legal**).]

**illegible** *adjective* (th)
Writing or print that is **illegible** is difficult or impossible to read. **illegibly** *adverb.*
[**Illegible** comes from Latin *il-* 'not' and **legible**.]

**illicit** *adjective* (th)
Something that is **illicit** happens secretly because it is against the law or against certain rules. **illicitly** *adverb.*
[**Illicit** comes via French from Latin *il-* 'not' and *licitus* 'allowed'.]

**illiterate** *adjective*
**1** Someone who is **illiterate** cannot read or write.
**2** Someone who is **illiterate** is very badly educated.
[**Illiterate** comes from Latin *il-* 'not' and *litteratus* 'learned' (ancestor of **literate**).]

**illness** *noun* **illnesses** (th)
**1** An **illness** is something that makes you unwell: *A cold is not a serious illness.*
**2** **Illness** is being unwell: *He's had time off school through illness.*

**illogical** *adjective*
Something that is **illogical** does not make sense because it has not been thought out properly. **illogically** *adverb.*
[**Illogical** comes from *il-* 'not' and **logical**.]

**illuminate** *verb* **illuminates, illuminating, illuminated** (th)
**1** To **illuminate** something is to light it up: *Spotlights illuminate the building at night.*

**2** To **illuminate** something is to explain it or make it clear: *These instructions aren't very illuminating.*
[**Illuminate** comes from Latin *lumen* 'light'.]

**illusion** *noun* **illusions** (th)
**1** An **illusion** is a false idea or belief about a thing or a person.
**2** An **illusion** is something that looks real but is not.
[**Illusion** comes from Latin *illudere* 'to make a fool of someone'.]

**illustrate** *verb* **illustrates, illustrating, illustrated**
**1** To **illustrate** something is to explain it by using examples and pictures.
**2** To **illustrate** a book or magazine is to add pictures to it.
[**Illustrate** comes from Latin.]

**imaginary** *adjective* (th)
Something that is **imaginary** is not real: *imaginary monsters.*
[**Imaginary** comes via French from the same Latin word as **imagine**.]

**imagination** *noun* **imaginations**
**Imagination** is the ability to form pictures and ideas in your mind.
[**Imagination** comes via French from the same Latin word as **imagine**.]

**imagine** *verb* **imagines, imagining, imagined** (th)
**1** If you **imagine** something, you have an idea or picture of it in your mind: *Imagine you are on a desert island.*
**2** If you **imagine** something, you think it exists when it doesn't: *Did I hear a scream or did I imagine it?*
[**Imagine** comes from Latin *imaginari* 'to form a picture in your mind'.]

**imitate** *verb* **imitates, imitating, imitated** (th)
**1** If you **imitate** something, you copy it.
**2** If you **imitate** someone, you copy the way s/he talks or behaves because you want to be like him/her or in order to make other people laugh. [**Imitate** comes from Latin.]

**immaculate** *adjective* (th)
Something that is **immaculate** is perfect or very clean. **immaculately** *adverb.*
[**Immaculate** comes from Latin *immaculatus* 'spotless, unstained'.]

a b c d e f g h **i** j k l m

**immaterial** *adjective* (th)
Something that is **immaterial** is not important or not relevant.
[**Immaterial** comes from Latin *im-* 'not' and *materialis* 'to do with matter' (ancestor of **material**).]

**immature** *adjective* (th)
A person who is **immature** thinks or behaves in a way that is normal for someone younger. **immaturely** *adverb*.
[**Immature** comes from Latin *im-* 'not' and *maturus* 'ripe'.]

**immediately** *adverb* (th)
If something happens **immediately**, it happens at once or straight away.
[**Immediately** comes via French from Latin *im-* 'not' and *mediatus* 'in the middle'.]

**immense** *adjective* (th)
**Immense** means very big or very great: *Look at the size of this – it's immense!* **immensely** *adverb*.
[**Immense** comes from Latin *im-* 'not' and *mensus* 'measured'.]

**immerse** *verb* **immerses, immersing, immersed** (th)
**1** If you **immerse** yourself **in** something, you give it all your attention: *She's immersed in a book.*
**2** To **immerse** something or someone is to put that thing or person deep into a liquid so they are completely covered.
[**Immerse** comes from Latin.]

**immigrant** *noun* **immigrants**
An **immigrant** is a person who has come into a foreign country to live there permanently.
[**Immigrant** comes from the same Latin words as **immigration**.]

**immigration** *noun*
**Immigration** is coming to a foreign country to live there permanently.
[**Immigration** comes from Latin *im-* 'in' and *migrare* 'to migrate' (ancestor of **migrate**).]

**imminent** *adjective* (th)
Something that is **imminent** is about to happen and it is usually unpleasant: *Look at those black clouds – a huge storm is imminent.* **imminently** *adverb*.
[**Imminent** comes from Latin *imminere* 'to hang over'.]

**immobile** *adjective* (th)
Something or someone that is **immobile** doesn't move.
[**Immobile** comes from Latin *im-* 'not' and **mobile**.]

**immobilise** *verb* **immobilises, immobilising, immobilised** *Also* **immobilize** (th)
To **immobilise** something or someone is to stop them from moving or working: *The car alarm immobilises the engine; He was immobilised after breaking both his legs.*

**immovable** *adjective* (th)
Something that is **immovable** cannot move or be moved. **immovably** *adverb*.
[**Immovable** comes from *im-* 'not' and *movable*.]

**immune** *adjective*
If you are **immune** to something, it cannot affect you: *Once you've had chickenpox you're immune to it.*
[**Immune** comes from Latin.]

**immunity** *noun*
If you have **immunity** to or from something, you are immune to it: *One injection gives immunity to typhoid and cholera; The informer had been granted immunity from prosecution.*

**impact** *noun* **impacts**
**1** The **impact** of something is the force with which it hits something else.
**2** The **impact** of something is the effect it has on something or someone.
**3 On impact** means the moment when one thing hits another: *The bomb will explode on impact.*
[**Impact** comes from Latin *im-* 'into' and *pactum* 'driven'.]

**impatient** *adjective* (th)
**1** A person who is **impatient** cannot wait calmly for something to happen.
**2** Someone who gets annoyed easily is **impatient**. **impatiently** *adverb*.
[**Impatient** comes via French from Latin *im-* 'not' and *patiens* (ancestor of **patient**).]

**impeccable** *adjective* (th)
Something that is **impeccable** is perfect: *He's French but he speaks impeccable English.* **impeccably** *adverb*.
[**Impeccable** comes from Latin *im-* 'not'

and *peccare* 'to sin'.]

**impediment** *noun* (th)
An **impediment** is a problem that makes it difficult for something to happen or to continue: *Lack of medicine is an impediment to good health.*
[**Impediment** comes from Latin *impedire* 'to chain someone's feet'.]

**impenetrable** *adjective* (th)
1 Something that is **impenetrable** is impossible to enter or get through.
2 Something that is **impenetrable** is impossible to understand: *impenetrable legal documents.*
[**Impenetrable** comes from Latin *im-* 'not' and *penetrare* 'to go into' (ancestor of **penetrate**).]

**imperfect** *adjective* (th)
Something that is **imperfect** has mistakes or faults. **imperfectly** *adverb*.
[**Imperfect** comes via French from Latin *im-* 'not' and *perfectus* (ancestor of **perfect**).]

**imperial** *adjective*
1 **Imperial** means to do with or having an empire: *When Britain had an empire it was an imperial power.*
2 The **imperial** system of measurement uses inches, pounds, yards, miles, pints and gallons. The **imperial** system of measurement was used before the metric system, which uses centimetres, kilometres and litres.
[**Imperial** comes from Latin.]

**impersonate** *verb* **impersonates, impersonating, impersonated**
To **impersonate** someone is to copy the way that person talks, looks and behaves, in order to deceive or amuse people: *He's a comedian who impersonates politicians.*
[**Impersonate** comes from Latin *im-* 'in, into' and *persona* (ancestor of **person**).]

**impertinent** *adjective* (th)
Someone who is **impertinent** is rude or does not show respect to someone who deserves it. **impertinently** *adverb*.
[**Impertinent** comes from Latin.]

**impervious** *adjective*
1 Something that is **impervious** does not let water pass through it: *impervious rock.*
2 Someone who is **impervious** to something is not affected by it.

[**Impervious** comes from Latin.]

**impetuous** *adjective*
Someone who is **impetuous** acts without thinking first. **impetuously** *adverb*. **impetuousness** *noun*.
[**Impetuous** comes from Latin via French.]

**implausible** *adjective*
Something that is **implausible** is not easy to believe. **implausibly** *adverb*.
[**Implausible** comes from *im-* 'not' and **plausible**.]

**implement** *noun* **implements** (th)
An **implement** is a tool, especially one used for outdoor work.
[**Implement** comes from Latin.]

**implement** *verb* **implements, implementing, implemented**
When you **implement** something such as a plan, a system or a reform, you start using it.

**implicate** *verb* **implicates, implicating, implicated**
To **implicate** someone is to show that s/he is involved in a crime or is responsible for something bad that has happened: *There is evidence to implicate him in the robbery.*
[**Implicate** comes from Latin *implicare* 'to fold in' or 'to entangle'.]

**implication** *noun* **implications**
1 An **implication** is the effect that something will have on something else in the future.
2 An **implication** is something that is suggested but is not said openly.

**imply** *verb* **implies, implying, implied** (th)
If you **imply** something, you suggest it in an indirect way but you do not actually say it: *She didn't actually call me a liar but she implied that I was lying.*
[**Imply** comes from the same Latin word as **implicate**.]

**impolite** *adjective*
Someone who is **impolite** is rude or bad-mannered: *It's impolite to ignore someone who is speaking to you.* **impolitely** *adverb*.
[**Impolite** comes from Latin *im-* 'not' and *politus* (ancestor of **polite**).]

**import** *verb* **imports, importing, imported**
To **import** is to buy goods from another

country and bring them into your own country in order to sell them: *Supermarkets import lots of fruit from Central America.* [**Import** comes from Latin *importare* 'to bring in'.]

**import** *noun* **imports**
Imports are goods bought in a foreign country and brought into your own country in order to sell them.

**important** *adjective* (th)
1 If something is **important**, it should be taken seriously or it has great value: *Listen, I'm about to tell you something important; What's more important – money or good health?*
2 An **important** person is someone with power who people respect.
**importantly** *adverb*. **importance** *noun*.
[**Important** comes from Latin.]

**impose** *verb* **imposes, imposing, imposed**
1 When governments or people with power **impose** something, they officially order it to happen: *The government imposed an extra tax on cigarettes.*
2 If you **impose** on someone, you expect that person to do something that might be unreasonable: *I could ask him to help me again but I don't want to impose.*
3 If you **impose** your beliefs or ideas on someone, you force that person to think like you because you have some power over him/her: *Parents shouldn't impose their ideas on their children.*
[**Impose** comes via French from Latin *im-* 'on' and *positum* 'placed'.]

**impossible** *adjective*
1 Something that is not possible is **impossible**.
2 An **impossible** situation or person is very annoying or hard to deal with.
**impossibly** *adverb*.
[**Impossible** comes from Latin *im-* 'not' and *possibilis* (ancestor of **possible**).]

**impostor** *noun* **impostors** *Also* **imposter**
An **impostor** is someone who pretends to be someone s/he is not in order to trick people.
[**Impostor** comes from Latin via French.]

**impractical** *adjective* (th)
1 Something that is **impractical** is not sensible or not useful in a certain situation.
2 An **impractical** person cannot do ordinary simple things that most people can do easily.
[**Impractical** comes from *im-* 'not' and **practical**.]

**imprecise** *adjective* (th)
Something that is **imprecise** is not clear or exact: *These directions are a bit imprecise – I hope we don't get lost.*
[**Imprecise** comes from *im-* 'not' and **precise**.]

**impress** *verb* **impresses, impressing, impressed**
1 To **impress** someone means to make that person feel admiration or respect.
2 If you **impress** something on someone, you make it very clear to that person that it is important.
[**Impress** comes from French *empresser* 'to press in'.]

**impression** *noun* **impressions** (th)
1 An **impression** is a feeling you get about something or someone.
2 An **impression** of someone is an imitation of the way that person speaks or behaves that people usually find funny.
3 An **impression** is a mark made in a surface by pressing an object into it.
[**Impression** comes from the same French word as **impress**.]

**impressive** *adjective* (th)
If something is **impressive**, you admire it because it is very grand or it seems to be very important.
[**Impressive** comes from **impress**.]

**imprison** *verb* **imprisons, imprisoning, imprisoned** (th)
To **imprison** someone is to put that person in prison.
[**Imprison** comes from an old French word.]

**imprisonment** *noun* (th)
**Imprisonment** is being sent to prison: *She was sentenced to three years' imprisonment.*

**improve** *verb* **improves, improving, improved** (th)
To **improve** is to get better or to make something better.
[**Improve** comes from an old French word.]

**improvement** *noun* **improvements** (th)
An **improvement** is a change that makes something better.

**improvise** *verb* **improvises, improvising, improvised**
1 To **improvise** is to do the best you can with the things you have got.
2 When someone such as an actor or a musician **improvises**, s/he makes up the words or music as s/he goes along.
[**Improvise** comes from Latin *im-* 'not' and *provisus* 'provided for'.]

**impudent** *adjective* (th)
An **impudent** person or remark is rude or cheeky.
**impudently** *adverb*. **impudence** *noun*.
[**Impudent** comes from Latin *im-* 'not' and *pudens* 'ashamed'.]

**impulse** *noun* **impulses**
1 An **impulse** is a sudden desire to do something: *On impulse she decided to call the radio station.*
2 An **impulse** is a small burst of energy: *Electrical impulses travel through the wires.*
[**Impulse** comes from Latin *impulsus* 'driven towards'.]

**impure** *adjective* (th)
An **impure** substance is a mixture of things and so is not the best quality.
[**Impure** comes from Latin *im-* 'not' and *purus* (ancestor of **pure**).]

**inability** *noun* **inabilities** (th)
If you have an **inability** to do something, you do not have the power or skill needed to do it.
[**Inability** comes from *in-* 'not' and **ability**.]

**inaccurate** *adjective* (th)
Something that is **inaccurate** is not correct or not very precise.
[**Inaccurate** comes from *in-* 'not' and **accurate**.]

**inadequate** *adjective* (th)
1 If something is **inadequate**, it is not enough or not good enough.
2 A person who feels **inadequate** thinks that s/he is not as good as other people and cannot do things as well.
**inadequately** *adverb*.
[**Inadequate** comes from *in-* 'not' and **adequate**.]

**inanimate** *adjective*
An **inanimate** object is not living: *A chair is an inanimate object.* **inanimately** *adverb*.
[**Inanimate** comes from Latin.]

**inarticulate** *adjective*
If you are **inarticulate**, you find it hard to say what you mean because you cannot find the right words.
**inarticulately** *adverb*.
[**Inarticulate** comes from *in-* 'not' and **articulate**.]

**inaudible** *adjective*
Something that is **inaudible** cannot be heard. **inaudibly** *adverb*.
[**Inaudible** comes from Latin *in-* 'not' and *audibilis* (ancestor of **audible**).]

**incapacitate** *verb* **incapacitates, incapacitating, incapacitated**
To **incapacitate** someone is to take away that person's ability to move or do something normally: *She was incapacitated by flu.*
[**Incapacitate** comes from Latin via French.]

**incense** *noun*
**Incense** is a substance that is burned to give off a sweet smell.
[**Incense** comes via French from Latin *incendere* 'to set fire to'.]

**incense** *verb* **incenses, incensing, incensed** (th)
To be **incensed** is to be very angry.

**incentive** *noun* **incentives**
An **incentive** is something that encourages you to do something: *The bank gives students free CD tokens as an incentive to open an account.*
[**Incentive** comes from Latin *incentivum* 'something that incites'.]

**incessant** *adjective* (th)
Something that is **incessant** never stops.
**incessantly** *adverb*.
[**Incessant** comes from Latin *in-* 'not' and *cessare* 'to stop' (ancestor of **cease**).]

**inch** *noun* **inches**
An **inch** is a measurement in the imperial system of length, equal to about 2.5 centimetres.
[**Inch** comes from Old English.]

**inch** *verb* **inches, inching, inched**
To **inch** is to move a short distance in a

a b c d e f g h **i** j k l m

very careful way.

**incidence** *noun* **incidences**
The **incidence** of something is how often it happens.
[**Incidence** comes from Latin *incidens* 'happening'.]

**incident** *noun* **incidents** (th)
An **incident** is something that happens, especially something unpleasant but not very important: *Police were called to an incident outside a nightclub.*
[**Incident** comes from Latin *incidere* 'to happen to'.]

**incinerate** *verb* **incinerates, incinerating, incinerated**
To **incinerate** something is to burn it in order to destroy it.
[**Incinerate** comes from Latin *incinerare* 'to turn into ashes'.]

**incision** *noun* **incisions**
An **incision** is a cut that is carefully made into something.
[**Incision** comes from Latin *incidere* 'to cut into'.]

**incisor** *noun* **incisors**
An **incisor** is a sharp tooth at the front of the mouth.
[**Incisor** comes from the same Latin word as **incision**.]

**incite** *verb* **incites, inciting, incited** (th)
To **incite** is to encourage people to cause trouble, fight or argue, for example, by making them very angry or excited: *incite the crowd to violence.*
[**Incite** comes from Latin *incitare* 'to rouse' (ancestor of **incentive**).]

**inclination** *noun* **inclinations**
An **inclination** is a feeling that you want to have or do something: *an inclination to travel.*
[**Inclination** comes from the same Latin word as **incline**.]

**incline** *verb* **inclines, inclining, inclined** (th)
**1** If someone is **inclined** to do something, s/he wants to do it or has a feeling that it is the right thing to do.
**2** To **incline** is to slope or lean: *The building inclines towards the left; The road had a steep incline.*
[**Incline** comes via French from Latin

*inclinare* 'to bend towards'.]

**include** *verb* **includes, including, included** (th)
If something **includes** something or someone, that thing or person is part of it: *Does the price include postage?; We want to include everyone in our plans.*
[**Include** comes from Latin *includere* 'to hold in'.]

**inclusive** *adjective*
Something that is **inclusive**, especially a price, includes everything: *The price is inclusive of postage.*

**incognito** *adverb*
Someone who does something **incognito** does it in a way that means people will not find out his/her real identity: *Many famous people like to travel incognito.*
[**Incognito** comes via Italian from Latin *in-* 'not' and *cognitus* 'known'.]

**income** *noun* **incomes**
Someone's **income** is the money that s/he gets for working or from investments.

**incompatible** *adjective*
Two people who cannot get on with each other or two things that do not work together are **incompatible**.
**incompatibly** *adverb*.
[**Incompatible** comes from Latin.]

**incompetent** *adjective* (th)
Someone who is **incompetent** does not have the skill needed to do a job well.
**incompetently** *adverb*.
[**Incompetent** comes from Latin *incompetentus* 'not suitable'.]

**incomprehensible** *adjective* (th)
Something that is **incomprehensible** is impossible to understand.
**incomprehensibly** *adverb*.
[**Incomprehensible** comes from Latin *in-* 'not' and *comprehendere* 'to take in' (ancestor of **comprehension**).]

**inconceivable** *adjective* (th)
Something that is **inconceivable** is impossible or very hard to imagine or believe. **inconceivably** *adverb*.
[**Inconceivable** comes from *in-* 'not' and **conceive**.]

**inconclusive** *adjective*
Something that is **inconclusive** does not prove or decide anything.

**inconclusively** *adverb*.
[**Inconclusive** comes from Latin *in-* 'not' and *claudere* 'to shut'.]

**incongruous** *adjective*
Something that is **incongruous** seems strange or looks out of place in a certain situation. **incongruously** *adverb*.
[**Incongruous** comes from Latin *in-* 'not' and *congruus* 'suitable'.]

**inconvenient** *adjective* (th)
Something that is **inconvenient** causes difficulty or trouble, or does not fit in with your plans. **inconveniently** *adverb*.
[**Inconvenient** comes from Latin *in-* 'not' and *convenire* 'to go together' (ancestor of **convenient**).]

**incorporate** *verb* **incorporates, incorporating, incorporated**
To **incorporate** something is to make it a part of something else.
[**Incorporate** comes from Latin.]

**increase** *verb* **increases, increasing, increased** (th)
To **increase** is to become or to make something larger in size or amount. **increasingly** *adverb*.
[**Increase** comes from Latin *in-* 'into', 'towards' and *crescere* 'to grow'.]

**incubate** *verb* **incubates, incubating, incubated**
To **incubate** something is to keep it in the right conditions for it to grow and develop. [**Incubate** comes from Latin.]

**incubation** *noun*
1 **Incubation** is the process of keeping eggs warm so that they will hatch.
2 The **incubation** period of an illness is the time between catching the disease and the time when the symptoms show.

**incubator** *noun* **incubators**
An **incubator** is a special device used for keeping small or weak babies alive or for keeping eggs warm so that they will hatch.

**indebted** *adjective*
If you are **indebted** to someone, you are very grateful for that person's help.
[**Indebted** comes from an old French word.]

**indecisive** *adjective* (th)
1 Someone who is **indecisive** cannot

make decisions.
2 Something that is **indecisive** does not prove or decide anything.
**indecisively** *adverb*.
[**Indecisive** comes from *in-* 'not' and **decisive**.]

**indelible** *adjective*
Something that is **indelible** cannot be removed or washed out: *indelible ink*.
**indelibly** *adverb*.
[**Indelible** comes from Latin *in-* 'not' and *delere* (ancestor of **delete**).]

**indent** *verb* **indents, indenting, indented**
To **indent** a line of writing or text is to start it further from the left side of the page than the other lines.
[**Indent** comes from Latin via French.]

**index** *noun* **indexes** *or* **indices**
An **index** is an alphabetical list of names or topics at the end of a book that tells you where to find them in the main part of the book.
[**Index** comes from Latin *index* 'pointer'.]

**indicate** *verb* **indicates, indicating, indicated** (th)
1 To **indicate** is to show or point to something: *The cabin crew will indicate the emergency exit closest to you.*
2 To **indicate** is to give a general idea about something: *The tests indicate nothing serious is wrong.*
3 If the driver of a vehicle **indicates**, s/he makes a signal to show that the vehicle is going to move to the left or right: *Drivers should always indicate before turning.*
[**Indicate** comes from Latin.]

**indifference** *noun* (th)
**Indifference** is a lack of interest or feeling towards a thing or person.
[**Indifference** comes from Latin *in-* 'not' and *differe* 'to separate' (ancestor of **difference**).]

**indifferent** *adjective* (th)
1 If you feel **indifferent** to something or someone, you are not interested in him/her or it or you do not care about him/her or it.
2 Something that is **indifferent** is not very good. **indifferently** *adverb*.
[**Indifferent** comes via French from Latin *in-* 'not' and *differe* (ancestor of **different**).]

a b c d e f g h **i** j k l m

**indigenous** *adjective*
A plant, animal or person that is **indigenous** to a particular place comes from there originally.
[**Indigenous** comes from Latin *indigena* 'a native'.]

**indigestion** *noun*
If you have **indigestion**, you have a pain in your stomach or chest because you are not digesting your food properly.
[**Indigestion** comes from Latin *in-* 'not' and *digerere* (ancestor of **digest**).]

**indignant** *adjective* (th)
Someone who is **indignant** is shocked or angry because s/he feels insulted or badly treated. **indignantly** *adverb*.
[**Indignant** comes from Latin *indignari* 'to be offended'.]

**indignity** *noun* **indignities**
An **indignity** is something that makes you feel humiliated or embarrassed.
[**Indignity** comes from the same Latin word as **indignant**.]

**indispensable** *adjective* (th)
If a person or a thing is **indispensable**, you cannot do without him/her or it. **indispensably** *adverb*.
[**Indispensable** comes from Latin.]

**indisposed** *adjective*
Someone who is **indisposed** is slightly ill.
[**Indisposed** comes from *in-* 'not' and *to be disposed* 'to feel like'.]

**individual** *adjective*
1 Something that is **individual** is single or separate: *Can you buy individual cans or do they only come in packs of six?*
2 Something that is **individual** is just for one person and is not shared: *I had individual lessons with the instructor.* **individually** *adverb*.
[**Individual** comes from Latin *individualis* 'not able to be divided'.]

**individual** *noun* **individuals**
An **individual** is one person.

**indoctrinate** *verb* **indoctrinates, indoctrinating, indoctrinated** (th)
To **indoctrinate** someone is to train that person to accept certain ideas or religious or political beliefs.
[**Indoctrinate** comes from *in-* 'into' and *doctrine* 'religious or political beliefs',

which comes from Latin.]

**indoor** *adjective*
used, or designed to be used, inside a building: *indoor fireworks.*

**indoors** *adverb*
in or into a building: *Let's go indoors.*

**induce** *verb* **induces, inducing, induced** (th)
1 To **induce** something means to make it happen: *These drugs induce sleep.*
2 To **induce** someone to do something means to influence or persuade him/her to do it.
[**Induce** comes from Latin *inducere* 'to lead in'.]

**indulge** *verb* **indulges, indulging, indulged** (th)
1 To **indulge** someone is to let that person have his/her own way: *Those parents indulge their children so much that they're spoiled brats.*
2 If you **indulge** yourself or **indulge in** something, you do something or treat yourself to something that gives you a lot of pleasure. **indulgently** *adverb*.
[**Indulge** comes from Latin.]

**industrious** *adjective* (th)
An **industrious** person works very hard. **industriously** *adverb*.
[**Industrious** comes via French from the same Latin word as **industry**.]

**industry** *noun* **industries**
1 **Industry** is the production of goods, especially in factories: *Shipbuilding is a heavy industry.*
2 An **industry** is a particular business that supplies goods and services: *Tourism is one of Spain's biggest industries.*
[**Industry** comes from Latin *industria* 'hard work'.]

**inedible** *adjective*
Something that is **inedible** is not suitable to be eaten.
[**Inedible** comes from *in-* 'not' and **edible**.]

**inefficient** *adjective* (th)
Something or someone that is **inefficient** does not work very well and wastes time and money. **inefficiently** *adverb*.
[**Inefficient** comes from *in-* 'not' and *efficient* 'effective', which comes from

Latin.]

**inert** *adjective*
1 Someone or something that is **inert** does not move or cannot move.
2 An **inert** substance does not react with other chemicals. **inertly** *adverb*.
[**Inert** comes from Latin *iners* 'idle'.]

**inertia** *noun* (th)
1 **Inertia** is the feeling of being unable to move or do something, especially because you feel weak, lazy or tired.
2 The **inertia** of an object is its resistance to a change in motion, which means that it is hard to make the object move when it is still, or hard to make it stop when it is moving.
[**Inertia** comes from the same Latin word as **inert**.]

**inevitable** *adjective* (th)
If something is **inevitable**, it is certain to happen: *Death is inevitable.*
**inevitably** *adverb*.
[**Inevitable** comes from Latin.]

**inexpensive** *adjective* (th)
Something that is **inexpensive** is cheap.
**inexpensively** *adverb*.
[**Inexpensive** comes from *in-* 'not' and **expensive**.]

**infallible** *adjective* (th)
1 Something that is **infallible** never fails.
2 Someone who is **infallible** never makes a mistake. **infallibly** *adverb*.
[**Infallible** comes from Latin.]

**infamous** *adjective* (th)
Something or someone that is **infamous** has a bad reputation: *an infamous criminal.*
[**Infamous** comes from Latin.]

**infant** *noun* **infants**
An **infant** is a very young child.
[**Infant** comes from Latin *infans* 'unable to speak'.]

**infantry** *noun* **infantries**
The **infantry** is the soldiers in the army who fight on foot.
[**Infantry** comes from Italian *infante* 'young man'.]

**infatuated** *adjective*
If you are **infatuated** with someone, you have strong feelings of love for that person which stop you from thinking sensibly.

[**Infatuated** comes from Latin *infatuare* 'to be made foolish'.]

**infection** *noun* **infections**
1 An **infection** is an illness caused by a germ or a virus that can be passed from one person or animal to another.
2 **Infection** is when a germ or virus gets into your body, or is passed from one person or animal to another: *the risk of infection in dirty and overcrowded houses.*
[**Infection** comes from Latin *inficere* 'to poison' or 'to stain'.]

**infectious** *adjective*
An **infectious** illness is one that you can catch from someone else. Flu, chickenpox and measles are all **infectious.**
[**Infectious** comes from the same Latin word as **infection**.]

**inferior** *adjective*
Something that is **inferior** is not as good as something similar.
[**Inferior** comes from Latin *inferior* 'lower'.]

**inflate** *verb* **inflates, inflating, inflated**
If you **inflate** something or if something **inflates**, it gets bigger because it is being filled with air or gas.
[**Inflate** comes from Latin *inflare* 'to blow into'.]

**inflation** *noun*
**Inflation** is when prices keep rising so that your money is not worth as much.
[**Inflation** comes from the same Latin word as **inflate**.]

**inflict** *verb* **inflicts, inflicting, inflicted**
If you **inflict** something unpleasant on someone, you make him/her suffer it: *It is wrong to inflict pain on animals; My sister's inflicting her horrible kids on me.*
[**Inflict** comes from Latin.]

**influence** *noun* **influences**
1 If you have **influence**, you have the power to persuade people to do what you want them to: *Her father used his influence to get her a job.*
2 An **influence** is an example that affects you or the way you do something: *She's a bad influence on you; My poetry was influenced by Wordsworth.*
3 If you are **under the influence** of something, it affects how you behave: *Under her aunt's influence she became a polite*

and charming young woman; driving while under the influence of drink.
[**Influence** comes from Latin *influentia* 'flowing in'.]

**influence** *verb* **influences, influencing, influenced**
To **influence** someone or something means to have an effect on them: *The teacher's advice influenced his decision.*

**inform** *verb* **informs, informing, informed**
To **inform** someone of something is to tell him/her about it formally or firmly: *She informed me that she had no intention of coming with me; You will be informed by letter when you are required to attend.*
[**Inform** comes from Latin.]

**information** *noun* (th)
**Information** is facts or knowledge: *Please tell the police if you have any information about the crime.*
[**Information** comes from the same Latin word as **inform**.]

**informative** *adjective*
Something that is **informative** gives you useful knowledge or information.
**informatively** *adverb*.
[**Informative** comes from the same Latin word as **inform**.]

**inhabitant** *noun* **inhabitants** (th)
An **inhabitant** of a place is someone who lives there.
[**Inhabitant** comes from Latin via French.]

**inhale** *verb* **inhales, inhaling, inhaled**
When you **inhale**, you breathe in: *Inhale through your nose; He had inhaled some smoke.*

**injure** *verb* **injures, injuring, injured** (th)
To **injure** means to hurt or harm a person, an animal or a part of the body: *Was anyone injured in the accident?*
[**Injure** comes from Latin.]

**ink** *noun* **inks**
**Ink** is the coloured liquid in pens used for writing and drawing.
[**Ink** comes from Greek via French and Latin.]

**in-laws** *plural noun*
Your **in-laws** are the family of your husband or wife.

**inn** *noun* **inns**
An **inn** is a small hotel or an old pub, especially in the country.
[**Inn** comes from Old English.]

**innocent** *adjective* (th)
**1** Someone who is **innocent** has not done anything bad.
**2** Someone who is **innocent** is not aware of unpleasant or bad things or people, and is easily shocked or fooled.
[**Innocent** comes from Latin.]

**inquire** *verb* **inquires, inquiring, inquired**
If you **inquire** about something, you ask for information about it.
[**Inquire** comes from Latin *in-* 'into' and *quaerere* 'to seek' (ancestor of **query**).]

**inquiry** *noun* **inquiries**
**1** An **inquiry** is a question you ask in order to get information about something.
**2** An **inquiry** is an official investigation into something.

**inscription** *noun* **inscriptions**
An **inscription** is words that are carved or engraved on something.
[**Inscription** comes from Latin.]

**insect** *noun* **insects**
**Insects** are small animals with no backbone, six legs, two pairs of wings, and a body that is divided into three parts. [**Insect** comes from Latin.]

**insensitive** *adjective* (th)
Someone who is **insensitive** does not notice or care about other people's feelings. **insensitively** *adverb*.
[**Insensitive** comes from *in-* 'not' and **sensitive**.]

**insensitivity** *noun*
**Insensitivity** is lack of concern about other people's feelings.

**insert** *verb* **inserts, inserting, inserted**
To **insert** something means to put it into something else: *insert the key in the lock; He inserted an extra paragraph in the letter.*
[**Insert** comes from Latin.]

**inside** *noun*
The **inside** of something is its inner part or surface: *I'll open the door from the inside.*

**inside** *adjective*
in or on the inner part or surface of something: *the inside pocket of my jacket.*

## inside *preposition*
within something else: *What's inside the box?*

## inside *adverb*
in or to the inner part of something: *Let's go inside – it's cold out here.*

## insist *verb* **insists, insisting, insisted**
1 To **insist** means to say very firmly that something is true, even though other people say that it isn't: *He insists that he is innocent.*
2 To **insist** or **insist on** something is to say firmly that it must happen or be done, even though someone else doesn't want it to: *The teacher insists on discipline in the school; We didn't want him to come, but he insisted.* [**Insist** comes from Latin.]

## inspect *verb* **inspects, inspecting, inspected**
To **inspect** something means to look at every part of it very carefully, especially to see whether anything is wrong. [**Inspect** comes from Latin.]

## inspire *verb* **inspires, inspiring, inspired**
1 To **inspire** someone to do something good means to make that person really want to do it: *A spell in hospital inspired her to be a nurse.*
2 To **inspire** something good is to be the reason that it happens or is made: *The case inspired a change in the law; The film was inspired by a true story.*
[**Inspire** comes via French from Latin *inspirare* 'to breathe into'.]

## instead *adverb* (th)
in place of something or someone else. [**Instead** comes from *in* and *stead* 'a place', which comes from Old English.]

## instep *noun* **insteps**
Your **instep** is the top part of your foot between your toes and your ankle. [No one knows where **instep** comes from.]

## instinct *noun* **instincts**
An **instinct** is behaviour that comes naturally and does not have to be learned. **instinctively** *adverb*. [**Instinct** comes from Latin.]

## instruction *noun* **instructions** (th)
1 **Instruction** is teaching: *They receive instruction in Mathematics and English.*
2 **Instructions** are words or diagrams that tell you how to do something. [**Instruction** comes from Latin *instruere* 'to prepare or equip'.]

## instrument *noun* **instruments**
1 An **instrument** is an object that you use to make musical sounds. Violins, trumpets and pianos are all musical instruments.
2 An **instrument** is a tool used for doing delicate or scientific work. [**Instrument** comes from the same Latin word as **instruction**.]

## insufficient *adjective* (th)
If something is **insufficient**, it is not enough or there is not enough of it. **insufficiently** *adverb*. [**Insufficient** comes from Latin via French.]

## insulate *verb* **insulates, insulating, insulated**
To **insulate** something is to cover it with material so that heat or electricity cannot escape from it. [**Insulate** comes from the same Latin word as **isolate**.]

## insult *verb* **insults, insulting, insulted** (th)
To **insult** someone is to do or say something that s/he finds rude and upsetting. **insultingly** *adverb*. [**Insult** comes from Latin *insultare* 'to jump or trample on'.]

## insurance *noun*
If you take out **insurance**, you pay money to a company so that it will give you money if something bad happens, for example if you are ill or if things get damaged or stolen. [**Insurance** comes from *insure*, an old spelling of **ensure**.]

## intelligence *noun*
**Intelligence** is the ability to think and to learn. [**Intelligence** comes from Latin *intelligere* 'to understand'.]

## intelligent *adjective* (th)
An **intelligent** person is clever and quick to learn. **intelligently** *adverb*.

## intelligible *adjective*
If something, especially speech or writing, is **intelligible**, it is possible to

understand it. **intelligibly** *adverb*.
[**Intelligible** comes from the same Latin word as **intelligence**.]

**intend** *verb* **intends, intending, intended** (th)
If you **intend** to do something, you mean to do it or plan to do it.
[**Intend** comes from Latin *intendere* 'to stretch or reach for'.]

**intense** *adjective* (th)
**1** A sensation or a feeling that is **intense** is very strong: *intense heat; intense happiness*.
**2** A person who is **intense** has very strong feelings about things.
[**Intense** comes from the same Latin word as **intend**.]

**intent** *adjective* (th)
If you are **intent on** doing something, you are determined to do it.
[**Intent** comes from the same Latin word as **intend**.]

**intentional** *adjective* (th)
If something is **intentional**, it is done on purpose: *I didn't mean to upset you – it wasn't intentional*. **intentionally** *adverb*.
[**Intentional** comes from the same Latin word as **intend**.]

**intercept** *verb* **intercepts, intercepting, intercepted**
To **intercept** something or someone is to stop them or catch them while they are moving from one place to another: *The police intercepted the terrorist at the airport*.
[**Intercept** comes from Latin.]

**interest** *verb* **interests, interesting, interested**
If something **interests** you, or if you are **interested in** something, you want to know more about it or to be more involved with it.
[**Interest** comes via French from Latin *interesse* 'to be important'.]

**interfere** *verb* **interferes, interfering, interfered** (th)
To **interfere** means to get involved with something that is someone else's business and not yours.
[**Interfere** comes from French.]

**interminable** *adjective*
Something that is **interminable** goes on and on and seems to have no end.

**interminably** *adverb*.
[**Interminable** comes from Latin *in-* 'not' and *terminare* 'to end' (ancestor of **terminal**).]

**international** *adjective*
Something that is **international** involves two or more countries.
**internationally** *adverb*.
[**International** comes from Latin *inter-* 'between' and English *national*, which comes from **nation**.]

**Internet** *noun* Also **internet**
The **Internet** is many small computer networks that connect together to form a larger network that covers the whole world. The **Internet** is often called the **Net** for short.
[**Internet** comes from Latin *inter-* 'between' and **net**.]

**interrupt** *verb* **interrupts, interrupting, interrupted** (th)
**1** To **interrupt** someone is to say or do something while s/he is speaking so that s/he has to stop.
**2** To **interrupt** is to stop something or someone for a short time: *The movie was interrupted by a newsflash*.
[**Interrupt** comes from Latin.]

**interview** *verb* **interviews, interviewing, interviewed**
To **interview** someone is to ask that person questions about a particular subject. [**Interview** comes from French.]

**intestine** *noun* **intestines**
Your **intestine** is the tube that carries food from your stomach after it has been digested. [**Intestine** comes from Latin.]

**into** *preposition*
To go **into** something is to go inside it, to go in its direction or to hit it. *They went into the shop to shelter from the rain*.

**intrepid** *adjective*
Someone who is **intrepid** is brave, adventurous and does not show fear.
[**Intrepid** comes from Latin *in-* 'not' and *trepidus* 'afraid'.]

**introduce** *verb* **introduces, introducing, introduced**
**1** To **introduce** people, or to **introduce** someone to someone else, means to bring them together for the first time and tell

them each other's names.

**2** To **introduce** something or someone means to tell an audience what they will see next: *Let me introduce the next act.*
[**Introduce** comes from Latin *intro-* 'towards' and *ducere* 'to lead'.]

**invent** *verb* **invents, inventing, invented** (th)
**1** To **invent** something means to create something, such as a machine or a way of doing something, that did not exist before.
**2** To **invent** something means to make up something that is not true: *He invented some excuse, but we didn't believe him.*
[**Invent** comes from Latin.]

**invention** *noun* **inventions**
An **invention** is something that has been created by someone for the first time.

**inventor** *noun* **inventors**
An **inventor** is a person who creates something that has never been created before.

**invertebrate** *noun* **invertebrates**
An **invertebrate** is an animal without a backbone. Insects and creatures like slugs and snails are **invertebrates**.
[**Invertebrate** comes from Latin.]

**investigate** *verb* **investigates, investigating, investigated** (th)
To **investigate** something is to find out all the facts about it or the causes of it.
[**Investigate** comes from Latin.]

**invisible** *adjective*
Something that is **invisible** cannot be seen. **invisibly** *adverb*.
[**Invisible** comes from *in-* 'not' and **visible**.]

**invitation** *noun* **invitations**
An **invitation** is a request to go somewhere or do something.
[**Invitation** comes from Latin.]

**invite** *verb* **invites, inviting, invited**
To **invite** someone is to ask him/her to come somewhere or do something.
[**Invite** comes from the same Latin word as **invitation**.]

**iron** *noun* **irons**
**1 Iron** is a hard grey metal that is used to make steel.
**2** An **iron** is a household appliance that

you use to get the creases out of clothes.
[**Iron** comes from Old English.]

**irregular** *adjective* (th)
**1** Something that is **irregular** is not even or regular.
**2** Something that is **irregular** does not follow the usual rules. **irregularly** *adverb*.
[**Irregular** comes from Latin *ir-* 'not' and *regularis* (ancestor of **regular**).]

**irrelevant** *adjective*
Something that is **irrelevant** is not important or has nothing to do with a particular thing.
[**Irrelevant** comes from Latin *ir-* 'not' and **relevant**.]

**irresponsible** *adjective* (th)
A person who you cannot trust to be responsible is **irresponsible**.
[**Irresponsible** comes from *ir-* 'not' and **responsible**.]

**irrigate** *verb* **irrigates, irrigating, irrigated**
To **irrigate** means to supply water to land using channels or pipes.
[**Irrigate** comes from Latin *rigare* 'to water'.]

**irrigation** *noun*
**Irrigation** is supplying water to land using channels or pipes.

**Islam** *noun*
**Islam** is the religion of the Muslims, based on the teachings of the Prophet Muhammad. Muslims believe in one God, who is called Allah.
[**Islam** comes from Arabic *islam* 'submission to God'.]

**island** *noun* **islands**
An **island** is land with water all round it.
[**Island** comes from Old English.]

**isolate** *verb* **isolates, isolating, isolated** (th)
To **isolate** means to keep someone or something separate from other people or things.
[**Isolate** comes via French and Italian from Latin *insulare* 'to make into an island'.]

**isosceles** *adjective*
An **isosceles** triangle is a triangle that has two sides of equal length.
[**Isosceles** comes from Greek *iso-* 'equal'

and *skelos* 'leg'.]

**isthmus** *noun* **isthmuses**
An **isthmus** is a narrow strip of land that connects two larger areas of land.
[**Isthmus** comes from Greek.]

**it** *pronoun*
**1** You use **it** to talk about something that has already been mentioned. **It** can be the subject or the object of a verb: *I'd like a holiday but it would cost too much.*
**2** You use **it** to talk about the weather: *Is it going to rain?* [**It** comes from Old English.]

**italic** *noun, adjective*
**Italic** is a style of writing or printing in which the letters slope to the right, *like this.*
[**Italic** comes via Latin from Greek *Italikos* 'Italian', because italic writing was first used in Italy.]

**itinerary** *noun* **itineraries** (th)
An **itinerary** is a list of all the details of a journey such as how, where and when you are travelling.
[**Itinerary** comes from Latin.]

**its** *pronoun*
belonging or to do with it: *The shop has cut its prices.*

**it's** *abbreviation*
**It's** is short for **it is**.

**itself** *pronoun*
**1** You use **itself** when you are talking about something that is the object of a verb of which it is also the subject: *The company has made itself very unpopular.*
**2** You can use **itself** to emphasise something or to make it clear what you are talking about: *The house itself is lovely, but the garden's a mess.*
[**Itself** comes from Old English.]

**ivory** *noun*
**1 Ivory** is the hard substance that elephants' tusks are made of. It was used in the past to make piano keys and other things.
**2 Ivory** is the creamy white colour of elephants' tusks.
[**Ivory** comes from Latin via French.]

**ivory** *adjective*
**1** made of ivory: *an ivory handle.*
**2** of the colour of ivory: *a dress of ivory satin.*

**ivy** *noun* **ivies**
**Ivy** is an evergreen plant with pointed leaves that climbs up walls or buildings.
[**Ivy** comes from Old English.]

# Dictionary Fun

**Work it out**
These words are anagrams: one, beginning with 'i' which means a religious painting, the other beginning with 'c' is a metal disc used as money. What are they?

**Etymology**
Why are the words **impractical** and **implicate** related to each other but not to **imperfect**?

Which word comes from Latin *inficere* 'to poison' or 'to stain'?

**Complete the simile**
As cold as i_____.

**Did you know?**
◆ The word **italic** comes from the Greek word *Italikos* which means 'Italian', because the sloping writing was first used in Italy.

**Brainteaser**
Some months have 30 days. Some have 31 days. How many have 28 days?

# Jj

**jab** *verb* **jabs, jabbing, jabbed** (th)
To **jab** means to poke something roughly.
[No one knows where **jab** comes from.]

**jack** *noun* **jacks**
1 A **jack** is a tool for raising a car or other vehicle, often to change a tyre.
2 A **jack** is a playing card with a picture of a young man on it. The value of a **jack** is between a ten and a queen.
[**Jack** comes from the name *Jack*, short for *John*.]

**jackal** *noun* **jackals**
A **jackal** is a kind of wild dog from Africa and Asia that eats dead animals.
[**Jackal** comes via Turkish from Persian (the language spoken in Iran).]

**jacket** *noun* **jackets**
1 A **jacket** is a kind of short coat.
2 A **jacket** is something that you put over or around something to protect it: *a book jacket.*
[**Jacket** comes from an old French word.]

**jackpot** *noun* **jackpots**
The **jackpot** is the biggest prize in a competition.
[A **jackpot** was originally a prize in a card game that you could only win if you played two jacks.]

**jade** *noun*
**Jade** is a valuable hard green stone that is used to make jewellery and ornaments.
[**Jade** comes from Spanish.]

**jagged** *adjective* (th)
Something that is **jagged** has a sharp, uneven or rough edge.
[**Jagged** comes from Scots *jag* 'to stab'.]

**jaguar** *noun* **jaguars**
A **jaguar** is a large wild animal of the cat family from South or Central America. It has a brown or yellow coat with black spots and is similar to a leopard.
[**Jaguar** comes via Portuguese from Tupi-Guarani (a South American Indian language).]

**jail** *noun* **jails** *Also* **gaol**
A **jail** is a prison where people must stay as a punishment.
[**Jail** comes from an old French word.]

**jam** *noun* **jams**
1 **Jam** is food made from fruit boiled with sugar.
2 A **jam** is a lot of people or cars crowded together so that they can hardly move.
[No one knows where **jam** comes from.]

**jam** *verb* **jams, jamming, jammed**
To **jam** means to become fixed or stuck tight: *The window is jammed.*

**jangle** *verb* **jangles, jangling, jangled**
To **jangle** means to make a hard ringing sound like a lot of metal objects banging lightly together.
[**Jangle** comes from an old French word.]

**jar¹** *noun* **jars**
A **jar** is a container, usually made of glass.
[**Jar¹** comes from Arabic via French.]

**jar²** *verb* **jars, jarring, jarred**
To **jar** means to have an unpleasant effect or make an unpleasant sound.
[The word **jar²** is probably an imitation of the sound.]

**jargon** *noun*
**Jargon** is words and phrases used about a particular subject or in a particular job that other people cannot easily understand: *technical jargon.*
[**Jargon** comes from Italian via French.]

**javelin** *noun* **javelins**
A **javelin** is a long light spear. Throwing the **javelin** is an athletics event.
[**Javelin** comes from an old French word.]

**jaw** *noun* **jaws**
Your **jaw** is a bone in the lower part of your face that holds your teeth.
[**Jaw** comes from an old French word.]

**jazz** *noun*
**Jazz** is a type of music with strong lively rhythms that was first created by African Americans in the United States.
[No one knows where the word **jazz** comes from.]

**jealous** *adjective*
If you are **jealous**, you feel bad because you want what someone else has.
[**Jealous** comes from Latin via French.]

**jealousy** *noun*
**Jealousy** is a bad feeling of wanting what someone else has.

**jeans** *plural noun*
**Jeans** are strong casual trousers made of a blue cotton material called denim.
[**Jeans** comes from *Genoa*, the name of a city in Italy where a similar kind of cloth was made.]

**Jeep** *noun* **Jeeps**
A **Jeep** is the tradename of a vehicle for driving over rough roads or through the country.
[**Jeep** comes from the initials *GP*, which stood for *general purpose*.]

**jeer** *verb* **jeers, jeering, jeered** (th)
To **jeer** means to make fun of someone in an unpleasant or noisy way.
[No one knows where **jeer** comes from.]

**jelly** *noun* **jellies**
**Jelly** is a soft pudding, usually coloured and flavoured with fruit. **Jelly** can be moulded into shapes.
[**Jelly** comes from Latin *gelare* 'to freeze'.]

**jellyfish** *noun* **jellyfish**
A **jellyfish** is a creature that lives in the sea. It has a body like jelly and tentacles that can sting you.

**jeopardy** *noun* (th)
Someone or something that is **in jeopardy** is in danger or at risk.
[**Jeopardy** comes from an old French word.]

**jerk** *verb* **jerks, jerking, jerked** (th)
To **jerk** means to move suddenly and not smoothly.
[No one knows where **jerk** comes from.]

**jersey** *noun* **jerseys**
A **jersey** is a knitted jumper.
[**Jersey** was originally a kind of woollen cloth made on the island of *Jersey*.]

**jester** *noun* **jesters**
A **jester** was a person in the Middle Ages who entertained a royal court with stories, jokes and music.
[**Jester** comes from *jest* 'joke', which comes from Latin.]

**jet** *noun* **jets**
**1** A **jet** is a liquid or gas that comes forcefully out of a small opening.
**2** A **jet** is a plane powered by engines that push hot air and gases out at the back to make the plane move forward.
[**Jet** comes from French *jeter* 'to throw'.]

**jetty** *noun* **jetties** (th)
A **jetty** is a platform that stretches into the sea and is used as a place for people to get on or off boats.
[**Jetty** comes from French.]

**Jew** *noun* **Jews**
A **Jew** is a person whose ancestors came from the ancient tribes of Israel, or whose religion is Judaism.
[**Jew** comes via French, Latin and Greek from Hebrew *jehudah* 'Judah', the name of one of the tribes of Israel. Hebrew is the language spoken in Israel.]

**jewel** *noun* **jewels**
A **jewel** is a precious beautiful stone such as a diamond or a ruby.
[**Jewel** comes from an old French word.]

**jeweller** *noun* **jewellers**
A **jeweller** is a person whose job is making or selling jewellery.

**jewellery** *noun* Also **jewelry**
**Jewellery** is ornaments that people wear such as rings, bracelets or necklaces.
[**Jewellery** comes from the same old French word as **jewel**.]

**jig** *noun* **jigs**
A **jig** is a lively folk dance: *an Irish jig*.
[No one knows where **jig** comes from.]

**jigsaw** *noun* **jigsaws**
A **jigsaw** is a puzzle made of pieces that fit together to form a picture.
[**Jigsaw** comes from **jig** (in the sense 'to jerk up and down or from side to side') and **saw¹**.]

**jingle** *noun* **jingles**
**1** A **jingle** is the tinkling or clinking sound made by a small bell or by small metal objects such as keys shaken together.
**2** A **jingle** is a short song that is easy to remember, used to advertise something on radio or television.
[The word **jingle** is an imitation of the sound.]

**jingle** *verb* **jingles, jingling, jingled** (th)
To **jingle** means to make a tinkling or clinking sound like a small bell or like coins being shaken together.

**jinx** *noun* **jinxes**
A **jinx** is something that someone believes brings bad luck.

[No one knows where **jinx** comes from.]

**job** *noun* **jobs** (th)
1 Your **job** is the work that you do to earn money.
2 A **job** is a piece of work that a person has to do.
[No one knows where **job** comes from.]

**jockey** *noun* **jockeys**
A **jockey** is a person who rides horses in horse races.
[**Jockey** comes from the name *Jock*, the Scots form of *Jack*.]

**jodhpurs** *plural noun*
**Jodhpurs** are trousers that you wear for riding horses. They are loose around the top of the leg and tight below the knee.
[**Jodhpurs** are named after the city of *Jodhpur* in India, where similar trousers are worn.]

**jog** *verb* **jogs, jogging, jogged**
1 To **jog** means to run at a slow steady pace, especially as a form of physical exercise.
2 To **jog** means to accidentally knock or bump someone or something.
3 If something **jogs your memory**, it makes you remember something.
[**Jog** is a different spelling of Scots *jag* 'to stab' (ancestor of **jagged**).]

**join** *verb* **joins, joining, joined**
1 To **join** two things means to fasten or fix them together.
2 To **join** a group or club means to become a member of it.
3 To **join** means to go somewhere so that you can be with or do something with someone else: *I'll join you later.*
4 To **join** means to meet or connect: *Where do the two rivers join?*
[**Join** comes from Latin via French.]

**joint** *noun* **joints**
1 A **joint** is a point in the body where two bones fit together: *the knee joint.*
2 A **joint** of meat is a large piece of it.
[**Joint** comes from the same French word as **join**.]

**joint** *adjective* (th)
Something that is **joint** is shared or done by two people equally. **jointly** *adverb*.

**joist** *noun* **joists**
A **joist** is a beam of wood or metal that is used to support a floor or a ceiling.
[**Joist** comes from an old French word.]

**joke** *noun* **jokes**
A **joke** is something that someone says or does in order to make people laugh.
[**Joke** probably comes from Latin.]

**joke** *verb* **jokes, joking, joked**
To **joke** means to say or do something in order to make people laugh.

**joker** *noun* **jokers**
A **joker** is a playing card that does not belong to any of the four suits, and has a special value in some card games.
[The **joker** is so called because it usually has a picture of a jester on it.]

**jolt** *verb* **jolts, jolting, jolted** (th)
1 To **jolt** means to move suddenly and sharply, causing bumps and knocks.
2 If something **jolts** you, it gives you an unpleasant surprise.
[No one knows where **jolt** comes from.]

**jostle** *verb* **jostles, jostling, jostled** (th)
To **jostle** means to push and bump into people as you are moving forward.
[**Jostle** comes from *jost*, an old spelling of **joust**.]

**joule** *noun* **joules**
A **joule** is a unit that measures energy or the amount of work done.
[**Joule** is named after J. P. *Joule*, a scientist who studied energy and heat.]

**journal** *noun* **journals**
1 A **journal** is a diary in which you write each day about your activities and feelings.
2 A **journal** is a weekly or monthly magazine that deals with a serious subject.
[**Journal** comes via French from Latin *diurnal* 'by day'.]

**journalist** *noun* **journalists** (th)
A **journalist** is a person whose job is writing articles for newspapers and magazines.

**journey** *noun* **journeys** (th)
If you go on a **journey**, you travel from one place to another.
[**Journey** comes from old French *jornee* 'a day's travel'.]

**joust** *noun* **jousts**
A **joust** was a contest in the Middle Ages

between two knights on horseback who were armed with long weapons called lances.
[**Joust** comes from an old French word.]

**joy** *noun* **joys** (th)
**1 Joy** is a feeling of great happiness.
**2** A **joy** is something that makes you feel very happy.
[**Joy** comes from an old French word.]

**jubilant** *adjective* (th)
Someone who is **jubilant** is very happy because s/he has been successful at something.
[**Jubilant** comes from Latin *jubilare* 'to shout with joy'.]

**jubilee** *noun* **jubilees**
A **jubilee** is a celebration that takes place on the anniversary of something important that happened in the past.
[**Jubilee** comes via French and Latin from Hebrew *yobel*, a year in which slaves were freed and some property was returned to its former owners, held once every fifty years in ancient Israel, where Hebrew was spoken. *Yobel* originally meant 'ram'; a ram's horn was blown at the beginning of the jubilee year.]

**Judaism** *noun*
**Judaism** is the religion of the Jewish people. It is based on the belief that there is one God who revealed his laws to the ancient Israelites, whose story is told in the Old Testament of the Bible.
[**Judaism** comes via Latin from Greek *Ioudaios* 'Jew'.]

**judge** *noun* **judges**
A **judge** is a person who decides the result either in a court of law or in a competition. [**Judge** comes from Latin.]

**judge** *verb* **judges, judging, judged** (th)
To **judge** means to decide the result in a court of law, a competition or an argument.

**judgement** *noun* **judgements** *Also* **judgment** (th)
**1** A **judgement** is a decision made by a judge in a court or in a competition.
**2 Judgement** is the ability to decide the result of something.
**3** A **judgement** is an opinion that you give after thinking carefully about something.

**judo** *noun*
**Judo** is a Japanese sport or form of self-defence in which two people fight each other with controlled movements and try to throw each other to the ground.
[**Judo** comes from Japanese *ju do* 'the gentle way', because the fighters are not supposed to hurt each other.]

**jug** *noun* **jugs**
A **jug** is a container used for holding and pouring liquids.
[**Jug** may come from the name *Joan* or *Jenny*.]

**juggernaut** *noun* **juggernauts**
A **juggernaut** is a very large truck.
[**Juggernaut** comes from the name of a Hindu god whose statue was pulled through the streets on a heavy cart.]

**juggle** *verb* **juggles, juggling, juggled**
To **juggle** means to keep several objects moving in the air by throwing them up and catching them one after the other.
[**Juggle** comes from Latin via French.]

**juggler** *noun* **jugglers**
A **juggler** is someone who entertains people by juggling balls, clubs or other objects.

**juice** *noun* **juices**
**Juice** is the liquid that comes out of fruit and vegetables. [**Juice** comes from Latin.]

**juicy** *adjective* **juicier, juiciest**
A fruit that is **juicy** has lots of juice.

**jukebox** *noun* **jukeboxes**
A **jukebox** is a machine that plays a record when you put money into it.
[**Juke** comes from Gullah (a West African language).]

**jumbo jet** *noun* **jumbo jets**
A **jumbo jet** is a very large plane that can carry hundreds of passengers.
[**Jumbo** was the name of a huge elephant at London Zoo in the 19th century, and so came to be used for something that is very big.]

**jump** *verb* **jumps, jumping, jumped** (th)
**1** To **jump** means to move into the air quickly by bending your knees and pushing with your legs: *She jumped off the wall; The cat jumped onto my lap.*
**2** If you **jump up** or **jump to your feet**, you get up suddenly and quickly.

**3** If something **makes you jump**, it startles you so that you make a sudden movement.
[No one knows where **jump** comes from.]

**junction** *noun* **junctions**
A **junction** is a place where roads or railway lines meet or cross each other.
[**Junction** comes from Latin.]

**jungle** *noun* **jungles**
A **jungle** is a thick forest in a hot country.
[**Jungle** comes from Hindi (an Indian language).]

**junior** *adjective*
**1** A person who is **junior** to someone else is younger or in a less important position.
**2** Something that is for children or young people up to the age of 16 is **junior**: *a junior tennis champion*.
[**Junior** comes from Latin *junior* 'younger'.]

**junk¹** *noun* (th)
**Junk** is things that you do not want.
[No one knows where **junk¹** comes from.]

**junk²** *noun* **junks**
A **junk** is a Chinese sailing boat.
[**Junk²** comes via French or Portuguese from Malay (a language spoken in Malaysia).]

**jury** *noun* **juries**
A **jury** is a group of people who have been chosen to listen to a trial in a court of law and decide whether the person accused of a crime is guilty or innocent.
[**Jury** comes from Latin.]

**just** *adjective* (th)
Something that is **just** is fair: *a just verdict*.
[**Just** comes from Latin via French.]

**just** *adverb* (th)
**1** exactly: *That present was just what I wanted!*
**2** recently or at this moment: *The plane's just landed.*
**3** only: *There's just one ticket left.*

**justice** *noun* (th)
**1 Justice** is the process of law that makes sure things are done in a fair way.
**2 Justice** is when something is fair and right.
[**Justice** comes from Latin via French.]

**justify** *verb* **justifies, justifying, justified** (th)
To **justify** something means to give a reason to show why it is fair or necessary.
[**Justify** comes via French from the same Latin word as **justice**.]

**juvenile** *adjective*
Something that is **juvenile** involves young people who are not yet legally adults: *juvenile crime*.
[**Juvenile** comes from Latin *juvenis* 'a young person'.]

---

# Dictionary Fun

## Etymology
The word **jodhpur** is named after a town in Asia: which country in Jodhpur in? Use an atlas if you do not know!

## Did you know?
◆ The phrase Jack the Lad, which means a carefree young man, was the nickname of Jack Sheppard, an 18th century thief in Britain.

◆ The word **judo** comes from Japanese *ju + do*, which means *gentle way*.

◆ The word **jubilee** comes from a Hebrew word which means ram. Originally a ram's horn was blown at the beginning of the jubilee.

## Brainteaser
Two girls played badminton. They played three games. Each girl won two games. How do you explain this?

a b c d e f g h i **j** k l m

# Kk

**kaleidoscope** *noun* **kaleidoscopes**
A **kaleidoscope** is a tube with mirrors and loose coloured pieces that you look through and see pretty patterns that change when you turn it.
[**Kaleidoscope** comes from Greek.]

**kangaroo** *noun* **kangaroos**
A **kangaroo** is a large Australian animal that carries its young in a pouch and moves by jumping along on its strong back legs.
[**Kangaroo** comes from an Australian Aboriginal word.]

**karaoke** *noun*
**Karaoke** is a form of entertainment where people sing well-known songs to a pre-recorded background.
[**Karaoke** comes from Japanese *kara oke* 'empty orchestra'.]

**karate** *noun*
**Karate** is a Japanese sport or form of self-defence in which two people fight each other with controlled movements, especially kicks with the feet and chopping movements with the hands.
[**Karate** comes from Japanese *kara te* 'empty hand'.]

**kayak** *noun* **kayaks**
A **kayak** is a narrow covered canoe that one person can sit in and move through the water by using a paddle with a blade at each end.
[**Kayak** comes from an Inuit word. The Inuit are the native people of Greenland and north-west Canada.]

**keen** *adjective* **keener, keenest**
If you are **keen** on something, you are enthusiastic about it: *a keen football fan.*
**keenly** *adverb.* **keenness** *noun.*
[**Keen** comes from Old English.]

**keep** *verb* **keeps, keeping, kept** (th)
**1** To **keep** means to have something and not give it away: *Are you going to keep these books?*
**2** To **keep** doing something means to continue doing it: *The phone kept ringing all day.*
**3** To **keep** means to make something stay the same: *The drinks will keep cool in the ice-box.* [**Keep** comes from Old English.]

**keg** *noun* **kegs** (th)
A **keg** is a round container like a small barrel for storing liquids.
[**Keg** comes from Old Norse.]

**kennel** *noun* **kennels**
A **kennel** is a small hut for a dog to live in.
[**Kennel** comes via French from Latin *canis* 'dog' (ancestor of **canine**).]

**kerb** *noun* **kerbs**
A **kerb** is the line of stones or concrete along the edge of a pavement.
[**Kerb** comes from an old French word.]

**ketchup** *noun*
**Ketchup** is a thick sauce, usually made from tomatoes, vinegar and vegetables: *tomato ketchup.*
[**Ketchup** probably comes from Cantonese, a Chinese language.]

**kettle** *noun* **kettles**
A **kettle** is a container for boiling water.
[**Kettle** comes from Old English.]

**key** *noun* **keys**
**1** A **key** is a piece of metal that you fit into a lock and turn to undo it.
**2** A **key** is a kind of button or bar that you press on a piano, typewriter or computer.
**3** A **key** is a set of musical notes based around one note: *the key of C.*
[**Key** comes from Old English.]

**key** *verb* **keys, keying, keyed**
To **key** means to write on a computer by pressing the letters on the keyboard.

**keyboard** *noun* **keyboards**
A **keyboard** is the set of keys that you press on a piano, typewriter or computer.

**keyhole** *noun* **keyholes**
A **keyhole** is the hole which you put a key in to open or close a lock.

**khaki** *noun*
**Khaki** is a yellowish-brown colour, like mud, that is often used in soldiers' uniforms.
[**Khaki** comes from Urdu (a language spoken in India and Pakistan).]

**khaki** *adjective*
of a muddy yellowish-brown colour: *soldiers in khaki uniforms.*

**kick** *verb* **kicks, kicking, kicked**
To **kick** means to hit out or hit something

with one or both feet.
[No one knows where **kick** comes from.]

**kid** *noun* **kids**
1 A **kid** is a young goat.
2 A **kid** is a child. The word **kid** is mainly used in speaking.
[**Kid** comes from Old Norse.]

**kid** *verb* **kids, kidding, kidded**
To **kid** means to tell someone something that is not true, as a joke: *He tried to kid me that there's no school today.*

**kidnap** *verb* **kidnaps, kidnapping, kidnapped** (th)
To **kidnap** someone means to take that person away by force and keep him/her as a prisoner until some money is paid or a demand is met.
[**Kidnap** comes from **kid** and an old word *napper* 'thief'.]

**kidney** *noun* **kidneys**
A **kidney** is one of a pair of organs in your body that remove waste from your blood and turn it into urine.
[No one knows where **kidney** comes from.]

**kill** *verb* **kills, killing, killed** (th)
To **kill** means to make someone or something die.
[**Kill** probably comes from Old English.]

**kilogram** *noun* **kilograms**
A **kilogram** is a unit of weight in the metric system that is equal to 1000 grams.
[**Kilogram** comes from Greek *khilioi* 'a thousand' and **gram**.]

**kilometre** *noun* **kilometres**
A **kilometre** is a unit of distance in the metric system that is equal to 1000 metres.
[**Kilometre** comes from Greek *khilioi* 'a thousand' and **metre**.]

**kilt** *noun* **kilts**
A **kilt** is a pleated skirt made of tartan material that is often worn in Scotland.
[**Kilt** probably comes from a Scandinavian language.]

**kind** *noun* **kinds** (th)
A **kind** of something is a sort or type of that thing: *What kind of music do you like?*
[**Kind** comes from Old English.]

**kind** *adjective* (th)
Someone who is helpful and loving is

**kind**: *He is always kind to animals.*
**kindly** *adverb*.

**kindness** *noun* (th)
**Kindness** is when someone is helpful and loving: *Peter showed me great kindness when my cat died.*

**king** *noun* **kings** (th)
1 A **king** is a man who has been crowned as ruler of a country.
2 A **king** is a playing card with a picture of a man on it. It is worth one more point than a queen.
3 The **king** is the most important piece in the game of chess.
[**King** comes from Old English.]

**kingdom** *noun* **kingdoms** (th)
1 A **kingdom** is a country that has a king or queen as its ruler.
2 A **kingdom** is one of the large groups of things in nature: *the animal kingdom.*
[**Kingdom** comes from Old English.]

**kingfisher** *noun* **kingfishers**
A **kingfisher** is a small brightly coloured bird that dives into water to catch fish for food.

**kiosk** *noun* **kiosks**
A **kiosk** is a stall that sells newspapers, food, tickets or other things, in the street or inside a building such as a cinema.
[**Kiosk** comes via French and Turkish from Persian (the language spoken in Iran).]

**kiss** *verb* **kisses, kissing, kissed**
To **kiss** means to touch someone with your lips as a greeting or to show that you like or love that person.
[**Kiss** comes from Old English.]

**kit** *noun* **kits** (th)
1 A **kit** is a set of tools, clothing or things that you need for a sport or activity: *football kit.*
2 A **kit** is a set of pieces or parts that you fix together to make something: *The dolls' house comes in a kit.*
[**Kit** comes from an old Dutch word.]

**kitchen** *noun* **kitchens**
A **kitchen** is a room where food is stored, prepared and cooked.
[**Kitchen** comes from Old English.]

**kite** *noun* **kites**
A **kite** is a frame covered with a light

material and joined to a long piece of string so that it can be flown in the wind. [**Kite** comes from Old English.]

**kitten** *noun* **kittens**
A **kitten** is a young cat.
[**Kitten** comes from an old French word.]

**kiwi fruit** *noun* **kiwi fruits**
A **kiwi fruit** is an oval fruit with thin, brown, furry skin and sweet green flesh. [The **kiwi fruit** was named after the *kiwi*, a New Zealand bird, because the fruit was originally imported from New Zealand.]

**knack** *noun* (th)
A **knack** is a special skill or way of doing something: *She has the knack of always saying the right thing.*
[No one knows where **knack** comes from.]

**knead** *verb* **kneads, kneading, kneaded** (th)
To **knead** bread dough means to stretch and punch it so that it is smooth before leaving it to rise.
[**Knead** comes from Old English.]

**knee** *noun* **knees**
Your **knee** is the joint in the middle of your leg where it bends.
[**Knee** comes from Old English.]

**kneel** *verb* **kneels, kneeling, kneeled**
To **kneel** means to bend your legs and rest your weight on your knees.
[**Kneel** comes from Old English.]

**knew** *verb*
**Knew** is the past tense of **know**.

**knick-knack** *noun* **knick-knacks** (th)
A **knick-knack** is a small object used as an ornament or souvenir.
[**Knick-knack** probably comes from an old Dutch word.]

**knife** *noun* **knives**
A **knife** is a tool with a sharp blade for cutting things.
[**Knife** comes from Old English.]

**knight** *noun* **knights**
**1** A **knight** was a man in the Middle Ages who fought on horseback and wore armour.
**2** A **knight** is a piece in chess with a horse's head.

[**Knight** comes from Old English.]

**knit** *verb* **knits, knitting, knitted**
To **knit** means to make clothing out of wool by looping it round a pair of pointed thin sticks called knitting needles. [**Knit** comes from Old English.]

**knitwear** *noun*
**Knitwear** is clothing made out of knitted material, especially wool.

**knob** *noun* **knobs**
A **knob** is a round handle.
[**Knob** comes from an old German word.]

**knobbly** *adjective* **knobblier, knobbliest** (th)
Something that is **knobbly** is bony and bumpy: *knobbly knees.*

**knock** *verb* **knocks, knocking, knocked** (th)
**1** To **knock** means to hit something or bump into it.
**2** To **knock** someone **out** means to hit that person so hard that s/he becomes unconscious.
[**Knock** comes from Old English.]

**knot** *noun* **knots**
**1** A **knot** is a place in a piece of string, rope or ribbon where the end has been passed through a loop and pulled tight. A **knot** can be used to join two pieces of string, rope or ribbon together.
**2** A **knot** is a small hard area in a tree or a piece of wood where a branch used to grow. [**Knot** comes from Old English.]

**knot** *verb* **knots, knotting, knotted**
To **knot** something means to fasten it with a knot: *She knotted the scarf round her neck.*

**know** *verb* **knows, knowing, knew, known** (th)
**1** To **know** something means to have learned something and have it in your mind.
**2** If you **know** someone, you have met that person before.
[**Know** comes from Old English.]

**knowledge** *noun* (th)
**Knowledge** is information that you have learned and remembered.
[**Knowledge** comes from Old English.]

**knowledgeable** *adjective*
If you are **knowledgeable** about

something, you know a lot about it: *He is very knowledgeable about aircraft.*

**knuckle** *noun* **knuckles**
Your **knuckles** are the joints in your fingers, especially where your fingers join your hands.
[**Knuckle** comes from an old German word.]

**koala** *noun* **koalas**
A **koala** is a furry Australian animal that lives in trees and looks like a small bear.
[**Koala** is an Australian Aboriginal word.]

**Koran** *noun* *Also* **Qur'an**
The **Koran** is the holy book of Islam, the Muslim religion.
[**Koran** comes from Arabic *kur'an* 'reading aloud'.]

**kosher** *adjective*
Food that is **kosher** has been prepared according to the laws of the Jewish religion.
[**Kosher** comes from Hebrew *kasher* 'proper'. Hebrew is the language spoken in Israel.]

---

# Dictionary Fun

**What do these idioms mean?**
1. Keep your hair on!
2. A kick in the teeth
3. Dressed to kill

**Etymology**
Which word comes via French from Latin *canis* 'dog'?

**Riddles**
What 'k' word has a head like a cat and a tail like a cat but is not a cat?

I may look a hero
But I sound like the night
I may fight with a sword
But a move has more bite
Which 'k' word am I?

**Work it out**
1. What do these words have in common? **knit, knight, know**
2. There are two Australian animals in the 'k' section. What are they?

**Did you know?**
♦ **Kiwi fruit** is also called *Chinese gooseberry.*
♦ People are born with two **kidneys,** but we can live with just one. Surgeons can remove one kidney and give it to someone else who needs it.

**Brainteaser**
Barbara always tells the truth, her sister, Melissa, never tells the truth. One sister says, "My sister says she's Barbara." Which one was it?

a b c d e f g h i j **k** l m

# Ll

**label** *noun* **labels** (th)

A **label** is a piece of card or paper with writing on it that is put on something to show what it is, what it costs, whose it is or where it is going.
[**Label** comes from an old French word.]

**label** *verb* **labels, labelling, labelled**

To **label** something means to attach a label to it.

**laboratory** *noun* **laboratories**

A **laboratory** is a place where scientific experiments are done.
[**Laboratory** comes from Latin *laboratorium* 'workplace'.]

**labour** *noun* (th)

**1 Labour** is hard physical work.
**2 Labour** is the process of giving birth to a baby.
[**Labour** comes from Latin via French.]

**labourer** *noun* **labourers**

A **labourer** is a person whose job is doing physical work usually outdoors.

**Labrador** *noun* **Labradors**

A **Labrador** is a breed of dog with a black or golden coat.
[The **Labrador** was named after *Labrador* in eastern Canada, where it was bred.]

**labyrinth** *noun* **labyrinths**

A **labyrinth** is a set of tunnels or passages where it is easy to get lost.
[**Labyrinth** was the name of the maze that Theseus had to go into (look under **clue**).]

**lace** *noun* **laces**

**1 Lace** is a delicate pretty material with a pattern of small holes in it.
**2 Laces** are thin cords for tying up shoes.
[**Lace** comes from Latin via French.]

**lack** *noun* (th)

A **lack** of something is when there is not enough of it: *a lack of water.*
[**Lack** comes from an old German or Dutch word.]

**ladder** *noun* **ladders**

A **ladder** is two long pieces of wood or metal with bars going across it, used for climbing up or down.
[**Ladder** comes from Old English.]

**laden** *adjective*

Someone or something that is laden with things is carrying a lot: *The ship was laden with treasure.*
[**Laden** comes from Old English.]

**ladle** *noun* **ladles**

A **ladle** is a very large spoon used for serving soup.
[**Ladle** comes from Old English.]

**lady** *noun* **ladies**

**1** A **lady** is a polite word for a woman: *Ask that lady where the bus stop is.*
**2** A **lady** is a woman who is very polite and dignified: *She's a real lady!*
**3** A **lady/Lady** is the wife or widow of a lord, or a woman with a rank equal to that of a lord.
[**Lady** comes from Old English.]

**ladybird** *noun* **ladybirds**

A **ladybird** is a small, usually red insect with black spots.
[**Ladybird** comes from *Our Lady's bird* (*Our Lady* is Mary, the mother of Christ), because it eats harmful insects.]

**lagoon** *noun* **lagoons**

A **lagoon** is a large pool of water that is separated from the sea by a bank of sand.
[**Lagoon** comes from Latin.]

**laid** *verb*

**Laid** is the past tense and past participle of **lay**[1].

**lain** *verb*

**Lain** is the past participle of **lie**[1].

**lair** *noun* **lairs** (th)

A **lair** is a place where a wild animal lives. [**Lair** comes from Old English.]

**lake** *noun* **lakes**

A **lake** is a large area of water with land all around it.
[**Lake** comes from Latin via French.]

**lamb** *noun* **lambs**

**1** A **lamb** is a young sheep.
**2 Lamb** is the meat from a lamb.
[**Lamb** comes from Old English.]

**lamp** *noun* **lamps**

A **lamp** is something that uses electricity or other fuel to produce light.
[**Lamp** comes from Greek *lampein* 'to shine'.]

# lance

### lance *noun* **lances**
A **lance** is a long spear used by knights or soldiers on horseback.
[**Lance** comes from Latin via French.]

### land *noun* **lands** (th)
1 **Land** is all the dry parts of the earth, not the sea.
2 A **land** is a country: *our native land.*
[**Land** comes from Old English.]

### land *verb* **lands, landing, landed** (th)
To **land** means to arrive on land, often from a boat or plane.

### landlady *noun* **landladies**
1 A **landlady** is a woman who rents a room, flat or house to someone.
2 A **landlady** is a woman who runs a pub.
[A **landlady** was originally a woman who controlled or rented out land.]

### landlord *noun* **landlords**
1 A **landlord** is a man who rents a room, flat or house to someone.
2 A **landlord** is a man who runs a pub.
[A **landlord** was originally a man who controlled or rented out land.]

### landmark *noun* **landmarks**
A **landmark** is a building or natural object that you can see from a distance and that helps you find out where you are.

### landscape *noun* **landscapes**
1 The **landscape** is the land or scenery that exists in a particular place.
2 A **landscape** is a picture of scenery.
[**Landscape** comes from Dutch.]

### landslide *noun* **landslides**
A **landslide** is a sudden fall of rocks and earth down the side of a mountain.

### lane *noun* **lanes**
1 A **lane** is a narrow road, often in the country.
2 A **lane** is a strip marked off on a main road, an athletics track or in a swimming pool so that cars or people can go along beside each other.
[**Lane** comes from Old English.]

### language *noun* **languages**
1 **Language** is the words spoken or written by people.
2 A **language** is the form of speaking in a particular country: *French is the language of France.*
3 A **language** is a set of signs or symbols that show a particular meaning: *a computer language.*
[**Language** comes via French from Latin *lingua* 'tongue'.]

### lantern *noun* **lanterns**
A **lantern** is a glass, metal or paper case that you can see through, and is used for holding a candle.
[**Lantern** comes via French and Latin from the same Greek word as **lamp**.]

### lap[1] *noun* **laps**
Your **lap** is the firm area formed by your thighs when you sit down.
[**Lap**[1] comes from Old English *laeppa*.]

### lap[2] *noun* **laps**
A **lap** is one circuit of a sports track.
[**Lap**[2] comes from an old word *lap* 'to fold or coil', which comes from **lap**[1].]

### lap[3] *verb* **laps, lapping, lapped**
To **lap** means to drink with the tongue, like a cat.
[**Lap**[3] comes from Old English *lapian*.]

### lapel *noun* **lapels**
A **lapel** is the part of a collar that folds back onto the rest of a shirt, jacket or coat.
[**Lapel** comes from **lap**[1].]

### laptop *noun* **laptops**
A **laptop** is a small light computer that you can carry and use on your lap.

### large *adjective* **larger, largest** (th)
Something that is **large** is big.
[**Large** comes from Latin via French.]

### lark *noun* **larks**
A **lark** is a small bird with a lovely song.
[**Lark** comes from Old English.]

### larva *noun* **larvae**
A **larva** is an insect at the stage between an egg and an adult. Maggots and caterpillars are both kinds of **larva**.
[**Larva** comes from Latin.]

### larynx *noun* **larynxes**
Your **larynx** is the part of the passage from your throat to your lungs that contains the vocal cords.
[**Larynx** comes from Greek.]

### lasagne *noun*
**Lasagne** is an Italian dish made with layers of pasta, meat or vegetables, and cheese sauce.
[**Lasagne** comes via Italian from Latin

*lasanum* 'cooking pot'.]

### laser *noun* **lasers**

A **laser** is a very narrow beam of strong light that is used in science, for example in surgery for cutting very hard things. [**Laser** comes from the initial letters of *light amplification (by) stimulated emission (of) radiation.*]

### lash *noun* **lashes** (th)

1 Your **lashes** are the small hairs that grow along your eyelids.
2 The **lash** of a whip is the flexible part that you strike with.
3 A **lash** is a stroke with a whip: *sentenced to twenty lashes.*
[No one knows where **lash** comes from.]

### lash *verb* **lashes, lashing, lashed** (th)

1 To **lash** means to beat down hard: *Rain lashed against the windows.*
2 To **lash** means to hit something or someone violently with a whip.
3 To **lash** something means to tie it firmly with a rope: *The lifeboat was lashed to the deck.*

### lasso *noun* **lassos or lassoes**

A **lasso** is a long rope with a loop at the end that is used for catching horses and cattle.
[**Lasso** comes via Spanish from the same Latin word as **lace**.]

### last *noun* (th)

The **last** of something comes at the end: *the last of the milk.*
[**Last** comes from Old English.]

### last *verb* **lasts, lasting, lasted** (th)

To **last** means to go on for an amount of time: *The circus lasts for two hours.*

### last *adjective*

1 Something that is **last** comes after all the others: *I bought the last banana in the shop.*
2 The most recent in a series of things is the **last** one: *last Monday.*

### last *adverb*

If something happens **last**, it happens after everything else: *I painted the door last.*

### latch *noun* **latches**

A **latch** is a bar on a gate or door that keeps it fastened shut.
[**Latch** comes from Old English.]

### late *adjective* **later, latest** (th)

1 Someone who comes or something that happens after the expected time is **late**.
2 **Late** means near the end of the day, season or some other period of time: *late summer.*
3 Someone described as **late** is no longer alive: *her late husband.*
[**Late** comes from Old English.]

### lately *adverb* (th)

recently: *He has not been well lately.*

### later *adverb*

You use **later** or **later on** to talk about something that happened or that will happen after some time: *I can't come now, I'll come later; We went shopping and then later on we went to the beach.*

### latest *adjective*

1 **Latest** is the superlative of **late**.
2 The **latest** means the most recent: *the latest fashion.*
3 You say **at the latest** to make it clear that what you are talking about must happen or must be done by the time you say: *Your work must be in by Thursday at the latest.*

### lathe *noun* **lathes**

A **lathe** is a machine that is used for turning and shaping pieces of wood.
[**Lathe** comes from Old English.]

### lather *noun*

**Lather** is the mass of bubbles made by soap mixed with water.
[**Lather** comes from Old English.]

### Latin *noun*

**Latin** is the language spoken by the ancient Romans. Italian, French, Spanish and Portuguese come from **Latin**, and many English words also come from it.
[**Latin** comes from *Latium*, the name of an ancient district of Italy that included Rome.]

### latitude *noun* **latitudes**

**Latitude** is the position of a place measured by how far south or north of the equator it is.
[**Latitude** comes from Latin *latitudo* 'breadth'.]

### latter *adjective*

If you talk about two things, the **latter** is the second one you mention: *They offered red or white wine, and he chose the latter.*

[**Latter** comes from the same Old English word as **late**.]

## lattice noun lattices
A **lattice** is a pattern of diagonal lines.
[**Lattice** comes from an old French word.]

## laugh verb laughs, laughing, laughed (th)
To **laugh** means to make happy or amused sounds with your voice.
[**Laugh** comes from Old English.]

## launch¹ noun launches
A **launch** is a motor boat.
[**Launch**¹ comes from Spanish.]

## launch² verb launches, launching, launched
To **launch** means to slide a ship into the water or send a spaceship into space.
[**Launch**² comes from the same French word as **lance**.]

## laundry noun
**Laundry** is clothes, towels and other things that you are going to wash or that have been washed.
[**Laundry** comes via French from the same Latin word as **lavatory**.]

## laurel noun laurels
A **laurel** is an evergreen bush with shiny smooth leaves. In ancient Rome, a crown of **laurel** leaves was given to heroes.
[**Laurel** comes from Latin via French.]

## lava noun
**Lava** is the hot liquid that pours out of a volcano and cools into rock.
[**Lava** comes from Latin via Italian.]

## lavatory noun lavatories
A **lavatory** is a toilet.
[**Lavatory** comes from Latin *lavare* 'to wash'.]

## lavender noun
**Lavender** is a bush with narrow leaves and pale purple flowers that produce a pleasant smell.
[**Lavender** comes from Latin via French.]

## lavish verb lavishes, lavishing, lavished
If you **lavish** something like affection or money on someone, you give that person a lot of it in a very generous way.
[**Lavish** comes from old French *lavasse* 'heavy rain'.]

## law noun laws (th)
**1** A **law** is a rule made by the government that everybody in a country must obey.
**2 Law** is the system of rules made by the government: *It's against the law to sell cigarettes to children; You are obliged by law to pay taxes.*
**3** A **law** in science is something that will always happen or be true: *the law of gravity.*
[**Law** comes from Old Norse.]

## lawn noun lawns
A **lawn** is an area of a garden or park covered in short grass.
[**Lawn** comes from an old French word.]

## lawyer noun lawyers
A **lawyer** is a person whose job is to advise people about their legal matters and speak for them in court.

## lay¹ verb lays, laying, laid (th)
**1** To **lay** something or to **lay** something **down** means to put something down somewhere: *She laid the baby in her cot.*
**2** To **lay** means to produce an egg.
[**Lay**¹ comes from Old English.]

## lay² verb
**Lay**² is the past tense of **lie**¹.

## layer noun layers (th)
A **layer** is a quantity of something or a flat piece of something that lies on or inside another surface: *a layer of snow on the grass.* [**Layer** comes from **lay**¹.]

## lazy adjective lazier, laziest (th)
Someone who is **lazy** is not willing to work. **lazily** *adverb.* **laziness** *noun.*
[**Lazy** probably comes from an old German word.]

## lead¹ noun
**Lead** is a soft, very heavy metal.
[**Lead**¹ comes from Old English *lead*.]

## lead² verb leads, leading, led (th)
**1** To **lead** means to go in front of other people to show them the way.
**2** To **lead** means to be in charge of a group of people.
[**Lead**² comes from Old English *laedan*.]

## lead² noun leads
A **lead** is a strap fastened to an animal's collar so that it can be controlled.

## leader noun leaders (th)
A **leader** is someone who leads a group of people.

**leaf** *noun* **leaves**
A **leaf** is one of the flat, usually green, parts of a tree or other plant that grow on its stem or branch. Plants breathe through their **leaves**.
[**Leaf** comes from Old English.]

**leaflet** *noun* **leaflets**
A **leaflet** is a sheet of paper printed with information.
[**Leaflet** comes from **leaf**.]

**leak** *noun* **leaks**
A **leak** is when liquid or gas escapes through a crack or hole in something.
[**Leak** probably comes from an old German or Dutch word.]

**leak** *verb* **leaks, leaking, leaked**
If a liquid or gas **leaks**, it escapes through a crack or hole in something.

**lean¹** *verb* **leans, leaning, leaned** *or* **leant** (th)
**1** To **lean** means to be in a sloping position, or to put something in a sloping position.
**2** To **lean** means to rest against something.
[**Lean** comes from Old English *hleonian*.]

**lean²** *adjective* **leaner, leanest** (th)
Something that has no fat on it is **lean**: *lean meat*.
[**Lean** comes from Old English *hlaene*.]

**leap** *verb* **leaps, leaping, leaped** *or* **leapt** (th)
To **leap** means to jump forward.
[**Leap** comes from Old English.]

**leap year** *noun* **leap years**
A **leap year** is a year with an extra day in it on 29 February. A **leap year** happens every four years.
[A **leap year** is probably so called because the dates after 29 February seem to 'leap' a day; a date that would fall on a Monday in a normal year will be on Tuesday in a leap year.]

**learn** *verb* **learns, learning, learned** *or* **learnt** (th)
To **learn** means to find out about something, or to get new skills.
[**Learn** comes from Old English.]

**lease** *noun* **leases**
A **lease** is a legal agreement for someone to rent a house, office or piece of land for a certain period of time.
[**Lease** comes from Latin via French.]

**least** *noun*
The **least** is the smallest amount: *Choose the meat with the least fat on it.*
[**Least** comes from Old English.]

**least** *adverb*
**1** **Least** means less than all the others: *History is my least favourite subject.*
**2** You use **at least** to say that something is the least that it could be, or the least that should be done: *If you can't go and see her you should at least write to her.*

**leather** *noun*
**Leather** is a strong material made from animal skins.
[**Leather** comes from Old English.]

**leave** *verb* **leaves, leaving, left** (th)
**1** To **leave** means to go away from somewhere: *We left at six o'clock.*
**2** To **leave** means to let something stay somewhere: *You can leave your things in this locker.*
[**Leave** comes from Old English.]

**leave** *noun*
**Leave** is time that you have away from a job for holidays or because you are ill.

**lecture** *noun* **lectures** (th)
A **lecture** is a serious talk that someone gives to a class or an audience in order to teach something.
[**Lecture** comes from Latin.]

**led** *verb*
**Led** is the past tense and past participle of **lead²**.

**ledge** *noun* **ledges**
**1** A **ledge** is a narrow shelf, for example along the bottom of a window.
**2** A **ledge** is a narrow, flat place on the side of a mountain or cliff.
[No one knows where **ledge** comes from.]

**leech** *noun* **leeches**
A **leech** is a kind of worm that sticks onto the skin of animals and sucks their blood.
[**Leech** comes from Old English.]

**leek** *noun* **leeks**
A **leek** is a long white vegetable that has green leaves.
[**Leek** comes from Old English.]

**left¹** *adjective*
The **left** side is one of the two sides of something. In the word *as*, the *a* is on the **left** side of the *s*.
[**Left¹** comes from Old English.]

**left¹** *noun*
The **left** is the left side of something: *In Britain people drive on the left.*

**left¹** *adverb*
towards the left side: *Turn left at the crossroads.*

**left²** *verb*
**Left²** is the past tense and past participle of **leave**.

**left-hand** *adjective*
The **left-hand** side of something is the side on the left.

**left-handed** *adjective*
If you are **left-handed**, you hold the pen or pencil in your left hand when you write.

**leg** *noun* **legs**
1 Your **leg** is one of the parts of your body you use for standing and walking.
2 A **leg** is one of the supports on a table or other pieces of furniture.
[**Leg** comes from Old Norse.]

**legal** *adjective* (th)
1 Something that is **legal** is allowed by law.
2 **Legal** means to do with law: *legal advice.*
**legally** *adverb.*
[**Legal** comes from Latin.]

**legend** *noun* **legends**
1 A **legend** is a very old and well-known story about something that is supposed to have happened long ago.
2 A **legend** is a piece of writing on a map or chart that explains the symbols used on it.
[**Legend** comes from Latin *legenda* 'things to be read'.]

**legible** *adjective* (th)
If writing is **legible**, you can read it easily.
[**Legible** comes from Latin *legere* 'to read'.]

**legion** *noun* **legions**
1 A **legion** is a section of an army, especially of the ancient Roman army.
2 A **legion** is a large number of people.

[**Legion** comes from Latin via French.]

**legislate** *verb* **legislates, legislating, legislated**
To **legislate** means to pass a law about something.
[**Legislate** comes from **legislation**.]

**legislation** *noun*
**Legislation** is laws that a government has passed.
[**Legislation** comes from Latin *legis latio* 'the making of laws'.]

**legitimate** *adjective*
Something that is **legitimate** is allowed or acceptable according to the law.
[**Legitimate** comes from Latin *legitimare* 'to make something lawful'.]

**leisure** *noun*
**Leisure** is free time that you spend away from school or work doing things you enjoy.
[**Leisure** comes from an old French word.]

**lemon** *noun* **lemons**
A **lemon** is a yellow fruit with a sour taste.
[**Lemon** comes via French from Arabic *limun* 'citrus fruit'.]

**lend** *verb* **lends, lending, lent** (th)
To **lend** means to let someone have something for a while before returning it.
[**Lend** comes from Old English.]

**length** *noun* **lengths** (th)
1 The **length** of something is the distance from one end to the other.
2 The **length** of something is the time from the beginning of it to the end.
3 If you swim a **length** of a swimming pool, you swim from one end to the other.
[**Length** comes from Old English.]

**lengthen** *verb* **lengthens, lengthening, lengthened** (th)
To **lengthen** something means to make it longer.

**lenient** *adjective* (th)
If someone is **lenient**, s/he is not strict.
[**Lenient** comes from Latin *lenire* 'to soothe or soften'.]

**lens** *noun* **lenses**
A **lens** is a curved piece of glass or plastic used in things like glasses, telescopes and cameras. [**Lens** comes from Latin.]

**Lent** *noun*
> **Lent** is the period of 40 days before Easter in the Christian religion. During **Lent** some Christians fast or give up something they enjoy.
> [**Lent** comes from Old English.]

**lent** *verb*
> **Lent** is the past tense and past participle of **lend**.

**leopard** *noun* **leopards**
> A **leopard** is a large wild animal of the cat family. **Leopards** have yellow fur with black spots and live in Africa and Asia.
> [**Leopard** comes from Greek via French and Latin.]

**leotard** *noun* **leotards**
> A **leotard** is a piece of clothing worn by dancers and gymnasts. It looks like a swimming costume with sleeves.
> [The **leotard** is named after a French acrobat, Jules *Léotard*, who designed it.]

**leprechaun** *noun* **leprechauns**
> A **leprechaun** is a small goblin from Irish stories.
> [**Leprechaun** comes from Irish *leipreachan* 'a small body'.]

**less** *adjective, adverb*
> **Less** means not so much: *My sister gets less pocket money than me.*
> [**Less** comes from Old English.]

**lesson** *noun* **lessons** (th)
> 1 A **lesson** is a period of time in school when something is taught.
> 2 A **lesson** is something that you learn or an experience that makes you realise something.
> [**Lesson** comes from Latin via French.]

**let** *verb* **lets, letting, let** (th)
> To **let** means to allow: *Let the dog out; She let us borrow her car.*
> [**Let** comes from Old English.]

**lethal** *adjective* (th)
> Something that is **lethal** can kill you.
> [**Lethal** comes from Latin *let(h)um* 'death'.]

**letter** *noun* **letters**
> 1 A **letter** is one of the symbols used to write words. *A, b and c are the first three letters of the alphabet.*
> 2 A **letter** is a message that someone writes and sends by post to another person.
> [**Letter** comes via French from Latin *lit(t)era* (ancestor of **literate**).]

**lettuce** *noun* **lettuces**
> A **lettuce** is a green vegetable with large leaves that you eat raw in salads.
> [**Lettuce** comes from Latin via French.]

**leukaemia** *noun*
> **Leukaemia** is a disease in which the blood produces too many white cells.
> [**Leukaemia** comes from Greek *leukos haima* 'white blood'.]

**level** *noun* **levels**
> 1 The **level** of something is the height or depth of it: *100 metres above/below sea level.*
> 2 The **level** of something is where it is on a scale: *There are classes for every level from beginners to advanced.*
> 3 A **level** is a tool for checking whether something is horizontal.
> [**Level** comes from Latin via French.]

**level** *adjective* (th)
> 1 Something that is **level** is flat.
> 2 Things that are **level** are equal.

**lever** *noun* **levers**
> A **lever** is a bar that is pulled down to lift up a heavy object or to work a machine.
> [**Lever** comes from Latin *levare* 'to lift up'.]

**liable** *adjective* (th)
> If you are **liable** for something, you are legally responsible for it.
> [**Liable** probably comes from an old French word.]

**liar** *noun* **liars**
> A **liar** is someone who tells lies.

**liberal** *adjective*
> Someone who has **liberal** views accepts other people's ideas easily.
> [**Liberal** comes via French from the same Latin word as **liberty**.]

**liberate** *verb* **liberates, liberating, liberated** (th)
> To **liberate** means to set someone free.
> [**Liberate** comes from the same Latin word as **liberty**.]

**liberty** *noun* **liberties** (th)
> **Liberty** is freedom from being controlled or being a prisoner.
> [**Liberty** comes via French from Latin *liber*

'free'.]

**library** *noun* **libraries**
A **library** is a collection of books, kept for people to read or borrow.
[**Library** comes from Latin *libraria* 'bookshop'.]

**lice** *plural noun* **louse** *singular*
**Lice** are small insects that live on the skin or hair of people or animals.
[**Lice** comes from Old English.]

**licence** *noun* **licences** (th)
A **licence** is a document that proves you are allowed to do something: *a driving licence.*
[**Licence** comes from Latin *licere* 'to be allowed'.]

**license** *verb* **licenses, licensing, licensed** (th)
To **license** something means to give official permission or a licence for it.
[**License** comes from **licence.**]

**lichen** *noun* **lichens**
**Lichen** is a flat yellow or green plant that looks like moss and grows on rocks and tree trunks.
[**Lichen** comes from Greek via Latin.]

**lick** *verb* **licks, licking, licked**
To **lick** means to touch something with the tongue.
[**Lick** comes from Old English.]

**licorice** *noun*
**Licorice** is another way to spell **liquorice.**

**lid** *noun* **lids**
A **lid** is a cover for a box or other container. [**Lid** comes from Old English.]

**lie¹** *verb* **lies, lying, lay, lain** (th)
To **lie** means to be in a flat position or put yourself in a flat position: *She's lying on the floor; He lay on the bed and fell asleep.*
[**Lie¹** comes from Old English *licgan.*]

**lie²** *verb* **lies, lying, lied** (th)
To **lie** means to say something that you know is not true.
[**Lie²** comes from Old English *leogan.*]

**lie²** *noun* **lies**
A **lie** is something that someone says that is not true.

**lieutenant** *noun* **lieutenants**
A **lieutenant** is an officer in the armed forces. [**Lieutenant** comes from French.]

**life** *noun* **lives**
1 Someone's **life** is the time s/he is alive between birth and death.
2 A **life** is the experiences someone has: *They lead an exciting life.*
3 **Life** is living things: *the plant life of the Arctic.*
4 The **life** of something is how long it exists or continues to work: *These batteries have the longest life of any brand.*
[**Life** comes from Old English.]

**lifeguard** *noun* **lifeguards**
A **lifeguard** is someone who is trained to save swimmers if they get into danger.

**lifeline** *noun* **lifelines**
A **lifeline** is something that connects people to the outside world: *For many old people, a telephone is their lifeline.*
[A **lifeline** was originally a line thrown from a boat to someone in the water so that s/he could be pulled out.]

**lift** *noun* **lifts**
1 A **lift** is a machine for taking people and things from one floor of a building to another.
2 A **lift** is a free ride in someone's car: *Can you give me a lift to the station?*
[**Lift** comes from Old Norse.]

**lift** *verb* **lifts, lifting, lifted** (th)
1 To **lift** means to move something to a higher position: *Lift the ball above your head.*
2 To **lift** means to pick something up: *I can't lift this bag – it's too heavy.*

**ligament** *noun* **ligaments**
A **ligament** is a strong band of tissue that holds bones together.
[**Ligament** comes from Latin *ligare* 'to bind'.]

**light¹** *noun* **lights** (th)
1 **Light** is brightness that allows you to see things: *These big windows let in a lot of light.*
2 A **light** is an object such as a lamp that gives out light: *It's dark – put the light on!*
[**Light¹** comes from Old English *leoht.*]

**light¹** *adjective* **lighter, lightest** (th)
Something that is **light** is bright or pale, not dark: *light green.*

**a b c d e f g h i j k l m**

**light¹** *verb* **lights, lighting, lit** (th)
**1** To **light** something means to make it start burning: *Light the fire – I'm cold!*
**2** To **light** something means to make it bright with lights: *The building is lit with floodlights at night.*

**light²** *adjective* **lighter, lightest**
Something that is **light** does not weigh very much and is not heavy.
[**Light²** comes from Old English *liht*.]

**lighthouse** *noun* **lighthouses**
A **lighthouse** is a tower in or near the sea with a bright flashing light on top that warns ships of dangerous rocks nearby.

**lightning** *noun*
**Lightning** is electric flashes in the sky during a thunderstorm.
[**Lightning** comes from **light¹**.]

**light year** *noun* **light years**
**1** A **light year** is the distance that light travels in one year, which is used as a measurement of the distance between stars and planets in space.
**2** A **light year** is an extremely long time: *Scientists are light years away from creating a computer that can think.*

**like¹** *verb* **likes, liking, liked** (th)
**1** To **like** someone or something means to think that person or thing is pleasant: *Do you like school?*
**2** To **like** is to want: *You can do what you like; What would you like to eat?*
[**Like¹** comes from Old English.]

**like²** *preposition* (th)
similar to something or someone: *That cat is just like ours.*
[**Like²** comes from Old Norse.]

**likely** *adjective* **likelier, likeliest** (th)
Something that is **likely** is probably true or will probably happen.
[**Likely** comes from **like²**.]

**lilac** *noun*
**1 Lilac** is a tall garden plant with heart-shaped leaves and white, purple or pink flowers with a strong smell.
**2 Lilac** is a pale purple colour.
[**Lilac** comes via French, Spanish and Arabic from Persian (the language spoken in Iran).]

**lilac** *adjective*
a pale purple colour: *a lilac shirt.*

**limb** *noun* **limbs**
**1** A **limb** is one of your arms or legs.
**2** A **limb** of a tree is one of its branches.
[**Limb** comes from Old English.]

**lime¹** *noun* **limes**
**1** A **lime** is an oval green fruit that tastes similar to a lemon.
**2 Lime** or **lime-green** is a yellowish-green colour.
[**Lime¹** comes via French and Spanish from the same Arabic word as **lemon**.]

**lime¹** *adjective* Also **lime-green**
of a yellowish-green colour: *a lime-green jumper.*

**lime²** *noun*
**Lime** is a white powder that is used to make cement or is spread on fields as a fertiliser.
[**Lime²** comes from Old English.]

**limelight** *noun*
Something or someone that is **in the limelight** is the centre of attention.
[**Limelight** comes from **lime²**, which gives out a bright light when it is heated and which used to be used to light the stage in a theatre.]

**limerick** *noun* **limericks**
A **limerick** is a silly poem that has five lines, two long ones that rhyme, then two short ones that rhyme, then a long one that rhymes with the first two.
[**Limerick** is named after the town of *Limerick* in Ireland.]

**limestone** *noun*
**Limestone** is a pale chalky rock.
[**Limestone** is so called because it contains **lime²**.]

**limit** *noun* **limits** (th)
**1** A **limit** is the greatest amount of something that is allowed: *The speed limit is too high.*
**2** A **limit** of a place is the furthest point or edge of it: *This wall marks the old city limits.*
[**Limit** comes from Latin.]

**limousine** *noun* **limousines**
A **limousine** is a large comfortable car: *a chauffeur-driven limousine.*
[A **limousine** was originally a cape with a hood which was worn in *Limousin* in France; the car was so called because the first ones had a canvas roof to protect the

driver.]

**limp** *verb* **limps, limping, limped** (th)
To **limp** is to walk in an uneven way by putting more weight on one leg than the other: *The injured player limped off the field.*
[No one knows where **limp** comes from.]

**limp** *adjective* **limper, limpest** (th)
Something that is **limp** is not stiff or strong: *a limp lettuce leaf.*

**limpet** *noun* **limpets**
A **limpet** is a shellfish with a cone-shaped shell that clings tightly to rock.
[**Limpet** comes from Latin via Old English.]

**line¹** *noun* **lines** (th)
1 A **line** is a long, thin mark on a surface.
2 A **line** is a row of people or things: *a long line of people waiting for the bus.*
3 A **line** is a long piece of rope, string or wire: *a telephone line.*
[**Line¹** comes from Old English.]

**line²** *verb* **lines, lining, lined**
To **line** something is to cover its inside surface with material: *This jacket is lined with fleecy material.*
[**Line²** comes from **linen**, which was often used to line clothes.]

**linen** *noun*
1 **Linen** is a material like rough cotton that is made from the flax plant: *a linen shirt.*
2 **Linen** is cloth items for the house, such as tablecloths, sheets and tea towels: *All the linen is in the cupboard.*
[**Linen** comes from Latin *linum* 'flax'.]

**linger** *verb* **lingers, lingering, lingered** (th)
Something or someone that **lingers** stays somewhere or goes on for a long time: *The smell of fried food lingers for ages.*
[**Linger** comes from Old English.]

**link** *noun* **links** (th)
1 A **link** is one ring or loop in a chain.
2 A **link** is something that connects things or people: *There's a strong link between smoking and lung cancer.*
[**Link** comes from Old Norse.]

**link** *verb* **links, linking, linked** (th)
To **link** two or more people or things is to make a connection between them: *The Channel Tunnel links England and France.*

**lint** *noun*
**Lint** is a soft material that soaks up liquid and is used for covering wounds.
[**Lint** probably comes from French *lin* 'flax', which lint used to be made from.]

**lion** *noun* **lions**
A **lion** is a large wild animal that is part of the cat family and lives in Africa and parts of southern Asia. Male **lions** have a mane.
[**Lion** comes from Greek via French and Latin.]

**lioness** *noun* **lionesses**
A **lioness** is a female lion.

**lip** *noun* **lips**
1 Your **lip** is one of the soft pink parts on the outside of your mouth.
2 A **lip** is the edge of a cup or something shaped like a cup.
[**Lip** comes from Old English.]

**lip-read** *verb* **lip-reads, lip-reading, lip-read**
To **lip-read** is to understand what someone says by looking at the way his/her lips move because you cannot hear what that person is saying.

**liqueur** *noun* **liqueurs**
A **liqueur** is a strong alcoholic drink that is usually quite sweet.
[**Liqueur** comes from French *liqueur* 'liquor'.]

**liquid** *noun* **liquids**
A **liquid** is a wet substance that you can pour. Water and oil are both liquids.
[**Liquid** comes from Latin.]

**liquor** *noun*
**Liquor** is a strong alcoholic drink such as whisky, gin or brandy.
[**Liquor** comes from Latin via French.]

**liquorice** *noun* Also **licorice**
**Liquorice** is a black substance with a strong taste that is used to make sweets.
[**Liquorice** comes from Greek via French and Latin.]

**list¹** *noun* **lists** (th)
A **list** is words or numbers that are written down one underneath the other: *a shopping list.*
[**List¹** comes from an Old French word.]

a b c d e f g h i j k **l** m

**list²** *verb* **lists, listing, listed** (th)
When a ship **lists**, it leans to one side: *The tanker was listing in high seas.*
[No one knows where **list²** comes from.]

**listen** *verb* **listens, listening, listened** (th)
To **listen** means to pay attention in order to hear something.
[**Listen** comes from Old English.]

**lit** *verb*
**Lit** is the past tense and past participle of **light**.

**literate** *adjective*
Someone who is **literate** can read and write.
[**Literate** comes from Latin *lit(t)era* 'letter, literature' (ancestor of **letter**).]

**literature** *noun*
**1 Literature** is books, especially novels, plays and poems: *Shakespeare's plays are some of the best in English literature.*
**2 Literature** is the printed documents that give you information about something: *There's lots of literature with this new fax machine.*
[**Literature** comes from the same Latin word as **literate**.]

**litre** *noun* **litres**
A litre is a unit of measurement for liquids in the metric system. There are 1000 millilitres in a **litre**.
[**Litre** comes from Greek via Latin and French.]

**little** *adjective* **littler, littlest** *or* **less, least** (th)
**1** Something or someone that is **little** is small or short: *a little dog; We only live a little way from the station.*
**2** Someone who is **little** is young, or younger than you: *My little sister is nearly 15.*
**3** If you have a **little** of something, you have a small amount: *just a little piece of cake.* [**Little** comes from Old English.]

**live¹** *verb* **lives, living, lived** (th)
**1** To **live** means to be alive or to stay alive.
**2** The place where you **live** is where you have your home: *She lives in Paris.*
**3** The way people **live** is the kind of life they have: *We've got enough money and we live very well.*
[**Live¹** comes from Old English.]

**live²** *adjective* (th)
**1** Something that is **live** is alive or living: *There are real live tigers in the zoo.*
**2** A **live** programme comes to your radio or television the moment it is happening.
**3** Anything electrical that is **live** is carrying electricity that could give you a shock. [**Live** comes from **alive**.]

**livelihood** *noun* **livelihoods** (th)
A person's **livelihood** is the job s/he does to earn money: *Farming is his livelihood.*
[**Livelihood** comes from Old English.]

**livestock** *noun*
**Livestock** is the animals such as pigs, sheep and cows that are kept on farms.

**living** *noun*
A **living** is a way of earning money: *She cleans houses for a living.*
[**Living** comes from **live¹**.]

**living room** *noun* **living rooms**
A **living room** is the main room in a house, which usually has comfortable chairs.

**lizard** *noun* **lizards**
A **lizard** is a reptile with four legs, scaly skin and a long tail: *An iguana is a type of lizard.*
[**Lizard** comes from Latin via French.]

**load** *noun* **loads** (th)
A **load** is something that is carried: *The lorry was carrying a wide load.*
[**Load** comes from Old English.]

**load** *verb* **loads, loading, loaded**
**1** To **load** is to put things into a vehicle or container so that they can be taken somewhere: *Luggage was loaded into the plane: We loaded the car with the bags.*
**2** To **load** a camera is to put a film into it, and to **load** a gun is to put bullets into it.

**loaf** *noun* **loaves**
A **loaf** is bread that is shaped and baked in a single piece.
[**Loaf** comes from Old English.]

**loam** *noun*
**Loam** is rich fertile soil containing sand, clay and decayed plants.
[**Loam** comes from Old English.]

**loan** *noun* **loans**
A **loan** is money that you borrow: *a bank loan.* [**Loan** comes from Old Norse.]

**loan** *verb* **loans, loaning, loaned**
If you **loan** someone something,
especially money, you lend it to him/her.

**loathe** *verb* **loathes, loathing,
loathed** (th)
If you **loathe** something, you hate or
detest it.
[**Loathe** comes from Old English.]

**lob** *verb* **lobs, lobbing, lobbed** (th)
To **lob** something is to throw it through
the air.
[**Lob** probably comes from an old German
or Dutch word.]

**lobster** *noun* **lobsters**
A **lobster** is a large shellfish with eight
legs and two large claws. **Lobsters** are a
dark blue colour when they are alive but
turn red when they are cooked.
[**Lobster** comes from Latin via Old
English.]

**local** *adjective*
Something that is **local** is near your house
or belongs to the area you live in: *a local
church; the local newspaper.*
[**Local** comes from Latin *locus* 'a place'.]

**locate** *verb* **locates, locating, located** (th)
**1** When you **locate** something, you find
out where it is.
**2** If something is **located** in a place, it is at
or in that place: *The offices are located in
Queen Street.*
[**Locate** comes from the same Latin word
as **local**.]

**loch** *noun* **lochs**
A **loch** is a Scottish lake: *Is there a monster
in Loch Ness?* [**Loch** comes from Gaelic.]

**lock¹** *noun* **locks** (th)
**1** A **lock** is a device that fastens a door or
a container and can only be opened with
a key.
**2** A **lock** is part of a canal with gates at
either end so that water can be let in or
out and boats raised or lowered to
different water levels.
[**Lock¹** comes from Old English *loc*.]

**lock¹** *verb* **locks, locking, locked** (th)
To **lock** means to close something with a
key: *Did you lock the front door?*

**lock²** *noun* **locks** (th)
A **lock²** is a piece of hair: *A lock of hair
curled over her forehead; curly blond locks.*

[**Lock²** comes from Old English *locc*.]

**locker** *noun* **lockers**
A **locker** is a type of cupboard that can be
locked. **Lockers** are often found in schools
and changing rooms.

**locket** *noun* **lockets**
A **locket** is a piece of jewellery that opens
up and usually contains a picture of
someone or a piece of someone's hair. You
wear a **locket** on a chain around your
neck.
[**Locket** comes from an old French word.]

**locust** *noun* **locusts**
A **locust** is an insect from Africa and Asia
that looks like a grasshopper and
destroys crops by eating them: *a swarm of
locusts.*
[**Locust** comes from Latin via French.]

**loft** *noun* **lofts**
A **loft** is the space under the roof of a
building. [**Loft** comes from Old Norse.]

**log** *noun* **logs**
**1** A **log** is a piece of a tree that has fallen
down or has been cut down.
**2** A **log** is a daily written record of
something, especially a voyage.
[No one knows where **log** comes from.]

**log** *verb* **logs, logging, logged**
**1** If you **log on** to a computer or a
network, you put in your password so
you can begin to use it.
**2** If you **log off** a computer or a network,
you put in a command to stop it working.

**logical** *adjective*
If something is **logical** it is sensible and
properly thought out. **logically** *adverb*.
[**Logical** comes via Latin from Greek *logos*
'reason'.]

**lonely** *adjective* **lonelier, loneliest** (th)
**1** If you are **lonely**, you are sad because
you are by yourself.
**2** A place that is **lonely** is far away from
other people or things: *a lonely hut in the
middle of nowhere.* **loneliness** *noun*.
[**Lonely** comes from **alone**.]

**long¹** *adjective* **longer, longest**
**1** Something that is **long** is more than
average in length, distance or time: *The
concert was a bit long and boring; Twenty
kilometres is a long way to walk.*
**2** You use **long** after a distance or a time

to say that something measures that much or lasts for that amount of time: *The beach is five kilometres long.*
[**Long**¹ comes from Old English *lang*.]

**long² verb longs, longing, longed (th)**
To **long** for something means to want it very much.
[**Long**² comes from Old English *langian*.]

**longitude noun longitudes**
**Longitude** is the position of a place east or west of an imaginary line round the earth that runs from the North Pole to the South Pole through the Greenwich Observatory in London.
[**Longitude** comes from Latin *longitudo* 'length'.]

**look verb looks, looking, looked (th)**
1 To **look** is to use your eyes to see things.
2 To **look** is to seem or appear: *You look tired; It looks as though it might rain.*
[**Look** comes from Old English.]

**loom noun looms**
A **loom** is a machine for weaving cloth.
[**Loom** comes from Old English.]

**loose adjective (th)**
1 Something that is **loose** is not tight: *Loose clothes are comfortable.*
2 Something that is **loose** is not tightly fixed to something else: *a loose tooth.*
3 Items that are **loose** are not in a packet: *You can buy apples in a bag or loose.*
[**Loose** comes from Old Norse.]

**lord noun lords**
1 A **lord/Lord** is a nobleman or a man who has been given the title 'Lord'.
2 The **Lord** is another name for God.
[**Lord** comes from Old English.]

**lose verb loses, losing, lost (th)**
1 To **lose** something means to be unable to find it.
2 If you **lose** something, you do not have it any more: *He lost his job.*
3 To **lose** means to be beaten in a game: *We lost to a better team.*
[**Lose** comes from Old English.]

**lot noun lots (th)**
1 A **lot** or **lots** is a large number or a large amount: *What a lot of people!; We've had lots of rain this year.*
2 The **lot** is the whole amount of something or a whole group of people or set of things: *He bought a litre of cola and he drank the lot.*
[**Lot** comes from Old English.]

**loud adjective louder, loudest (th)**
Something that is **loud** is noisy and not quiet: *loud music; a loud voice.*
**loudly** adverb. **loudness** noun.
[**Loud** comes from Old English.]

**loudspeaker noun loudspeakers**
A **loudspeaker** is a piece of equipment that turns electrical signals into sound, from CD players or microphones, for example.

**lounge noun lounges**
1 A **lounge** is the main room in a house or hotel that usually has comfortable chairs.
2 A **lounge** is an area with chairs where you wait at an airport: *the departure lounge.*
[No one knows where **lounge** comes from.]

**louse noun**
**Louse** is the singular of **lice**.

**love verb loves, loving, loved (th)**
To **love** something or someone means to like that thing or person very much: *I love chocolate; Do you love your boyfriend?*
[**Love** comes from Old English.]

**lovely adjective lovelier, loveliest (th)**
1 Someone who is **lovely** is pretty or good-looking or has a very nice personality: *I think that new boy in our class is lovely.*
2 If you think something is **lovely**, you like it or enjoy it very much: *The food was lovely; We had a lovely time.*
[**Lovely** comes from **love**.]

**low adjective lower, lowest (th)**
1 Something that is **low** is close to the ground or close to the bottom, and not high: *low prices; a low voice.*
2 Something that is **low** is short and not tall: *These shoes have low heels.*
[**Low** comes from Old Norse.]

**loyal adjective (th)**
Someone who is **loyal** can always be relied on and trusted.
[**Loyal** comes from an old French word.]

**luck noun (th)**
1 **Luck** is something that happens by chance: *You don't need skill to win the*

*lottery, just luck.*
**2 Luck** or **good luck** is good things that happen to you that are not planned: *We wish you luck on your travels.*
[**Luck** comes from an old German or Dutch word.]

**lucky** *adjective* **luckier, luckiest** (th)
**1** If you are **lucky**, good things happen to you by chance.
**2** If something is **lucky**, you believe that it brings you good luck: *my lucky rabbit's foot.*

**luggage** *noun*
Your **luggage** is the bags and suitcases you take with you when you travel.
[**Luggage** comes from *lug* 'to drag or carry something', which comes from a Scandinavian word.]

**lullaby** *noun* **lullabies**
A **lullaby** is a slow, gentle song that you sing to help a baby go to sleep.
[The word **lullaby** is an imitation of the soft sound that you make to soothe a child.]

**lunch** *noun* **lunches**
**Lunch** is a meal eaten in the middle of the day.
[**Lunch** is short for **luncheon**. No one knows where **luncheon** comes from.]

**lung** *noun* **lungs**
Your **lungs** are the two organs inside your chest that you use for breathing.
[**Lung** comes from Old English.]

**lurch** *verb* **lurches, lurching, lurched**
To **lurch** is to move in an uncontrolled, jerky way: *The drunken man lurched along the road.*
[No one knows where **lurch** comes from.]

**lynx** *noun* **lynxes**
A **lynx** is a wild cat with spotted fur, long legs and heavy paws: *A bobcat is a type of lynx.* [**Lynx** comes from Greek via Latin.]

**lyric** *noun* **lyrics**
**1** A **lyric** is a short poem about the poet's thoughts and feelings.
**2** The **lyrics** of a song are its words.
[**Lyric** comes from Greek.]

## Dictionary Fun

**Etymology**
1. Which 'l' word is made from the initial letters of a description of its use?
2. Which 'l' word comes from Greek *logos* 'reason'?

**What do these idioms mean?**
1. To lead someone up the garden path
2. To take a leap in the dark
3. To not have a leg to stand on

**Complete the proverbs**
1. He who l_____ last l_____ longest.
2. Look before you l_____.

3. A l_____ does not change its spots.

**Complete the simile**
As gentle as a l_____.

**Did you know?**
◆ The word **limousine** comes from the name of the French district *Limousin*, where the inhabitants used to wear special hooded cloaks. The French then gave an early chauffeur-driven car this name because it had a hood which protected the driver as well as the passengers.

a b c d e f g h i j k **l** m

# Mm

**machine** *noun* **machines**
A **machine** is a piece of equipment that uses electricity or other power to do a certain job: *a sewing machine.*
[**Machine** comes from Greek via French and Latin.]

**machinery** *noun*
1 You use **machinery** to talk about machines in general, or about all the machines in a particular place or of a particular kind: *The new machinery means that the work only takes half as long; farm machinery.*
2 The **machinery** is the working parts of a machine or engine.

**macro** *noun* **macros**
A **macro** is a set of computer instructions that are stored as if they were a single instruction.
[**Macro** comes from Greek *makros* 'large'.]

**mad** *adjective* **madder, maddest** (th)
1 A **mad** person is mentally ill.
2 Something or someone that is **mad** is crazy or very silly.
3 Someone who is **mad** is very angry.
4 If someone is **mad about** something, they like it very much.
**madly** *adverb.* **madness** *noun.*
[**Mad** comes from Old English.]

**made** *verb*
**Made** is the past tense and past participle of **make**.

**magazine** *noun* **magazines** (th)
A **magazine** is a thin book with stories, articles and pictures that comes out each week or month.
[**Magazine** comes via French and Italian from Arabic *makhazin* 'storehouse', because a magazine contains many different items.]

**maggot** *noun* **maggots**
A **maggot** is the larva that hatches from the eggs of certain flies.
[No one knows where **maggot** comes from.]

**magic** *noun*
1 **Magic** is the power to make impossible things happen, especially in stories. Witches and fairies use **magic**.
2 **Magic** is the skill magicians use to do tricks to entertain people.
[**Magic** comes from Greek via French and Latin.]

**magician** *noun* **magicians**
1 A **magician** is a person in stories who can do things by magic.
2 A **magician** is a person who does amazing tricks that seem impossible in order to entertain people: *The magician sawed a woman in half.*

**magnate** *noun* **magnates**
A **magnate** is a rich and powerful business person: *a shipping magnate.*
[**Magnate** comes from Latin *magnus* 'great'.]

**magnet** *noun* **magnets**
A **magnet** is a piece of metal that can make other pieces of metal stick to it. **Magnets** have two ends, or poles, called the north pole and the south pole.
[**Magnet** comes from Greek via Latin.]

**magnify** *verb* **magnifies, magnifying, magnified**
To **magnify** something is to make it seem larger than it really is by using an instrument such as a magnifying glass or a microscope.
[**Magnify** comes via French from Latin *magnificare* 'to make great'.]

**mail** *noun*
1 **Mail** is the letters and parcels delivered to your house: *Did the postman deliver any mail?*
2 **Mail** is the system for delivering letters and parcels: *The card is in the mail.*
3 **Mail** is short for e-mail: *I'll log on and check for new mail.*
[**Mail** comes from an old French word.]

**mail** *verb* **mails, mailing, mailed**
1 To **mail** a letter to someone is to send it through the post.
2 To **mail** something or someone is to send an e-mail.

**maim** *verb* **maims, maiming, maimed** (th)
To **maim** someone is to injure that person so badly that s/he will never completely recover.
[**Maim** comes from an old French word.]

**main** *adjective* (th)
**Main** means most important: *What's your main reason for coming today?*
[**Main** comes from Old English.]

**mainframe** *noun* **mainframes**
A **mainframe** is a large and powerful computer that is often at the centre of a network.

**mainland** *noun*
The **mainland** is the main land area of a country that does not include the islands around it: *You can cross from the mainland to the Isle of Wight on a ferry.*

**mains** *plural noun*
The **mains** are the pipes or wires that bring gas, water and electricity into a building: *Turn off the water at the mains.*

**maize** *noun*
**Maize** is a cereal crop that produces sweetcorn.
[**Maize** comes via French and Spanish from Taino (a South American Indian language).]

**major** *adjective* (th)
**Major** means important or more important: *a major road; Smoking is a major cause of cancer.*
[**Major** comes from Latin *major* 'larger or greater'.]

**major** *noun* **majors**
A **major** is an officer in the army.

**make** *verb* **makes, making, made** (th)
**1** to build or produce something: *The factory makes cars.*
**2** to do something: *make a speech; make a phonecall; make a mistake.*
**3** to cause an action or feeling: *It made me cry; You make me angry!*
**4** to force someone to do something: *He made her eat her vegetables.*
**5** to add up to a particular amount: *11 and 12 make 23.*
[**Make** comes from Old English.]

**make** *noun* **makes**
A **make** of something is a brand: *What make are your trainers?*

**makeshift** *adjective*
Something that is **makeshift** is used for a short time until something better can take its place: *The homeless people were living in makeshift housing.*

[**Makeshift** comes from an old phrase *to make shift* 'to manage somehow'.]

**malaria** *noun*
**Malaria** is a disease that causes a high fever. You can get **malaria** if you are bitten by a mosquito that is carrying it.
[**Malaria** comes from Italian *mal aria* 'bad air', which people used to think was the cause of the disease.]

**male** *noun* **males**
A **male** is a man or boy, or a male animal.
[**Male** comes via French from the same Latin word as **masculine**.]

**male** *adjective*
A **male** animal can fertilise the eggs of a female and a **male** plant fertilises female seeds.

**malfunction** *verb* **malfunctions, malfunctioning, malfunctioned** (th)
A machine that **malfunctions** stops working properly.
[**Malfunction** comes from Latin *male* 'badly' and English *function* 'to work', which comes from Latin.]

**malnutrition** *noun*
**Malnutrition** is an illness that is caused by not eating enough food, or by eating food that does not contain enough of the things, such as vitamins and protein, that your body needs.
[**Malnutrition** comes from Latin *male* 'bad' and English *nutrition* 'the art or study of proper feeding', which comes from the same Latin word as **nutritious**.]

**mammal** *noun* **mammals**
A **mammal** is any animal that gives birth to live young that can feed on its mother's milk. Human beings are **mammals**.
[**Mammal** comes from Latin *mamma* 'breast'.]

**mammoth** *noun* **mammoths**
A **mammoth** is an extinct animal that looked like a huge hairy elephant with long curved tusks.
[**Mammoth** comes from Russian.]

**man** *noun* **men** (th)
**1** A **man** is a fully grown male human being.
**2** You can use **man** to refer to the whole human race: *Stone Age man.* Many people

a b c d e f g h i j k l **m**

now prefer to use the word 'humans' or 'people' instead of **man**.
[**Man** comes from Old English.]

**manage** *verb* **manages, managing, managed** (th)
**1** Someone who **manages** someone or something controls that person or thing.
**2** If you **manage** to do something, you succeed in doing something that was not very easy: *I managed to get tickets for the big game.*
[**Manage** comes from Italian *maneggiare* 'to handle'.]

**manager** *noun* **managers** (th)
**1** A **manager** is someone who is in charge of a business or a sports team: *a restaurant manager.*
**2** A **manager** is someone who looks after the business affairs of famous people: *The rock band sacked their manager.*

**mane** *noun* **manes**
A **mane** is the long thick hair on the neck of, for example, a lion or a horse.
[**Mane** comes from Old English.]

**manger** *noun* **mangers**
A **manger** is an open box that holds food for horses and cows.
[**Manger** comes from French *manger* 'to eat'.]

**mangle** *verb* **mangles, mangling, mangled** (th)
To **mangle** something is to twist or pull it out of shape.
[**Mangle** comes from an old French word.]

**mango** *noun* **mangos** *or* **mangoes**
A **mango** is a yellowish-red tropical fruit.
[**Mango** comes via Portuguese from Tamil (a southern Indian language.]

**maniac** *noun* **maniacs**
A **maniac** is someone who is mad or someone who acts in a wild or violent way.
[**Maniac** comes from Greek *mania* 'madness'.]

**manipulate** *verb* **manipulates, manipulating, manipulated** (th)
To **manipulate** someone is to trick or influence him/her to behave in a certain way. [**Manipulate** comes from Latin.]

**mankind** *noun*
**Mankind** is the human race now and in the past. Many people now prefer to use the word 'humankind' instead of **mankind**.

**manoeuvre** *noun* **manoeuvres**
A **manoeuvre** is a difficult movement that requires skill.
[**Manoeuvre** comes from French.]

**manoeuvre** *verb* **manoeuvres, manoeuvring, manoeuvred** (th)
To **manoeuvre** something is to move or turn it skilfully.

**manslaughter** *noun*
**Manslaughter** is the crime of killing someone without meaning or planning to.

**manual** *noun* **manuals**
A **manual** is a book that tells you how to do something or how something works.
[**Manual** comes from Latin *manus* 'hand'.]

**manual** *adjective*
**1** **Manual** means worked by hand, instead of automatically or by electricity or a motor: *a manual gearbox; a manual typewriter.*
**2** **Manual** work is work in which you use your hands or your strength rather than your brain.

**manufacture** *verb* **manufactures, manufacturing, manufactured**
To **manufacture** things means to make them, especially to make a lot of them in a factory: *The company manufactures trucks and buses.*
[**Manufacture** comes via French from Latin *manu factum* 'made by hand'.]

**manure** *noun*
**Manure** is animal faeces spread on the land or mixed into the soil to make plants grow better.
[**Manure** comes from an old French word.]

**many** *adjective* (th)
a large number of people or things: *There are so many people here.*
[**Many** comes from Old English.]

**map** *noun* **maps**
A **map** is a plan of an area that shows the things that are there, such as its mountains, rivers, roads, towns and buildings.

n o p q r s t u v w x y z

[**Map** comes from Latin.]

## maple *noun* **maples**

A **maple** is a kind of tree whose leaf is the emblem of Canada.
[**Maple** comes from Old English.]

## marathon *noun* **marathons**

1 A **marathon** is a race that is 42 km long.
2 A **marathon** is an activity that lasts a very long time: *a dance marathon*.
[The **marathon** is named after *Marathon* in Greece. After a battle there a messenger is supposed to have run to Athens (about 40 kilometres away) with the news that the Greeks had won.]

## marble *noun* **marbles**

1 **Marble** is a type of coloured limestone that is used in buildings and for sculptures.
2 A **marble** is a small glass ball used in games played by children.
[**Marble** comes from Greek via French and Latin.]

## march *verb* **marches, marching, marched** (th)

1 To **march** means to walk in step with a group of people: *The soldiers marched*.
2 To **march** is to walk quickly with determination: *She marched up to the manager to complain*.
[**March** comes from French *marcher* 'to walk'.]

## march *noun* **marches**

A **march** is a large group of people who walk somewhere together to protest about something.

## mare *noun* **mares**

A **mare** is an adult female horse.
[**Mare** comes from Old English.]

## margarine *noun*

**Margarine** is a substitute for butter. It is made from vegetable oils or animal fat.
[**Margarine** comes from Greek via French.]

## margin *noun* **margins**

A **margin** is the blank space that runs down the side of a page: *Scribble notes in the margin*.
[**Margin** comes from Latin.]

## mark *noun* **marks** (th)

1 A **mark** is a scratch or stain on something that spoils it: *a dirty mark*.
2 A **mark** is a number or letter put on a piece of work to show how well it has been done: *a low mark*.
[**Mark** comes from Old English.]

## market *noun* **markets**

1 A **market** is a group of stalls, especially in the open air, where things are sold.
2 A **market** is a place where goods are bought and sold: *the international market*.
3 If there is a **market** for something, people want to buy it: *There's a huge market for designer clothes*.
[**Market** comes via French from the same Latin word as **merchant**.]

## marmalade *noun*

**Marmalade** is a kind of jam made from oranges, lemons or grapefruits.
[**Marmalade** comes from Portuguese via French.]

## maroon *noun*

**Maroon** is a dark brownish-red colour.
[**Maroon** comes from French *marron* 'chestnut'.]

## maroon *adjective*

of a dark brownish-red colour: *maroon suede shoes*.

## marooned *adjective*

Someone who is **marooned** is in a place that s/he cannot get away from: *The shipwrecked sailors were marooned on a desert island*.
[**Marooned** comes from Spanish via French.]

## marriage *noun* **marriages**

1 A **marriage** is a wedding ceremony: *The marriage took place in Jamaica*.
2 **Marriage** is the state of being husband and wife: *They divorced after only three years of marriage*.
[**Marriage** comes from the same French word as **marry**.]

## marrow *noun* **marrows**

1 **Marrow** is the soft substance inside your bones that makes red and white blood cells.
2 A **marrow** is a long green vegetable that looks like a very big cucumber.
[**Marrow** comes from Old English.]

## marry *verb* **marries, marrying, married**

To **marry** means to become someone's husband or wife: *Will you marry me?*

[**Marry** comes via French from Latin *maritus* 'married'.]

**marsh** *noun* **marshes** (th)
A **marsh** is an area of low wet ground. [**Marsh** comes from Old English.]

**marsupial** *noun* **marsupials**
A **marsupial** is a mammal such as a kangaroo or wombat. Baby marsupials are born very small and undeveloped, and their mother carries them in a pouch on her stomach.
[**Marsupial** comes via Latin from Greek *marsupion* 'pouch'.]

**Martian** *noun*
In stories, a **Martian** is an alien from the planet Mars.

**Martian** *adjective*
connected with or from the planet Mars: *Can the Martian climate support life?*

**martyr** *noun* **martyrs**
A **martyr** is someone who is killed or made to suffer for something s/he believes in very strongly.
[**Martyr** comes from Greek via Old English.]

**marvellous** *adjective* (th)
Something that is **marvellous** is wonderful or very good.
**marvellously** *adverb*.
[**Marvellous** comes via French from the same Latin word as **miracle**.]

**mascot** *noun* **mascots**
A **mascot** is an object, an animal or a person that is supposed to bring good luck: *The team's mascot is a goat.*
[**Mascot** comes from French.]

**masculine** *adjective*
1 Something that is **masculine** is considered typical of men or suitable for men: *Motor racing is traditionally a masculine sport.*
2 In some languages, such as French, some words are classed as **masculine**.
[**Masculine** comes via French from Latin *masculus* 'male' (ancestor of **male**).]

**mash** *verb* **mashes, mashing, mashed**
If you **mash** food, you break it up until it is soft. [**Mash** comes from Old English.]

**mash** *noun*
**Mash** is mashed potatoes: *sausages and mash.*

**mask** *noun* **masks**
A **mask** is a covering for the face to protect or disguise it.
[**Mask** comes from Italian via French.]

**mason** *noun* **masons**
A **mason** is someone who cuts and carves stone for buildings or gravestones.
[**Mason** comes from an old French word.]

**masonry** *noun*
**Masonry** is the parts of a building that are made of stone: *A chunk of masonry fell from the roof.*

**mass¹** *noun* Also **Mass**
In the Roman Catholic Church, **mass** is a service in which people share bread and wine which has been consecrated.
[**Mass¹** comes from Greek via Old English.]

**mass²** *noun* **masses**
1 A **mass**, or **masses**, of something is a lot of it: *There were masses of people at the party.*
2 A **mass** of something is a large, shapeless lump or heap of it: *His desk was covered with a mass of papers; a great mass of rock blocked the road.*
3 The **mass** of a substance is the amount of matter it contains: *a litre of liquid has more mass than a litre of gas.* **Mass** is a word used in science and mathematics.
[**Mass²** comes from Greek via French and Latin.]

**mass²** *adjective*
**Mass** means to do with a large number of people: *the mass media; a mass protest in Trafalgar Square.*

**massive** *adjective*
Something that is **massive** is huge: *the massive walls of the castle.*
[**Massive** comes via French from the same Latin word as **mass**.]

**mast** *noun* **masts**
A **mast** is a tall pole to hold up a sail, aerial or flag.
[**Mast** comes from Old English.]

**mat** *noun* **mats**
1 A **mat** is a small piece of carpet or other floor covering.
2 A **mat** is a piece of material that is used to put plates on to protect a table: *a place mat.*

[**Mat** comes from Old English.]

**match¹** *noun* **matches**
A **match** is a small wooden stick with a head that bursts into flames when you strike it.
[**Match¹** comes from an old French word.]

**match²** *noun* **matches** (th)
1 A **match** is a game between two people or teams: *a tennis match.*
2 If something is a **match** for something else, it is like it or equal to it: *The hat is a perfect match for the shoes.*
[**Match²** comes from Old English.]

**match²** *verb* **matches, matching, matched** (th)
1 If things **match¹** they have the same colour or pattern.
2 If something **matches** something else, it is equal to it.
3 If you **match** something, you find something else that is equal to it or that has the same colour or pattern.

**material** *noun* **materials**
1 A **material** is any substance that can be used to make things: *raw materials.*
2 **Material** is fabric or cloth.
[**Material** comes from the same Latin word as **matter**.]

**mathematics** *noun*
**Mathematics** is the study of numbers, measurements, quantities and shapes.
[**Mathematics** comes via French and Latin from Greek *mathema* 'science'.]

**matter** *noun* **matters** (th)
1 **Matter** is any kind of substance: *waste matter; printed matter.*
2 A **matter** is a subject or a situation that you must think about or do something about: *I don't want to make matters too complicated.*
3 **Matter** is the materials that make up everything.
[**Matter** comes via French from Latin *materia* 'substance' (ancestor of **material**).]

**matter** *verb* **matters, mattering, mattered** (th)
If something **matters**, it is important.

**mattress** *noun* **mattresses**
A **mattress** is a thick, soft pad for sleeping on.
[**Mattress** comes via French and Italian

from Arabic *matrah* 'cushion'.]

**maximum** *adjective*
The **maximum** amount of something is the largest possible amount.
[**Maximum** comes from Latin *maximum* 'the largest thing'.]

**may** *verb* **might**
1 **May** is used to say that something is possible: *I may be wrong.*
2 **May** is used as a polite way of asking permission or giving permission: *May I leave the table? You may use the phone.*
[**May** comes from Old English.]

**maybe** *adverb*
**Maybe** means perhaps or possibly: *Maybe she'll come, I'm not sure.*

**mayonnaise** *noun*
**Mayonnaise** is a cold, creamy sauce made with eggs and olive oil, usually eaten with salad.
[**Mayonnaise** comes from French.]

**mayor** *noun* **mayors**
A **mayor** is the person who is elected to be the leader of a council or a city.
[**Mayor** comes via French from the same Latin word as **major**.]

**me** *pronoun*
You use **me** to talk about yourself when you are the object of a verb: *Give me some sweets; Would you like me to help?*
[**Me** comes from Old English.]

**meadow** *noun* **meadows** (th)
A **meadow** is a field of grass where horses or cattle often graze.
[**Meadow** comes from Old English.]

**meal** *noun* **meals**
A **meal** is the food that you eat at breakfast, lunch, dinner, tea or supper.
[**Meal** comes from Old English.]

**mean¹** *verb* **means, meaning, meant** (th)
1 To **mean** means to have a certain explanation, to express a certain idea, or to be a sign of something: *The sign means 'Stop!'; Black clouds mean rain.*
2 If you **mean** to do something, you plan to do it: *I mean to get all my homework done by teatime; I didn't mean to hurt you.*
3 If something **means** something to you, it is important: *My family means a lot to me.*
[**Mean¹** comes from Old English *maenan.*]

a b c d e f g h i j k l **m**

**mean²** *adjective* **meaner, meanest** (th)
Someone who is not generous or will not share what s/he has is **mean**.
**meanly** *adverb.* **meanness** *noun.*
[**Mean²** comes from Old English *maena*.]

**meander** *verb* **meanders, meandering, meandered** (th)
To **meander** means to wander or wind slowly along.
[**Meander** comes via Latin and Greek from the name of the River Mendere in Turkey, which has a meandering course.]

**meaning** *noun* **meanings** (th)
**1** A **meaning** is an explanation of a word or idea.
**2** If something has **meaning**, it is important and has a purpose.
[**Meaning** comes from **mean¹**.]

**meaningful** *adjective* (th)
**1** Something that is **meaningful** is serious or important.
**2** A **meaningful** look is a look that is trying to tell someone something.
**meaningfully** *adverb.*

**meant** *verb*
**Meant** is the past participle of **mean**.

**meaningless** *adjective* (th)
Something that is **meaningless** seems to have no meaning.

**measles** *noun*
**Measles** is an illness that makes red spots appear on your skin. You catch **measles** from someone else who has it, but once you have had it you will not get it again.
[**Measles** probably comes from an old Dutch word.]

**measure** *noun* **measures**
**1** A **measure** is a unit in a measuring system, such as a metre for measuring length or a kilogram for measuring weight.
**2** A **measure** is an action that is taken for a particular purpose: *government measures to help the poor.*
[**Measure** comes from Latin via French.]

**measure** *verb* **measures, measuring, measured**
**1** To **measure** something means to find out how big it is, or how much of it there is.
**2** If something **measures** a certain size, it

is that big: *The room measures 11 metres by 12 metres.*

**measurement** *noun* **measurements**
A **measurement** is the length, width or height of something found by measuring it: *The builder checked the measurements of the room.*

**meat** *noun* **meats**
**Meat** is animal flesh used as food.
[**Meat** comes from Old English.]

**meatball** *noun* **meatballs**
A **meatball** is a cooked ball of mince and breadcrumbs, usually in gravy or a sauce. You sometimes eat **meatballs** with spaghetti.

**mechanic** *noun* **mechanics**
A **mechanic** is a person whose job is to repair machines.
[**Mechanic** comes via Latin from the same Greek word as **machine**.]

**mechanical** *adjective*
**1** Something that is **mechanical** uses a machine to make it work.
**2** If you do something in a **mechanical** way, you do it automatically, without thinking about it. **mechanically** *adverb.*
[**Mechanical** comes from the same Greek word as **machine**.]

**medal** *noun* **medals**
A **medal** is a small shaped piece of metal that you get for winning a race, or for being very brave or doing something very well.
[**Medal** comes from Latin via French and Italian.]

**medallist** *noun* **medallists**
A **medallist** is someone who has won a medal.

**media** *plural noun*
The **media** means newspapers, television, and radio: *I'd like a job in the media.*
[**Media** is the plural of **medium**.]

**mediaeval** *adjective*
**Mediaeval** is another way to spell **medieval**.

**medical** *adjective*
**Medical** means to do with people's health or with treating illness: *a medical centre.*
[**Medical** comes via French from Latin *medicus* 'doctor'.]

**medicine** *noun* **medicines** (th)
A **medicine** is a liquid or tablet that you take when you are ill.
[**Medicine** comes via French from the same Latin word as **medical**.]

**medieval** *adjective Also* **mediaeval**
Something that is **medieval** comes from the time in history called the Middle Ages.
[**Medieval** comes from Latin *medium aevum* 'middle age'.]

**medium** *noun*
1 A **medium** is something you can use to tell other people about your ideas: *Television is the most popular medium for news and entertainment.* The plural is **media**.
2 A **medium** is a person who believes that s/he can pass on messages from people who have died. The plural is **mediums**.
[**Medium** comes from Latin *medium* 'middle'.]

**medium** *adjective*
Something that is **medium** is of average or middle size.

**meet** *verb* **meets, meeting, met** (th)
To **meet** means to come together with someone or something.
[**Meet** comes from Old English.]

**meeting** *noun* **meetings** (th)
A **meeting** is a group of people who have come together for a particular purpose.

**megabyte** *noun* **megabytes**
A **megabyte** is one million bytes of data. **Megabytes** are used to talk about how much memory a computer has.
[**Megabyte** comes from Greek *megas* 'great' and **byte**.]

**melody** *noun* **melodies**
A **melody** is a tune.
[**Melody** comes from Greek.]

**melon** *noun* **melons**
A **melon** is a large, round or oval fruit with a thick green or yellow skin and many pips.
[**Melon** comes from Greek via French and Latin.]

**melt** *verb* **melts, melting, melted** (th)
When something **melts**, it changes from a solid into a liquid as it gets warmer: *The ice melted in the heat of the sun.*

[**Melt** comes from Old English.]

**member** *noun* **members**
A **member** is someone who belongs to a group or a club.
[**Member** comes from Latin.]

**membrane** *noun* **membranes**
A **membrane** is a very thin layer of skin in a part of a plant or an animal.
[**Membrane** comes from Latin.]

**memento** *noun* **mementos** *or* **mementoes**
A **memento** is something that you keep to remind you of a place or a person.
[**Memento** comes from Latin *memento* 'remember'.]

**memorable** *adjective* (th)
Something that is memorable is unusual or special, and easy to remember: *a memorable experience.*
[**Memorable** comes from the same Latin word as **memory**.]

**memorise** *verb* **memorises, memorising, memorised** *Also* **memorize**
To **memorise** something means to learn it by heart so that you will remember it.
[**Memorise** comes from **memory**.]

**memory** *noun* **memories**
1 **Memory** is being able to remember things: *She has a good memory.*
2 A **memory** is something that you remember from the past.
3 A computer's **memory** is the part that stores information.
[**Memory** comes via French from Latin *memor* 'keeping in your mind'.]

**mend** *verb* **mends, mending, mended** (th)
To **mend** something that is damaged or broken means to repair it so that it can be used again.
[**Mend** comes from *amend* 'to alter or put right', which comes from Latin *menda* 'a fault'.]

**menstruation** *noun*
**Menstruation** is when a girl or woman has her period, and blood comes from her womb.
[**Menstruation** comes from Latin *menstruus* 'monthly'.]

**mental** *adjective*
Mental means to do with thinking or your mind: *We had a mental arithmetic test today.* **mentally** *adverb.*
[Mental comes from Latin.]

**mention** *verb* **mentions, mentioning, mentioned**
To **mention** something means to say it, or say something about it, in a few words: *The article mentioned our school.*
[Mention comes from Latin.]

**menu** *noun* **menus**
1 A **menu** is a list of the food and drinks that you can choose in a restaurant.
2 On a computer, the **menu** shows you a list of what you can do.
[Menu comes from French.]

**merchant** *noun* **merchants**
A **merchant** is a person who buys and sells things, especially things from other countries.
[Merchant comes via French from Latin *mercari* 'to buy and sell' (ancestor of **market**).]

**merciful** *adjective* (th)
Someone who is **merciful** is kind and forgiving. **mercifully** *adverb.*
[Merciful comes from **mercy**.]

**merciless** *adjective* (th)
Someone who is **merciless** is very cruel. **mercilessly** *adverb.*
[Merciless comes from **mercy**.]

**mercury** *noun*
Mercury is a silver-coloured liquid metal.
[Mercury is named after the Roman god *Mercury*.]

**mercy** *noun* (th)
Mercy means kindness and forgiveness.
[Mercy comes from Latin via French.]

**merge** *verb* **merges, merging, merged** (th)
1 When two things **merge**, they come together to make one thing.
2 When something **merges into** something else, it gradually blends into it.
[Merge comes from Latin.]

**meringue** *noun* **meringues**
A **meringue** is a sweet, cream-coloured cake made from egg-whites and sugar.
[Meringue comes from French.]

**mermaid** *noun* **mermaids**
A **mermaid** is a creature in stories with a woman's body and a fish's tail instead of legs.
[Mermaid comes from Old English *mere* 'sea' and *maid* 'girl'.]

**merrily** *adverb*
If you do something **merrily**, you do it in a merry way: *laughing merrily.*

**merry** *adjective* **merrier, merriest** (th)
Merry means cheerful and happy.
[Merry comes from Old English.]

**mess** *noun* **messes** (th)
If you say that something is a **mess** or **in a mess**, you mean that it is untidy or dirty.
[Mess comes from French *mes* 'a helping of food'.]

**mess** *verb* **messes, messing, messed** (th)
1 To **mess about** or **mess around** means to act in a silly way, or to do pointless things.
2 To **mess** something **up** means to spoil it or make it untidy.

**message** *noun* **messages**
A **message** is a piece of information that you send to another person.
[Message comes from Latin via French.]

**messenger** *noun* **messengers**
A **messenger** is a person who takes a message to someone.
[Messenger comes from the same French word as **message**.]

**messy** *adjective* **messier, messiest** (th)
Messy means untidy or dirty.
[Messy comes from **mess**.]

**met** *verb*
Met is the past tense of **meet**.

**metal** *noun* **metals**
A **metal** is a hard substance such as gold and copper. **Metals** are good at conducting heat and electricity.
[Metal comes from Greek via French or Latin.]

**meteor** *noun* **meteors**
A **meteor** is a piece of rock from space that burns very brightly when it enters the earth's atmosphere.
[Meteor comes from Greek *meteoros* 'high in the air'.]

**meteorite** *noun* **meteorites**
A **meteorite** is a piece of rock from space that falls to earth.
[**Meteorite** comes from **meteor**.]

**meteorology** *noun*
If you study **meteorology**, you learn about the weather and the climate. People use **meteorology** to make weather forecasts.
[**Meteorology** comes from the same Greek word as **meteor**.]

**meter** *noun* **meters**
A **meter** is a machine that measures the amount of something you have used: *reading the electricity meter.*
[**Meter** comes an old word *mete* 'to measure', which comes from Old English.]

**method** *noun* **methods** (th)
A **method** is a way of doing something.
[**Method** comes from Greek via Latin.]

**methodical** *adjective* (th)
If you do something in a **methodical** way, you do it carefully and thoroughly.
**methodically** *adverb.*
[**Methodical** comes from the same Greek word as **method**.]

**metre** *noun* **metres**
1 A **metre** is a unit that we use to measure length. There are 100 centimetres in a **metre**.
2 In poetry, **metre** is the way that the words and syllables are arranged so that they have rhythm.
[**Metre** comes via French from Greek *metron* 'measure'.]

**metric** *adjective*
**Metric** measurements are based on units of ten. Litres, metres, and grams are used in the **metric** system.
[**Metric** comes from the same French word as **metre**.]

**miaow** *noun* **miaows**
A **miaow** is the noise that a cat makes.
[The word **miaow** is an imitation of the sound.]

**miaow** *verb* **miaows, miaowing, miaowed**
To **miaow** means to make the noise that a cat makes.

**mice** *noun*
**Mice** is the plural of mouse.

**microchip** *noun* **microchips**
A **microchip** acts as the brain of a computer. Although **microchips** are usually only 0.5cm long and 0.05cm, thick, they can handle a lot of information.
[**Microchip** comes from *micro-* 'small' and **chip**.]

**microphone** *noun* **microphones**
A **microphone** is a machine for picking up sound waves for recording or sending through loudspeakers.
[**Microphone** comes from *micro-* 'small' and Greek *phone* 'sound'.]

**microprocessor** *noun* **microprocessors**
A **microprocessor** is the main chip in a small computer.
[**Microprocessor** comes from *micro-* 'small' and *processor* 'something that carries out a process'.]

**microscope** *noun* **microscopes**
A **microscope** is an instrument that you use in science. It has lenses that make tiny things look bigger so that you can study them.
[**Microscope** comes from Greek *mikros* 'small' and *skopein* 'to look at'.]

**microwave** *noun* **microwaves**
A **microwave** is an electronic wave, used in various ways including in telecommunications and microwave ovens.
[**Microwave** comes from *micro-* 'small' and **wave**.]

**midday** *noun*
**Midday** is 12 o'clock in the daytime.
[**Midday** comes from Old English.]

**middle** *noun* **middles** (th)
The **middle** of something is the same distance from both ends or edges.
[**Middle** comes from Old English.]

**Middle Ages** *plural noun*
The time in history between about AD 1000 and about AD 1500 is called the **Middle Ages**.

**midnight** *noun*
**Midnight** is 12 o'clock in the night-time.
[**Midnight** comes from Old English.]

**midwife** *noun* **midwives**
A **midwife** is a person whose job is to look after and help women who are having a baby.
[**Midwife** comes from Old English *mid wyf* 'with the woman'.]

**might** *verb*
**1 Might** is the past tense of **may**.
**2** If you say that you **might** do something, you mean that there is a chance that you will do it: *I might go out later.*

**mighty** *adjective* **mightier, mightiest** (th)
**Mighty** means strong, large or powerful: *a mighty king; a mighty river.*
[**Mighty** comes from Old English *miht* 'strength or power'.]

**migrate** *verb* **migrates, migrating, migrated**
**1** To **migrate** means to move from one place to another, especially to find a job.
**2** When birds and animals **migrate**, they go to another part of the world at certain times of the year to find food or to breed.
[**Migrate** comes from Latin *migrare* 'to move'.]

**mild** *adjective* **milder, mildest** (th)
**1** Someone who is **mild** is gentle and good-tempered.
**2** A food that is **mild** does not have a strong taste.
**3** Weather that is **mild** is not too hot or too cold. **mildly** *adverb*. **mildness** *noun*.
[**Mild** comes from Old English.]

**mile** *noun* **miles**
**1** A **mile** is a measurement of length in the imperial system, equal to about 1.609 kilometres.
**2** You use **miles** to mean a very long way: *We had to park miles from the shops.*
[**Mile** comes via Old English from Latin *milles passus* 'one thousand paces', the length of a Roman mile.]

**military** *adjective*
You use **military** to talk about things that are to do with armies and soldiers: *military training; military action.*
[**Military** comes from Latin *miles* 'soldier'.]

**milk** *noun*
**Milk** is a white liquid that female mammals feed their babies with.
[**Milk** comes from Old English.]

**milk** *verb* **milks, milking, milked**
If you **milk** an animal, you get milk from its udder.

**mill** *noun* **mills**
**1** A **mill** is a building where corn, rice or wheat is ground into flour.
**2** A **mill** is a kind of factory: *Paper is made in a paper mill.*
[**Mill** comes via Old English from Latin *molere* 'to grind'.]

**millennium** *noun* **millenniums or millennia**
A **millennium** is one thousand years.
[**Millennium** comes from Latin *mille* 'a thousand' and *annus* 'year'.]

**milligram** *noun* **milligrams**
A **milligram** is a unit that we use to measure weight. There are 1,000 **milligrams** in one gram.
[**Milligram** comes from Latin *mille* 'a thousand' and **gram**.]

**millilitre** *noun* **millilitres**
A **millilitre** is a unit that we use to measure the volume of a liquid. There are 1,000 **millilitres** in one litre.
[**Millilitre** comes from Latin *mille* 'a thousand' and **litre**.]

**millimetre** *noun* **millimetres**
A **millimetre** is a unit that we use to measure length. There are ten **millimetres** in one centimetre and 1,000 millimetres in one metre.
[**Millimetre** comes from Latin *mille* 'a thousand' and **metre**.]

**million** *noun* **millions**
A **million** is the number 1,000,000.
[**Million** comes from Italian via French.]

**millionaire** *noun* **millionaires**
A **millionaire** is a very rich person who has at least a million dollars or pounds.
[**Millionaire** comes from the same French word as **million**.]

**millipede** *noun* **millipedes**
A **millipede** is a small creature with a long, thin body and a lot of legs.
[**Millipede** comes from Latin *mille* 'a thousand' and *pedes* 'feet'.]

**mime** *noun* **mimes**
A **mime** is a kind of play, or a kind of acting, in which the actors use gestures and expressions instead of speaking.

[**Mime** comes from Greek via Latin.]

**mime** *verb* **mimes, miming, mimed**
When you **mime**, you act something out without using your voice.

**mimic** *verb* **mimics, mimicking, mimicked** (th)
If you **mimic** someone, you copy what s/he says or does.
[**Mimic** comes from the same Greek word as **mime**.]

**minaret** *noun* **minarets**
A **minaret** is a thin tower on a mosque.
[**Minaret** comes from Arabic via French and Turkish.]

**minbar** *noun* **minbars** *Also* **mimbar**
A **minbar** is a platform for speaking to people in a mosque.

**mince** *noun*
**Mince** is meat that has been cut up very small.
[**Mince** comes via French from Latin *minutia* 'smallness'.]

**mince** *verb* **minces, mincing, minced**
When you **mince** meat, you use a machine to cut it very small.

**mincemeat** *noun*
**Mincemeat** is a mixture of dried fruit, suet, spices and sugar.
[**Mincemeat** comes from **mince** and **meat** in an old sense 'food'.]

**mince pie** *noun* **mince pies**
A **mince pie** is a small pastry case filled with mincemeat. People often eat **mince pies** at Christmas.

**mind** *noun* **minds**
**1** Your **mind** is the way you think, and what is in your thoughts.
**2** If you **change your mind**, you change the way that you feel about something, or make a different decision.
[**Mind** comes from Old English.]

**mind** *verb* **minds, minding, minded** (th)
**1** If you **mind** something, you care about it, or are not happy about it: *Do you mind if I smoke?*
**2** To **mind** a person or a thing means to look after that person or thing.
**3** To **mind** or **mind out** means to be careful of something: *Mind you don't fall!*

**mine**[1] *noun* **mines**
**1** A **mine** is a very deep hole dug to get coal, metal or rock out of the ground.
**2** A **mine** is a bomb hidden underground or in the sea to blow up things that pass over it.
[**Mine**[1] comes from an old French word.]

**mine**[2] *pronoun*
Something that belongs to me is **mine**.
[**Mine**[2] comes from Old English.]

**miner** *noun* **miners**
A **miner** is someone who works down a mine.

**mineral** *noun* **minerals**
A **mineral** is something that people dig out of the ground, such as coal, oil or salt.
[**Mineral** comes from Latin.]

**mineral water** *noun*
**Mineral water** is water that comes out of the ground at a spring.

**miniature** *adjective* (th)
Something that is **miniature** is a very small version of a bigger thing: *a dolls' house with miniature tables and chairs.*
[**Miniature** comes from Latin via Italian.]

**minimum** *adjective*
The **minimum** amount of something is the smallest or least amount.
[**Minimum** comes from Latin *minimum* 'the smallest thing'.]

**minister** *noun* **ministers**
**1** The priest in some churches is called a **minister**.
**2** A **minister** is someone who is in charge of a part of the government: *the Minister of Transport.*
[**Minister** comes via French from Latin *minister* 'servant'.]

**minor** *adjective* (th)
Something that is **minor** is smaller or less important.
[**Minor** comes from Latin *minor* 'smaller' or 'less'.]

**minstrel** *noun* **minstrels**
A **minstrel** was a singer or a poet in medieval times.
[**Minstrel** comes from an old French word.]

**mint**[1] *noun* **mints**
**1 Mint** is a herb with leaves that have a

strong smell and flavour.
2 A **mint** is a sweet that tastes of mint.
[**Mint**[1] comes from Old English.]

**mint**[2] *noun* **mints**
A **mint** is a building where coins are
made.
[**Mint**[2] comes via Old English from the
same Latin word as **money**.]

**minus** *preposition*
**Minus** means that you are taking one
number away from another number. The
symbol for **minus** is – : $9 - 2 = 7$; *Nine
minus two is seven.*
[**Minus** comes from Latin *minus* 'less'.]

**minute**[1] *noun* **minutes**
A **minute** is 60 seconds. There are 60
**minutes** in an hour.
[**Minute**[1] comes via French from the same
Latin word as **minute**[2].]

**minute**[2] *adjective* (th)
Something that is tiny is **minute**.
[**Minute**[2] comes from Latin *minutus* 'made
small'.]

**miracle** *noun* **miracles**
A **miracle** is something wonderful that
happens, which people did not think was
possible.
[**Miracle** comes from Latin *mirari* 'to look
at' or 'to wonder at' (ancestor of
**marvellous**).]

**miraculous** *adjective* (th)
**Miraculous** means very surprising and
lucky: *We had a miraculous escape.*
**miraculously** *adverb.*
[**Miraculous** comes via French from the
same Latin word as **miracle**.]

**mirage** *noun* **mirages**
A **mirage** is something that you think you
can see in the distance that is not really
there.
[**Mirage** comes via French from the same
Latin word as **miracle**.]

**mirror** *noun* **mirrors**
A **mirror** is a piece of glass that reflects
things very clearly.
[**Mirror** comes via French from the same
Latin word as **miracle**.]

**misbehave** *verb* **misbehaves,
misbehaving, misbehaved** (th)
If you **misbehave**, you are naughty or
silly.

[**Misbehave** comes from *mis-* 'badly or
wrongly' and **behave**.]

**miscarriage** *noun* **miscarriages**
If a woman has a **miscarriage**, her baby
dies and comes out of her body before it
is ready to be born.
[**Miscarriage** comes from *mis-* 'badly or
wrongly' and **carriage** in the sense
'carrying'.]

**miscellaneous** *adjective* (th)
**Miscellaneous** things are mixed, or of
different kinds: *I found miscellaneous items
under her bed.*
[**Miscellaneous** comes from Latin
*miscellus* 'mixed'.]

**mischief** *noun* (th)
**Mischief** is silly or naughty behaviour.
[**Mischief** comes from an old French
word.]

**mischievous** *adjective* (th)
Someone who is **mischievous** likes to
play tricks on other people and make
trouble. **mischievously** *adverb.*
[**Mischievous** comes from the same old
French word as **mischief**.]

**miser** *noun* **misers** (th)
A **miser** is a person who does not like to
spend money.
[**Miser** comes from Latin *miser* 'unhappy
or pitiful'.]

**miserable** *adjective* (th)
Someone who is **miserable** is very
unhappy. **miserably** *adverb.*
[**Miserable** comes via French from the
same Latin word as **miser**.]

**misery** *noun* (th)
**Misery** is great unhappiness.
[**Misery** comes via French from the same
Latin word as **miser**.]

**miss** *verb* **misses, missing, missed** (th)
1 If you **miss** something, you do not
manage to do it, see it, catch it or hit it:
*She missed the ball; We missed the train; I
went to meet my sister but I missed her.*
2 To **miss** a person means to be sad
because s/he has gone away.
3 If you **miss** something, you realise that
you have lost it.
[**Miss** comes from Old English.]

**missile** *noun* **missiles**
A **missile** is a weapon that is thrown by a

person or shot from a rocket.
[**Missile** comes from Latin *missum* 'sent'.]

**missing** *adjective* (th)
If someone or something is **missing** s/he or it is lost.
[**Missing** comes from **miss**.]

**mist** *noun* **mists** (th)
A **mist** is damp air that is difficult to see through. [**Mist** comes from Old English.]

**mistake** *noun* **mistakes** (th)
A **mistake** is something that is wrong or not correct.
[**Mistake** comes from *mis-* 'badly or wrongly' and Old Norse *taka* 'to take'.]

**mistletoe** *noun*
**Mistletoe** is an evergreen plant with white berries that grows on other trees.
[**Mistletoe** comes from Old English.]

**misty** *adjective* **mistier, mistiest** (th)
When it is **misty**, there is a lot of mist.

**misunderstand** *verb* **misunderstands, misunderstanding, misunderstood**
If you **misunderstand** something, you get it wrong because you do not understand it.
[**Misunderstand** comes from *mis-* 'badly or wrongly' and **understand**.]

**misunderstanding** *noun* **misunderstandings**
A **misunderstanding** is when someone has not understood something properly.

**mix** *verb* **mixes, mixing, mixed** (th)
To **mix** things means to put them together and stir or shake them.
[**Mix** comes from the same Latin word as **miscellaneous**.]

**mixture** *noun* **mixtures**
A **mixture** is something you make by mixing different things together.

**moan** *verb* **moans, moaning, moaned** (th)
1 To **moan** means to make a long, soft, low sound. You might **moan** when you are hurt or very sad.
2 To **moan** means to grumble or complain: *always moaning about the food at school.*
[**Moan** probably comes from Old English.]

**moan** *noun* **moans**
A **moan** is a long, soft, low sound.

**moat** *noun* **moats**
A **moat** is a wide ditch filled with water. People made **moats** around castles to stop other people getting in.
[**Moat** comes from an old French word.]

**mob** *noun* **mobs** (th)
A **mob** is a big crowd of noisy or violent people. [**Mob** comes from Latin.]

**mobile** *noun* **mobiles**
A **mobile** is a decoration that hangs from a ceiling: *They hung a mobile above the baby's cot.* [**Mobile** comes from Latin.]

**mobile** *adjective* (th)
Something that is **mobile** can move around: *a mobile library; Now I've got a car, I'm more mobile.*

**model** *noun* **models** (th)
1 A **model** of something is a small copy of it: *We're making a model of the church.*
2 A **model** is one version of a machine or a car: *The cheaper model has no sunroof.*
3 A **model** is a person who wears new clothes for people who might want to buy them or take photographs of them.
[**Model** comes from Latin *modulus* 'a small measure or amount' (ancestor of **mould²**).]

**model** *verb* **models, modelling, modelled**
1 To **model** is to wear new clothes for people who might want to buy them or take photographs of them.
2 To **model** an object is to make it from something such as clay.

**modem** *noun* **modems**
A **modem** is a piece of equipment that you need if you want to join a computer to a telephone system.
[**Modem** comes from *modulator* and *demodulator*. The modem *modulates* (changes) the electric signal from the computer to send it through the telephone system, and another modem *demodulates* it (changes it back) so that the computer that receives it can understand it.]

**modern** *adjective* (th)
Something that is **modern** is in use at the present time and is not old.
[**Modern** comes from Latin *modo* 'just now'.]

**modest** *adjective* (th)
1 If you are **modest**, you do not like to tell other people about the good things that

a b c d e f g h i j k l **m**

you have done.
**2** Something that is **modest** is not very
big. **modestly** adverb.
[**Modest** comes from Latin via French.]

**moist** adjective **moister, moistest** (th)
Something that is damp is **moist**.
**moistly** adverb. **moistness** noun.
[**Moist** comes from an old French word.]

**moisture** noun
**Moisture** is damp air that condenses on
surfaces.
[**Moisture** comes from the same old
French word as **moist**.]

**molar** noun **molars**
A **molar** is a large flat tooth that you use
for chewing food.
[**Molar** comes from Latin *mola*
'millstone'.]

**mole**[1] noun **moles**
A **mole** on your skin is a raised brown
spot like a big freckle.
[**Mole**[1] comes from Old English.]

**mole**[2] noun **moles**
A **mole** is a small, furry animal that
burrows underground.
[**Mole**[2] probably comes from an old
German or Dutch word.]

**molecule** noun **molecules**
A **molecule** is the smallest amount of a
substance that can exist by itself.
[**Molecule** comes from Latin *molecula*
'little mass'.]

**moment** noun **moments** (th)
A **moment** is a very small amount of time.
[**Moment** comes from Latin.]

**monarch** noun **monarchs**
A **monarch** is a ruler such as a king or a
queen.
[**Monarch** comes via Latin from Greek
*monarches* 'someone who rules alone'.]

**monarchy** noun **monarchies**
If a country is a **monarchy**, it has a king or
a queen.

**monastery** noun **monasteries**
A **monastery** is a building where monks
live and work.
[**Monastery** comes from Greek *monazein*
'to live separately'.]

**money** noun (th)
**Money** is the metal coins and paper notes
that we use to buy and sell things.
[**Money** comes from Latin.]

**monitor** noun **monitors**
A **monitor** is a screen that is linked to a
computer, or a screen in a television
studio that shows what the camera is
seeing.
[**Monitor** comes from Latin *monere* 'to
warn'.]

**monk** noun **monks**
A **monk** is a man who lives with other
**monks** in a building called a monastery.
**Monks** live in a simple way and pray to
God several times a day.
[**Monk** comes from Greek.]

**monkey** noun **monkeys**
A **monkey** is an animal with long arms
and a long tail. **Monkeys** live in trees in
tropical countries.
[No one knows where **monkey** comes
from.]

**monsoon** noun **monsoons**
A **monsoon** is when there is a strong
wind and heavy rain for many weeks.
**Monsoons** occur in India and other
countries in Asia.
[**Monsoon** comes from Arabic via Dutch.]

**monster** noun **monsters**
A **monster** is a huge, frightening animal
in stories. [**Monster** comes from Latin.]

**month** noun **months**
A **month** is one of the 12 parts into which
a year is divided.
[**Month** comes from Old English.]

**monthly** adverb
If something happens **monthly**, it
happens every month.

**monthly** adjective
A **monthly** magazine comes out once a
month.

**monument** noun **monuments** (th)
A **monument** is a statue or a building,
especially one that is built to remind
people of something that has happened
or someone who has died.
[**Monument** comes from Latin.]

**mood** noun **moods**
**1** A **mood** is a way that you are feeling:
*He's in a good mood.*
**2** If you are **in the mood** to do something,
you feel like doing it.
[**Mood** comes from Old English.]

**moon** noun *Also* **Moon**
The **moon** is a small planet that goes

round the earth and shines at night.
[**Moon** comes from Old English.]

**moose** *noun* **moose**
A **moose** is a large North American deer.
[**Moose** comes from Abnaki (a North
American Indian language).]

**moral** *noun* **morals**
**1** The **moral** of a story is the lesson that
you are supposed to learn from it.
**2** Your **morals** are your ideas and beliefs
about what is right and wrong.
[**Moral** comes from Latin.]

**more** *adjective*
**1** larger in number or amount: *have some
more cereal; I need more time.*
**2** extra: *Add more cheese.*
[**More** comes from Old English.]

**more** *adverb*
**1** again: *He did it once more.*
**2** to a greater extent: *This book is more
suitable; I like meat more than fish.*

**morning** *noun* **mornings**
**Morning** is the early part of the day
before midday.
[**Morning** comes from old English.]

**mortal** *adjective*
To be **mortal** means that you cannot live
for ever and that one day you have to die.
[**Mortal** comes from Latin *mortis* 'to do
with death'.]

**mortar** *noun*
**Mortar** is a mixture of sand, cement and
water used to stick bricks together in
buildings.
[**Mortar** comes from Latin via French.]

**mortgage** *noun* **mortgages**
A **mortgage** is a way of buying a house.
You borrow the money from a bank or a
building society and pay it back over
many years.
[**Mortgage** comes from an old French
word.]

**mosaic** *noun* **mosaics**
A **mosaic** is a picture or a pattern made
by putting together lots of small pieces of
tile or glass.
[**Mosaic** comes from Italian via French.]

**Moslem** *noun* **Moslems**
**Moslem** is another way to spell **Muslim**.

**mosque** *noun* **mosques**
A **mosque** is a building where Muslims
worship.

[**Mosque** comes from Arabic via French,
Spanish and Italian.]

**mosquito** *noun* **mosquitoes**
A **mosquito** is an insect that bites.
[**Mosquito** comes via Spanish or
Portuguese from Latin *mosca* 'a fly'.]

**moss** *noun* **mosses**
**Moss** is a very small, furry plant that
grows in damp places.
[**Moss** comes from Old English.]

**most** *adjective*
**1** the largest amount: *I ate most of the
chocolate.*
**2** more than the other people or things: *He
was the most friendly of the neighbours.*
[**Most** comes from Old English.]

**moth** *noun* **moths**
A **moth** is an insect like a butterfly that
usually flies at night.
[**Moth** comes from Old English.]

**mother** *noun* **mothers**
Your **mother** is your female parent.
[**Mother** comes from Old English.]

**mother-in-law** *noun* **mothers-in-law**
Your **mother-in-law** is the mother of your
husband or wife.

**motive** *noun* **motives**
Your **motive** for doing something is your
reason for doing it.
[**Motive** comes via French from Latin
*movere* 'to move' (ancestor of **move**).]

**motor** *noun* **motors**
A **motor** is a machine that makes
something move or work.
[**Motor** comes from Latin *motor* 'someone
or something that moves'.]

**motorbike** *noun* **motorbikes**
A **motorbike** is a motorcycle. **Motorbike**
is an informal word.

**motorcycle** *noun* **motorcycles**
A **motorcycle** is a two-wheeled vehicle
with an engine.

**mould**[1] *noun*
**Mould** is a furry fungus that grows in
damp places and on old food.
[**Mould**[1] comes from Old Norse.]

**mould**[2] *noun* **moulds**
A **mould** is a container that gives a shape
to a liquid so that it can set into a solid.
[**Mould**[2] comes from the same Latin word
as **model**.]

a b c d e f g h i j k l **m**

**moult** *verb* **moults, moulting, moulted**
If an animal **moults**, its fur, feathers or skin falls off and a new layer grows back. [**Moult** comes via Old English from Latin *mutare* 'to change'.]

**mountain** *noun* **mountains**
A **mountain** is a very high hill. [**Mountain** comes from French.]

**mountaineer** *noun* **mountaineers**
A **mountaineer** is a person who climbs mountains.

**mourn** *verb* **mourns, mourning, mourned** (th)
To **mourn** means to feel and show your sadness when someone has died. [**Mourn** comes from Old English.]

**mouse** *noun* **mice**
1 A **mouse** is a small animal with a long tail.
2 A **mouse** is a small device that is attached to a computer. You move the **mouse** about and click its buttons to control what the computer does. [**Mouse** comes from Old English.]

**moustache** *noun* **moustaches**
A **moustache** is hair that grows on a man's upper lip. [**Moustache** comes from Greek via French and Italian.]

**mouth** *noun* **mouths**
Your **mouth** is the part of your face that opens to speak and eat. [**Mouth** comes from Old English.]

**move** *verb* **moves, moving, moved** (th)
To **move** means to go or take something from one place to another. [**Move** comes from Latin.]

**movement** *noun* **movements**
1 A **movement** is a change of position or place.
2 A **movement** is a section of a long piece of classical music.

**movie** *noun* **movies**
A **movie** is a film shown at a cinema or on television. [**Movie** is short for *moving picture*.]

**mow** *verb* **mows, mowing, mowed**
To **mow** grass or a crop in a field means to cut it. [**Mow** comes from Old English.]

**much** *adverb* (th)
a lot or greatly: *Thank you very much.* [**Much** comes from Old English.]

**mucus** *noun*
**Mucus** is the wet substance that comes out of the nose when you have a cold. [**Mucus** comes from Latin.]

**mud** *noun* (th)
**Mud** is wet earth. [**Mud** probably comes from an old German word.]

**muddle** *verb* **muddles, muddling, muddled** (th)
To **muddle** things means to mix them up and get them in a mess. [**Muddle** probably comes from an old Dutch word.]

**muesli** *noun* **mueslis**
**Muesli** is a breakfast cereal made from oats, nuts, and dried fruit that you eat with milk. [**Muesli** comes from the form of German spoken in Switzerland.]

**mug** *noun* **mugs**
A **mug** is a deep cup with straight sides and a handle. [**Mug** probably comes from a Scandinavian language.]

**mulberry** *noun* **mulberries**
A **mulberry** is a tree with purple berries that can be eaten. [**Mulberry** comes from Old English.]

**mule** *noun* **mules**
A **mule** is an animal produced by a female horse and a male donkey. [**Mule** comes from Old English.]

**multimedia** *adjective*
Computer games and programs that are **multimedia** include text, sound, pictures and video. [**Multimedia** comes from Latin *multus* 'many' and **media**.]

**multiplication** *noun*
**Multiplication** is the process of multiplying numbers. [**Multiplication** comes via French from the same Latin word as **multiply**.]

**multiply** *verb* **multiplies, multiplying, multiplied**
1 To **multiply** a number means to add that number to itself a particular number of times: The symbol for multiplying one number by another is x: *10 x 10 = 100; 10 multiplied by 10 is 100.*
2 To **multiply** means to grow in number: *The weeds in the garden are multiplying.*

[**Multiply** comes from Latin via French.]

**mumble** *verb* **mumbles, mumbling, mumbled** (th)
To **mumble** means to speak quietly and unclearly so that you cannot easily be heard or understood.
[**Mumble** comes from Old English.]

**mummy¹** *noun* **mummies**
**Mummy** is a child's word for mother.
[**Mummy¹** is probably an imitation of the sounds a baby makes when it first tries to speak.]

**mummy²** *noun* **mummies**
A **mummy** is the body of a dead person that was preserved and wrapped in cloth by the ancient Egyptians.
[**Mummy²** comes via French and Latin from Arabic.]

**mumps** *noun*
**Mumps** is an illness that makes the sides of your face and neck swell. You catch **mumps** from someone else who has it, but once you have had it you will not get it again.
[**Mumps** comes from an old word *mump* 'to pull a face'.]

**mundane** *adjective* (th)
Something that is **mundane** is boring and ordinary. [**Mundane** comes from Latin.]

**murder** *verb* **murders, murdering, murdered** (th)
To **murder** means to kill someone deliberately.
[**Murder** comes from Old English.]

**murmur** *verb* **murmurs, murmuring, murmured** (th)
To **murmur** means to speak in a very quiet voice.
[**Murmur** comes from Latin via French.]

**muscle** *noun* **muscles**
A **muscle** is one of the parts inside the body that produce movement.
[**Muscle** comes via French from Latin *musculus* 'little mouse' (because the shape of some **muscles** reminded people of mice).]

**museum** *noun* **museums**
A **museum** is a place where old or interesting objects are kept for people to go and see.
[**Museum** comes via Latin from Greek *mouseion* 'the home of the Muses'; the Muses were the Greek goddesses of the arts and sciences.]

**mushroom** *noun* **mushrooms**
A **mushroom** is a fungus. Some mushrooms can be eaten.
[**Mushroom** comes from Latin via French.]

**music** *noun*
1 **Music** is pleasing sounds made by singing or playing a musical instrument.
2 **Music** is the signs and symbols that represent musical sounds.
[**Music** comes via French and Latin from Greek *mousike* 'to do with the Muses' (look under **museum**).]

**musical** *noun* **musicals**
A **musical** is a play or film that tells a story using songs and dancing.
[**Musical** comes via French from the same Latin word as **music**.]

**musical** *adjective*
1 A person who is **musical** is good at playing a musical instrument or singing.
2 Something that is **musical** is to do with music: *musical instruments.*

**musician** *noun* **musicians**
A **musician** is someone who plays or composes music, especially as a job.
[**Musician** comes via French from the same Latin word as **music**.]

**Muslim** *noun* **Muslims** *Also* **Moslem**
A **Muslim** is a person who follows the religion of Islam.
[**Muslim** comes from Arabic *muslim* 'someone who submits to God.]

**muslin** *noun*
**Muslin** is a fine, soft cotton material.
[**Muslin** was named after *Mosul*, a place in Iraq where it was made.]

**mussel** *noun* **mussels**
A **mussel** is a kind of shellfish that can be cooked and eaten from the shell.
[**Mussel** comes from Old English.]

**must** *verb*
**Must** means to have to: *You must go.*
[**Must** comes from Old English.]

**mustard** *noun*
**Mustard** is a yellow powder or paste made from mustard seeds. It is used to add a strong flavour to food.
[**Mustard** comes from Latin via French.]

**mute** *adjective*
A person who does not or cannot speak is

mute.
[**Mute** comes from Latin via French.]

**mutilate** *verb* **mutilates, mutilating, mutilated** (th)
To **mutilate** means to injure or damage someone or something very badly, especially by cutting it to pieces or by cutting parts of it off.
[**Mutilate** comes from Latin *mutilare* 'to maim'.]

**mutiny** *noun* **mutinies** (th)
A **mutiny** is when sailors or soldiers rebel against the people in charge of them.
[**Mutiny** comes from an old French word.]

**mutter** *verb* **mutters, muttering, muttered** (th)
To **mutter** means to speak quietly so that people cannot understand you properly.
[The word **mutter** is an imitation of the sound.]

**my** *pronoun*
belonging to me: *This is my book, not yours.*
[**My** was originally the form **mine²** that was used before consonants.]

**myself** *pronoun*
**1** You use **myself** for the object of a verb when the subject is **I** and the object is the same person: *I saw myself in the mirror.*
**2** If I do something **myself** or **by myself**, I do it alone.
[**Myself** comes from **me** and **self**.]

**mysterious** *adjective* (th)
Something that is **mysterious** is strange and cannot be explained.
[**Mysterious** comes from the same French word as **mystery**.]

**mystery** *noun* **mysteries**
A **mystery** is something strange that you cannot explain.
[**Mystery** comes via French or Latin from Greek *mysterion* 'a secret' or 'a secret ceremony'.]

**myth** *noun* **myths**
A **myth** is a very old well-known story about gods and heroes, especially one that seems to explain natural events.
[**Myth** comes via Latin from Greek *mythos* 'story'.]

**mythology** *noun*
**Mythology** is a group of myths from a particular country or culture.

---

## Dictionary Fun

### What do these idioms mean?
1. To make a meal of (*something*)
2. To take one's medicine
3. To make ends meet
4. To give somebody a piece of your mind

### Complete the proverbs
1. While the cat's away the m_____ will play.
2. A m____ is as good as a mile.

### Complete the similes
1. As stubborn as a m_____.
2. As poor as a church m_____.

### Work it out
Which 'm' word describes all of these: a human being, a dog and a whale?

### Did you know?
◆ The word **muscle** comes from the Latin *musculus* word, which means *little mouse*, because some muscles were thought to look like a mouse!

# Nn

**nail** *noun* **nails**
1 A **nail** is the hard part that covers the tip of each finger and toe.
2 A **nail** is a short metal spike used to hammer pieces of wood together.
[**Nail** comes from Old English.]

**naked** *adjective* (th)
If you are **naked**, you have no clothes on.
[**Naked** comes from Old English.]

**name** *noun* **names**
A **name** is what someone or something is called: *My name is Sam; What's the name of the road?* [**Name** comes from Old English.]

**name** *verb* **names, naming, named** (th)
To **name** someone or something means to give that person or thing a name.

**nanny** *noun* **nannies**
A **nanny** is a woman whose job is to look after someone else's children at their home.
[**Nanny** is a form of the name *Ann*.]

**nap** *verb* **naps, napping, napped** (th)
To **nap** means to have a short sleep.
[**Nap** comes from Old English.]

**nape** *noun*
The **nape** of the neck is the back of it.
[No one knows where **nape** comes from.]

**narrate** *verb* **narrates, narrating, narrated** (th)
To **narrate** means to tell a story.
[**Narrate** comes from Latin.]

**narrow** *adjective* **narrower, narrowest** (th)
Something that is not wide is **narrow**.
[**Narrow** comes from Old English.]

**nasal** *adjective*
**Nasal** means to do with the nose.
[**Nasal** comes from Latin *nasus* 'nose'.]

**nasty** *adjective* **nastier, nastiest** (th)
1 Something that is **nasty** is unpleasant: *a nasty smell.*
2 Someone who is **nasty** is unkind: *Don't be nasty!*
[No one knows where **nasty** comes from.]

**nation** *noun* **nations**
A **nation** is a country and the people who live there.

[**Nation** comes via French from Latin *nasci* 'to be born'.]

**nationality** *noun* **nationalities**
A **nationality** is being a member of a particular nation: *My parents are from Poland, but I have British nationality because I was born here.*

**native** *noun* **natives**
A **native** of a place is a person who was born there.
[**Native** comes from the same Latin word as **nation**.]

**nativity** *noun* **nativities**
In the Christian religion, the **Nativity** is the birth of Jesus Christ.
[**Nativity** comes from the same Latin word as **nation**.]

**natural** *adjective* (th)
1 Something that is **natural** exists in nature and is not made by people.
2 Something that is **natural** is normal and usual. **naturally** *adverb*.
[**Natural** comes via French from the same Latin word as **nation**.]

**nature** *noun* (th)
1 **Nature** is everything in the universe not made by people, such as plants, animals, rocks and stars.
2 A person's **nature** is his/her character.
[**Nature** comes via French from the same Latin word as **nation**.]

**naughty** *adjective* **naughtier, naughtiest** (th)
Someone who behaves badly is **naughty**.
[**Naughty** comes from Old English.]

**nausea** *noun*
**Nausea** is a feeling that you are going to be sick.
[**Nausea** comes via Latin from Greek *nausia* 'seasickness'.]

**nautical** *adjective*
**Nautical** means to do with sailing and ships.
[**Nautical** comes via French or Latin from Greek *nautes* 'sailor'.]

**naval** *adjective*
**Naval** means to do with the navy.
[**Naval** comes from the same Latin word as **navy**.]

**nave** *noun* **naves**
The **nave** is the long, narrow central part of a church.
[**Nave** comes from the same Latin word as **navy**.]

**navel** *noun* **navels**
The **navel** is the small round hollow in the stomach where the umbilical cord joined your body before you were born.
[**Navel** comes from Old English.]

**navigate** *verb* **navigates, navigating, navigated** (th)
**1** To **navigate** means to make sure a ship or aircraft is going in the right direction.
**2** To **navigate** means to find your way somewhere.
[**Navigate** comes from Latin *navis* 'ship' and *agere* 'to drive'.]

**navy** *noun* **navies**
**1** A **navy** is the ships and sailors that defend a country at sea.
**2 Navy** or **navy blue** is the dark blue colour of a sailor's uniform.
[**Navy** comes via French from Latin *navis* 'ship'.]

**navy** *adjective* Also **navy blue**
of the dark colour of a sailor's uniform: *a white suit with navy shoes and handbag.*

**near** *adjective* **nearer, nearest** (th)
Something that is **near** is close or close by: *the near future; My house is quite near.*
[**Near** comes from Old Norse.]

**near** *preposition*
not far away: *The dog stayed near its master.*

**nearly** *adverb* (th)
not quite: *We're nearly there; Nearly 500 people came.*

**neat** *adjective* **neater, neatest** (th)
Something that is **neat** is tidy.
[**Neat** comes from Latin via French.]

**necessary** *adjective* (th)
Something that you really need to have or do is **necessary**.
[**Necessary** comes from Latin.]

**necessity** *noun* **necessities**
A **necessity** is something that you really need to have.
[**Necessity** comes via French from the same Latin word as **necessary**.]

**neck** *noun* **necks**
Your **neck** is the part of your body that joins your head to your shoulders.
[**Neck** comes from Old English.]

**necklace** *noun* **necklaces**
A **necklace** is a chain of beads, jewels, gold or silver worn round the neck.
[**Necklace** comes from **neck** and **lace** in the sense 'a string'.]

**nectar** *noun*
**Nectar** is the sweet liquid that bees collect from flowers to make into honey.
[**Nectar** comes via Latin from Greek *nektar* 'drink of the gods.']

**need** *verb* **needs, needing, needed**
**1** To **need** means to be without something that is necessary.
**2** To **need to do** something means to have to do it because it is necessary: *We need to talk.* [**Need** comes from Old English.]

**needle** *noun* **needles**
A **needle** is a thin pointed piece of metal or plastic used for stitching or knitting.
[**Needle** comes from Old English.]

**negative** *noun* **negatives**
**1** A **negative** is the word 'no' or 'not'.
**2** A **negative** is the film that photographs are printed from.
[**Negative** comes from Latin *negare* 'to deny'.]

**neglect** *verb* **neglects, neglecting, neglected**
To **neglect** means to fail to look after someone or something properly.
[**Neglect** comes from Latin *negligare* 'to leave out'.]

**negotiate** *verb* **negotiates, negotiating, negotiated** (th)
To **negotiate** means to discuss something so that you can come to an agreement with someone.
[**Negotiate** comes from Latin *negotium* 'business'.]

**neigh** *verb* **neighs, neighing, neighed**
When a horse **neighs**, it opens its mouth and makes a loud sound.
[The word **neigh** is an imitation of the sound.]

**neighbour** *noun* **neighbours**
A **neighbour** is someone who lives next to or near someone else.

[**Neighbour** comes from Old English.]

**neither** *pronoun*
**Neither** means not one thing or person nor another: *Neither of us likes oranges.*
[**Neither** comes from Old English.]

**neither** *adverb*
If you say that one person or thing does not do something, or one thing is not so, you use **neither**: *He never goes there on Sundays; neither does she.*

**neon** *noun*
**Neon** is a gas used in lights and street signs that glows when electricity is passed through it.
[**Neon** comes from Greek.]

**nephew** *noun* **nephews**
Your **nephew** is the son of your brother or sister or of your brother-in-law or sister-in-law.
[**Nephew** comes from Latin via French.]

**nerve** *noun* **nerves**
A **nerve** is one of the fibres in the body that sends messages of feeling and movement between the brain and other parts of the body.
[**Nerve** comes from Latin.]

**nervous** *adjective* (th)
Someone who is **nervous** is afraid or easily frightened.
**nervously** *adverb.* **nervousness** *noun.*
[**Nervous** comes from the same Latin word as **nerve**.]

**nest** *noun* **nests**
A **nest** is a place made by birds and some animals for their babies.
[**Nest** comes from Old English.]

**net** *noun* **nets**
1 A **net** is a web or fabric made of strings or threads knotted together: *a fishing net.*
2 The **Net** is short for the Internet.
[**Net** comes from Old English.]

**nettle** *noun* **nettles**
A **nettle** is a plant with leaves that sting when you touch them.
[**Nettle** comes from Old English.]

**neuter** *adjective*
1 Something that is **neuter** is neither male nor female.
2 In some languages, a word that is **neuter** belongs to a class of words which are neither masculine nor feminine.
[**Neuter** comes via French from Latin *neuter* 'neither'.]

**neuter** *verb* **neuters, neutering, neutered** (th)
To **neuter** an animal means to operate on it so that it can no longer produce young.

**neutral** *adjective*
1 A person or a country that is **neutral** does not support either side in a war or disagreement.
2 A **neutral** colour is not bright or strong, and goes with many other colours.
[**Neutral** comes from the same Latin word as **neuter**.]

**neutron** *noun* **neutrons**
A **neutron** is a tiny part of an atom that does not have an electrical charge.
[**Neutron** comes from **neutral**.]

**never** *adverb*
not ever or at no time: *I've never been to Paris; She never eats meat.*
[**Never** comes from Old English.]

**new** *adjective* **newer, newest** (th)
Something that has just been bought, made or discovered is **new**.
[**New** comes from Old English.]

**news** *noun*
**News** is information about things that have just happened.
[**News** comes from **new**.]

**newspaper** *noun* **newspapers**
A **newspaper** is large sheets of paper folded together, printed each day or week with the news.

**newt** *noun* **newts**
A **newt** is an amphibian that looks like a small lizard. Some **newts** spend most of their lives on land, but some live in water even when they are adult.
[**Newt** comes from Old English.]

**next** *adjective* (th)
1 Something that is nearest to something else is the **next** one: *They live in the next street.*
2 Something that comes straight after something else is **next**: *I'm going next month; When's the next train?*
[**Next** comes from Old English.]

**nib** *noun* **nibs**
A **nib** is the pointed part of a pen that is used to write with.
[**Nib** comes from an old German or Dutch word.]

**nibble** *verb* **nibbles, nibbling, nibbled**
To **nibble** means to eat by taking tiny bites.
[**Nibble** comes from an old German or Dutch word.]

**nice** *adjective* **nicer, nicest** (th)
Something or someone that is **nice** is pleasant. [**Nice** comes from Latin.]

**nickel** *noun*
**Nickel** is a silver-coloured metal that is mixed with other metals to make them harder. [**Nickel** comes from German.]

**nickname** *noun* **nicknames**
A **nickname** is a name used instead of someone's real name.
[**Nickname** comes from an old phrase *an eke name* 'an extra name'.]

**niece** *noun* **nieces**
Your **niece** is the daughter of your brother or sister or of your brother-in-law or sister-in-law.
[**Niece** comes via French from the same Latin word as *nephew*.]

**night** *noun* **nights**
**Night** is the time it is dark, between sunset and sunrise.
[**Night** comes from Old English.]

**nightingale** *noun* **nightingales**
A **nightingale** is a small brown bird that sings at night.
[**Nightingale** comes from Old English *nihtegala* 'night-singer'.]

**nightmare** *noun* **nightmares**
A **nightmare** is a very frightening dream.
[**Nightmare** comes from **night** and Old English *maere* 'an evil spirit'.]

**nimble** *adjective* **nimbler, nimblest**
Someone who is **nimble** moves quickly and easily.
[**Nimble** comes from Old English.]

**nitrogen** *noun*
**Nitrogen** is a gas with no smell or colour that makes up four-fifths of the earth's atmosphere.
[**Nitrogen** comes from French.]

**no** *adverb*
You use **no** to show that you do not agree with something or approve of something.
[**No** comes from **none**.]

**noble** *adjective* **nobler, noblest**
Someone who is **noble** is brave, dignified and kind.
[**Noble** comes from Latin via French.]

**nobody** *pronoun*
**Nobody** means no person.

**nocturnal** *adjective*
A bird or animal that is active at night is **nocturnal**. [**Nocturnal** comes from Latin.]

**nod** *verb* **nods, nodding, nodded**
To **nod** means to move the head up and down, to show agreement or because you are sleepy.
[No one knows where **nod** comes from.]

**noise** *noun* **noises** (th)
A **noise** is a sound.
[**Noise** comes from Latin via French.]

**noisy** *adjective* **noisier, noisiest** (th)
Someone or something that makes a lot of noise is **noisy**.

**nomad** *noun* **nomads**
A **nomad** is a member of a tribe or group that travels from place to place and has no permanent home.
[**Nomad** comes via French and Latin from Greek *nomas* 'roaming in search of pasture'.]

**none** *pronoun*
When there is not any of something, there is **none**. [**None** comes from Old English.]

**nonsense** *noun* (th)
**Nonsense** is something that does not mean anything.
[**Nonsense** comes from *non* 'not' and **sense**.]

**nonstop** *adverb*
Something that happens or that you do **nonstop** happens or is done without a break or without stopping.

**noon** *noun*
**Noon** is 12 o'clock in the daytime.
[**Noon** comes from Latin via Old English.]

**no one** *pronoun*
**No one** means no person.

**noose** *noun* **nooses**
A **noose** is a large loop at the end of a rope that can be pulled tight.
[No one knows where **noose** comes from.]

**normal** *adjective* (th)
Something that is usual and what you expect is **normal**.
[**Normal** comes from Latin *norma* 'a pattern or rule'.]

**north** *noun*
**North** is the direction to which one end of a compass needle always points. If you face the rising sun, **north** is to your left.
[**North** comes from Old English.]

**north-east** *noun*
The **north-east** is the point of the compass midway between north and east.

**northerly** *adjective*
**1** to the north or towards the north: *The river flows in a northerly direction.*
**2** A **northerly** wind blows from the north.

**northern** *adjective*
in the north or from the north: *Normandy is in northern France.*

**north-west** *noun*
The **north-west** is the point of the compass midway between north and west.

**nose** *noun* **noses**
Your **nose** is the part of your face used for breathing and smelling.
[**Nose** comes from Old English.]

**nostalgic** *adjective*
Someone who is **nostalgic** thinks about the past in an affectionate way.
[**Nostalgic** comes from Greek.]

**nostril** *noun* **nostrils**
A **nostril** is one of the two openings at the end of the nose.
[**Nostril** comes from Old English.]

**nosy** *adjective* **nosier, nosiest** *Also* **nosey** (th)
Someone who is **nosy** is too interested in what other people are doing.
[**Nosy** comes from *sticking your nose in* 'interfering in someone else's business'.]

**not** *adverb*
You use **not** to change the meaning of something to its opposite: *I'm not a child; "Will it rain?" "I hope not."*
[**Not** comes from **nought**.]

**note** *noun* **notes**
**1** A **note** is a short letter or message.
**2** A **note** is a single sound in music.
[**Note** comes from Latin *nota* 'a mark'.]

**nothing** *noun*
**Nothing** means not anything.

**notice** *noun* **notices**
A **notice** is something written and put up somewhere for people to read.

**notice** *verb* **notices, noticing, noticed** (th)
To **notice** means to see something or realise it is there.
[**Notice** comes from Latin via French.]

**nought** *noun* **noughts**
**Nought** is the number 0 or zero.
[**Nought** comes from Old English *nowiht* 'nothing'.]

**noun** *noun* **nouns**
A **noun** is a word which gives the name of something. *Table, freedom* and *Mary* are all **nouns**.
[**Noun** comes from Latin *nomen* 'name'.]

**novel** *noun* **novels**
A **novel** is a book that tells a long story that someone has made up.
[**Novel** comes from Italian *novella storia* 'a new story'.]

**now** *adverb*
at this time or at this moment: *Divorce is quite common now.*
[**Now** comes from Old English.]

**nowhere** *adverb*
When something is **nowhere**, it is not anywhere.

**nuclear** *adjective*
Something that is **nuclear** uses the power that is created when atoms are split: *nuclear power; nuclear weapons.*
[**Nuclear** comes from **nucleus**.]

**nucleus** *noun* **nuclei**
**1** A **nucleus** is the part in the centre of an atom.
**2** A **nucleus** is the central part of a cell of an animal or plant.
[**Nucleus** comes from Latin.]

**nude** *adjective* (th)
If you are **nude**, you are not wearing any clothes.
[**Nude** comes from Latin.]

a b c d e f g h i j k l m

**nuisance** *noun* **nuisances** (th)
A **nuisance** is someone or something that causes trouble.
[**Nuisance** comes via French from Latin *nocere* 'to hurt or harm'.]

**numb** *adjective* **number**
If a part of your body is **numb**, you cannot feel it or move it.
[**Numb** comes from Old English.]

**number** *noun* **numbers**
A **number** is a word or figure showing how many. *1, 100, three* and *two million* are all **numbers**.
[**Number** comes via French from the same Latin word as **numeral**.]

**numeral** *noun* **numerals**
A **numeral** is a sign or symbol that represents a number. V is the Roman **numeral** for the number five, but we use the Arabic **numeral** 5.
[**Numeral** comes from Latin *numerus* 'number'.]

**numerator** *noun* **numerators**
A **numerator** is the number in a fraction that is above the line. It shows how many of the parts that the whole is divided into are being used: *In the fraction ¾, 3 is the numerator.*
[**Numerator** comes from **numeral**.]

**numerous** *adjective* (th)
If people or things are **numerous**, there are many of them.

[**Numerous** comes from the same Latin word as **numeral**.]

**nun** *noun* **nuns**
A **nun** is a woman who is a member of a religious group. Many nuns live and work together in a convent.
[**Nun** comes from Latin via Old English.]

**nurse** *noun* **nurses**
A **nurse** is someone whose job is to look after people who are ill or hurt.
[**Nurse** comes from Latin.]

**nursery** *noun* **nurseries**
A **nursery** is a room or building where young children play and are looked after.
[**Nursery** comes via French from the same Latin word as **nurse**.]

**nut** *noun* **nuts**
**1** A **nut** is a kind of fruit with a hard shell.
**2** A **nut** is a piece of metal that is screwed on to a bolt.
[**Nut** comes from Old English.]

**nutritious** *adjective*
Food that is **nutritious** contains things that are good for your body such as protein and vitamins.
[**Nutritious** comes from Latin.]

**nylon** *noun*
**Nylon** is a very strong material used for making clothes and many other things such as rope.
[**Nylon** is a made-up word.]

## Dictionary Fun

**Etymology**
Which word comes from Latin *navis* 'ship' and *agere* 'to drive'?

**What do these idioms mean?**
1. To be up to your neck in something
2. A needle in a haystack

**Complete the proverbs**
1. No n____ is good news.
2. N_____ is the mother of invention.

**Think about it**
Which 'n' word reads the same forwards as backwards? Clue: it's a part of the day.

**Riddle**
What's black and white and read all over?

**Did you know?**
In Greek and Roman mythology, **nectar** was the name of the drink of the gods.

# Oo

**oak** *noun* **oaks**
An **oak** is a large tree whose seeds are called acorns.
[**Oak** comes from Old English.]

**oar** *noun* **oars**
An **oar** is a pole with a flat blade at the end used to row a boat.
[**Oar** comes from Old English.]

**oasis** *noun* **oases**
An **oasis** is a place in a desert with water and plants.
[**Oasis** comes via Latin from Greek, probably from an Egyptian word.]

**oat** *noun* **oats**
**Oats** are the grains from a cereal plant that are used to make porridge.
[**Oat** comes from Old English.]

**oath** *noun* **oaths**
1 An **oath** is a very serious or formal promise that someone makes.
2 If you are **on oath** or **under oath**, you have made a solemn promise to tell the truth in a court, and you can be punished if you tell lies.
[**Oath** comes from Old English.]

**oatmeal** *noun*
**Oatmeal** is a kind of coarse flour made of ground oats.
[**Oatmeal** comes from **oat** and Old English *melu* 'coarse flour'.]

**obedient** *adjective*
Someone who is **obedient** does what s/he is told.
[**Obedient** comes via French from the same Latin word as **obey**.]

**obelisk** *noun* **obelisks**
An **obelisk** is a tall column or monument with four sides and a top shaped like a pyramid.
[**Obelisk** comes from Greek via Latin.]

**obey** *verb* **obeys, obeying, obeyed** (th)
To **obey** means to do what you are told to do. [**Obey** comes from Latin via French.]

**obituary** *noun* **obituaries**
An **obituary** is a piece of writing about a person's life and what s/he has achieved. An **obituary** is published when s/he dies.
[**Obituary** comes from Latin *obitus*

'death'.]

**object** *noun* **objects** (th)
1 An **object** is something that you can see or touch.
2 The **object** of what someone is doing is the purpose or aim.
3 An **object** in grammar is the noun that is affected by the action of the verb in a sentence. In the sentence 'Monkeys like bananas', *bananas* is the **direct object** of the verb *like*. [**Object** comes from Latin.]

**object** *verb* **objects, objecting, objected** (th)
To **object** means to say that you do not agree with something.

**objection** *noun* **objections**
An **objection** is a reason why you do not like or agree with something.

**objective** *noun* **objectives** (th)
Your **objective** is what you are trying to achieve.
[**Objective** comes via French from the same Latin word as **object**.]

**objective** *adjective* (th)
Something that is **objective** is based on facts and not on opinions or feelings.

**obligation** *noun* **obligations** (th)
An **obligation** is something that you must do because it is your duty.
[**Obligation** comes via French from the same Latin word as **oblige**.]

**oblige** *verb* **obliges, obliging, obliged** (th)
1 If you are **obliged** to do something, you have to do it.
2 To **oblige** or **oblige someone** means to help someone by doing something that s/he needs or that s/he asks you to do: *Would you oblige me by posting this letter?; If you need a babysitter? I'd be happy to oblige.*
[**Oblige** comes from Latin *ligare* 'to bind'.]

**obliterate** *verb* **obliterates, obliterating, obliterated** (th)
To **obliterate** something means to destroy or remove it completely.
[**Obliterate** comes from Latin *obliterare* 'to cross out'.]

**oblivious** *adjective* (th)
Someone who is **oblivious** to something is not aware of it.
[**Oblivious** comes from Latin *oblivisci* 'to

**forget'.]**

**oblong** *noun* **oblongs**
An **oblong** is a shape with two long
straight sides, two shorter straight sides
and four right angles.
[**Oblong** comes from Latin *oblongus* 'fairly
long'.]

**obnoxious** *adjective* (th)
If a person or a person's behaviour is
**obnoxious**, it is very unpleasant.
[**Obnoxious** comes from Latin.]

**oboe** *noun* **oboes**
An **oboe** is a musical instrument in the
woodwind family. It is shaped like a long
tube and has a reed in the mouthpiece
that you blow through.
[**Oboe** comes from Italian or French.]

**obscure** *adjective* **obscurer, obscurest**
(th)
1 Someone or something that is **obscure** is
not known by many people.
2 Something that is **obscure** is difficult to
understand because it is strange or
complicated.
[**Obscure** comes from Latin *obscurus*
'dark'.]

**observation** *noun* **observations**
1 An **observation** is something that you
have learned by watching something
carefully: *scientific observations.*
2 **Observation** is the ability to watch or
notice something carefully: *He has good
powers of observation.*
3 **Observation** is the process of watching
something carefully: *the observation of the
stars.*
[**Observation** comes from the same Latin
word as **observe**.]

**observatory** *noun* **observatories**
An **observatory** is a building with a large
telescope where you can watch the
planets and stars.
[**Observatory** comes from the same Latin
word as **observe**.]

**observe** *verb* **observes, observing,
observed** (th)
To **observe** means to watch or look at
something carefully.
[**Observe** comes from Latin *observare* 'to
watch' or 'to pay attention to'.]

**obsession** *noun* **obsessions** (th)

An **obsession** is something that someone
cannot stop thinking about.
[**Obsession** comes from Latin.]

**obsolete** *adjective* (th)
Something that is **obsolete** is no longer
used or is out of date.
[**Obsolete** comes from Latin *obsoletus* 'old,
worn out'.]

**obstacle** *noun* **obstacles** (th)
An **obstacle** is something that gets in
your way when you are trying to do
something or go somewhere.
[**Obstacle** comes from Latin.]

**obstruct** *verb* **obstructs, obstructing,
obstructed**
To **obstruct** means to get in someone's or
something's way.
[**Obstruct** comes from Latin *obstruere* 'to
block up'.]

**obtain** *verb* **obtains, obtaining, obtained**
If you **obtain** something, you get it,
especially by making an effort: *We need
four of them, but so far we have managed to
obtain only three; Olive oil is obtained by
pressing olives.* [**Obtain** comes from Latin.]

**obvious** *adjective* (th)
If something is **obvious**, it is easy to see
or understand.
[**Obvious** comes from Latin.]

**occasion** *noun* **occasions** (th)
1 An **occasion** is an important event or
celebration: *a special occasion.*
2 An **occasion** is a time when something
happens: *He's been skiing on several
occasions.* [**Occasion** comes from Latin.]

**occasional** *adjective* (th)
Something that is **occasional** happens
sometimes but not often: *an occasional trip
to the theatre.* **occasionally** *adverb.*
[**Occasional** originally meant 'happening
on or made for a particular occasion'.]

**occupation** *noun* **occupations** (th)
Someone's **occupation** is his/her job.
[**Occupation** comes via French from the
same Latin word as **occupy**.]

**occupy** *verb* **occupies, occupying,
occupied** (th)
1 To **occupy** means to take up an amount
of space or time: *The bed occupies one side of
the room.*
2 To **occupy** means to live or work in a

building: *Who occupies the top floor?*
**3** To **occupy** someone means to keep him/
her busy and happy: *The game occupied the
children all afternoon.*
**4** If an army **occupies** a country, it moves
into it and takes control of it.
[**Occupy** comes from Latin via French.]

**occur** *verb* **occurs, occurring, occurred**
(th)
**1** If something **occurs**, it happens: *The
accident occurred at midnight.*
**2** If something **occurs to** you, you think of
it suddenly: *It occurs to me that I owe you
some money.* [**Occur** comes from Latin.]

**ocean** *noun* **oceans**
An **ocean** is a very large area of sea.
[**Ocean** comes via French and Latin from
Greek *Okeanos*, the name of a great river
which the Greeks thought went right
round the edge of the world.]

**o'clock** *adverb*
You use **o'clock** after the hour when you
are telling the time: *It's six o'clock.*
[**O'clock** is short for 'of the clock'.]

**octagon** *noun* **octagons**
An **octagon** is a shape with eight straight
sides and eight angles.
[**Octagon** comes from Greek *okto* 'eight'
and *gonia* 'angle'.]

**octave** *noun* **octaves**
An **octave** is a gap of eight notes in a
musical scale.
[**Octave** comes from Latin *octavus*
'eighth'.]

**octopus** *noun* **octopuses**
An **octopus** is a creature with eight arms
that lives in the sea.
[**Octopus** comes from Greek *okto* 'eight'
and *pous* 'foot'.]

**odd** *adjective* **odder, oddest** (th)
**1** Something that is **odd** is strange.
**2** Things that are **odd** are not exactly
alike: *He's wearing odd socks.*
**3** An **odd** number cannot be divided
exactly by two. 7, 15 and 313 are **odd**
numbers. [**Odd** comes from Old Norse.]

**ode** *noun* **odes**
An **ode** is a poem that praises someone or
something.
[**Ode** comes from Greek *oide* 'song'.]

**odour** *noun* **odours** (th)
An **odour** is a smell.
[**Odour** comes from Latin.]

**offal** *noun*
**Offal** is the liver, kidney and heart of
animals when they are cooked and eaten.
[**Offal** originally meant the parts that
were thrown away, and comes from *off*
and **fall**.]

**offence** *noun* **offences**
**1** An **offence** is a crime.
**2** If someone **takes offence**, s/he is upset
by what someone has said or done.
[**Offence** comes via French from the same
Latin word as **offend**.]

**offend** *verb* **offends, offending, offended**
(th)
**1** To **offend** means to commit a crime.
**2** To **offend** someone means to do
something that makes him/her feel angry
and upset.
[**Offend** comes from Latin *fendere* 'to hit'
(ancestor of **defend**).]

**offensive** *noun* **offensives** (th)
An **offensive** is a military attack.
[**Offensive** comes via French from the
same Latin word as **offend**.]

**offensive** *adjective* (th)
Something that is **offensive** upsets people
and is very unpleasant.

**offer** *verb* **offers, offering, offered**
**1** To **offer** means to ask someone if s/he
would like something: *She offered me a
drink.*
**2** To **offer** means to say that you are
willing to do something: *He offered to help.*
[**Offer** comes from Old English.]

**office** *noun* **offices**
**1** An **office** is a room where someone or a
group of people do work such as writing
letters and keeping records and accounts.
**2** If someone is **in office** or **holds office**,
s/he has a powerful or responsible job,
especially in the government.
[**Office** comes from Latin *officium* 'service'
or 'duty'.]

**officer** *noun* **officers**
An **officer** is someone in the army, navy
or air force who is in charge of others.
[**Officer** comes via French from the same
Latin word as **office**.]

a b c d e f g h i j k l m

**official** *noun* **officials**
An **official** is someone who has a job of responsibility in an organisation.
[**Official** comes via French from the same Latin word as **office**.]

**official** *adjective*
Something that is **official** comes from or is approved by someone in authority.

**off-peak** *adjective*
**Off-peak** means at a time that is not very busy: *Phone calls are cheaper at off-peak times.*

**often** *adverb* (th)
When something happens **often**, it happens many times.
[**Often** comes from Old English.]

**ogre** *noun* **ogres**
An **ogre** is a frightening cruel giant in fairy stories. [**Ogre** comes from French.]

**oil** *noun* **oils**
**Oil** is a thick liquid. There are different types used in machines and in cooking, or for burning fuel.
[**Oil** comes from Latin via French.]

**oil paint** *noun* **oil paints** *or* **oils**
**Oil paint** is thick coloured paint containing oil that is used by artists for painting pictures.

**oily** *adjective* **oilier, oiliest**
Something that is **oily** contains, or is covered with, a lot of oil.

**ointment** *noun* **ointments**
An **ointment** is a cream used to heal cuts and sore skin.
[**Ointment** comes from Latin via French.]

**old** *adjective* **older, oldest** (th)
**1** Someone who has lived a long time is **old**.
**2** Something that is **old** was made a long time ago. [**Old** comes from Old English.]

**old-fashioned** *adjective* (th)
Something that is **old-fashioned** was popular or fashionable in the past but is not used much any more: *old-fashioned clothes; old-fashioned ideas.*

**olive** *noun* **olives**
An **olive** is a small black or green bitter fruit that can be eaten.
[**Olive** comes from Greek via French and Latin.]

**olive oil** *noun* **olive oils**
**Olive oil** is a pale yellow or greeny-yellow oil obtained by pressing olives. **Olive oil** is used in cooking and can be sprinkled on salad.

**omelette** *noun* **omelettes**
An **omelette** is a dish made by cooking beaten eggs in a flat pan.
[**Omelette** is a French word.]

**omen** *noun* **omens**
An **omen** is something that is believed to be a sign of good luck or a warning of bad luck in the future.
[**Omen** comes from Latin.]

**ominous** *adjective* (th)
Something that is **ominous** is worrying because it makes you think something bad will happen: *Those storm clouds look ominous.*
[**Ominous** comes from the same Latin word as **omen**.]

**omit** *verb* **omits, omitting, omitted**
**1** To **omit** something means to leave it out: *His name was omitted from the list.*
**2** To **omit** to do something means to fail to do it: *She omitted to mention that she'd been in prison.* [**Omit** comes from Latin.]

**omnibus** *noun* **omnibuses**
**1** An **omnibus** is an old-fashioned word for a bus.
**2** An **omnibus edition** or **omnibus volume** is a book that contains several works by the same author that have already been published separately.
[**Omnibus** comes from Latin *omnibus* 'for all'.]

**omnivore** *noun* **omnivores**
An **omnivore** is an animal that eats a mixed diet of both meat and plants.
[**Omnivore** comes from Latin *omnis* 'all' and *vorare* 'to devour'.]

**once** *adverb* (th)
**1** only one time: *I only hit him once.*
**2** some time in the past: *The family once lived in Africa; We had a dog once, but it died.*
**3** If you do something **at once**, you do it immediately.
**4** If things happen **at once**, or **all at once**, they happen at the same time.
[**Once** comes from **one**, which comes from Old English.]

**one-way** *adjective*
Something that is **one-way** may be used in only one direction: *a one-way street; a one-way ticket.*

**onion** *noun* **onions**
An **onion** is a round vegetable with many layers and a strong taste.
[**Onion** comes from French.]

**only** *adverb* (th)
not more than: *There was only one seat left on the coach.*
[**Only** comes from Old English.]

**onomatopoeia** *noun*
**Onomatopoeia** is when a word sounds like the noise of the thing it is describing: *Buzz* and *hiss* are examples of **onomatopoeia**.
[**Onomatopoeia** comes from Greek via Latin.]

**onset** *noun*
The **onset** of something, especially something unpleasant, is the beginning of it: *the onset of winter.*

**ooze** *verb* **oozes, oozing, oozed** (th)
If a thick liquid **oozes**, it flows out slowly from somewhere.
[**Oozes** comes from Old English.]

**opal** *noun* **opals**
An **opal** is a milky white precious stone that reflects other colours.
[**Opal** comes via French or Latin from Sanskrit (a very old Indian language).]

**opaque** *adjective* (th)
If something is **opaque**, you cannot see through it. [**Opaque** comes from Latin.]

**open** *adjective* (th)
**1** Something that is **open** is not shut, enclosed or folded up: *an open window; an open field; an open umbrella.*
**2** A shop or business that is **open** is ready to serve its customers.
[**Open** comes from Old English.]

**open** *verb* **opens, opening, opened** (th)
To **open** means become open or to make something open: *Open your eyes; Her eyes opened; The bank opens at nine.*

**opening** *noun* **openings** (th)
**1** An **opening** is a hole or gap that something can get through: *an opening in the fence.*

**2** The **opening** of a book, play or film is the first part of it.
**3** An **opening** is an opportunity, especially an opportunity to take up a career.

**opera** *noun* **operas**
An **opera** is a kind of musical play in which all the words are sung.
[**Opera** comes from Latin via Italian.]

**operate** *verb* **operates, operating, operated**
**1** To **operate** a machine means to make it work.
**2** To **operate** means to perform a medical operation on someone's body.
[**Operate** comes from Latin.]

**operation** *noun* **operations**
**1** An **operation** is the process of cutting open a part of the body usually in order to remove a diseased part or repair something that is damaged.
**2** If a machine is **in operation**, it is working.

**operator** *noun* **operators**
An **operator** is a person who controls or works a machine or a telephone system.

**opinion** *noun* **opinions** (th)
Your **opinion** is what you think or believe about something: *He has strong opinions about animal cruelty.*
[**Opinion** comes via French from Latin *opinari* 'to think or believe'.]

**opponent** *noun* **opponents** (th)
**1** An **opponent** is the person you are playing against in a contest or game.
**2** An **opponent** is someone who is against a person or an idea: *Opponents of animal testing say it is cruel.*
[**Opponent** comes from the same Latin word as **oppose**.]

**opportunity** *noun* **opportunities**
An **opportunity** is a chance to do something.
[**Opportunity** comes from Latin.]

**oppose** *verb* **opposes, opposing, opposed** (th)
To **oppose** something means to be against it: *She opposes the new road scheme.*
[**Oppose** comes from Latin *opponere* 'to set against'.]

**opposite** *noun* **opposites**
The **opposite** of something is as different from it as it is possible to be: *Day is the opposite of night.*
[**Opposite** comes via French from the same Latin word as **oppose**.]

**opposite** *adjective* (th)
Something that is **opposite** something else is completely different from it: *They ran off in opposite directions.*

**opposite** *preposition*
Someone or something that is facing something is **opposite** it: *Our house is opposite the park.*

**oppress** *verb* **oppresses, oppressing, oppressed** (th)
To **oppress** people means to treat them in a cruel way and prevent them from having any freedom.
[**Oppress** comes from Latin.]

**opt** *verb* **opts, opting, opted** (th)
To **opt** to do something means to choose to do it.
[**Opt** comes via French from the same Latin word as **optional**.]

**optical** *adjective*
**Optical** means to do with the eyes or eyesight.
[**Optical** comes via French and Latin from Greek *optos* 'seen'.]

**optician** *noun* **opticians**
An **optician** is someone whose job is to look after people's eyes and give them the glasses or contact lenses they need.
[**Optician** comes via French and Latin from the same Greek word as **optical**.]

**optimism** *noun*
**Optimism** is a feeling of hope that good things will happen.
[**Optimism** comes via French from Latin *optimum* 'the best thing'.]

**optimist** *noun* **optimists**
An **optimist** is someone who always believes that good things will happen.

**optimistic** *adjective* (th)
Someone who is **optimistic** believes that good things will happen.

**optional** *adjective*
If something is **optional**, you do not have to have it or do it: *All the cars have a radio,*

but the CD player is an optional extra.
[**Optional** comes via French from Latin *optare* 'to choose'.]

**or** *conjunction*
You use **or** to talk about two or more possibilities, only one of which is true or will happen: *You can have chicken or pizza; Shall we go this week or next?; Hurry up or you'll be late.* [**Or** comes from **other**.]

**oral** *adjective*
**1** to do with or using the mouth: *The dentist will advise you on oral hygiene.*
**2** spoken, not written: *oral exams.*
**orally** *adverb.* [**Oral** comes from Latin.]

**orange** *noun* **oranges**
**1** An **orange** is a round sweet juicy fruit with a thick orange peel.
**2 Orange** is a bright colour between red and yellow.
[**Orange** comes via French and Arabic from Persian (the language spoken in Iran).]

**orange** *adjective*
of the colour of an orange: *bright orange marigolds.*

**orangutan** *noun* **orangutans** Also **orang-utan**
An **orangutan** is a large ape with long reddish-brown hair that lives in the forests of Borneo and Sumatra in Indonesia.
[**Orangutan** comes from Malay *orang hutan* 'person of the forest'. Malay is the language spoken in Malaysia.]

**orbit** *noun* **orbits** (th)
An **orbit** is the path in space of a planet or satellite moving around another planet.
[**Orbit** comes from Latin *orbis* 'circle'.]

**orchard** *noun* **orchards**
An **orchard** is a large area where fruit trees grow.
[**Orchard** comes from Old English.]

**orchestra** *noun* **orchestras**
An **orchestra** is a large group of people playing different musical instruments together.
[**Orchestra** comes from Greek via Latin.]

**orchid** *noun* **orchids**
An **orchid** is a plant with colourful flowers.
[**Orchid** comes from Greek via Latin.]

**ordain** *verb* **ordains, ordaining, ordained**
To **ordain** someone means to make that person a priest in a religious ceremony.
[**Ordain** comes via French from the same Latin word as **order**.]

**ordeal** *noun* **ordeals**
An **ordeal** is a difficult and unpleasant experience.
[**Ordeal** comes from Old English.]

**order** *noun* **orders** (th)
**1** An **order** is something that you are told to do by someone in authority: *Soldiers must obey orders.*
**2** An **order** is a request for a shop or a restaurant to get you something: *You can place your order over the phone.*
**3 Order** is when everything is in the correct place or done in the right way: *The books are in alphabetical order.*
**4** If a machine is **out of order**, it is not working.
[**Order** comes via French from Latin *ordo* 'a row or series'.]

**order** *verb* **orders, ordering, ordered** (th)
**1** To **order** means to tell someone to do something.
**2** To **order** means to ask a shop or restaurant to get you something: *Are you ready to order, Sir?*
**3** To **order** things means to arrange them properly.

**ordinal number** *noun* **ordinal numbers**
An **ordinal number** is a number that tells you where something comes in a series of things. *First*, *second* and *tenth* are all **ordinal numbers**.
[**Ordinal** comes from the same Latin word as **order**.]

**ordinary** *adjective* (th)
Something that is **ordinary** is usual and not special in any way.
[**Ordinary** comes from Latin *ordinarius* 'in order'.]

**ore** *noun* **ores**
**Ore** is the rock that metals are found in.
[**Ore** comes from Old English.]

**oregano** *noun*
**Oregano** is a herb with small round leaves that is used in cooking.
[**Oregano** comes from Greek via Spanish.]

**organ** *noun* **organs**
**1** An **organ** is a large musical instrument similar to a piano. It has a keyboard and a lot of pedals, and the sound comes through pipes.
**2** An **organ** is a part of the body that does a special job: *The heart, lungs and kidneys are vital organs.*
[**Organ** comes via Latin from Greek *organon* 'a tool or instrument'.]

**organic** *adjective*
**Organic** farming does not use any chemicals. **Organic** fruit, vegetables and other crops have been grown without using chemicals.
[**Organic** comes via Latin from Greek *organikos* 'to do with an organism'.]

**organisation** *noun* **organisations** *Also* **organization** (th)
An **organisation** is a group of people who work together.
[**Organisation** comes from **organise**.]

**organise** *verb* **organises, organising, organised** *Also* **organize** (th)
**1** To **organise** means to plan and arrange an event.
**2** To **organise** means to get people working together well.
[**Organise** comes via Latin from the same Greek word as **organ**.]

**organism** *noun* **organisms**
An **organism** is a living thing.
[**Organism** comes from **organise**.]

**orient** *noun*
The **orient** is the countries of eastern Asia, especially China and Japan.
[**Orient** comes via French from Latin *oriens* 'the rising sun' or 'the east'.]

**oriental** *adjective*
Something that comes from eastern Asian countries such as China and Japan is **oriental**.

**orienteering** *noun*
**Orienteering** is a sport in which you have to find your way somewhere using a map and a compass.
[**Orienteering** comes from Swedish.]

**origami** *noun*
**Origami** is a Japanese art in which you fold paper into shapes such as flowers or birds.

**a b c d e f g h i j k l m**

[**Origami** comes from Japanese *ori* 'fold' and *kami* 'paper'.]

**origin** *noun* **origins** (th)
1 The **origin** of something is the cause of something or the beginning of something.
2 A person's **origin** is the country, race or social class s/he had when s/he was born, or of his/her parents or ancestors: *people of Asian origin; He's proud of his humble origin.*
[**Origin** comes from Latin *oriri* 'to rise'.]

**original** *adjective* (th)
1 Something that is **original** came first or happened earliest: *the original inhabitants of North America.*
2 Something that is **original** is not a copy: *an original work of art.*
3 Something that is **original** is new and interesting: *an original idea.*
[**Original** comes via French from the same Latin word as **origin**.]

**originate** *verb* **originates, originating, originated** (th)
To **originate** means to begin to happen or exist: *The breed originated in Australia.*
[**Originate** comes from the same Latin word as **origin**.]

**ornament** *noun* **ornaments**
An **ornament** is an object used to make a place look more attractive.
[**Ornament** comes via French from Latin *ornare* 'to decorate'.]

**ornate** *adjective* (th)
Something that has a lot of decoration on it is **ornate**.
[**Ornate** comes from the same Latin word as **ornament**.]

**ornithology** *noun*
**Ornithology** is the study of birds.
[**Ornithology** comes from Greek via Latin.]

**orphan** *noun* **orphans**
An **orphan** is a child whose parents have both died.
[**Orphan** comes from Greek via Latin.]

**orphanage** *noun* **orphanages**
An **orphanage** is a home where orphans live and are looked after.

**orthodox** *adjective*
1 **Orthodox** beliefs are ones that are accepted by most people.

2 A person who follows the rules of his/her religion very closely is **orthodox**.
[**Orthodox** comes from Greek *ortho* 'straight' and *doxa* 'opinion'.]

**ostrich** *noun* **ostriches**
An **ostrich** is a very large bird that cannot fly but can run very quickly.
[**Ostrich** comes from an old French word.]

**other** *adjective, pronoun*
Something that is not the same as the one being discussed is the **other** one: *I don't want that dress, I want the other one.*
[**Other** comes from Old English.]

**otter** *noun* **otters**
An **otter** is an animal that lives near rivers and eats fish.
[**Otter** comes from Old English.]

**ought** *verb*
1 If you **ought** to do something, you should do it because it is your duty or because it is a good idea: *We ought to go and see Granny more often; You ought to take your umbrella, it looks like rain.*
2 If you say something **ought** to happen or **ought** to be true, you expect it to happen or be true: *He's worked hard for the exams and he ought to do well; They ought to be home by now.*
[**Ought** comes from Old English.]

**ounce** *noun* **ounces**
An **ounce** is a unit for measuring weight in the imperial system. An **ounce** is equal to about 29 grams.
[**Ounce** comes from Latin via French.]

**our** *adjective*
belonging to us: *These are our seats; We're going to visit our uncle.*
[**Our** comes from Old English.]

**ours** *pronoun*
belonging to us: *His daughter is older than ours; Fishing is a hobby of ours.*
[**Ours** comes from **our**.]

**ourselves** *pronoun*
1 You use **ourselves** for the object of a verb when the subject is **we** and the object is the same people: *We treated ourselves to a bottle of champagne.*
2 When we do something **ourselves** or **by ourselves**, we do it and no one does it with us: *Our parents gave us permission to go to the beach by ourselves.*

[**Ourselves** comes from Old English.]

**out** *adverb* (th)
Someone or something that is not in is **out**. [**Out** comes from Old English.]

**outback** *noun*
The **outback** is the parts of Australia that are far from any towns and far from the sea.

**outbreak** *noun* **outbreaks**
An **outbreak** is the sudden beginning of something that affects a lot of people: *the outbreak of war; an outbreak of chickenpox.*

**outburst** *noun* **outbursts** (th)
An **outburst** is a sudden expression of strong feelings: *There was a huge outburst from the crowd when they found out that the singer was ill.*

**outcome** *noun* **outcomes** (th)
An **outcome** is a result of something.

**outdoor** *adjective*
used, or designed to be used, outside and not in a building: *an outdoor ice-rink.*

**outfit** *noun* **outfits** (th)
An **outfit** is a set of clothes that you wear: *I bought myself a new outfit today to cheer myself up.*
[**Outfit** comes from *to fit out* 'to equip'.]

**outlaw** *noun* **outlaws** (th)
An **outlaw** is a criminal, especially someone in the past who was hiding from the law.
[An **outlaw** was someone who was outside the protection of the law; anyone could attack an outlaw without being punished.]

**outline** *noun* **outlines** (th)
1 An **outline** is the line that shows the shape or edge of something.
2 An **outline** of something is the main facts about it, but with no details.

**out-of-date** *adjective* (th)
Something that is **out-of-date** is not useful or fashionable because it is too old.

**outpatient** *noun* **outpatients**
An **outpatient** is someone who goes to a hospital for treatment but does not stay the night there.

**outpost** *noun* **outposts**
An **outpost** is a settlement or a military fort that is a long way from anywhere.
[**Outpost** comes from **out** and **post**² in the sense 'a place where someone is on duty'.]

**output** *noun*
1 The amount that a factory or business produces is its **output**.
2 The amount of information that a computer produces is its **output**.

**outset** *noun* (th)
The **outset** of something is the beginning or the start of it: *From the outset, I knew everything would go wrong.*

**outside** *noun* **outsides**
The **outside** is the outer part of something: *We painted the outside of the house white.*

**outside** *adjective*
Something that is **outside** is near the outer edge or furthest from the centre: *the outside lane of the running track.*

**outside** *adverb* (th)
Something that is not inside a building is **outside**: *The children were playing outside.*

**outskirts** *plural noun* (th)
The **outskirts** of a town or city are the parts that are on the edge: *My house is on the outskirts of the city.*
[**Outskirts** comes from **out** and *skirt* 'to go round the outside'.]

**outstanding** *adjective* (th)
1 Something that is **outstanding** is extremely good or of unusually high quality.
2 An **outstanding** bill has not been paid.

**oval** *adjective*
Something that is **oval** is shaped something like an egg, but with both ends the same.
[**Oval** comes from Latin *ovum* 'egg'.]

**ovation** *noun* **ovations** (th)
An **ovation** is loud applause and cheering.
[**Ovation** comes from Latin *ovare* 'to rejoice'.]

**oven** *noun* **ovens**
An **oven** is the closed part of a cooker where food is baked or roasted: *Cook the cake at the top of a hot oven.*
[**Oven** comes from Old English.]

abcdefghijklm

**over** *adverb* (th)
**1** Something that is **over** or **left over**
remains after you have used all you need:
*I posted all my cards and had some stamps left
over.*
**2** When something has ended, it is **over**.
[**Over** comes from Old English.]

**over** *preposition* (th)
**1** Something that is above or covering an
object is **over** it: *The bird flew over the tree-
tops; She wore a cardigan over her blouse.*
**2** When there is **over** a certain number or
amount, there is more: *There were over 100
guests; She left over an hour ago.*

**overalls** *plural noun*
**Overalls** are a piece of clothing that
covers your clothes to protect them while
you are working.

**overboard** *adverb*
Someone who goes **overboard** goes over
the side of a boat into the water.
[**Overboard** comes from **over** and **board**
in an old sense 'the side of a ship'.]

**overcast** *adjective* (th)
If the weather is **overcast**, the sky is full of
grey clouds.
[**Over** comes from **over** and the past
participle of **cast**.]

**overcrowded** *adjective* (th)
If a place is **overcrowded**, there are too
many people there: *an overcrowded beach.*

**overdose** *noun* **overdoses**
An **overdose** is an amount of a drug that
is too large and that can make someone
very ill or die.

**overdue** *adjective*
If something is **overdue**, it should have
arrived or should have been done earlier:
*Your library book is overdue.*

**overflow** *verb* **overflows, overflowing,
overflowed**
To **overflow** means to flow over the edges
of a container because it is too full: *Watch
what you're doing – the milk is overflowing!*

**overgrown** *adjective*
An **overgrown** garden has not been
looked after and is full of weeds and
plants that have grown too big.

**overhear** *verb* **overhears, overhearing,
overheard**
To **overhear** means to hear what someone
else is saying when s/he does not know
you are listening: *I overheard her saying
that she doesn't want to come to my party any
more.*

**overlap** *verb* **overlaps, overlapping,
overlapped**
To **overlap** means to cover part of
something else.
[**Overlap** comes from **over** and an old
word *lap* 'to fold or coil', which comes
from **lap**[1].]

**overnight** *adverb*
for the night: *We slept overnight on the boat.*

**overseas** *adverb*
**1** If you live **overseas**, you live in another
country.
**2** If you **go overseas**, you go to another
country.

**overtake** *verb* **overtakes, overtaking,
overtook**
To **overtake** means to go past another
person or moving vehicle in order to get
in front.

**overture** *noun* **overtures**
An **overture** is a piece of music that is
played at the start of an opera or musical.
[**Overture** comes from old French *overture*
'opening'.]

**owe** *verb* **owes, owing, owed**
**1** If you **owe** money, you have to pay
money to someone because s/he has lent
it to you or has sold you something that
you have not yet paid for: *I owe him money
for my theatre ticket.*
**2** If you **owe** something to someone or
something, they helped you to get it: *I owe
my good health to regular exercise and a good
diet.* [**Owe** comes from Old English.]

**owl** *noun* **owls**
An **owl** is a bird that flies at night and
eats small animals.
[**Owl** comes from Old English.]

**own** *verb* **owns, owning, owned** (th)
**1** If you **own** something, it is yours: *She
owns a sports car.*
**2** If you **own up** to a bad deed, you admit
that you did it: *The person who smashed the
window must own up by the end of the day!*

[**Own** comes from Old English.]

**oxygen** *noun*
Oxygen is one of the gases in the air which animals and plants need to stay alive. [**Oxygen** comes from French.]

**oyster** *noun* **oysters**
An **oyster** is a kind of shellfish. [**Oyster** comes from Greek via French and Latin.]

**ozone** *noun*
Ozone is a form of oxygen that has a strong smell and is poisonous. [**Ozone** comes via German from Greek *ozein* 'to smell'.]

**ozone layer** *noun*
The **ozone layer** is a layer of ozone high above the earth's surface that protects it from the sun's harmful rays.

# Dictionary Fun

## Etymology
1. Which word is from Malay *orang hutan* 'forest person'?
2. Which word comes from Japanese *ori* 'fold' + *kami* 'paper'?

## What do these idioms mean?
1. To be out of pocket
2. Out of this world
3. To be over the hill

## Riddle
My first is in *root* but not in *tree*
My second is in *leaf* but not in *flee*
My last is in *bark* but not in *twig*
When I'm grown I am sturdy and really quite big!
What am I?

## Complete the simile
As o____ as the hills.

## Did you know?
◆ Sometimes a person who refuses to accept facts is called an **ostrich**, because ostriches were thought to bury their heads in the sand when they were being chased.
◆ An **outlaw** is so called because an outlaw used to be someone who was outside the protection of the law; anyone could attack an outlaw without being punished.

## Complete the proverb
O_____ bitten, twice shy.

## Brainteaser
If a doctor gave you three pills and told you to take one every half-hour, how long would it be before they were all gone?

a b c d e f g h i j k l m

# Pp

**pace** *noun* **paces** (th)
1 A **pace** is a step: *Walk forward three paces.*
2 A **pace** is a speed of walking or running: *a slow pace.*
[**Pace** comes via French from the same Latin word as **pass**[1].]

**pace** *verb* **paces, pacing, paced**
To **pace** means to walk forwards and backwards: *He paced up and down.*

**pacifist** *noun* **pacifists**
A **pacifist** is someone who believes that war and violence are wrong and who refuses to fight.
[**Pacifist** comes from Latin *pacis* 'to do with peace'.]

**pack** *noun* **packs** (th)
1 A **pack** is a group of wolves or dogs.
2 A **pack** is a set of things in one packet.
[**Pack** comes from an old German or Dutch word.]

**pack** *verb* **packs, packing, packed** (th)
1 To **pack** means to put things into containers such as bags, suitcases or boxes.
2 To **pack** a place means to fill it tightly with people.

**package** *noun* **packages**
1 A **package** is a parcel or packet.
2 A **package** is a number of things that are offered together: *The package includes a computer, printer and a range of software.*
[**Package** comes from **pack**.]

**packaging** *noun*
**Packaging** is the wrapping on things you buy. [**Packaging** comes from **package**.]

**packet** *noun* **packets**
A **packet** is a small parcel.
[**Packet** comes from **pack**.]

**pact** *noun* **pacts** (th)
A **pact** is a promise or agreement, often between two countries.
[**Pact** comes from Latin via French.]

**pad**[1] *noun* **pads**
1 A **pad** is a set of sheets of writing paper held together along one edge.
2 A **pad** is a soft, thick piece of material.
[No one knows where **pad**[1] comes from.]

**pad**[2] *verb* **pads, padding, padded**
To **pad** means to walk softly.
[**Pad**[2] comes from an old German word.]

**paddle**[1] *noun* **paddles**
A **paddle** is a short oar with a wide flat end that is used to move a small boat or canoe through water.
[No one knows where **paddle**[1] comes from.]

**paddle**[2] *verb* **paddles, paddling, paddled**
To **paddle** means to walk in shallow water.
[**Paddle**[2] may come from an old German or Dutch word.]

**paddle steamer** *noun* **paddle steamers**
A **paddle steamer** is a ship that is moved through the water by two large wheels that act as paddles and are driven by a steam engine.

**paddock** *noun* **paddocks** (th)
A **paddock** is a small field, especially one near a house where horses are kept.
[No one knows where **paddock** comes from.]

**padlock** *noun* **padlocks**
A **padlock** is a lock that you can fix onto something and take off again.
[**Padlock** comes from an old word *pad* and **lock**[1].]

**paediatrician** *noun* **paediatricians**
A **paediatrician** is a doctor who treats children's illnesses.
[**Paediatrician** comes from Greek via Latin.]

**page**[1] *noun* **pages** (th)
A **page** is one side of a piece of paper in a book. [**Page**[1] comes from Latin via French.]

**page**[2] *noun* **pages**
1 A **page** is a small boy who walks behind the bride at a wedding.
2 A **page** is a boy or young man who works in a hotel running errands and calling guests to tell them that someone wants to see them or speak to them.
[**Page**[2] comes via French from Greek *paidion* 'small boy'.]

**pageant** *noun* **pageants**
A **pageant** is a show where people wear costumes and walk in a procession, often to act out a historical event.

[No one knows where **pageant** comes from.]

**pager** *noun* **pagers**
A **pager** is an electronic device that can receive, but not send, messages from a telephone. [**Pager** comes from **page²**.]

**pagoda** *noun* **pagodas**
A **pagoda** is a building where Buddhists worship. A **pagoda** looks like a tower with lots of storeys that have decorated roofs.
[**Pagoda** comes from a Portuguese word which may come from Persian (the language spoken in Iran).]

**paid** *verb*
**Paid** is the past tense and past participle of **pay**.

**pain** *noun* **pains** (th)
A **pain** is an unpleasant feeling in part of the body because of illness or injury.
[**Pain** comes via French from the same Latin word as **penalty** and **punishment**.]

**painful** *adjective* (th)
Something that hurts is **painful**.

**paint** *noun* **paints**
**Paint** is a liquid that is put on paper or on an object to colour it.
[**Paint** comes from Latin via French.]

**paint** *verb* **paints, painting, painted**
1 To **paint** means to put paint on a surface: *paint the walls*.
2 To **paint** means to make a picture using paint: *paint a portrait*.

**painting** *noun* **paintings**
A **painting** is a picture that has been painted.

**pair** *noun* **pairs** (th)
A **pair** is two of the same kind of thing.
[**Pair** comes via French from Latin *paria* 'equal things'.]

**palace** *noun* **palaces**
A **palace** is a very large house in which an important person lives.
[**Palace** comes from *Palatium*, the Latin name of a hill in Rome where the emperor's palace once stood.]

**palate** *noun* **palates**
Your **palate** is the top of the inside of your mouth. [**Palate** comes from Latin.]

**pale** *adjective* **paler, palest** (th)
1 Something that is a very light colour is **pale**.
2 Someone who is **pale** does not have very much colour in his/her face, sometimes because s/he is ill.
[**Pale** comes from Latin via French.]

**palette** *noun* **palettes**
A **palette** is a board that an artist mixes colours on.
[**Palette** comes from Latin via French.]

**palindrome** *noun* **palindromes**
A **palindrome** is a word or phrase that is spelled the same forwards or backwards. The word *noon* is a **palindrome**.
[**Palindrome** comes from Greek *palindromos* 'running back again'.]

**pallbearer** *noun* **pallbearers**
A **pallbearer** is someone who helps to carry a coffin at a funeral.
[**Pallbearer** comes from *pall* 'a cloth spread over a coffin', which comes from Latin *pallium* 'cloak'.]

**pallet** *noun* **pallets**
A **pallet** is a flat platform that goods can be stacked on and easily moved.
[**Pallet** comes via French from the same Latin word as **palette**.]

**palm¹** *noun* **palms**
A **palm** is the inside part of the hand between the wrist and the fingers.
[**Palm¹** comes from Latin via French.]

**palm²** *noun* **palms**
A **palm** is a tree with large leaves but no branches that grows in hot countries.
[**Palm²** comes via Old English from Latin *palma* 'palm of the hand', because the leaves of the tree look like an open hand.]

**palpitate** *verb* **palpitates, palpitating, palpitated**
If someone's heart **palpitates**, it beats faster than normal.
[**Palpitate** comes from Latin.]

**pamper** *verb* **pampers, pampering, pampered** (th)
To **pamper** means to give someone a lot of care and attention or special treats that are not really necessary.
[**Pamper** probably comes from an old German or Dutch word.]

**pamphlet** noun **pamphlets**
A **pamphlet** is a small booklet.
[**Pamphlet** comes from *Pamphilet*, the name of a long Latin poem that filled a small booklet.]

**pan** noun **pans**
A **pan** is a round metal dish with a handle that you use to cook food.
[**Pan** comes from Old English.]

**pancake** noun **pancakes**
A **pancake** is a thin flat cake made from a batter of milk, eggs and flour, and fried in a pan.

**panda** noun **pandas**
A **panda** is a large animal like a black and white bear that lives in China and eats bamboo.
[**Panda** comes from Nepali (the language spoken in Nepal).]

**pane** noun **panes**
A **pane** is a piece of glass for a window or door. [**Pane** comes from Latin.]

**panel** noun **panels**
**1** A **panel** is a flat section of wood or other material for a door or wall.
**2** A **panel** is a board or surface that has controls on it for operating a vehicle or machine.
**3** A **panel** is a group of people who decide or discuss something, especially in front of an audience.
[**Panel** comes via French from the same Latin word as **pane**.]

**pang** noun **pangs**
A **pang** is a sudden feeling or pain: *hunger pangs; a pang of guilt*.
[**Pang** may come from **prong**.]

**panic** noun (th)
A **panic** is a sudden fear that is difficult to control.
[**Panic** comes from *Pan*, the name of a Greek god who could terrify people and animals.]

**panic** verb **panics, panicking, panicked** (th)
If you **panic**, you suddenly become so frightened that you cannot control yourself and you act in a stupid way.

**panorama** noun **panoramas**
A **panorama** is a complete view of a place from one side to the other.

[**Panorama** comes from Greek *pan* 'all' and *horama* 'a view'.]

**pant** verb **pants, panting, panted**
To **pant** means to take short quick breaths.
[**Pant** comes from Greek via French.]

**panther** noun **panthers**
A **panther** is a leopard, usually with black fur.
[**Panther** comes from Greek via French and Latin.]

**pantomime** noun **pantomimes**
A **pantomime** is a musical play based on a fairy story and performed at Christmas time.
[**Pantomime** comes from Greek via Latin and French.]

**pants** plural noun
**1 Pants** are the piece of clothing you wear on your bottom under your clothes.
**2 Pants** are trousers.
[**Pants** is short for **pantaloons**, a kind of baggy trousers worn by *Pantaloon*, a character in an Italian comedy.]

**paper** noun **papers**
**1 Paper** is a thin material that you can write or draw on.
**2** A **paper** is a newspaper.
[**Paper** comes via French from the same Latin word as **papyrus**.]

**paperback** noun **paperbacks**
A **paperback** is a book with a thin cover.

**papier-mâché** noun
**Papier-mâché** is a mixture of pieces of paper that are soaked in glue and used to make objects such as models.
[**Papier-mâché** is a French word that means 'chewed paper'.]

**papyrus** noun
**Papyrus** is a tall grassy plant that grows in Africa and was used in the past to make a type of paper.
[**Papyrus** comes from Greek via Latin.]

**parable** noun **parables**
A **parable** is a short story that teaches a religious or moral lesson.
[**Parable** comes from Greek via French and Latin.]

**parachute** noun **parachutes**
A **parachute** is a large piece of cloth that

opens like an umbrella and is used so that someone can drop safely from a plane. [**Parachute** comes from Latin *parare* 'to protect from' and French *chute* 'a fall'.]

**parade** *noun* **parades** (th)
A **parade** is a group of people marching or walking along while others watch. [**Parade** comes from Latin via French, Spanish and Italian.]

**parade** *verb* **parades, parading, paraded**
To **parade** means to march or walk in a group while people watch.

**paradise** *noun*
1 **Paradise** is a beautiful or wonderful place.
2 **Paradise** is heaven.
[**Paradise** comes via French, Latin and Greek from Avestan *pairideisos* 'park, garden'. Avestan is a very old language that used to be spoken in Iran.]

**paradox** *noun* **paradoxes**
A **paradox** is a true statement or situation that seems to contradict itself. [**Paradox** comes from Greek *paradoxon* 'opposite opinion'.]

**paraffin** *noun*
**Paraffin** is a liquid that is used for heating and lighting. [**Paraffin** comes from Latin via German.]

**paragraph** *noun* **paragraphs**
A **paragraph** is a section of a piece of writing. [**Paragraph** comes from Greek via French and Latin.]

**parakeet** *noun* **parakeets**
A **parakeet** is a kind of small parrot. [**Parakeet** comes from French.]

**parallel** *adjective*
Lines or rows that are **parallel** are always the same distance apart. [**Parallel** comes via French and Latin from Greek *parallelos* 'beside each other'.]

**parallelogram** *noun* **parallelograms**
A **parallelogram** is a shape with four sides, in which each side is equal and parallel to the side opposite it. [**Parallelogram** comes via French and Latin from Greek *parallelos* 'beside each other' (ancestor of **parallel**) and *gramme* 'line'.]

**paralyse** *verb* **paralyses, paralysing, paralysed**
If someone is **paralysed**, s/he cannot feel or move a part of his/her body. [**Paralyse** comes from Greek via French and Latin.]

**paramount** *adjective*
Something that is **paramount** is of the greatest importance. [**Paramount** comes from old French *paramont* 'above'.]

**parapet** *noun* **parapets**
A **parapet** is a low wall along the edge of a bridge, roof or balcony. [**Parapet** comes from French or Italian.]

**paraphernalia** *noun* (th)
**Paraphernalia** is a lot of pieces of equipment or belongings that people think are unnecessary. [**Paraphernalia** comes from Greek.]

**paraphrase** *verb* **paraphrases, paraphrasing, paraphrased** (th)
To **paraphrase** something means to say or write it again using different words. [**Paraphrase** comes from Greek via Latin.]

**paraplegic** *noun* **paraplegics**
A **paraplegic** is someone who cannot feel or move his/her legs or the lower part of his/her body. [**Paraplegic** comes from Greek.]

**parasite** *noun* **parasites**
A **parasite** is a plant or animal that lives on or in another plant or animal, called its host. It gets its food from the host but doesn't do anything in return. [**Parasite** comes from Greek via Latin *parasitos* 'eating at someone else's table'.]

**parasol** *noun* **parasols**
A **parasol** is a small umbrella used to protect you from the sun. [**Parasol** comes from Italian via French.]

**paratrooper** *noun* **paratroopers**
A **paratrooper** is a soldier who is trained to use a parachute and is dropped from an aircraft into an enemy area. [**Paratrooper** comes from **parachute** and **troop**.]

**parcel** *noun* **parcels** (th)
A **parcel** is something wrapped up ready to post or carry. [**Parcel** comes from Latin via French.]

**parched** *adjective* (th)
**1** If you are **parched**, you are very thirsty.
**2** If the ground or a plant is **parched**, it is very dry and needs water.
[No one knows where **parched** comes from.]

**parchment** *noun*
**Parchment** is material made from the skin of a sheep or goat that was used in the past as paper.
[**Parchment** comes from Latin via French.]

**pardon** *verb* **pardons, pardoning, pardoned** (th)
To **pardon** means to forgive.
[**Pardon** comes from Latin via French.]

**parent** *noun* **parents**
Your **parents** are your mother and father.
[**Parent** comes via French from Latin *parere* 'to bear children'.]

**parish** *noun* **parishes**
A **parish** is an area that has its own church.
[**Parish** comes from Greek via French and Latin.]

**park** *noun* **parks**
A **park** is a large area of ground like a garden that anyone can walk or play in.
[**Park** comes from an old French word.]

**park** *verb* **parks, parking, parked**
To **park** means to leave a vehicle somewhere for a while.

**parliament** *noun* **parliaments**
A **parliament** is a group of people who decide the laws for the country.
[**Parliament** comes from French *parler* 'to speak'.]

**parody** *noun* **parodies**
A **parody** is a funny piece of music or drama that imitates another well-known piece.
[**Parody** comes from Greek via Latin.]

**parole** *noun*
**Parole** is when a prisoner is released early from prison for good behaviour.
[**Parole** comes from French.]

**parquet** *noun*
**Parquet** is a floor covering made of a pattern of small blocks of wood.
[**Parquet** comes from French.]

**parrot** *noun* **parrots**
A **parrot** is a brightly coloured bird that can learn to speak by copying.
[**Parrot** comes from French.]

**parsley** *noun*
**Parsley** is a herb with small leaves that is used to give flavour to food or to decorate it.
[**Parsley** comes from Latin via Old English.]

**parsnip** *noun* **parsnips**
A **parsnip** is a plant with a long cream-coloured root that is eaten as a vegetable.
[**Parsnip** comes from Latin via French.]

**part** *noun* **parts** (th)
**1** A **part** is some but not all of something.
**2** A **part** is a small piece of a machine or piece of equipment: *spare parts*.
**3** A **part** in a play or film is a character in it played by an actor.
[**Part** comes from Latin via Old English or French.]

**part** *verb* **parts, parting, parted** (th)
**1** To **part** means to divide or separate into parts: *The clouds parted and the sun came out; She parts her hair in the centre.*
**2** To **part** means to leave another person or go different ways.

**partial** *adjective* (th)
Something that is not complete or total is **partial**: *a partial success*.
[**Partial** comes via French from the same Latin word as **part**.]

**participate** *verb* **participates, participating, participated**
If you **participate** in an activity, you join in with it.
[**Participate** comes from Latin *pars* 'part' and *capere* 'to take'.]

**participle** *noun* **participles**
A **participle** is a part of a verb that you use with *to have* or *to be* to form certain tenses. The **past participle** usually ends in *-ed*, and is used for an action that has been completed: *I have already packed; He had visited her before.* The **present participle** ends in *-ing*, and is used for an action that is still going on, or that was going on at the time you are speaking about: *I am studying French this year; She was going home when she saw him.* You also use the **present participle** for something

that will happen in the near future: *I am going tomorrow; He's taking his driving test next week.*
[**Participle** comes from Latin via French.]

**particle** *noun* **particles** (th)
A **particle** is a tiny amount or part of something.
[**Particle** comes from Latin *particula* 'small part'.]

**particular** *adjective*
A **particular** thing is the one you are talking about and not anything else: *This particular animal is only found in the wild.*
[**Particular** comes from Latin *particularis* 'to do with a small part'.]

**parting** *noun* **partings**
1 A **parting** is a line where you brush your hair into different sections.
2 A **parting** is when two people leave each other. [**Parting** comes from **part**.]

**partition** *noun* **partitions**
1 A **partition** is a screen that separates two parts of a room.
2 **Partition** is when a country is divided into more than one part because the people that live in the different parts cannot agree.
[**Partition** comes from Latin *partiri* 'to divide or share'.]

**partly** *adverb* (th)
When part of something is done but not all of it, it is done **partly**.

**partner** *noun* **partners** (th)
1 A **partner** is someone who you do something with: *my dancing partner.*
2 A **partner** is a husband or wife, or a person someone lives with as a husband or wife.
[**Partner** comes from the same Latin word as **partition**.]

**part of speech** *noun* **parts of speech**
A **part of speech** is the type of word something is, such as a noun, adjective or verb.

**part-time** *adjective*
A job that you do for a few hours a day or a few days a week only is **part-time**.

**party** *noun* **parties** (th)
1 A **party** is a happy occasion when a group of people meet to celebrate something and enjoy themselves.

2 A **party** is a group of people travelling or working together.
3 A **party** is an organisation of people who have similar opinions.
[**Party** comes via French from the same Latin word as **partition**.]

**pass¹** *noun* **passes** (th)
1 A **pass** is a document or card that allows you to do something: *a security pass.*
2 A **pass** is a successful result in an exam.
[**Pass¹** comes from Latin *passus* 'pace' (ancestor of **pace**).]

**pass¹** *verb* **passes, passing, passed** (th)
1 To **pass** something to someone means to give it to him/her.
2 To **pass** something means to go past it.
3 To **pass** an exam or test means to be successful in it.
4 If you say that someone has **passed away** or **passed on**, you mean that s/he has died.

**pass²** *noun* **passes**
A **pass** is a narrow passage between two mountains. [**Pass²** comes from **pace**.]

**passage** *noun* **passages** (th)
1 A **passage** is a corridor.
2 A **passage** is a short part of a piece of writing or music.
[**Passage** comes via French from the same Latin word as **pass¹**.]

**passenger** *noun* **passengers**
A **passenger** is someone who is travelling in a vehicle but not driving it.
[**Passenger** comes from the same French word as **passage**.]

**passer-by** *noun* **passers-by** (th)
A **passer-by** is a person in the street who happens to be going past something.

**passion** *noun* **passions** (th)
1 **Passion** is a very strong feeling such as love or hate.
2 A **passion** is a very strong love for something.
[**Passion** comes via French from Latin *passio* 'suffering'.]

**passionate** *adjective* (th)
Someone who is **passionate** feels very strongly about someone or something.

**passive** *adjective*
1 Someone who is **passive** lets things happen rather than taking action.

**a b c d e f g h i j k l m**

**2 Passive smoking** is breathing in the smoke from other people's cigarettes. [**Passive** comes from Latin *passivus* 'capable of suffering'.]

**Passover** *noun*
Passover is a Jewish festival held in March or April that remembers when, Jews believe, the Israelites were rescued by God from slavery in Egypt. At **Passover**, Jewish families have a meal at which they eat special foods, say special prayers and tell the story of the Israelites' escape.
[**Passover** comes from the belief that the angel of death 'passed over' the Israelites but killed many Egyptians.]

**passport** *noun* **passports**
A **passport** is an official document containing your photograph and personal details that you must show when you travel to another country.
[**Passport** comes from French.]

**password** *noun* **passwords**
A **password** is a secret word that you use to enter a locked building or a computer system.

**past** *noun*
The **past** is the time that has gone.
[**Past** is a different spelling of **passed**, the past tense and past participle of **pass**.]

**past** *adjective* (th)
Something that is gone or finished is **past**: *a past tennis champion; The past few days have been very busy.*

**past** *preposition* (th)
after or beyond: *She ran past me; The shop is on the left, past the church.*

**pasta** *noun*
**Pasta** is a dough made with flour and water that is made into shapes and cooked in water. Spaghetti is a kind of **pasta**.
[**Pasta** comes via Italian from the same Latin word as **paste**.]

**paste** *noun* **pastes**
**Paste** is a wet mixture used to stick things together.
[**Paste** comes from Latin via French.]

**paste** *verb* **pastes, pasting, pasted**
To **paste** means to stick something with glue: *I pasted the picture onto a card.*

**pastel** *noun* **pastels**
1 A **pastel** is a soft coloured crayon.
2 **Pastels** are pale soft colours.
[**Pastel** comes from Latin.]

**pasteurised** *adjective* Also **pasteurized**
Milk that is **pasteurised** has been heated to a very high temperature to kill germs.
[**Pasteurised** comes from the name of Louis *Pasteur*, a French scientist, who invented the process.]

**pastime** *noun* **pastimes** (th)
A **pastime** is a hobby or something you enjoy doing in your spare time.
[**Pastime** comes from **pass¹** and **time**.]

**pastor** *noun* **pastors**
A **pastor** is a minister of a church.
[**Pastor** comes from Latin *pastor* 'shepherd'.]

**past participle** *noun*
To find **past participle**, look under **participle**.

**pastry** *noun* **pastries**
**Pastry** is a mixture of flour, fat and water that is rolled out and used to make pies and pastries. [**Pastry** comes from **paste**.]

**pasture** *noun* **pastures** (th)
**Pasture** is land covered in grass used to graze cattle and sheep.
[**Pasture** comes from Latin via French.]

**pasty** *noun* **pasties**
A **pasty** is an envelope of pastry that is filled with meat or vegetables.
[**Pasty** comes via French from the same Latin word as **paste**.]

**pat** *verb* **pats, patting, patted** (th)
To **pat** means to hit gently.
[The word **pat** may be an imitation of the sound.]

**patch** *noun* **patches** (th)
1 A **patch** is a small piece of material sewn over a hole in a piece of clothing.
2 A **patch** is a small piece of ground.
[**Patch** probably comes from the same French word as **piece**.]

**patch** *verb* **patches, patching, patched**
To **patch** means to cover a hole in a piece of clothing with a piece of material.

**patchwork** *noun*
**Patchwork** material is made of lots of small pieces of different coloured fabric

that are sewn together.

**patchy** *adjective* **patchier, patchiest**
Something that is uneven and exists only in some places is **patchy**: *patchy fog*.
[**Patchy** comes from **patch**.]

**paté** *noun* **patés**
**Paté** is a soft paste made of meat, fish or vegetables that is eaten with bread or toast.
[**Paté** is the French word for **paste**.]

**patent** *noun* **patents**
A **patent** is an official right to be the only person allowed to make or sell a product for a period of time.
[**Patent** comes from Latin.]

**path** *noun* **paths** (th)
A **path** is a narrow way to walk along.
[**Path** comes from Old English.]

**pathetic** *adjective* (th)
**1** Someone who is sad or helpless and makes you feel sorry for him/her is **pathetic**.
**2** Something that is weak or useless and makes you feel cross is **pathetic**.
[**Pathetic** comes via Latin from Greek *pathos* 'suffering'.]

**patience** *noun*
**Patience** is the ability to wait or deal with problems without getting angry or upset.
[**Patience** comes via French from the same Latin word as **patient**.]

**patient** *noun* **patients**
A **patient** is someone who is being looked after by a doctor or nurse.
[**Patient** comes via French from Latin *patiens* 'suffering'.]

**patient** *adjective*
Someone who is **patient** can wait or deal with problems without getting angry or upset.

**patio** *noun* **patios**
A **patio** is an area with a hard surface next to or behind a house, where you can sit and relax.
[**Patio** comes from Spanish *patio* 'courtyard'.]

**patriot** *noun* **patriots**
A **patriot** is someone who loves his/her country and is willing to fight for it.
[**Patriot** comes via Latin from Greek *patris*

'native country'.]

**patriotism** *noun*
**Patriotism** is love for your country and willingness to fight for it.

**patrol** *noun* **patrols**
A **patrol** is a group of people who are guarding an area.
[**Patrol** comes from French.]

**patrol** *verb* **patrols, patrolling, patrolled** (th)
To **patrol** a place is to guard it by walking around and checking that everything is safe.

**patronise** *verb* **patronises, patronising, patronised** *Also* **patronize** (th)
To **patronise** someone means to treat that person in a way that seems friendly, but actually shows that you think s/he is less important or not as clever as you.
[**Patronise** comes from Latin via French.]

**pattern** *noun* **patterns** (th)
**1** A **pattern** is a design of lines, shapes and colours.
**2** A **pattern** is a design that you can copy in order to make something.
[**Pattern** comes from Latin via French.]

**pauper** *noun* **paupers**
A **pauper** is a very poor person.
[**Pauper** comes from Latin *pauper* 'poor' (ancestor of **poor** and **poverty**).]

**pause** *noun* **pauses**
A **pause** is a short period when you stop talking or doing something.
[**Pause** comes via French and Latin from Greek *pausien* 'to stop'.]

**pavement** *noun* **pavements**
A **pavement** is the hard surface next to a road where people can walk.
[**Pavement** comes via French from Latin *pavimentum* 'a floor hardened by treading on it'.]

**pavilion** *noun* **pavilions**
**1** A **pavilion** is a building at a sports ground for players to rest or change their clothes.
**2** A **pavilion** is a large tent used for outdoor public events.
[**Pavilion** comes from old French *pavillon* 'tent'.]

**paw** *noun* **paws**
A **paw** is an animal's foot.
[**Paw** comes from an old French word.]

**pawn** *noun* **pawns**
A **pawn** is a chess piece with the lowest value.
[**Pawn** comes via French from Latin *pedo* 'foot soldier'.]

**pay** *verb* **pays, paying, paid** (th)
To **pay** means to give money for something.
[**Pay** comes from Latin via French.]

**payment** *noun* **payments**
A **payment** is an amount of money that you pay for something.

**PC** *noun* **PCs**
A **PC** is a computer designed to be used by one person. **PC** is short for **Personal Computer**.

**pea** *noun* **peas**
**Peas** are small, round, green vegetables that grow in pods.
[**Pea** comes from Old English.]

**peace** *noun* (th)
**1 Peace** is a time when there is no war.
**2 Peace** is a time of quiet and rest.
[**Peace** comes from Latin via French.]

**peach** *noun* **peaches**
A **peach** is a round soft fruit with a furry orange skin and a large stone.
[**Peach** comes from Latin via French.]

**peacock** *noun* **peacocks**
A **peacock** is a large male bird with a huge colourful tail that it can spread out like a fan. The female is called a **peahen**.
[**Peacock** comes from Old English.]

**peak** *noun* **peaks** (th)
**1** A **peak** is the pointed tip or highest point of something: *mountain peaks*.
**2** A **peak** is the part of a cap that sticks out in front.
[No one knows where **peak** comes from.]

**peal** *verb* **peals, pealing, pealed**
If a set of bells **peal**, they ring.
[**Peal** comes from an old French word.]

**peanut** *noun* **peanuts**
A **peanut** is a kind of nut that grows in a pod underground.
[The word **peanut** comes from **pea**, to which the peanut is related.]

**pear** *noun* **pears**
A **pear** is a juicy fruit with yellow, brown or green skin that is round at the base and narrower at the top.
[**Pear** comes from Latin via Old English.]

**pearl** *noun* **pearls**
A **pearl** is a small hard ball that grows in the shell of some oysters. It is shiny and white, and is used to make jewellery.
[**Pearl** comes from French.]

**peasant** *noun* **peasants**
A **peasant** is a poor person who works on the land.
[**Peasant** comes from Latin via French.]

**peat** *noun*
**Peat** is dark brown material like earth that is made of rotted plants. **Peat** is found in wet cool land, and is used in gardening or burned as fuel.
[**Peat** comes from Latin.]

**pebble** *noun* **pebbles**
A **pebble** is a small round stone.
[No one knows where **pebble** comes from.]

**peck** *verb* **pecks, pecking, pecked**
To **peck** means to bite something with the beak.
[No one knows where **peck** comes from.]

**peculiar** *adjective* (th)
Something that is odd or strange is **peculiar**. [**Peculiar** comes from Latin.]

**pedal** *noun* **pedals**
A **pedal** is a thing on a bicycle, piano, car or machine that you press with your foot to make it work.
[**Pedal** comes from Latin *pedis* 'for a foot'.]

**pedal** *verb* **pedals, pedalling, pedalled**
To **pedal** means to push the pedals on a bicycle to make it move.

**pedestal** *noun* **pedestals**
A **pedestal** is the base that a statue stands on.
[**Pedestal** comes from Italian via French.]

**pedestrian** *noun* **pedestrians**
A **pedestrian** is someone who is walking, not travelling in a vehicle.
[**Pedestrian** comes via French from Latin *pedester* 'going on foot'.]

**peel** *noun*
**Peel** is the skin or rind on some fruit and

vegetables. [**Peel** comes from Latin.]

**peel** *verb* **peels, peeling, peeled**
1 To **peel** a fruit or vegetable is to take the peel off.
2 If you **peel**, the thin top layer of your skin gradually comes off because it has been burned by the sun.

**peep** *verb* **peeps, peeping, peeped**
To **peep** means to look quickly for a short time.
[No one knows where **peep** comes from.]

**peer¹** *noun* **peers**
1 Your **peers** are people who are the same age or of the same social class as you.
2 A **peer** is a man who has a title, such as *lord*, *earl* or *duke*.
[**Peer¹** comes via French from Latin *par* 'equal'.]

**peer²** *verb* **peers, peering, peered**
To **peer** means to look hard or closely at something: *We peered through the window.*
[No one knows where **peer²** comes from.]

**peg** *noun* **pegs**
1 A **peg** is a wooden or plastic clip used for hanging washing on a line.
2 A **peg** is a pointed piece of wood or metal used to fasten or pin something down: *tent pegs*.
[**Peg** probably comes from an old German word.]

**pelican** *noun* **pelicans**
A **pelican** is a large bird with a very long beak that it uses for catching fish.
[**Pelican** comes from Greek via Latin.]

**pellet** *noun* **pellets**
A **pellet** is a small ball of something such as food, paper or metal.
[**Pellet** comes via French from Latin *pila* 'ball'.]

**pelt** *verb* **pelts, pelting, pelted** (th)
To **pelt** means to throw things at someone or something: *pelted with snowballs*.
[No one knows where **pelt** comes from.]

**pelvis** *noun* **pelvises**
Your **pelvis** is the wide curved set of bones at the bottom of your spine.
[**Pelvis** comes from Latin *pelvis* 'basin', because of its shape.]

**pen¹** *noun* **pens** (th)
A **pen¹** is used for writing with ink.

[**Pen¹** comes from Latin *penna* 'feather', because people used to write with a pen made from a feather.]

**pen²** *noun* **pens** (th)
A **pen** is a small fenced-off piece of land for keeping in animals.
[**Pen²** comes from Old English.]

**penalty** *noun* **penalties** (th)
A **penalty** is a punishment for breaking a law, rule or contract.
[**Penalty** comes from Latin *poena* 'punishment' (ancestor of **pain** and **punishment**).]

**pence** *plural noun*
**Pence** is one of the plurals of **penny**.

**pencil** *noun* **pencils**
A **pencil** is a writing and drawing instrument containing a very thin stick of black or coloured material inside it.
[**Pencil** comes from Latin *penicillum* 'paint brush'.]

**pendulum** *noun* **pendulums**
A **pendulum** is a rod with a weight on the end that swings from side to side.
[**Pendulum** comes from Latin *pendulum* 'something that hangs down'.]

**penetrate** *verb* **penetrates, penetrating, penetrated** (th)
To **penetrate** something means to go inside or pass through it.
[**Penetrate** comes from Latin.]

**pen friend** *noun* **pen friends** *Also* **pen pal**
A **pen friend** is a friend who you write letters to regularly.

**penguin** *noun* **penguins**
A **penguin** is a black and white seabird, which cannot fly but swims. Most **penguins** live in the Antarctic.
[No one knows where **penguin** comes from.]

**penicillin** *noun*
**Penicillin** is a substance used as a medicine that can kill bacteria.
[**Penicillin** comes from Latin.]

**peninsula** *noun* **peninsulas**
A **peninsula** is a piece of land that is surrounded by water on three sides.
[**Peninsula** comes from Latin *paene* 'almost' and *insula* 'island'.]

**penis** *noun* **penises**
The **penis** is the part of the body of a man or a male animal that he uses to pass urine and to pass sperm to the female during sexual intercourse.
[**Penis** comes from Latin.]

**penny** *noun* **pennies** *or* **pence**
A **penny** is a British unit of currency. There are 100 **pennies** in a pound.
[**Penny** comes from Old English.]

**pen pal** *noun* **pen pals**
**Pen pal** is another word for **pen friend**.

**pension** *noun* **pensions**
A **pension** is an amount of money that is paid to someone regularly after they have retired from work.
[**Pension** comes via French from Latin *pensio* 'payment'.]

**pentagon** *noun* **pentagons**
A **pentagon** is a shape with five sides and five angles.
[**Pentagon** comes from Greek *penta* 'five' and *gonia* 'angle'.]

**people** *plural noun*
**People** are men, women and children.
[**People** comes via French from Latin *populus* 'the people'.]

**pepper** *noun* **peppers**
**Pepper** is a powder made from peppercorns that is used to give food a strong, hot taste.
[**Pepper** comes from Latin via Old English.]

**peppercorn** *noun* **peppercorns**
A **peppercorn** is a small white or black seed that pepper is made from.

**peppermint** *noun* **peppermints**
**1 Peppermint** is a plant with dark green leaves and mauve flowers. It has a strong taste that is used to flavour sweets and toothpaste.
**2 Peppermints** are sweets flavoured with peppermint.
[**Peppermint** comes from **pepper** and **mint**[1].]

**per cent** *adverb* *Also* **percent**
One **per cent** is one part out of every hundred: *100 per cent cotton T-shirts.*
[**Per cent** comes from Latin.]

**percentage** *noun* **percentages**
A **percentage** is an amount of something expressed as a number out of a hundred: *Meat has a high percentage of protein.*
[**Percentage** comes from **per cent**.]

**perceptive** *adjective* (th)
Someone who is **perceptive** is quick to notice or realise something.
[**Perceptive** comes from Latin.]

**perch** *noun* **perches**
A **perch** is something, such as a branch, that a bird rests on when it is not flying.
[**Perch** comes via French from Latin *pertica* 'pole'.]

**perch** *verb* **perches, perching, perched**
To **perch** means to sit on something that might not be very comfortable.

**percussion** *noun*
**Percussion** instruments are musical instruments that you play by hitting or shaking them. Drums and tambourines are percussion instruments.
[**Percussion** comes from Latin *percussio* 'hitting'.]

**perennial** *adjective*
**1** A **perennial** plant lives for several years and has flowers every year.
**2** A **perennial** problem or situation often happens or keeps happening.
[**Perennial** comes from Latin.]

**perfect** *adjective* (th)
Something that is **perfect** has no faults.
[**Perfect** comes from Latin *perfectum* 'completed'.]

**perfectly** *adverb*
Something that has been done completely and with no faults has been done **perfectly**.

**perforate** *verb* **perforates, perforating, perforated**
To **perforate** something means to make small holes in it.
[**Perforate** comes from Latin.]

**perform** *verb* **performs, performing, performed** (th)
**1** To **perform** means to act, dance, sing or play music in front of an audience.
**2** To **perform** means to carry out or do something: *He performed his task well.*
[**Perform** comes from an old French word.]

**performance** *noun* **performances**
A **performance** is something such as a play, dancing, singing or music performed in front of an audience.

**perfume** *noun* **perfumes**
A **perfume** is a liquid with a beautiful smell.
[**Perfume** comes from Italian via French.]

**perhaps** *adverb* (th)
You use **perhaps** to say that something may happen but is not certain.
[**Perhaps** comes from Latin *per* 'through' and an old word *hap* 'luck' (ancestor of **haphazard**, **happen** and **happy**).]

**period** *noun* **periods** (th)
1 A **period** is a length of time.
2 A woman's **period** is a few days every month when blood comes from her womb.
[**Period** comes from Greek via French and Latin.]

**periscope** *noun* **periscopes**
A **periscope** is an instrument with mirrors at each end that allows you to see what is going on above you, for example from a submarine.
[**Periscope** comes from Greek *peri* 'around' and *skopein* 'to look at'.]

**permanent** *adjective* (th)
Something that is **permanent** lasts for a long time and is not going to change.
[**Permanent** comes from Latin.]

**permission** *noun* (th)
If you have **permission** to do something, someone in authority allows you to do it.
[**Permission** comes from the same Latin word as **permit**.]

**permit** *verb* **permits, permitting, permitted** (th)
To **permit** someone to do something means to allow him/her to do it.
[**Permit** comes from Latin.]

**perpetuate** *verb* **perpetuates, perpetuating, perpetuated**
Something that **perpetuates** goes on for ever.
**perpetual** *adjective*. **perpetually** *adverb*.
[**Perpetuate** comes from Latin.]

**person** *noun* **people** *or* **persons**
1 A **person** is a man, woman or child.
2 In grammar, **person** refers to the three groups of personal pronouns that go with verbs. The **first person** refers to whoever is speaking, and is shown by the pronouns *I, we, us*. The **second person** refers to whoever is being spoken to, and is shown by the pronoun *you*. The **third person** refers to whoever is being spoken about, and is shown by the pronouns *he, him, she, her, it, they* and *them*.
[**Person** comes from Latin.]

**personal** *adjective* (th)
Something that is to do with or for one person only is **personal**: *your personal belongings*.
[**Personal** comes via French from the same Latin word as **person**.]

**personality** *noun* **personalities**
1 Your **personality** is your character and the way you behave with other people.
2 A **personality** is a famous person who is often seen by the public, for example on television.
[**Personality** comes via French from the same Latin word as **person**.]

**perspective** *noun* **perspectives**
1 **Perspective** in a picture is the way that objects are drawn to look nearer or further away from each other, as they are in real life.
2 Your **perspective** is the way that you look at or understand something.
[**Perspective** comes from Latin *perspicere* 'to look at closely'.]

**perspiration** *noun*
**Perspiration** is sweat, the liquid that comes out of your skin when you are hot.
[**Perspiration** comes from the same French word as **perspire**.]

**perspire** *verb* **perspires, perspiring, perspired**
If you **perspire**, you sweat.
[**Perspire** comes from Latin via French.]

**persuade** *verb* **persuades, persuading, persuaded** (th)
To **persuade** means to make someone do or believe something by giving him/her reasons why it is a good idea or why it is true. [**Persuade** comes from Latin.]

**persuasion** *noun*
**Persuasion** is when someone persuades another person to do something.
[**Persuasion** comes from the same Latin word as **persuade**.]

**pessimism** *noun*
**Pessimism** is a feeling that things will turn out badly.
[**Pessimism** comes from Latin *pessimus* 'worst'.]

**pessimist** *noun* **pessimists**
A **pessimist** is someone who always believes that things will turn out badly.

**pessimistic** *adjective*
Someone who is **pessimistic** always believes that things will turn out badly.

**pest** *noun* **pests**
1 A **pest** is an animal or an insect that damages crops or goods. Locusts and rats are **pests**.
2 A **pest** is a person who is being a nuisance.
[**Pest** comes from Latin *pestis* 'plague'.]

**pesticide** *noun* **pesticides**
A **pesticide** is a chemical that farmers put on crops to kill harmful insects.
[**Pesticide** comes from **pest** and Latin *caedere* 'to kill'.]

**pet** *noun* **pets**
A **pet** is an animal kept for company.
[No one knows where **pet** comes from.]

**petal** *noun* **petals**
A **petal** is one of the coloured parts of a flower.
[**Petal** comes from Greek *petalos* 'spread out'.]

**petrified** *adjective* (th)
If you are **petrified**, you are extremely frightened so that you cannot think or move.
[**Petrified** comes via French and Latin from Greek *petra* 'rock'.]

**petrol** *noun*
**Petrol** is the liquid that is used as fuel for cars and other vehicles.
[**Petrol** comes via French from Greek *petra* 'rock' and Lastin *oleum* 'oil'.]

**phantom** *noun* **phantoms** (th)
A **phantom** is a ghost.
[**Phantom** comes from Greek via French.]

**Pharaoh** *noun* **Pharaohs**
A **Pharaoh** was a ruler in ancient Egypt.
[**Pharaoh** comes from Egyptian via Latin and Greek.]

**pharmacist** *noun* **pharmacists**
A **pharmacist** is a person whose job is to prepare and sell medicines and drugs.
[**Pharmacist** comes via Latin from Greek *pharmakon* 'drug'.]

**phase** *noun* **phases**
A **phase** is a stage in the development or process of something: *phases of the moon*.
[**Phase** comes from Greek via French.]

**pheasant** *noun* **pheasants**
A **pheasant** is a low-flying bird with a long tail. **Pheasants** are shot for sport and food.
[**Pheasant** comes from Greek via French and Latin.]

**phenomenon** *noun* **phenomena**
A **phenomenon** is something very interesting or unusual that can be seen.
[**Phenomenon** comes via Latin from Greek *phainomenon* 'something that appears'.]

**philosophy** *noun* **philosophies** (th)
1 **Philosophy** is the study of ideas about thinking and knowledge.
2 A person's **philosophy** is the set of beliefs and ideas s/he has about how to live.
[**Philosophy** comes via French and Latin from Greek *philosophia* 'love of wisdom'.]

**phlegm** *noun*
**Phlegm** is the thick substance produced in the nose and throat when you have a cold.
[**Phlegm** comes from Greek via French and Latin.]

**phobia** *noun* **phobias**
A **phobia** is a very strong fear of something, especially of something that is not dangerous or harmful: *She has a phobia about spiders*.
[**Phobia** comes from Greek via Latin.]

**phone** *noun* **phones**
**Phone** is short for **telephone**.

**phosphorous** *noun*
**Phosphorous** is the chemical used in matches that burns on contact with air.
[**Phosphorous** comes via Latin from Greek *phos* 'light' and *-phoros* 'bringing'.]

**photo** *noun* **photos**
**Photo** is short for **photograph**.

**photocopy** *noun* **photocopies**
A **photocopy** is a copy of a document made by quickly photographing it in a machine.
[**Photocopy** comes from **photograph** and **copy**.]

**photogenic** *adjective*
Someone who is **photogenic** looks good in photographs.
[**Photogenic** comes from **photograph** and *-genic* 'producing', which comes from Greek.]

**photograph** *noun* **photographs**
A **photograph** is a picture taken with a camera and then printed on paper.
[**Photograph** comes from *photo-* 'light' and Greek *graphein* 'to draw'.]

**photographer** *noun* **photographers**
A **photographer** is someone whose job is to take photographs.

**photosynthesis** *noun*
**Photosynthesis** is the process in which green plants use light from the sun to turn carbon dioxide and water into energy.
[**Photosynthesis** comes from *photo-* 'light' and *synthesis* 'putting differerent things together to make something', which comes from Greek.]

**phrase** *noun* **phrases**
A **phrase** is a few words that form part of a sentence or that have a particular meaning. *Died of a broken heart* is a phrase.
[**Phrase** comes via Latin from Greek *phrazein* 'to declare'.]

**physical** *adjective*
1 Activities that are **physical** are to do with the body: *physical exercise.*
2 **Physical** means to do with things that you can touch and see.
[**Physical** comes via Latin from the same Greek word as **physics**.]

**physics** *noun*
**Physics** is the science that studies energy, heat, movement and light.
[**Physics** comes via Latin from Greek *physika* 'natural things'.]

**piano** *noun* **pianos**
A **piano** is a large musical instrument with black and white keys. When you press a key a tiny hammer hits a string and produces a note.
[**Piano** is short for **pianoforte**, which comes from Italian *piano e forte* 'soft and loud'.]

**pick** *verb* **picks, picking, picked** (th)
1 To **pick** something or **pick** something **out** means to choose it.
2 To **pick** means to collect flowers or fruit from plants or trees.
3 To **pick** something **up** means to take hold of it and lift it up.
[No one knows where **pick** comes from.]

**pickles** *plural noun*
**Pickles** are a strong-tasting food made from vegetables and vinegar.
[**Pickles** comes from an old German or Dutch word.]

**pickpocket** *noun* **pickpockets**
A **pickpocket** is someone who steals from people's pockets or bags.

**picnic** *noun* **picnics**
A **picnic** is a meal eaten in the open air.
[**Picnic** comes from French.]

**picture** *noun* **pictures**
A **picture** is a drawing, painting or photo.
[**Picture** comes from Latin.]

**picture** *verb* **pictures, picturing, pictured**
To **picture** something is to form an idea in your mind of what it might be like: *He pictured himself scoring the winning goal.*

**picturesque** *adjective* (th)
A place that is **picturesque** is lovely to look at.
[**Picturesque** comes via French and Italian from the same Latin word as **picture**.]

**pie** *noun* **pies**
A **pie** is meat or fruit covered in pastry and baked.
[No one knows where the word **pie** comes from.]

**piece** *noun* **pieces** (th)
1 A **piece** is a part of or an amount of something: *a piece of cake; a piece of wood.*
2 A **piece** is one of a set of things used in a game: *a chess piece.*
3 A **piece** is something that someone has written or made: *a piece of music.*
[**Piece** comes from French.]

a b c d e f g h i j k l m

**pier** *noun* **piers**
A **pier** is a long structure built out into the sea for people to walk on.
[**Pier** comes from Latin.]

**pierce** *verb* **pierces, piercing, pierced** (th)
To **pierce** something means to make a hole in it.
[**Pierce** comes from Latin via French.]

**piercing** *adjective* (th)
A **piercing** sound is loud and shrill.
[**Piercing** comes from **pierce**.]

**pig** *noun* **pigs**
A **pig** is an animal with bristly skin and a blunt snout, kept on a farm for its meat.
[**Pig** probably comes from Old English.]

**pigeon** *noun* **pigeons**
A **pigeon** is a bird like a dove. **Pigeons** are good at finding their way home, and are sometimes kept for racing or to carry messages.
[**Pigeon** comes from Latin via French.]

**pile** *noun* **piles** (th)
A **pile** is a number of things one on top of the other in a heap.
[**Pile** comes via French from Latin *pila* 'pillar'.]

**pilgrim** *noun* **pilgrims**
A **pilgrim** is a person who goes on a pilgrimage. [**Pilgrim** comes from Latin.]

**pilgrimage** *noun* **pilgrimages**
A **pilgrimage** is a journey that you make for religious reasons, for example, to worship at a holy place: *go on a pilgrimage to Mecca.*

**pill** *noun* **pills**
A **pill** is a small tablet of medicine.
[**Pill** comes from Latin *pilula* 'little ball'.]

**pillar** *noun* **pillars**
A **pillar** is a large post that helps to hold up a building or structure.
[**Pillar** comes via French from the same Latin word as **pile**.]

**pillow** *noun* **pillows**
A **pillow** is a cushion for your head to rest on in bed.
[**Pillow** comes from Old English.]

**pilot** *noun* **pilots**
1 A **pilot** is the person who steers an aircraft.

2 A **pilot** is someone who guides a ship in and out of a harbour.
[**Pilot** comes from Greek via French and Latin.]

**pin** *noun* **pins**
A **pin** is a thin device with a sharp point used to fasten things.
[**Pin** comes from Latin via Old English.]

**pinch** *verb* **pinches, pinching, pinched**
1 To **pinch** means to squeeze painfully.
2 To **pinch** something means to steal it.
[**Pinch** comes from an old French word.]

**pine**[1] *noun* **pines**
A **pine** is an evergreen tree with small hard leaves, called needles.
[**Pine**[1] comes from Latin.]

**pine**[2] *verb* **pines, pining, pined** (th)
To **pine** means to be very sad and feel ill with longing for someone or something.
[**Pine**[2] comes from Old English.]

**pineapple** *noun* **pineapples**
A **pineapple** is a large, yellow tropical fruit.
[**Pineapple** comes from **pine**[1] and **apple**, because the fruit looks something like a pine cone.]

**pink** *noun*
1 **Pink** is a pale red colour.
2 A **pink** is a garden plant with small pink, white or red flowers.
[No one knows where **pink** comes from.]

**pink** *adjective*
of a pale red colour: *a pink rose.*

**pint** *noun* **pints**
A **pint** is a unit of measurement in the imperial system for liquids, equal to 0.568 of a litre.
[**Pint** comes from an old French word.]

**pipe** *noun* **pipes** (th)
1 A **pipe** is a tube for carrying gas or liquid.
2 A **pipe** is a tube with a small bowl at one end used for smoking tobacco.
[**Pipe** comes from Old English.]

**pirate** *noun* **pirates**
A **pirate** is someone who attacks and robs ships at sea.
[**Pirate** comes via Latin from Greek *peirein* 'to attack'.]

**pistol** *noun* **pistols**
A **pistol** is a small gun that you hold in one hand.
[**Pistol** comes via French and German from Czech.]

**pit** *noun* **pits**
1 A **pit** is a deep hole in the ground.
2 A **pit** is a coal mine.
3 The **pits** is the area beside a motor-racing track where the cars are refuelled and repaired.
[**Pit** comes from Old English.]

**pitch¹** *noun* **pitches**
1 A **pitch** is an area of ground marked out for a game: *a football pitch*.
2 The **pitch** of a musical note is how high it is.
[No one knows where **pitch¹** comes from.]

**pitch¹** *verb* **pitches, pitching, pitched** (th)
1 To **pitch** a tent means to put it up.
2 To **pitch** means to throw.

**pitch²** *noun*
**Pitch** is a thick black liquid made from tar. [**Pitch²** comes from Old English.]

**pitiful** *adjective* (th)
Something or someone that is **pitiful** is so weak or miserable that you feel pity: *a pitiful cry*. **pitifully** *adverb*.

**pitiless** *adjective* (th)
Someone or something that is **pitiless** shows no pity or mercy: *a pitiless dictator*.

**pity** *noun* (th)
**Pity** is a feeling of being sorry for someone in pain or trouble.
[**Pity** comes from Latin via French.]

**place** *noun* **places** (th)
1 A **place** is a particular area or position.
2 If something is **in place**, it is where it should be.
[**Place** comes from Greek via Latin and French.]

**place** *verb* **places, placing, placed** (th)
To **place** means to put something in a particular spot.

**plain** *noun* **plains**
A **plain** is a large area of flat land.
[**Plain** comes via French from Latin *planus* 'flat' or 'clear'.]

**plain** *adjective* **plainer, plainest** (th)
1 Something that is **plain** is not fancy, decorated, or patterned.
2 Someone or something that is **plain** looks ordinary, and not beautiful or ugly.
3 Something that is **plain** is simple and easy to understand.

**plan** *noun* **plans** (th)
1 A **plan** is an arrangement to do something.
2 A **plan** is a map of a building or area of land. [**Plan** comes from French.]

**plan** *verb* **plans, planning, planned** (th)
To **plan** means to arrange to do something, or to decide how you are going to do it.

**plane¹** *noun* **planes**
A **plane** is a vehicle with wings that flies in the sky.
[**Plane¹** is short for **aeroplane**.]

**plane²** *noun* **planes**
1 A **plane** is a flat surface. A cube has six **planes**.
2 A **plane** is a tool that carpenters use to give wood a smooth surface.
[**Plane²** comes from the same Latin word as **plain**.]

**planet** *noun* **planets**
A **planet** is a sphere in space that travels around another, such as the earth around the sun.
[**Planet** comes via Latin from Greek *planetes* 'wanderer', because the planets seem to move in relation to the stars.]

**plank** *noun* **planks**
A **plank** is a long, flat piece of wood.
[**Plank** comes from Latin via French.]

**plant** *noun* **plants**
A **plant** is any living thing that is not an animal. Flowers, trees, seaweed and fungi are all **plants**.
[**Plant** comes from Latin via Old English.]

**plaster** *noun* **plasters**
1 A **plaster** is a strip of material for sticking over a cut.
2 **Plaster** is a mixture that is spread over walls and ceilings and sets hard.
[**Plaster** comes from Latin via Old English.]

**plastic** *noun* **plastics**
**Plastic** is a light, strong substance made from chemicals which can be moulded into many shapes and used to make all kinds of things.

[**Plastic** comes from Greek via French and Latin.]

**Plasticine** *noun*
**Plasticine** is a soft substance used to make models.
[**Plasticine** comes from **plastic**.]

**plate** *noun* **plates**
A **plate** is a flat dish for food.
[**Plate** comes from Latin *platus* 'broad' or 'flat'.]

**plateau** *noun* **plateaus** or **plateaux**
A **plateau** is a large, high area of flat land.
[**Plateau** comes via French from the same Latin word as **plate**.]

**platform** *noun* **platforms**
**1** A **platform** is the raised area in a station where people stand waiting for a train.
**2** A **platform** is a flat, raised surface such as a stage.
[**Platform** comes from French.]

**plausible** *adjective* (th)
Something that is **plausible** is easy to believe, although it may not be true.
[**Plausible** comes from Latin *plausibilis* 'deserving applause'.]

**play** *noun* **plays**
A **play** is a story acted on a stage or on television. [**Play** comes from Old English.]

**play** *verb* **plays, playing, played** (th)
**1** To **play** means to take part in a game or to have fun.
**2** To **play** means to make music with an instrument.

**player** *noun* **players** (th)
A **player** is someone who plays in a game or on a musical instrument.

**pleasant** *adjective* (th)
**1** Something that is **pleasant** is enjoyable.
**2** Someone who is **pleasant** is friendly and easy to like.
[**Pleasant** comes via French from the same Latin word as **please**.]

**please** *verb* **pleases, pleasing, pleased** (th)
**1** To **please** means to make someone happy.
**2** You use **please** to ask for something politely.
[**Please** comes from Latin via French.]

**pleased** *adjective* (th)
If you are **pleased**, you are happy or satisfied with something.

**pleasure** *noun* **pleasures** (th)
**Pleasure** is the feeling of being happy.
[**Pleasure** comes via French from the same Latin word as **please**.]

**plenty** *noun* (th)
**Plenty** is as much or more than is needed.
[**Plenty** comes via French from Latin *plenus* 'full'.]

**plot** *noun* **plots** (th)
**1** The **plot** of a novel or play is its story.
**2** A **plot** is a secret plan.
**3** A **plot** is a small piece of land.
[No one knows where **plot** comes from.]

**plot** *verb* **plots, plotting, plotted**
**1** To **plot** means to make a secret plan.
**2** To **plot** means to mark out the path of something on a graph or map.

**pluck** *verb* **plucks, plucking, plucked** (th)
**1** To **pluck** means to pull the feathers off a bird, or to pull a hair out of the skin.
**2** To **pluck** means to pick flowers or fruit.
**3** To **pluck** means to play a musical instrument by pulling a string and letting it go quickly.
[**Pluck** comes from Old English.]

**plug** *noun* **plugs** (th)
**1** A **plug** is a part on the end of a wire that fits into an electric socket.
**2** A **plug** is something used to fill a hole.
[**Plug** comes from an old German or Dutch word.]

**plum** *noun* **plums**
A **plum** is a small, soft fruit with a purple or orange skin and a small stone.
[**Plum** comes from Latin via Old English.]

**plumage** *noun*
A bird's **plumage** is its feathers.
[**Plumage** comes from Latin *pluma* 'feather'.]

**plunge** *verb* **plunges, plunging, plunged**
To **plunge** means to jump into water or put something into water suddenly.
[**Plunge** comes from Latin via French.]

**plural** *noun* **plurals**
A **plural** is the form of a word used to mean there is more than one.
[**Plural** comes from the same Latin word as **plus**.]

**plus** *preposition*
**Plus** means that something is being added: The sign for **plus** is +: *4 + 3 = 7;*

*Four plus three is seven.*
[**Plus** comes from Latin *plus* 'more'.]

**p.m.** *abbreviation*
You write **p.m.** after a time to show that it is after noon: *4 p.m.*
[**P.M.** is short for Latin *post meridiem*, 'after noon'.]

**pocket** *noun* **pockets**
A **pocket** is a small pouch or patch sewn onto a piece of clothing to carry things in.
[**Pocket** comes from the same French word as **pouch**.]

**pod** *noun* **pods**
On some plants a **pod** is a long case which contains seeds.
[No one knows where **pod** comes from.]

**poem** *noun* **poems** (th)
A **poem** is a piece of writing, laid out in lines, that has a rhythm. Many **poems** rhyme.
[**Poem** comes via French and Latin from Greek *poiein* 'to create'.]

**poetry** *noun*
**Poetry** is poems.
[**Poetry** comes via French and Latin from the same Greek word as **poem**.]

**point** *noun* **points** (th)
1 A **point** is the sharp end of something such as a pin.
2 A **point** is a mark scored when playing a game.
3 The **point** is the main reason for something or the most important idea in something: *Get to the point!*
[**Point** comes from Latin via French.]

**point** *verb* **points, pointing, pointed**
1 To **point** means to show the position of something using a finger.
2 To **point** a weapon means to aim it.
3 To **point out** something means to draw someone's attention to it.

**poison** *noun* **poisons** (th)
A **poison** is a substance that causes death or harm to living things if they eat it, breathe it in or get it on them.
[**Poison** comes via French from Latin *potio* 'a magic drink'.]

**poke** *verb* **pokes, poking, poked** (th)
1 To **poke** means to push someone or something with your finger or with something sharp.
2 To **poke out** or **through** something means to appear or show something through it: *She poked her head outside.*
[**Poke** comes from an old German or Dutch word.]

**polar** *adjective*
**Polar** means to do with the North or South Pole.
[**Polar** comes from the same Latin word as **pole¹**.]

**polar bear** *noun* **polar bears**
A **polar bear** is a large white bear that lives in the Arctic.

**pole¹** *noun* **poles**
1 A **pole** is one of the two ends (the **North Pole** and the **South Pole**) of the imaginary axis on which the earth turns.
2 A **pole** is one of the two opposite ends of a magnet.
[**Pole¹** comes from Latin *polus* 'the end of an axis'.]

**pole²** *noun* **poles**
A **pole** is a long, round, smooth stick or post: *a telegraph pole.*
[**Pole²** comes from Old English.]

**police** *plural noun*
The **police** are the people whose job is to make sure everyone obeys the law and catch those that do not.
[**Police** comes via French from Latin *politia* 'government'.]

**polish** *verb* **polishes, polishing, polished**
To **polish** means to rub something to make it shine.
[**Polish** comes from Latin via French.]

**polite** *adjective* **politer, politest** (th)
Someone who is **polite** has good manners and is not rude to people.
[**Polite** comes from Latin *politus* 'polished'.]

**politician** *noun* **politicians**
A **politician** is someone who is involved in the way the country is run, either as a member of the government or as one of its opponents.
[**Politician** comes from the same Latin word as **police**.]

**pollen** *noun*
**Pollen** is the powder inside a flower that is carried to other flowers by insects or the wind so that the flowers can reproduce.

[**Pollen** comes from Latin *pollen* 'fine powder'.]

**pollute** *verb* **pollutes, polluting, polluted** (th)
To **pollute** something means to make it dirty or dangerous by letting harmful substances get into it.
[**Pollute** comes from Latin.]

**pond** *noun* **ponds**
A **pond** is a small area of fresh water.
[No one knows where **pond** comes from.]

**ponder** *verb* **ponders, pondering, pondered** (th)
To **ponder** means to think about something seriously.
[**Ponder** comes via French from Latin *ponderare* 'to weigh or weigh up'.]

**pony** *noun* **ponies**
A **pony** is a small kind of horse.
[**Pony** comes from Latin via French *poulenet* 'little foal'.]

**pool**[1] *noun* **pools**
A **pool** is a pond or puddle.
[**Pool**[1] comes from Old English.]

**pool**[2] *noun*
**Pool** is a game like snooker.
[**Pool**[2] comes from French.]

**poor** *adjective* **poorer, poorest** (th)
1 Someone who is **poor** has very little money.
2 Something that is **poor** is not of a good standard or quality.
3 You use **poor** to say that you are sorry for a person or animal.
[**Poor** comes via French from the same Latin word as **pauper**.]

**poorly** *adverb* (th)
1 If something is done **poorly**, it is done badly.
2 If someone is **poorly**, s/he is ill.

**poppy** *noun* **poppies**
A **poppy** is a flower that usually has red petals.
[**Poppy** comes from Latin via Old English.]

**popular** *adjective*
Someone or something that is **popular** is liked by a lot of people.
[**Popular** comes from the same Latin word as **people**.]

**population** *noun* **populations**
The **population** of a place is the total number of people living there.
[**Population** comes from the same Latin word as **people**.]

**pore** *noun* **pores**
A **pore** is one of the tiny holes in your skin. You sweat through your **pores**.
[**Pore** comes via French and Latin from Greek *poros* 'a passage'.]

**pork** *noun*
**Pork** is meat from a pig.
[**Pork** comes via French from Latin *porcus* 'pig'.]

**porpoise** *noun* **porpoises**
A **porpoise** is a sea animal like a small whale.
[**Porpoise** comes from Latin *porcus* 'pig' and *piscis* 'fish', because of its plump, round body.]

**porridge** *noun*
**Porridge** is a food made from boiling oats in milk or water.
[**Porridge** comes from an old word *pottage* 'soup or stew', which comes from old French.]

**port**[1] *noun* **ports** (th)
A **port** is a harbour where ships come to shore.
[**Port**[1] comes from Latin via Old English.]

**port**[1] *adjective*
The **port** side of a boat or plane is the left-hand side, if you are looking towards the front.
[The **port**[1] side is so called because it was the side next to the quay when the boat was being loaded or unloaded.]

**port**[2] *noun*
**Port** is a kind of strong, sweet wine.
[**Port**[2] is named after *Oporto*, a city in Portugal where it was made.]

**porthole** *noun* **portholes**
A **porthole** is a small, round window in the side of a ship.
[**Porthole** comes from Latin *porta* 'gate' and **hole**.]

**position** *noun* **positions** (th)
1 A **position** is the place where something is or should be.
2 A **position** is the way something is arranged or someone is sitting or standing.

[Position comes from Latin via French.]

**possess** *verb* **possesses, possessing, possessed** (th)
To **possess** something is to own it or have it. [**Possess** comes from Latin via French.]

**possession** *noun* **possessions** (th)
1 A **possession** is something that you own.
2 If something is **in your possession**, you own it or have it.
[**Possession** comes via French from the same Latin word as **possess**.]

**possible** *adjective* (th)
Something that is **possible** can be done or can happen. **possibly** *adverb*.
[**Possible** comes from Latin *posse* 'to be able'.]

**post¹** *noun* **posts**
A **post** is a long piece of wood, concrete or metal fixed in the ground.
[**Post¹** comes from Latin.]

**post²** *noun* **posts**
A **post** is a particular job: *the post of coach to the football team*.
[**Post²** comes via French and Italian from Latin *positum* 'placed'.]

**post³** *noun*
1 The **post** is the system of sending and receiving letters and parcels.
2 **Post** is letters or parcels that are sent or received: *Is there any post for me?*
[**Post³** comes via French from the same Italian word as **post²**.]

**post³** *verb* **posts, posting, posted**
To **post** means to send a letter, postcard or parcel.

**postcard** *noun* **postcards**
A **postcard** is a card, often with a picture on one side, on which a message can be written and then sent by post.

**poster** *noun* **posters**
A **poster** is a large sheet of paper with pictures and writing on it to display on the wall. [**Poster** comes from **post¹**.]

**post office** *noun* **post offices**
A **post office** is a place where stamps are sold and letters and parcels are sorted.

**postpone** *verb* **postpones, postponing, postponed** (th)
To **postpone** something means to put it off until later.

[**Postpone** comes from Latin *post* 'after' and *ponere* 'to place'.]

**pot** *noun* **pots**
A **pot** is a round container such as a saucepan or a flower pot.
[**Pot** comes from Old English.]

**potato** *noun* **potatoes**
A **potato** is a vegetable that grows underground.
[**Potato** comes via Spanish from Taino (a South American Indian language).]

**pottery** *noun*
**Pottery** is pots and other items made from clay which is baked.
[**Pottery** comes from French.]

**pouch** *noun* **pouches**
1 A **pouch** is a small bag.
2 A **pouch** is a kind of pocket some animals, such as kangaroos, have in their skin.
[**Pouch** comes from French *poche* 'bag'.]

**poultry** *plural noun*
**Poultry** are birds such as chickens, ducks and geese that are kept for their eggs and meat.
[**Poultry** comes from an old French word.]

**pound¹** *noun* **pounds**
1 A **pound** is the British unit of money, equal to 100 pence.
2 A **pound** is a unit for measuring weight in the imperial system, equal to 16 ounces or about 454 grams.
[**Pound²** comes from Old English *pund*.]

**pound²** *verb* **pounds, pounding, pounded** (th)
1 To **pound** means to keep hitting something heavily and noisily: *Waves pounded the shore*.
2 To **pound** means to crush something to powder by hitting it hard many times.
[**Pound²** comes from Old English *pundian*.]

**pour** *verb* **pours, pouring, poured**
1 To **pour** a liquid means to make it flow out of something: *pour the tea*.
2 When something **pours**, it flows down or off or out of something: *Blood poured from the wound*.
3 When it is **pouring**, it is raining hard.
[No one knows where **pour** comes from.]

**pout** *verb* **pouts, pouting, pouted**
When you **pout**, you stick out your lips to show that you are sulking or

a b c d e f g h i j k l m

disappointed.
[**Pout** probably comes from a Scandinavian language.]

**poverty** *noun* (th)
People who are living in **poverty** are poor.
[**Poverty** comes via French from the same Latin word as **pauper**.]

**powder** *noun* **powders**
**Powder** is the crushed grains of something solid: *powder paint*.
[**Powder** comes from Latin via French.]

**power** *noun* **powers** (th)
**1** Someone who has **power** is in charge or in control of other people.
**2** If you have the **power** to do something, you are able to do it.
**3 Power** is energy. Electricity is a form of **power**.
**4 Power** is the strength that your body has.
[**Power** comes from an old French word.]

**powerful** *adjective* (th)
Someone who is very strong or important is **powerful**. **powerfully** *adverb*.

**powerless** *adjective* (th)
If you are **powerless**, you can't do anything to change a situation or stop something happening.
**powerlessness** *noun*.

**practicable** *adjective* (th)
**1** A **practicable** idea or plan makes sense and should work.
**2** A **practicable** task is something that you can actually do.
[**Practicable** comes via French from the same Greek word as **practical**.]

**practical** *adjective* (th)
**1** Something that is **practical** uses real situations or experiences, and not just ideas.
**2 Practical** clothes, shoes, or other things are sensible rather than fashionable.
**3** A **practical** person is good at doing things with his/her hands.
[**Practical** comes via French and Latin from Greek *praktikos* 'to do with action'.]

**practically** *adverb* (th)
**1 Practically** means in a practical or useful way.
**2** almost: *I've practically finished*.

**practice** *noun* **practices** (th)
**1 Practice** is when you do something

many times so that you get better at it.
**2** A **practice** is the business of a doctor, lawyer or dentist.
**3** A **practice** is a habit or custom.
[**Practice** comes from **practise**.]

**practise** *verb* **practises, practising, practised** (th)
**1** To **practise** means to do something over and over so that you get better at it.
**2** To **practise** a religion means to believe in it, to obey its rules and to take part in its customs and ceremonies.
**3** To **practise** medicine, law or dentistry means to work as a doctor, lawyer or dentist.
[**Practise** comes via French or Latin from the same Greek word as **practical**.]

**prairie** *noun* **prairies**
A **prairie** is a large flat area covered in grass, with few trees.
[**Prairie** comes from Latin via French.]

**praise** *verb* **praises, praising, praised** (th)
**1** When you **praise** a person, you say good things about him/her.
**2** When you **praise** God, you say prayers or sing hymns to give thanks for what you believe God has done.
[**Praise** comes from Latin via French.]

**praise** *noun*
**Praise** is the good things that you say or write about someone: *My school report was full of praise*.

**pram** *noun* **prams**
A **pram** is a small bed on wheels for carrying a baby.
[**Pram** is short for **perambulator**, which comes from Latin *perambulare* 'to walk about'.]

**prance** *verb* **prances, prancing, pranced** (th)
To **prance** means to dance or walk with high steps.
[No one knows where **prance** comes from.]

**prawn** *noun* **prawns**
A **prawn** is a small shellfish that you can eat.
[No one knows where **prawn** comes from.]

**pray** *verb* **prays, praying, prayed**
To **pray** means to talk to God.
[**Pray** comes via French from the same

Latin word as **prayer**.]

**prayer** noun **prayers**
A **prayer** is what you say when you are talking to God.
[**Prayer** comes from Latin via French.]

**preach** verb **preaches, preaching, preached**
1 To **preach** means to talk to people as part of a church service.
2 To **preach** means to talk to people about how they should behave.
[**Preach** comes from Latin via French.]

**precious** adjective (th)
Something that is very valuable or that you love very much is **precious**.
[**Precious** comes from the same Latin word as **price** and **prize**.]

**precious stone** noun **precious stones**
A **precious stone** is a valuable stone such as a diamond or ruby. **Precious stones** are often polished and used in jewellery.

**precipice** noun **precipices**
A **precipice** is the steep side of a cliff or a mountain.
[**Precipice** comes via French from Latin *praeceps* 'steep'.]

**precise** adjective (th)
**Precise** means exact or accurate.
**precisely** adverb.
[**Precise** comes from Latin via French.]

**predict** verb **predicts, predicting, predicted** (th)
To **predict** means to say what you think will happen: *I predicted he would get the job.*
[**Predict** comes from Latin *prae-* 'before' and *dicere* 'to say'.]

**prediction** noun **predictions** (th)
When you make a **prediction**, you say what you think will happen.

**prefer** verb **prefers, preferring, preferred** (th)
To **prefer** means to like one thing more than another: *I prefer strawberry ice cream.*
[**Prefer** comes from Latin via French.]

**prefix** noun **prefixes**
A **prefix** is a part added on to the beginning of a word to make a new word. *Un-, non-* and *re-* are **prefixes**.
[**Prefix** comes via French from Latin *praefixus* 'fixed in front'.]

**pregnant** adjective
To be **pregnant** means that a baby is growing inside your womb.
[**Pregnant** comes from Latin.]

**prehistoric** adjective
Something that is **prehistoric** existed or happened a very long time ago, before things were written down.
[**Prehistoric** comes from *pre-* 'before' and **historic**.]

**prejudice** noun **prejudices** (th)
1 A **prejudice** is a fixed idea or opinion that you don't want to change.
2 **Prejudice** is when people are treated unfairly because of something such as their colour, religion, sex or age.
[**Prejudice** comes from Latin *prae* 'before' and *judicium* 'judgement'.]

**prejudiced** adjective
To be **prejudiced** against people means that you don't like them even though you do not know them.

**prepare** verb **prepares, preparing, prepared** (th)
To **prepare** means to get something ready.
[**Prepare** comes from Latin via French.]

**preposition** noun **prepositions**
A **preposition** is a word that shows how things in a sentence are related to each other. *By, for, up* and *on* are **prepositions**.
[**Preposition** comes from Latin *praepositio* 'putting in front'.]

**prescription** noun **prescriptions**
A **prescription** is a note from a doctor saying what medicine you need, and how much you should take.
[**Prescription** comes via French from Latin *praescribere* 'to tell in writing'.]

**present** noun **presents** (th)
1 A **present** is something special that you give to someone or get from someone.
2 The **present** means now, not the future or the past: *The story is set in the present.*
[**Present** comes from Latin via French.]

**present** verb **presents, presenting, presented** (th)
1 When you give someone something special, you **present** it: *She presented me with a trophy.*
2 A person who introduces a television or radio programme **presents** it.

**present** *adjective*
Someone who is **present** is here.

**present participle** *noun*
To find **present participle**, look under
**participle**.

**preservative** *noun* **preservatives**
A **preservative** is something that stops
things from going bad or rotting.
[**Preservative** comes via French from the
same Latin word as **preserve**.]

**preserve** *verb* **preserves, preserving,
preserved**
To **preserve** something means to keep it
safe or in good condition.
[**Preserve** comes from Latin via French.]

**preside** *verb* **presides, presiding,
presided**
Someone who **presides** over a formal
assembly is in charge of it.
[**Preside** comes via French from Latin
*praesidere* 'to sit in front'.]

**president** *noun* **presidents**
1 A **president** is the head of a country that
does not have a king or queen.
2 A **president** is the person in charge of a
club or organisation.

**press** *verb* **presses, pressing, pressed**
1 To **press** means to push hard on
something.
2 To **press** means to make something
smooth and flat: *pressing flowers*.
[**Press** comes from Latin via French.]

**press** *plural noun*
The press means newspapers and
journalists: *The actor spoke to the press*.

**pressure** *noun* **pressures**
1 **Pressure** is weight or force that is
pressing on something.
2 If you are **under pressure** to do
something, you feel as though it is
important or urgent to do it.
[**Pressure** comes via French from the same
Latin word as **press**.]

**pretend** *verb* **pretends, pretending,
pretended** (th)
To **pretend** means to imagine that
something is true, or to behave as if
something is true.
[**Pretend** comes from Latin *praetendere* 'to
claim'.]

**pretty** *adjective* **prettier, prettiest** (th)
**Pretty** means attractive to look at: *a pretty
village*. [**Pretty** comes from Old English.]

**prevent** *verb* **prevents, preventing,
prevented** (th)
To **prevent** something means to stop it
from happening.
[**Prevent** comes from Latin *praevenire* 'to
anticipate'.]

**previous** *adjective*
1 **Previous** means happening before the
thing you are talking about: *We met on a
previous occasion*.
2 The **previous** person who did a job is
the person who did it just before whoever
is doing it now: *the previous chef*.
[**Previous** comes from Latin *praevius*
'going before'.]

**prey** *noun*
An animal that is hunted by another
animal for food is its **prey**.
[**Prey** comes from Latin via French.]

**price** *noun* **prices** (th)
A **price** is the sum of money that you
have to pay for something.
[**Price** comes from Latin *pretium* 'reward'
or 'value' (ancestor of **precious** and
**prize**).]

**priceless** *adjective* (th)
Something that is **priceless** is very
valuable and precious.

**prick** *verb* **pricks, pricking, pricked** (th)
To **prick** something means to make a
small hole in it with a sharp point.
[**Prick** comes from Old English.]

**prickle** *verb* **prickles, prickling, prickled**
When something **prickles** you, it feels as
though sharp points are touching your
skin. [**Prickle** comes from Old English.]

**prickly** *adjective* **pricklier, prickliest**
1 A plant that is **prickly** has sharp points
or thorns on it.
2 Something that feels **prickly** is
uncomfortable and prickles your skin.

**pride** *noun* (th)
1 When you feel **pride**, you feel happy
and pleased with what you have done.
You can also feel **pride** when someone
connected with you does well.
2 **Pride** is the feeling that you are better or
more important than other people.
[**Pride** comes from Old English.]

**priest** *noun* **priests**
A **priest** is a person who leads religious services and ceremonies.
[**Priest** comes from Old English.]

**primary** *adjective* (th)
Something that is first or most important is **primary**: *Our primary concern is safety.*
[**Primary** comes from Latin *primus* 'first'.]

**prime number** *noun* **prime numbers**
A **prime number** is a number that can only be divided by itself or 1.
[**Prime** comes from the same Latin word as **primary**.]

**primitive** *adjective*
1 We use **primitive** to describe people who live in a simple way, without modern inventions and ideas.
2 Things that are **primitive** are simple and roughly made: *primitive stone tools.*
[**Primitive** comes via French from the same Latin word as **primary**.]

**prince** *noun* **princes**
A **prince** is a boy or a man in a royal family, especially the son of a king or a queen.
[**Prince** comes via French from Latin *princeps* 'first' or 'chief'.]

**princess** *noun* **princesses**
A **princess** is a girl or a woman in a royal family, especially the daughter of a king or a queen.
[**Princess** comes from the same French word as **prince**.]

**principal** *adjective* (th)
The **principal** person or thing is the most important person or thing.
[**Principal** comes from the same Latin word as **prince**.]

**principal** *noun* **principals**
The **principal** of a college or other organisation is the head of it.

**principle** *noun* **principles** (th)
1 A **principle** is a rule that helps you decide how to behave.
2 In science, a **principle** is a rule that describes how something works.
[**Principle** comes via French from the same Latin word as **prince**.]

**print** *verb* **prints, printing, printed**
1 To **print** means to write with letters that are not joined together.
2 To **print** means to put words or pictures onto paper using a machine.
[**Print** comes via French from Latin *premere* 'to press'.]

**print** *noun* **prints**
1 A **print** is a mark left by something.
2 A **print** is a copy of a painting or a photograph.
3 **Print** is the letters and numbers that are printed on something such as a book or a newspaper.

**priority** *noun* **priorities**
A **priority** is something important that you should do first.
[**Priority** comes from Latin via French.]

**prise** *verb* **prises, prising, prised**
To **prise** something means to force it to open, come away or come off by using a lever.
[**Prise** comes from an old French word.]

**prism** *noun* **prisms**
1 A **prism** is a solid shape with two sides that are parallelograms, and two ends that are parallel.
2 A **prism**, is a clear solid shape with many faces. When you look through a **prism**, you see a rainbow.
[**Prism** comes from Greek via Latin.]

**prison** *noun* **prisons** (th)
A **prison** is a place where criminals are kept.
[**Prison** comes from Latin via French.]

**private** *adjective* (th)
1 Something that is **private** is secret.
2 Something that is **private** belongs to just one person or one group of people.
[**Private** comes from Latin.]

**privilege** *noun* **privileges**
A **privilege** is something special that you are allowed to do or have.
[**Privilege** comes via French from Latin *privilegium* 'a law affecting one person'.]

**prize** *noun* **prizes** (th)
A **prize** is something that you get when you win a competition or a race.
[**Prize** comes from **price**.]

**probable** *adjective* (th)
If something is **probable**, it is likely to happen or likely to be true.
[**Probable** comes via French from Latin *probare* 'to prove' (ancestor of **proof** and **prove**).]

**a b c d e f g h i j k l m**

**probably** *adverb*
If something will **probably** happen, it is likely to happen.

**problem** *noun* **problems** (th)
1 A **problem** is a difficult situation: *We have a problem – there aren't enough chairs!*
2 A **problem** is a puzzle or a question that you have to solve.
[**Problem** comes from Greek via French and Latin.]

**process** *noun* **processes**
A **process** is a series of steps that you go through to make something or change something: *Making bread is a simple process.*
[**Process** comes via French from Latin *procedere* 'to go forward'.]

**procession** *noun* **processions** (th)
A **procession** is a long moving line of people or vehicles.
[**Procession** comes via French from the same Latin word as **process**.]

**prod** *verb* **prods, prodding, prodded** (th)
To **prod** means to poke or push a person or an animal, especially when you want to make him/her do something.
[No one knows where **prod** comes from.]

**produce** *verb* **produces, producing, produced**
1 To **produce** something means to make it: *The factory produces cheese.*
2 To **produce** a result means to make it happen: *The teacher's shout produced the effect she wanted.*
3 To **produce** something such as a film, a CD, a radio or television programme, or a magazine means to be in charge of making it. [**Produce** comes from Latin.]

**product** *noun* **products**
1 A **product** is something that has been made: *the new cleaning product.*
2 In mathematics, the **product** is the answer that you get when you multiply two numbers: *10 is the product of 2 and 5.*
[**Product** comes from the same Latin word as **produce**.]

**production** *noun* **productions**
1 Making or growing something is called **production**.
2 A **production** is a play or a show: *an exciting new production of Snow White.*
[**Production** comes via French from the same Latin word as **produce**.]

**profession** *noun* **professions**
A **profession** is a job that you need to study or train for a long time. Teaching and being a lawyer or doctor are **professions**.
[**Profession** comes from Latin.]

**professional** *adjective*
1 **Professional** means that you get paid to do it, rather than doing it for fun.
2 If you do something in a **professional** way, you do it well. **professionally** *adverb.*

**professor** *noun* **professors**
A **professor** is an important teacher in a university.
[**Professor** comes from the same Latin word as **profession**.]

**profile** *noun* **profiles**
1 Your **profile** is the side view of your face.
2 A **profile** is a short account of the main facts of someone's life or progress.
[**Profile** comes from old Italian *profilare* 'to draw in outline'.]

**profit** *noun* **profits**
**Profit** is money that you get if you buy something and then sell it at a higher price: *The cake stall made a profit.*
[**Profit** comes from Latin via French.]

**program** *noun* **programs**
A **program** for a computer is a list of instructions that tell it to do something.
[**Program** is the American way of spelling **programme**.]

**programme** *noun* **programmes**
1 A **programme** is a show, play or other item on the radio or television.
2 A **programme** is a leaflet giving details of a play or other event.
[**Programme** comes via Latin from Greek *prographein* 'to announce in writing'.]

**progress** *noun* (th)
1 If you make **progress**, you improve or move forward in some way.
2 Something that is **in progress** is happening. [**Progress** comes from Latin.]

**project** *noun* **projects** (th)
A **project** is a plan that you have.
[**Project** comes from Latin.]

**prominent** *adjective* (th)
1 Something that is **prominent** stands out and is easy to see.
2 Someone who is **prominent** is important or famous. **prominently** *adverb.*

[**Prominent** comes from Latin *prominere* 'to stick out'.]

**promise** *noun* **promises** (th)
1 When you make a **promise**, you say that you will definitely do, or not do, something.
2 If someone **shows promise**, s/he shows signs that s/he will be good at something. [**Promise** comes from Latin.]

**promise** *verb* **promises, promising, promised** (th)
To **promise** means to say that you will definitely do, or not do, something.

**promote** *verb* **promotes, promoting, promoted**
1 To **promote** someone means to give that person a more important job.
2 To **promote** something means to help it or to help make it more popular.
[**Promote** comes from Latin *promovere* 'to move forward.']

**pronoun** *noun* **pronouns**
A **pronoun** is a word that you use in place of a noun, especially so that you do not have to repeat a noun that you have already used. *I, you, we* and *it* are **pronouns**.
[**Pronoun** comes from *pro-* 'in place of' and **noun**.]

**pronounce** *verb* **pronounces, pronouncing, pronounced**
To **pronounce** a word means to say it. [**Pronounce** comes from Latin via French.]

**proof** *noun* (th)
1 To have **proof** means to be able to show that something happened or that something is true: *Do you have proof?*
2 A **proof** is a first copy of a book or document that is printed so that it can be checked for mistakes.
[**Proof** comes via French from the same Latin word as **probable** and **prove**.]

**proofread** *verb* **proofreads, proofreading, proofread**
When you **proofread** a piece of writing, you read it very carefully to find all the mistakes.

**prop** *verb* **props, propping, propped** (th)
1 When you rest or lean one thing on another, you **prop** it or **prop** it **up**.
2 To **prop** something **up** means to support it.

[**Prop** probably comes from an old Dutch word.]

**prop** *noun* **props**
In a play, the **props** are the things on the stage that the actors use, such as furniture or weapons. [**Prop** is short for **property**.]

**propeller** *noun* **propellers**
A **propeller** is a device with blades attached to a boat or an aircraft. When the blades go round, the boat or aircraft can move.
[**Propeller** comes from Latin *propellere* 'to drive forward'.]

**proper** *adjective* (th)
1 Something that is **proper** is real and good: *You should have a proper breakfast.*
2 Something that is **proper** is correct or suitable: *That isn't the proper way to eat.*
[**Proper** comes via French from Latin *proprius* 'your own' or 'special'.]

**properly** *adverb* (th)
If you do something **properly**, you do it well or in the right way: *Make sure the burgers are properly cooked.*

**property** *noun* **properties** (th)
1 If something is your **property**, you own it.
2 A **property** is a building and the land around it.
[**Property** comes via French from the same Latin word as **proper**.]

**prophecy** *noun* **prophecies** (th)
When you make a **prophecy**, you say that something will happen in the future.
[**Prophecy** comes via French and Latin from the same Greek word as **prophet**.]

**prophesy** *verb* **prophesies, prophesying, prophesied** (th)
To **prophesy** means to say what will happen in the future.
[**Prophesy** comes from the same French word as **phrophecy**.]

**prophet** *noun* **prophets**
1 A **prophet** is a person who says what will happen in the future.
2 A **prophet** is someone who people think God has spoken to, and who can tell them what God wants them to do.
[**Prophet** comes via French and Latin from Greek *prophetes* 'someone who speaks for someone else'.]

**propose** *verb* **proposes, proposing, proposed** (th)
**1** To **propose** something means to suggest it.
**2** To **propose** to someone means to ask him/her to marry you.
[**Propose** comes from Latin via French.]

**prose** *noun*
**Prose** is writing that is not a poem or a play.
[**Prose** comes via French from Latin *prosus* 'straightforward'.]

**prosecute** *verb* **prosecutes, prosecuting, prosecuted**
To **prosecute** means to send a person to court to be tried because s/he may have done something that is against the law.
[**Prosecute** comes from Latin.]

**prosper** *verb* **prospers, prospering, prospered**
To **prosper** means to do well or become rich.
[**Prosper** comes from Latin via French.]

**prosperous** *adjective* (th)
Someone who is **prosperous** is successful and rich.
[**Prosperous** comes via French from the same Latin word as **prosper**.]

**protect** *verb* **protects, protecting, protected** (th)
**1** To **protect** something means to cover it or keep it safe.
**2** To **protect** someone means to guard that person and make sure that s/he is safe.
[**Protect** comes from Latin.]

**protein** *noun* **proteins**
We get **protein** from the food that we eat, especially from meat, cheese and milk. Our bodies need **protein** to grow and stay healthy.
[**Protein** comes via French and German from Greek *proteios* 'most important'.]

**protest** *verb* **protests, protesting, protested** (th)
To **protest** means to say that you do not agree with something, or that you are not happy about it.
[**Protest** comes from Latin via French.]

**protest** *noun* **protests** (th)
A **protest** is when you complain about something, especially when a large group of people complain together.

**protractor** *noun* **protractors**
A **protractor** is a tool that you measure angles with.
[**Protractor** comes from Latin.]

**proud** *adjective* **prouder, proudest** (th)
**1** A person who is **proud** feels happy because s/he has done something well, or because someone s/he is connected with has done something well.
**2** A person who is **proud** thinks that s/he is better than other people.
**3** A person who is **proud** does not like to ask for help or advice. **proudly** *adverb*.
[**Proud** comes from French via Old English.]

**prove** *verb* **proves, proving, proved** (th)
If you **prove** something, you show that it is true: *I proved that I can sing*.
[**Prove** comes from the same Latin word as **probable** and **proof**.]

**proverb** *noun* **proverbs**
A **proverb** is an old saying that gives a piece of advice or makes a comment about life. *Look before you leap* is a **proverb**.
[**Proverb** comes from Latin via French.]

**provide** *verb* **provides, providing, provided** (th)
To **provide** something means to give it or sell it to someone who needs it.
[**Provide** comes from Latin.]

**provoke** *verb* **provokes, provoking, provoked** (th)
To **provoke** someone means to annoy or irritate him/her on purpose.
[**Provoke** comes via French from Latin *provocare* 'to challenge'.]

**prow** *noun* **prows**
A **prow** is the front part of a boat or a ship.
[**Prow** comes from an old French word.]

**prowl** *verb* **prowls, prowling, prowled**
To **prowl** means to move around quietly and secretly, the way an animal does when it is trying to catch something.
[No one knows where **prowl** comes from.]

**prune¹** *noun* **prunes**
A **prune** is a dried plum.
[**Prune¹** comes via French and Latin from Greek *prounon* 'plum'.]

**prune²** *verb* **prunes, pruning, pruned**
You **prune** a tree or a bush by cutting

some of its branches off so that it will grow better.
[**Prune**² comes from an old French word.]

**psalm** *noun* **psalms**
A **psalm** is a song, prayer or poem in the Bible.
[**Psalm** comes via Old English and Latin from Greek *psalmos* 'song sung to the harp'.]

**puberty** *noun*
**Puberty** is the time when your body starts to change so that it is more like an adult's body.
[**Puberty** comes from Latin *pubes* 'an adult'.]

**public** *noun* (th)
The **public** is all people: *This swimming pool is open to the public*.
[**Public** comes from Latin via French.]

**public** *adjective*
Something that is **public** is open to anybody: *the public library*.

**publicity** *noun* (th)
**Publicity** is information or an advertisement that tells you about something that is happening.
[**Publicity** comes from the same French word as **public**.]

**publish** *verb* **publishes, publishing, published** (th)
To **publish** a book or a magazine means to print copies of it to be sold.
[**Publish** comes via French from Latin *publicare* 'to make public'.]

**pudding** *noun* **puddings**
A **pudding** is a sweet food that you eat after the main course of a meal.
[**Pudding** comes from Latin via French.]

**puddle** *noun* **puddles**
A **puddle** is a small pool made by rain.
[**Puddle** comes from Old English.]

**puff** *noun* **puffs**
A **puff** of smoke is a small cloud of it.
[**Puff** comes from Old English.]

**puff** *verb* **puffs, puffing, puffed** (th)
1 To **puff** means to breathe quickly: *puffing and panting*.
2 To **puff** means to blow out air, smoke or steam in quick bursts.

**puffin** *noun* **puffins**
A **puffin** is a black and white bird with a

coloured beak. **Puffins** live near the sea.
[No one knows where **puffin** comes from.]

**pull** *verb* **pulls, pulling, pulled** (th)
1 To **pull** something means to get hold of it and try to make it move towards you.
2 To **pull** something means to drag it or tow it behind you: *a car pulling a caravan*.
[**Pull** comes from Old English.]

**pulley** *noun* **pulleys**
A **pulley** is a machine that can lift heavy weights. It uses a wheel and a rope or a chain.
[**Pulley** comes from an old French word.]

**pulp** *noun* (th)
**Pulp** is something that has been mashed up or crushed so that it is soft.
[**Pulp** comes from Latin.]

**pulpit** *noun* **pulpits**
A **pulpit** is the place in a church where the priest stands to speak to and be seen by everyone present.
[**Pulpit** comes from Latin.]

**pulse** *noun* **pulses**
Your **pulse** is the beating of the blood going round your body. You can feel your **pulse** by pressing inside your wrist.
[**Pulse** comes from Latin *pulsus* 'beating'.]

**puma** *noun* **pumas**
A **puma** is a large wild cat with brownish-grey fur.
[**Puma** comes via Spanish from Quechua (a South American Indian language).]

**pump** *noun* **pumps**
A **pump** is a machine that makes liquid or air go in a particular direction.
[No one knows where **pump** comes from.]

**pump** *verb* **pumps, pumping, pumped**
1 If you **pump up** something, you fill it with air.
2 A machine that **pumps** liquid or air makes it move in a particular direction.

**pumpkin** *noun* **pumpkins**
A **pumpkin** is a very large, round, yellow or orange fruit. You can eat **pumpkin** as a vegetable or in a pie.
[**Pumpkin** comes from Greek via French and Latin.]

**pun** *noun* **puns**
A **pun** is a kind of joke that uses two

words that sound the same but have different meanings. An example is: *Why couldn't the pony sing? Because it was a little hoarse!*
[No one knows where **pun** comes from.]

**punch** *verb* **punches, punching, punched** (th)
To **punch** means to hit something or someone very hard with your fist.
[No one knows where **punch** comes from.]

**punctual** *adjective* (th)
**Punctual** means arriving exactly at the right time, not late or early.
**punctually** *adverb*.
[**Punctual** comes from the same Latin word as **punctuation**.]

**punctuation** *noun*
The marks that we use when we write, such as full stops, commas, and question marks, are **punctuation** marks. **Punctuation** helps you to read and understand the writing by dividing it into sentences and by showing you, for example, when a sentence is a question or when it is something that someone said.
[**Punctuation** comes from Latin *punctum* 'a point'.]

**puncture** *noun* **punctures**
A **puncture** is a hole in a tyre.
[**Puncture** comes from Latin.]

**punish** *verb* **punishes, punishing, punished** (th)
You **punish** someone who has done something bad or wrong.
[**Punish** comes via French from Latin *poena* 'penalty' (ancestor of **penalty** and **pain**).]

**punishment** *noun* **punishments** (th)
A **punishment** is something that you have to do if you have done something bad or wrong: *I had to miss football as a punishment for being rude.*
[**Punishment** comes via French from the same Latin word as **punish**.]

**pupil** *noun* **pupils**
1 A **pupil** is a child at school.
2 Your **pupils** are the round, dark openings in the centre of your eyes.
[**Pupil** comes via French from Latin *pupa* 'girl' or 'doll'.]

**puppet** *noun* **puppets**
A **puppet** is a kind of doll that you can move by using your hands inside it or using rods or strings attached to it.
[**Puppet** comes from the same Latin word as **pupil**.]

**puppy** *noun* **puppies**
A **puppy** is a young dog.
[No one knows where **puppy** comes from.]

**pure** *adjective* **purer, purest** (th)
1 Something that is **pure** is clean and has nothing else mixed with it: *pure water; pure gold.*
2 **Pure** means complete or total: *It was pure luck that we found it.* **purely** *adverb*.
[**Pure** comes from Latin via French.]

**purée** *noun* **purées**
A **purée** is a soft smooth sauce made by putting fruit or vegetables through a sieve or a liquidiser. [**Purée** is a French word.]

**purify** *verb* **purifies, purifying, purified**
To **purify** something means to make it pure by removing any dirty or unwanted substances from it.
[**Purify** comes via French from the same Latin word as **pure**.]

**purple** *noun*
**Purple** is a reddish-blue colour.
[**Purple** comes via Old English and Latin from Greek *porphura*, a kind of shellfish used to make purple dye.]

**purple** *adjective*
of the colour **purple**: *purple plums.*

**purpose** *noun* **purposes** (th)
1 The **purpose** of something is the reason for it or the point of it.
2 To do something **on purpose** means to do it deliberately, not by mistake.
[**Purpose** comes from Latin via French.]

**purr** *verb* **purrs, purring, purred**
To **purr** means to make the soft noise that a cat makes when it is happy.
[The word **purr** is an imitation of the sound.]

**purse** *noun* **purses**
A **purse** is a small bag that you can keep money in.
[**Purse** comes via Latin from Greek *bursa* 'leather'.]

**push** *verb* **pushes, pushing, pushed** (th)
When you **push** something, you put your hands on it and try to move it away from you. [**Push** comes from Latin via French.]

**put** *verb* **puts, putting, put** (th)
**1** To **put** means to place something in a particular position.
**2** To **put** an animal **down** means to kill it because it is ill and suffering, and it will not get better.
**3** To **put** something **off** means to do it later.
**4** To **put** a person **off** means to distract him/her so that s/he cannot concentrate. [**Put** comes from Old English.]

**puzzle** *noun* **puzzles**
A **puzzle** is a problem or a game that you have to think about and try to solve: *a jigsaw puzzle; a crossword puzzle.* [No one knows where **puzzle** comes from.]

**puzzle** *verb* **puzzles, puzzling, puzzled** (th)
**1** If you **puzzle** over a problem, you think very hard to try to find the answer.
**2** If something **puzzles** you, it makes you feel confused because you can't explain it.

**puzzled** *adjective* (th)
If you cannot understand or explain something, you are **puzzled**.

**pyjamas** *plural noun*
**Pyjamas** are a top and trousers that you wear in bed.
[**Pyjamas** comes from Persian or Urdu *pay* 'leg' and *jamah* 'clothing'. Persian is the language spoken in Iran, and Urdu is a language spoken in India and Pakistan which has taken many words from Persian.]

**pyramid** *noun* **pyramids**
**1** A **pyramid** is a solid shape with a square base and sloping sides that meet in a point.
**2** A **pyramid** is a large stone building in the shape of a pyramid. The ancient Egyptians made **pyramids** for the body of a dead king or queen.
[**Pyramid** comes from Greek via Latin.]

**python** *noun* **pythons**
A **python** is a large snake. **Pythons** kill small animals by squeezing them to death.
[**Python** comes from *Python*, the name of a huge snake or monster in Greek mythology.]

## Dictionary Fun

**Complete the idioms**
1. To put someone through their p_____ (*To test someone out*)
2. To p_____ the town red (*To go out and enjoy yourself a lot*)

**Complete the proverbs**
1. P_____ is better than cure.
2. He who p____ the p_____ calls the tune.

**Complete the similes**
1. As bright as a new p____.
2. As p____ as a peacock.

**Work it out**
Which 'p' word describes these words? madam, deed, noon

**Did you know?**
The word parasite comes from the Greek word *parasitos* which means 'eating at someone else's table'.

**Brainteaser**
A woman goes on a journey which lasts an hour, but she arrives at the same time as she left. How did she do this?

a b c d e f g h i j k l m

# Qq

**quack** *verb* **quacks, quacking, quacked**
To **quack** means to make a sound like a duck.
[The word **quack** is an imitation of the sound.]

**quadrilateral** *noun* **quadrilaterals**
A **quadrilateral** is any flat shape that has four straight sides. Squares and oblongs are **quadrilaterals**.
[**Quadrilateral** comes from Latin.]

**quail¹** *noun* **quails**
A **quail** is a small bird. You can eat **quails** and their eggs.
[**Quail¹** comes from Latin via French.]

**quail²** *verb* **quails, quailing, quailed** (th)
To **quail²** means to look very frightened.
[No one knows where **quail²** comes from.]

**qualification** *noun* **qualifications**
**Qualifications** are exams that you have passed that show that you can do a job or that you have learned about a subject.
[**Qualification** comes from Latin.]

**qualified** *adjective* (th)
Someone who is **qualified** to do a job has studied or trained and passed exams.
[**Qualified** comes via French from the same Latin word as **qualification**.]

**quality** *noun* **qualities** (th)
1 The **quality** of something is how good or bad it is: *We only sell top-quality meat.*
2 Your **qualities** are the things that you are good at or the good parts of your nature: *He has the qualities of a good teacher.*
[**Quality** comes from Latin via French.]

**quantity** *noun* **quantities** (th)
A **quantity** is an amount of something.
[**Quantity** comes from Latin *quantus* 'how much?']

**quarrel** *verb* **quarrels, quarrelling, quarrelled** (th)
To **quarrel** means to argue with someone in an angry way.
[**Quarrel** comes via French from Latin *querela* 'complaint'.]

**quarrel** *noun* **quarrels** (th)
A **quarrel** is an angry argument.

**quarry** *noun* **quarries**
A **quarry** is a place where clay, stone or slate is dug out of the ground.
[**Quarry** comes from Latin via French.]

**quarter** *noun* **quarters**
When you cut or divide something into four equal parts, the parts are called **quarters**.
[**Quarter** comes from Latin via French.]

**quartz** *noun*
**Quartz** is a very hard mineral. Watches and clocks sometimes have **quartz** crystals in them.
[**Quartz** comes from Polish via German.]

**quay** *noun* **quays**
A **quay** is a place in a harbour where people load and unload ships.
[**Quay** comes from an old French word.]

**queen** *noun* **queens**
1 A **queen** is a woman who rules a country, or the wife of a king.
2 A **queen** is a playing card with a picture of a woman on it. The value of a **queen** is between a jack and a king.
3 A **queen** is a piece in the game of chess that can move in any direction.
[**Queen** comes from Old English.]

**queer** *adjective* **queerer, queerest** (th)
Something that is **queer** is strange or odd. **queerly** *adverb*.
[No one knows where **queer** comes from.]

**quench** *verb* **quenches, quenching, quenched** (th)
1 You **quench** your thirst by having a drink.
2 You **quench** a fire by putting it out.
[**Quench** comes from Old English.]

**query** *noun* **queries**
A **query** is a question.
[**Query** comes from Latin *quaerere* 'to seek' (ancestor of **enquire** and **inquire**).]

**quest** *noun* **quests** (th)
A **quest** is a long search for something special: *The knights set out on a quest.*
[**Quest** comes via French from the same Latin word as **query**.]

**question** *noun* **questions** (th)
A **question** is something that you ask when you want to know the answer.
[**Question** comes via French from the same Latin word as **query**.]

## question mark noun question marks

A **question mark** is a mark that you put at the end of a question when you are writing, like this ?

## queue noun queues (th)

A **queue** is a line of people or vehicles waiting in turn for something.
[**Queue** comes from Latin via French.]

## quiche noun quiches

A **quiche** is a kind of tart with a pastry base and a filling of cheese, eggs, cream and sometimes bacon or vegetables.
[**Quiche** is a French word.]

## quick adjective quicker, quickest (th)

**1** Something that is moving fast is **quick**.
**2** Someone who is **quick** does something in less time than expected.
[**Quick** comes from Old English.]

## quickly adverb (th)

If you do something **quickly**, you do it fast: *Don't drink so quickly.*

## quicksand noun quicksands

**Quicksand** is deep, wet sand that you can sink into.
[**Quicksand** comes from **quick** in an old sense 'alive', because the sand moves and swallows things as if it were alive.]

## quiet adjective quieter, quitest (th)

**1** Someone who is **quiet** does something without making much noise.
**2** A **quiet** place is peaceful without much

happening. **quietly** adverb. **quietness** noun.
[**Quiet** comes from Latin via French.]

## quill noun quills

A **quill** is a kind of pen made from a bird's feather.
[**Quill** probably comes from an old German word.]

## quilt noun quilts

A **quilt** is a padded cover for a bed.
[**Quilt** comes via French from Latin *culcita* 'mattress or cushion'.]

## quite adverb (th)

**1** completely or definitely: *I haven't quite finished*; *Are you quite sure?*
**2** fairly: *quite good*; *quite hot*.
[**Quite** comes from Latin via French.]

## quiver[1] noun quivers

A **quiver** is a bag for holding arrows.
[**Quiver**[1] comes from an old French word.]

## quiver[2] verb quivers, quivering, quivered (th)

To **quiver** means to shake or tremble.
[**Quiver**[2] comes from Old English.]

## quiz noun quizzes (th)

A **quiz** is a set of questions to see how much someone knows.
[No one knows where **quiz** comes from.]

## Qur'an noun

**Qur'an** is another way to spell **Koran**.

---

# Dictionary Fun

**Etymology**
Which three 'q' words come from Latin *quaerere* 'to seek'?

**Riddle**
I have no mouth
But I can eat
If you stand on me
You may lose your feet!
What am I? Clue: Don't be slow
because I am quick!

**Think about it**
What does every 'q' word have in common?

**Did you know?**
◆ Shakespeare wrote his plays with a **quill.**

**Brainteaser**
Can you find a word that follows the pattern below?
queer error orange gentle lemon

---

a b c d e f g h i j k l m

# Rr

**rabbit** *noun* **rabbits**
A **rabbit** is a furry animal that lives in a burrow in the wild.
[No one knows where **rabbit** comes from.]

**rabble** *noun* **rabbles** (th)
A **rabble** is a noisy crowd of people.
[**Rabble** probably comes from an old German or Dutch word.]

**raccoon** *noun* **raccoons** *Also* **racoon**
A **raccoon** is a small, furry North American animal with black rings on its bushy tail and black patches around its eyes.
[**Raccoon** comes from Algonquian (a North American Indian language).]

**race¹** *noun* **races**
A **race** is a competition between people, cars or animals to see which is the fastest: *a horse race; a 200m race.*
[**Race¹** comes from Old Norse.]

**race¹** *verb* **races, racing, raced**
1 To **race** is to have a competition with someone to see who is the fastest: *I'll race you to the end of the road.*
2 To **race** is to go very fast: *They raced to catch the plane; Her heart raced.*

**race²** *noun* **races**
**Race** is one of the main groups that people can be divided into, according to where they come from and the colour of their skin.
[**Race²** comes from Italian via French.]

**race relations** *noun*
**Race relations** are how people from different races get on together when they all live in the same community.

**racism** *noun*
**Racism** is treating people from a particular race badly because you do not believe they are as good as people from other races or your own race.

**racist** *noun*
A **racist** is someone who believes that some races are better than others and that people of his/her race are the best.

**rack** *noun* **racks**
A **rack** is a type of shelf made from bars

that things can be stored or carried on: *a roof rack; a spice rack.*
[**Rack** comes from an old German or Dutch word.]

**racket¹** *noun* **rackets** *Also* **racquet**
A **racket** is a piece of sports equipment that is used for hitting balls in games such as tennis, squash and badminton.
[**Racket¹** comes via French and Italian from Arabic *rahat* 'the palm of the hand'.]

**racket²** *noun* (th)
1 A **racket** is a loud noise: *Be quiet! You're making such a racket!*
2 A **racket** is a way of making money that is dishonest or illegal: *a Mafia protection racket.*
[No one knows where **racket²** comes from.]

**racoon** *noun*
**Racoon** is another way to spell **raccoon**.

**racquet** *noun* **racquets**
**Racquet** is another way to spell **racket¹**.

**radar** *noun*
**Radar** is a system for finding solid objects that cannot be seen by bouncing radio waves off them. It is used by aircraft and ships.
[**Radar** comes from the initial letters of *radio detection and ranging*.]

**radiant** *adjective* (th)
A **radiant** smile is a very happy smile, and someone who looks **radiant** is glowing with health and happiness.
[**Radiant** comes from the same Latin word as **radiate**.]

**radiate** *verb* **radiates, radiating, radiated** (th)
1 To **radiate** means to send out rays of light or heat.
2 Something that **radiates** goes out in all directions from a central point: *Many roads radiate from London.*
3 If a person **radiates** health, charm or confidence, for example, these things seem to be sent out from that person.
[**Radiate** comes from Latin *radiare* 'to send out rays'.]

**radiation** *noun*
1 **Radiation** is the sending out of rays of light or heat.
2 **Radiation** is particles or waves that are

sent out from a radioactive substance, and that are very dangerous to animals and people.
[**Radiation** comes from the same Latin word as **radiate**.]

**radical** *adjective* (th)
1 A **radical** change or reform, for example, is very important and has many effects.
2 Someone with **radical** ideas, opinions or beliefs wants society to change completely. **radically** *adverb*.
[**Radical** comes from Latin *radix* 'root'.]

**radio** *noun* **radios**
1 A **radio** is a piece of equipment for sending or receiving messages or programmes by means of electrical waves: *Use the ship's radio to send a mayday signal; I listen to pop music on the radio.*
2 **Radio** is the sending and receiving of sound by means of electrical waves, or the industry that does this: *The police kept in touch by radio; My first job was in radio.*
[**Radio** comes from the same Latin word as **radius**.]

**radio** *verb* **radios, radioing, radioed**
To **radio** is to send a message by radio: *The police officer radioed for backup.*

**radioactive** *adjective*
A **radioactive** substance sends out harmful particles or waves as its atoms decay.

**radiography** *noun*
**Radiography** is the process of taking x-rays of people's bones or organs.
[**Radiography** comes from **radio** and **photography**.]

**radius** *noun* **radiuses** or **radii**
A **radius** is a straight line drawn from the centre of a circle to its outer edge.
[**Radius** comes from Latin *radius* 'a spoke or ray'.]

**raft** *noun* **rafts**
1 A **raft** is a flat boat that can be made by tying together logs or other things that will float together.
2 A **raft** is a plastic or rubber boat with a flat bottom: *a life raft.*
[**Raft** comes from Old Norse.]

**rag** *noun* **rags**
1 A **rag** is an old piece of cloth that is used for cleaning things.

2 **Rags** are old, dirty and torn clothes.
[**Rag** comes from Old Norse.]

**rage** *noun* (th)
**Rage** is great anger.
[**Rage** comes from Latin via French.]

**rage** *verb* **rages, raging, raged**
Something such as a storm or battle **rages** when it continues with force or violence: *The storm raged all night.*

**raid** *noun* **raids** (th)
A **raid** is a sudden attack on a place: *an air raid; a police raid.*
[**Raid** comes from Old English.]

**rail** *noun* **rails**
1 A **rail** is a bar or rod that is fixed to a wall: *a towel rail; a hand rail.*
2 **Rail** is the railway system: *travel by rail.*
3 **Rails** are the tracks that trains travel on: *The train came off the rails.*
[**Rail** comes via French from the same Latin word as **regular** and **rule**.]

**railing** *noun* **railings**
A **railing** or **railings** is a fence or barrier made of metal bars: *Don't chain bikes to the railings.* [**Railing** comes from **rail**.]

**railway** *noun* **railways**
1 A **railway** is the track a train runs on.
2 The **railway** is trains and tracks as a system for transporting goods or people.

**rain** *noun*
**Rain** is drops of water that fall from clouds. [**Rain** comes from Old English.]

**rain** *verb* **rains, raining, rained** (th)
When it **rains**, drops of water fall from the clouds.

**rainbow** *noun* **rainbows**
A **rainbow** is an arch of colours in the sky caused by the sun shining through raindrops.
[**Rainbow** comes from **rain** and **bow**[1].]

**rainfall** *noun*
**Rainfall** is the total amount of rain that falls in a place during a certain amount of time: *total annual rainfall.*

**raise** *verb* **raises, raising, raised** (th)
1 To **raise** something means to lift it up or make it higher: *raise your hand; raise prices.*
2 To **raise** money is to collect it, especially for a charity or good cause.

**3** To **raise** a family is to look after children until they are old enough to leave home. [**Raise** comes from Old Norse.]

**raisin** noun **raisins**
A **raisin** is a dried grape.
[**Raisin** comes from French *raisin* 'grape'.]

**rake** noun **rakes**
A **rake** is a garden tool that is used for making patches of earth smooth or collecting leaves and grass.
[**Rake** comes from Old English.]

**rally** noun **rallies**
**1** A **rally** is a race for cars or motorbikes: *a speedway rally.*
**2** A **rally** is a large political meeting of people.
**3** A **rally** in tennis is hitting the ball backwards and forwards until a point is won. [**Rally** comes from French.]

**RAM** noun
**RAM** is computer memory, measured in bytes: *64 megabytes of RAM.* The more **RAM** a computer has, the faster it works. [**RAM** stands for *Random Access Memory*.]

**ram** noun **rams**
A **ram** is an adult male sheep.
[**Ram** comes from Old English.]

**ram** verb **rams, ramming, rammed** (th)
**1** To **ram** means to push something into place forcefully.
**2** To **ram** something is to crash into it with great force, especially on purpose.

**Ramadan** noun
**Ramadan** is the ninth month in the Islamic year, when Muslims must not eat or drink anything between sunrise and sunset. [**Ramadan** comes from Arabic.]

**ramble** verb **rambles, rambling, rambled** (th)
**1** To **ramble** is to walk for pleasure, especially in the countryside.
**2** If a person **rambles,** they talk all the time in a way that is boring or hard to understand.
[**Ramble** may come from an old Dutch word.]

**ramp** noun **ramps**
A **ramp** is a slope between two different levels.
[**Ramp** comes from old French *ramper* 'to climb'.]

**rampage** verb **rampages, rampaging, rampaged**
To **rampage** means to charge around in a noisy, destructive way: *The children are rampaging around the garden.*
[No one knows where **rampage** comes from.]

**rampage** noun (th)
If someone is **on the rampage**, s/he is charging around in a violent and destructive way: *a gunman on the rampage.*

**rampart** noun **ramparts**
A **rampart** is a bank of earth or a stone wall built around a castle or fort to protect it. [**Rampart** comes from French.]

**ram-raid** verb **ram-raids, ram-raiding, ram-raided**
To **ram-raid** a shop is to drive a vehicle through its window in order to steal the things inside.

**ran** verb
**Ran** is the past tense of **run.**

**ranch** noun **ranches**
A **ranch** is a large North American cattle-farm. [**Ranch** comes from Spanish.]

**rancid** adjective
**Rancid** fat or oil tastes or smells sour because it has gone off.
[**Rancid** comes from Latin *rancidus* 'stinking'.]

**random** adjective (th)
**1** Something that is **random** doesn't have any fixed order or is chosen by chance.
**2** Something that is done **at random** happens by chance or is not done in any special order.
[**Random** comes from an old French word.]

**rang** verb
**Rang** is the past tense of **ring.**

**range** noun **ranges**
**1** A **range** is a chain of mountains.
**2** A **range** is a series or collection of different things that belong in a group: *The shop has a wide range of sports equipment.*
**3** A **range** is everything within certain limits: *the 10 to 13 age range; The car is outside my price range.*
**4** A **range** is a limited distance: *The walkie-talkie has a range of 200 metres.*

[**Range** comes from an old French word.]

**rap** noun
**Rap** is a type of poetry where words are spoken very quickly to a strong rhythm or to music.
[The word **rap** is an imitation of the sound.]

**rape** verb **rapes, raping, raped**
To **rape** someone is to force that person to have sexual intercourse.
[**Rape** comes via French from Latin *rapere* 'to seize or take by force'.]

**rapid** adjective (th)
Something that happens quickly is **rapid**: *rapid progress*. **rapidly** adverb.
[**Rapid** comes from the same Latin word as **rape**.]

**rapids** plural noun
The part of a river where water flows quickly over rocks is called the **rapids**.

**rapist** noun **rapists**
A **rapist** is a person who rapes someone.

**rare¹** adjective **rarer, rarest** (th)
Something that is **rare** does not happen very often or does not exist in large numbers: *The bald eagle is quite a rare bird*. **rarely** adverb. [**Rare¹** comes from Latin.]

**rare²** adjective **rarer, rarest**
**Rare** meat is not cooked for very long: *I like my steak rare*.
[**Rare²** comes from Old English.]

**rash** noun **rashes**
A **rash** is an area of red or itchy spots that appears on your skin.
[**Rash** probably comes from an old French word.]

**raspberry** noun **raspberries**
A **raspberry** is a small, soft, red fruit with lots of pips.
[No one knows where the *rasp* of **raspberry** comes from.]

**rat** noun **rats**
1 A **rat** is an animal that looks like a large mouse.
2 If you call someone a **rat**, you think s/he is a bad person.
[**Rat** comes from Old English.]

**rate** noun **rates**
1 The **rate** of something is the speed at which it happens or travels: *At this rate*

we'll be finished in no time; We're cruising at a rate of 400 kph above the Atlantic ocean.
2 A **rate** is a measurement, percentage or amount: *a high success rate; a 10% tax rate*.
[**Rate** comes from Latin via French.]

**ratio** noun **ratios**
A **ratio** is a relation between numbers or amounts that shows how much bigger one is than the other: *In a class of 18 girls and 6 boys, the ratio of girls to boys is 3 to 1*.
[**Ratio** comes from Latin *ratio* 'reckoning'.]

**ration** verb **rations, rationing, rationed**
To **ration** something is to give it out in limited amounts because there is not very much of it.
[**Ration** comes via French from the same Latin word as **ratio**.]

**ration** noun **rations** (th)
1 A **ration** is a limited amount of something.
2 **Rations** is food provided for soldiers.

**rat race** noun
The **rat race** is a stressful way of life where everyone tries to become more successful than everyone else.

**rattle** noun **rattles**
A **rattle** is a baby's toy which makes a noise when it is shaken.
[The word **rattle** is an imitation of the sound.]

**rattle** verb **rattles, rattling, rattled**
Something that **rattles** makes a noise when it is shaken: *The wind makes the windows rattle*.

**rattlesnake** noun **rattlesnakes**
A **rattlesnake** is a poisonous American snake that has horny rings on its tail. When it shakes its tail, the rings rattle and warn people and animals to leave the snake alone.

**rave** verb **raves, raving, raved** (th)
1 To **rave about** something is to say how wonderful it is.
2 To **rave** is to talk in a wild and uncontrolled way, usually because you are ill or angry.
[**Rave** probably comes from an old French word.]

**rave** noun **raves**
A **rave** is a big event like a huge party for

many people.

**ravenous** *adjective* (th)
If you are **ravenous**, you are very hungry.
**ravenously** *adverb*.
[**Ravenous** comes from an old French word.]

**ravine** *noun* **ravines**
A **ravine** is a deep narrow valley with very steep sides.
[**Ravine** comes from Latin via French.]

**raw** *adjective*
1 Food that is **raw** is not cooked.
2 Materials or food that are **raw** are in their natural condition and have not been processed in a factory.
[**Raw** comes from Old English.]

**ray**¹ *noun* **rays**
A **ray** is a thin beam of light, heat or energy: *a ray of sunlight.*
[**Ray**¹ comes via French from the same Latin word as **radius**.]

**ray**² *noun* **rays**
A **ray** is a large flat fish with fins like wings, a long thin tail and a mouth on the underside of its body.
[**Ray**² comes via French from Latin *raia*.]

**razor** *noun* **razors**
A **razor** is an instrument with a sharp blade used for shaving.
[**Razor** comes from Latin via French.]

**reach** *verb* **reaches, reaching, reached** (th)
1 To **reach** a place or point is to get to it: *We'll reach the coast by evening; Summer temperatures reach as high as 30°C.*
2 To **reach** something is to stretch out your arm in order to get it or touch it: *I can't reach anything on that high shelf.*
[**Reach** comes from Old English.]

**react** *verb* **reacts, reacting, reacted**
1 To **react** to something is to respond to it: *She reacted angrily to the suggestion.*
2 If one substance **reacts** with another, a chemical change takes place when they are mixed.
[**React** comes from *re-* 'in return' and **act**.]

**reaction** *noun* **reactions**
1 A **reaction** is a response to something: *I don't know how he'll react to the idea; Alcohol slows down your reactions.*
2 A **reaction** is a chemical change when two or more substances are mixed together.

**read** *verb* **reads, reading, read**
To **read** means to be able to look at words and understand what they mean or to say them out loud.
[**Read** comes from Old English.]

**ready** *adjective* (th)
A thing or person that is **ready** is prepared for something: *We're ready to go; Breakfast's ready!*
[**Ready** comes from Old English.]

**real** *adjective* (th)
1 Something that is **real** is true or a fact: *'Gordon' isn't his real name.*
2 Something that is **real** is not artificial or a copy: *real leather.*
[**Real** comes from Latin via French.]

**realise** *verb* **realises, realising, realised**
Also **realize** (th)
To **realise** something is to understand it or know that it is true: *I realise you're busy, but could you help me?*
[**Realise** comes from **real**.]

**realistic** *adjective* (th)
1 Something that is **realistic** is not real but looks like the real thing: *The dinosaurs in the film were very realistic.*
2 Someone who is **realistic** understands how something is and accepts it: *I have to be realistic about my chances of passing the exam.* [**Realistic** comes from **real**.]

**really** *adverb* (th)
1 very or very much: *I'm really hungry; She really hates hot weather.*
2 in reality or truly: *Are you really 18?*
[**Really** comes from **real**.]

**rear**¹ *verb* **rears, rearing, reared**
1 To **rear** children or young animals means to give birth to them and care for them as they grow up.
2 To **rear** farm animals means to breed them and look after them until they are big enough to sell.
3 When a horse **rears**, it stands on its hind legs. [**Rear**¹ comes from Old English.]

**rear**² *noun* **rears** (th)
The **rear** is the back of something: *an emergency exit at the rear of the bus.*
[**Rear**² comes from Latin via French.]

**reason** *noun* **reasons** (th)
1 A **reason** is an explanation of why something happens or exists.
2 **Reason** is your ability to think sensibly and clearly.
[**Reason** comes via French from the same Latin word as **ratio**.]

**reason** *verb* **reasons, reasoning, reasoned** (th)
1 To **reason** means to think in a clear and logical way: *We reasoned it would be easier to take this route.*
2 If you **reason with** someone, you try to persuade that person to do a sensible thing that you have suggested.

**reasonable** *adjective*
1 Someone or something that is **reasonable** is sensible and fair.
2 Something that is **reasonable** is not too big or too small: *Their prices are very reasonable; The animals need a reasonable amount of space to move around.*
**reasonably** *adverb*.
[**Reasonable** comes from the same French word as **reason**.]

**reassure** *verb* **reassures, reassuring, reassured** (th)
To **reassure** someone is to do or say something that makes that person feel less nervous.
[**Reassure** comes from re- 'again' and **assure**.]

**rebel** *noun* **rebels**
1 A **rebel** is a person who refuses to obey authority.
2 A **rebel** is a person or a soldier who fights against the government in order to change things. [**Rebel** comes from Latin.]

**receive** *verb* **receives, receiving, received** (th)
To **receive** something means to get it: *Did you receive my letter?*
[**Receive** comes from Latin via French.]

**recent** *adjective*
Something that is **recent** happened a short time ago. **recently** *adverb*.
[**Recent** comes from Latin.]

**reception** *noun* **receptions**
1 A **reception** is a formal party: *a wedding reception.*
2 **Reception** is the place in a hotel or building where you go when you arrive

or where you make enquiries: *Tell someone at reception that you've arrived.*
3 **Reception** is the ability to receive radio and television signals: *Television reception is poor in this area.*
[**Reception** comes from the same Latin word as **receive**.]

**receptionist** *noun* **receptionists**
A **receptionist** is a person who works in the reception area of a building or hotel, answering the phone and dealing with guests and visitors.

**recession** *noun* **recessions**
A **recession** is a time when a country's economy is not very strong and people are unemployed.
[**Recession** comes from Latin.]

**recipe** *noun* **recipes**
A **recipe** is the list of ingredients and set of instructions for cooking something.
[**Recipe** comes from Latin.]

**recite** *verb* **recites, reciting, recited**
To **recite** something means to say something out loud that you have learned by heart: *recite a poem.*
[**Recite** comes from Latin *recitare* 'to read out loud'.]

**reckless** *adjective* (th)
A **reckless** person does dangerous things and does not care about safety: *a reckless driver.* **recklessly** *adverb*. **recklessness** *noun*.
[**Reckless** comes from Old English.]

**reckon** *verb* **reckons, reckoning, reckoned** (th)
1 To **reckon** is to count up or calculate: *We're reckoning on about 100 people coming to the party.*
2 To **reckon** is to think or believe something: *I reckon you're right.*
[**Reckon** comes from Old English.]

**recognise** *verb* **recognises, recognising, recognised** *Also* **recognize** (th)
If you **recognise** someone or something, you know who or what they are because you have seen them before.
[**Recognise** comes from Latin via French.]

**recollect** *verb* **recollects, recollecting, recollected** (th)
If you **recollect** something, you remember it from the past: *I can't recollect the time when we last met.*

a b c d e f g h i j k l m

[**Recollect** comes from Latin *recolligere* 'to gather again'.]

**recommend** *verb* **recommends, recommending, recommended** (th)
If you **recommend** something, you suggest it to someone because you think it is good. [**Recommend** comes from Latin.]

**record** *noun* **records**
1 A **record** is information that is written down or stored in a computer: *medical records; The school register is a record of attendance.*
2 A **record** is a plastic disc with recorded sound on it.
3 If you set a **record** in an activity, you do it better than anyone has ever done it: *break the world record.*
[**Record** comes via French from Latin *recordari* 'to remember'.]

**record** *verb* **records, recording, recorded**
1 To **record** something means to write it down or store it in a computer.
2 To **record** music or a television programme means to save it on a disc or tape.

**recover** *verb* **recovers, recovering, recovered** (th)
1 To **recover** is to start feeling better after an illness or bad experience.
2 To **recover** something is to get it back.
[**Recover** comes from Latin via French.]

**recreation** *noun* **recreations** (th)
**Recreation** is enjoying yourself and relaxing, or the things you do for enjoyment or relaxation.
[**Recreation** comes via French from Latin *recreare* 'to renew'.]

**recruit** *noun* **recruits**
A **recruit** is a person who has just joined an organisation.
[**Recruit** comes from Latin via French.]

**recruit** *verb* **recruits, recruiting, recruited**
To **recruit** someone is to get that person to join something: *We need to recruit three new members of staff.*

**rectangle** *noun* **rectangles**
A **rectangle** is a shape with four straight sides and four right angles.
[**Rectangle** comes from Latin *rectus*

'straight' or 'right' and *angulus* 'an angle'.]

**rectify** *verb* **rectifies, rectifying, rectified** (th)
To **rectify** something is to put right something that is wrong.
[**Rectify** comes via French from Latin *rectus* 'right'.]

**recur** *verb* **recurs, recurring, recurred** (th)
If something **recurs**, it happens again and again.
[**Recur** comes from Latin *recurrere* 'to run again'.]

**recurring** *adjective*
In mathematics, a **recurring** number occurs many times and will continue to recur to infinity: *The answer to 10÷3 is 3.33333 or 3.33 recurring.*

**recycle** *verb* **recycles, recycling, recycled**
To **recycle** materials such as glass, metal and paper is to collect and process them so they can be made into new things instead of throwing them away.
[**Recycle** comes from *re-* 'again' and **cycle**.]

**red** *noun*
**Red** is the colour of blood or of a ripe tomato. [**Red** comes from Old English.]

**red** *adjective* **redder, reddest**
of the colour of blood or a ripe tomato: *red cheeks.*

**reduce** *verb* **reduces, reducing, reduced** (th)
To **reduce** something is to make it less: *The price was reduced by 50%.*
[**Reduce** comes from Latin.]

**redundant** *adjective*
1 Someone who is **redundant** isn't needed to do a job any more and so is out of work: *When the factory closed, 300 people were made redundant.*
2 Something that is **redundant** is no longer necessary or useful: *Our record player is redundant now we've got CDs.*
[**Redundant** comes from Latin *redundare* 'to overflow'.]

**reed** *noun* **reeds**
1 A **reed** is a grass-like plant that grows in or near water.

**2** A **reed** in instruments such as the oboe or clarinet is the part in the mouthpiece that vibrates to make a musical sound when the player blows into it.
[**Reed** comes from Old English.]

**reef** *noun* **reefs**
A **reef** is a ridge of rocks or coral close to the surface of the sea.
[**Reef** comes from Old Norse.]

**reek** *verb* **reeks, reeking, reeked**
To **reek** is to smell strongly of something unpleasant: *He reeked of whisky.*
[**Reek** comes from Old English.]

**reel** *noun* **reels**
A **reel** is a cylinder on which things such as camera film or fishing line are wound.
[**Reel** comes from Old English.]

**reel** *verb* **reels, reeling, reeled** (th)
**1** To **reel** is to stagger around: *They reeled in from the party very drunk.*
**2** If you **reel** or your mind is **reeling**, you feel almost dizzy with shock or confusion.

**refectory** *noun* **refectories**
A **refectory** is a dining-hall in a school, college or monastery.
[**Refectory** comes from Latin.]

**refer** *verb* **refers, referring, referred** (th)
**1** To **refer** to someone or something is to mention or talk about them: *He sometimes refers to his wife as 'her indoors'.*
**2** If you **refer** to something, you have a look at it: *She made a speech without referring to her notes.*
**3** If you are **referred** to someone, you are sent to see that person: *The doctor referred him to a specialist.*
[**Refer** comes via French from Latin *referre* 'to bring back'.]

**referee** *noun* **referees**
A **referee** is a person in games such as football and boxing who makes sure the rules are obeyed.
[**Referee** comes from **refer**.]

**refine** *verb* **refines, refining, refined** (th)
To **refine** a substance is to process it in order to make it pure.
[**Refine** comes from an old word *fine* 'to make pure'.]

**refinery** *noun* **refineries**
A **refinery** is a place where a substance is processed in order to make it pure.

[**Refinery** comes from **refine**.]

**reflect** *verb* **reflects, reflecting, reflected**
**1** If you are **reflected** in a mirror or in water, you can see yourself in it.
**2** If something **reflects** light or heat, the light or heat bounces back from it and doesn't go through it.
**3** If you **reflect** on something, you think carefully about it.
[**Reflect** comes via French from Latin *reflectere* 'to bend back'.]

**reflection** *noun* **reflections**
**1** A **reflection** is an image in a mirror or a shiny surface.
**2** **Reflection** is thinking carefully about something, or the thoughts you have when you reflect.
[**Reflection** comes via French from the same Latin word as **reflect**.]

**reflex** *noun* **reflexes**
**1** A **reflex** is an action or movement that you do without thinking: *Breathing is a natural reflex.*
**2** Your **reflexes** are your ability to react to something: *Football players need to have fast reflexes.*
[**Reflex** comes from the same Latin word as **reflect**.]

**reform** *verb* **reforms, reforming, reformed** (th)
To **reform** something is to change it in order to make it better.

**reform** *noun* **reforms** (th)
A **reform** is a change that makes something better.
[**Reform** comes from Latin via French.]

**refrain** *verb* **refrains, refraining, refrained** (th)
To **refrain** from something is to stop yourself doing it: *Customers are requested to refrain from smoking.*
[**Refrain** comes via French from Latin *refrenare* 'to bridle'.]

**refrigerate** *verb* **refrigerates, refrigerating, refrigerated** (th)
To **refrigerate** something is to put it in the refrigerator to keep it cold.
[**Refrigerate** comes from Latin.]

**refrigerator** *noun* **refrigerators**
A **refrigerator** is a piece of kitchen

**a b c d e f g h i j k l m**

equipment like a cupboard that keeps food cold.

**refuse** *noun* (th)
**Refuse** is waste material such as left-over food or packaging that you throw away: *a refuse bin.*
[**Refuse** comes from an old French word.]

**refuse** *verb* **refuses, refusing, refused** (th)
To **refuse** is to say or show that you don't want something or you don't want to do something.

**regain** *verb* **regains, regaining, regained** (th)
To **regain** something is to get it back when it has been lost.
[**Regain** comes from French.]

**regard** *verb* **regards, regarding, regarded**
The way you **regard** a thing or person is the way you think of them.
[**Regard** comes from French.]

**regard** *noun* (th)
**Regard** is care or thought for people or things: *He shows no regard for the feelings of others.*

**regards** *plural noun*
If you send someone **regards**, you send them best wishes.

**regatta** *noun* **regattas**
A **regatta** is an event where there are boat races. [**Regatta** comes from Italian.]

**reggae** *noun*
**Reggae** is music from the Caribbean with a strong rhythm.
[**Reggae** probably comes from a Jamaican English word.]

**regime** *noun* **regimes**
A **regime** is a system of government: *a military regime.*
[**Regime** comes via French from Latin *regere* 'to rule'.]

**regiment** *noun* **regiments**
A **regiment** is a large group of soldiers controlled by a colonel.
[**Regiment** comes via French from the same Latin word as **regime**.]

**regimented** *adjective*
Something that is **regimented** is very strongly controlled.

[**Regimented** comes from *regiment* 'to form troops into a regiment'.]

**register** *noun* **registers**
A **register** is an official list or record of information.
[**Register** comes from Latin via French.]

**register** *verb* **registers, registering, registered**
1 To **register** something is to put it on an official list: *register a birth; I've registered for a French class.*
2 To **register** something is to show it: *The thermometer registered -15°C.*

**register office** *noun* **register offices**
A **register office** is a government building where births, marriages and deaths are officially recorded. People can also get married in a **register office**.

**regret** *noun* **regrets** (th)
**Regret** is a feeling of sadness about something that you can't change.
[**Regret** comes from French.]

**regret** *verb* **regrets, regretting, regretted** (th)
To regret something is to feel sad about something that you can't change: *I regret not travelling more when I was younger.*

**regular** *adjective* (th)
1 Something that is **regular** always happens at the same time: *a regular Monday morning meeting.*
2 Something that is **regular** is even or constant: *regular breathing.*
[**Regular** comes via French from Latin *regula* 'a rule' (ancestor of **rail** and **rule**).]

**rehearse** *verb* **rehearses, rehearsing, rehearsed**
To **rehearse** means to practise a play or a piece of music that you are going to perform later on.
[**Rehearse** comes from an old French word.]

**reign** *noun* **reigns**
A **reign** is a length of time when a king or queen is ruler of a country.
[**Reign** comes from Latin via French.]

**reign** *verb* **reigns, reigning, reigned**
When a king or queen **reigns** over a country, s/he is the ruler of that country.

**rein** *noun* **reins**
A **rein** is a long narrow strap fixed to a horse's bridle to control it.
[**Rein** comes via French from the same Latin word as **retain**.]

**reindeer** *noun* **reindeer**
A **reindeer** is a deer that lives in the Arctic. [**Reindeer** comes from Old Norse.]

**reinforce** *verb* **reinforces**, **reinforcing**, **reinforced** (th)
To **reinforce** something is to make it stronger. [**Reinforce** comes from French.]

**reject** *verb* **rejects**, **rejecting**, **rejected** (th)
To **reject** something or someone is to refuse to accept them.
[**Reject** comes from Latin *rejectus* 'thrown back'.]

**reject** *noun* **rejects**
A **reject** is a thing or a person who is not accepted because they are not good enough.

**rejoice** *verb* **rejoices**, **rejoicing**, **rejoiced** (th)
To **rejoice** is to feel or show great happiness.
[**Rejoice** comes from an old French word.]

**relapse** *noun* **relapses**
A **relapse** is a condition or situation that gets worse again after getting better: *The patient was recovering, but then had a relapse.*
[**Relapse** comes from Latin *relapsus* 'slipped back'.]

**relapse** *verb* **relapses**, **relapsing**, **relapsed**
To **relapse** is to get worse again after getting better.

**relate** *verb* **relates**, **relating**, **related** (th)
1 If something is **related** to something else, it is connected with it.
2 If someone is **related** to you, s/he is part of your family.
3 To **relate** to someone is to understand how that person thinks or feels: *Some people can't relate to children.*
4 If you **relate** a story, you tell it: *She related her experiences in Africa.*
[**Relate** comes from Latin.]

**relation** *noun* **relations** (th)
1 A **relation** is a connection between two or more things.
2 A **relation** is a member of your family.
[**Relation** comes via French from the same Latin word as **relate**.]

**relationship** *noun* **relationships**
1 A **relationship** is a friendship or a love affair: *They've just ended a three-year relationship.*
2 A **relationship** between people or groups is the way they get on together: *The teacher has a good relationship with the class.*
3 A **relationship** is a family connection: *"What's your relationship to him?" "We're cousins."*

**relative** *noun* **relatives**
A **relative** is a member of your family: *We've got relatives in Australia.*
[**Relative** comes via French from the same Latin word as **relate**.]

**relatively** *adverb* (th)
compared with similar things or with what is usual: *The car is relatively cheap to run; The neighbours were relatively quiet yesterday.*

**relax** *verb* **relaxes**, **relaxing**, **relaxed** (th)
1 To **relax** means to rest and become less tense.
2 If your muscles **relax**, they become less stiff and tense.
3 To **relax** a rule or law is to make it less strict.
[**Relax** comes from Latin *laxus* 'loose'.]

**relaxed** *adjective* (th)
Someone or something that is **relaxed** is calm or not tense: *I feel very relaxed after my holiday.*

**release** *verb* **releases**, **releasing**, **released** (th)
1 To **release** someone is to set that person free: *He was released from prison.*
2 To **release** a film or a CD is to let people see it or hear it: *Their new album will be released next month.*
[**Release** comes from the same Latin word as **relax**.]

**relegate** *verb* **relegates**, **relegating**, **relegated**
To **relegate** a person or team is to put them into a lower position: *The team was relegated to a lower division.*
[**Relegate** comes from Latin *relegare* 'to

send away'.]

**relevant** *adjective*
If a fact or something you say is **relevant**, it is directly connected with something that is happening or being talked about. [**Relevant** comes from Latin.]

**reliable** *adjective* (th)
A thing or person that is **reliable** won't let you down. **reliably** *adverb*.
[**Reliable** comes from Latin via French.]

**relic** *noun* **relics**
A **relic** is the remains of something from the distant past that survives today.
[**Relic** comes via French from Latin *reliquus* 'remaining'.]

**relief** *noun*
**Relief** is a feeling of freedom when something stops worrying you or hurting you: *My exams have finished – what a relief!*
[**Relief** comes via French from Latin *relevare* 'to lift up again'.]

**relieve** *verb* **relieves, relieving, relieved**
To **relieve** something is to make it better, especially by taking away worry or pain: *These tablets should relieve the pain; We were so relieved when the child was found.*
[**Relieve** comes via French from the same Latin word as **relief**.]

**religion** *noun* **religions**
**1 Religion** is a belief in God or gods.
**2** A **religion** is a set of beliefs about God or gods: *the Jewish religion; the Hindu religion.*
[**Religion** comes from Latin via French.]

**remain** *verb* **remains, remaining, remained** (th)
**1** To **remain** means to be left after others have gone: *This was a forest but now only a few trees remain.*
**2** To **remain** means to stay the same: *She remained calm; Only one wall remains standing.*
[**Remain** comes from Latin via French.]

**remark** *noun* **remarks**
A **remark** is a written or spoken comment.
[**Remark** comes from French.]

**remark** *verb* **remarks, remarking, remarked**
To **remark** is to comment on something.

**remarkable** *adjective* (th)
Something that is **remarkable** is unusual or special, which makes people notice it. **remarkably** *adverb*.
[**Remarkable** comes from the same French word as **remark**.]

**remedy** *noun* **remedies** (th)
A **remedy** is a cure for a problem or illness.
[**Remedy** comes from Latin via French.]

**remember** *verb* **remembers, remembering, remembered**
**1** To **remember** something is to keep something in your mind: *I'll always remember this house.*
**2** To **remember** something is to bring something to your mind: *I can't remember how to get there.*
[**Remember** comes from Latin via French.]

**remind** *verb* **reminds, reminding, reminded**
To **remind** someone is to make that person remember something.
[**Remind** comes from *re-* 'again' and **mind**.]

**reminisce** *verb* **reminisces, reminiscing, reminisced**
To **reminisce** is to talk about good things that happened in the past.
[**Reminisce** comes from Latin *reminisci* 'to remember'.]

**remnant** *noun* **remnants**
A **remnant** is a piece or amount of something that is left over: *The remnants of breakfast were still on the table.*
[**Remnant** comes from old French *remenant* 'remaining'.]

**remorse** *noun* (th)
**Remorse** is a feeling of sadness or guilt about something you have done wrong.
[**Remorse** comes from Latin via French.]

**remote** *adjective* **remoter, remotest** (th)
A **remote** place is far away from other places: *a remote Scottish farmhouse.*
[**Remote** comes from the same Latin word as **remove**.]

**remove** *verb* **removes, removing, removed** (th)
To **remove** something means to take it away.

[**Remove** comes from Latin via French.]

## rendezvous *noun* **rendezvous**

**1** A **rendezvous** is an arrangement to meet at a certain time and place.
**2** A **rendezvous** is a place where people meet: *The café is a rendezvous for artists and writers.*
[**Rendezvous** comes from French *rendez-vous!* 'present yourselves!']

## renew *verb* **renews, renewing, renewed**

**1** To **renew** an activity means to begin it again: *We renewed our efforts the next morning.*
**2** To **renew** something means to replace it with something similar but new: *Your pass must be renewed every year.*
**3** To **renew** a library book means to arrange to keep it for a longer time.
[**Renew** comes from *re-* 'again' and **new**.]

## renowned *adjective* (th)

**Renowned** means well known or famous: *a renowned pianist; She is renowned for her cooking.* [**Renowned** comes from French.]

## rent *verb* **rents, renting, rented**

When you **rent** something, such as a house or a television, you pay money to its owner to let you use it.
[**Rent** comes from an old French word.]

## rent *noun* **rents**

**Rent** is money that you pay to someone who is letting you stay in a house or letting you use something that s/he owns.

## repair *verb* **repairs, repairing, repaired** (th)

To **repair** something means to mend it.
[**Repair** comes via French from Latin *reparare* 'to get something ready again'.]

## repay *verb* **repays, repaying, repaid** (th)

To **repay** someone means to pay him/her back in some way: *I wanted to repay him for his kindness.* [**Repay** comes from French.]

## repeat *verb* **repeats, repeating, repeated**

To **repeat** something means to do it or say it again.
[**Repeat** comes from Latin via French.]

## repel *verb* **repels, repelling, repelled**

**1** If something **repels** you, you find it horrible or disgusting.
**2** To **repel** something means to drive it or push it away.
[**Repel** comes from Latin *repellere* 'to drive back'.]

## repent *verb* **repents, repenting, repented**

To **repent** means to be very sorry for something that you have done.
[**Repent** comes from an old French word.]

## repetition *noun* **repetitions**

A **repetition** is when something is done again, said again or happens again.
[**Repetition** comes via French from the same Latin word as **repeat**.]

## replace *verb* **replaces, replacing, replaced** (th)

**1** To **replace** something means to put it back.
**2** If you **replace** a person, you take over from him/her.
**3** To **replace** something that you have lost or broken means to get a similar thing to use instead.
[**Replace** comes from *re-* 'back, again' and **place**.]

## replay *noun* **replays**

**1** A **replay** is a match that has to be played again.
**2** A **replay** is when something on a video or a film is shown again.
[**Replay** comes from *re-* 'back, again' and **play**.]

## replica *noun* **replicas** (th)

A **replica** is an exact copy of something.
[**Replica** comes from Italian.]

## reply *verb* **replies, replying, replied** (th)

To **reply** means to answer: *Please reply to my letter.*
[**Reply** comes from Latin via French.]

## reply *noun* **replies**

A **reply** is an answer: *Did you get a reply when you knocked?*

## report *noun* **reports**

**1** A **report** is a piece of writing giving information about something.
**2** A **report** is a description of how well you are doing at school in each of the subjects.
[**Report** comes from Latin *reportare* 'to bring back'.]

**report** *verb* **reports, reporting, reported**
**1** To **report** means to tell someone formally or officially about something: *Did you report the accident to the police?*
**2** To **report** means to tell someone officially that you have arrived: *Report for duty at 13.00 hours.*

**reporter** *noun* **reporters**
A **reporter** is someone who collects news or information for a newspaper or radio or television programme.

**represent** *verb* **represents, representing, represented** (th)
**1** A person who **represents** other people speaks for them: *I represent my class on the school council.*
**2** To **represent** something means to stand for it: *This cross on my map represents the church.*
[**Represent** comes from Latin via French.]

**representative** *noun* **representatives** (th)
A **representative** is a person who speaks for other people.

**reproduce** *verb* **reproduces, reproducing, reproduced** (th)
**1** If you **reproduce** something, you make a copy of it.
**2** To **reproduce** means to have a baby or to have young.
**3** If a plant **reproduces**, it makes seeds or new plants.
[**Reproduce** comes from Latin re- 'again' and **produce**.]

**reproduction** *noun*
**Reproduction** is when people or animals have babies or young, and when plants produce new plants.

**reproductive** *adjective*
Your **reproductive** organs are the parts of your body that will help you to produce babies.

**reptile** *noun* **reptiles**
A **reptile** is a cold-blooded animal that has a scaly skin and lays eggs. Snakes and tortoises are **reptiles**.
[**Reptile** comes from Latin reptilis 'crawling'.]

**republic** *noun* **republics**
A **republic** is a country that doesn't have

a king or a queen, and usually has a president.
[**Republic** comes from Latin res publica 'thing that concerns the public'.]

**repugnant** *adjective* (th)
Something that is **repugnant** is disgusting.
[**Repugnant** comes from Latin via French.]

**repulsive** *adjective* (th)
Something that is **repulsive** is extremely ugly or disgusting.
[**Repulsive** comes from the same Latin word as **repel**.]

**reputable** *adjective* (th)
A **reputable** person or company is reliable and can be trusted.
[**Reputable** comes via French from the same Latin word as **reputation**.]

**reputation** *noun* **reputations**
**1** Your **reputation** is what people think or say about you: *Our teacher has a reputation for being very strict.*
**2** To have a **good reputation** means that people have a good opinion of you.
[**Reputation** comes from Latin reputare 'to think about'.]

**request** *noun* **requests**
If you make a **request**, you ask for something.
[**Request** comes via French from the same Latin word as **require**.]

**request** *verb* **requests, requesting, requested**
To **request** something means to ask for it.

**require** *verb* **requires, requiring, required**
**1** If you **require** something, you need it. **Require** is a formal word.
**2** If you are **required** to do something, you have to do it.
[**Require** comes from Latin.]

**requirement** *noun* **requirements**
**1** A **requirement** is something that you have to have or have to do: *It is a requirement that you must be fit to join the army.*
**2** **Requirements** are things that you need: *We can provide all your camping requirements.*

**rescue** *verb* **rescues, rescuing, rescued**
To **rescue** a person means to save him/her from danger.
[**Rescue** comes from Latin via French.]

**rescue** *noun* **rescues**
1 A **rescue** is when someone saves a person or people from danger.
2 To **go to** or **come to** someone's **rescue** means to try to help him/her.

**research** *noun*
If you do **research**, you find out about a subject by reading, asking questions or carrying out experiments.
[**Research** comes from an old French word.]

**research** *verb* **researches, researching, researched** (th)
To **research** something means to read or ask questions so that you find out about it: *He's researching his family history.*

**researcher** *noun* **researchers**
A **researcher** is a person whose job is to find out facts about things or people.

**resemblance** *noun* **resemblances** (th)
If you have a **resemblance** to another person, you look a bit like him/her.
[**Resemblance** comes from the same French word as **resemble**.]

**resemble** *verb* **resembles, resembling, resembled** (th)
To **resemble** something means to look like it or be like it in some way.
[**Resemble** comes via French from Latin *similis* 'like' (ancestor of **similar**).]

**resent** *verb* **resents, resenting, resented**
If you **resent** something, you feel annoyed or hurt about it.
[**Resent** comes from an old French word.]

**resentful** *adjective* (th)
If you are **resentful**, you feel annoyed or hurt about something.

**reservation** *noun* **reservations**
When you make a **reservation**, you book something, such as a ticket or a table at a restaurant.
[**Reservation** comes from the same Latin word as **reserve**.]

**reserve** *verb* **reserves, reserving, reserved** (th)
1 When you **reserve** something, you ask

someone to keep it for you.
2 If you **reserve** something or **keep** something **in reserve**, you save it in case you need it later.
[**Reserve** comes from Latin *reservare* 'to keep back'.]

**reserve** *noun* **reserves**
1 A **reserve** is an extra member of a team.
2 A **reserve** is a place that is kept for wild animals, birds or plants.

**reservoir** *noun* **reservoirs**
A **reservoir** is a large artificial lake where water is stored.
[**Reservoir** comes via French from the same Latin word as **reserve**.]

**resident** *noun* **residents** (th)
A **resident** of a house or a place is a person who lives there.
[**Resident** comes from Latin *residere* 'to stay'.]

**resign** *verb* **resigns, resigning, resigned**
1 To **resign** means to give up your job.
2 If you **resign yourself** or become **resigned** to something, you accept that it will happen although you do not like it.
[**Resign** comes from Latin.]

**resin** *noun*
**Resin** is a sticky liquid that comes out of trees. [**Resin** comes from Latin.]

**resist** *verb* **resists, resisting, resisted** (th)
1 To **resist** something means to fight against it or try to stop it happening.
2 If you **resist temptation**, you don't do something that you would really like to do.
[**Resist** comes from Latin *resistere* 'to stand firmly against something'.]

**resistance** *noun* (th)
1 If you put up **resistance**, you fight or struggle against something.
2 If you have **resistance** to an illness or a disease, your body can defend itself against it.
3 **Resistance** is a force that makes something that is moving slow down.
[**Resistance** comes via French from the same Latin word as **resist**.]

**resistant** *adjective*
A thing that is **resistant** to something is not damaged or affected by it.
[**Resistant** comes from **resist**.]

a b c d e f g h i j k l m

**resolution** *noun* **resolutions**
If you make a **resolution**, you decide that you will do something.
[**Resolution** comes from Latin.]

**resonate** *verb* **resonates, resonating, resonated**
When a sound **resonates**, it vibrates and makes a deep, echoing sound.
[**Resonates** comes from Latin.]

**resort** *noun* **resorts**
1 A **resort** is a town or a place where people stay on holiday.
2 If something is a **last resort**, you will only try it if nothing else works.
[**Resort** comes from French.]

**resource** *noun* **resources**
A **resource** is something that you can use.
[**Resource** comes from Latin.]

**resourceful** *adjective*
A **resourceful** person is good at making use of things and solving problems.

**respect** *verb* **respects, respecting, respected** (th)
1 To **respect** people means to admire and value them.
2 To **respect** other people's opinions or feelings means to accept them and not try to change them.
[**Respect** comes from Latin.]

**respect** *noun*
1 If you treat people with **respect**, you treat them politely because you have a good opinion of them.
2 If you treat things with **respect**, you are careful with them.

**respected** *adjective*
To be **respected** means that many people think that what you have done is good or important.

**respectful** *adjective*
If you are **respectful**, you are polite and treat people with respect.

**respond** *verb* **responds, responding, responded** (th)
To **respond** means to do something or say something when something happens to you.
[**Respond** comes from Latin via French.]

**response** *noun* **responses** (th)
A **response** is something that you say or do when something happens.
[**Response** comes via French from the same Latin word as **respond**.]

**responsibility** *noun* **responsibilities** (th)
1 A **responsibility** is something that it is up to you to do or take care of.
2 If you **take responsibility** for something that has happened, you say that it was your fault.
[**Responsibility** comes from **responsible**.]

**responsible** *adjective* (th)
1 Someone who is **responsible** can be trusted to do something or to behave properly.
2 If you are **responsible** for something, you are in charge and it is your fault if anything goes wrong.
[**Responsible** comes via French from the same Latin word as **respond**.]

**rest¹** *noun* **rests** (th)
1 A **rest** is a break from work.
2 A **rest** is a nap or a short sleep.
[**Rest¹** comes from Old English.]

**rest¹** *verb* **rests, resting, rested**
1 To **rest** means to have a break from work and relax by sitting or lying down.
2 To **rest** on something means to lie or lean on it: *The ladder rested against the wall; I rested my book on my knees.*

**rest²** *noun* **rests**
1 The **rest** is the part that is left: *She spent the rest of her life in London.*
2 The **rest** is the other people or things: *Some of us went by bus and the rest walked.*
[**Rest** comes via French from Latin *restare* 'to remain'.]

**restaurant** *noun* **restaurants**
A **restaurant** is a place where you can go to buy and eat a meal.
[**Restaurant** comes from French.]

**restful** *adjective* (th)
Something that is **restful** makes you feel relaxed and rested.

**restless** *adjective* (th)
If you are **restless**, you are bored or impatient and can't keep still.
**restlessly** *adverb.* **restlessness** *noun.*

**restore** *verb* **restores, restoring, restored** (th)
1 To **restore** a painting or a piece of furniture means to make it look how it

did when it was new.

**2** To **restore** something means to give it back or put it back.

[**Restore** comes from Latin via French.]

**restrain** *verb* **restrains, restraining, restrained**

**1** To **restrain** people or animals means to stop them from moving or doing something, usually by holding onto them or tying them up.

**2** If you **restrain yourself**, you stop yourself from doing something or saying something.

[**Restrain** comes from Latin via French.]

**restrict** *verb* **restricts, restricting, restricted** (th)

To **restrict** something means to say that people can only have a certain amount of it.

[**Restrict** comes from the same Latin word as **restrain**.]

**restricted** *adjective*

If an area or a place is **restricted**, only some people can go there.

**result** *noun* **results** (th)

**1** A **result** is something that happens because other things have happened: *The famine is a result of the drought.*

**2** A **result** is the final score in a game or a competition. [**Result** comes from Latin.]

**resume** *verb* **resumes, resuming, resumed** (th)

When something **resumes**, it carries on again after a break.

[**Resume** comes from Latin via French.]

**retain** *verb* **retains, retaining, retained** (th)

To **retain** something means to keep it.

[**Retain** comes via French from Latin *retenere* 'to hold back'.]

**retaliate** *verb* **retaliates, retaliating, retaliated** (th)

If you **retaliate**, you do something back when someone has hurt you or upset you.

[**Retaliate** comes from Latin.]

**retire** *verb* **retires, retiring, retired**

To **retire** means to stop working because you have reached a certain age.

[**Retire** comes from French *retirer* 'to draw back'.]

**retreat** *verb* **retreats, retreating, retreated**

To **retreat** means to go back, away from something or someone.

[**Retreat** comes via French from Latin *retrahere* 'to pull back'.]

**retrieve** *verb* **retrieves, retrieving, retrieved**

To **retrieve** something means to get it back. [**Retrieve** comes from French.]

**return** *verb* **returns, returning, returned** (th)

**1** To **return** means to come or go back somewhere.

**2** To **return** something means to give it back.

[**Return** comes from Latin via French.]

**reunion** *noun* **reunions**

A **reunion** is when people who haven't seen each other for a long time meet again.

[**Reunion** comes via French from the same Latin word as **reunite**.]

**reunite** *verb* **reunites, reuniting, reunited**

When two things or people are **reunited**, they come together after they have been apart.

[**Reunite** comes from Latin *reunire* 'to bring together again'.]

**reveal** *verb* **reveals, revealing, revealed** (th)

**1** If you **reveal** something that was hidden, you show it.

**2** If you **reveal** a secret, you tell people about it.

[**Reveal** comes from Latin via French.]

**revenge** *noun* (th)

**Revenge** is something that you do to hurt someone who has hurt you in some way.

[**Revenge** comes from Latin via French.]

**reverse** *verb* **reverses, reversing, reversed**

**1** If you **reverse** a vehicle, you drive it backwards.

**2** If you **reverse** the order of something, you change the order so that it is the other way round.

[**Reverse** comes via French from Latin *revertere* 'to turn back'.]

a b c d e f g h i j k l m

**review** *verb* **reviews, reviewing, reviewed**
When you **review** something such as a book or a play, you write a short article about what you thought of it for a newspaper or magazine.
[**Review** comes from an old French word.]

**revise** *verb* **revises, revising, revised**
To **revise** means to go over what you have already learned to prepare for an exam or a test.
[**Revise** comes via French from Latin *revisere* 'to look at again'.]

**revolt** *noun* **revolts** (th)
A **revolt** is when a group of people try to change the way that their country is run, often in a violent way.
[**Revolt** comes via French and Italian from the same Latin word as **revolve**.]

**revolting** *adjective* (th)
Something that is **revolting** is disgusting.
[**Revolting** comes from **revolt**.]

**revolution** *noun* **revolutions** (th)
**1** When there is a **revolution** in a country, a large group of people get together and get rid of the government usually by fighting.
**2** A **revolution** is a big, important change.
[**Revolution** comes via French from the same Latin word as **revolve**.]

**revolutionary** *adjective*
A **revolutionary** idea is one that is extremely new and different.

**revolve** *verb* **revolves, revolving, revolved**
To **revolve** means to turn in a circle round something: *The earth revolves round the sun; a revolving door.*
[**Revolve** comes from Latin *revolvere* 'to roll back or turn round'.]

**revolver** *noun* **revolvers**
A **revolver** is a small gun.
[A **revolver** is so called because the chamber (the part that holds the bullets) revolves so that the bullets go into the barrel one after another and you do not have to reload until the whole chamber is empty.]

**reward** *noun* **rewards**
A **reward** is a prize or present that you get for doing something well, or for finding something.
[**Reward** comes from an old French word.]

**reward** *verb* **rewards, rewarding, rewarded**
To **reward** someone means to give him/her a prize or present for doing something well, or for finding something.

**rewarding** *adjective* (th)
A **rewarding** job is a job that makes you feel satisfied and happy.

**rewind** *verb* **rewinds, rewinding, rewound**
When you **rewind** a cassette tape or a videotape, you make it go backwards to get to an earlier part.
[**Rewind** comes from Latin *re-* 'back or again' and **wind**[2].]

**rheumatism** *noun*
**Rheumatism** is an illness. If you have **rheumatism**, your joints and muscles get stiff and sore.
[**Rheumatism** comes from Greek via Latin or French.]

**rhinoceros** *noun* **rhinoceroses**
A **rhinoceros** is a very large animal with either one or two horns on its nose.
[**Rhinoceros** comes from Greek via Latin.]

**rhombus** *noun* **rhombuses** *or* **rhombi**
A **rhombus** is a flat shape that has four straight sides that are equal, and no right angles.
[**Rhombus** comes from Greek via Latin.]

**rhubarb** *noun*
**Rhubarb** is a plant that has long red stems and big leaves. You can cook **rhubarb** and eat it.
[**Rhubarb** comes from Latin via French.]

**rhyme** *noun* **rhymes**
**1** A **rhyme** is a word that has the same sound at the end as another word. A **rhyme** for *cat* is *mat*.
**2** A **rhyme** is a short song or poem: *a nursery rhyme.*
[**Rhyme** comes via French and Latin from the same Greek word as **rhythm**.]

**rhyme** *verb* **rhymes, rhyming, rhymed**
If two words **rhyme**, they have the same sound at the end. *Moon* **rhymes** with *June.*

**rhythm** *noun* **rhythms**
A **rhythm** is a pattern of sounds or beats in music, poetry or dancing.
[**Rhythm** comes from Greek via French or Latin.]

**rhythmic** *adjective* Also **rhythmical**
Something that is **rhythmic** has a regular pattern or beat. **rhythmically** *adverb*.

**rib** *noun* **ribs**
Your **ribs** are the thin curved bones that go across your chest.
[**Rib** comes from Old English.]

**ribbon** *noun* **ribbons**
A **ribbon** is a narrow strip of thin material that you use to decorate something.
[**Ribbon** comes from an old French word.]

**rice** *noun*
**Rice** is a cereal that grows in wet fields in hot climates.
[**Rice** comes from Greek via French and Italian.]

**rich** *adjective* **richer**, **richest** (th)
1 Someone who has a lot of money is **rich**.
2 **Rich** foods have a lot of fat or oil in them. [**Rich** comes from Old English.]

**riddle** *noun* **riddles**
A **riddle** is a question or puzzle, sometimes in rhyme, which has a clever or amusing answer.
[**Riddle** comes from Old English.]

**ride** *verb* **rides**, **riding**, **rode**, **ridden**
1 To **ride** a horse or a bicycle means to sit on it and control it as it moves.
2 To **ride** means to travel in a vehicle.
[**Ride** comes from Old English.]

**ride** *noun* **rides**
1 To **have a ride** or **go for a ride** means to go for a journey in a vehicle or on a horse or bicycle.
2 A **ride** at a fair is a kind of entertainment where you sit on or in something while it moves around.

**ridiculous** *adjective* (th)
**Ridiculous** means silly or foolish: *You look ridiculous in that hat.*
**ridiculously** *adverb*.
[**Ridiculous** comes from Latin.]

**rifle** *noun* **rifles**
A **rifle** is a long gun that you hold against your shoulder.
[**Rifle** comes from French.]

**rigging** *noun*
The **rigging** on a ship is the ropes that hold up the masts and the sails.
[**Rigging** probably comes from a Scandinavian language.]

**right** *adjective* (th)
1 Something that is **right** is correct or true.
2 Something that is **right** is fair.
3 The **right** side is one of the two sides of something. In the word *as*, the *s* is on the **right** side of the *a*.
[**Right** comes from Old English.]

**right** *noun* **rights**
1 The **right** is the right side of something: *In the USA, people drive on the right.*
2 Your **rights** are the things that you should be allowed to do or to have: *Women had to fight for the right to vote.*

**right** *adverb*
1 towards the right side: *turn right at the church.*
2 completely: *turn right round; go right to the end.*
3 exactly in that place: *You can park right outside; Stay right where you are!*
4 correctly or properly: *Did I guess right?; You were right to refuse.*

**right angle** *noun* **right angles**
A **right angle** is an angle that measures 90 degrees. The corner of a square is a **right angle**.

**right-hand** *adjective*
The **right-hand** side of something is the side on the right.

**right-handed** *adjective*
If you are **right-handed**, you hold the pen or pencil in your right hand when you write.

**rigid** *adjective*
Something that is **rigid** is hard and stiff.
[**Rigid** comes from Latin.]

**rim** *noun* **rims**
1 The **rim** of a wheel is the outer edge.
2 The **rim** of a cup or a glass is the circular top of it.
[**Rim** comes from Old English.]

**rind** *noun* **rinds**
Rind is hard skin, for example on cheese, bacon or fruit.
[**Rind** comes from Old English.]

**ring**[1] *noun* **rings**
1 A **ring** is a circle or something in the shape of a circle: *The children sat in a ring round their teacher.*
2 A **ring** is a piece of jewellery that you wear on your finger.
3 A **ring** is an area where a circus or a boxing match takes place.
[**Ring**[1] comes from Old English *hring*.]

**ring**[2] *verb* **rings, ringing, rang, rung**
1 If something **rings**, it makes the sound of a bell.
2 If you **ring** someone, you telephone him/her.
[**Ring**[2] comes from Old English *hringan*, which may be an imitation of the sound.]

**rink** *noun* **rinks**
A **rink** is a large space indoors where you can ice skate or roller skate.
[No one knows where **rink** comes from.]

**rinse** *verb* **rinses, rinsing, rinsed**
To **rinse** something means to wash it in clean water after you have put soap or shampoo on it.
[**Rinse** comes from an old French word.]

**riot** *noun* **riots**
A **riot** is when a large crowd of people behave in a noisy or violent way.
[**Riot** comes from an old French word.]

**rip** *verb* **rips, ripping, ripped**
To **rip** something means to tear it.
[No one knows where **rip** comes from.]

**ripe** *adjective* **riper, ripest**
Something that is **ripe** is ready to be picked or eaten.
[**Ripe** comes from Old English.]

**ripen** *verb* **ripens, ripening, ripened**
When fruit **ripens**, it becomes ripe.
[**Ripen** comes from **ripe**.]

**ripple** *noun* **ripples**
A **ripple** is a tiny movement or wave on the surface of water.
[No one knows where **ripple** comes from.]

**rise** *verb* **rises, rising, rose, risen** (th)
1 To **rise** means to go up: *The balloon rose in the air; Prices have risen this year.*
2 To **rise** means to get up: *She rose from her chair to welcome them; He never rises till noon.* [**Rise** comes from Old English.]

**risk** *noun* **risks**
1 A **risk** is a chance that something bad might happen.
2 If you take a **risk**, you do something that could be dangerous or bad.
[**Risk** comes via French from Italian *risco* 'danger'.]

**risk** *verb* **risks, risking, risked**
1 If you **risk** your life, you do something very dangerous that could kill you.
2 If you **risk** doing something, you do it even though you know that something bad could happen.

**risky** *adjective* **riskier, riskiest** (th)
Something that is dangerous or might lead to trouble is **risky**.

**rite** *noun* **rites**
A **rite** is a religious ceremony.
[**Rite** comes from Latin.]

**ritual** *noun* **rituals**
A **ritual** is something that has to be done in a fixed order or in a special way.
[**Ritual** comes from the same Latin word as **rite**.]

**rival** *noun* **rivals** (th)
A **rival** is an enemy, or a person in the same race or competition as you.
[**Rival** comes from Latin.]

**river** *noun* **rivers**
A **river** is a very large stream of water which flows into the sea or a lake.
[**River** comes from Latin via French.]

**road** *noun* **roads**
A **road** is a wide path with a hard surface for vehicles to go along.
[**Road** comes from Old English.]

**roam** *verb* **roams, roaming, roamed** (th)
To **roam** means to wander or walk about.
[No one knows where **roam** comes from.]

**roar** *noun* **roars**
A **roar** is a very loud, deep sound: *the lion's roar; the roar of traffic.*
[**Roar** comes from Old English *rarian*, which is an imitation of the sound.]

**roar** *verb* **roars, roaring, roared**
To **roar** means to make a very loud, deep

sound like a lion.

**roast** *verb* **roasts, roasting, roasted**
To **roast** meat or vegetables means to cook them in the oven or over a fire.
[**Roast** comes from an old French word.]

**rob** *verb* **robs, robbing, robbed** (th)
To **rob** someone means to steal something from him/her. To **rob** a place means to steal something from it.
[**Rob** comes from an old French word.]

**robbery** *noun* **robberies**
A **robbery** is when a thief steals money or other people's things.
[**Robbery** comes from the same old French word as **rob**.]

**robe** *noun* **robes**
A **robe** is a long gown or dress, especially one that is worn on special occasions or to show who you are: *the mayor's robe.*
[**Robe** comes from an old French word.]

**robin** *noun* **robins**
A **robin** is a small, brown bird with a red breast.
[**Robin** comes from French *Robin* 'little Robert'.]

**robot** *noun* **robots**
A **robot** is a machine that can move or do things automatically.
[**Robot** comes from Czech *robota* 'forced labour'.]

**rock¹** *noun* **rocks**
1 A **rock** is a very large stone.
2 **Rock** is the very hard substance that the earth is made of.
3 **Rock** is a hard kind of sweet, sometimes shaped like a stick.
[**Rock¹** comes from Latin via French.]

**rock²** *verb* **rocks, rocking, rocked**
1 To **rock** means to move gently backwards and forwards.
2 To **rock** something means to move it gently backwards and forwards.
[**Rock²** comes from Old English.]

**rock²** *noun*
**Rock** is music that has a strong beat and is usually played loudly: *a rock concert.*

**rockery** *noun* **rockeries**
A **rockery** is a part of a garden that has small plants growing in between rocks.

**rocket** *noun* **rockets**
1 A **rocket** is a long tube that flies through the air by expelling burning gas. **Rockets** are used to launch spacecraft and missiles.
2 A **rocket** is a firework that shoots high into the air and explodes.
[**Rocket** comes from Italian via French.]

**rod** *noun* **rods**
A **rod** is a long, thin stick or bar.
[**Rod** comes from Old English.]

**rode** *verb*
**Rode** is the past tense of **ride**.

**rodent** *noun* **rodents**
A **rodent** is an animal that has sharp teeth for gnawing. Mice and squirrels are **rodents**.
[**Rodent** comes from Latin *rodere* 'to gnaw'.]

**rodeo** *noun* **rodeos**
A **rodeo** is a show where you can watch people riding horses and catching calves.
[**Rodeo** comes from Spanish.]

**roe** *noun*
The eggs of a fish are called **roe**.
[**Roe** comes from an old German or Dutch word.]

**role** *noun* **roles**
A **role** is a part in a play or a film.
[**Role** comes from old French *roule* 'roll', because the actor's part was written on a roll of paper.]

**roll** *noun* **rolls**
1 A **roll** is something curled into a tube shape: *a roll of film.*
2 A **roll** is a very small, round loaf of bread.
[**Roll** comes from Latin via French.]

**roll** *verb* **rolls, rolling, rolled**
1 To **roll** means to turn over and over like a wheel moving along the ground.
2 When you **roll** something **up**, you make it into the shape of a tube.
3 To **roll** or **roll out** clay or pastry means to make it flat with a rolling pin.
4 When thunder **rolls**, it makes a long, rumbling sound.

**Rollerblade** *noun* **Rollerblades**
**Rollerblades** are boots like ice-skates, but with a line of wheels under them where the blades of the skates would be.

a b c d e f g h i j k l m

**rollercoaster** *noun* **rollercoasters**
A **rollercoaster** is a ride that goes very fast along a curving track that can be high off the ground.

**roller skate** *noun* **roller skates**
**Roller skates** are shoes that have small wheels on the bottom.
[**Skate** comes from French via Dutch.]

**rolling pin** *noun* **rolling pins**
A **rolling pin** is a wooden object in the shape of a cylinder that you use for rolling out pastry.

**romantic** *adjective* (th)
1 Something that is **romantic** is about love or people in love: *a romantic novel*.
2 A **romantic** idea is unrealistic and not practical.
[**Romantic** comes from an old French word.]

**roof** *noun* **roofs**
A **roof** is the part that covers the top of a building or vehicle.
[**Roof** comes from Old English.]

**rook**[1] *noun* **rooks**
A **rook** is a large black bird.
[**Rook**[1] comes from Old English.]

**rook**[2] *noun* **rooks**
**Rook** is another name for the **castle** in chess.
[**Rook**[2] comes from Arabic via French.]

**room** *noun* **rooms**
1 A **room** is a space with walls around it inside a building.
2 **Room** is space for someone or something: *Is there room in the car for our bags?* [**Room** comes from Old English.]

**rooster** *noun* **roosters**
A **rooster** is an adult male chicken. This word is used mainly in North America.
[**Rooster** comes from Old English.]

**root** *noun* **roots**
A **root** is the part of a plant that grows underground.
[**Root** comes from Old Norse.]

**root word** *noun* **root words**
A **root word** is a word to which you can add a prefix or suffix to make another word. For example, you can add *un* to the **root word** *happy* to make *unhappy*.

**rope** *noun* **ropes**
A **rope** is very thick string made from strong threads twisted together.
[**Rope** comes from Old English.]

**rose**[1] *noun* **roses**
A **rose** is a flower with a beautiful scent and thorns on its stem.
[**Rose**[1] comes from Latin via Old English.]

**rose**[2] *verb*
**Rose**[2] is the past tense of **rise**.

**rosy** *adjective* **rosier, rosiest**
If your cheeks are **rosy**, they are pink or red and look healthy.
[**Rosy** comes from **rose**[1].]

**rot** *verb* **rots, rotting, rotted** (th)
1 When food **rots**, it goes bad.
2 When wood **rots**, it goes soft and may break.
[**Rot** comes from Old English.]

**rotate** *verb* **rotates, rotating, rotated**
To **rotate** means to go round or turn like a wheel.
[**Rotate** comes from Latin *rota* 'a wheel'.]

**rotation** *noun*
**Rotation** is when something goes round: *You can't feel the rotation of the earth.*
[**Rotation** comes from the same Latin word as **rotate**.]

**rotten** *adjective* (th)
Something that is bad or falling to pieces is **rotten**: *rotten tomatoes; a rotten plank.*
[**Rotten** comes from Old Norse.]

**rough** *adjective* **rougher, roughest** (th)
1 Something that is **rough** is not smooth.
2 Someone who is **rough** is not gentle.
3 A **rough** figure or amount is not exact.
**roughly** *adverb*. **roughness** *noun*.
[**Rough** comes from Old English.]

**round** *adjective* **rounder, roundest** (th)
Something that is **round** is shaped like a circle or a ball. **roundness** *noun*.
[**Round** comes from Latin via French.]

**round** *preposition*
1 on all sides: *There is a high fence round the prison.*
2 to all parts: *She showed us round the house.*
3 in a circle around something: *The earth goes round the sun; He ran round the track.*

**round** *noun* **rounds**
1 A **round** is a part in a tournament or competition: *She was out in the first round.*
2 A **round** is a series of visits that a person such as a doctor or postal worker makes.

**roundabout** *noun* **roundabouts**
1 A **roundabout** is a place where roads meet and vehicles have to go round a circle.
2 A **roundabout** is an amusement at a fair. You sit on a model horse or vehicle and ride round and round.
3 A **roundabout** is something that you can sit on in a park and go round and round.

**rounders** *noun*
Rounders is a team game that you play outside. You have to hit a hard ball with a thin wooden bat and try to run round the pitch. [**Rounders** comes from **round**.]

**route** *noun* **routes**
A **route** is a way of getting somewhere: *Work out the shortest route.*
[**Route** comes from Latin via French.]

**routine** *noun* **routines** (th)
If you have a **routine** for doing something, you do it in a certain way every time.
[**Routine** comes from the same French word as **route**.]

**row¹** *noun* **rows** (th)
A **row** is a line of people or things.
[**Row¹** comes from Old English *raw.*]

**row²** *noun* **rows** (th)
1 A **row** is when there is too much noise: *Don't make such a row!*
2 A **row** is a quarrel: *He's had a row with his friend.*
[No one knows where **row²** comes from.]

**row³** *verb* **rows, rowing, rowed**
To **row** a boat means to move it along using oars.
[**Row³** comes from Old English *rowan.*]

**royal** *adjective*
Royal means to do with a king, queen, prince or princess.
[**Royal** comes from Latin via French.]

**royalty** *noun* **royalties**
1 Royalty are the members of a country's royal family.

2 A **royalty** is a sum of money that a person is paid so that his/her work can be used, performed or published.
[**Royalty** comes from the same French word as **royal**.]

**rub** *verb* **rubs, rubbing, rubbed**
1 To **rub** means to move something backwards and forwards against another thing.
2 To **rub** means to wipe or polish something hard.
[**Rub** may come from an old German word.]

**rubber** *noun* **rubbers**
1 Rubber is a material that stretches, bends and bounces. **Rubber** comes from the juice of the rubber tree.
2 A **rubber** is a piece of rubber used for removing pencil marks.
[**Rubber** comes from **rub**.]

**rubbish** *noun* (th)
1 Rubbish is things that you throw away because they are no longer useful or wanted.
2 Rubbish is nonsense.
[**Rubbish** may come from the same old French word as **rubble**.]

**rubble** *noun*
Rubble is pieces of broken stone, brick and metal.
[**Rubble** comes from an old French word.]

**ruby** *noun* **rubies**
A **ruby** is a dark red precious stone.
[**Ruby** comes from Latin *rubeus* 'red'.]

**rudder** *noun* **rudders**
A **rudder** is a flat piece of hinged wood or metal that is attached to the back of a boat or plane and is used for steering.
[**Rudder** comes from Old English.]

**rude** *adjective* **ruder, rudest** (th)
Someone or something that is **rude** is insulting or offensive and not polite.
[**Rude** comes from Latin *rudis* 'rough or raw'.]

**rug** *noun* **rugs**
1 A **rug** is a small carpet.
2 A **rug** is a blanket used for sitting on, or to keep you warm when you are on a journey.
[**Rug** probably comes from a Scandinavian language.]

**rugby** *noun*
**Rugby** is a game played with an oval ball, in which the players are allowed to carry and throw the ball as well as kick it. [**Rugby** is named after *Rugby School*, in the town of Rugby, England, where the game was first played.]

**ruin** *noun* **ruins**
A **ruin** is a building that has been destroyed or is falling down because it is very old. [**Ruin** comes from Latin via French.]

**ruin** *verb* **ruins, ruining, ruined** (th)
To **ruin** something means to spoil it so it cannot be used.

**rule** *noun* **rules**
A **rule** is a law or something that everyone should obey. [**Rule** comes via French from the same Latin word as **regular** and **rail**).]

**rule** *verb* **rules, ruling, ruled**
1 To **rule** means to be in charge of everyone in a country.
2 To **rule** means to draw a straight line with a ruler.

**ruler** *noun* **rulers**
1 A **ruler** is someone who is in charge of a country.
2 A **ruler** is a strip of wood, plastic or metal with straight edges for measuring and for drawing straight lines.

**rum** *noun*
**Rum** is a strong alcoholic drink made from sugar cane. [No one knows where the word **rum** comes from.]

**rumble** *verb* **rumbles, rumbling, rumbles**
To **rumble** means to make a deep long sound like thunder. [**Rumble** probably comes from an old Dutch word.]

**rummage** *verb* **rummages, rummaging, rummaged**
To **rummage** means to look for something by moving things around and making a mess: *I rummaged in my drawers for a clean pair of socks.* [**Rummage** comes via French from an old Dutch word.]

**rumour** *noun* **rumours**
A **rumour** is something that people are talking about that may or may not be true. [**Rumour** comes via French from Latin *rumor* 'noise'.]

**run** *verb* **runs, running, ran, run** (th)
1 To **run** means to move forward using fast steps: *I ran for the bus.*
2 If a machine is **running**, it is working: *He left the engine running.*
3 If you **run** something, you are in charge of it: *She runs her own business.*
4 If water **runs**, it flows or you make it flow: *She ran a bath.*
5 If colours **run**, they spread into each other. [**Run** comes from Old English.]

**rung**[1] *noun* **rungs**
A **rung** is one of the bars used as steps on a ladder. [**Rung**[1] comes from Old English.]

**rung**[2] *verb*
**Rung**[2] is the past participle of **ring**.

**runner** *noun* **runners**
A **runner** is someone who runs, especially in a race.

**runny** *adjective* **runnier, runniest**
Something that is **runny** flows like a liquid: *This sauce is too runny.*

**runt** *noun* **runts**
A **runt** is an animal that is the smallest in a group. [No one knows where **runt** comes from.]

**runway** *noun* **runways**
A **runway** is the strip of land used by planes when taking off or landing.

**rupture** *verb* **ruptures, rupturing, ruptured** (th)
To **rupture** means to burst or break open. [**Rupture** comes from Latin via French.]

**rural** *adjective*
**Rural** means to do with the countryside or living in the country. [**Rural** comes from Latin via French.]

**rush**[1] *noun* **rushes**
1 A **rush** is a sudden movement forward: *There was a rush to get to the front.*
2 A **rush** is when you are in a hurry: *I'm in a rush.* [**Rush**[1] comes from an old French word.]

**rush¹** *verb* **rushes, rushing, rushed** (th)
To **rush** means to move very quickly.

**rush²** *noun* **rushes**
A **rush** is a tall, slender plant that grows in or near water.
[**Rush²** comes from Old English.]

**rust** *noun*
**Rust** is the rough, reddish-brown substance that forms on iron after it gets wet. [**Rust** comes from Old English.]

**rustle** *verb* **rustles, rustling, rustled**
To **rustle** means to make a gentle sound like the wind blowing through dry leaves.
[The word **rustle** is an imitation of the sound.]

**rusty** *adjective* **rustier, rustiest**
If metal is **rusty**, it has rust on it.

**rut** *noun* **ruts**
**1** A **rut** is a deep track in the ground made by a wheel.
**2** If you are **in a rut**, you are bored because you are doing the same things all the time.
[**Rut** probably comes from the same French word as **route**.]

**ruthless** *adjective* (th)
A person who is **ruthless** is cruel and tries to get what s/he wants without caring about other people.
[**Ruthless** comes from an old word *ruth* 'pity'.]

**rye** *noun*
**Rye** is a type of grain that is grown in cool climates and is used to make flour and whisky.
[**Rye** comes from Old English.]

---

# Dictionary Fun

**Etymology**
Which word is taken from the following phrase: *radio detection and ranging*? Clue: look at the first letters in each word.

**What do these idioms mean?**
1. To read between the lines
2. To keep a tight rein on something or someone
3. As right as rain

**New words**
1. Clue: This is the memory that a computer has.
2. Clue: A phrase that sounds like a rodent but is actually a stressful way of living.

**Complete the proverbs**
1. A r_____ stone gathers no moss.
2. R_____ was not built in a day.

**Riddle**
I may be quiet or noisy
But never hear a sound
I'll disappear into the sea
Never to be found
What am I?

**Did you know?**
◆ The word **robot** comes from the Czech word *robota*, which means 'forced labour'.
◆ One of the most popular times to make a **resolution** is at the beginning of the year.

a b c d e f g h i j k l m

# Ss

**Sabbath** *noun*
The **Sabbath** is a day of the week that is kept for rest and worship in some religions.
[**Sabbath** comes from Hebrew *shabat* 'rest'. Hebrew is the language spoken in Israel.]

**saccharin** *noun*
**Saccharin** is a chemical that is very sweet and is used in food and drinks instead of sugar.
[**Saccharin** comes from Greek *saccharon* 'sugar'.]

**sachet** *noun* **sachets**
A **sachet** is a small closed packet or envelope containing something such as sugar or shampoo.
[**Sachet** comes from French *sachet* 'little bag'.]

**sack** *noun* **sacks**
A **sack** is a large bag made of strong material.
[**Sack** comes from Greek via Old English and Latin.]

**sack** *verb* **sacks, sacking, sacked** (th)
To **sack** someone means to tell that person that s/he no longer has a job and must leave.

**sacred** *adjective* (th)
Something that is holy or used in religious worship is **sacred**.
[**Sacred** comes via French from Latin *sacer* 'holy'.]

**sacrifice** *verb* **sacrifices, sacrificing, sacrificed**
**1** To **sacrifice** an animal means to kill it as an offering to God in a religious ceremony: *a sacrificed goat.*
**2** To **sacrifice** something that you value very much means to give it up for an important reason: *He sacrificed his career to look after his sick mother.*
[**Sacrifice** comes via French from the same Latin word as **sacred**.]

**sacrifice** *noun* **sacrifices**
**1** A **sacrifice** is when you offer something to a god, or when you give up something for an important reason: *My parents made a lot of sacrifices to send me to university.*

**2** A **sacrifice** is the animal or thing that you sacrifice.

**sad** *adjective* **sadder, saddest** (th)
Someone who is **sad** is unhappy.
[**Sad** comes from Old English.]

**saddle** *noun* **saddles**
A **saddle** is a seat for the rider of a bicycle or a horse.
[**Saddle** comes from Old English.]

**safari** *noun* **safaris**
A **safari** is an expedition to look at or hunt wild animals such as lions.
[**Safari** comes from Arabic *safar* 'a journey'.]

**safe**[1] *noun* **safes**
A **safe** is a strong box or cupboard in which you can lock away money and valuable things. [**Safe**[1] comes from **save**.]

**safe**[2] *adjective* **safer, safest** (th)
**1** Someone who is **safe** is free from danger.
**2** Something that is **safe** is not dangerous.
**safely** *adverb*.
[**Safe**[2] comes via French from the same Latin word as **save**.]

**safety** *noun*
**Safety** is when there is no danger: *A good car is designed for safety.*
[**Safety** comes via French from the same Latin word as **save**.]

**sag** *verb* **sags, sagging, sagged**
To **sag** means to hang or sink down in the middle.
[**Sag** probably comes from an old German or Dutch word.]

**saga** *noun* **sagas**
A **saga** is a very long story.
[**Saga** comes from Old Norse.]

**sage** *noun*
**Sage** is a herb with greyish-green leaves that is used in cooking.
[**Sage** comes via French from Latin *salvia* 'healing plant'.]

**said** *verb*
**Said** is the past tense and past participle of **say**.

**sail** *noun* **sails**
A **sail** is a large piece of material fixed to the mast of a boat. When the wind blows on the **sail**, it moves the boat along.

[**Sail** comes from Old English.]

**sail** *verb* **sails, sailing, sailed**
To **sail** means to travel in a boat.

**sailor** *noun* **sailors**
A **sailor** is one of a ship's crew.

**saint** *noun* **saints**
**Saint** is a title given to a very holy person in the Christian Church: *Saint Francis of Assisi.*
[**Saint** comes via French from Latin *sanctus* 'dedicated to God'.]

**sake** *noun*
If you do something for the **sake** of someone else, you do it to help, protect or please that person.
[**Sake** comes from Old English.]

**salad** *noun* **salads**
A **salad** is a mixture of raw or cold vegetables.
[**Salad** comes from Latin via French.]

**salamander** *noun* **salamanders**
A **salamander** is an amphibian that looks like a lizard.
[**Salamander** comes from Greek via French and Latin.]

**salary** *noun* **salaries**
A **salary** is an amount of money that someone receives regularly for work s/he does.
[**Salary** comes via French from Latin *salarium*, the money given to a Roman soldier to buy salt.]

**sale** *noun* **sales**
1 A **sale** is the selling of something: *laws to control the sale of alcohol.*
2 A **sale** is a time when things in a shop are sold at lower prices.
[**Sale** comes from Old Norse.]

**saline** *adjective*
Water or a liquid that is **saline** contains salt. [**Saline** comes from Latin *sal* 'salt'.]

**saliva** *noun*
**Saliva** is the liquid in your mouth that helps you chew food and swallow.
[**Saliva** comes from Latin.]

**salmon** *noun* **salmon**
A **salmon** is a large fish with a silver skin and pink flesh that is born in a river and swims out to the sea to live.
[**Salmon** comes from Latin via French.]

**salt** *noun* **salts**
1 **Salt** is a white powder used to flavour or preserve food.
2 A **salt** is a chemical compound that is formed from an acid and an alkali.
[**Salt** comes from Old English.]

**salute** *verb* **salutes, saluting, saluted**
To **salute** means to raise your hand to your forehead as a sign of respect in the army, navy, etc.
[**Salute** comes from Latin.]

**same** *adjective* (th)
1 When two or more things are like each other in every way, they are the **same**.
2 If someone or something has not changed, s/he or it is the **same**.
[**Same** comes from Old Norse.]

**sample** *noun* **samples** (th)
A **sample** is a small amount of something that you take in order to find out what the rest is like.
[**Sample** comes via French from Latin *exemplum* 'something taken out' (ancestor of **example**).]

**sample** *verb* **samples, sampling, sampled**
To **sample** something means to try a small amount of it.

**sanctuary** *noun* **sanctuaries** (th)
1 A **sanctuary** is a place where someone can escape to or feel safe.
2 A **sanctuary** is a holy place.
3 A **sanctuary** is a place where wild animals and birds are protected.
[**Sanctuary** comes via French from the same Latin word as **saint**.]

**sand** *noun*
**Sand** is the tiny grains of worn-down rock found on beaches and in deserts.
[**Sand** comes from Old English.]

**sandal** *noun* **sandals**
A **sandal** is a kind of open shoe with straps that go round and over the foot.
[**Sandal** comes via Latin from Greek *sandalion* 'little wooden shoe'.]

**sandpaper** *noun*
**Sandpaper** is paper with grains of sand glued to it that is used to make wood smooth.

**sandwich** *noun* **sandwiches**
A **sandwich** is two slices of bread and

butter with another food between them.
[The **sandwich** was invented in the
eighteenth century by the Earl of
Sandwich so that he could eat while
playing cards.]

**sandy** *adjective* **sandier, sandiest**
1 A **sandy** place is covered with sand.
2 Something that contains sand is **sandy**.

**sane** *adjective* **saner, sanest** (th)
Someone who is **sane** has a healthy mind
and is not crazy.
[**Sane** comes from Latin *sanus* 'healthy'.]

**sang** *verb*
Sang is the past tense of **sing**.

**sanity** *noun*
Sanity is having a healthy mind and not
being crazy.
[**Sanity** comes from the same Latin word
as **sane**.]

**sank** *verb*
Sank is the past tense of **sink**.

**sap** *noun*
Sap is the liquid inside a plant.
[**Sap** comes from Old English.]

**sapling** *noun* **saplings**
A **sapling** is a young tree.
[**Sapling** comes from **sap**.]

**sapphire** *noun* **sapphires**
A **sapphire** is a blue precious stone.
[**Sapphire** comes from Greek via French
and Latin.]

**sarcasm** *noun*
Sarcasm is when you say the opposite of
what you mean in order to be funny or to
make fun of someone.
[**Sarcasm** comes from Greek via French
and Latin.]

**sarcastic** *adjective*
If you are **sarcastic**, you say the opposite
of what you mean in order to be funny or
to make fun of someone.

**sardine** *noun* **sardines**
A **sardine** is a small fish. **Sardines** are
often cooked and sold in tins.
[**Sardine** comes from Greek via Latin or
French.]

**sari** *noun* **saris** *Also* **saree**
A **sari** is a piece of clothing worn
especially by Indian women. It is made of
a long piece of cloth that is folded round
the body to form a skirt with the other
end covering the shoulders.
[**Sari** comes from Hindi (a language
spoken in India).]

**sarong** *noun* **sarongs**
A **sarong** is a long piece of cloth wrapped
round the body like a skirt that is worn
especially by men and women in
Malaysia and other south-east Asian
countries.
[**Sarong** comes from Malay (a language
spoken in Malaysia).]

**sat** *verb*
Sat is the past tense and past participle of
**sit**.

**satellite** *noun* **satellites**
A **satellite** is something that moves in
space round the earth or another planet.
[**Satellite** comes via French from Latin
*satelles* 'attendant'.]

**satellite dish** *noun* **satellite dishes**
A **satellite dish** is a large metal dish that
is fixed to a roof or outside wall and can
receive television pictures from a satellite
in space.

**satellite television** *noun*
Satellite television is television
programmes that are transmitted via a
satellite above the earth and received by a
satellite dish.

**satin** *noun*
Satin is a type of material, often made
from silk, that is smooth and shiny on one
side.
[**Satin** comes from Arabic via French.]

**satire** *noun* **satires**
Satire is a type of humour, or a humorous
play or poem, that mocks ideas or people.
[**Satire** comes from Latin.]

**satisfaction** *noun* (th)
Satisfaction is a feeling of being pleased
with a situation or with something you
have done.
[**Satisfaction** comes via French from the
same Latin word as **satisfy**.]

**satisfactory** *adjective* (th)
Something that is **satisfactory** is of a good
enough standard.
[**Satisfactory** comes via French from the
same Latin word as **satisfy**.]

**satisfy** *verb* **satisfies, satisfying, satisfied** (th)
1 To **satisfy** means to please someone by giving him/her what s/he needs or wants.
2 To **satisfy** someone means to convince him/her that something is true: *I wasn't satisfied by his explanation.*
[**Satisfy** comes via French from Latin *satis* 'enough' or 'full'.]

**saturate** *verb* **saturates, saturating, saturated** (th)
To **saturate** something means to soak it thoroughly with a liquid.
[**Saturate** comes from the same Latin word as **satisfy**.]

**sauce** *noun* **sauces**
A **sauce** is a thick, tasty liquid added to or poured over food.
[**Sauce** comes via French from Latin *salsus* 'salty'.]

**saucepan** *noun* **saucepans**
A **saucepan** is a cooking pot with a handle.

**saucer** *noun* **saucers**
A **saucer** is a kind of small plate used to put a cup on.
[**Saucer** comes from an old French word.]

**sauna** *noun* **saunas**
A **sauna** is a room filled with dry heat that people sit in to sweat and clean their skin.
[**Sauna** comes from Finnish (the language spoken in Finland).]

**sausage** *noun* **sausages**
A **sausage** is a tube of thin skin filled with minced meat and other things such as cereal, herbs and spices.
[**Sausage** comes via French from the same Latin word as **sauce**.]

**savage** *adjective* (th)
A **savage** animal or person is wild and cruel.
[**Savage** comes via French from Latin *silvaticus* 'wild, living in the woods'.]

**savage** *verb* **savages, savaging, savaged** (th)
To **savage** means to attack a person or animal in a wild and fierce way: *The zoo keeper was savaged by a tiger.*

**save** *verb* **saves, saving, saved** (th)
1 To **save** means to rescue someone or something from danger: *A lifeguard saved the girl from drowning.*
2 To **save** means to keep something for use later: *How much money have you saved?*
3 To **save** something such as energy, time or space means not to waste it or use too much of it.
4 To **save** a ball in a game such as football means to stop it going into the goal.
[**Save** comes via French from Latin *salvus* 'safe' (ancestor of **safe²**).]

**savoury** *adjective*
Food that is **savoury** has a salty rather than a sweet taste.
[**Savoury** comes from Latin via French.]

**saw¹** *noun* **saws**
A **saw** is a tool with teeth along a metal blade that is used for cutting wood.
[**Saw** comes from Old English.]

**saw¹** *verb* **saws, sawing, sawed** or **sawn**
To **saw** something means to cut it using a saw.

**saw²** *verb*
**Saw²** is the past tense of **see**.

**sawdust** *noun*
**Sawdust** is the fine powder that is produced when you cut wood.

**saxophone** *noun* **saxophones**
A **saxophone** is a musical instrument made of brass that you blow into. It is often played in jazz and dance music.
[The **saxophone** was named after Adolphe *Sax*, a Belgian instrument maker, who invented it.]

**say** *verb* **says, saying, said** (th)
1 To **say** means to speak.
2 To **say** means to give information in words, pictures or numbers: *The sign says, 'No Smoking'.*
[**Say** comes from Old English.]

**saying** *noun* **sayings**
A **saying** is something that people often say as a piece of advice.

**scab** *noun* **scabs**
A **scab** is the hard layer that forms over a wound while it is healing.
[**Scab** comes from Old Norse.]

a b c d e f g h i j k l m

**scaffolding** *noun*
Scaffolding is the structure of metal poles and planks of wood that workers stand on while they are building or painting. [**Scaffolding** comes from an old French word.]

**scald** *verb* **scalds, scalding, scalded**
To **scald** means to burn your skin with hot liquid or steam. [**Scald** comes from Latin via French.]

**scale¹** *noun* **scales**
1 A **scale** is the set of marks used for measuring, found on instruments such as a ruler or thermometer.
2 A **scale** is a set of musical notes going up or down in order. [**Scale¹** comes from Old Norse.]

**scale²** *noun* **scales**
A **scale** is a small, hard circle of skin. The bodies of many kinds of fish and some reptiles are covered with **scales**. [**Scale²** comes from an old French word.]

**scales³** *noun*
Scales are an instrument for weighing things. [**Scales³** comes from **scale¹**.]

**scalp** *noun* **scalps**
Your **scalp** is the skin on the top of your head under your hair. [**Scalp** probably comes from a Scandinavian language.]

**scalpel** *noun* **scalpels**
A **scalpel** is a small sharp knife used by a surgeon during a medical operation. [**Scalpel** comes from Latin *scalpere* 'to scratch'.]

**scan** *verb* **scans, scanning, scanned** (th)
1 To **scan** means to look over an area carefully because you are looking for something.
2 To **scan** means to read something quickly because you are looking for information.
3 If a machine **scans** an object, it moves a beam of light over it to produce a picture of it. [**Scan** comes from Latin.]

**scanner** *noun* **scanners**
A scanner is a machine that moves a beam of light over something to produce a picture of it, which can then be viewed on a computer screen.

**scapegoat** *noun* **scapegoats**
A **scapegoat** is someone who gets the blame for something that another person has done. [**Scapegoat** comes from an old word *scape* 'to escape'. In ancient Israel a priest used to lay the blame for all the bad things that people had done on a goat, which was then allowed to escape into the desert.]

**scar** *noun* **scars**
A **scar** is the mark left on the skin after a cut has healed. [**Scar** comes from Greek via French and Latin.]

**scarce** *adjective* **scarcer, scarcest** (th)
If something is **scarce**, there is very little of it available. [**Scarce** comes from an old French word.]

**scare** *verb* **scares, scaring, scared** (th)
To **scare** means to frighten. [**Scare** comes from Old Norse.]

**scarecrow** *noun* **scarecrows**
A **scarecrow** is a model of a person that a farmer puts in a field to frighten birds away from the crops.

**scarf** *noun* **scarves**
A **scarf** is a strip of material that you wear round your neck or head. [**Scarf** comes from Old Norse via French.]

**scatter** *verb* **scatters, scattering, scattered** (th)
1 To **scatter** things means to throw them in different directions or across a wide area.
2 If people **scatter**, they run off in different directions. [**Scatter** probably comes from **shatter**.]

**scene** *noun* **scenes** (th)
1 A **scene** is the place where something has happened.
2 A **scene** is one of the parts of a play or film. [**Scene** comes via Latin from Greek *skene* 'stage'.]

**scenery** *noun* **sceneries**
1 Scenery is what is in the countryside such as trees, hills, mountains and rivers.
2 Scenery is the painted backgrounds that are on stage in a play, ballet or opera. [**Scenery** comes via Italian from the same Latin word as **scene**.]

**scenic** *adjective*
A place that has beautiful countryside around it is **scenic**.
[**Scenic** comes via Latin from the same Greek word as **scene**.]

**scent** *noun* **scents** (th)
1 A **scent** is a pleasant smell: *the scent of lavender.*
2 A **scent** is a liquid with a very pleasant smell that you can put on your skin.
3 A **scent** is an animal's smell: *The dog followed the fox's scent.*
[**Scent** comes from Latin via French.]

**schedule** *noun* **schedules** (th)
A **schedule** is a timetable or programme of things that are going to happen.
[**Schedule** comes from Greek via French and Latin.]

**scheme** *noun* **schemes** (th)
A **scheme** is a plan for doing something.
[**Scheme** comes from Greek via Latin.]

**scholarship** *noun* **scholarships**
A **scholarship** is a prize of money that is given to a student to pay for his/her place at a school or college.
[**Scholarship** comes via Old English from the same Latin word as **school**[1].]

**school**[1] *noun* **schools**
A **school** is a building where children go to learn.
[**School**[1] comes from Greek via Latin.]

**school**[2] *noun* **schools**
A **school** is a group of fish, whales, porpoises or dolphins swimming together.
[**School**[2] comes from old Dutch *schole* 'troop' (ancestor of **shoal**).]

**science** *noun* **sciences**
**Science** is the study of the natural world and the way it works through observing and experimenting.
[**Science** comes from Latin via French.]

**science fiction** *noun*
**Science fiction** is stories that show imaginary life in the future or on other planets.

**scientific** *adjective*
Something that is **scientific** is connected with science or uses the methods of science.
[**Scientific** comes from the same French

word as **science**.]

**scientist** *noun* **scientists**
A **scientist** is someone who studies science.
[**Scientist** comes from **science**.]

**scissors** *plural noun*
**Scissors** are a pair of sharp blades pivoted so that they can be brought together and used for cutting things.
[**Scissors** comes via French from the same Latin word as **chisel**.]

**scoff** *verb* **scoffs, scoffing, scoffed** (th)
To **scoff** means to laugh at someone or at an idea and say s/he or it is stupid.
[**Scoff** probably comes from a Scandinavian language.]

**scoop** *noun* **scoops**
1 A **scoop** is a deep round spoon.
2 A **scoop** of something is a deep spoonful of it.
3 A **scoop** in a newspaper is a story that no other paper has got.
[**Scoop** comes from an old German or Dutch word.]

**scoop** *verb* **scoops, scooping, scooped**
To **scoop** means to lift or pick up something with a scoop or a curved hand.

**scooter** *noun* **scooters**
1 A **scooter** is a child's toy with two wheels joined by a board.
2 A **scooter** is a small motorcycle.
[No one knows where **scooter** comes from.]

**scorch** *verb* **scorches, scorching, scorched** (th)
To **scorch** something means to burn the surface of it.
[No one knows where **scorch** comes from.]

**score** *noun* **scores**
1 A **score** is the number of points gained by each side in a game.
2 A **score** is a piece of music in its written form. [**Score** comes from Old Norse.]

**score** *verb* **scores, scoring, scored** (th)
1 To **score** means to get a point or goal in a game or competition.
2 To **score** means to cut a line along a surface.

**scorn** *noun* (th)
**Scorn** is a strong feeling that someone is stupid or worthless.
[**Scorn** comes from an old French word.]

**scorpion** *noun* **scorpions**
A **scorpion** is a creature of the spider family that lives in hot countries. It has a long body, claws and a poisonous sting in its tail.
[**Scorpion** comes from Greek via French and Latin.]

**scramble** *verb* **scrambles, scrambling, scrambled** (th)
To **scramble** means to climb awkwardly using your hands and feet.
[No one knows where **scramble** comes from.]

**scrap** *noun* **scraps** (th)
1 A **scrap** is a small piece of something.
2 **Scrap** is rubbish: *scrap metal*.
[**Scrap** comes from Old Norse.]

**scrape** *verb* **scrapes, scraping, scraped**
To **scrape** means to rub against something rough or hard.
[**Scrape** comes from Old English.]

**scratch** *noun* **scratches** (th)
A **scratch** is a mark made on a surface by something sharp.
[No one knows where **scratch** comes from.]

**scratch** *verb* **scratches, scratching, scratched** (th)
1 To **scratch** means to rub a part of your body with your nails.
2 To **scratch** means to mark or damage the surface of something using a sharp object.

**scrawl** *verb* **scrawls, scrawling, scrawled**
To **scrawl** means to write something very quickly and untidily.
[No one knows where **scrawl** comes from.]

**scream** *noun* **screams** (th)
A **scream** is a loud cry that you make if you are frightened or in pain.
[**Scream** may come from an old Dutch word.]

**scream** *verb* **screams, screaming, screamed** (th)
To **scream** means to make a loud cry because you are frightened or in pain.

**screech** *verb* **screeches, screeching, screeched**
To **screech** means to make an unpleasant high-pitched sound.
[The word **screech** is an imitation of the sound.]

**screen** *noun* **screens**
1 A **screen** is the front of a television or computer that you see pictures on.
2 A **screen** is the flat surface that films are shown on.
3 A **screen** is a flat object that is used to hide or protect people and things.
[**Screen** comes from an old French word.]

**screen** *verb* **screens, screening, screened** (th)
1 To **screen** something means to hide it with a screen or something like a screen: *Tall bushes screened the house from the road.*
2 To **screen** someone means to examine him or her carefully, for example to see if s/he has a certain disease or is suitable for a particular job.
3 To **screen** a film or television programme means to show it.

**screw** *noun* **screws**
A **screw** is a kind of nail with grooves that turns easily, used to fasten pieces of wood or metal together.
[**Screw** comes from an old French word.]

**screw** *verb* **screws, screwing, screwed**
1 To **screw** means to fasten something with a screw.
2 To **screw** means to turn or twist something: *Screw the lid on tightly.*

**screwdriver** *noun* **screwdrivers**
A **screwdriver** is a tool with a flat end for turning screws.

**scribble** *verb* **scribbles, scribbling, scribbled**
To **scribble** means to write or draw untidily and quickly.
[**Scribble** comes from Latin *scribere* 'to write'.]

**script** *noun* **scripts**
1 A **script** is the alphabet that a language uses: *the Arabic script*.
2 A **script** is the words of a play or film written down.
[**Script** comes via French from Latin *scriptum* 'something written'.]

**scroll** *noun* **scrolls**
A **scroll** is a long roll of paper with writing on it.
[**Scroll** comes from an old French word.]

**scrub** *verb* **scrubs, scrubbing, scrubbed**
To **scrub** means to rub something hard with a wet brush to clean it.
[**Scrub** probably comes from an old German or Dutch word.]

**scruffy** *adjective* **scruffier, scruffiest** (th)
Someone or something that is **scruffy** is untidy and quite dirty.
[**Scruffy** comes from Old English.]

**scuba diving** *noun*
**Scuba diving** is the sport of diving and swimming underwater while breathing through a tube that is connected to a tank of air on your back.
[**Scuba** stands for *self-contained underwater breathing apparatus*.]

**sculptor** *noun* **sculptors**
A **sculptor** is a person who makes statues or works of art out of stone, wood or metal.
[**Sculptor** comes from the same Latin word as **sculpture**.]

**sculpture** *noun* **sculptures**
A **sculpture** is a statue or work of art made from stone, wood, or metal.
[**Sculpture** comes from Latin *sculpere* 'to carve out'.]

**scum** *noun*
**Scum** is a dirty layer that forms on the top of a liquid.
[**Scum** comes from an old German or Dutch word.]

**scythe** *noun* **scythes**
A **scythe** is an old-fashioned tool with a large curved blade and a long handle, used for cutting grass or crops.
[**Scythe** comes from Old English.]

**sea** *noun* **seas**
A **sea** is a very large area of salt water.
[**Sea** comes from Old English.]

**seafaring** *adjective*
Someone or something that is **seafaring** travels on the sea.

**seagull** *noun* **seagulls**
**Seagull** is another word for **gull**.

**seahorse** *noun* **seahorses**
A **seahorse** is a small creature that lives in the sea. It has a head that looks like a horse's head and a long curling tail, and it swims upright.

**seal**[1] *noun* **seals**
A **seal** is a large furry animal that lives in the sea and on land.
[**Seal**[1] comes from Old English.]

**seal**[2] *verb* **seals, sealing, sealed**
To **seal** means to close something by sticking it up.
[**Seal**[2] comes via French from the same Latin word as **sign**.]

**sea level** *noun*
The **sea level** is the average height of the surface of the sea that is used for measuring other things: *The town is 500 metres above sea level.*

**sea lion** *noun* **sea lions**
A **sea lion** is a mammal like a large seal that lives in the ocean.

**seam** *noun* **seams**
A **seam** is a line of stitches that joins two pieces of material.
[**Seam** comes from Old English.]

**search** *verb* **searches, searching, searched** (th)
To **search** means to look for something very carefully.
[**Search** comes from Latin via French.]

**sea-shanty** *noun* **sea-shanties**
A **sea-shanty** is a song that sailors used to sing while they worked.
[**Shanty** probably comes from French *chanter* 'to sing'.]

**seashore** *noun*
The **seashore** is the land next to the sea.

**seasick** *adjective*
If you feel **seasick**, you feel ill because of the movement of a boat or ship.

**seaside** *noun*
The **seaside** is the coast or a town next to the sea where you can go for a holiday.

**season** *noun* **seasons**
**1** A **season** is one of the parts of the year, marked out by the weather. Most parts of the world have four **seasons**, spring, summer, autumn and winter. Some parts have two, a wet and a dry **season**.

a b c d e f g h i j k l m

**2** A **season** is a part of the year when something happens or something is available: *the football season.*
[**Season** comes from Latin via French.]

**seasoning** *noun*
Seasoning is salt, pepper, spice or herbs that you add to food to flavour it.
[**Seasoning** comes from **season**.]

**seat** *noun* **seats**
A **seat** is something to sit on.
[**Seat** comes from Old Norse.]

**seatbelt** *noun* **seatbelts**
A **seatbelt** is a strong belt that is fastened to a seat in a vehicle that you wear to keep you safe while travelling.

**seaweed** *noun*
Seaweed is a plant that grows in the sea. There are many different kinds of seaweed.

**secateurs** *plural noun*
Secateurs are strong scissors for cutting plants.
[**Secateurs** comes from French *secateur* 'cutter'.]

**secluded** *adjective* (th)
Somewhere that is quiet and away from other people and places is **secluded**.
[**Secluded** comes from Latin *secludere* 'to shut away'.]

**second** *noun* **seconds**
A **second** is a small unit of time. There are 60 **seconds** in a minute.
[A **second** is so called because an hour is divided into minutes, and then divided a second time into **seconds**.]

**second-hand** *adjective* (th)
Things that are **second-hand** have belonged to someone else first.

**second person** *noun*
To find **second person**, look under **person**.

**secret** *noun* **secrets**
A **secret** is something that you must not tell or show to anyone else.
[**Secret** comes via French from Latin *secretus* 'moved or kept apart'.]

**secret** *adjective*
If something is **secret**, you do not want anyone else to know about it.

**secretary** *noun* **secretaries**
A **secretary** is someone whose job is to write letters, answer the telephone, look after papers and make arrangements for other people.
[**Secretary** comes from Latin *secretarius* 'someone trusted to know your secrets'.]

**secrete** *verb* **secretes, secreting, secreted**
If an animal or plant **secretes** a substance or liquid, it produces it.
[**Secrete** comes from the same Latin word as **secret**.]

**section** *noun* **sections**
A **section** is one of the parts that something has been divided into.
[**Section** comes from Latin *secare* 'to cut'.]

**sector** *noun* **sectors**
**1** A **sector** is a part of a circle made by drawing two straight lines from the centre to the edge.
**2** A **sector** is one of the areas of activity that business is divided into: *the engineering sector.*
[**Sector** comes from the same Latin word as **section**.]

**secular** *adjective*
Something that is **secular** is not connected with or controlled by any religion.
[**Secular** comes from Latin via French.]

**secure** *adjective* **securer, securest** (th)
**1** If something is **secure**, it is safe or firmly fixed: *Make sure the gate is secure before you leave.*
**2** If a person is **secure**, s/he feels safe and loved.
**3** If a situation is **secure**, you can trust it because it is not likely to change: *a secure job.* [**Secure** comes from Latin.]

**security** *noun* (th)
**1** Security is a feeling of being safe.
**2** Security is action that makes sure that things and people are safe and protected.
[**Security** comes via French from the same Latin word as **secure**.]

**sedate** *adjective* (th)
A person or place that is **sedate** is calm or peaceful.
[**Sedate** comes from Latin *sedare* 'to settle'.]

**sedative** *noun* **sedatives**
A **sedative** is a drug that makes you calm

or sleepy.
[**Sedative** comes via French from the same Latin word as **sedate**.]

**sediment** *noun*
**Sediment** is a thick or solid substance that settles at the bottom of a liquid.
[**Sediment** comes from Latin *sedere* 'to sit'.]

**see** *verb* **sees, seeing, saw, seen** (th)
**1** To **see** means to use your eyes to recognise things.
**2** To **see** means to understand: *Do you see what I mean?*
[**See** comes from Old English.]

**seed** *noun* **seeds**
A **seed** is a small hard object, produced by a plant, that a new plant can grow from. [**Seed** comes from Old English.]

**seedling** *noun* **seedlings**
A **seedling** is a young plant that has been grown from a seed.

**seek** *verb* **seeks, seeking, sought** (th)
**1** To **seek** means to search or look for something.
**2** To **seek** help or advice means to try and get it: *You should seek medical attention immediately.*
[**Seek** comes from Old English.]

**seem** *verb* **seems, seeming, seemed** (th)
To **seem** means to appear to be something: *You seem tired; It seems like a complete waste of time to me.*
[**Seem** comes from Old Norse.]

**seen** *verb*
**Seen** is the past participle of **see**.

**seep** *verb* **seeps, seeping, seeped**
To **seep** means to ooze or trickle out slowly.
[**Seep** probably comes from Old English.]

**see-saw** *noun* **see-saws**
A **see-saw** is a piece of equipment for two children to play on, made of a plank balanced in the middle. A child sits on each end to make it move up and down.
[**See-saw** comes from an old song that people sawing wood used to sing to keep their rhythm, which was later used as a nursery rhyme and sung by children on a see-saw.]

**segment** *noun* **segments**
A **segment** is a part of something that naturally divides into pieces: *a segment of an orange.*
[**Segment** comes from the same Latin word as **section**.]

**seldom** *adverb* (th)
Something that happens **seldom** does not happen very often.
[**Seldom** comes from Old English.]

**select** *verb* **selects, selecting, selected** (th)
To **select** something means to choose it carefully. [**Select** comes from Latin.]

**self** *noun* **selves**
Your **self** is your real personality or nature: *She never lets you see her real self; He's much more like his old self.*
[**Self** comes from Old English.]

**self-centred** *adjective*
Someone who is **self-centred** only thinks about himself or herself.

**self-conscious** *adjective* (th)
If you are **self-conscious**, you are worried about what people are thinking about you.

**self-defence** *noun*
**Self-defence** is the ability to protect yourself if you are attacked.

**selfish** *adjective*
Someone who is **selfish** puts himself or herself first all the time.
[**Selfish** comes from **self**.]

**self-raising flour** *noun*
**Self-raising flour** is flour that contains baking powder to make bread and cakes rise.

**self-service** *adjective*
A **self-service** shop or garage is one where you take what you want and pay for it at a checkout.

**sell** *verb* **sells, selling, sold** (th)
To **sell** means to give something in exchange for money.
[**Sell** comes from Old English.]

**semicircle** *noun* **semicircles**
A **semicircle** is half a circle.
[**Semicircle** comes from Latin *semi* 'half' and **circle**.]

**a b c d e f g h i j k l m**

**semicolon** *noun* **semicolons**
A **semicolon** is a punctuation mark like this ;. It is used to show a pause between two parts of a sentence.
[**Semicolon** comes from Latin *semi* 'half' and **colon**.]

**semifinal** *noun* **semifinals**
A **semifinal** is a sports match or competition that is held to decide who will play in the final.
[**Semifinal** comes from Latin *semi* 'half' and **final**.]

**send** *verb* **sends, sending, sent**
**1** To **send** means to make someone or something go somewhere.
**2** To **send** means to make someone or something become something: *The noise sent him mad.*
**3** If you **send for** something or someone, you order them to come or be brought to you. [**Send** comes from Old English.]

**senior** *adjective*
A person who is **senior** to someone else is older or in a more important position.
[**Senior** comes from Latin *senior* 'older'.]

**senior citizen** *noun* **senior citizens**
A **senior citizen** is an elderly person who has retired from work.

**sensation** *noun* **sensations** (th)
**1** A **sensation** is a physical feeling: *a tingling sensation.*
**2** A **sensation** is something that makes everyone excited and interested: *The film caused a sensation.*
[**Sensation** comes from the same Latin word as **sense**.]

**sense** *noun* **senses**
**1** A **sense** is one of the five abilities of sight, hearing, smell, feeling and taste.
**2** A **sense** is the ability to feel and understand something: *a sense of humour.*
**3 Sense** is good judgement.
[**Sense** comes from Latin.]

**sense** *verb* **senses, sensing, sensed** (th)
To **sense** something means to be aware of it or to feel it: *I sensed that something was wrong.*

**senseless** *adjective* (th)
Something that is **senseless** has no meaning or purpose.

**sensible** *adjective* (th)
Someone who makes good decisions is **sensible**: *She was sensible to buy a warm coat for the winter.*
[**Sensible** comes via French from the same Latin word as **sense**.]

**sensitive** *adjective*
**1** Someone or something that is **sensitive** senses things easily or is easily affected by them: *She has sensitive fingers; A cat's eyes are very sensitive to light.*
**2** Someone who is **sensitive** thinks about how people feel and tries not to upset them.
**3** Someone who is **sensitive** is easily offended or upset. **sensitively** *adverb.*
[**Sensitive** comes via French from the same Latin word as **sense**.]

**sent** *verb*
**Sent** is the past tense and past participle of **send**.

**sentence** *noun* **sentences**
**1** A **sentence** is a group of words belonging together that begins with a capital letter and ends with a full stop, a question mark or an exclamation mark.
**2** A **sentence** is a punishment that a criminal is given in a court of law.
[**Sentence** comes from Latin via French.]

**sentence** *verb* **sentences, sentencing, sentenced**
To **sentence** someone means to give him or her a punishment in a court of law: *The judge sentenced him to six months in prison.*

**sentimental** *adjective*
Something that is **sentimental** shows, arouses, or appeals to tender emotions or feelings rather than reason: *My mother's bracelet isn't valuable – I keep it for sentimental reasons.*
[**Sentimental** comes via French from the same Latin word as **sense**.]

**sentry** *noun* **sentries**
A **sentry** is a soldier who keeps guard.
[No one knows where **sentry** comes from.]

**separate** *adjective* (th)
Things that are not joined together, not shared or not near each other are **separate**: *We slept in separate beds; Keep cooked meat and fresh meat separate.*
[**Separate** comes from Latin.]

**separate** *verb* **separates, separating, separated** (th)
1 To **separate** people or things means to divide them or keep them apart.
2 If a husband and wife **separate**, they stop living together but do not get a divorce.

**sequel** *noun* **sequels**
A **sequel** is a book or film that continues a story from an earlier book or film.
[**Sequel** comes via French from the same Latin word as **sequence**.]

**sequence** *noun* **sequences** (th)
A **sequence** is a series of things that follow in order.
[**Sequence** comes from Latin *sequi* 'to follow'.]

**serial** *noun* **serials**
A **serial** is a story on television, on radio or in a magazine that is told in several parts. [**Serial** comes from **series**.]

**series** *noun* **series** (th)
1 A **series** is a number of things that happen one after the other: *a series of mistakes*.
2 A television or radio **series** is a number of programmes that are linked together by the same characters or the same subject each week.
[**Series** comes from Latin *serere* 'to join up'.]

**serious** *adjective* (th)
1 Something that is not funny is **serious**.
2 A person who is **serious** is thoughtful and careful.
3 Something that is **serious** is very bad: *a serious illness*. [**Serious** comes from Latin.]

**sermon** *noun* **sermons**
A **sermon** is a religious talk often given by priests in religious services.
[**Sermon** comes via French from Latin *sermo* 'talk or conversation'.]

**servant** *noun* **servants**
A **servant** is someone who is paid to look after someone else or someone else's possessions. In the past many people had **servants**.
[**Servant** comes via French from the same Latin word as **serve**.]

**serve** *verb* **serves, serving, served**
1 To **serve** means to sell things to people in a shop.
2 To **serve** someone means to work for that person.
3 To **serve** means to give food to someone at a meal.
4 In the game of tennis, to **serve** means to throw the ball up in the air and hit it across the net to your opponent.
[**Serve** comes from Latin via French.]

**service** *noun* **services**
1 A **service** is an organisation that provides something for the public: *a bus service*.
2 **Service** is the help and attention you get in a shop or restaurant.
3 A **service** is the regular checks and repairs done to a car.
[**Service** comes via Old English from the same Latin word as **serve**.]

**set** *noun* **sets** (th)
A **set** is a group of things or people that belong together.
[**Set** comes from Old English.]

**set** *verb* **sets, setting, set** (th)
1 To **set** means to put or arrange something: *Please set the table for tea.*
2 To **set** means to give someone or yourself a piece of work to do: *The teacher sets homework every night.*
3 To **set** means to decide on a date or time to do something.
4 If a liquid **sets**, it becomes hard or solid.
5 When the sun **sets**, it goes down beyond the horizon and it becomes dark.

**several** *adjective, pronoun* (th)
**Several** is more than two but not very many: *They were gone for several days; Several of us went to look for them.*
[**Several** comes from Latin via French.]

**severe** *adjective* (th)
1 Something that is **severe** is very bad: *severe weather*.
2 A person who is **severe** is strict and hard. [**Severe** comes from Latin.]

**sew** *verb* **sews, sewing, sewed, sewn**
To **sew** means to join pieces of material together using a needle and thread.
[**Sew** comes from Old English.]

**sewage** *noun*
**Sewage** is solid waste and water that is carried out of houses in pipes.
[**Sewage** comes from **sewer**.]

a b c d e f g h i j k l m

**sewer** *noun* **sewers**
A **sewer** is an underground pipe that carries solid waste and water from houses.
[**Sewer** comes from an old French word.]

**sex** *noun* **sexes**
1 Your **sex** is whether you are male or female.
2 **Sex** is the physical activity between a man and a woman that can create a baby.
[**Sex** comes from Latin.]

**sexual intercourse** *noun*
**Sexual intercourse** is the physical activity between a man and a woman that can create a baby.

**shade** *noun* **shades**
1 **Shade** is a place with no direct sunlight on it.
2 A **shade** is the depth of a colour.
[**Shade** comes from Old English.]

**shade** *verb* **shades, shading, shaded**
1 To **shade** means to keep strong sunlight away from something.
2 To **shade** means to darken parts of a picture.

**shadow** *noun* **shadows**
A **shadow** is the dark shape that is made by something that blocks out the light.
[**Shadow** comes from the same Old English word as **shade**.]

**shake** *verb* **shakes, shaking, shook, shaken** (th)
1 To **shake** something means to move it very quickly up and down or from side to side.
2 To **shake** means to tremble or shiver: *He shook with fear.*
3 If something **shakes** you, it shocks or upsets you and makes you feel anxious or sad. [**Shake** comes from Old English.]

**shall** *verb* **should**
1 You use **shall** to say what you will do in the future, either by yourself or with someone else: *I shall go tomorrow; We shall arrive on Tuesday.*
2 You use **shall** to ask whether you should do something, or what you should do: *Shall I tell you a story?; Whatever shall we do?* [**Shall** comes from Old English.]

**shallow** *adjective* **shallower, shallowest**
Something that is not deep is **shallow**.

[No one knows where **shallow** comes from.]

**shame** *noun* (th)
1 **Shame** is a feeling of guilt or embarrassment because you have done something wrong or stupid.
2 If you say that something is **a shame**, you mean that it is a sad thing to have happened: *It's a shame that the children could not go on the trip.*
[**Shame** comes from Old English.]

**shampoo** *noun* **shampoos**
A **shampoo** is a liquid soap used for washing hair.
[**Shampoo** comes from Hindi (a language spoken in India).]

**shamrock** *noun* **shamrocks**
A **shamrock** is a small green plant with leaves that are divided into three. The **shamrock** is the national symbol of Ireland. [**Shamrock** comes from Irish.]

**shape** *noun* **shapes**
1 A **shape** is the outline of something.
2 The **shape** of something is its general condition: *The house is in good shape.*
[**Shape** comes from Old English.]

**share** *noun* **shares** (th)
1 A **share** of something is the amount of it that one person receives, or should receive.
2 A **share** is one of the equal parts that a company is divided into. You can buy **shares** in a company and benefit from any profit it makes.
[**Share** comes from Old English.]

**share** *verb* **shares, sharing, shared** (th)
1 To **share** something or **share** something **out** means to divide it into parts and give the parts to other people.
2 To **share** means to use something that someone else is also using.

**shark** *noun* **sharks**
A **shark** is a very large sea fish with sharp teeth.
[No one knows where **shark** comes from.]

**sharp** *adjective* **sharper, sharpest** (th)
1 Something that is **sharp** has a thin cutting edge or point.
2 Someone who is **sharp** is clever and quick to notice things.
3 Something that is **sharp** is not sweet

and tastes like vinegar or lemon juice.
4 Something that is **sharp** is quick or
sudden and short, not gradual: *a sharp
bend*.
[**Sharp** comes from Old English.]

**sharpen** *verb* **sharpens, sharpening,
sharpened**
To **sharpen** something means to make it
sharper. [**Sharpen** comes from **sharp**.]

**shatter** *verb* **shatters, shattering,
shattered**
To **shatter** means to break into a lot of
very small pieces.
[No one knows where **shatter** comes
from.]

**shave** *verb* **shaves, shaving, shaved**
To **shave** means to cut off the hair very
close to the skin with a razor.
[**Shave** comes from Old English.]

**she** *pronoun*
You use **she** when you are talking about a
female person or animal that has already
been mentioned and that is the subject of
a verb: *I saw Mary but she didn't see me.*
[**She** comes from Old English.]

**shears** *plural noun*
**Shears** are a tool like very large strong
scissors.
[**Shears** comes from Old English.]

**shed¹** *noun* **sheds**
A **shed** is a small hut used for keeping
things in or as a workshop.
[**Shed¹** comes from **shade**.]

**shed²** *verb* **sheds, shedding, shed**
To **shed** means to let something fall off.
[**Shed²** comes from Old English.]

**sheep** *noun* **sheep**
A **sheep** is a farm animal kept for its wool
and meat.
[**Sheep** comes from Old English.]

**sheer** *adjective* **sheerer, sheerest** (th)
1 Something that is **sheer** is very steep.
2 Material that is **sheer** is thin and nearly
see-through.
[**Sheer** comes from Old English.]

**sheet** *noun* **sheets**
1 A **sheet** is a large piece of cloth,
especially one that covers a bed.
2 A **sheet** is a flat thin piece of something
such as paper or glass.

[**Sheet** comes from Old English.]

**shelf** *noun* **shelves**
A **shelf** is a long piece of wood, glass or
metal fixed to a wall for putting things
on.
[**Shelf** comes from an old German word.]

**shell** *noun* **shells**
1 A **shell** is the hard outer covering of an
egg or nut, or of an animal such as a snail
or crab.
2 A **shell** is a large bullet which explodes
when it hits something.
[**Shell** comes from Old English.]

**shellfish** *noun* **shellfish**
A **shellfish** is a creature that lives in the
sea that has a shell. Many **shellfish**, such
as crabs, lobsters and mussels, can be
eaten.

**shelter** *noun* **shelters**
A **shelter** is a place which gives protection
from the weather or from danger.
[**Shelter** probably comes from Old
English.]

**shield** *noun* **shields**
A shield is a large piece of metal, leather
or plastic carried by soldiers or police for
protection.
[**Shield** comes from Old English.]

**shield** *verb* **shields, shielding, shielded**
(th)
To **shield** something or someone is to
protect them from something unpleasant
or damaging: *Umbrellas shield you from the
rain.*

**shift** *noun* **shifts**
A **shift** is the number of hours someone
works in one go: *a night shift.*
[**Shift** comes from Old English.]

**shift** *verb* **shifts, shifting, shifted**
To **shift** something is to move it from one
place to another.

**shimmer** *verb* **shimmers, shimmering,
shimmered** (th)
Something that **shimmers** shines with a
flickering light: *Sun shimmered on the
water.*
[**Shimmer** comes from Old English.]

**shin** *noun* **shins**
Your **shin** is the bone that runs down the
front of your leg from the knee to the

ankle. [**Shin** comes from Old English.]

**shine** *verb* **shines, shining, shone** (th)
To **shine** means to give out light or to point a light at something: *The sun is shining; The doctor shone a light in his eyes.* [**Shine** comes from Old English.]

**ship** *noun* **ships**
A **ship** is a large boat for carrying passengers or cargo.
[**Ship** comes from Old English.]

**shipwreck** *noun* **shipwrecks**
A **shipwreck** is the destruction of a ship at sea by rocks or a storm.

**shirt** *noun* **shirts**
A **shirt** is a piece of clothing made of light material and worn on the top half of the body. A **shirt** usually has buttons down the front, a collar and long or short sleeves. [**Shirt** comes from Old English.]

**shiver** *verb* **shivers, shivering, shivered** (th)
To **shiver** means to shake with cold or fear.
[**Shiver** may come from Old English.]

**shoal** *noun* **shoals**
A **shoal** of fish is a large group of fish that swim together.
[**Shoal** comes from the same old Dutch word as **school**[2].]

**shock** *noun* **shocks**
**1** A **shock** is the feeling of surprise that you get when something unpleasant happens suddenly: *His death was such a shock.*
**2** An electric **shock** is a dangerous amount of electricity that flows through your body, and which causes a lot of pain or can kill you.
**3** A **shock** is violent shaking caused by an explosion or an earthquake.
**4 Shock** is a medical condition which makes people very weak because they have had a very bad experience: *Four people were suffering from shock after the accident.*
[**Shock** comes from French.]

**shock** *verb* **shocks, shocking, shocked** (th)
If something **shocks** someone, it gives him or her a feeling of being surprised or upset by something unpleasant: *We were*

*shocked by her bad language.*

**shoe** *noun* **shoes**
A **shoe** is something you wear on your foot and which is usually made of leather or plastic: *a pair of shoes; What size shoes do you take?* [**Shoe** comes from Old English.]

**shone** *verb*
**Shone** is the past tense and past participle of **shine**.

**shook** *verb*
**Shook** is the past tense of **shake**.

**shoot** *noun* **shoots**
A **shoot** is the tip of a growing plant.
[**Shoot** comes from Old English.]

**shoot** *verb* **shoots, shooting, shot**
**1** To **shoot** means to fire a weapon such as a gun.
**2** To **shoot** a person or animal is to injure or kill them by firing a weapon such as a gun at them.
**3** To **shoot** means to move very quickly in one direction: *The racing cars shot past the flag; The price of houses has shot up.*
**4** To **shoot** a film or television programme is to record it using a camera: *The film was shot in Scotland.*

**shop** *noun* **shops**
A **shop** is a building where things are bought and sold.
[**Shop** comes from an old French word.]

**shop** *verb* **shops, shopping, shopped**
To **shop** means to buy things: *Many people shop at supermarkets.*

**shoplifter** *noun* **shoplifters**
A **shoplifter** is someone who steals things from shops.

**shore** *noun* **shores**
The **shore** is the land along the edge of a sea or lake.
[**Shore** comes from an old German or Dutch word.]

**short** *adjective* **shorter, shortest** (th)
**1** Something that is **short** is not long: *short hair; a short letter; a short walk.*
**2** Someone who is **short** is not as tall as most people.
**3** Something that is **short** does not last a long time: *a short holiday.* **shortness** *noun.*
[**Short** comes from Old English.]

**shortage** *noun* **shortages** (th)
If there is a **shortage** of something, there is not enough of it.
[**Shortage** comes from **short**.]

**shorthand** *noun*
**Shorthand** is a system for writing quickly in which signs or short forms of words are used instead of whole words.

**shortly** *adverb* (th)
**Shortly** means soon: *They'll be here shortly.*
[**Shortly** comes from Old English.]

**short-sighted** *adjective*
Someone who is **short-sighted** cannot see things clearly when they are far away.
**short-sightedness** *noun.*

**shot**[1] *noun* **shots**
1 A **shot** is the firing of a gun: *Shots were fired into the air.*
2 A **shot** is a photograph or a frame in a film: *We got some great shots of the mountains.*
3 A **shot** is an injection of a medicine or vaccine: *a shot of morphine.*
4 **Shot** is the metal pellets that are fired from a shotgun.
[**Shot** comes from Old English.]

**shot**[2] *verb*
**Shot** is the past tense and past participle of **shoot**.

**shotgun** *noun* **shotguns**
A **shotgun** is a long gun that fires metal pellets and is often used to shoot birds and small animals: *a double-barrelled shotgun.*

**should** *verb*
1 **Should** is the past tense of **shall**.
2 **Should** means ought to: *We should visit Paul more often; They should be home by now.*

**shoulder** *noun* **shoulders**
Your **shoulder** is the part of your body between the top of your arm and your neck: *shrug your shoulders.*
[**Shoulder** comes from Old English.]

**shoulder blade** *noun* **shoulder blades**
Your **shoulder blades** are the bones at the top of your back below your shoulders.

**shout** *verb* **shouts, shouting, shouted** (th)
To **shout** means to speak in a very loud voice.

[No one knows where **shout** comes from.]

**shove** *verb* **shoves, shoving, shoved** (th)
To **shove** means to push in a rough way: *He shoved his way through the crowd; She shoved the money into the bag.*
[**Shove** comes from Old English.]

**shovel** *noun* **shovels**
A **shovel** is a type of spade that is used for moving sand, snow or earth.
[**Shovel** comes from Old English.]

**show** *verb* **shows, showing, showed, shown** (th)
1 To **show** something is to let people see it.
2 To **show** someone something means to point out something or take someone to something.
3 To **show** someone something is to explain or demonstrate how to do it.
[**Show** comes from Old English.]

**show** *noun* **shows**
1 A **show** on television or at the theatre is a performance that entertains people.
2 A **show** is a collection of things for people to look at: *a dog show; a motor show.*

**shower** *noun* **showers**
1 A **shower** is when it rains or snows for a short time.
2 A **shower** is something in a bathroom that sprays water on you so you can wash yourself: *have a shower.*
[**Shower** comes from Old English.]

**showjumping** *noun*
**Showjumping** is a sport where horses and riders jump over fences. They lose points if they knock the fence down or if the horse will not jump it.
[**Showjumping** is jumping done at a horse show, rather than when racing or hunting.]

**showroom** *noun* **showrooms**
A **showroom** is a large area in a building where people can look at things for sale.

**shrank** *verb*
**Shrank** is the past tense of **shrink**.

**shrapnel** *noun*
**Shrapnel** is the small bits of metal that fly around when a bomb explodes.
[**Shrapnel** is named after Henry *Shrapnel*, a British soldier who invented this kind of bomb.]

**shriek** *noun* **shrieks**
A **shriek** is a short sharp scream.
[The word **shriek** is an imitation of the sound.]

**shriek** *verb* **shrieks, shrieking, shrieked**
To **shriek** is to let out a short sharp scream.

**shrimp** *noun* **shrimps**
A **shrimp** is a small long shellfish that turns pink when it is cooked.
[**Shrimp** probably comes from an old German word.]

**shrine** *noun* **shrines**
A **shrine** is a holy place for religious people. [**Shrine** comes from Old English.]

**shrink** *verb* **shrinks, shrinking, shrank, shrunk** (th)
1 To **shrink** is to become smaller or to make something smaller.
2 If you **shrink** from something, you try to avoid it because you are afraid or because you think it is bad: *She shrank back as the dog came nearer; They would not shrink from stealing.*
[**Shrink** comes from Old English.]

**shrivel** *verb* **shrivels, shrivelling, shrivelled** (th)
When something **shrivels**, it dries out and becomes wrinkled: *Leaves shrivel in the autumn.*
[**Shrivel** probably comes from Old Norse.]

**shrub** *noun* **shrubs**
A **shrub** is a small bush.
[**Shrub** comes from Old English.]

**shrubbery** *noun* **shrubberies**
**Shrubbery** is an area planted with small bushes.

**shrunk** *verb*
**Shrunk** is the past participle of **shrink**.

**shudder** *verb* **shudders, shuddering, shuddered** (th)
To **shudder** is to shake from cold, fear or the thought of something horrible.
[**Shudder** comes from an old German or Dutch word.]

**shut** *verb* **shuts, shutting, shut**
1 To **shut** something means to move something such as a door or a lid across an opening so that nothing can go through it.
2 If you **shut** something such as a book or an umbrella, you bring the parts of it together.
3 If a shop **shuts**, it closes its doors and does not let any more customers in.
[**Shut** comes from Old English.]

**shutter** *noun* **shutters**
1 A **shutter** is a cover for the outside of a window that is closed to keep out the light.
2 A **shutter** is the part of a camera that opens to let light onto the film.
[**Shutter** comes from **shut**.]

**shuttle** *noun* **shuttles**
1 In weaving, a **shuttle** carries the thread across the material and then back again.
2 A **shuttle** is a bus or train that goes backwards and forwards along the same route.
3 A **shuttle** is a spaceship for short journeys to and from the earth.
[**Shuttle** comes from Old English.]

**shy** *adjective* **shyer, shyest** (th)
Someone who is **shy** is afraid of meeting or talking to new people.
[**Shy** comes from Old English.]

**sibling** *noun* **siblings**
Your **sibling** is your brother or sister.
[**Sibling** comes from Old English.]

**sick** *adjective* **sicker, sickest** (th)
1 Someone who is **sick** is ill: *She's sick so she's off work.*
2 If you feel **sick**, you feel as though you want to vomit: *I feel sick after eating all that chocolate.*
3 If you are **sick** of something, you are tired of it and bored with it: *I'm sick of school!* [**Sick** comes from Old English.]

**sickle** *noun* **sickles**
A **sickle** is a large knife with a curved blade and a short handle that is used for cutting long grass.
[**Sickle** comes from Old English.]

**side** *noun* **sides** (th)
1 The **side** of something is an outside surface that is not the top or the bottom.
2 A **side** is an edge of something: *A rectangle has four sides.*
3 Your **side** is the left or right part of your body from under your arm to the top of your leg.

**4** A **side** is one of two teams or groups of people who play against each other or fight each other.
[**Side** comes from Old English.]

**siege** *noun* **sieges**
A **siege** is when an army or the police surround a place and cut off supplies to it until the people inside surrender.
[**Siege** comes from an old French word.]

**siesta** *noun* **siestas**
A **siesta** is a short sleep, especially in the afternoon after lunch.
[**Siesta** comes via Spanish from Latin *sexta hora* 'the sixth hour, midday'.]

**sieve** *noun* **sieves**
A **sieve** is a kitchen tool that has lots of small holes in it to strain or sift things.
[**Sieve** comes from Old English.]

**sift** *verb* **sift, sifting, sifted**
To **sift** something is to put it through a sieve in order to remove lumps and add air. [**Sift** comes from Old English.]

**sigh** *verb* **sighs, sighing, sighed**
To **sigh** is to breathe out heavily, especially because you are sad or relieved.
[**Sigh** probably comes from Old English.]

**sight** *noun* **sights**
**1 Sight** is the ability to see.
**2** A **sight** is something interesting that can be seen: *The Eiffel Tower is a famous sight in Paris.* [**Sight** comes from Old English.]

**sightseeing** *noun*
**Sightseeing** is travelling around to look at interesting places and buildings.

**sign** *noun* **signs** (th)
**1** A **sign** is a mark or symbol that means something: *$ is a dollar sign.*
**2** A **sign** is a board or notice that gives you information.
**3** A **sign** is any movement you make that has a particular meaning.
[**Sign** comes via French from Latin *signum* 'a sign, symbol or token'.]

**sign** *verb* **signs, signing, signed** (th)
**1** To **sign** means to write your name in your own special way: *She signed the letter.*
**2** To **sign** means to use sign language: *Many deaf people communicate by signing to each other.*

**signal** *noun* **signals**
**1** A **signal** is a sound, an action or a movement that means something.
**2** A **signal** is an electrical wave that carries pictures and sounds to televisions and radios.
[**Signal** comes via French from the same Latin word as **sign**.]

**signature** *noun* **signatures**
Your **signature** is the way you write your name in your own special way.
[**Signature** comes from the same Latin word as **sign**.]

**significant** *adjective*
If something is **significant**, it is important or it has a certain meaning.
[**Significant** comes via French from the same Latin word as **sign**.]

**sign language** *noun*
**Sign language** is signs people make with their hands as a way of communicating without speaking. **Sign language** is used especially by people who are deaf or who cannot speak.

**signpost** *noun* **signposts**
A **signpost** is a sign by the road that gives you directions.

**Sikh** *noun* **Sikhs**
A **Sikh** is a member of a religion founded in northern India. Sikh men adopt the name *Singh*, do not cut their hair and often wear a turban; Sikh women adopt the name *Kaur*.
[**Sikh** comes from Punjabi (a language spoken in northern India).]

**Sikhism** *noun*
**Sikhism** is the religion of the Sikhs and grew out of Hinduism and Islam. Sikhs worship only one God.

**silence** *noun* **silences** (th)
**Silence** is when there is no noise.
[**Silence** comes via French from the same Latin word as **silent**.]

**silent** *adjective* (th)
Someone or something that is **silent** makes no sound.
[**Silent** comes from Latin.]

**silhouette** *noun* **silhouettes**
A **silhouette** is the dark shape or outline of something that has light behind it.
[**Silhouette** comes from the name of a

French politician, Étienne de *Silhouette*, but no one really knows why.]

**silicon** *noun*
Silicon is a common metal element. It is used to make glass and also **silicon chips**.
[**Silicon** comes from Latin.]

**silicon chip** *noun* **silicon chips**
A **silicon chip** is a microchip. Many microchips are made of silicon.

**silk** *noun*
Silk is a soft cloth that is made from threads spun by a kind of caterpillar called a silkworm.
[**Silk** comes from Greek via Old English and Latin.]

**silly** *adjective* **sillier, silliest** (th)
1 Something or someone that is **silly** is funny and makes you laugh: *a silly joke; The clown did lots of silly things.*
2 Something or someone that is **silly** is foolish and not sensible.
[**Silly** comes from Old English.]

**silo** *noun* **silos**
1 A **silo** is a large tower for storing grain.
2 A **silo** is a place underground that a missile is fired from.
[**Silo** comes from Greek via Spanish and Latin.]

**silt** *noun*
Silt is the mud that is carried by a river and is dropped when the river flows more slowly.
[**Silt** probably comes from a Scandinavian language.]

**silver** *noun*
Silver is greyish-white shiny metal that is used for making jewellery.
[**Silver** comes from Old English.]

**silver** *adjective*
1 made of silver: *a silver bracelet.*
2 of the colour of silver: *silver hair.*

**silver-plated** *adjective*
Something that is **silver-plated** is covered with a thin layer of silver.

**similar** *adjective* (th)
Things or people that are **similar** are like each other in many ways but are not exactly the same.
[**Similar** comes from Latin *similis* 'like'.]

**simmer** *verb* **simmers, simmering, simmered**
To **simmer** means to boil gently: *Bring the soup to the boil and simmer it for 10 minutes.*
[No one knows where **simmer** comes from.]

**simple** *adjective* **simpler, simplest** (th)
1 Something that is **simple** is easy to understand or not difficult to do.
2 Something that is **simple** is plain and does not have extra things that you do not need.
[**Simple** comes from Latin via French.]

**simplify** *verb* **simplifies, simplifying, simplified**
To **simplify** something means to make it simpler.
[**Simplify** comes from the same Latin word as **simple**.]

**simultaneous** *adjective*
If two or more things are **simultaneous**, they happen at the same time.
**simultaneously** *adverb*.
[**Simultaneous** comes from Latin.]

**sin** *noun* **sins**
A **sin** is something bad that you do, especially if it breaks a religious law.
[**Sin** comes from Old English.]

**since** *preposition*
Since means from a time in the past until now: *It's been raining since Thursday.*
[**Since** comes from Old English.]

**since** *conjunction*
Since means because or as: *Since you're here you can help with the dinner.*

**sincere** *adjective* (th)
Something or someone that is **sincere** is honest and truthful.
[**Sincere** comes from Latin *sincerus* 'clean or pure'.]

**sincerely** *adverb*
1 in an honest or truthful way.
2 You end a letter with *Yours sincerely* when you start the letter with the name of the person.

**sing** *verb* **sings, singing, sang, sung**
To sing means to make a musical noise with your voice.
[**Sing** comes from Old English.]

**singe** *verb* **singes, singeing, singed** (th)
To **singe** something is to burn it slightly but not set it on fire.
[**Singe** comes from Old English.]

**singer** *noun* **singers**
A **singer** is someone who sings, especially as a job: *an opera singer.*

**single** *adjective*
**1** only one: *There was a single biscuit on the plate.*
**2** Someone who is **single** is not married: *Is he married or single?*
**3** A **single** ticket or a **single** fare is to a place, but not back from it.
**4** for one person: *a single bed; a single room.*
[**Single** comes from Latin via French.]

**singular** *noun*
The **singular** is the form of a word used to mean that there is only one.
[**Singular** comes via French from the same Latin word as **single**.]

**singular** *adjective*
**1** When there is one of something, it is **singular**.
**2** If something is **singular**, it is outstanding or unusual.

**sinister** *adjective*
A **sinister** thing or person seems evil or frightening.
[**Sinister** comes from Latin *sinister* 'on the left'.]

**sink** *noun* **sinks**
A **sink** is a fixed, open container for water in a kitchen or bathroom that has taps and a drain.
[**Sink** comes from Old English.]

**sink** *verb* **sinks, sinking, sank, sunk** (th)
**1** To **sink** means to go under the surface of the water: *The ship sank in the storm.*
**2** To **sink** means to get lower: *The sun sank over the horizon.*

**sinus** *noun* **sinuses**
Your **sinuses** are the hollow spaces in your skull on either side of your nose and above your eyes.
[**Sinus** comes from Latin.]

**sip** *verb* **sips, sipping, sipped**
To **sip** a drink means to drink only a small amount at a time: *He sipped the hot tea.*

[**Sip** probably comes from Old English.]

**siphon** *noun* **siphons** *Also* **syphon**
A **siphon** is a tube through which liquid moves up and then down to a lower level.
[**Siphon** comes via French or Latin from Greek *siphon* 'a pipe'.]

**siren** *noun* **sirens**
A **siren** is something that makes a loud warning sound.
[**Siren** is named after the *Sirens* in Greek legend, who were women who sang to lure sailors onto the rocks.]

**sister** *noun* **sisters**
Your **sister** is a female child of your parents. [**Sister** comes from Old English.]

**sister-in-law** *noun* **sisters-in-law**
Your **sister-in-law** is the sister of your husband or wife, or the wife of your brother.

**sit** *verb* **sits, sitting, sat**
To **sit** is to be in a position on a chair, for example, where most of your weight is supported by your buttocks.
[**Sit** comes from Old English.]

**sitar** *noun* **sitars**
A **sitar** is an Indian musical instrument with strings.
[**Sitar** comes from Persian (the language spoken in Iran).]

**site** *noun* **sites**
**1** A **site** is a place where something happened or existed in the past, or will happen or exist in the future: *Hastings was the site of a famous battle in 1066.*
**2** A **site** is a piece of land where a particular thing happens: *a building site; a caravan site.*
[**Site** comes from Latin *situs* 'position'.]

**situation** *noun* **situations** (th)
**1** A **situation** is the way something is: *People without enough food or water are in a difficult situation.*
**2** A **situation** is the place where something is: *The hotel is in a beautiful situation overlooking the lake.*
[**Situation** comes from the same Latin word as **site**.]

**size** *noun* **sizes** (th)
The **size** of something is how big or small it is: *What size are the rooms?*
[**Size** comes from an old French word.]

**sizzle** *verb* **sizzles, sizzling, sizzled**
Things **sizzle** when they get very hot and sometimes make a hissing noise: *Bacon sizzled in the frying pan.*
[The word **sizzle** is an imitation of the sound.]

**skate** *noun* **skates**
**Skate** is short for **ice-skate** or **roller skate**.

**skate** *verb* **skates, skating, skated**
To **skate** means to move on ice-skates or roller skates.
[**Skate** comes from French via Dutch.]

**skateboard** *noun* **skateboards**
A **skateboard** is a piece of wood or plastic with wheels underneath that you ride on.

**skeleton** *noun* **skeletons**
**1** Your **skeleton** is the framework of bones in your body.
**2** A **skeleton** is a dead body when all the flesh has rotted away and only the bones are left.
[**Skeleton** comes from Greek *skeletos* 'dried up'.]

**sketch** *noun* **sketches**
**1** A **sketch** is a quick drawing without much detail.
**2** A **sketch** is a short comedy scene that is usually part of a television or radio programme.
[**Sketch** comes from Italian via Dutch or German.]

**skewer** *noun* **skewers**
A **skewer** is a long thin piece of wood or metal that pieces of food are pushed onto to hold them together while they are cooked.
[No one knows where **skewer** comes from.]

**ski** *noun* **skis**
A **ski** is a long thin piece of metal or plastic on the bottom of a boot that is used for travelling over snow.
[**Ski** comes from Norwegian.]

**ski** *verb* **skies, skiing, skied**
To **ski** means to travel over snow on skis.

**skid** *verb* **skids, skidding, skidded**
To **skid** means to slide out of control on a slippery surface.
[**Skid** probably comes from a Scandinavian language.]

**skilful** *adjective* (th)
Someone who is **skilful** is very good at doing something. **skilfully** *adverb*.
[**Skilful** comes from **skill**.]

**skill** *noun* **skills** (th)
**1 Skill** is the ability to do something well: *It takes a lot of skill to drive racing cars.*
**2** A **skill** is something that you can do well: *You need good computer skills for this job.* [**Skill** comes from Old English.]

**skim** *verb* **skims, skimming, skimmed** (th)
**1** To **skim** liquid is to take something off its surface: *Skim the cream off the milk.*
**2** To **skim** is to glide over the surface of water: *Insects skimmed over the pond.*
**3** To **skim** something means to read it very quickly: *She skims the newspapers every morning.*
[**Skim** comes from an old French word.]

**skimmed milk** *noun*
**Skimmed milk** is milk that has had most of the fat removed from it.

**skin** *noun* **skins**
**1 Skin** is the outer covering of a person or an animal's body.
**2 Skin** is the outer layer of some fruits and vegetables: *a banana skin.*
[**Skin** comes from Old Norse.]

**skin** *verb* **skins, skinning, skinned**
To **skin** something is to remove its skin.

**skinny** *adjective* **skinnier, skinniest**
A **skinny** person is too thin.
[**Skinny** comes from **skin**.]

**skip¹** *verb* **skips, skipping, skipped** (th)
**1** To **skip** means to move along quickly hopping or jumping from one foot to the other.
**2** To **skip** means to jump over a turning rope.
**3** To **skip** something means to miss it out: *I skipped my class this morning; Skip the next chapter and go to page 35.*
[**Skip¹** probably comes from a Scandinavian language.]

**skip²** *noun* **skips**
A **skip** is a large metal container that holds rubbish, especially from building sites. [**Skip²** comes from Old Norse.]

**skipper** *noun* **skippers**
A **skipper** is a captain, especially of a ship

or a sports team.
[**Skipper** comes from old Dutch or German *schip* 'ship'.]

**skirt** *noun* **skirts**
A **skirt** is a piece of clothing that is worn by women and hangs from the waist.
[**Skirt** comes from Old Norse.]

**skive** *verb* **skives, skiving, skived**
To **skive** is to not do work when you should do it.
[**Skive** may come from French *esquiver* 'to creep away'.]

**skull** *noun* **skulls**
A **skull** is the bony part of a person's or animal's head.
[**Skull** probably comes from a Scandinavian language.]

**skunk** *noun* **skunks**
A **skunk** is a small animal found in North America that has black fur with white stripes on its back and head. A **skunk** sprays a liquid with a very bad smell at anything that tries to attack it.
[**Skunk** comes from Abnaki (a North American Indian language).]

**sky** *noun* **skies**
The **sky** is the space above the earth that is part of the earth's atmosphere.
[**Sky** comes from Old Norse.]

**skydiving** *noun*
**Skydiving** is jumping out of planes and doing stunts before opening the parachute.

**skylight** *noun* **skylights**
A **skylight** is a window in a roof.

**skyscraper** *noun* **skyscrapers**
A **skyscraper** is a very tall building.

**slab** *noun* **slabs**
A **slab** is a thick square piece of stone: *paving slabs.*
[No one knows where **slab** comes from.]

**slack** *adjective* **slacker, slackest** (th)
1 Something that is **slack** is loose or not pulled tight: *a slack rope.*
2 Someone who is **slack**, or whose work is **slack**, does not do very much or does not do a very good job.
3 If a shop or business is **slack**, there are not many customers: *Hotels are slack in the winter.* [**Slack** comes from Old English.]

**slacks** *plural noun*
**Slacks** are trousers for casual wear.
[**Slacks** comes from **slack**.]

**slag heap** *noun* **slag heaps**
A **slag heap** is a hill made of waste material from a coal mine.
[**Slag** comes from an old German word.]

**slain** *verb*
**Slain** is the past participle of **slay**.

**slalom** *noun*
A **slalom** is a race where skiers have to ski downhill zigzagging between poles.
[**Slalom** comes from Norwegian.]

**slam** *verb* **slams, slamming, slammed**
To **slam** means to shut something very noisily.
[**Slam** probably comes from a Scandinavian language.]

**slang** *noun*
**Slang** is very informal language that is usually spoken but not written. **Slang** is often used by certain groups of people and is sometimes only fashionable for a short time.
[No one knows where the word **slang** comes from.]

**slant** *verb* **slants, slanting, slanted** (th)
To **slant** is to slope or lean in one direction.
[**Slant** comes from a Scandinavian language.]

**slap** *verb* **slaps, slapping, slapped**
To **slap** someone is to hit him or her with your hand open, rather than with your fist.
[The word **slap** is an imitation of the sound.]

**slapdash** *adjective* (th)
Something that is **slapdash** is done quickly and carelessly.
[**Slapdash** comes from *slap* and *dash* 'a blow or splash', which is an imitation of the sound.]

**slapstick** *noun*
**Slapstick** is a type of comedy full of practical jokes with people running around noisily and falling over.
[**Slapstick** originally meant a device that clowns used to make a loud noise.]

**slash** *verb* **slashes, slashing, slashed**
To **slash** something is to make a long cut in it with one movement.
[**Slash** probably comes from an old French word.]

**slate** *noun* **slates**
1 **Slate** is a soft grey rock that is easily split into thin pieces.
2 A **slate** is a roof tile made of slate.
[**Slate** comes from an old French word.]

**slaughter** *verb* **slaughters, slaughtering, slaughtered** (th)
1 To **slaughter** an animal is to kill it for food.
2 If people are **slaughtered**, they are killed ruthlessly or in large numbers, for example, during a war.
[**Slaughter** comes from Old Norse.]

**slave** *noun* **slaves**
A **slave** is a person who is owned by another person and has to work for that person. [**Slave** comes from Latin.]

**slay** *verb* **slays, slaying, slew, slain** (th)
To **slay** someone means to kill him or her. The word **slay** is mainly used in stories.
[**Slay** comes from Old English.]

**sledge** *noun* **sledges** *Also* **sled**
A **sledge** is a flat board with runners underneath that is used for moving over snow.
[**Sledge** come from an old Dutch word.]

**sleep** *verb* **sleeps, sleeping, slept** (th)
To **sleep** means to rest with your eyes closed when your mind is practically unconscious.
[**Sleep** comes from Old English.]

**sleet** *noun*
**Sleet** is a mixture of rain and snow.
[**Sleet** comes from Old English.]

**sleeve** *noun* **sleeves**
A **sleeve** is part of a piece of clothing that covers the arms.
[**Sleeve** comes from Old English.]

**sleigh** *noun* **sleighs**
A **sleigh** is a large sledge that is usually pulled by dogs or horses.
[**Sleigh** comes from Dutch.]

**slender** *adjective* (th)
A **slender** person is slim.
[No one knows where **slender** comes from.]

**slept** *verb*
**Slept** is the past tense and past participle of **sleep**.

**sleuth** *noun* **sleuths**
A **sleuth** is a detective. The word **sleuth** is mainly used in stories.
[**Sleuth** comes from Old Norse.]

**slew** *verb*
**Slew** is the past tense of **slay**.

**slice** *noun* **slices** (th)
A **slice** is a piece of food that is cut from a larger piece: *a slice of cake; a slice of bread*.
[**Slice** comes from an old French word.]

**slice** *verb* **slices, slicing, sliced** (th)
To **slice** something is to cut it into smaller pieces: *slice the potatoes*.

**slide** *noun* **slides**
1 A **slide** is a long smooth piece of plastic or metal in a playground that children can slide down.
2 A **slide** is a photograph in a piece of glass or plastic that can be seen with the help of a projector.
3 A **slide** is a small piece of glass on which something is put so it can be looked at under a microscope.
4 A **slide** is a hair clip.
[**Slide** comes from Old English.]

**slide** *verb* **slides, sliding, slid** (th)
To **slide** means to move smoothly over a surface.

**slight** *adjective* **slighter, slightest** (th)
1 Something that is **slight** is small or not very important: *a slight problem; a slight cold*.
2 A **slight** person is small and thin.
[**Slight** comes from Old Norse.]

**slim** *adjective* **slimmer, slimmest** (th)
A **slim** person is thin in an attractive way.
[**Slim** comes from an old German or Dutch word.]

**slim** *verb* **slims, slimming, slimmed**
To **slim** means to become thinner, usually by going on a diet.

**slime** *noun*
**Slime** is any thick, sticky, unpleasant liquid. [**Slime** comes from Old English.]

**sling** *noun* **slings**
1 A **sling** is a bandage that you put under your arm and tie round your neck to support a broken arm or wrist.
2 A **sling** is a strap or a piece of rope or cloth hung in a loop so that something can be held in it or lifted by it.
[**Sling** comes from an old German word.]

**sling** *verb* **slings, slinging, slung** (th)
1 To **sling** something is to lift it or move it by using a sling.
2 To **sling** something is to throw it somewhere in a careless way.

**slip** *noun* **slips**
1 A **slip** is a small mistake.
2 A **slip** is a small piece of paper.
[**Slip** probably comes from an old German or Dutch word.]

**slip** *verb* **slips, slipping, slipped** (th)
To **slip** means to slide or fall on a slippery surface.

**slippers** *plural noun*
**Slippers** are soft, comfortable shoes that are worn indoors.
[**Slippers** comes from **slip**.]

**slippery** *adjective*
Something that is **slippery** is hard to hold or walk on because it is wet, greasy or smooth.
[**Slippery** comes from **slip**.]

**slit** *noun* **slits** (th)
A **slit** is a long cut or a narrow opening in something.
[**Slit** comes from Old English.]

**slither** *verb* **slithers, slithering, slithered**
To **slither** means to slide along the ground in an unsteady way.
[**Slither** comes from Old English.]

**sliver** *noun* **slivers**
A **sliver** is a small, thin piece of something.
[**Sliver** comes from an old word *slive* 'to split something' or 'to cut a piece off'.]

**slope** *noun* **slopes** (th)
A **slope** is a surface that goes upwards or downwards gradually.
[No one knows where **slope** comes from.]

**slope** *verb* **slopes, sloping, sloped** (th)
If something **slopes**, it stands or lies at an angle: *a sloping roof.*

**slot** *noun* **slots**
A **slot** is a narrow opening or groove, such as a hole in a machine for coins.
[**Slot** comes from an old French word.]

**sloth** *noun* **sloths**
1 A **sloth** is a mammal that lives in South America. **Sloths** hang upside down in trees, and move very slowly.
2 **Sloth** is extreme laziness.
[**Sloth** comes from **slow**.]

**slothful** *adjective*
Someone who is **slothful** is lazy and slow.

**slouch** *verb* **slouches, slouching, slouched**
If you **slouch**, you sit or stand with your shoulders and your head drooping.
[No one knows where **slouch** comes from.]

**slow** *adjective* **slower, slowest**
1 Something that is **slow** takes a long time.
2 A clock that is **slow** is behind the correct time. **slowly** *adverb.* **slowness** *noun.*
[**Slow** comes from Old English.]

**slug** *noun* **slugs**
A **slug** is a soft brown or black creature like a snail without a shell.
[**Slug** probably comes from a Scandinavian language.]

**slum** *noun* **slums**
A **slum** is a part of a city where very poor people live in bad conditions.
[No one knows where **slum** comes from.]

**slung** *verb*
**Slung** is the past tense and past participle of **sling**.

**sly** *adjective* **slyer, slyest** (th)
Someone who is **sly** is good at tricking other people or doing secret things.
**slyly** *adverb.* [**Sly** comes from Old Norse.]

**smack** *verb* **smacks, smacking, smacked**
To **smack** someone means to hit him or her with the palm of your hand.
[**Smack** comes from Old English.]

**small** *adjective* **smaller, smallest** (th)
Something that is **small** is not big, or is less than the usual size.
[**Small** comes from Old English.]

**smart** *adjective* **smarter, smartest** (th)
1 **Smart** means neat and clean: *He always*

came to work looking *smart*.
**2 Smart** means clever: *She was smart enough to know what to do.*
**smartly** *adverb.* **smartness** *noun.*
[**Smart** comes from Old English.]

**smash** *verb* **smashes, smashing, smashed** (th)
To **smash** something means to break it into tiny pieces noisily.
[The word **smash** is an imitation of the sound.]

**smear** *verb* **smears, smearing, smeared** (th)
When you **smear** something such as paint or food, you spread it on a surface.
[**Smear** comes from Old English.]

**smell** *noun* **smells** (th)
**1** A **smell** is something that you sense with your nose.
**2 Smell** is the ability to sense things with your nose.
[No one knows where **smell** comes from.]

**smell** *verb* **smells, smelling, smelled** *or* **smelt** (th)
**1** To **smell** something means to use your nose to sense it: *I can smell something burning.*
**2** If something **smells**, it gives off a good or a bad smell: *This garden smells of lemons.*

**smile** *noun* **smiles**
A **smile** is your expression when you are happy or pleased.
[**Smile** probably comes from a Scandinavian language.]

**smile** *verb* **smiles, smiling, smiled**
When you **smile**, your mouth turns up at the corners because you are pleased or happy.

**smog** *noun*
**Smog** is a kind of fog that has smoke and petrol fumes in it.
[**Smog** comes from **smoke** and **fog**.]

**smoke** *noun*
**Smoke** is the white or grey gas that is given off when something is burning.
[**Smoke** comes from Old English.]

**smoke** *verb* **smokes, smoking, smoked**
**1** To **smoke** means to take in smoke from a cigarette, cigar or pipe through your mouth and breathe it out.
**2** To **smoke** food means to hang it in

smoke so that it keeps well and has a pleasant flavour: *smoked mackerel.*

**smoky** *adjective* **smokier, smokiest**
**1** A **smoky** room is one that is filled with smoke.
**2** A **smoky** fire makes a lot of smoke.

**smooth** *adjective* **smoother, smoothest**
**1** Something that is **smooth** has no lumps or holes or rough parts.
**2** A **smooth** journey or ride is one that is comfortable because there are no bumps and jolts.
**smoothly** *adverb.* **smoothness** *noun.*
[**Smooth** comes from Old English.]

**smother** *verb* **smothers, smothering, smothered** (th)
**1** To **smother** someone means to stop that person breathing by covering his or her face.
**2** To **smother** something means to cover it completely: *strawberries smothered with cream.*
**3** To **smother** someone means to protect that person too much so that s/he does not learn to do things or to look after himself or herself.
[**Smother** comes from Old English.]

**smoulder** *verb* **smoulders, smouldering, smouldered**
To **smoulder** means to burn slowly, without any flames.
[No one knows where **smoulder** comes from.]

**smudge** *noun* **smudges** (th)
A **smudge** is a dirty mark.
[No one knows where **smudge** comes from.]

**smudge** *verb* **smudges, smudging, smudged** (th)
To **smudge** ink, chalk or paint means to smear or rub it so that it makes a mark where you do not want it.

**smug** *adjective* **smugger, smuggest** (th)
If you are **smug**, you are pleased with yourself or with what you have in an unpleasant way.
**smugly** *adverb.* **smugness** *noun.*
[**Smug** comes from an old German word.]

**smuggler** *noun* **smugglers**
A **smuggler** is someone who brings something into a country secretly and

against the law.
[**Smuggler** comes from an old German or Dutch word.]

**snack** *noun* **snacks** (th)
A **snack** is a small meal.
[**Snack** comes from an old Dutch word.]

**snag** *noun* **snags**
A **snag** is a small problem.
[**Snag** probably comes from a Scandinavian language.]

**snail** *noun* **snails**
A **snail** is a small creature that moves very slowly and has a shell on its back.
[**Snail** comes from Old English.]

**snake** *noun* **snakes**
A **snake** is a long reptile with no legs. Some **snakes** are poisonous.
[**Snake** comes from Old English.]

**snap** *verb* **snaps, snapping, snapped** (th)
1 To **snap** means to break suddenly.
2 To **snap** means to take a sudden bite.
3 To **snap** shut means to shut quickly with a click or a sharp sound.
4 To **snap at** someone means to talk in a quick, angry way.
[**Snap** probably comes from an old German or Dutch word.]

**snarl** *verb* **snarls, snarling, snarled**
When a dog **snarls**, it growls and shows its teeth.
[The word **snarl** is an imitation of the sound it makes.]

**snatch** *verb* **snatches, snatching, snatched** (th)
If you **snatch** something, you take it suddenly or rudely.
[No one knows where **snatch** comes from.]

**sneak** *verb* **sneaks, sneaking, sneaked** (th)
To **sneak** means to move in a quiet way so that no one will see or hear you.
[No one knows where **sneak** comes from.]

**sneeze** *verb* **sneezes, sneezing, sneezed**
To **sneeze** means to make a sudden noise as air rushes out of your nose and mouth.
[**Sneeze** probably comes from Old English *fneosan*, an imitation of the sound.]

**sniff** *verb* **sniffs, sniffing, sniffed**
To **sniff** means to take in air noisily through your nose.
[The word **sniff** is an imitation of the sound.]

**snigger** *verb* **sniggers, sniggering, sniggered**
To **snigger** means to laugh quietly in an unkind or rude way.
[The word **snigger** is an imitation of the sound.]

**snip** *verb* **snips, snipping, snipped**
If you **snip** something, you cut it with scissors, using short strokes.
[**Snip** comes from an old German or Dutch word.]

**snivel** *verb* **snivels, snivelling, snivelled**
To **snivel** means to cry and sniff at the same time.
[**Snivel** comes from Old English.]

**snob** *noun* **snobs**
A **snob** is someone who thinks that s/he is better than other people.
[No one knows where **snob** comes from.]

**snooker** *noun*
**Snooker** is an indoor game played on a special table. You use a long stick called a cue to knock coloured balls into pockets around the table.
[No one knows where **snooker** comes from.]

**snoop** *verb* **snoops, snooping, snooped** (th)
If you **snoop**, you look around secretly, trying to find something out.
[**Snoop** comes from Dutch.]

**snooze** *noun*
A **snooze** is a short sleep, especially in the daytime.
[No one knows where **snooze** comes from.]

**snore** *noun* **snores**
A **snore** is a loud sound made by breathing noisily in your sleep.
[The word **snore** is an imitation of the sound.]

**snore** *verb* **snores, snoring, snored**
To **snore** means to breathe very noisily while you are asleep.

**snorkel** *noun* **snorkels**
A **snorkel** is a tube that sticks up so that you can breathe through it while you are swimming under water.
[**Snorkel** comes from German.]

**snort** *verb* **snorts, snorting, snorted**
To **snort** means to make a grunting sound as you breathe out through your nose.
[The word **snort** is an imitation of the sound.]

**snout** *noun* **snouts**
A **snout** is an animal's nose, or its nose and mouth: *a pig's snout.*
[**Snout** comes from an old German or Dutch word.]

**snow** *noun*
**Snow** is small white flakes of frozen water that fall from clouds in cold weather. [**Snow** comes from Old English.]

**snow** *verb* **snows, snowing, snowed**
When it **snows**, flakes of snow fall.

**snowdrop** *noun* **snowdrops**
A **snowdrop** is a flower with a white, drooping head.

**snowman** *noun* **snowmen**
A **snowman** is a model of a person made out of snow.

**snowy** *adjective* **snowier, snowiest**
When it is **snowy**, there is a lot of snow.

**snug** *adjective* **snugger, snuggest** (th)
**Snug** means warm and comfortable.
**snugly** *adverb.*
[**Snug** probably comes from Dutch.]

**snuggle** *verb* **snuggles, snuggling, snuggled**
To **snuggle** means to curl up or cuddle up closely to someone.
[**Snuggle** comes from Dutch.]

**soak** *verb* **soaks, soaking, soaked** (th)
**1** To **soak** something means to make it very wet.
**2** If something **soaks up** a liquid, the liquid goes into it.
[**Soak** comes from Old English.]

**soap** *noun* **soaps**
**Soap** is something that you use for washing: *a bar of soap; liquid soap.*
[**Soap** comes from Old English.]

**soar** *verb* **soars, soaring, soared** (th)
**1** To **soar** means to go up high into the air.
**2** When prices or temperatures **soar**, they go up very quickly.
[**Soar** comes from an old French word.]

**sob** *noun* **sobs**
A **sob** is a gasping noise that you make when you cry.
[**Sob** probably comes from an old German or Dutch word.]

**sob** *verb* **sobs, sobbing, sobbed**
To **sob** means to make a gasping noise when you cry.

**sober** *adjective*
Someone who is **sober** is not drunk.
[**Sober** comes from Latin via French.]

**soccer** *noun*
**Soccer** is another word for football.
[**Soccer** is short for *Association* in *Association Football.*]

**sociable** *adjective* (th)
If you are **sociable**, you are friendly and enjoy talking to people.
[**Sociable** comes from the same Latin word as **social.**]

**social** *adjective*
**1 Social** means to do with life in a community: *social problems such as drug abuse and bad housing.*
**2 Social** means to do with meeting people and enjoying their company: *a social club; a busy social life.*
**3 Social** animals, birds and insects live together in large communities, not alone or just with their families. Ants and bees are **social** insects.
[**Social** comes from Latin *socius* 'friend or partner'.]

**society** *noun* **societies** (th)
**1** A **society** is all the people who live in a country.
**2** A **society** is a club for people who like doing the same things.
[**Society** comes via French from the same Latin word as **social.**]

**sock** *noun* **socks**
A **sock** is a soft covering for your foot.
[**Sock** comes from Old English.]

**socket** *noun* **sockets**
**1** A **socket** is a hollow place that something fits into: *an eye socket.*

**2** A **socket** is a device in a wall or on the end of a wire that an electric plug or a light bulb fits into.
[**Socket** comes from an old French word.]

**sofa** *noun* **sofas**
A **sofa** is a comfortable seat with a back for more than one person.
[**Sofa** comes from Arabic *suffa* 'a stone bench'.]

**soft** *adjective* **softer, softest** (th)
**1** Something that is **soft** is not hard or firm.
**2** A sound that is not at all loud is **soft**.
**3** Something that is **soft** is gentle: *a soft breeze*. **softly** *adverb*. **softness** *noun*.
[**Soft** comes from Old English.]

**software** *noun*
**Software** is the programs that make a computer work and tell it what to do.
[**Software** comes from **soft** and *ware* 'goods' (which comes from Old English).]

**soggy** *adjective* **soggier, soggiest** (th)
Something that is **soggy** is wet or full of water.
[**Soggy** comes from an old word *sog* 'a swamp'.]

**soil** *noun*
**Soil** is the top layer of earth. Plants grow in **soil**.
[**Soil** comes from an old French word.]

**solar** *adjective*
**1** **Solar** means using light or heat from the sun: *solar power*.
**2** **Solar** means to do with the sun: *a solar eclipse*. [**Solar** comes from Latin *sol* 'sun'.]

**solar system** *noun*
The **solar system** is the sun and the planets that move around it.

**sold** *verb*
**Sold** is the past tense and past participle of **sell**.

**soldier** *noun* **soldiers**
A **soldier** is a person in an army.
[**Soldier** comes from Latin via French.]

**sole**[1] *noun* **soles**
A **sole** is the bottom part of a foot or shoe.
[**Sole**[1] comes via Old English and old French from Latin *solum* 'bottom'.]

**sole**[2] *noun* **sole** *or* **soles**
A **sole** is a flat sea fish that you can eat.
[**Sole**[2] comes via French from the same

Latin word as **sole**[1].]

**sole**[3] *adjective*
**Sole** means only: *His sole aim was to cause trouble.*
[**Sole**[3] comes via French from Latin *sola* 'alone'.]

**solemn** *adjective* (th)
To do something in a **solemn** way means to do it seriously and without smiling.
**solemnly** *adverb*.
[**Solemn** comes from Latin via French.]

**solicitor** *noun* **solicitors**
A **solicitor** is a lawyer who gives people advice about the law.
[**Solicitor** comes from Latin via French.]

**solid** *noun* **solids**
**1** A **solid** is a substance that is hard and firm, and not liquid.
**2** A **solid** is a shape that is not flat and has length, breadth and height.
[**Solid** comes from Latin.]

**solid** *adjective* (th)
**1** Something that is **solid** is not hollow and has no empty space inside it: *a table made from solid oak.*
**2** Something that is **solid** is hard and firm, and not liquid.

**solidify** *verb* **solidifies, solidifying, solidified** (th)
When a liquid **solidifies**, it becomes hard and firm. [**Solidify** comes from **solid**.]

**solitary** *adjective* (th)
**1** A **solitary** person spends a lot of time alone.
**2** If there is only one of something, you can say that it is **solitary**: *a solitary tree.*
[**Solitary** comes from the same Latin word as **sole**[3].]

**solo** *noun* **solos**
A **solo** is a song or a piece of music sung or played by one person.
[**Solo** comes via Italian from the same Latin word as **sole**[3].]

**soloist** *noun* **soloists**
A **soloist** is someone who sings or plays a solo.

**soluble** *adjective*
If you can dissolve something in liquid, it is **soluble**.
[**Soluble** comes via French from the same Latin word as **solve**.]

**solution** *noun* **solutions**
**1** The **solution** to a problem is a way of solving it.
**2** A **solution** is a liquid with something dissolved in it.
[**Solution** comes via French from the same Latin word as **solve**.]

**solve** *verb* **solves, solving, solved**
To **solve** a puzzle, a problem or a mystery means to find the answer to it.
[**Solve** comes from Latin *solvere* 'to loosen or undo'.]

**some** *adjective*
a little of something or a few of something: *Add some pepper; Some children were playing outside.*
[**Some** comes from Old English.]

**somebody** *pronoun*
You say **somebody** when you want to talk about a person but you cannot or do not want to say who it is: *I saw somebody in the garden.*

**somehow** *adverb*
in some way: *Somehow, she managed to escape; He seemed different somehow.*

**someone** *pronoun*
**Someone** means somebody: *Can someone give me a hand with this table?*

**somersault** *noun* **somersaults**
If you do a **somersault**, you roll forwards or backwards so that your feet go over your head.
[**Somersault** comes from an old French word.]

**something** *pronoun*
You say **something** when you want to talk about a thing but you cannot or do not want to say what it is: *I wanted something to drink; There's something in my soup.*

**sometimes** *adverb* (th)
Something that happens **sometimes** does not happen all the time or every time: *It sometimes snows in May.*

**somewhere** *adverb*
You say **somewhere** when you want to talk about a place but you cannot or do not want to say where it is: *I put my cup down somewhere.*

**son** *noun* **sons**
Your **son** is your male child.
[**Son** comes from Old English.]

**song** *noun* **songs**
A **song** is music with words that you can sing. [**Song** comes from Old English.]

**sonic** *adjective*
If something is **sonic**, it makes sounds or uses sounds.
[**Sonic** comes from the same Latin word as **sound**.]

**son-in-law** *noun* **sons-in-law**
Your **son-in-law** is your daughter's husband.

**soon** *adverb* **sooner** (th)
Something that will happen in a short time from now will happen **soon**.
[**Soon** comes from Old English.]

**soot** *noun*
**Soot** is a black powder left by smoke.
[**Soot** comes from Old English.]

**soothing** *adjective*
Something that is **soothing** makes you feel better or calmer.
[**Soothing** comes from Old English.]

**sorcerer** *noun* **sorcerers**
A **sorcerer** is a man who does magic, especially bad magic. **Sorcerers** are usually found in stories.
[**Sorcerer** comes from an old French word.]

**sorceress** *noun* **sorceresses**
A **sorceress** is a woman who does magic, especially bad magic. **Sorceresses** are usually found in stories.

**sorcery** *noun*
**Sorcery** is magic, especially bad magic.
[**Sorcery** comes from **sorcerer**.]

**sore** *adjective* **sorer, sorest** (th)
A part of your body that is painful is **sore**. **soreness** *noun*.
[**Sore** comes from Old English.]

**sorrow** *noun* (th)
**Sorrow** means sadness.
[**Sorrow** comes from Old English.]

**sorry** *adjective* **sorrier, sorriest** (th)
**1** You are **sorry** if you feel sad because of something wrong that you did.
**2** You feel **sorry** for someone if you feel

sad about something that has happened
to him/her.
[**Sorry** comes from Old English.]

**sort** *noun* **sorts** (th)
**Sort** means kind or type: *What sort of cake
shall we make?*
[**Sort** comes from Latin via French.]

**sort** *verb* **sorts, sorting, sorted** (th)
**1** If you **sort** things, you arrange them in
groups or put them in order.
**2** If you **sort out** a problem, you do
something so that it is not a problem any
more.

**sought** *verb*
**Sought** is the past tense and past
participle of **seek**.

**soul** *noun* **souls**
Your **soul** is the part of you that is not
your body and that some people believe
goes on living after your body dies. Your
feelings and your character are a part of
your **soul**.
[**Soul** comes from Old English.]

**sound** *noun* **sounds**
A **sound** is something that you can hear.
[**Sound** comes from Latin via French.]

**sound** *verb* **sounds, sounding, sounded**
**1** If something **sounds**, it makes a noise.
**2** If you **sound** angry or happy, you make
people think that you are angry or happy
by the way you speak.

**soundtrack** *noun* **soundtracks**
A **soundtrack** is the sound and music that
goes with a film.

**soup** *noun* **soups**
**Soup** is a hot liquid food made from meat
or vegetables.
[**Soup** comes from an old French word.]

**sour** *adjective* **sourer, sourest**
**1** A taste that is **sour** is sharp or bitter.
**2** Milk that is **sour** is not fresh and has
gone bad. **sourness** *noun*.
[**Sour** comes from Old English.]

**source** *noun* **sources**
**1** The **source** of something is where it
comes from or where you get it from.
**2** The **source** of a river or a stream is the
place where it starts.
[**Source** comes from Latin via French.]

**south** *noun*
**South** is the direction opposite north. If
you look towards the rising sun, **south** is
on your right.
[**South** comes from Old English.]

**south-east** *noun*
**South-east** is the point of the compass
midway between south and east.

**southerly** *adjective*
**1** to the south or towards the south: *We
travelled in a southerly direction for two days.*
**2** A **southerly** wind blows from the south.

**southern** *adjective*
in the south or from the south: *the
southern half of the country.*

**south-west** *noun*
**South-west** is the point of the compass
midway between south and west.

**souvenir** *noun* **souvenirs**
A **souvenir** is something that reminds
you of a place, person or event.
[**Souvenir** comes from French *se souvenir*
'to remember or to remind yourself'.]

**sovereign** *noun* **sovereigns**
A **sovereign** is a king or a queen.
[**Sovereign** comes via French from the
same Latin word as **super**.]

**sow**[1] *verb* **sows, sowing, sowed, sown**
To **sow** seeds means to plant them in the
ground.
[**Sow**[1] comes from Old English *sawan*.]

**sow**[2] *noun* **sows**
A **sow** is a female pig.
[**Sow**[2] comes from Old English *sugu*.]

**soya** *noun*
**Soya** is a kind of bean. You can use **soya**
beans for making oil, butter, flour, and
other foods.
[**Soya** comes via Dutch from Malay (the
language spoken in Malaysia).]

**space** *noun* **spaces** (th)
**1** A **space** is the distance between things.
**2** A **space** is an area that is empty.
**3** Space is all the area in which the
planets and stars move.
[**Space** comes from Latin via French.]

**spacecraft** *noun* **spacecraft**
A **spacecraft** is a rocket or another vehicle
that travels in space.

**a b c d e f g h i j k l m**

**spaceship** *noun* **spaceships**
A **spaceship** is a vehicle that takes people into space.

**space shuttle** *noun* **space shuttles**
A **space shuttle** is a spacecraft that can be used many times.

**spacious** *adjective* (th)
Something that is **spacious** has plenty of room in it.
[**Spacious** comes via French from the same Latin word as **space**.]

**spade¹** *noun* **spades**
A **spade** is a tool with a long handle that you use for digging.
[**Spade¹** comes from Old English.]

**spade²** *noun* **spades**
**Spades** is one of the four suits in a pack of playing cards. A **spade** is a black shape like an upside-down heart with a stalk.
[**Spade²** comes from Italian.]

**spaghetti** *noun*
**Spaghetti** is a long thin kind of pasta.
[**Spaghetti** comes from Italian *spaghetti* 'little strings'.]

**span** *noun* **spans**
A **span** is the width of something like a bird's wings or a bridge.
[**Span** comes from Old English.]

**spaniel** *noun* **spaniels**
A **spaniel** is a small kind of dog with drooping ears and a silky coat.
[**Spaniel** comes from old French *espaigneul* 'Spanish', because spaniels originally came from Spain.]

**spank** *verb* **spanks, spanking, spanked**
To **spank** means to hit someone hard, usually on his or her bottom, because s/he has been naughty.
[The word **spank** is an imitation of the sound of spanking someone.]

**spanner** *noun* **spanners**
A **spanner** is a tool that you use to undo or tighten a nut.
[**Spanner** comes from German.]

**spare** *adjective*
**1 Spare** means extra: *Have you got a spare pencil?*
**2** Your **spare** time is time when you can do what you like.
[**Spare** comes from Old English.]

**spare** *verb* **spares, sparing, spared** (th)
**1** To **spare** something, such as time or money, means to give it or save it for a particular purpose.
**2** To **spare** someone's life means to decide not to kill him or her.

**spark** *noun* **sparks**
A **spark** is a small bright flash.
[**Spark** comes from Old English.]

**sparkle** *verb* **sparkles, sparkling, sparkled** (th)
To **sparkle** means to shine with a lot of tiny sparks. [**Sparkle** comes from **spark**.]

**sparkler** *noun* **sparklers**
A **sparkler** is a kind of firework that you hold in your hand. You light the end and wave it as it sparkles.

**sparrow** *noun* **sparrows**
A **sparrow** is a small brown bird that is very common.
[**Sparrow** comes from Old English.]

**spat** *verb*
**Spat** is the past tense and past participle of **spit**.

**spatula** *noun* **spatulas**
A **spatula** is a tool with a flat blade that you use in the kitchen for smoothing or lifting. [**Spatula** comes from Latin.]

**spawn** *noun*
**Spawn** is the eggs of a fish, or of an amphibian such as a frog.
[**Spawn** comes from an old French word.]

**spay** *verb* **spays, spaying, spayed**
To **spay** a female animal means to operate on her so that she cannot have young.
[**Spay** comes from Latin via French.]

**speak** *verb* **speaks, speaking, spoke, spoken**
**1** To **speak** means to use your voice to make words.
**2** To **speak** a language means to be able to understand and use that language: *She speaks Russian.*
[**Speak** comes from Old English.]

**spear** *noun* **spears**
A **spear** is a sharp metal point on the end of a long pole, used as a weapon.
[**Spear** comes from Old English.]

**special** *adjective* (th)
1 Something that is **special** is unusual and different, usually in a good way.
2 Something that is **special** is for a particular event, person or activity.
**specially** *adverb*.
[**Special** comes from Latin via French.]

**species** *noun* **species**
A **species** is a group of plants or animals that are the same in most ways and can breed together: *an endangered species.*
[**Species** comes from the same Latin word as **special**.]

**speck** *noun* **specks** (th)
A **speck** is a tiny spot or piece.
[**Speck** comes from Old English.]

**spectator** *noun* **spectators** (th)
A **spectator** is a person who is watching something happening.
[**Spectator** comes from Latin *spectare* 'to look at'.]

**spectrum** *noun* **spectra** *or* **spectrums**
The colours of the **spectrum** are all the colours that you can see in a rainbow, or when light shines through a prism.
[**Spectrum** comes from Latin.]

**speech** *noun* **speeches**
1 **Speech** is the ability to speak.
2 A **speech** is a talk that someone gives to a group of people.
3 **Speech** is what someone says. In writing, **direct speech** is the actual words that someone says, which have **speech marks** around them: *"I'm going to France,"* *he said.* **Indirect speech** or **reported speech** is when the writer tells you what someone has said but does not use the same words: *He said he was going to France.*
[**Speech** comes from Old English.]

**speechless** *adjective* (th)
If you are **speechless**, you cannot talk because of a strong emotion.

**speed** *noun* **speeds** (th)
1 The **speed** of something is how quickly it moves.
2 **Speed** is very fast movement.
[**Speed** comes from Old English.]

**speed** *verb* **speeds, speeding, sped** (th)
1 To **speed** means to move very quickly.
2 To **speed** means to drive a vehicle faster than the law allows.

3 To **speed up** means to get faster.

**spell**[1] *noun* **spells**
A **spell** is magic words that someone says to make something happen.
[**Spell**[1] comes from Old English.]

**spell**[2] *verb* **spells, spelling, spelled** *or* **spelt**
To **spell** means to put the letters of a word in the right order.
[**Spell**[2] comes from an old French word.]

**spend** *verb* **spends, spending, spent**
1 To **spend** money means to pay money for something: *He spent his pocket money on a pair of trainers.*
2 To **spend** time means to pass time: *We spent three weeks in Italy.*
[**Spend** comes from Old English.]

**sperm** *noun* **sperms** *or* **sperm**
A **sperm** is a cell made in the body of a male animal or person. If the **sperm** meets a female's egg a baby will start to grow.
[**Sperm** comes via Latin from Greek *sperma* 'seed'.]

**sphere** *noun* **spheres**
A **sphere** is a round shape like a ball.
[**Sphere** comes via French and Latin from Greek *sphaira* 'ball'.]

**spherical** *adjective*
Something that is **spherical** is shaped like a ball.
[**Spherical** comes from the same Greek word as **sphere**.]

**spice** *noun* **spices**
A **spice** is a substance from a plant used to flavour food.
[**Spice** comes from Latin via French.]

**spicy** *adjective* **spicier, spiciest**
**Spicy** food has strong spices in it.

**spider** *noun* **spiders**
A **spider** is a small creature with eight legs that spins a web to catch its prey. Most **spiders** eat insects.
[**Spider** comes from Old English *spithra* 'spinner'.]

**spike** *noun* **spikes**
A **spike** is a sharp, metal point.
[No one knows where **spike** comes from.]

**spill** *verb* **spills, spilling, spilled** *or* **spilt**
To **spill** something means to knock it over or tip it out so that it makes a mess.

[**Spill** comes from Old English.]

**spin** *verb* **spins, spinning, spun** (th)
**1** To **spin** means to turn round and round very quickly.
**2** To **spin** means to twist wool or cotton into a thread.
[**Spin** comes from Old English.]

**spinach** *noun*
**Spinach** is a vegetable with dark green leaves.
[**Spinach** comes via French and Arabic from Persian (the language spoken in Iran).]

**spine** *noun* **spines**
**1** Your **spine** is the long series of bones down the centre of your back.
**2** A **spine** is a thorn or a prickle.
**3** The **spine** of a book is the stiff part where the pages are joined together.
[**Spine** comes from Latin.]

**spiral** *noun* **spirals**
A **spiral** is a pattern or a shape that curves in bigger and bigger circles.
[**Spiral** comes from Latin.]

**spire** *noun* **spires**
A **spire** is a tall conical or pyramid-shaped tower on the top of a church.
[**Spire** comes from Old English.]

**spirit** *noun* **spirits**
**1** A **spirit** is a ghost.
**2** Your **spirit** is the part of you that is not your body, for example your mind and your thoughts. [**Spirit** comes from Latin.]

**spit**[1] *verb* **spits, spitting, spat**
To **spit** means to make something such as saliva or water come out of your mouth.
[**Spit** comes from Old English *spittan*.]

**spit**[1] *noun*
**Spit** is saliva that you spit out.

**spit**[2] *noun* **spits**
A **spit** is a rod over or in front of a fire or gas flame. You put meat on a **spit**, and it turns round and round so that all the parts of the meat are cooked.
[**Spit**[2] comes from Old English *spitu*.]

**spite** *noun* (th)
**Spite** is a feeling that you want to hurt or be nasty to someone.
[**Spite** comes from French.]

**spiteful** *adjective*
Someone who is **spiteful** deliberately tries to upset or be mean to people.
**spitefully** *adverb*.

**splash** *noun* **splashes**
**1** A **splash** is liquid flying about because something has been dropped into it.
**2** A **splash** is the sound of something falling into liquid.
**3** A **splash** of colour is a patch of it.
[The word **splash** is an imitation of the sound.]

**splash** *verb* **splashes, splashing, splashed** (th)
To **splash** means to make liquid fly about in drops.

**splendid** *adjective* (th)
Something that looks very grand or is excellent is **splendid**: *a splendid palace; splendid work*. **splendidly** *adverb*.
[**Splendid** comes from Latin *splendidus* 'shining'.]

**splinter** *noun* **splinters**
A **splinter** is a tiny, sharp piece of something.
[**Splinter** comes from an old Dutch word.]

**split** *verb* **splits, splitting, split** (th)
**1** To **split** something means to break it into pieces or divide it.
**2** When something **splits**, it breaks or divides.
**3** To **split up** means to separate.
[**Split** comes from Dutch.]

**splutter** *verb* **splutters, spluttering, spluttered**
To **splutter** means to have trouble talking because you are upset or angry.
[The word **splutter** is an imitation of the sound.]

**spoil** *verb* **spoils, spoiling, spoiled** *or* **spoilt** (th)
**1** To **spoil** something means to damage or ruin it.
**2** To **spoil** a child means to give him or her everything that s/he wants.
**3** If food **spoils**, it goes bad.
[**Spoil** comes from Latin via French.]

**spoke**[1] *noun* **spokes**
A **spoke** is one of the wires or rods that joins the centre of a wheel to the rim.
[**Spoke**[1] comes from Old English.]

**spoke² *verb***
Spoke² is the past tense of **speak**.

**spoken *verb***
Spoken is the past participle of **speak**.

**sponge *noun* sponges**
1 A **sponge** is a sea creature with a soft body that has little holes in it.
2 A **sponge** is a soft cloth or pad with little holes in it, used for washing or wiping something.
3 A **sponge** is a light, sweet cake or pudding: *a chocolate sponge.*
[**Sponge** comes from Greek via Old English and Latin.]

**sponsor *verb* sponsors, sponsoring, sponsored**
1 If you **sponsor** someone, you say that you will give money to charity if s/he does something such as a long walk or a parachute jump.
2 If a company **sponsors** people or events, it gives them money, usually in return for advertising the company or its products.
[**Sponsor** comes from Latin *spondere* 'to promise'.]

**spontaneous *adjective***
1 Something that is **spontaneous** happens naturally, without anything making it happen.
2 A **spontaneous** action is one that you do without anyone telling you to and without thinking about it before you do it.
**spontaneously** *adverb.*
[**Spontaneous** comes from Latin.]

**spooky *adjective* spookier, spookiest**
A **spooky** place is a frightening place where you might hear strange sounds.
**Spooky** is an informal word.
[**Spooky** comes from *spook* 'a ghost', which comes from Dutch.]

**spoon *noun* spoons**
A **spoon** is something that you use for eating or serving food. It has a handle and a bowl-shaped end.
[**Spoon** comes from Old English.]

**sport *noun* sports**
A **sport** is a game such as football, tennis or basketball, or an activity such as athletics, in which you compete against another player or another team. **Sports** are played for enjoyment or as a good way of keeping fit.

[**Sport** comes from an old French word.]

**spot *noun* spots (th)**
1 A **spot** is a small round dot.
2 A **spot** is a place that is special in some way: *a perfect spot for a picnic.*
3 A **spot** is a small, raised, coloured mark on your skin.
[**Spot** probably comes from an old Dutch word.]

**spot *verb* spots, spotting, spotted (th)**
To **spot** something means to notice it.

**spotted *adjective***
Something that is **spotted** has spots on it.

**spout *noun* spouts**
A **spout** is a tube or narrow part of a container such as a teapot or a watering-can for pouring liquid out of it.
[**Spout** comes from an old Dutch word.]

**sprain *verb* sprains, spraining, sprained**
If you **sprain** a joint in your body, you injure it by twisting it.
[No one knows where **sprain** comes from.]

**sprang *verb***
Sprang is the past tense of **spring**.

**sprawl *verb* sprawls, sprawling, sprawled (th)**
1 To **sprawl** means to sit with your legs and arms spread out in a careless way.
2 To **sprawl** means to spread out in every direction.
[**Sprawl** comes from Old English.]

**spray *verb* sprays, spraying, sprayed**
To **spray** means to scatter tiny drops of liquid over something.
[No one knows where **spray** comes from.]

**spray *noun* sprays**
1 **Spray** is tiny drops of liquid propelled through the air: *Spray from the wet road covered the windscreen.*
2 A **spray** is a container or device for sending out liquid in tiny drops: *a perfume spray.*

**spread *verb* spreads, spreading, spread (th)**
1 To **spread** means to lay or stretch something out to its full size: *I spread the map on the table.*
2 To **spread** means to cover a surface with something soft: *He spread the bread with*

a b c d e f g h i j k l m

*honey.*

**3** To **spread** means to increase and affect more and more people or more and more of a place: *The fire quickly spread.*

**4** To **spread** news or information means to tell a lot of people about it.

[**Spread** comes from Old English.]

**spreadsheet** *noun* **spreadsheets**

A **spreadsheet** is a computer program that allows data, especially numbers, to be manipulated.

**spring** *noun* **springs**

**1 Spring** is the season of the year after winter when the weather gets warmer and leaves grow back on the trees.

**2** A **spring** is a place where water flows out of the ground.

**3** A **spring** is a piece of metal wound in rings so that it can stretch and then return to its normal shape.

[**Spring** comes from Old English.]

**spring** *verb* **springs, springing, sprang, sprung** (th)

To **spring** means to jump up suddenly.

**sprinkle** *verb* **sprinkles, sprinkling, sprinkled**

To **sprinkle** means to scatter a small amount of a powder or liquid over someone or something.

[**Sprinkle** probably comes from an old Dutch word.]

**sprint** *verb* **sprints, sprinting, sprinted**

To **sprint** means to run very quickly over a small distance.

[**Sprint** comes from Old Norse.]

**sprout** *noun* **sprouts**

**1** A **sprout** is a new small shoot growing from a plant.

**2 Sprout** is short for **Brussels sprout**.

[**Sprout** probably comes from Old English.]

**sprout** *verb* **sprouts, sprouting, sprouted** (th)

To **sprout** means to begin to grow.

**sprung** *verb*

**Sprung** is the past participle of **spring**.

**spun** *verb*

**Spun** is the past tense and past participle of **spin**.

**spurt** *noun* **spurts** (th)

**1** A **spurt** is a sudden gush of liquid.

**2** A **spurt** is a sudden burst of effort, movement or growth.

[No one knows where **spurt** comes from.]

**spurt** *verb* **spurts, spurting, spurted** (th)

To **spurt** means suddenly to gush out.

**spy** *noun* **spies**

A **spy** is a person who tries to find out secret information.

[**Spy** comes from an old French word.]

**spy** *verb* **spies, spying, spied** (th)

**1** To **spy** means to find out secret information from one organisation or country and give it to another.

**2** To **spy** on someone means to watch him or her secretly.

**3** To **spy** something means to notice or see it.

**squabble** *verb* **squabbles, squabbling, squabbled** (th)

To **squabble** means to have a silly argument.

[No one knows where **squabble** comes from.]

**squad** *noun* **squads** (th)

**1** A **squad** is a team of people working together.

**2** A **squad** is a group of soldiers.

[**Squad** comes from Italian via French.]

**square** *noun* **squares**

A **square** is a shape with four sides of equal length and four right angles.

[**Square** comes from an old French word.]

**square** *adjective*

**1** Something that is **square** has four sides of equal length and four right angles.

**2** A **square** measurement is a measurement of area equal to a length multiplied by itself. A **square metre** measures 1 metre x 1 metre; five square metres measures 5 x 1 metre x 1 metre. **Five metres square** equals 5 metres x 5 metres, or 25 square metres.

**square** *verb* **squares, squaring, squared**

**1** To **square** a number means to multiply it by itself. The sign for a number that has been **squared** is $^2$. $10^2$ means 10 **squared**, or 10 x 10.

**2 Squared** paper has lines on it that divide it into squares.

### squash[1] noun
**1 Squash** is a fruit flavoured drink.
**2 Squash** is an indoor game played with rackets and a small rubber ball.
[**Squash[1]** comes from Latin.]

### squash[1] verb squashes, squashing, squashed (th)
To **squash** something means to crush it.

### squash[2] noun squashes
A **squash** is a vegetable like a pumpkin.
[**Squash[2]** comes from Narragansett (a North American Indian language).]

### squat verb squats, squatting, squatted
**1** To **squat** means to lower your body into a sitting position with your legs bent, your bottom close to the ground and your weight on your feet.
**2** To **squat** means to live in an empty house without permission.
[**Squat** comes from an old French word.]

### squeak verb squeaks, squeaking, squeaked
To **squeak** means to make a short high-pitched sound like a mouse.
[The word **squeak** is an imitation of the sound.]

### squeeze verb squeezes, squeezing, squeezed (th)
To **squeeze** means to crush or press something hard.
[No one knows where **squeeze** comes from.]

### squelch verb squelches, squelching, squelched
To **squelch** means to make a sucking noise when you are walking on wet or muddy ground, or because there is water in your shoes.
[The word **squelch** is an imitation of the sound.]

### squid noun squids or squid
A **squid** is a sea creature with a long soft body and ten arms.
[No one knows where **squid** comes from.]

### squire noun squires
A **squire** was a young man in medieval times who served a knight.
[**Squire** comes via French from Latin *scutarius* 'shield-bearer'.]

### squirrel noun squirrels
A **squirrel** is a small animal with a long bushy tail that lives in trees.
[**Squirrel** comes from Greek via French and Latin.]

### squirt verb squirts, squirting, squirted (th)
To **squirt** means to send out a thin stream of liquid under pressure.
[The word **squirt** is an imitation of the sound.]

### stable[1] noun stables
**1** A **stable** is a building in which horses are kept.
**2** A **stable** is a number of horses kept in the same place or owned or trained by the same person: *a racing stable.*
[**Stable[1]** comes via French from Latin *stabulum* 'a place to stand or stay'.]

### stable[2] adjective (th)
**1** Something that is **stable** is firm and does not move or change.
**2** Someone who is **stable** is sensible and not easily upset.
[**Stable[2]** comes via French from Latin *stabilis* 'able to stand'.]

### stack noun stacks
A **stack** is an orderly pile of things.
[**Stack** comes from Old Norse.]

### stack verb stacks, stacking, stacked
To **stack** things means to pile them carefully on top of each other.

### stadium noun stadiums or stadia
A **stadium** is a sports ground with rows of seats all round the edge.
[**Stadium** comes from Greek via Latin.]

### staff noun staffs (th)
**1** The **staff** of a shop or company are the people who work there.
**2** A **staff** is a long thick wooden stick.
[**Staff** comes from Old English.]

### stag noun stags
A **stag** is an adult male deer.
[**Stag** probably comes from Old English.]

### stage noun stages (th)
**1** A **stage** is a raised floor in a hall or theatre.
**2** A **stage** is a point reached in the development or progress of something.
[**Stage** comes from Latin via French.]

**stagger** *verb* **staggers, staggering, staggered**
1 To **stagger** means to walk unsteadily.
2 To **stagger** events means to arrange them so that they do not all take place at the same time.
[**Stagger** comes from Old Norse.]

**stagnant** *adjective*
Water that is **stagnant** does not flow and smells bad.
[**Stagnant** comes from Latin *stagnum* 'a pool'.]

**stain** *noun* **stains** (th)
A **stain** is a dirty mark on something.
[**Stain** comes from an old French word.]

**stain** *verb* **stains, staining, stained**
1 To **stain** something means to leave a mark on it that is hard to get rid of.
2 To **stain** wood or glass means to colour it with dye.

**stainless steel** *noun*
**Stainless steel** is a type of strong shiny metal that does not get rust on it.

**staircase** *noun* **staircases**
A **staircase** is a set of stairs with rails that you can hold onto.

**stairs** *plural noun*
**Stairs** are steps going from one floor to another in a building.
[**Stairs** comes from Old English.]

**stake** *noun* **stakes**
A **stake** is a piece of wood with a pointed end that can be pushed into the ground to mark or support something.
[**Stake** comes from Old English.]

**stalactite** *noun* **stalactites**
A **stalactite** is a long thin piece of rock hanging down from the roof of a cave, formed by minerals and dripping water.
[**Stalactite** comes via Latin from Greek *stalaktos* 'dripping', because the water drips off the end of it.]

**stalagmite** *noun* **stalagmites**
A **stalagmite** is a long thin piece of rock that sticks up from the floor of a cave, formed by minerals and dripping water.
[**Stalagmite** comes via Latin from Greek *stalagma* 'a drop', because drops of water fall onto it from the stalactite above.]

**stale** *adjective*
Something that is **stale** is not fresh: *stale bread; stale air*.
[**Stale** comes from an old French word.]

**stalk**[1] *noun* **stalks**
A **stalk** is a thin stem on a plant.
[**Stalk**[1] probably comes from an old word *stale* 'a long handle'.]

**stalk**[2] *verb* **stalks, stalking, stalked** (th)
To **stalk** means to follow a person or animal secretly and silently.
[**Stalk**[2] comes from Old English.]

**stall**[1] *noun* **stalls**
1 A **stall** is a table or stand that things are sold from in a market or fair.
2 A **stall** is a section in a stable or shed where one animal is kept.
3 The **stalls** in a theatre or cinema are the seats downstairs.
[**Stall**[1] comes from Old English.]

**stall**[2] *verb* **stalls, stalling, stalled**
1 If a car **stalls**, it suddenly stops moving.
2 If you **stall**, you try to delay something.
[**Stall**[2] comes from an old French word.]

**stallion** *noun* **stallions**
A **stallion** is an adult male horse.
[**Stallion** comes from an old French word.]

**stamina** *noun*
**Stamina** is the strength to keep doing something for a long time.
[**Stamina** comes from Latin.]

**stamp** *noun* **stamps**
1 A **stamp** is a small piece of coloured paper which is stuck on a letter or parcel before posting it.
2 A **stamp** is a device which has writing or a design on it. You press the **stamp** onto an inky pad and then onto an object, and the object is marked with whatever is on the **stamp**.
[**Stamp** probably comes from Old English.]

**stamp** *verb* **stamps, stamping, stamped**
1 To **stamp** means to bang your foot heavily on the ground.
2 To **stamp** a letter or parcel is to put a stamp on it.
3 To **stamp** something is to mark it using a stamp.

**stampede** *noun* **stampedes**
A **stampede** is a rush of frightened animals or people.
[**Stampede** comes from Spanish.]

**stand** *noun* **stands**
1 A **stand** is a support to rest things on or in: *a music stand*.
2 A **stand** is a table or small shop where things can be sold outside.
[**Stand** comes from Old English.]

**stand** *verb* **stands, standing, stood**
1 To **stand** means to be upright on your feet without moving.
2 To **stand** means to be upright or remain in a place: *No buildings were left standing after the earthquake.*
3 If you cannot **stand** something, you dislike it very much.
4 If letters **stand for** a name or word, you write them or say them for short, instead of writing or saying the whole word: *UK stands for United Kingdom.*

**standard** *noun*
A **standard** is something that other things can be measured by.
[**Standard** comes from an old French word.]

**standard** *adjective* **standards**
Something that is accepted as usual or average is **standard**: *I wear a standard size.*

**stank** *verb*
**Stank** is a past tense of **stink**.

**staple**[1] *noun* **staples**
A **staple** is a small piece of wire that holds papers together.
[**Staple**[1] comes from Old English *stapol* 'a U-shaped nail'.]

**staple**[2] *adjective*
A **staple** food or crop is the main one that people in a country eat or produce.
[**Staple**[2] comes from an old french word.]

**star** *noun* **stars**
1 A **star** is a small bright light seen in the sky at night.
2 A **star** is a famous entertainer.
[**Star** comes from Old English.]

**starboard** *adjective*
The **starboard** side of a boat or plane is the right-hand side, if you are looking towards the front.
[**Starboard** comes from Old English *steor* 'a paddle for steering' (usually on the right-hand side) and **board**, in an old sense 'the side of a boat'.]

**stare** *verb* **stares, staring, stared** (th)
To **stare** means to look at someone or something continuously for a long time.
[**Stare** comes from Old English.]

**starfish** *noun* **starfishes** *or* **starfish**
A **starfish** is a sea creature shaped like a five-pointed star.

**start** *verb* **starts, starting, started** (th)
1 To **start** means to begin or to begin doing something: *School starts at 9 o'clock.*
2 To **start** means to make something begin or happen: *Someone started the fire.*
[**Start** comes from Old English.]

**startle** *verb* **startles, startling, startled** (th)
To **startle** means to frighten someone by doing something unexpected.
[**Startle** comes from Old English.]

**starve** *verb* **starves, starving, starved**
To **starve** means to become ill or die because of lack of food.
[**Starve** comes from Old English.]

**state** *noun* **states**
1 A **state** is the condition of a person or thing: *a good state of health.*
2 A **state** is an area of a country that has its own laws: *The states of the USA.*
3 The **State** is the government of a country. [**State** comes from Latin.]

**state** *verb* **states, stating, stated** (th)
To **state** something is to say it or write it formally.

**statement** *noun* **statements**
1 A **statement** is something that someone says or writes in a formal situation: *She had to give a statement to the police.*
2 A **statement** is a list of the sums of money paid in and out of a bank account, or that someone owes and has paid to a company. [**Statement** comes from **state**.]

**static** *adjective*
1 Something that is **static** does not change or move.
2 **Static** electricity is electricity that is in the air or that has collected on the surface of things. [**Static** comes from Greek.]

**station** *noun* **stations**
1 A **station** is a place with buildings where trains or buses stop.

a b c d e f g h i j k l m

**2** A **station** is a building for police officers and firefighters.
[**Station** comes via French from Latin *statio* 'standing'.]

**stationary** *adjective*
Something that is **stationary** is not moving.
[**Stationary** comes from the same Latin word as **station**.]

**stationery** *noun*
**Stationery** is things used for writing such as paper, envelopes and pens.
[**Stationery** comes from Latin.]

**statue** *noun* **statues**
A **statue** is a model of a person made out of stone or metal.
[**Statue** comes from Latin via French.]

**stave** *noun* **staves**
A **stave** is the set of five lines that musical notes are written on.
[**Stave** comes from **staves**, the old plural of **staff**.]

**stay** *verb* **stays**, **staying**, **stayed** (th)
**1** To **stay** means to remain in the same place.
**2** To **stay** means to live somewhere while visiting a place: *We stayed at the new hotel.*
[**Stay** comes from Latin via French.]

**stay** *noun* **stays**
A **stay** is a period of time spent visiting a place.

**steady** *adjective* **steadier**, **steadiest** (th)
**1** Something that is **steady** is not moving or shaking.
**2** If something is **steady**, it is regular and seems likely to go on without changing: *a steady rise in prices; a steady job.*
[**Steady** comes from *stead* 'a place', which comes from Old English.]

**steak** *noun* **steaks**
A **steak** is a thick slice of meat or fish.
[**Steak** comes from Old Norse.]

**steal** *verb* **steals**, **stealing**, **stole**, **stolen** (th)
To **steal** means to take something that belongs to somebody else and keep it without his or her permission.
[**Steal** comes from Old English.]

**steam** *noun*
**Steam** is the vapour coming from boiling water. [**Steam** comes from Old English.]

**steel** *noun*
**Steel** is a strong metal made from iron.
[**Steel** comes from Old English.]

**steep** *adjective* **steeper**, **steepest** (th)
Something that slopes sharply is **steep**.
[**Steep** comes from Old English.]

**steeple** *noun* **steeples**
A **steeple** is the pointed tower on the roof of a church.
[**Steeple** comes from Old English.]

**steer** *verb* **steers**, **steering**, **steered**
To **steer** means to control the direction in which something moves.
[**Steer** comes from Old English.]

**stem** *noun* **stems**
**1** A **stem** is the main part of a plant growing up from the ground.
**2** A **stem** is the thin part of a plant that joins a leaf, flower or fruit to the rest of the plant. [**Stem** comes from Old English.]

**stencil** *noun* **stencils**
A **stencil** is a piece of card, plastic or metal with a design cut out of it that can be painted over or drawn around in order to transfer the design onto something else.
[**Stencil** comes from an old French word.]

**step** *noun* **steps**
**1** A **step** is the movement made by one leg when you walk.
**2** A **step** is a flat place to put your foot when walking from one level to another.
**3** A **step** is one action in a series of actions done for a particular purpose: *first steps in learning French.*
[**Step** comes from Old English *staepe*.]

**step** *verb* **steps**, **stepping**, **stepped** (th)
To **step** means to lift and move your foot forward when you walk.

**stepbrother** *noun* **stepbrothers**
Your **stepbrother** is the son of your stepfather or stepmother.
[**Step** comes from Old English *stop-* 'orphaned'.]

**stepfather** *noun* **stepfathers**
Your **stepfather** is a man who is married to your mother but is not your father.

**stepmother** *noun* **stepmothers**
A **stepmother** is a woman who is married to your father but is not your mother.

**stepsister** *noun* **stepsisters**
Your **stepsister** is the daughter of your

stepfather or stepmother.

**stereo** *noun* **stereos**
1 A **stereo** is equipment that plays recorded music.
2 **Stereo** is sound that comes from two directions at the same time.
[**Stereo** is short for *stereophonic*, which comes from Greek *stereos* 'solid' and *phone* 'sound'.]

**stereotype** *noun* **stereotypes**
A **stereotype** is an idea of what someone or something is like that is very fixed and simple.
[A **stereotype** was originally a kind of printing that looked three-dimensional; the word comes from Greek *stereos* 'solid' and **type**.]

**sterile** *adjective*
Something that is **sterile** is completely free of germs. [**Sterile** comes from Latin.]

**stern¹** *noun* **sterns**
The **stern** of a boat or ship is the back end of it. [**Stern¹** comes from Old Norse.]

**stern²** *adjective* **sterner, sternest** (th)
Someone or something that is **stern** is strict or severe: *a stern teacher; She gave me a stern look.* **sternly** *adverb*.
[**Stern²** comes from Old English.]

**stethoscope** *noun* **stethoscopes**
A **stethoscope** is an instrument that doctors use to listen to a person's breathing or heartbeat.
[**Stethoscope** comes from Greek via French.]

**stew** *noun* **stews**
A **stew** is a dish of meat or vegetables that is cooked slowly in liquid.
[**Stew** comes from an old French word.]

**steward** *noun* **stewards**
A **steward** is someone whose job is to look after passengers on a ship or plane.
[**Steward** comes from Old English.]

**stick¹** *noun* **sticks**
1 A **stick** is a long thin piece of wood.
2 A **stick** is a long thin piece of something: *a stick of chalk.*
[**Stick¹** comes from Old English *sticca*.]

**stick²** *verb* **sticks, sticking, stuck**
1 To **stick** means to push something pointed into something else: *He stuck his finger in my eye!*

2 To **stick** means to fix something somewhere, especially with glue.
[**Stick²** comes from Old English *stician*.]

**sticker** *noun* **stickers**
A **sticker** is a sign or label with a sticky back that you can attach to something.

**sticky** *adjective* **stickier, stickiest**
1 Something that has glue on it is **sticky**.
2 Something that sticks easily to things and feels like glue when you touch it is **sticky**.

**stiff** *adjective* **stiffer, stiffest** (th)
Something that does not bend easily is **stiff**. [**Stiff** comes from Old English.]

**stiffen** *verb* **stiffens, stiffening, stiffened**
To **stiffen** means to make something become stiff. [**Stiffen** comes from **stiff**.]

**stile** *noun* **stiles**
A **stile** is a wooden step that you use to help you climb over a fence, especially in a field. [**Stile** comes from Old English.]

**still** *adjective* (th)
1 Something that is not moving is **still**.
2 A drink that is **still** is not fizzy.
[**Still** comes from Old English.]

**still** *adverb*
When something is the same as it was, it is **still** like that.

**stimulate** *verb* **stimulates, stimulating, stimulated**
To **stimulate** means to make someone feel interested or excited.
[**Stimulate** comes from Latin.]

**sting** *noun* **stings**
A **sting** is the part of some animals, insects or plants that can pierce your skin and put poison in it.
[**Sting** comes from Old English.]

**sting** *verb* **stings, stinging, stung**
1 To **sting** means to hurt someone with a sting.
2 To **sting** means to hurt with a sharp pain: *The smoke stung our eyes.*

**stingray** *noun* **stingrays**
A **stingray** is a flat fish with large fins and a long poisonous tail.
[**Stingray** comes from **sting** and **ray²**.]

**stink** *verb* **stinks, stinking, stank, stunk**
To **stink** means to smell very bad.
[**Stink** comes from Old English.]

**stir** *verb* **stirs, stirring, stirred**
1 To **stir** means to move a liquid or soft mixture round and round.
2 To **stir** means to move slightly.
[**Stir** comes from Old English.]

**stitch** *noun* **stitches**
1 A **stitch** is a loop of thread made when sewing or knitting.
2 A **stitch** is a pain in your side when you run. [**Stitch** comes from Old English.]

**stock** *noun* **stocks**
1 **Stock** is all the goods that are kept in a factory or shop to sell.
2 **Stock** is a liquid made from cooking meat or vegetables that is used in making soups and stews.
3 **Stocks** are a wooden frame with holes in that a criminal's ankles were locked into as a punishment in the past.
[**Stock** comes from Old English.]

**stock** *verb* **stocks, stocking, stocked**
1 If a shop **stocks** a particular thing, it keeps that thing to sell.
2 If you **stock up** on something, you buy a lot of it to use in the future.

**stodgy** *adjective* **stodgier, stodgiest**
Food that is heavy and filling is **stodgy**.
[**Stodgy** probably comes from **stuff** and *podgy* 'fat'.]

**stoke** *verb* **stokes, stoking, stoked**
To **stoke** means to poke a fire and put fuel on it. [**Stoke** comes from Dutch.]

**stole** *verb*
Stole is the past tense of steal.

**stomach** *noun* **stomachs**
The **stomach** is the part of the body where food is digested after you swallow it.
[**Stomach** comes from Greek via French and Latin.]

**stone** *noun* **stones**
1 **Stone** is rock.
2 A **stone** is a piece of rock.
3 A **stone** is the large hard seed in the middle of some fruits.
4 A **stone** is a unit in the imperial system for measuring weight, equal to 14 pounds or 6.35 kilograms.
[**Stone** comes from Old English.]

**Stone Age** *noun*
The **Stone Age** is a very early period of history thousands of years ago when people made things out of stone.

**stood** *noun*
**Stood** is the past tense and past participle of **stand**.

**stool** *noun* **stools**
A **stool** is a small seat with no back.
[**Stool** comes from Old English.]

**stoop** *verb* **stoops, stooping, stooped**
1 To **stoop** means to bend your head and body forward.
2 To **stoop** means to walk with your head and back bent forward.
[**Stoop** comes from Old English.]

**stop** *verb* **stops, stopping, stopped** (th)
1 To **stop** means to end.
2 To **stop** means to cease moving or working, or to make something cease moving or working.
3 If you **stop** something, you do not do it any more or you do not let it happen
4 To **stop** means to stay somewhere for a while. [**Stop** comes from Old English.]

**storage** *noun*
**Storage** is putting things somewhere and keeping them there until you need them.
[**Storage** comes from **store**.]

**store** *noun* **stores**
A **store** is a large shop.
[**Store** comes from Latin via French.]

**store** *verb* **stores, storing, stored** (th)
To **store** means to keep things in a safe place until you need them.

**storey** *noun* **storeys**
A **storey** is a level or floor of a building.
[**Storey** comes from Latin.]

**stork** *noun* **storks**
A **stork** is a large bird with long legs and a long beak.
[**Stork** comes from Old English.]

**storm** *noun* **storms** (th)
A **storm** is a time of very strong winds and heavy rain or snow.
[**Storm** comes from Old English.]

**story** *noun* **stories** (th)
A **story** is a written or spoken description of a real or imaginary event.
[**Story** comes via French and Latin from the same Greek word as **history**.]

**stowaway** *noun* **stowaways**
A **stowaway** is someone who hides on a ship or a plane so that they can travel without paying for a ticket.

[**Stowaway** comes from *stow* 'to put away carefully' and **away**.]

**straight** *adjective* **straighter, straightest**
Something that does not bend or curve is **straight**.
[**Straight** is the old past participle of **stretch**.]

**straightaway** *adverb* (th)
If you do something **straightaway**, you do it immediately.

**strain** *noun* **strains**
**1** Strain is tension or injury in a muscle caused by stretching it too much.
**2** Strain is when there is too much to do or too many responsibilities: *Many working mothers suffer from nervous strain.*
[**Strain** comes from Latin via French.]

**strain** *verb* **strains, straining, strained**
**1** To **strain** a muscle means to stretch it too much and cause tension or injury.
**2** To **strain** means to make a lot of physical effort to do something.
**3** To **strain** means to separate the water from a mixture of solids and liquid, for example by pouring through a sieve or colander.

**strait** *noun* **straits**
A **strait** is a narrow strip of sea between two areas of land or between two seas.
[**Strait** comes via French from the same Latin word as **strict**.]

**strand** *noun* **strands**
A **strand** is a single hair, thread or piece of wire.
[No one knows where **strand** comes from.]

**stranded** *adjective*
A person, animal or vehicle that is **stranded** is stuck somewhere and cannot move or leave that place.
[**Stranded** comes from Old English.]

**strange** *adjective* **stranger, strangest** (th)
**1** Something that is **strange** is unusual and hard to understand.
**2** If something is **strange**, you did not know about it before: *At first a new school is a strange place with strange people.*
[**Strange** comes from Latin via French.]

**stranger** *noun* **strangers**
**1** A **stranger** is someone who is not known to you.
**2** A **stranger** is someone who is in a place

s/he does not know.
[**Stranger** comes from the same French word as **strange**.]

**strangle** *verb* **strangles, strangling, strangled**
To **strangle** means to kill someone by squeezing the throat and stopping him or her breathing.
[**Strangle** comes from Greek via French and Latin.]

**strap** *noun* **straps**
A **strap** is a strip of material or leather that is used to hold or fasten something in position.
[**Strap** probably comes from Latin.]

**straw** *noun* **straws**
**1** Straw is dry stalks of corn.
**2** A **straw** is a thin tube for drinking through. [**Straw** comes from Old English.]

**strawberry** *noun* **strawberries**
A **strawberry** is a small red summer fruit that grows on a bush near the ground.
[A **strawberry** is so called because you put straw round the plants to keep slugs away from the fruit.]

**stray** *verb* **strays, straying, strayed**
To **stray** means to get lost or wander away from a group.
[**Stray** comes from an old French word.]

**stray** *noun* **strays**
A **stray** is an animal that has wandered away from its home and got lost.

**stream** *noun* **streams**
**1** A **stream** is a small river.
**2** A **stream** is a flow of liquid.
**3** A **stream** is a line of moving people or cars. [**Stream** comes from Old English.]

**street** *noun* **streets**
A **street** is a road in a town with buildings along it.
[**Street** comes via Old English from Latin *via strata* 'paved road'.]

**strength** *noun* **strengths** (th)
**1** Strength is being strong, or how strong someone or something is.
**2** A **strength** is a good quality that you have, or something that you can do well.
[**Strength** comes from Old English.]

**strengthen** *verb* **strengthens, strengthening, strengthened**
To **strengthen** means to make something

stronger.

**strenuous** *adjective* (th)
An activity that is **strenuous** needs a lot of strength and effort.
[**Strenuous** comes from Latin.]

**stress** *noun* **stresses** (th)
**Stress** is worry and mental pressure caused by work or problems.
[The word **stress** comes from **distress**.]

**stretch** *noun* **stretches** (th)
**1** A **stretch** is the action of stretching a part of the body.
**2** A **stretch** is a continuous period of time.
**3** A **stretch** of water or land is an area of it. [**Stretch** comes from Old English.]

**stretch** *verb* **stretches, stretching, stretched**
**1** To **stretch** means to become or to make something longer, wider or tighter.
**2** When you **stretch**, you straighten your body and limbs and make them as long as you can.
**3** To **stretch** means to extend or spread out: *The sands stretched far into the distance.*

**stretcher** *noun* **stretchers**
A **stretcher** is a piece of canvas or other material attached to two poles or a metal frame that is used to carry an injured person.
[**Stretcher** comes from **stretch**.]

**strict** *adjective* **stricter, strictest** (th)
A person who is **strict** always wants rules obeyed correctly.
[**Strict** comes from Latin *strictus* 'pulled tight' (ancestor of **strait**).]

**stride** *noun* **strides**
A **stride** is a long step.
[**Stride** comes from Old English.]

**stride** *verb* **strides, striding, strode**
To **stride** means to walk with long steps.

**strike** *noun* **strikes**
**1** A **strike** is when people refuse to work because they have a disagreement with their employer.
**2** A **strike** is the action of hitting something.
[**Strike** comes from Old English.]

**strike** *verb* **strikes, striking, struck** (th)
**1** To **strike** means to refuse to work because of a disagreement with an employer.

**2** To **strike** something means to hit it.
**3** If a clock **strikes**, it gives the time by making a sound for each hour.

**string** *noun* **strings**
**1** **String** is very thin rope or cord.
**2** A **string** is a thin piece of wire on a guitar, violin or other musical instrument.
[**String** comes from Old English.]

**strip**[1] *noun* **strips**
A **strip** is a long narrow piece of something.
[**Strip**[1] probably comes from Old English.]

**strip**[2] *verb* **strips, stripping, stripped**
To **strip** means to remove something that covers something else: *First, we have to strip the wallpaper.*
[**Strip**[2] probably comes from an old Dutch word.]

**stripe** *noun* **stripes**
A **stripe** is a long narrow band of colour.
[**Stripe** comes from an old German or Dutch word.]

**stroke**[1] *noun* **strokes**
**1** A **stroke** is a hit or a hitting movement.
**2** A **stroke** is a style of swimming.
**3** A **stroke** is a sudden illness that damages a part of a person's brain so that s/he may find it difficult to move or speak. [**Stroke**[1] comes from **strike**.]

**stroke**[2] *verb* **strokes, stroking, stroked** (th)
To **stroke** means to move your hand gently over something.
[**Stroke**[2] comes from Old English.]

**stroll** *noun* **strolls** (th)
A **stroll** is a relaxed short walk.
[**Stroll** comes from German.]

**strong** *adjective* **stronger, strongest** (th)
**1** Someone or something that is **strong** has a lot of energy or power.
**2** Something that is **strong** is not easily broken.
**3** Food or drink that is **strong** has a lot of flavour or taste.
**4** An alcoholic drink that is **strong** has a lot of alcohol in it.
[**Strong** comes from Old English.]

**struck** *verb*
**Struck** is the past tense and past participle of **strike**.

## structure *noun* **structures** (th)
1 A **structure** is something that has been built such as a building or a bridge.
2 The **structure** of something is the way that the parts of it are connected together.
[**Structure** comes from Latin via French.]

## struggle *noun* **struggles** (th)
1 A **struggle** is a hard fight to achieve something you want: *the country's struggle for independence.*
2 A **struggle** is a fight between two or more people.
[No one knows where **struggle** comes from.]

## struggle *verb* **struggles, struggling, struggled** (th)
1 To **struggle** means to fight to defend yourself or to get free.
2 To **struggle** means to make a lot of effort to achieve something that is very difficult for you.

## strum *verb* **strums, strumming, strummed**
To **strum** means to play a guitar or similar instrument by moving your fingers over the strings.
[The word **strum** is an imitation of the sound.]

## stub *noun* **stubs**
A **stub** is the short end left on something.
[**Stub** comes from Old English.]

## stubborn *adjective* (th)
A **stubborn** person is determined not to change his/her mind.
[No one knows where **stubborn** comes from.]

## stuck *verb*
**Stuck** is the past tense and past participle of **stick**.

## student *noun* **students**
A **student** is a person who is studying.
[**Student** comes from the same Latin word as **study**.]

## studio *noun* **studios**
1 A **studio** is a place where an artist, musician or dancer works or practises.
2 A **studio** is a place where films are made or music is recorded.
[**Studio** comes via Italian from the same Latin word as **study**.]

## study *noun* **studies**
A **study** is a room where someone studies.
[**Study** comes from Latin.]

## study *verb* **studies, studying, studied** (th)
1 To **study** means to spend time learning about something.
2 To **study** means to look at something very carefully.

## stuff *noun* (th)
1 **Stuff** is a kind of material or substance.
2 **Stuff** is things in general or things that you use for a particular purpose: *Don't forget your swimming stuff.*
[**Stuff** comes from Greek via French.]

## stuff *verb* **stuffs, stuffing, stuffed** (th)
To **stuff** means to pack tightly or fill with something.

## stuffing *noun*
1 **Stuffing** is a mixture of chopped bread, onions or other food that is put inside a chicken or a vegetable before it is cooked.
2 **Stuffing** is the material that is used to fill something such as a cushion.
[**Stuffing** comes from **stuff**.]

## stuffy *adjective* **stuffier, stuffiest** (th)
A place that is **stuffy** does not have enough fresh air in it.
[**Stuffy** comes from **stuff**.]

## stumble *verb* **stumbles, stumbling, stumbled**
To **stumble** means to trip or almost fall over something.
[**Stumble** comes from Old Norse.]

## stump *noun* **stumps**
1 A **stump** is the part of a tree that is left after it has been cut down.
2 A **stump** is the part of something that is left after the main part has been cut off or used.
3 A **stump** is one of the three wooden rods of a wicket in the game of cricket.
[**Stump** comes from an old German or Dutch word.]

## stung *verb*
**Stung** is the past tense and past participle of **sting**.

## stunk *verb*
**Stunk** is a past tense and the past participle of **stink**.

## stunt *noun* **stunts**
A **stunt** is a difficult or dangerous trick or act that someone performs.
[No one knows where **stunt** comes from.]

**stupid** *adjective* (th)
**1** Someone or something that is **stupid** is very silly.
**2** Someone who is **stupid** is not clever.
[**Stupid** comes from Latin *stupidus* 'dazed'.]

**sturdy** *adjective* **sturdier, sturdiest** (th)
Something that is **sturdy** is well made and strong.
[**Sturdy** comes from an old French word.]

**stutter** *verb* **stutters, stuttering, stuttered**
To **stutter** means to repeat the first sound of a word several times before managing to say the whole word.
[No one knows where **stutter** comes from.]

**sty**[1] *noun* **sties**
A **sty** is a pen for pigs to live in.
[**Sty**[1] comes from Old English *sti*.]

**sty**[2] *noun* **sties**
A **sty** is a painful red swelling on the eye.
[**Sty**[2] comes from Old English *stigend*.]

**style** *noun* **styles**
**1** The **style** of something is the way it is made or designed.
**2** A **style** is a way of doing something.
[**Style** comes from Latin via French.]

**subconscious** *noun*
The **subconscious** is the part of your mind that you are not aware of but that affects the way you behave.
[**Subconscious** comes from *sub* 'under' and **conscious**.]

**subconsciously** *adverb*
If you do something **subconsciously**, you do it without realising why.

**subject** *noun* **subjects**
**1** A **subject** is a person, thing or idea being talked, written or learned about.
**2** A **subject** is a member of a particular country.
**3** The **subject** of a sentence is the person or thing that does the action of the verb. In the sentence *The monkey likes bananas*, 'the monkey' is the **subject**.
[**Subject** comes from Latin *subjectus* 'brought under'.]

**submarine** *noun* **submarines**
A **submarine** is a kind of ship that can travel under water.
[**Submarine** comes from *sub* 'under' and *marine* 'to do with the sea'.]

**submerge** *verb* **submerges, submerging, submerged** (th)
To **submerge** means to go, or to make something go, completely under water.
[**Submerge** comes from Latin.]

**subscription** *noun* **subscriptions**
A **subscription** is an amount of money that you pay in advance to receive a newspaper or magazine regularly.
[**Subscription** comes from Latin.]

**substance** *noun* **substances**
A **substance** is a liquid or solid that things consist of.
[**Substance** comes from Latin via French.]

**substitute** *noun* **substitutes** (th)
A **substitute** is a person or thing that is used instead of another.
[**Substitute** comes from Latin.]

**subtitles** *noun*
**Subtitles** are words printed on a television or film screen. People who cannot hear, or who do not speak the language that the programme or film is in, can read the **subtitles** to find out what is being said.
[**Subtitles** comes from *sub* 'under' and **title**.]

**subtle** *adjective* **subtler, subtlest**
Something that is **subtle** is not easy to notice or understand immediately.
[**Subtle** comes from Latin via French.]

**subtract** *verb* **subtracts, subtracting, subtracted**
To **subtract** means to take one number away from another.
[**Subtract** comes from Latin.]

**suburb** *noun* **suburbs**
A **suburb** is an area of a city or town that is far from the centre.
[**Suburb** comes from Latin *sub* 'near to' and *urbis* 'city'.]

**subway** *noun* **subways**
A **subway** is a tunnel for people to walk under somewhere safely.
[**Subway** comes from *sub* 'under' and **way**.]

**succeed** *verb* **succeeds, succeeding, succeeded**
To **succeed** means to do what you wanted or set out to do.

n o p q r **s** t u v w x y z

[**Succeed** comes from Latin via French.]

**success** *noun* **successes**
1 A **success** is something that has a good result.
2 A **success** is when someone achieves what s/he wanted or set out to do. [**Success** comes from the same Latin word as **succeed**.]

**such** *adjective*
1 of the same kind that is being described: *I have never seen such a terrible thing.*
2 so much: *We had such fun at the fair.* [**Such** comes from Old English.]

**suck** *verb* **sucks, sucking, sucked**
1 To **suck** means to draw liquid into your mouth.
2 To **suck** means to hold something in the mouth without biting it.
3 To **suck** means to pull something in strongly. [**Suck** comes from Old English.]

**suction** *noun*
**Suction** is the force created when air is removed from a space so that another substance can be pulled into it. [**Suction** comes from Latin.]

**sudden** *adjective* (th)
Something that happens quickly and unexpectedly is **sudden**. [**Sudden** comes from Latin via French.]

**suddenly** *adverb* (th)
When something happens quickly and unexpectedly, it happens **suddenly**.

**sue** *verb* **sues, suing, sued**
To **sue** someone means to claim money from that person in a court because s/he has done something against you. [**Sue** comes from Latin via French.]

**suede** *noun*
**Suede** is soft leather with a surface that can be brushed like velvet. [**Suede** comes from French *Suède* 'Sweden'; suede gloves from Sweden were fashionable in France in the 19th century.]

**suffer** *verb* **suffers, suffering, suffered** (th)
To **suffer** means to feel pain or unhappiness. [**Suffer** comes from Latin.]

**suffix** *noun* **suffixes**
A **suffix** is a group of letters that is added to the end of a word to make a new word

that is related. *-less, -ness* and *-ly* are **suffixes**. [**Suffix** comes from Latin.]

**suffocate** *verb* **suffocates, suffocating, suffocated**
1 To **suffocate** means to stop someone from breathing so s/he dies.
2 To **suffocate** means to be unable to breathe. [**Suffocate** comes from Latin.]

**sugar** *noun*
**Sugar** is a sweet-tasting substance used in food. [**Sugar** comes via French, Italian, Latin and Arabic from Persian (the language spoken in Iran).]

**sugar beet** *noun*
**Sugar beet** is a plant with a round white root that sugar comes from. [**Beet** comes from Old English *bete* (ancestor of **beetroot**).]

**sugar cane** *noun*
**Sugar cane** is a tall plant that grows in warm countries and that sugar comes from.

**suggest** *verb* **suggests, suggesting, suggested**
To **suggest** means to give someone an idea to think about. [**Suggest** comes from Latin.]

**suicide** *noun*
If a person **commits suicide**, s/he kills himself or herself. [**Suicide** comes from Latin *sui* 'of yourself' and *caedere* 'to kill'.]

**suit** *noun* **suits**
A **suit** is a jacket and a pair of trousers or a skirt that are made out of the same material. [**Suit** comes from Latin via French.]

**suit** *verb* **suits, suiting, suited**
1 To **suit** means to be convenient for someone: *Would it suit you to come on Thursday?*
2 To **suit** means to look right on someone: *That colour really suits you.*

**suitable** *adjective* (th)
Something that is what is wanted is **suitable**. [**Suitable** comes from **suit**.]

**sulk** *verb* **sulks, sulking, sulked**
To **sulk** means to be silent and moody because you are angry. [No one knows where **sulk** comes from.]

**sulphur** noun
Sulphur is a yellow chemical element that burns easily.
[**Sulphur** comes from Latin via French.]

**sultana** noun **sultanas**
A **sultana** is a dried grape.
[**Sultana** comes from Italian.]

**sum** noun **sums**
1 A **sum** is a problem to be solved using numbers.
2 A **sum** is the total when numbers are added together.
3 A **sum** is an amount of money.
[**Sum** comes from Latin *summa* 'total'.]

**summary** noun **summaries**
A **summary** is a short account of something that includes the main points.
[**Summary** comes from the same Latin word as **sum**.]

**summer** noun **summers**
Summer is the season after spring and before autumn when the weather is sunny and warm.
[**Summer** comes from Old English.]

**summit** noun **summits** (th)
A **summit** is the top of a mountain.
[**Summit** comes from Latin *summus* 'highest'.]

**summon** verb **summons, summoning, summoned** (th)
To **summon** means to send for someone or order someone to come somewhere: *The judge summoned him to appear in court.*
[**Summon** comes from Latin.]

**summons** noun
A **summons** is an official order for someone to go somewhere: *a summons from the court.*
[**Summons** comes via French from the same Latin word as **summon**.]

**sun** noun
The **sun** is the star that gives the earth heat and light.
[**Sun** comes from Old English.]

**sunbathe** verb **sunbathes, sunbathing, sunbathed**
To **sunbathe** means to lie in the sun in order to make your skin go darker.

**sunburn** noun
Sunburn is red painful skin caused by staying too long in the sun.

**sunflower** noun **sunflowers**
A **sunflower** is a very large yellow flower that grows on a tall stem.
[The **sunflower** is so called because it turns to follow the path of the sun.]

**sung** verb
Sung is the past participle of **sing**.

**sunglasses** plural noun
Sunglasses are glasses with dark lenses that protect your eyes from the sun's light.

**sunk** verb
Sunk is the past participle of **sink**.

**sunny** adjective **sunnier, sunniest**
When the sun shines, it is **sunny**.

**sunrise** noun **sunrises**
Sunrise is the time when the sun appears in the sky early in the morning.

**sunset** noun **sunsets**
Sunset is the time when the sun disappears below the horizon at the end of the day.

**sunshine** noun
Sunshine is the warm light from the sun.

**suntan** noun
Suntan is the darker shade your skin has when you have been in the sun.

**super** adjective
1 If you say that someone or something is **super**, you like them very much or think they are very good: *She's a super teacher.* **Super** is an informal word.
2 **Super** means bigger or better than other similar things: *Super tankers can carry vast amounts of oil.*
[**Super** comes from Latin *super* 'over'.]

**superb** adjective (th)
Something that is **superb** is very good or magnificent.
[**Superb** comes from Latin *superbus* 'proud'.]

**superior** adjective (th)
Something that is **superior** is better than anything similar.
[**Superior** comes from Latin *superior* 'higher'.]

**superlative** adjective
1 Something that is **superlative** is the best or of the highest quality: *a superlative performance that won him an Oscar.*

**2** You use the **superlative** form of an adjective or adverb to show that the noun or verb it describes is more or greater in some way than other things, or than anything or anyone else. **Superlative** forms usually end in *-est*: if the adjective or adverb has no **superlative** form, you use *most* in front of it.
[**Superlative** comes via French from Latin *superlatus* 'carried above'.]

**supermarket** *noun* **supermarkets**
A **supermarket** is a large shop where people take what they want and pay as they leave.
[**Supermarket** comes from **super** and **market**.]

**supernatural** *adjective*
Something that is **supernatural** is mysterious and cannot be explained by nature or science.
[**Supernatural** comes from Latin *super* 'above' and **natural**.]

**supersonic** *adjective*
Something that travels faster than the speed of sound is **supersonic**.
[**Supersonic** comes from Latin *super* 'above' and **sonic**.]

**superstition** *noun* **superstitions**
A **superstition** is something that some people believe although there is no reason to do so: *It's an old superstition that walking under a ladder is unlucky.*
[**Superstition** comes from Latin.]

**superstitious** *adjective*
If you are **superstitious**, you believe that luck and magic influence things that happen.

**supervise** *verb* **supervises, supervising, supervised** (th)
To **supervise** means to make sure that work is done properly.
[**Supervise** comes from Latin *supervidere* 'to look over'.]

**supper** *noun* **suppers**
A **supper** is an evening meal or snack.
[**Supper** comes from an old French word.]

**supple** *adjective* **suppler, supplest** (th)
A **supple** person is able to bend and twist parts of the body easily.
[**Supple** comes from Latin via French.]

**supply** *noun* **supplies** (th)
**1** A **supply** of something is an amount of

it that is provided or that you have: *the water supply.*
**2 Supplies** are food and equipment that you take with you on a trip.
[**Supply** comes via French from Latin *supplere* 'to fill up'.]

**supply** *verb* **supplies, supplying, supplied** (th)
To **supply** something means to provide it to people when they want or need it.

**support** *noun* **supports** (th)
**1** A **support** is something that helps to hold a thing up.
**2 Support** is helping someone and showing your approval.
[**Support** comes from Latin via French.]

**support** *verb* **supports, supporting, supported** (th)
**1** To **support** means to hold something up so that it does not fall over.
**2** To **support** means to give help or approval to someone or something.

**suppose** *verb* **supposes, supposing, supposed** (th)
**1** To **suppose** means to imagine that something is true.
**2** If you are **supposed** to do something, a rule says you should do it: *You're not supposed to park there.*
[**Suppose** comes from Latin via French.]

**sure** *adjective* **surer, surest** (th)
**1** Someone who is certain about something is **sure**.
**2** Something that is **sure** to happen will certainly happen.
[**Sure** comes via French from the same Latin word as **secure**.]

**surf** *noun*
**Surf** is large white waves breaking on the shore.
[No one knows where **surf** comes from.]

**surface** *noun* **surfaces**
**1** A **surface** is the outside of something.
**2** A **surface** is a flat area on the top or outside of something.
[**Surface** comes from French.]

**surfing** *noun*
**Surfing** is standing or lying on a board and riding on waves as they are breaking.
[**Surfing** comes from **surf**.]

**surgeon** *noun* **surgeons**
A **surgeon** is a doctor who performs

operations.
[**Surgeon** comes from Greek via French and Latin.]

**surgery** *noun* **surgeries**
1 **Surgery** is an operation on part of the body that is damaged or diseased.
2 A **surgery** is a place where you go to see a doctor or dentist.
[**Surgery** comes from the same French word as **surgeon**.]

**surname** *noun* **surnames**
Your **surname** is your family name: *Clark's surname is Kent.*
[**Surname** comes from French.]

**surprise** *noun* **surprises** (th)
1 A **surprise** is something that was not expected.
2 **Surprise** is the feeling you get when something unexpected happens.
[**Surprise** comes from Latin via French.]

**surprise** *verb* **surprises, surprising, surprised** (th)
To **surprise** someone means to do or say something that s/he does not expect.

**surrender** *verb* **surrenders, surrendering, surrendered** (th)
To **surrender** means to stop fighting and give in to the enemy.
[**Surrender** comes from an old French word.]

**surround** *verb* **surrounds, surrounding, surrounded** (th)
To **surround** means to go or be all round something.
[**Surround** comes via French from Latin *superundare* 'to flow over'.]

**survive** *verb* **survives, surviving, survived** (th)
1 To **survive** means to stay alive after you have been in danger: *He survived in the jungle for a week after the plane crash.*
2 To **survive** means to continue to exist after a long time or after danger: *Only one part of the old castle has survived.*
[**Survive** comes from Latin via French.]

**survivor** *noun* **survivors**
A **survivor** is someone who is still alive after an accident, war or dangerous situation.

**suspect** *verb* **suspects, suspecting, suspected**
1 To **suspect** someone means that you

think s/he is probably guilty of a crime.
2 To **suspect** something means to think that it is probably true.
[**Suspect** comes from Latin.]

**suspend** *verb* **suspends, suspending, suspended** (th)
1 To **suspend** something means to hang it from somewhere so that it can move freely.
2 To **suspend** someone means to stop him/her taking part in something for a short time: *She was suspended from school.*
3 To **suspend** something means to stop it or stop doing it for a short time: *The train service has been suspended due to flooding.*
[**Suspend** comes from Latin via French.]

**suspense** *noun* (th)
**Suspense** is a worried feeling when you are not sure what is going to happen next.
[**Suspense** comes from the same Latin word as **suspend**.]

**suspicious** *adjective*
If you feel **suspicious**, you think that someone might have done something wrong or cannot be trusted.
[**Suspicious** comes from the same Latin word as **suspect**.]

**swallow**[1] *noun* **swallows**
A **swallow** is a small bird with a long forked tail.
[**Swallow**[1] comes from Old English *swealwe*.]

**swallow**[2] *verb* **swallows, swallowing, swallowed** (th)
To **swallow** means to make something go down your throat.
[**Swallow**[2] comes from Old English *swelgan*.]

**swam** *verb*
**Swam** is the past tense of **swim**.

**swamp** *noun* **swamps** (th)
A **swamp** is an area of very wet ground.
[No one knows where **swamp** comes from.]

**swan** *noun* **swans**
A **swan** is a large white or black bird with a long neck. **Swans** live on or near water.
[**Swan** comes from Old English.]

**swap** *verb* **swaps, swapping, swapped** (th)
To **swap** something means to exchange it for something else.

[**Swap** originally meant to seal a bargain by slapping hands with the other person, and the word **swap** is an imitation of the sound.]

**swarm** *noun* **swarms**
A **swarm** is a large number of insects clustered together.
[**Swarm** comes from Old English.]

**sway** *verb* **sways, swaying, swayed** (th)
**1** To **sway** means to move slowly from side to side.
**2** To **sway** someone or someone's opinion means to make that person think differently.
[No one knows where **sway** comes from.]

**swear** *verb* **swears, swearing, swore**
**1** To **swear** means to make a solemn promise.
**2** To **swear** means to use rude words.
[**Swear** comes from Old English.]

**sweat** *verb* **sweats, sweating, sweated**
To **sweat** means to give off liquid through the skin when you are hot or ill.
[**Sweat** comes from Old English.]

**sweater** *noun* **sweaters**
A **sweater** is a knitted jumper.
[**Sweater** comes from **sweat**.]

**sweep** *noun* **sweeps**
A **sweep** is a person whose job is to clean chimneys.
[**Sweep** comes from Old English.]

**sweep** *verb* **sweeps, sweeping, swept**
To **sweep** means to clean something using a brush or broom.

**sweet** *noun* **sweets**
**1** A **sweet** is a small piece of food made from sugar or chocolate.
**2** A **sweet** is a pudding.
[**Sweet** comes from Old English.]

**sweet** *adjective* **sweeter, sweetest**
**1** Something that tastes of sugar is **sweet**.
**2** Something that is **sweet** is very pleasant or attractive.

**sweetcorn** *noun*
**Sweetcorn** is the yellow seeds of the maize plant that you eat as a vegetable.

**sweeten** *verb* **sweetens, sweetening, sweetened**
To **sweeten** something means to make it sweet.

**swell** *verb* **swells, swelling, swelled, swollen** (th)
To **swell** means to get bigger.
[**Swell** comes from Old English.]

**swept** *verb*
**Swept** is the past tense and past participle of **sweep**.

**swerve** *verb* **swerves, swerving, swerved**
To **swerve** means to change direction suddenly to avoid something while moving.
[**Swerve** comes from Old English.]

**swift** *adjective* **swifter, swiftest** (th)
Someone or something that is quick is **swift**. [**Swift** comes from Old English.]

**swift** *noun* **swifts**
A **swift** is a small bird with a forked tail that flies very quickly.

**swim** *verb* **swims, swimming, swam, swum**
**1** To **swim** means to move your body through water.
**2** To **swim** means to cross something by swimming.
[**Swim** comes from Old English.]

**swimmer** *noun* **swimmers**
A **swimmer** is someone who swims: *a good swimmer; an Olympic swimmer.*

**swindle** *verb* **swindles, swindling, swindled** (th)
To **swindle** people means to get their money or something they own by tricking them.
[**Swindle** comes from German *Schwindler* 'a cheat'.]

**swine** *noun* **swine**
**Swine** is another word for pig.
[**Swine** comes from Old English.]

**swing** *noun* **swings**
A **swing** is a seat fixed to a frame that you sit on in order to move backwards and forwards. [**Swing** comes from Old English.]

**swing** *verb* **swings, swinging, swung** (th)
To **swing** means to move freely through the air backwards and forwards or from side to side.

**swipe** *verb* **swipes, swiping, swiped**
**1** To **swipe** someone or something means to hit that thing or person by swinging your arm at them.

a b c d e f g h i j k l m

**2** To **swipe** a plastic card means to pull it through a special machine that can read the details on it.
[**Swipe** comes from **sweep**.]

**swirl** *verb* **swirls, swirling, swirled** (th)
To **swirl** means to move in circles: *Her skirt swirled as she danced.*
[**Swirl** probably comes from an old German or Dutch word.]

**switch** *noun* **switches**
A **switch** is a device on a piece of electrical equipment that lets electricity flow into it if you move it one way, or stops the electricity if you move it the other way.
[**Switch** probably comes from an old German word.]

**switch** *verb* **switches, switching, switched**
**1** To **switch** means to change from one thing to another: *She switched from being very calm to very angry.*
**2** To **switch** something **on** is to make it start by moving a switch.
**3** To **switch** something **off** is to make it stop by moving a switch.

**swivel** *verb* **swivels, swivelling, swivelled**
To **swivel** means to move round on a fixed central point.
[**Swivel** comes from Old English.]

**swollen** *verb*
**Swollen** is the past participle of **swell**.

**swoop** *verb* **swoops, swooping, swooped**
**1** When a bird or an aircraft **swoops**, it moves quickly down through the air, especially in order to attack something.
**2** If soldiers or police **swoop**, they arrive somewhere very suddenly and unexpectedly.
[**Swoop** probably comes from the same Old English word as **sweep**.]

**sword** *noun* **swords**
A **sword** is a weapon with a long sharp blade. [**Sword** comes from Old English.]

**swore** *verb*
**Swore** is the past tense and past participle of **swear**.

**swot** *verb* **swots, swotting, swotted**
To **swot** means to study hard, especially for a test or an exam.
[**Swot** is an old spelling of **sweat**.]

**swum** *verb*
**Swum** is the past participle of **swim**.

**swung** *verb*
**Swung** is the past tense and past participle of **swing**.

**syllable** *noun* **syllables**
A **syllable** is part of a word that contains a single sound. The word *television* has four **syllables**.
[**Syllable** comes from Greek via French and Latin.]

**syllabus** *noun* **syllabuses**
A **syllabus** is the list of subjects and topics that are taught in a school, college or university.
[**Syllabus** comes from Greek via Latin.]

**symbol** *noun* **symbols**
A **symbol** is a sign or an object that represents something else: *The symbol @ stands for the word 'at'.*
[**Symbol** comes via Latin from Greek *symbolon* 'a mark or token'.]

**symmetrical** *adjective*
A **symmetrical** shape or object has two halves that are exactly the same size and shape.
[**Symmetrical** comes from Greek via French or Latin.]

**sympathetic** *adjective* (th)
A **sympathetic** person is someone, who listens to other people's problems and tries to understand them and help them.
**sympathetically** *adverb*.
[**Sympathetic** comes from **sympathy**.]

**sympathy** *noun* **sympathies** (th)
If you feel **sympathy** for someone, you feel sorry for that person because s/he is ill or in a difficult situation.
[**Sympathy** comes from Greek via Latin.]

**symphony** *noun* **symphonies**
A **symphony** is a long piece of music that is played by an orchestra.
[**Symphony** comes via French and Latin from Greek *symphonos* 'in harmony'.]

**symptom** *noun* **symptoms**
A **symptom** is a change in your body that shows you are ill.
[**Symptom** comes from Greek via Latin.]

**synagogue** *noun* **synagogues**
A **synagogue** is a building where Jews worship.

[**Synagogue** comes via French and Latin from Greek *synagoge* 'an assembly'.]

**synchronise** *verb* **synchronises, synchronising, synchronised** *Also* **synchronize**
1 To **synchronise** two or more things means to make them happen at the same time or work at the same speed.
2 To **synchronise** clocks or watches means to make them show exactly the same time.
[**Synchronise** comes from Greek via Latin.]

**syndrome** *noun* **syndromes**
A **syndrome** is a group of signs or changes in your body that show you have an illness.
[**Syndrome** comes from Greek *syndrome* 'happening together'.]

**synonym** *noun* **synonyms**
A **synonym** is a word that means the same or almost the same as another word. *Slim* is a synonym of *slender*.
[**Synonym** comes from Greek via Latin.]

**synthetic** *adjective*
Something that is **synthetic** does not occur naturally in the world and is made by people: *Nylon is a synthetic material.*
[**Synthetic** comes via French or Latin from Greek *syntithenai* 'to put together'.]

**syphon** *verb*
**Syphon** is another way to spell **siphon**.

**syringe** *noun* **syringes**
A **syringe** is a tube with a needle attached to it that is used for giving injections or taking blood.
[**Syringe** comes via Latin from Greek *syrinx* 'a pipe'.]

**syrup** *noun*
**Syrup** is a thick, sticky sweet liquid.
[**Syrup** comes from Arabic via French or Latin.]

**system** *noun* **systems**
1 A **system** is a group of things or parts of things which work together in an organised way: *a computer system.*
2 A **system** is the way something is organised or done: *a filing system.*
[**System** comes from Greek via French and Latin.]

## Dictionary Fun

### Complete the idioms
1. A s_____ in a teacup (*a lot of excitement over nothing*)
2. The s_____ of the earth (*someone who is reliable and honest*)
3. S_____ your breath (*don't waste time talking*)

### Complete the proverbs
1. A s_____ in time saves nine.
2. S_____ waters run deep.
3. Let s_____ dogs lie.

### New words
Clue: This enables you to watch more television channels.

### Complete the similes
1. As s_____ as an eel.
2. As s_____ as honey.
3. As white as s_____.

### Did you know?
◆ **Sandwich** is named after the 4th Earl of Sandwich, who is said to have invented the snack so that he could eat while playing cards.
◆ The word **siren** is named after the Sirens from Greek mythology, whose singing led sailors onto the rocks.

# Tt

**ta b** *noun* **tabs**
A **tab** is a small label, flap or loop.
[No one knows where **tab** comes from.]

**table** *noun* **tables**
1 A **table** is a piece of furniture with a flat top and legs.
2 A **table** is a list of information in columns.
3 **Tables** are lists of numbers multiplied by other numbers: *the seven times table.*
[**Table** comes from Latin.]

**tablespoon** *noun* **tablespoons**
A **tablespoon** is a large spoon used for serving or measuring food.

**tablet** *noun* **tablets**
A **tablet** is a tiny block of medicine that is small enough to swallow.
[**Tablet** comes via French from the same Latin word as **table**.]

**taboo** *adjective*
If something is **taboo**, you are not allowed to do it or talk about it because you will upset many people.
[**Taboo** comes from Tongan *tabu* 'sacred' or 'forbidden'. Tongan is the language spoken in a group of islands in the South Pacific.]

**tack** *noun* **tacks**
A **tack** is a small nail.
[**Tack** probably comes from an old French word.]

**tack** *verb* **tacks, tacking, tacked**
1 To **tack** something is to pin it up with tacks: *The notice was tacked to the tree.*
2 To **tack** a piece of material means to sew it roughly with large stitches so that it is ready to be properly sewn with smaller stitches.

**tackle** *verb* **tackles, tackling, tackled** (th)
1 To **tackle** someone in games such as football means to try to get the ball from a player in the other team.
2 To **tackle** something difficult is to start to do it.
[**Tackle** comes from an old German word.]

**tact** *noun* (th)
**Tact** is the ability to deal with people without upsetting them, especially in difficult situations.
[**Tact** comes from Latin via French.]

**tactful** *adjective* (th)
Someone who is **tactful** is able to deal with people in a way that does not upset them, especially in difficult situations.
**tactfully** *adverb.*

**tactics** *plural noun*
**Tactics** are a method or system for winning a game or a battle.
[**Tactics** comes from Greek.]

**tadpole** *noun* **tadpoles**
A **tadpole** is a small black creature that lives in water. **Tadpoles** eventually grow legs and lose their tails, and turn into frogs or toads.
[**Tadpole** comes from Old English *tada* 'toad' and an old word *poll* 'head', probably because a young tadpole seems to be just a large head and a tail.]

**tag** *noun* **tags**
A **tag** is a small label: *a price tag.*
[No one knows where **tag** comes from.]

**tail** *noun* **tails**
1 A **tail** is the long thin part at the end of the body of an animal, bird or fish: *The dog is wagging his tail.*
2 **Tails** is the side of the coin that does not have a head on it.
3 The **tail** of something is the end of it: *the tail of the queue.*
[**Tail** comes from Old English.]

**tailor** *noun* **tailors**
A **tailor** is a person whose job is making clothes.
[**Tailor** comes via French from Latin *taliare* 'to cut'.]

**tailor** *verb* **tailors, tailoring, tailored** (th)
To **tailor** something is to design it for a particular person or purpose: *You can tailor the language course to suit your needs.*

**tainted** *adjective* (th)
Something that is **tainted** is spoilt by something unpleasant.
[**Tainted** comes via French from the same Latin word as **tint**.]

**take** *verb* **takes, taking, took, taken** (th)
1 to carry something: *She took her suitcase to the car.*
2 to hold something: *Could you take the baby for a moment?*

**3** to remove or steal something: *Someone's taken my money!*
**4** to accept something: *Do you take cheques?* [**Take** comes from Old Norse.]

**takeaway** *noun* **takeaways**
**1** A **takeaway** is a shop that sells meals for you to eat somewhere else.
**2** A **takeaway** is a meal that you buy from a shop and eat somewhere else.

**takings** *plural noun*
The **takings** of places such as shops are the money that they get from everything that is sold: *the day's takings.*
[**Takings** comes from **take**.]

**talk** *verb* **talks, talking, talked** (th)
To **talk** means to say things to someone.
[**Talk** comes from Middle English.]

**talk** *noun* **talks** (th)
**1** A **talk** is a lecture or a speech: *They gave a talk on the town's history.*
**2** **Talks** are discussions between countries or groups of people: *peace talks.*

**tall** *adjective* **taller, tallest**
**1** A **tall** person is of more than average height: *Basketball players are really tall.*
**2** Something that is **tall** is high.
[**Tall** comes from Old English.]

**talon** *noun* **talons**
A **talon** is a sharp claw, such as a bird of prey has.
[**Talon** comes from Latin via French.]

**tambourine** *noun* **tambourines**
A **tambourine** is a round musical instrument with a skin stretched over it like a drum and metal discs round the edge. [**Tambourine** comes from French.]

**tame** *adjective* **tamer, tamest** (th)
**1** A **tame** animal is not wild and can live safely with people.
**2** Something that is **tame** is not very exciting: *It was a very tame movie – nothing happened.* [**Tame** comes from Old English.]

**tamper** *verb* **tampers, tampering, tampered** (th)
To **tamper** with something means to do something to it that breaks or spoils it.
[**Tamper** comes from **temper**.]

**tampon** *noun* **tampons**
A **tampon** is a specially designed piece of cotton wool that a woman can put inside

her vagina to collect blood during her period. [**Tampon** comes from French.]

**tan** *noun* **tans**
**1** A **tan** or **suntan** is the brown colour that your skin goes when you have been in the sun.
**2** **Tan** is a light brown colour.
[**Tan** comes from Old English.]

**tan** *adjective*
of a light brown colour: *tan shoe polish.*

**tandem** *noun* **tandems**
A **tandem** is a bicycle for two people.
[**Tandem** comes from Latin *tandem* 'at length'.]

**tandoori** *adjective*
**Tandoori** food is Indian food that has been baked in a clay oven called a tandoor: *chicken tandoori.*
[**Tandoori** comes from Persian (the language spoken in Iran).]

**tangent** *noun* **tangents**
A **tangent** is a straight line that touches a curve but does not cross it.
[**Tangent** comes from Latin *tangens* 'touching'.]

**tangerine** *noun* **tangerines**
A **tangerine** is a small sweet orange.
[The **tangerine** is named after *Tangier*, a city in Morocco, from which it was exported to Europe.]

**tangle** *noun* **tangles**
A **tangle** of things such as threads or hair is a knotted mass that cannot easily be separated.
[**Tangle** probably comes from a Scandinavian language.]

**tank** *noun* **tanks**
**1** A **tank** is a container for holding liquid: *a petrol tank.*
**2** A **tank** is a large, heavy, armoured vehicle that runs on tracks and fires shells.
[**Tank** comes from Gujarati or Marathi (languages spoken in India).]

**tanker** *noun* **tankers**
A **tanker** is a large lorry or ship that carries oil or other liquids.
[**Tanker** comes from **tank**.]

**tantrum** *noun* **tantrums**
A **tantrum** is a sudden burst of anger or

temper.
[No one knows where **tantrum** comes from.]

**tap¹** *noun* **taps**
A **tap** is a type of handle that you turn to control the flow of water or gas.
[**Tap¹** comes from Old English.]

**tap²** *noun* **taps** (th)
A **tap** is a gentle touch or hit: *He heard a tap at the door.*
[**Tap²** comes from an old French word.]

**tap²** *verb* **taps**, **tapping**, **tapped** (th)
To **tap** someone or something means to hit or touch them gently: *She tapped him on the shoulder.*

**tap-dancing** *noun*
**Tap-dancing** is dancing with special shoes that click when they touch the floor.

**tape** *noun* **tapes**
**1 Tape** is cloth or plastic in a long, thin strip. **Tape** has many uses: for example, you can use it to tie things up or you can write your name on it and sew it to something to show that it belongs to you.
**2** A **tape** is a cassette of magnetic material that contains sound or video recordings: *a music tape.*
**3 Tape** is a thin strip of magnetic material for recording sound or pictures.
**4 Tape** is sticky plastic that comes on a reel and is used for sticking things.
[**Tape** comes from Old English.]

**tape** *verb* **tapes**, **taping**, **taped**
To **tape** something is to record it on a video or audio cassette.

**tape measure** *noun* **tape measures**
A **tape measure** is a long thin strip of material or metal that is marked in centimetres or inches and is used for measuring things.

**tapestry** *noun* **tapestries**
A **tapestry** is a large piece of heavy cloth that has pictures and designs woven or sewn into it.
[**Tapestry** comes from French *tapis* 'carpet'.]

**tapeworm** *noun* **tapeworms**
A **tapeworm** is a long flat worm that lives in the guts of some people and animals.

**tar** *noun*

**1 Tar** is a thick, black, sticky liquid that is used for making roads.
**2 Tar** is a thick, black, sticky liquid that is formed when tobacco is burned and that collects in the lungs.
[**Tar** comes from Old English.]

**target** *noun* **targets**
A **target** is a person or thing that you aim at when you are shooting or attacking.
[**Target** comes from Old English.]

**tarnish** *verb* **tarnishes**, **tarnishing**, **tarnished**
If a metal **tarnishes**, it changes from being shiny to dull.
[**Tarnish** comes from French.]

**tarpaulin** *noun* **tarpaulins**
A **tarpaulin** is a heavy waterproof cloth sheet.
[**Tarpaulin** comes from **tar** and *pall* 'a cloth spread over a coffin', which comes from Latin *pallium* 'cloak'.]

**tart** *noun* **tarts**
A **tart** is an open pie: *treacle tart.*
[**Tart** comes from Latin.]

**tartan** *noun*
**Tartan** is a traditional Scottish pattern of coloured squares, or cloth of this pattern.
[**Tartan** probably comes from an old French word.]

**task** *noun* **tasks** (th)
A **task** is a job or piece of work that is sometimes difficult or not very nice to do.
[**Task** comes via French from the same Latin word as **tax**.]

**taste** *noun* **tastes** (th)
**1** The **taste** of something is whether it is sweet, sour, spicy, salty etc.
**2** Your sense of **taste** tells you what food you are eating and what it is like.
**3 Taste** is the ability to choose or judge what is attractive or suitable: *She has very good taste.*
[**Taste** comes from an old French word.]

**taste** *verb* **tastes**, **tasting**, **tasted**
**1** If you **taste** food or drink, you put it in your mouth to find out what its flavour is like.
**2** If food **tastes** sweet, sour, salty etc., it has that taste.

**tattoo** *noun* **tattoos**
A **tattoo** is words or pictures that are

made on someone's body with needles and ink.
[**Tattoo** comes from a Polynesian word. Polynesia is a region in the Pacific Ocean with many islands where various related languages are spoken.]

**taught** *verb*
**Taught** is the past tense and past participle of **teach**.

**taunt** *verb* **taunts**, **taunting**, **taunted** (th)
To **taunt** someone means to tease him/her in order to upset him/her.
[**Taunt** comes from French *tant pour tant* 'tit for tat'.]

**tax** *noun* **taxes**
**Tax** is money people pay to the government that the government spends on running the country.
[**Tax** comes via French from Latin *taxare* 'to calculate'.]

**taxi** *noun* **taxis**
A **taxi** is a car with a driver who you pay to drive you somewhere.
[**Taxi** comes from French.]

**taxi** *verb* **taxis**, **taxiing**, **taxied**
When a plane **taxis**, it moves along the runway.

**tea** *noun*
**1 Tea** is a drink made from pouring boiling water on dried leaves of the tea plant.
**2 Tea** is a meal eaten in the afternoon or evening.
[**Tea** comes from Chinese via Dutch.]

**teach** *verb* **teaches**, **teaching**, **taught** (th)
To **teach** means to help someone to understand something or do something.
[**Teach** comes from Old English.]

**teacher** *noun* **teachers**
A **teacher** is a person whose job is to teach, especially in a school.

**team** *noun* **teams** (th)
A **team** is a group of people who work together or play a game together on the same side.
[**Team** comes from Old English.]

**teapot** *noun* **teapots**
A **teapot** is a container with a spout and a lid that tea is made in.

**tear¹** *noun* **tears**
A **tear** is a drop of water that comes out of your eye when you cry.
[**Tear¹** comes from Old English *taeher*.]

**tear²** *verb* **tears**, **tearing**, **tore**, **torn** (th)
To **tear** something means to rip it or to pull one part of it away from another part.
[**Tear²** comes from Old English *teran*.]

**tease** *verb* **teases**, **teasing**, **teased** (th)
If you **tease** someone, you say unkind things to him/her.
[**Tease** comes from Old English.]

**teaspoon** *noun* **teaspoons**
A **teaspoon** is a small spoon used for stirring drinks or measuring food.

**technical** *adjective*
involving a lot of knowledge of things such as computers, science or machines: *Programming computers is a technical job.*
**technically** *adverb*.
[**Technical** comes via Latin from Greek *techne* 'an art or craft'.]

**technique** *noun* **techniques**
A **technique** is a particular way of doing something.
[**Technique** comes via French from the same Latin word as **technical**.]

**technology** *noun*
**Technology** is the use of science to do practical things.
[**Technology** comes from the same Greek word as **technical**.]

**teddy bear** *noun* **teddy bears**
A **teddy bear** is a soft, furry, toy bear.
[The **teddy bear** is named after an American President, Theodore Roosevelt, who liked hunting bears. *Teddy* is short for *Theodore*.]

**teenager** *noun* **teenagers**
A **teenager** is someone who is aged between 13 and 19.
[**Teenager** comes from -*teen* in the numbers thirteen to nineteen, which comes from Old English.]

**tee-shirt** *noun* **tee-shirts**
**Tee-shirt** is another way to spell **T-shirt**.

**teeth** *noun*
**Teeth** is the plural of **tooth**.

**a b c d e f g h i j k l m**

**teething** *adjective*
1 If a baby or a child is **teething**, new teeth are coming through his/her gums.
2 **Teething troubles** are small problems at the start of something new.
[**Teething** comes from **teeth**.]

**teetotal** *adjective*
If a person is **teetotal**, s/he never drinks alcohol.
[**Teetotal** comes from **total**, with *tee* added to make people notice the word.]

**telecommunications** *noun*
**Telecommunications** is the sending of messages over long distances by satellite, telephone or radio.
[**Telecommunications** comes from Greek *tele* 'far away' and **communication**.]

**telephone** *noun* **telephones**
A **telephone** is a device that allows you to speak to someone who is in another place.
[**Telephone** comes from Greek *tele* 'far away' and *phone* 'sound'.]

**telephone** *verb* **telephones, telephoning, telephoned**
To **telephone** means to use a telephone in order to speak to someone.

**telescope** *noun* **telescopes**
A **telescope** is a long thin instrument with lenses which is used for looking at things in the distance.
[**Telescope** comes from Greek *tele* 'far away' and *skopein* 'to see'.]

**teletext** *noun*
**Teletext** is written information that some televisions can receive and show on screen: *The news is on page 110 of teletext.*
[**Teletext** comes from Greek *tele* 'far away' and **text**.]

**television** *noun* **televisions**
A **television** is a piece of equipment that receives signals that it shows as moving pictures and sound.
[**Television** comes from Greek *tele* 'far away' and **vision**.]

**tell** *verb* **tells, telling, told** (th)
1 To **tell** someone something is to give him/her information: *Tell me your phone number.*
2 If you **tell** someone to do something, you order him/her to do it: *The teacher*

told us to be quiet.
3 If you can **tell** something, you can say what something is or who someone is: *I can't tell what's in this soup.*
[**Tell** comes from Old English.]

**temper** *noun* **tempers** (th)
If someone is in a **temper**, s/he is angry.
[**Temper** comes via Old English from Latin *temperare* 'to mix', because people believed that a person's temperament was due to the mixture of fluids in his or her body.]

**temperament** *noun* **temperaments** (th)
A person or an animal's **temperament** is how they usually behave or feel: *a dog with a gentle temperament.*
[**Temperament** comes from the same Latin word as **temper**.]

**temperate** *adjective* (th)
A **temperate** climate or part of the world has temperatures that are never very high and never very low.
[**Temperate** comes from the same Latin word as **temper**.]

**temperature** *noun* **temperatures**
1 The **temperature** of something is how hot or cold it is.
2 If you have a **temperature**, your body is warmer than it normally is because you are ill.
[**Temperature** comes from the same Latin word as **temper**, and used to mean the same as **temperament**.]

**temple** *noun* **temples**
A **temple** is a building where Buddhists, Hindus and some other religious groups worship. [**Temple** comes from Latin.]

**tempo** *noun* **tempos** or **tempi**
The **tempo** of a piece of music is its speed.
[**Tempo** comes from the same Latin word as **temporary**.]

**temporary** *adjective* (th)
Something that is **temporary** only lasts for a short time. **temporarily** *adverb*.
[**Temporary** comes from Latin *tempus* 'time'.]

**tempt** *verb* **tempts, tempting, tempted** (th)
If something **tempts** you, you feel that you want to have it or do it because it will

be nice: *Can I tempt you to a cake?*
[**Tempt** comes from Latin *temptare* 'to test or try' (ancestor of **attempt**).]

**tenant** *noun* **tenants**
A **tenant** is someone who pays rent to live in a house or use a building.
[**Tenant** comes via French from Latin *tenir* 'to hold'.]

**tender** *adjective* **tenderer, tenderest** (th)
1 **Tender** food, especially meat, is easy to cut and chew.
2 If a part of your body is **tender**, it hurts when you touch it.
3 Someone who is **tender** is kind and loving.
[**Tender** comes from Latin via French.]

**tendon** *noun* **tendons**
A **tendon** is like a strong thick muscle that joins muscles to bones.
[**Tendon** comes from the same Latin word as **tense²**.]

**tennis** *noun*
Tennis is a game played with rackets and balls over a net on a court.
[**Tennis** comes from French *tenez* 'take', which the person serving called to his or her opponent when s/he was about to serve.]

**tense¹** *noun* **tenses**
Tense is a form of a verb that shows whether something happens in the past, the present or the future: *'Ate' is the past tense of 'eat'.*
[**Tense¹** comes via French from the same Latin word as **temporary**.]

**tense²** *adjective* (th)
1 Someone who is **tense** is worried and cannot relax.
2 If you have **tense** muscles, they are stiff because you cannot relax them.
[**Tense²** comes from Latin *tendere* 'to stretch'.]

**tension** *noun* (th)
1 **Tension** is a feeling of worry or nervousness.
2 The **tension** of a rope or wire is how tightly it is stretched.
[**Tension** comes from the same Latin word as **tense²**.]

**tent** *noun* **tents**
A **tent** is a shelter made out of canvas or

nylon that is used for camping.
[**Tent** comes via French from the same Latin word as **tense²**.]

**tepid** *adjective*
Something that is **tepid** is slightly warm.
[**Tepid** comes from Latin *tepere* 'to be warm'.]

**term** *noun* **terms**
1 A **term** is part of a year when a school, college or university is open: *the summer term.*
2 A **term** is a certain amount of time: *The job is for a six-month term.*
3 A **term** is a word or group of words, especially ones that are used for talking about a particular subject: *medical terms.*
[**Term** comes via French from Latin *terminus* 'limit or end'.]

**terminal** *noun* **terminals**
1 A **terminal** is a large building at a railway station, airport or port where a journey begins or ends.
2 A **terminal** is a screen and keyboard that is linked to a computer network.
[**Terminal** comes from the same Latin word as **term**.]

**terminal** *adjective*
If someone has a **terminal** illness, s/he will die from it because it cannot be cured.

**termite** *noun* **termites**
A **termite** is a small creature like an ant that lives in a colony and eats wood.
[**Termite** comes from Latin.]

**terracotta** *noun*
Terracotta is a brownish-red clay that is used especially for making plant pots and roof tiles.
[**Terracotta** comes from Italian *terra cotta* 'baked earth'.]

**terrain** *noun*
Terrain is a large area of land. You use **terrain** when you are saying what the land is like: *desert terrain.*
[**Terrain** comes from the same Latin word as **terrier**.]

**terrapin** *noun* **terrapins**
A **terrapin** is a reptile that looks like a small turtle and lives in water.
[**Terrapin** comes from Algonquian (a North American Indian language).]

**a b c d e f g h i j k l m**

**terrestrial** *adjective*
to do with or living on the earth: *Humans are terrestrial beings.*
[**Terrestrial** comes from the same Latin word as **terrier**.]

**terrible** *adjective* (th)
**Terrible** means very bad or awful: *a terrible accident; The flu makes you feel terrible.*
[**Terrible** comes via French from the same Latin word as **terror**.]

**terrier** *noun* **terriers**
A **terrier** is a kind of small, lively dog. There are many different breeds of **terrier**: *a Highland terrier.*
[**Terrier** comes via French from Latin *terra* 'earth or land', because terriers were used to dig rabbits, foxes and badgers out of their holes.]

**terrific** *adjective* (th)
1 **Terrific** means very good or very enjoyable: *That was a terrific film!*
2 **Terrific** means very great: *a terrific noise; a terrific storm.* **terrifically** *adverb.*
[**Terrific** comes from the same Latin word as **terror**.]

**terrify** *verb* **terrifies, terrifying, terrified** (th)
To **terrify** someone means to make him/her very afraid.
[**Terrify** comes from the same Latin word as **terror**.]

**territory** *noun* **territory** (th)
A **territory** is an area of land, especially one that belongs to a person or an animal.
[**Territory** comes from the same Latin word as **terrier**.]

**terror** *noun* **terrors** (th)
**Terror** is great fear.
[**Terror** comes from Latin *terrere* 'to frighten'.]

**terrorism** *noun*
**Terrorism** is violent acts that are done by people to try to force governments to make changes.
[**Terrorism** comes from **terror**.]

**terrorist** *noun* **terrorists**
A **terrorist** is someone who uses violence to try to force governments to make changes.

**test** *noun* **tests** (th)
1 A **test** is like an exam to find out how much someone knows about a subject or how well s/he can do something: *a driving test; a science test.*
2 A **test** is an experiment to find out more about how something works, or to find out what it is made of.
3 A **test** is a medical examination of part of your body: *a hearing test.*
[**Test** comes from Latin via French.]

**test** *verb* **tests, testing, tested** (th)
1 To **test** someone means to find out how much s/he knows about something or how well s/he can do something.
2 To **test** something means to do certain things to it in order to find any problems with it, or to find out what it is made of.

**testicle** *noun* **testicles**
A **testicle** is one of the two parts of a male person's or animal's body that produces sperm. [**Testicle** comes from Latin.]

**testify** *verb* **testifies, testifying, testified**
To **testify** means to give evidence to a law court. [**Testify** comes from Latin.]

**test tube** *noun* **test tubes**
A **test tube** is a thin glass tube that is used in chemical experiments.

**text** *noun* **texts**
1 **Text** is the written words in a book, magazine or newspaper.
2 A **text** is a book or a piece of writing that students study for an exam.
[**Text** comes from Latin.]

**textbook** *noun* **textbooks**
A **textbook** is a school book that is studied in class or as part of a course.

**textile** *noun* **textiles**
A **textile** is a cloth or a fabric that is made by weaving.
[**Textile** comes from Latin *texere* 'to weave'.]

**texture** *noun* **textures**
The **texture** of something is how it feels when you touch it: *Silk has a smooth texture.*
[**Texture** comes from the same Latin word as **textile**.]

**than** *conjunction*
You use **than** when you are comparing two things: *Jack is taller than Jill.*

[**Than** comes from Old English.]

**thank** *verb* **thanks, thanking, thanked**
If you **thank** someone, you tell him/her
you are pleased because s/he has helped
you or given you something.
[**Thank** comes from Old English.]

**thankful** *adjective* (th)
If you are **thankful**, you feel pleased or
show that you are pleased because
someone has helped you or given you
something.

**that** *adjective*
The person or thing further away from
you is **that** one. The plural of **that** is
**those**.
[**That** comes from Old English.]

**that** *adverb*
1 You use **that** to say something is as big,
as much, or as far as you have already
said or suggested: *I'd pay as much as that,
but no more.*
2 **Not that** means not very: *He's not that
fast; I didn't like the book that much.*

**that** *conjunction*
1 You use **that** to say what someone says,
thinks or hopes: *She thought that he looked
like her brother; He promised us that he would
come.*
2 You can use **that** to say what the cause
or the result of something is: *His problem is
that he has no money; It rained so hard that
the river flooded.*

**theatre** *noun* **theatres**
1 A **theatre** is a place where people go to
watch plays.
2 A **theatre** is a place in a hospital where
surgeons operate.
[**Theatre** comes from Greek via French
and Latin.]

**theft** *noun* **thefts** (th)
**Theft** is the crime of stealing.
[**Theft** comes from Old English.]

**their** *pronoun*
**Their** means belonging to them.
[**Their** comes from Old Norse.]

**them** *pronoun*
You say **them** when you are talking about
people, animals or things that have
already been mentioned and that are the
object of a verb: *I wrote to my cousins to ask
if I could visit them.*

[**Them** comes from Old Norse.]

**theme** *noun* **themes**
1 The **theme** of a talk or a piece of writing
is what it is about: *The theme of my talk
tonight is the future of the Third World.*
2 A **theme** is a short, simple tune that is
used over and over again in a longer
piece of music.
[**Theme** comes from Greek via French and
Latin.]

**themselves** *pronoun*
1 You use **themselves** when you are
talking about people, animals or things
that are the object of a verb of which they
are also the subject: *They have only
themselves to blame.*
2 If people do something **themselves** or
**by themselves**, they do it without help
from anyone else.
[**Themselves** comes from **them** and
**selves**, plural of **self**.]

**then** *adverb*
1 at that time: *We were living in London
then; Come tomorrow, he'll be here then.*
2 after that: *Finish what you're doing and
then come and help me.*
3 in that case: *If she's 15, then her brother
must be 17.*
[**Then** comes from Old English.]

**therapy** *noun* **therapies**
**Therapy** is treatment for an illness that
does not usually involve drugs or
operations. [**Therapy** comes from Greek.]

**there** *adverb*
in, at or to that place: *We'll go there
tomorrow; He's lived there for years.*
[**There** comes from Old English.]

**thermometer** *noun* **thermometers**
A **thermometer** is an instrument for
measuring temperature.
[**Thermometer** comes from Greek *therme*
'heat' and Latin *metrum* 'a measure'.]

**thesaurus** *noun* **thesauruses** or **thesauri**
A **thesaurus** is a kind of dictionary that
groups words according to what they
mean. You use a **thesaurus** to find words
with the same or similar meanings so that
you do not have to use the same word all
the time.
[**Thesaurus** comes from the same Greek
word as **treasure**.]

**these** *adjective*
The people or things nearer to you are **these** ones. **These** is the plural of **this**.

**they** *pronoun*
**1** You say **they** when you are talking about people, animals or things that have already been mentioned and that are the subject of a verb: *I went to see my friends but they were out; He made some cakes and they were delicious.*
**2** You use **they** to talk about people in general: *They say it will be a hot summer.*
[**They** comes from Old Norse.]

**thick** *adjective* **thicker, thickest** (th)
**1** Something that is **thick** has a big distance between opposite surfaces: *a thick slice of bread.*
**2** Something that is **thick** is dense or is made up of things packed closely together: *thick cream; a thick forest.*
**thickly** *adverb.* **thickness** *noun.*
[**Thick** comes from Old English.]

**thief** *noun* **thieves** (th)
A **thief** is someone who steals.
[**Thief** comes from Old English.]

**thigh** *noun* **thighs**
Your **thigh** is the top part of your leg above your knee.
[**Thigh** comes from Old English.]

**thimble** *noun* **thimbles**
A **thimble** is a cover that you wear on the end of your finger to protect it when you are sewing.
[**Thimble** comes from Old English.]

**thin** *adjective* **thinner, thinnest** (th)
**1** A **thin** person or animal does not have much fat on their bones: *a poor thin kitten.*
**2** Something that is **thin** has only a small distance between opposite surfaces: *thin cloth; The ice was dangerously thin.*
**3** Something that is **thin** is not thick or dense: *thin soup.*
[**Thin** comes from Old English.]

**thing** *noun* **things**
A **thing** is an object, an action or a fact: *What's that thing in the corner?; What a stupid thing to do!*
[**Thing** comes from Old English.]

**think** *verb* **thinks, thinking, thought** (th)
To **think** is to use your mind to have ideas and opinions.

[**Think** comes from Old English.]

**third** *noun* **thirds**
A **third** is one of three equal parts.
[**Third** comes from Old English.]

**third person** *noun*
To find **third person**, look under **person**.

**Third World** *noun*
The **Third World** is the group of poorer countries in the world.

**thirsty** *adjective* **thirstier, thirstiest** (th)
If you are **thirsty**, you feel you want to drink something.
[**Thirsty** comes from Old English.]

**this** *adjective*
The person or thing nearer to you is **this** one. The plural of **this** is **these**. [**This** comes from Old English.]

**thistle** *noun* **thistles**
A **thistle** is a wild plant with prickly leaves and purple flowers.
[**Thistle** comes from Old English.]

**thorn** *noun* **thorns**
A **thorn** is a prickle that grows on the stem of some plants.
[**Thorn** comes from Old English.]

**those** *adjective*
The people or things further from you are **those** ones. **Those** is the plural of **that**.

**though** *conjunction*
**1** **Though** means in spite of the fact that. *The sky was very black though it did not rain.*
**2** **Though** means but: *He hopes he can come though he's not sure.*
[**Though** comes from Old English.]

**thought¹** *noun* **thoughts** (th)
A **thought** is an idea or an opinion.
[**Thought** comes from Old English.]

**thought²** *verb*
**Thought** is the past tense and past participle of **think**.

**thread** *noun* **threads**
A **thread** is a long, thin piece of cotton, wool or nylon.
[**Thread** comes from Old English.]

**thread** *verb* **threads, threading, threaded**
If you **thread** a needle, you put a piece of wool or cotton thread through the hole at the end of it.

**threadbare** *adjective*
Something that is **threadbare** is very worn: *The old carpet was threadbare.*

**threaten** *verb* **threatens, threatening, threatened** (th)
If someone **threatens** you, s/he frightens you by telling you that s/he will do something bad to you.
[**Threaten** comes from Old English.]

**three-dimensional** *adjective*
Something that is **three-dimensional** has, or seems to have, length, width and depth.

**throat** *noun* **throats**
Your **throat** is the front part of your neck or the tubes inside your neck that food and drink and air pass through.
[**Throat** comes from Old English.]

**through** *preposition*
1 from one end or side to the other: *We walked through the house.*
2 from the beginning to the end: *He slept through the film.*
[**Through** comes from Old English.]

**throw** *verb* **throws, throwing, threw, thrown** (th)
1 To **throw** something means to make it move through the air using your arm.
2 To **throw** something **away** means to get rid of it because you do not need it.
[**Throw** comes from Old English.]

**thrush** *noun* **thrushes**
A **thrush** is a bird with a speckled breast. **Thrushes** sing beautifully.
[**Thrush** comes from Old English.]

**thrust** *verb* **thrusts, thrusting, thrust** (th)
When you **thrust** something, you push it somewhere hard or quickly: *He thrust his book at me.*
[**Thrust** comes from Old Norse.]

**thud** *noun* **thuds**
A **thud** is the sound that something heavy makes when it falls onto the ground.
[**Thud** probably comes from Old English.]

**thumb** *noun* **thumbs**
Your **thumbs** are the short, thick fingers that you have at the side of each hand.
[**Thumb** comes from Old English.]

**thump** *verb* **thumps, thumping, thumped** (th)
1 To **thump** something means to hit it.
2 To **thump** a person means to hit him/her.
3 If your heart **thumps**, you can feel it beating quickly.
[The word **thump** is an imitation of the sound.]

**thunder** *noun*
**Thunder** is the loud, crashing sound that you hear after lightning in a storm.
[**Thunder** comes from Old English.]

**thyme** *noun*
**Thyme** is a herb that has small leaves and a strong smell.
[**Thyme** comes from Old English.]

**tiara** *noun* **tiaras**
A **tiara** is a small crown of jewels.
[**Tiara** comes from Greek via Latin.]

**tick** *noun* **ticks**
1 A **tick** is a mark you can make to show that something is correct, or that you have done something on a list of jobs.
2 A **tick** is the regular sound that a clock makes.
[**Tick** probably comes from an old German or Dutch word.]

**tick** *verb* **ticks, ticking, ticked**
1 To **tick** something means to mark it with a tick.
2 To **tick** means to make the sound of a clock.

**ticket** *noun* **tickets**
A **ticket** is a small piece of paper or card with writing on it. You buy a **ticket** if you want to travel on a bus or train or get into a cinema.
[**Ticket** comes via French from an old Dutch word.]

**tickle** *verb* **tickles, tickling, tickled**
To **tickle** someone means to touch his/her skin very lightly so that s/he laughs.
[No one knows where **tickle** comes from.]

**ticklish** *adjective*
If you are **ticklish**, you laugh a lot when someone tickles you.

**tidal** *adjective*
**Tidal** means to do with or having tides.

a b c d e f g h i j k l m

**tide** *noun* **tides**
A **tide** is the regular movement of the sea up and down the shore.
[**Tide** comes from Old English.]

**tidily** *adverb*
If you do something **tidily**, you do it in a tidy way.

**tidy** *adjective* **tidier, tidiest** (th)
Things that are neatly arranged are **tidy**.
[**Tidy** comes from **tide**, and used to mean 'at the right time'.]

**tidy** *verb* **tidies, tidying, tidied**
To **tidy** a room or a cupboard means to put all the things that are in it in their proper place.

**tie** *noun* **ties**
**1** A **tie** is a strip of material that you wear round your neck. **Ties** go under the collar of a shirt and hang down at the front.
**2** A **tie** is when two people in a race finish at the same time, or when two people in a competition get the same score.
[**Tie** comes from Old English.]

**tie** *verb* **ties, tying, tied**
**1** To **tie** something means to fasten it with a knot.
**2** If two people **tie**, they finish a race at the same time or get the same score in a competition.

**tiger** *noun* **tigers**
A **tiger** is a large animal with yellow fur and black stripes which lives in parts of Asia. **Tigers** are members of the cat family.
[**Tiger** comes from Greek via French and Latin.]

**tight** *adjective* **tighter, tightest** (th)
**1** Something that is a bit small for you is **tight**: *My shoes are too tight.*
**2** Something that is firm and hard to move is **tight**: *She did her laces in a tight bow.*
**3** Something that is pulled or stretched hard is **tight**: *Make sure the rope is tight.*
**tightly** *adverb*. **tightness** *noun*.
[**Tight** comes from Old English.]

**tight** *adverb*
**1** If you hold something **tight**, you hold it firmly and do not let go.
**2** Something that is shut **tight** is shut very firmly.

**tighten** *verb* **tightens, tightening, tightened**
To **tighten** something means to make it tight.

**tightrope** *noun* **tightropes**
A **tightrope** is a high rope that an acrobat balances on.
[A **tightrope** is so called because it is tied very tightly so that it cannot move about.]

**tights** *plural noun*
**Tights** are made of nylon or wool and they cover your lower body.
[**Tights** are so called because they fit very tightly.]

**tile** *noun* **tiles**
A **tile** is a flat, usually square piece of a strong substance that is used to cover a wall or a floor: *cork tiles; ceramic tiles.*
[**Tile** comes from Latin via Old English.]

**till¹** *noun* **tills**
A **till** is a drawer for money in a shop, usually part of a machine that records the amount of money that comes in. This machine is often called a **till**, although its proper name is a **cash register**.
[No one knows where **till¹** comes from.]

**till²** *preposition*
until: *I can't go till Friday.*
[**Till²** comes from Old English.]

**tilt** *verb* **tilts, tilting, tilted** (th)
To **tilt** means to tip or lean to one side.
[No one knows where **tilt** comes from.]

**timber** *noun*
**Timber** is wood that is ready to be used to make things.
[**Timber** comes from Old English.]

**time** *noun* **times**
**1** Time is the passing of seconds, minutes, days and years.
**2** Time is a certain moment in time: *What time is it?*
**3** A **time** is a period of time: *We had a good time on holiday; It happened in the time of Elizabeth I.*
**4** A **time** is an occasion when something happens: *That's the third time I've asked you.* [**Time** comes from Old English.]

**time** *verb* **times, timing, timed**
**1** To **time** something means to measure how long it takes.
**2** To **time** something means to work out

when would be the best moment to do it.

**times** *noun*
**Times** means multiplied by: *Five times two is ten.* The symbol for **times** is x: *5 x 2 = 10.*

**timetable** *noun* **timetables**
A **timetable** is a table showing when things will happen, such as when buses should arrive and leave, or showing which lessons you have at school each day.

**timid** *adjective* (th)
If you are **timid**, you are shy and not brave. **timidly** *adverb.*
[**Timid** comes from Latin *timidus* 'nervous'.]

**tin** *noun* **tins**
1 **Tin** is a soft, grey metal.
2 A **tin** is a metal container.
[**Tin** comes from Old English.]

**tingle** *verb* **tingles, tingling, tingled** (th)
When a part of your body **tingles**, it feels as though something is pricking or stinging it.
[**Tingle** probably comes from **tinkle**.]

**tinkle** *verb* **tinkles, tinkling, tinkled** (th)
To **tinkle** means to make a soft, ringing sound like a small bell.
[The word **tinkle** is an imitation of the sound.]

**tinsel** *noun*
**Tinsel** is shiny ribbon used for decoration, especially at Christmas.
[**Tinsel** comes from old French *estinceler* 'to sparkle'.]

**tint** *noun* **tints**
A **tint** is a small amount of a colour: *brown with a tint of orange.*
[**Tint** comes from Latin *tingere* 'to dye or stain'.]

**tiny** *adjective* **tinier, tiniest**
Something that is **tiny** is very small.
[No one knows where **tiny** comes from.]

**tip¹** *noun* **tips**
A **tip** is the very end of something: *sucking the tip of his pencil.*
[**Tip¹** comes from Old Norse.]

**tip²** *noun* **tips**
A **tip** is a place where people throw rubbish.
[**Tip²** probably comes from a

Scandinavian word.]

**tip²** *verb* **tips, tipping, tipped**
1 To **tip** something means to move it so that it is leaning.
2 To **tip** something means to pour it out: *tipped the dirty laundry onto the floor.*
3 If something **tips up**, it leans or slopes.

**tip³** *noun* **tips**
A **tip** is a small present of money that you give to a waiter or someone who has helped you.
[**Tip³** may come from **tip¹**.]

**tip³** *verb* **tips, tipping, tipped**
If you **tip** a waiter or someone who has helped you, you give them a small present of money.

**tiptoe** *verb* **tiptoes, tiptoeing, tiptoed**
To **tiptoe** means to walk quietly on your toes.

**tire** *verb* **tires, tiring, tired** (th)
1 If you **tire**, you get tired.
2 If something **tires** you, it makes you tired. [**Tire** comes from Old English.]

**tired** *adjective* (th)
1 You feel **tired** when you have been working or doing exercise and you need to rest.
2 If you are **tired of** something, you have had enough of it or you are bored with it. **tiredness** *noun.*

**tiresome** *adjective* (th)
1 A **tiresome** person is irritating or annoying.
2 A **tiresome** thing is boring or annoying.
[**Tiresome** comes from **tire**.]

**tissue** *noun* **tissues**
1 A **tissue** is a piece of soft thin paper that you use for wiping your nose.
2 **Tissue** is the cells that make up different parts of plants and animals: *muscle tissue.*
[**Tissue** comes via French from the same Latin word as **textile**.]

**tissue paper** *noun*
**Tissue paper** is thin, coloured paper used for wrapping things.

**title** *noun* **titles**
1 A **title** is the name of a book, play, film, picture or piece of music.
2 A **title** is a word in front of a person's name, such as *Mrs, Dr* or *Rev.*

**a b c d e f g h i j k l m**

[**Title** comes from Latin via Old English.]

**to ad** *noun* **toads**

A **toad** is a creature like a large frog. **Toads** have rough dry skin.
[**Toad** comes from Old English.]

**toadstool** *noun* **toadstools**

A **toadstool** is a kind of fungus like a mushroom. Many **toadstools** are poisonous.
[**Toadstools** are so called because people used to believe that toads sat on them.]

**toast** *noun* **toasts**

**1 Toast** is bread that you heat so that it is crisp and brown.
**2** If you drink a **toast** to someone, you have a special drink and say that you hope s/he has luck and happiness.
[**Toast** comes from Latin *tostum* 'dried up'.]

**toast** *verb* **toasts, toasting, toasted**

**1** To **toast** bread means to make it into toast.
**2** To **toast** someone means to drink a toast to him/her.

**toaster** *noun* **toasters**

A **toaster** is an electrical appliance for making toast in.

**tobacco** *noun*

**Tobacco** is the leaves that are used to make cigarettes and other products.
[**Tobacco** comes from Spanish, probably from a Central American Indian language.]

**toboggan** *noun* **toboggans**

A **toboggan** is a sledge that you sit on to slide over snow.
[**Toboggan** comes via Canadian French from Micmac (a North American Indian language).]

**today** *noun*

**Today** is this day.
[**Today** comes from Old English.]

**today** *adverb*

on or during this day: *I saw her today*.

**toddler** *noun* **toddlers**

A **toddler** is a young child who is learning to walk.
[**Toddler** comes from *toddle* 'to walk with short, unsteady steps', but no one knows where *toddle* comes from.]

**toe** *noun* **toes**

Your **toes** are the five parts at the end of each of your feet.
[**Toe** comes from Old English.]

**toffee** *noun* **toffees**

A **toffee** is a sweet made from butter and sugar.
[No one knows where the word **toffee** comes from.]

**toga** *noun* **togas**

A **toga** is a loose robe that goes round the body and over the shoulder. **Togas** were worn in ancient Rome.
[**Toga** comes from Latin.]

**together** *adverb*

with another person or thing: *They danced together all night; Mix everything together*.
[**Together** comes from Old English.]

**toggle** *noun* **toggles**

A **toggle** is a piece of wood or plastic that fits through a loop and is used like a button to fasten a coat or bag.
[No one knows where **toggle** comes from.]

**toilet** *noun* **toilets**

**1** A **toilet** is a large bowl with a pipe leading to a drain that is used to get rid of urine and faeces.
**2** A **toilet** is a room or building containing a toilet. [**Toilet** comes from French.]

**token** *noun* **tokens**

**1** A **token** is a piece of plastic or metal that you can use in a machine.
**2** A **token** is something that you can use instead of money: *a book token*.
[**Token** comes from Old English.]

**told** *verb*

**Told** is the past tense and past participle of **tell**.

**tolerate** *verb* **tolerates, tolerating, tolerated** (th)

**1** To **tolerate** something means to stand it or put up with it.
**2** To **tolerate** what someone does or thinks means not to argue or protest although s/he does not behave or think as you do. [**Tolerate** comes from Latin.]

**toll** *noun* **tolls**

A **toll** is money that you pay to cross a bridge or use a road.
[**Toll** comes via Old English and Latin

from Greek *telos* 'a tax'.]

**tomato** *noun* **tomatoes**
A **tomato** is a soft, juicy, round, red fruit. You can eat it raw in salads, or use it cooked in sauces and stews.
[**Tomato** comes via French, Spanish or Portuguese from Nahuatl (a South American Indian language).]

**tomb** *noun* **tombs**
A **tomb** is someone's grave or a monument built at his/her grave.
[**Tomb** comes from Greek via French and Latin.]

**tombstone** *noun* **tombstones**
A **tombstone** is a block of stone with writing carved on it, put up at someone's grave.

**tomorrow** *noun*
**Tomorrow** is the day after today.
[**Tomorrow** comes from Middle English *to morrow* 'in the morning'.]

**tone** *noun* **tones**
**1** The **tone** of your voice is how it sounds: *I could tell by his tone that he was annoyed.*
**2** A **tone** is the particular sound of a musical instrument.
[**Tone** comes from Greek via Latin and French.]

**tongs** *plural noun*
**Tongs** are a tool that you use to pick up or hold something with. They have two long parts joined at one end.
[**Tongs** comes from Old English.]

**tongue** *noun* **tongues**
Your **tongue** is the long, soft part inside your mouth which moves when you speak or eat.
[**Tongue** comes from Old English.]

**tonight** *noun*
**Tonight** is this night.
[**Tonight** comes from Old English.]

**tonne** *noun* **tonnes**
A **tonne** is a measure of weight in the metric system, equal to 1000 kilograms.
[**Tonne** comes from French.]

**tonsillitis** *noun*
**Tonsillitis** is an infection that makes your tonsils swell up and your throat hurt.

**tonsils** *plural noun*
Your **tonsils** are the soft lumps in your

throat, at the back of your mouth.
[**Tonsils** comes from Latin via French.]

**too** *adverb*
**1** as well: *I'd like some juice too.*
**2** very, or more than you want or need: *too silly; too late.*
[**Too** comes from Old English.]

**took** *verb*
**Took** is the past tense of **take**.

**tool** *noun* **tools** (th)
A **tool** is an instrument that you use to do a job: *garden tools; a carpenter's tools.*
[**Tool** comes from Old English.]

**tooth** *noun* **teeth**
A **tooth** is one of the hard, white parts in your mouth that you use for biting and chewing.
[**Tooth** comes from Old English.]

**toothache** *noun*
**Toothache** is when you have a pain in a tooth.

**toothbrush** *noun* **toothbrushes**
A **toothbrush** is a small brush with a long handle that you clean your teeth with.

**toothpaste** *noun* **toothpastes**
**Toothpaste** is a flavoured paste that you put on your toothbrush. It helps to clean your teeth.

**top**[1] *noun* **tops** (th)
**1** The **top** is the highest part of something.
**2** A **top** is a cover or a lid.
**3** A **top** is something that you wear above your waist: *a pyjama top.*
[**Top**[1] comes from Old English.]

**top**[1] *adjective* (th)
The **top** thing is the highest thing: *the top drawer.*

**top**[2] *noun* **tops**
A **top** is a toy that spins round very quickly.
[No one knows where **top**[2] comes from.]

**topic** *noun* **topics**
A **topic** is a subject that people are talking about, learning about or thinking about.
[**Topic** comes from Greek.]

**topple** *verb* **topples, toppling, toppled**
To **topple** means to wobble and fall over.
[**Topple** comes from **top**[1].]

**topsy-turvy** *adjective* (th)
Something that is **topsy-turvy** is mixed up or upside-down.
[**Topsy-turvy** probably comes from **top**[1] and an old word *terve* 'to turn upside down'.]

**torch** *noun* **torches**
A **torch** is an electric light run on batteries that you can carry around.
[**Torch** comes from Latin via French.]

**tore** *verb*
**Tore** is the past tense of **tear**.

**torn** *verb*
**Torn** is the past participle of **tear**.

**tornado** *noun* **tornadoes** *or* **tornados**
A **tornado** is a storm with very strong winds that go round in a circle.
[**Tornado** comes from Spanish.]

**torpedo** *noun* **torpedoes**
A **torpedo** is a bomb that travels underwater and explodes when it hits something.
[**Torpedo** is the Latin name of a fish something like the stingray that can give you an electric shock.]

**torrent** *noun* **torrents** (th)
A **torrent** is a stream of water that is flowing fast or falling heavily.
[**Torrent** comes via French and Italian from Latin *torrens* 'boiling' or 'roaring'.]

**torrential** *adjective*
**Torrential** rain is rain that is pouring down hard.

**tortoise** *noun* **tortoises**
A **tortoise** is a reptile that has a shell. **Tortoises** move very slowly and live for many years.
[**Tortoise** comes from Latin via French or Spanish.]

**torture** *verb* **tortures, torturing, tortured**
To **torture** someone means to hurt him/her, sometimes over and over again, especially when you are trying to make the person tell you something.
[**Torture** comes via French from Latin *tortura* 'twisting'.]

**toss** *verb* **tosses, tossing, tossed** (th)
To **toss** something means to throw it.
[No one knows where **toss** comes from.]

**total** *noun* **totals**
The **total** is the amount you get when you add everything up.
[**Total** comes via French from Latin *totus* 'whole'.]

**total** *adjective*
1 complete: *a total disaster*.
2 including everything: *the total cost has to be paid in 30 days*. **totally** *adverb*.

**totem pole** *noun* **totem poles**
A **totem pole** is a carved pole with special designs on it. Native Americans make **totem poles** showing the symbols of their tribe.
[**Totem** comes from Ojibwa (a North American Indian language).]

**totter** *verb* **totters, tottering, tottered** (th)
To **totter** means to sway or walk in an unsteady way.
[**Totter** comes from an old Dutch word.]

**toucan** *noun* **toucans**
A **toucan** is a large bird that has a big, brightly coloured beak.
[**Toucan** comes via French and Portuguese from Tupi (a South American Indian language).]

**touch** *verb* **touches, touching, touched** (th)
1 To **touch** something means to feel it with your fingers or your hand.
2 If one thing **touches** another thing, it is right next to it with no space in between.
[**Touch** comes from an old French word.]

**touch** *noun*
Your sense of **touch** is the way that you can feel things and know what they are like.

**touchdown** *noun* **touchdowns**
**Touchdown** is when an aircraft or spacecraft lands.

**tough** *adjective* **tougher, toughest** (th)
1 Something or someone that is **tough** is strong and hardy.
2 Something that is **tough** is hard to cut or chew.
3 Something that is **tough** is difficult or hard to do. **toughness** *noun*.
[**Tough** comes from Old English.]

**tour** *noun* **tours**
1 A **tour** is a journey where you travel to

several places to look at things.
**2** A **tour** is a walk round a place: *a guided tour of the palace.*
[**Tour** comes from Greek via French and Latin.]

**tourist** *noun* **tourists**
A **tourist** is someone who is on holiday in a place where s/he does not live.

**tournament** *noun* **tournaments**
A **tournament** is a series of contests or games to find a final winner.
[**Tournament** comes via French from the same Latin word as **tour**.]

**tow** *verb* **tows, towing, towed** (th)
To **tow** something means to pull it along.
[**Tow** comes from Old English.]

**towards** *preposition*
**Towards** means in the direction of something: *She moved towards the fire because she was cold.*
[**Towards** comes from Old English.]

**towel** *noun* **towels**
A **towel** is a piece of cloth for drying things.
[**Towel** comes from an old French word.]

**tower** *noun* **towers**
A **tower** is a tall narrow building or part of a building.
[**Tower** comes from Old English.]

**tower** *verb* **towers, towering, towered**
If something is much taller than another thing, it **towers over** or **above** it.

**town** *noun* **towns**
A **town** is a place with many houses, shops, schools and offices.
[**Town** comes from Old English.]

**towpath** *noun* **towpaths**
A **towpath** is a path that runs along the edge of a canal or a river.
[The **towpath** was where the horses that towed the boats used to walk.]

**toxic** *adjective*
If something is **toxic**, it is poisonous.
[**Toxic** comes from Greek via Latin.]

**toy** *noun* **toys**
**Toys** are things to play with.
[No one knows where **toy** comes from.]

**trace** *noun* **traces** (th)
**1** A **trace** is a very small amount of

something.
**2** A **trace** is a mark that shows where something has been.
[**Trace** comes from Latin via French.]

**trace** *verb* **traces, tracing, traced** (th)
**1** If you **trace** someone, you find out where they are.
**2** You **trace** a shape by going over the outline with a pencil onto very thin paper.

**track** *noun* **tracks** (th)
**1** A **track** is a path.
**2** A **track** is a set of railway lines or tram lines.
**3** A **track** is the marks left by someone or something passing through a place.
**4** The **track** of a tank or tractor is a continuous band that is turned by a set of wheels and enables the vehicle to cross rough ground.
[**Track** comes from an old French word.]

**track** *verb* **tracks, tracking, tracked** (th)
To **track** people or animals means to follow the marks that they have left.

**tracksuit** *noun* **tracksuits**
A **tracksuit** is a warm, comfortable top and trousers that you wear for doing exercise.

**tractor** *noun* **tractors**
A **tractor** is a vehicle used on farms.
[**Tractor** comes from Latin.]

**trade** *noun* **trades**
**Trade** is buying and selling things.
[**Trade** comes from an old German word.]

**trade** *verb* **trades, trading, traded**
To **trade** is to buy and sell things.

**trademark** *noun* **trademarks**
A **trademark** is a special sign or mark that a company puts on the things it makes.

**trader** *noun* **traders**
A **trader** is someone who buys and sells things.

**tradition** *noun* **traditions**
A **tradition** is a custom or a way of doing things that has stayed the same for many years.
[**Tradition** comes from Latin *traditio* 'handing on'.]

**traditional** *adjective*
If something is **traditional**, people have been doing it for many years.

**traditionally** *adverb*.
[**Traditional** comes from **tradition**.]

**traffic** *noun*
**Traffic** is vehicles travelling on the road.
[**Traffic** comes from French, Spanish or Italian.]

**traffic jam** *noun* **traffic jams**
A **traffic jam** is a long queue of vehicles that is not moving because the road is blocked.

**traffic light** *noun* **traffic lights**
A **traffic light** is a sign for drivers. **Traffic lights** use red, amber and green lights to show drivers when to go and stop.

**tragedy** *noun* **tragedies** (th)
1 A **tragedy** is something very sad that happens.
2 A **tragedy** is a play that has a sad ending.
[**Tragedy** comes from Greek via French and Latin.]

**tragic** *adjective* (th)
Something that is **tragic** is very sad.
[**Tragic** comes via French and Latin from the same Greek word as **tragedy**.]

**trail** *noun* **trails**
A **trail** is a track or a path: *a nature trail*.
[**Trail** comes from the same Latin word as **train**.]

**trail** *verb* **trails, trailing, trailed**
1 To **trail** means to drag along behind someone or something.
2 To **trail** someone means to follow him/her.

**trailer** *noun* **trailers**
A **trailer** is a vehicle that is pulled behind another vehicle.
[**Trailer** comes from **trail**.]

**train** *noun* **trains**
A **train** is a set of railway coaches pulled by an engine.
[**Train** comes via French from Latin *trahere* 'to pull along'.]

**train** *verb* **trains, training, trained** (th)
1 To **train** people or animals means to teach them to do something.
2 If you **train**, you practise doing something: *training for the big race*.

**trainers** *plural noun*
**Trainers** are soft, light shoes that you wear for sport.
[**Trainers** comes from **train**.]

**traitor** *noun* **traitors**
A **traitor** is a person who helps another country or an enemy instead of being loyal to his/her own country or friends.
[**Traitor** comes from Latin via French.]

**tram** *noun* **trams**
A **tram** is a vehicle like a bus that runs on tracks in the road. **Trams** are connected to electric wires above the tracks.
[**Tram** comes from an old German or Dutch word.]

**tramp** *noun* **tramps**
A **tramp** is a person who has no home and travels around looking for work or food and shelter.
[**Tramp** probably comes from an old German word.]

**trample** *verb* **tramples, trampling, trampled**
If you **trample** something, you squash it with your feet.
[**Trample** comes from *tramp* 'to walk with heavy steps', which comes from the same old German word as **tramp**.]

**trampoline** *noun* **trampolines**
A **trampoline** is a large strong piece of fabric joined to a frame by springs. You can bounce up and down on it.
[**Trampoline** comes from Italian.]

**trance** *noun* (th)
If you are in a **trance**, you are awake but are in a kind of dream.
[**Trance** comes from Latin via French.]

**transfer** *verb* **transfers, transferring, transferred** (th)
1 To **transfer** something means to move it to another place.
2 To **transfer** something means to give it to someone else.
[**Transfer** comes via French from Latin *transferre* 'to carry across'.]

**transform** *verb* **transforms, transforming, transformed** (th)
To **transform** something means to change it completely.
[**Transform** comes from Latin via French.]

**translate** *verb* **translates, translating, translated**
To **translate** means to hear or read words

in one language and say or write what they mean in another language: *I translated the letter into German.* [**Translate** comes from Latin.]

**translucent** *adjective*
If something is **translucent**, light passes through it but you cannot see through it clearly. [**Translucent** comes from Latin *translucere* 'to shine through'.]

**transmit** *verb* **transmits, transmitting, transmitted**
If you **transmit** something, you send it or pass it to other people: *Insects can transmit dangerous diseases; transmit a message by radio.* [**Transmit** comes from Latin *transmittere* 'to send through'.]

**transparent** *adjective*
Something that is clear enough to see through is **transparent**. [**Transparent** comes via French from Latin *transparere* 'to be seen through something'.]

**transplant** *noun* **transplants**
A **transplant** is a part that is taken from one person's body and put into another person's body: *a heart transplant; a bone marrow transplant.* [**Transplant** comes from Latin *transplantare* 'to plant across'.]

**transport** *noun*
**Transport** means carrying people or goods from one place to another, or the vehicles or other means that you use to do this: *a good transport system.* [**Transport** comes from Latin *transportare* 'to carry across'.]

**trap** *noun* **traps** (th)
1 A **trap** is a device for catching animals.
2 A **trap** is a plan or trick to capture or cheat someone. [**Trap** comes from Old English.]

**trap** *verb* **traps, trapping, trapped**
1 To **trap** an animal means to catch it in a trap.
2 To **trap** someone means to trick or catch him/her.

**trapdoor** *noun* **trapdoors**
A **trapdoor** is a small door in a floor or ceiling.

**trapeze** *noun* **trapezes**
A **trapeze** is a bar hanging from two ropes for acrobats to swing on. [**Trapeze** comes via French from the same Latin word as **trapezium**, because of its shape.]

**trapezium** *noun* **trapeziums** *or* **trapezia**
A **trapezium** is a flat shape that has four sides, with two of the sides being parallel but not equal. [**Trapezium** comes from Greek via Latin.]

**travel** *verb* **travels, travelling, travelled** (th)
To **travel** means to move from one place to another. [**Travel** comes from French *travail* 'hard work'.]

**traveller** *noun* **travellers** (th)
1 A **traveller** is someone who is on holiday or visiting places.
2 **Travellers** are people who do not live in one place but move around with their families.

**tray** *noun* **trays**
A **tray** is a board with a raised edge used for carrying things such as cups and saucers. [**Tray** comes from Old English.]

**treacle** *noun*
**Treacle** is sweet, dark, sticky syrup made from sugar. [**Treacle** comes from Greek via French and Latin.]

**tread** *verb* **treads, treading, trod, trodden**
To **tread** on something means to step on it. [**Tread** comes from Old English.]

**treasure** *noun* **treasures** (th)
1 **Treasure** is a collection of gold, jewels or money.
2 Your **treasure** is someone or something that is very precious to you. [**Treasure** comes via French from Greek *thesauros* 'a storehouse or place for keeping money or treasure' (ancestor of **thesaurus**).]

**treasurer** *noun* **treasurers**
A **treasurer** is a person who looks after the money for a club or a group of people. [**Treasurer** comes from the same French word as **treasure**.]

**treat** *noun* **treats**
A **treat** is something special that you can have or do as a present or a reward.
[**Treat** comes from Latin via French.]

**treat** *verb* **treats, treating, treated** (th)
1 To **treat** someone who is ill or hurt means to try to make him/her better.
2 To **treat** someone in a particular way means to behave towards him/her in that way: *He treats his children fairly.*
3 To **treat** someone means to do something nice or special for him/her: *I'll treat you to an ice cream.*

**treble** *verb* **trebles, trebling, trebled**
If you **treble** a number, you multiply it by three.
[**Treble** comes via French from the same Latin word as **triple**.]

**tree** *noun* **trees**
A **tree** is a tall plant with a woody trunk and branches. Oaks and willows are kinds of **tree**.
[**Tree** comes from Old English.]

**trek** *noun* **treks**
A **trek** is a long, hard walk.
[**Trek** comes from Dutch.]

**trek** *verb* **treks, trekking, trekked**
To **trek** means to make a long or difficult journey on foot.

**tremble** *verb* **trembles, trembling, trembled** (th)
To **tremble** means to shake because you are cold or frightened.
[**Tremble** comes via French from the same Latin word as **tremor**.]

**tremendous** *adjective* (th)
1 very big: *We heard a tremendous crash.*
2 very good: *a tremendous performance.*
**tremendously** *adverb*.
[**Tremendous** comes from the same Latin word as **tremor**.]

**tremor** *noun* **tremors**
A **tremor** is when something shakes, especially when the ground shakes during an earthquake.
[**Tremor** comes from Latin *tremere* 'to shake'.]

**trench** *noun* **trenches** (th)
A **trench** is a long, narrow, deep hole dug in the ground.

[**Trench** comes from Latin via French.]

**trend** *noun* **trends**
1 A **trend** is the general way in which something is changing: *a trend towards two-car families.*
2 A **trend** is a fashion: *The trend this winter is for longer skirts.*
[**Trend** comes from Old English.]

**trespass** *verb* **trespasses, trespassing, trespassed**
To **trespass** means to go onto someone else's land without asking if you can.
[**Trespass** comes from an old French word.]

**trespasser** *noun* **trespassers**
A **trespasser** is someone who goes onto another person's land without asking first.

**trial** *noun* **trials**
1 A **trial** is a kind of meeting in a court, where a judge or a jury decide whether a person has done something that is against the law.
2 A **trial** is a test.
[**Trial** comes from an old French word.]

**triangle** *noun* **triangles**
1 A **triangle** is a shape with three straight sides and three angles.
2 A **triangle** is a percussion instrument. It is made of steel bent into the shape of a triangle.
[**Triangle** comes via French from Latin *triangulus* 'three-cornered'.]

**triangular** *adjective*
Something that is **triangular** is shaped like a triangle.

**tribe** *noun* **tribes**
A **tribe** is a group of people or families who speak the same language and belong to the same race.
[**Tribe** comes from Latin.]

**tributary** *noun* **tributaries**
A **tributary** is a stream or a river that flows into a bigger river.
[**Tributary** comes from Latin.]

**trick** *noun* **tricks**
1 A **trick** is a clever way that a person or animal has learned to do something.
2 A **trick** is a plan to fool someone.
[**Trick** comes from an old French word.]

**trick** *verb* **tricks, tricking, tricked** (th)
1 If you **trick** someone, you fool or cheat him/her.
2 To **trick** someone means to make that person believe something that is not true or did not happen.

**trickle** *verb* **trickles, trickling, trickled** (th)
To **trickle** means to flow very slowly in a thin stream.
[The word **trickle** is an imitation of the sound of water trickling.]

**tricky** *adjective* **trickier, trickiest** (th)
Something that is **tricky** is difficult or awkward to do.
[**Tricky** comes from **trick**.]

**tricycle** *noun* **tricycles**
A **tricycle** is a vehicle that you pedal. It has three wheels.
[**Tricycle** comes from Greek *tri-* 'three' and **cycle**.]

**trifle** *noun* **trifles**
1 A **trifle** is a dessert made from layers of cake, fruit, custard and cream.
2 A **trifle** is something that is small or not important.
[**Trifle** comes from an old French word.]

**trigger** *noun* **triggers**
A **trigger** is the part of a gun which is pulled when it is fired.
[**Trigger** comes from Dutch.]

**trim** *verb* **trims, trimming, trimmed** (th)
1 To **trim** something such as hair means to make it shorter or a better shape by cutting off a small amount.
2 To **trim** something such as clothing means to decorate it: *a hat trimmed with a feather.* [**Trim** comes from Old English.]

**trio** *noun* **trios**
A **trio** is a group of three people, especially musicians or singers.
[**Trio** comes via Italian from Latin *tres* 'three'.]

**trip** *noun* **trips** (th)
A **trip** is a journey or outing.
[**Trip** comes via French from an old Dutch word.]

**trip** *verb* **trips, tripping, tripped**
1 To **trip** means to stumble or fall over something.
2 To **trip** someone or **trip** someone **up** means to make them stumble or fall over something.

**triple** *adjective*
**Triple** means having or involving three parts.
[**Triple** comes from Greek via Latin.]

**triple** *verb* **triples, tripling, tripled**
To **triple** something means to multiply it by three.

**triplet** *noun* **triplets**
A **triplet** is one of three children who are born at the same time to the same mother.
[**Triplet** comes from **triple**.]

**tripod** *noun* **tripods**
A **tripod** is a stand with three legs used to support something such as a camera.
[**Tripod** comes via Latin from Greek *tri-* 'three' and *podos* 'foot'.]

**triumph** *noun* **triumphs**
A **triumph** is a very great success.
[**Triumph** comes from Greek via French and Latin.]

**trivial** *adjective* (th)
Something that is not at all important is **trivial**. [**Trivial** comes from Latin.]

**trod** *verb*
**Trod** is the past tense of **tread**.

**trodden** *verb*
**Trodden** is the past participle of **tread**.

**troll** *noun* **trolls**
A **troll** is a giant or a dwarf with magic powers in old Scandinavian stories. Some **trolls** were friendly and helpful but others were bad and spiteful.
[**Troll** comes from Old Norse.]

**trombone** *noun* **trombones**
A **trombone** is a large brass musical instrument that you blow into. It has a sliding tube that you move in and out to change the notes.
[**Trombone** comes from Italian *tromba* 'trumpet'.]

**troop** *noun* **troops**
A **troop** is a group of soldiers.
[**Troop** comes via French from Latin *troppus* 'a flock'.]

a b c d e f g h i j k l m

**troop** verb **troops, trooping, trooped**
To **troop** means to walk together in a group.

**trophy** noun **trophies**
A **trophy** is a special cup, plate or other award that is given as a prize.
[**Trophy** comes from Greek via French and Latin.]

**tropic** noun **tropics**
The **tropics** are the area on each side of the equator where the sun is directly overhead on at least one day of the year. The **Tropic of Cancer** is an imaginary line that marks the northern limit of the **tropics**, and the **Tropic of Capricorn** is an imaginary line that marks the southern limit.
[**Tropic** comes from Greek *trope* 'turning', because when the sun reaches one of the tropics it appears to turn back.]

**tropical** adjective
**Tropical** means to do with or belonging to the tropics: *a tropical rainstorm.*

**trot** verb **trots, trotting, trotted**
If a horse **trots**, it moves at a pace between walking and cantering.
[**Trot** comes from an old French word.]

**trouble** noun **troubles** (th)
A **trouble** is a difficulty or worry.
[**Trouble** comes from an old French word.]

**trouble** verb **troubles, troubling, troubled** (th)
If something **troubles** you, it worries or disturbs you.

**trough** noun **troughs**
A **trough** is a long, narrow container that animals can drink or feed from.
[**Trough** comes from Old English.]

**trousers** plural noun
**Trousers** are a piece of clothing with two legs worn on the lower part of the body.
[**Trousers** comes from a Gaelic word.]

**trout** noun **trout**
A **trout** is a fish that lives in rivers and is good to eat.
[**Trout** comes from Greek via Latin.]

**trowel** noun **trowels**
1 A **trowel** is a small curved spade used for digging in the garden.

2 A **trowel** is a tool with a flat blade used for spreading plaster or cement.
[**Trowel** comes from Latin via French.]

**truant** noun **truants**
1 If you **play truant**, you stay away from school without permission.
2 A **truant** is a child who stays away from school without permission.
[**Truant** comes from an old French word.]

**truce** noun **truces** (th)
A **truce** is an agreement between two sides to stop fighting for a time.
[**Truce** comes from Old English.]

**truck** noun **trucks**
1 A **truck** is a kind of large vehicle.
2 A **truck** is a railway wagon.
[**Truck** probably comes from Latin via French.]

**true** adjective (th)
Something that is correct or real is **true**.
[**True** comes from Old English.]

**trumpet** noun **trumpets**
A **trumpet** is a small brass musical instrument.
[**Trumpet** comes from an old French word.]

**trunk** noun **trunks**
1 A **trunk** is the thick stem of a tree.
2 A **trunk** is a very large case.
3 A **trunk** is an elephant's long nose.
[**Trunk** comes from Latin via French.]

**trust** verb **trusts, trusting, trusted** (th)
To **trust** means to believe that someone will be honest and not let you down.
[**Trust** comes from Old Norse.]

**trustworthy** adjective (th)
Someone who is **trustworthy** is honest and will not let you down.

**truth** noun **truths**
**Truth** is what is true.
[**Truth** comes from Old English.]

**try** verb **tries, trying, tried** (th)
1 To **try** means to make an effort to do something.
2 To **try** something means to test it to see how it works or whether you like it.
[**Try** comes from an old French word.]

**T-shirt** noun **T-shirts** Also **tee-shirt**
A **T-shirt** is a piece of casual clothing, usually with a plain round neck and short

sleeves, for the upper part of your body.
[The **T-shirt** is so called because when you
lay it out flat, it makes the shape of a
capital **T**.]

**tub** *noun* **tubs**
A **tub** is a plastic container for storing
food: *a tub of yoghurt.*
[**Tub** probably comes from an old
German or Dutch word.]

**tuba** *noun* **tubas**
A **tuba** is a large brass instrument with a
very low sound.
[**Tuba** comes from Latin via Italian.]

**tube** *noun* **tubes**
**1** A **tube** is a hollow cylinder like a pipe.
**2** A **tube** is a narrow flexible container for
soft substances: *a tube of toothpaste.*
[**Tube** comes from Latin.]

**tubular** *adjective*
**Tubular** means shaped like a tube.
[**Tubular** comes from Latin *tubulus* 'a
small tube'.]

**tuck** *verb* **tucks, tucking, tucked**
To **tuck** means to push or fold something
into or under something else to keep it in
place: *Tuck your T-shirt into your shorts.*
[**Tuck** comes from Old English.]

**tuft** *noun* **tufts**
A **tuft** is a small bunch of grass, hair or
something similar.
[**Tuft** comes from an old French word.]

**tug** *noun* **tugs**
A **tug** is a boat for pulling ships.
[**Tug** may come from the same Old
English word as **tow**.]

**tug** *verb* **tugs, tugging, tugged** (th)
To **tug** means to pull hard.

**tug-of-war** *noun* **tugs-of-war**
A **tug-of-war** is a contest between two
teams who each pull as hard as they can
at opposite ends of a rope to see which
team is the stronger.

**tulip** *noun* **tulips**
A **tulip** is a spring flower that grows from
a bulb.
[**Tulip** comes from Persian *dulband*
'turban', because of the shape of the
flower. Persian is the language spoken in
Iran.]

**tumble** *verb* **tumbles, tumbling,
tumbled**
To **tumble** means to fall by rolling over.
[**Tumble** comes from an old German
word.]

**tumour** *noun* **tumours**
A **tumour** is a lump that grows inside a
part of the body.
[**Tumour** comes from Latin *tumere* 'to
swell'.]

**tuna** *noun* **tuna**
A **tuna** is a large fish that lives in the sea
and is good to eat.
[**Tuna** comes from Spanish.]

**tundra** *noun*
The **tundra** is a large area in the Arctic
where it is very cold and there are no
trees.
[**Tundra** comes from Lappish (the
language spoken in Lapland).]

**tune** *noun* **tunes**
**1** A **tune** is an arrangement of musical
notes.
**2** If singing or a musical instrument is **in
tune**, all the notes sound correct.
[**Tune** comes from **tone**.]

**tune** *verb* **tunes, tuning, tuned**
To **tune** a musical instrument means to
adjust the notes so that they sound
correct.

**tunic** *noun* **tunics**
A **tunic** is a loose piece of clothing that
covers most of the body and usually has
no sleeves.
[**Tunic** comes from Latin via French or
Old English.]

**tunnel** *noun* **tunnels**
A **tunnel** is a passage made under the
ground or through a hill.
[**Tunnel** comes from an old French word.]

**turban** *noun* **turbans**
A **turban** is a covering for the head made
by wrapping a long piece of cloth round
it.
[**Turban** comes from Persian (the
language spoken in Iran).]

**turbine** *noun* **turbines**
A **turbine** is an engine in which the
pressure of gas, water or steam makes the
blades of one or more wheels turn round.
[**Turbine** comes from Latin *turbo* 'a

whirlwind'.]

**turbulent** *adjective*
Something that is **turbulent** is stormy and changes a lot: *a turbulent sea.*
[**Turbulent** comes from Latin.]

**turf** *noun*
**Turf** is earth that is covered with a layer of grass. [**Turf** comes from Old English.]

**turkey** *noun* **turkeys**
1 A **turkey** is a large bird kept for its meat.
2 **Turkey** is the meat from a turkey.
[**Turkey** was originally the name of a different bird that came from Turkey.]

**turn** *noun* **turns**
A **turn** is the time when one person in a group does something.
[**Turn** comes from Greek via Old English and Latin.]

**turn** *verb* **turns, turning, turned** (th)
1 To **turn** means to move or make something move round in a circle: *The wheel is turning; I turned the key.*
2 To **turn** means to change the direction you are going or facing: *Turn left; She turned round to look.*
3 To **turn** means to become or change: *My socks turned pink in the wash.*
4 To **turn** something **on** or **off** means to switch it on or off.

**turnip** *noun* **turnips**
A **turnip** is a round white vegetable that grows under the ground.
[**Turnip** comes from Latin via Old English.]

**turquoise** *noun*
1 A **turquoise** is a blue-green stone that is sometimes used in jewellery.
2 **Turquoise** is a blue-green colour.
[**Turquoise** comes from French *pierre turquoise* 'Turkish stone', because it was first found in the Turkish empire.]

**turquoise** *adjective*
1 made of turquoise or with a turquoise: *a turquoise ring.*
2 blue-green in colour: *a swimming pool with turquoise tiles.*

**turtle** *noun* **turtles**
A **turtle** is a sea creature with a hard shell.
[**Turtle** comes from the same French word as **tortoise**.]

**tusk** *noun* **tusks**
A **tusk** is one of the two, long, pointed teeth that an elephant has.
[**Tusk** comes from Old English.]

**tutu** *noun* **tutus**
A **tutu** is a short skirt made of stiff net that female ballet dancers wear.
[**Tutu** comes from French.]

**twice** *adverb*
When something is done **twice**, it is done two times.
[**Twice** comes from Old English.]

**twig** *noun* **twigs**
A **twig** is a small branch of a tree.
[**Twig** comes from Old English.]

**twilight** *noun*
**Twilight** is the dim light in the evening before it gets dark.
[**Twilight** comes from Old English.]

**twin** *noun* **twins**
A **twin** is one of two children who are born at the same time to the same mother.
[**Twin** comes from Old English *twi* 'two'.]

**twinkle** *verb* **twinkles, twinkling, twinkled** (th)
To **twinkle** means to sparkle or shine with tiny flickering lights.
[**Twinkle** comes from Old English.]

**twirl** *verb* **twirls, twirling, twirled** (th)
To **twirl** means to turn round and round quickly.
[No one knows where **twirl** comes from.]

**twist** *verb* **twists, twisting, twisted** (th)
1 To **twist** means to turn or bend round.
2 To **twist** means to wind things round each other.
[**Twist** comes from Old English.]

**type** *noun* **types** (th)
1 A **type** is one kind of something: *What type of music do you like?*
2 **Type** is printed letters, numbers and symbols: *Headlines in newspapers are printed in large type.*
[**Type** comes from Greek via French and Latin.]

**type** *verb* **types, typing, typed**
To **type** means to write with a typewriter.

**typewriter** *noun* **typewriters**
A **typewriter** is a machine with keys

which print letters and numbers when pressed.

**typhoon** *noun* **typhoons** (th)
A **typhoon** is a very strong, windy storm.
[**Typhoon** comes from Chinese *tai fung* 'great wind'.]

**typical** *adjective* (th)
**Typical** means having the usual features of a particular thing: *a typical English breakfast*.
[**Typical** comes via Latin from the same Greek word as **type**.]

**tyrant** *noun* **tyrants**
A **tyrant** is a cruel ruler who has total power.
[**Tyrant** comes from Greek via French and Latin.]

**tyre** *noun* **tyres**
A **tyre** is a thick ring of rubber that goes round the wheel of a bicycle, car or other vehicle.
[**Tyre** may come from *attire* 'clothes', because the tyre goes round the wheel and protects it like clothing.]

## Dictionary Fun

**What do these idioms mean?**
1. To turn over a new leaf
2. To take your breath away
3. To talk the hind leg off a donkey

**Complete the proverbs**
1. Time and t_____ wait for no man.
2. A liar is not believed when he speaks the t_____.

**Riddle**
I have four legs
but I cannot walk
I stand all day
and I cannot talk.
What am I?

**Find out**
1. Which animal, beginning with 't', is the subject of a famous poem by William Blake? Try to learn the poem.
2. Which creature, beginning with 't', was featured in a famous story by Kenneth Grahame?

**Did you know?**
◆ The word **tulip** comes from the Persian word *dulband*, which means 'turban', because of the shape of the flower.

a b c d e f g h i j k l m

# Uu

**udder** *noun* **udders**
An **udder** is the part of a cow that hangs down like a bag under its body and produces milk.
[**Udder** comes from Old English.]

**UFO** *noun* **UFOs**
A **UFO** is a strange object in the sky that some people believe may be a spaceship from another planet.
[**UFO** stands for *unidentified flying object*.]

**ugly** *adjective* **uglier, ugliest** (th)
Something that is **ugly** is not pretty or pleasant to look at.
[**Ugly** comes from Old Norse *uggligr* 'to be dreaded'.]

**ultimate** *adjective*
**Ultimate** means final and most important: *Our ultimate aim is to win the contest.*
[**Ultimate** comes from Latin *ultimus* 'last'.]

**ultimatum** *noun* **ultimatums**
An **ultimatum** is a final threat that someone must do something or accept what happens if s/he does not do it.
[**Ultimatum** comes from Latin *ultimare* 'to come to an end', because you are not going to talk any more before taking action.]

**ultraviolet** *adjective*
**Ultraviolet** light comes from the sun. It cannot be seen and can burn your skin.
[**Ultraviolet** comes from Latin *ultra* 'beyond' and **violet**.]

**umbilical cord** *noun* **umbilical cords**
An **umbilical cord** is a tube that joins an unborn baby to its mother's body and supplies it with oxygen and food.
[**Umbilical** comes from Latin *umbilicus* 'navel'.]

**umbrella** *noun* **umbrellas**
An **umbrella** is a frame covered with cloth which can be folded up or opened and held over your head to keep off the rain.
[**Umbrella** comes via Italian from Latin *umbra* 'shade'.]

**umpire** *noun* **umpires**
An **umpire** is a person who makes sure that players in a sport such as tennis follow the rules.
[**Umpire** comes from French.]

**un-** *prefix*
**Un-** means 'not'. You add **un-** to a word to make it mean the opposite: *Someone who is not happy is unhappy; The door is locked at night and unlocked in the morning.*
[**Un-** comes from Old English.]

**unable** *adjective* (th)
Someone who is **unable** to do something cannot do it.

**unanimous** *adjective*
If a decision is **unanimous**, everyone agrees with it. **unanimously** *adverb*.
[**Unanimous** comes from Latin *unanimus* 'of one mind'.]

**unaware** *adjective* (th)
Someone who is **unaware** of something cannot see it or does not know about it.

**unbelievable** *adjective* (th)
Something that is **unbelievable** is so strange or surprising that you cannot believe it is true.

**uncanny** *adjective* **uncannier, uncanniest** (th)
Something that is **uncanny** is strange and cannot easily be explained.
**uncannily** *adverb*.
[**Uncanny** comes from *un-* 'not' and Scots *canny* 'possible to know or understand'.]

**uncertain** *adjective* (th)
If you are **uncertain** about something, you are not sure about it.

**uncle** *noun* **uncles**
Your **uncle** is a brother of your mother or father, or the husband of your aunt.
[**Uncle** comes from French or Latin.]

**unconcerned** *adjective* (th)
If you are **unconcerned** about something, you do not care or worry about it.

**unconscious** *adjective*
Someone who is **unconscious** is in a state when s/he cannot move, see or feel anything, usually because of an accident or illness.

**uncover** *verb* **uncovers, uncovering, uncovered** (th)
**1** To **uncover** means to take the covering off something.
**2** To **uncover** something means to find out

about something that was kept secret.

**undecided** *adjective* (th)
If you are **undecided** about something, you have not yet made up your mind.

**under** *preposition*
**1** below or beneath something: *The tunnel goes under the river.*
**2** less than: *children under the age of six.*
**3** ruled or controlled by: *The supervisor had 12 men under him.*
[**Under** comes from Old English.]

**underarm** *adverb*
If you throw a ball **underarm**, you throw it without lifting your arm above the shoulder.

**undercarriage** *noun* **undercarriages**
The **undercarriage** of a plane is the structure and wheels that support its weight on the ground.

**undercurrent** *noun* **undercurrents**
An **undercurrent** is a hidden current of water that flows in a different direction to the water on the surface of the sea or a river and is often dangerous.

**underestimate** *verb* **underestimates, underestimating, underestimated**
To **underestimate** means to say or guess that something is worth less or is smaller than it is.

**underground** *noun*
The **underground** is a railway that runs through tunnels below ground level.

**underground** *adjective, adverb*
below the ground: *an underground train; Rabbits burrow underground.*

**undergrowth** *noun*
**Undergrowth** is bushes and plants that grow together under trees in a wood or forest.

**underline** *verb* **underlines, underlining, underlined**
To **underline** something means to draw a line under it.

**underneath** *adverb, preposition*
If one thing is **underneath** something else, it is below or covered by it.
[**Underneath** comes from Old English.]

**underpants** *plural noun*
**Underpants** are pants worn by boys and men beneath their trousers.

**understand** *verb* **understands, understanding, understood** (th)
**1** To **understand** means to know what something means, how it works or what it is.
**2** To **understand** means to know or realise how someone feels.
[**Understand** comes from Old English.]

**undertaker** *noun* **undertakers**
An **undertaker** is a person whose job is to arrange funerals when people die.
[**Undertaker** comes from *undertake* 'to agree to do something', especially something difficult or unpleasant.]

**underwater** *adjective, adverb*
under the surface of water: *underwater exploration; Otters can swim underwater.*

**underwear** *noun*
**Underwear** is clothes that you wear next to your skin, under your other clothes.

**undo** *verb* **undoes, undoing, undone** (th)
**1** To **undo** something means to unfasten or unwrap it.
**2** To **undo** what someone has done means to destroy the result or effect of it: *He's undone all our hard work.*

**undress** *verb* **undresses, undressing, undressed**
To **undress** means to take off your clothes.

**unemployed** *adjective*
Someone who is **unemployed** does not have a job.

**unequal** *adjective* (th)
**1** Things that are **unequal** are not the same size, number or value as something else.
**2** People who are **unequal** are not treated fairly or in the same way.

**unexpected** *adjective* (th)
Something that you did not expect to happen is **unexpected**.

**unfair** *adjective* (th)
Something that is not right, equal or just is **unfair**.

**unfamiliar** *adjective* (th)
Something that you have not known about or seen before is **unfamiliar**.
[**Unfamiliar** comes from **un-** and *familiar* 'well known, often seen', which comes

from the same Latin word as **family**.]

**unfit** *adjective* (th)
1 Someone who is **unfit** does not do enough exercise to keep his/her body in a good physical condition.
2 Someone who is **unfit** to do something is not suitable or good enough to do it.
[**Unfit** comes from *un-* 'not' and **fit²**.]

**unfold** *verb* **unfolds, unfolding, unfolded**
To **unfold** means to spread or open out something that is folded or closed up.

**unfortunately** *adverb*
If something happens **unfortunately**, it is bad or unlucky that it happens.

**unfriendly** *adjective* (th)
Someone who is **unfriendly** does not want to make friends and be kind.

**ungrateful** *adjective*
Someone who is **ungrateful** does not show any thanks for something.

**unhappy** *adjective* **unhappier, unhappiest** (th)
Someone who is **unhappy** is miserable and not happy.
**unhappily** *adverb*. **unhappiness** *noun*.

**unhealthy** *adjective* **unhealthier, unhealthiest** (th)
1 Something that is **unhealthy** is not good for you.
2 Someone who is **unhealthy** is not in a good physical condition.

**unhurt** *adjective*
Someone who is **unhurt** was not hurt in an accident.

**unhygienic** *adjective*
Something that is **unhygienic** is dirty and full of germs.

**unicorn** *noun* **unicorns**
A **unicorn** is an imaginary animal that looks like a horse with a long straight horn in the middle of its forehead.
[**Unicorn** comes via French from Latin *uni-* 'one, single' and *cornu* 'horn'.]

**uniform** *noun* **uniforms**
A **uniform** is a special set of clothes worn by all members of a group, such as soldiers.
[**Uniform** comes from Latin *uniformus* 'having one form'.]

**unimportant** *adjective* (th)
Something that you do not have to worry about is **unimportant**.

**uninhabitable** *adjective*
A place that is **uninhabitable** is not fit to live in.
[**Uninhabitable** comes from *un-* 'not' and *inhabit* 'to live in a place', which comes from the same French word as **inhabitant**.]

**uninhabited** *adjective* (th)
A place that is **uninhabited** has no one living there.
[**Uninhabited** comes from *un-* 'not' and *inhabit* 'to live in a place', which comes from the same French word as **inhabitant**.]

**uninterested** *adjective* (th)
If you are **uninterested** in something, you do not want to know about it.

**union** *noun* **unions** (th)
1 A **union** is when people or things are joined together.
2 A **union** is a group of workers who join together in order to protect their rights.
[**Union** comes via French from the same Latin word as **unit**.]

**unique** *adjective*
If something is **unique**, nothing else is exactly like it.
[**Unique** comes via French from the same Latin word as **unit**.]

**unisex** *adjective*
Something that either men or women can use or wear is **unisex**.
[**Unisex** comes from Latin *uni-* 'one, single' and **sex**.]

**unit** *noun* **units**
1 A **unit** is the number one or a single thing.
2 A **unit** is an amount used for measuring or counting. A metre is a **unit** of length and a litre is a **unit** of volume.
[**Unit** comes from Latin *unus* 'one'.]

**unite** *verb* **unites, uniting, united** (th)
To **unite** means to join together to form a whole.
[**Unite** comes from the same Latin word as **unit**.]

**universal** *adjective* (th)
Something that is **universal** happens or is

understood by people all over the world. [**Universal** comes from the same Latin word as **universe**.]

**universe** *noun*
The **universe** is the whole of space and everything in it.
[**Universe** comes via French from Latin *universus* 'made into one'.]

**university** *noun* **universities**
A **university** is a place where some people go to study for degrees or qualifications after leaving school.
[**University** comes via French from the same Latin word as **universe**.]

**unkind** *adjective* **unkinder, unkindest** (th)
Someone who is **unkind** is nasty to other people.

**unknown** *adjective* (th)
Something that nobody knows about is **unknown**: *The cause of his illness is unknown.*

**unless** *conjunction*
**Unless** means except, or if not: *I will wear my new winter coat unless the weather is very warm.*
[**Unless** comes from a Middle English word.]

**unlike** *preposition*
If one thing is **unlike** another, it is completely different from it.

**unlikely** *adjective* **unlikelier, unlikeliest** (th)
Something that is **unlikely** probably will not happen or is probably not true.

**unload** *verb* **unloads, unloading, unloaded**
To **unload** means to remove things from a vehicle.

**unlucky** *adjective* **unluckier, unluckiest** (th)
1 If someone is **unlucky**, something bad happens to him/her by chance.
2 If something is **unlucky**, it happens because of bad luck.

**unnatural** *adjective*
Something that is **unnatural** does not normally happen or exist in nature.

**unnecessary** *adjective* (th)
If something is **unnecessary**, you do not need it.

**unoccupied** *adjective* (th)
A seat, room or house that is **unoccupied** has no one in it.

**unofficial** *adjective* (th)
Something that does not have the permission of someone in authority is **unofficial**.

**unpack** *verb* **unpacks, unpacking, unpacked**
To **unpack** means to take things out of a suitcase, bag or box.

**unplanned** *adjective*
Something that you did not plan to happen is **unplanned**.

**unpleasant** *adjective* (th)
1 Something that is not enjoyable is **unpleasant**.
2 Someone who is **unpleasant** is rude or unfriendly.

**unplug** *verb* **unplugs, unplugging, unplugged**
To **unplug** means to take a plug out of an electrical socket.

**unpopular** *adjective* (th)
Someone or something that is **unpopular** is not liked by many people.

**unprepared** *adjective*
If you are not ready for something you have to do, you are **unprepared**.

**unreasonable** *adjective* (th)
1 Someone who is **unreasonable** behaves in an unfair way.
2 If something is **unreasonable**, it is unfair to ask for it or ask someone to do it.

**unreliable** *adjective* (th)
Someone or something you cannot trust or rely on is **unreliable**.

**unripe** *adjective*
A fruit, vegetable or crop that is **unripe** is not yet ready to be picked or eaten.

**unsafe** *adjective*
Something that is **unsafe** is dangerous.

**unstable** *adjective* (th)
1 A thing that is **unstable** is likely to fall over because it is not balanced properly.
2 A person who is **unstable** changes his/ her mood often.
3 A situation that is **unstable** can

suddenly change or get worse.
[**Unstable** comes from *un-* 'not' and
**stable**$^2$.]

**unsteady** *adjective*
Something that is **unsteady** rocks or
shakes because it is not held or placed
firmly.

**unsuccessful** *adjective*
If you are **unsuccessful**, you fail in
something or do not get what you want.
[**Unsuccessful** comes from *un-* 'not',
**success** and *-ful* 'full of'.]

**unsuitable** *adjective* (th)
Something that is **unsuitable** is not the
right thing for a particular situation or
purpose.

**unsure** *adjective* (th)
If you are **unsure**, you do not feel certain
about what to do or decide.

**unsweetened** *adjective*
A food that is **unsweetened** has no sugar
added to it.

**unsympathetic** *adjective* (th)
A person who is **unsympathetic** does not
show that s/he cares about or
understands another person's problems.

**untidy** *adjective* **untidier, untidiest** (th)
1 Something that is **untidy** is in a mess
and is not neat.
2 A person who is **untidy** never keeps
his/her things in order.

**untie** *verb* **unties, untying, untied** (th)
To **untie** means to undo the knots or bows
that tie something.

**until** *preposition, conjunction*
When something is done up to a
particular time, it is done **until** then: *He
worked until bedtime; Don't come until I call
you.*
[**Until** comes from Old Norse.]

**unusual** *adjective* (th)
Something that is **unusual** is not seen or
does not happen very often.

**unwanted** *adjective*
Something that you do not want or need
is **unwanted**.

**unwieldy** *adjective* (th)
Something that is **unwieldy** is difficult to
hold, carry or use.

[**Unwieldy** comes from *un-* 'not' and an
old word *wieldy* 'handy, easy to use',
which comes from **wield**.]

**unwilling** *adjective* (th)
If you are **unwilling** to do something,
you do not want to do it.

**unwind** *verb* **unwinds, unwinding,
unwound** (th)
1 To **unwind** means to undo something
that has been wrapped or wound around
something else.
2 To **unwind** means to relax and stop
worrying.
[**Unwind** comes from *un-* 'to undo' and
**wind**$^2$.]

**unwrap** *verb* **unwraps, unwrapping,
unwrapped**
To **unwrap** means to take off the paper or
packaging that something is wrapped in.

**up** *preposition*
from a lower to a higher place: *We ran up
the hill.* [**Up** comes from Old English.]

**up** *adverb*
1 to or in a higher place or level: *She's up
in her bedroom; Prices are going up; Pick up
your books.*
2 into an upright position: *Stand up!*
3 out of bed: *It's time to get up; She's never
up before noon.*
4 completely or completely finished: *Eat
up your vegetables; He's used up all the milk;
Time's up!*
5 along or towards: *He walked straight up
to her.*

**upbringing** *noun*
Your **upbringing** is the way that you are
cared for by your parents and what they
teach you.

**update** *verb* **updates, updating, updated**
To **update** something means to add the
most recent information to it or change it
so that it is more modern.

**upgrade** *verb* **upgrades, upgrading,
upgraded**
To **upgrade** something means to improve
it.

**upheaval** *noun* **upheavals**
An **upheaval** is a very big change that is
disturbing or causes problems.
[**Upheaval** comes from **up** and *heave* 'to

lift or move something heavy', which comes from Old English.]

**uphill** *adverb*
going up a slope: *The road winds uphill to the summit.*

**upholstery** *noun*
**Upholstery** is the materials that are used to make soft covers for chairs and sofas. [**Upholstery** comes from *uphold* in the sense 'to keep in good condition'.]

**upper** *adjective*
Something that is higher than something else is in an **upper** position: *the upper branches of the tree.*
[**Upper** comes from **up**.]

**upright** *adjective* (th)
1 Someone or something that stands straight up is **upright**.
2 Someone who is **upright** is honest and always tries to do what is right.
[**Upright** comes from Old English.]

**uproar** *noun* (th)
**Uproar** is noise, shouting and confusion.

**uproot** *verb* **uproots, uprooting, uprooted**
1 To **uproot** a plant means to pull it right out of the ground.
2 To **uproot** yourself means to move from a place where you are settled.

**upset** *verb* **upsets, upsetting, upset** (th)
1 To **upset** someone means to make that person worried and unhappy.
2 To **upset** something means to spill it or tip it over.

**upset** *adjective*
If you are **upset**, something has made you feel unhappy and worried.

**upside down** *adjective, adverb*
Something that is **upside down** has turned over so that the top is at the bottom.

**upstairs** *adverb*
on or to an upper floor or floors: *There are two bedrooms upstairs; She went upstairs to the attic.*

**upstairs** *adjective*
on an upper floor: *the upstairs rooms.*

**up-to-date** *adjective*
Something that is **up-to-date** includes the most recent information or is the most modern version.

**uranium** *noun*
**Uranium** is a metal that is radioactive and is used to make nuclear power and nuclear weapons.
[**Uranium** is named after the planet *Uranus*.]

**urban** *adjective*
**Urban** means to do with a town or city and not the countryside.
[**Urban** comes from Latin *urbs* 'a city'.]

**urge** *verb* **urges, urging, urged**
To **urge** means to persuade or encourage someone strongly to do something.
[**Urge** comes from Latin.]

**urgent** *adjective*
Something that is **urgent** needs to be done immediately.
[**Urgent** comes via French from the same Latin word as **urge**.]

**urine** *noun*
**Urine** is the waste liquid from your body.
[**Urine** comes from Latin via French.]

**urn** *noun* **urns**
An **urn** is a vase with two handles used as a container, especially for the ashes of a dead person. [**Urn** comes from Latin.]

**use** *noun* **uses**
1 The **use** that something has is what you can use it for.
2 **Use** is when you use something: *Use of the gym is free to members.*
[**Use** comes from Latin via French.]

**use** *verb* **uses, using, used** (th)
1 To **use** something means to perform an action or do a job with it: *The burglars used a brick to break the window.*
2 To **use** something **up** means to use all of it so that there is none left.

**used to** *adjective*
If you are **used to** something, you have experienced it before many times.
[**Used to** comes from **use** in an old sense 'to make someone familiar with'.]

**useful** *adjective*
Something that is helpful is **useful**.

**useless** *adjective*
Something that is **useless** is not helpful or useful at all.

a b c d e f g h i j k l m

**user-friendly** *adjective* **user-friendlier, user-friendliest**

Something, such as a machine, that is **user-friendly** is easy to understand and use.

**usher** *noun* **ushers**

An **usher** is someone who shows people to their seats in a theatre, cinema or at a wedding.
[**Usher** comes from Latin via French.]

**usherette** *noun* **usherettes**

An **usherette** is a woman who shows people to their seats in a cinema.
[**Usherette** comes from **usher**.]

**usual** *adjective* (th)

Something that is **usual** is normal or happens often.
[**Usual** comes via French from the same Latin word as **use**.]

**usually** *adverb* (th)

If something **usually** happens, it happens often or most of the time.

**utensil** *noun* **utensils**

A **utensil** is a tool used in the kitchen.
[**Utensil** comes via French from the same Latin word as **use**.]

**utility** *noun* **utilities**

A **utility** is a necessary service like water, gas or electricity.
[**Utility** comes via French from the same Latin word as **use**.]

**utter** *verb* **utters, uttering, uttered**

To **utter** means to make a sound with the voice.
[**Utter** comes from an old Dutch word.]

**utter** *adjective*

An **utter** disaster or failure is a complete and total disaster or failure.
[**Utter** comes from Old English.]

**U-turn** *noun* **U-turns**

A **U-turn** is a turn made in the road by a vehicle, in order to go back in the other direction.
[**U-turn** comes from the shape of the letter **U**.]

---

# Dictionary Fun

**Etymology**
Which word comes from Latin *ultimare* 'to come to an end'?

**What does this idiom mean?**
It's right under your nose

**New words**
Clue: It's easy to use!

**Work it out**
What does the *uni-* in **unicorn** and **uniform** mean? Explain how this relates to the words.

**Find out**
Which 'u' word is associated with Oxford, Cambridge and Yale?

**Did you know?**
◆ The word **ugly** comes from the Old Norse word *uggligr*, which means 'to be dreaded'.

◆ Thousands of **UFOs** have been reported by people, but most can be easily explained. No scientific evidence of real UFOs exists, although some people believe in them.

**Brainteaser**
If two mothers and two daughters went shopping and each bought a dress, why did they come home with only three dresses?

# Vv

**vacant** *adjective* (th)
**1** A place that is **vacant** is empty and available for someone to use.
[**Vacant** comes from Latin *vacare* 'to be empty or idle'.]

**vacation** *noun* **vacations**
A **vacation** is a holiday.
[**Vacation** comes via French from the same Latin word as **vacant**.]

**vaccinate** *verb* **vaccinates, vaccinating, vaccinated**
To **vaccinate** means to give someone an injection in order to protect him/her against a disease.
[**Vaccinate** comes from **vaccine**.]

**vaccination** *noun* **vaccinations**
A **vaccination** is an injection that protects you against a disease.

**vaccine** *noun* **vaccines**
A **vaccine** is a substance containing a tiny amount of what causes a disease. It is given to someone as an injection to protect him/her from that disease.
[**Vaccine** comes from Latin *vacca* 'a cow', because the first vaccine was made from a substance that caused a disease in cows that could be caught by humans.]

**vacuum** *noun* **vacuums**
A **vacuum** is a space that has had all the air or gas removed from it.
[**Vacuum** comes from Latin *vacuus* 'empty'.]

**vacuum cleaner** *noun* **vacuum cleaners**
A **vacuum cleaner** is a machine that cleans by sucking up dirt and dust.

**vagina** *noun* **vaginas**
A woman's **vagina** is a part of her body like a tube that leads down from her womb to the area between the top of her legs. [**Vagina** comes from Latin.]

**vague** *adjective* **vaguer, vaguest** (th)
If something is **vague**, it is not clear or definite.
[**Vague** comes from Latin *vagus* 'wandering'.]

**vaguely** *adverb*
**Vaguely** means slightly but not clearly: *I vaguely remember her.*

**vain** *adjective* **vainer, vainest**
Someone who is **vain** believes s/he is very attractive and is very proud of himself or herself.
[**Vain** comes via French from Latin *vanus* 'empty or meaningless'.]

**valid** *adjective*
Something that is legal or acceptable is **valid**: *a valid ticket.*
[**Valid** comes via French from Latin *validus* 'strong'.]

**valley** *noun* **valleys**
A **valley** is a stretch of low land between hills.
[**Valley** comes from Latin via French.]

**valuable** *adjective*
Something that is **valuable** is very important to you or is worth a lot of money. [**Valuable** comes from **value**.]

**value** *noun* **values** (th)
**1** The **value** of something is what it is worth.
**2** If something is **good value** or **value for money**, it is worth the price being asked for it.
**3** Your **values** are the things you believe are most important in life.
[**Value** comes via French from Latin *valere* 'to be worth'.]

**value** *verb* **values, valuing, valued**
**1** To **value** something means to believe it is important: *I value our friendship.*
**2** To **value** something means to work out what it is worth.

**valve** *noun* **valves**
A **valve** is a device that opens and closes to control the flow of a liquid or gas through a pipe or tube.
[**Valve** comes from Latin.]

**vampire** *noun* **vampires**
A **vampire** is a person in horror stories who has died but rises from the grave at night to suck the blood of living people.
[**Vampire** probably comes from Turkish via French and Hungarian.]

**van** *noun* **vans**
A **van** is a vehicle with closed sides for carrying goods.
[**Van** comes from **caravan**.]

**vandal** *noun* **vandals**
A **vandal** is someone who breaks or

a b c d e f g h i j k l m

damages property for no reason.
[The **Vandals** were a tribe that attacked
Rome in the 5th century and destroyed
many works of art.]

**vanilla** *noun*
**Vanilla** is the pod of a climbing plant that
grows in hot countries and is used to
flavour some sweet foods such as cakes.
[**Vanilla** comes from Spanish.]

**vanish** *verb* **vanishes, vanishing,
vanished**
To **vanish** means to disappear out of
sight.
[**Vanish** comes from Latin via French.]

**vanity** *noun*
**Vanity** is when someone feels too proud
of himself or herself, especially of his/her
appearance.
[**Vanity** comes via French from the same
Latin word as **vain**.]

**vapour** *noun*
**Vapour** is a gas such as steam that
contains tiny drops of water and hangs in
the air.
[**Vapour** comes from Latin via French.]

**variety** *noun* **varieties** (th)
**1 Variety** is when there are a lot of things
that are different from each other: *a variety
of colours*.
**2** A **variety** is a different type of
something: *several varieties of tomato*.
[**Variety** comes via French from the same
Latin word as **various**.]

**various** *adjective* (th)
If there are **various** kinds of something,
there are several different kinds.
[**Various** comes from Latin *varius*
'changing or different'.]

**varnish** *noun* **varnishes**
A **varnish** is a liquid that is painted on
something to make it hard and give it a
smooth or shiny surface.
[**Varnish** comes via French from Latin or
Greek.]

**vary** *verb* **varies, varying, varied**
**1** To **vary** something means to change it
often or make it different from other
similar things.
**2** If things that are similar **vary**, they are
different from each other.
[**Vary** comes from the same Latin word as

**various**.]

**vase** *noun* **vases**
A **vase** is a container for holding flowers.
[**Vase** comes from Latin via French.]

**vast** *adjective* (th)
Something that is **vast** is very large or has
a wide area: *a vast desert*.
[**Vast** comes from Latin.]

**VDU** *noun* **VDUs**
A **VDU** is a screen that displays
information from a computer.
[**VDU** stands for *visual display unit*.]

**veal** *noun*
**Veal** is the meat from a calf.
[**Veal** comes from Latin *vitulus* 'a calf'.]

**vegan** *noun* **vegans**
A **vegan** is a person who does not eat
anything that comes from an animal,
including milk, eggs and cheese.
[**Vegan** comes from **vegetarian**.]

**vegetable** *noun* **vegetables**
A **vegetable** is a plant or part of a plant
that is used as food.
[**Vegetable** comes from Latin *vegetare* 'to
grow or develop'.]

**vegetarian** *noun* **vegetarians**
A **vegetarian** is someone who does not
eat meat or fish.
[**Vegetarian** comes from **vegetable**.]

**vegetation** *noun*
**Vegetation** is plants, especially the ones
that are growing in a particular area: *lush
tropical vegetation*.
[**Vegetation** comes from the same Latin
word as **vegetable**.]

**vehicle** *noun* **vehicles**
A **vehicle** is something such as a car or a
train for carrying people or things.
[**Vehicle** comes from Latin *vehiculum*
'something that carries'.]

**veil** *noun* **veils**
A **veil** is a piece of fine material that some
women wear to cover their faces.
[**Veil** comes from Latin via French.]

**vein** *noun* **veins**
A **vein** is a thin tube in the body that
carries blood to the heart.
[**Vein** comes from Latin via French.]

**velvet** *noun*
Velvet is a kind of material that is very soft on one side.
[**Velvet** comes from Latin via French.]

**venom** *noun*
Venom is a poisonous substance produced by some snakes and spiders and used when they bite.
[**Venom** comes via French from Latin *venenum* 'poison'.]

**ventilate** *verb* **ventilates, ventilating, ventilated**
To ventilate a place means to let fresh air into it.
[**Ventilate** comes from Latin *ventus* 'wind'.]

**veranda** *noun* **verandas**
A veranda is a platform, usually with a roof, around the outside of a house where you can sit.
[**Veranda** comes from Portuguese via Hindi (a language spoken in India).]

**verb** *noun* **verbs**
A verb is a word that says what someone or something does. *Sing, think* and *eat* are verbs.
[**Verb** comes from Latin.]

**verdict** *noun* **verdicts**
A verdict is the decision by a judge or jury in a court of law.
[**Verdict** comes from old French *verdit* 'speaking the truth'.]

**verge** *noun* **verges**
1 A verge is a strip of grass at the side of the road.
2 If you are **on the verge** of doing something, you are going to do it soon.
[**Verge** comes from Latin via French.]

**verruca** *noun* **verrucae** *or* **verrucas**
A verruca is a small growth on the sole of the foot, caused by a virus.
[**Verruca** comes from Latin.]

**versatile** *adjective*
Something that is useful in many different ways is versatile.
[**Versatile** comes from Latin.]

**verse** *noun* **verses**
1 A verse is a section of a poem or song.
2 Verse is poetry.
[**Verse** comes from Latin.]

**vertebra** *noun* **vertebrae**
A vertebra is one of the bones that make up the spine in the back.
[**Vertebra** comes from Latin.]

**vertebrate** *noun* **vertebrates**
A vertebrate is an animal that has a backbone.
[**Vertebrate** comes from the same Latin word as **vertebra**.]

**vertical** *adjective* (th)
Something that is upright is vertical.
**vertically** *adverb*.
[**Vertical** comes from Latin via French.]

**very** *adjective*
exact or actual: *It's the very thing we need!*
[**Very** comes via French from Latin *verus* 'true'.]

**very** *adverb*
1 especially or extremely: *She's a very nice girl; Thank you very much.*
2 You use **very** to add force to what you are saying: *They came the very next day.*

**vest** *noun* **vests**
A vest is a piece of clothing that you wear over the top half of your body under your other clothes.
[**Vest** comes from Latin *vestis* 'a piece of clothing'.]

**vet** *noun* **vets**
A vet is a doctor who treats sick animals.
[**Vet** is short for **veterinary surgeon**; **veterinary** comes from Latin *veterinae* 'cattle'.]

**via** *preposition*
Via means through or by way of: *The train goes to Liverpool via Crewe; These television pictures come via satellite.*
[**Via** comes from Latin *via* 'by the road or way'.]

**viaduct** *noun* **viaducts**
A viaduct is a bridge that carries a road or railway across a valley.
[**Viaduct** comes from Latin *via* 'road' and *ducere* 'to lead'.]

**vibrant** *adjective* (th)
Something that is very bright or full of life is vibrant: *vibrant colours.*
[**Vibrant** comes from the same Latin word as **vibrate**.]

**vibrate** *verb* **vibrates, vibrating, vibrated** (th)
To **vibrate** means to shake or move quickly backwards and forwards.
[**Vibrate** comes from Latin.]

**vicar** *noun* **vicars**
A **vicar** is a priest in the Anglican Church.
[**Vicar** comes from Latin.]

**vicarage** *noun* **vicarages**
A **vicarage** is a vicar's house and is usually near his/her church.

**vice-captain** *noun* **vice-captains**
A **vice-captain** is a deputy who helps a captain and is responsible when s/he is not there.
[**Vice** comes from Latin *vice* 'in place of'.]

**vice-president** *noun* **vice-presidents**
A **vice-president** is a deputy who helps a president and is responsible when s/he is not there.
[**Vice** comes from Latin *vice* 'in place of'.]

**vice versa** *adverb*
**Vice versa** means the other way around: *Any music I like, my sister hates, and vice versa.*
[**Vice versa** is Latin for 'the position being turned'.]

**vicinity** *noun* **vicinities**
The **vicinity** is the area surrounding a particular place.
[**Vicinity** comes from Latin *vicinus* 'neighbour'.]

**victim** *noun* **victims**
A **victim** is someone who suffers as the result of someone else's actions or of a disease or disaster: *the murderer's victim.*
[**Victim** comes from Latin *victima* 'a person sacrificed to a god'.]

**victory** *noun* **victories**
A **victory** is winning a fight or competition.
[**Victory** comes from Latin via French.]

**video** *noun* **videos**
1 **Video** is recorded pictures and sound that can be broadcast or used on a computer.
2 A **video** or **video tape** is a magnetic tape with recorded pictures and sound on it. When the **video** is played in a video recorder the pictures and sound are produced on a television screen.
[**Video** comes from Latin *video* 'I see'.]

**video** *verb* **videos, videoing, videoed**
To **video** means to record a television programme or make a film on video tape.

**view** *noun* **views** (th)
1 A **view** is what you can see from a place: *a beautiful view of the beach.*
2 Your **view** is your opinion.
[**View** comes via French from Latin *videre* 'to see'.]

**view** *verb* **views, viewing, viewed**
To **view** means to look at something you are interested in buying.

**vigorous** *adjective* (th)
Something that is **vigorous** is full of activity or energy: *vigorous exercise.*
[**Vigorous** comes from Latin via French.]

**Viking** *noun* **Vikings**
The **Vikings** were people from Scandinavia who attacked Northern Europe in the 8th to 10th centuries AD and settled there.
[**Viking** comes from Old Norse.]

**vile** *adjective* **viler, vilest** (th)
Something that is very nasty and unpleasant is **vile**: *This tastes vile.*
[**Vile** comes via French from Latin *vilis* 'cheap'.]

**villa** *noun* **villas**
1 A **villa** is a large house with a garden.
2 A **villa** in Roman times was a large house with a courtyard in the middle.
[**Villa** comes from Latin.]

**village** *noun* **villages**
A **village** is a group of houses and other buildings in the country.
[**Village** comes from the same Latin word as **villa**.]

**villain** *noun* **villains** (th)
A **villain** is a person who does bad or wicked things.
[**Villain** comes from Latin via French.]

**vine** *noun* **vines**
A **vine** is a plant that grapes grow on.
[**Vine** comes via French from Latin *vinum* 'wine'.]

**vinegar** *noun*
**Vinegar** is a sour liquid used to flavour food such as chips.

[**Vinegar** comes from old French *vyn egre* 'sour wine'.]

**vineyard** *noun* **vineyards**
A **vineyard** is a farm where grapes are grown for making wine.
[**Vineyard** comes from **vine** and **yard**[1].]

**viola** *noun* **violas**
A **viola** is a stringed instrument like a violin, but larger and with a lower tone.
[**Viola** comes from Spanish or Italian.]

**violence** *noun* (th)
**Violence** is the use of physical force to hurt people.
[**Violence** comes from Latin via French.]

**violent** *adjective* (th)
Someone or something that is very strong and rough is **violent**: *a violent criminal*.
[**Violent** comes via French from the same Latin word as **violence**.]

**violet** *noun* **violets**
1 A **violet** is a small bluish-purple or white spring flower.
2 **Violet** is the bluish-purple colour of a violet.
[**Violet** comes from Latin via French.]

**violet** *adjective*
of the bluish-purple colour of a violet.

**violin** *noun* **violins**
A **violin** is a musical instrument with strings. You play a **violin** with a bow.
[**Violin** comes from Italian *violino* 'little viola'.]

**viper** *noun* **vipers**
A **viper** is a poisonous snake. An adder is a kind of **viper**.
[**Viper** comes from Latin.]

**virgin** *noun* **virgins**
A **virgin** is someone who has never had sexual intercourse.
[**Virgin** comes from Latin *virgo* 'a young woman'.]

**virtual reality** *noun*
**Virtual reality** is an environment created by a computer that appears to be real. To experience it, you wear a special helmet that is attached to the computer.
[**Virtual** means 'almost, more or less', and comes from Latin.]

**virus** *noun* **viruses**
1 A **virus** is something that can grow in the cells of your body and make you ill.
2 A **virus** is a program that damages data in a computer.
[**Virus** comes from Latin *virus* 'poison'.]

**visa** *noun* **visas**
A **visa** is a stamp in a passport that allows a person to go into a country.
[**Visa** comes from Latin via French.]

**visibility** *noun*
**Visibility** means how well you can see things: *Fog has reduced visibility*.
[**Visibility** comes via French from the same Latin word as **visible**.]

**visible** *adjective* (th)
If something is **visible**, it means that you can see it.
[**Visible** comes from Latin.]

**vision** *noun*
1 Your **vision** is your sight: *Glasses can help your vision*.
2 A **vision** is something strange that you see in your mind.
[**Vision** comes from Latin via French.]

**visit** *verb* **visits, visiting, visited** (th)
1 To **visit** a place means to go to see it.
2 To **visit** people means to go to see them or stay with them for a short time.
[**Visit** comes from Latin.]

**visit** *noun* **visits** (th)
A **visit** is when you go to see a place or stay with someone.

**visitor** *noun* **visitors**
A **visitor** is someone who goes to see a person or a place.

**visor** *noun* **visors**
A **visor** is the part at the front of a helmet or a cap. It comes down to cover or shade your eyes.
[**Visor** comes from Latin via French.]

**visual** *adjective*
**Visual** means to do with seeing or sight.
**visually** *adverb*.
[**Visual** comes from Latin *visus* 'sight'.]

**visualise** *verb* **visualises, visualising, visualised** *Also* **visualize**
To visualise something means to imagine it or picture it.
[**Visualise** comes from **visual**.]

**vital** *adjective* (th)
Something that is **vital** is very important.

a b c d e f g h i j k l m

**vitally** *adverb.*
[**Vital** comes via French from Latin *vita* 'life'.]

**vitamin** *noun* **vitamins**
**Vitamins** are substances that we need to keep us healthy, and that we get from our food: *Carrots contain vitamin A, which is good for your eyes.*
[**Vitamin** comes from Latin *vita* 'life' and English *amine*, a kind of chemical which people used to think vitamins contained.]

**vivacious** *adjective*
If you are **vivacious**, you are lively and cheerful. **vivaciously** *adverb.*
[**Vivacious** comes from Latin *vivere* 'to live'.]

**vivid** *adjective* (th)
**1 Vivid** colours are bright and strong.
**2** A **vivid** memory of something is a clear memory of it.
**3** A **vivid** description of something is full of details. **vividly** *adverb.* **vividness** *noun.*
[**Vivid** comes from the same Latin word as **vivacious**.]

**vixen** *noun* **vixens**
A **vixen** is a female fox.
[**Vixen** comes from Old English.]

**vocabulary** *noun* **vocabularies**
Your **vocabulary** is all the words that you can understand and use.
[**Vocabulary** comes from Latin.]

**vocal** *adjective*
to do with or using the voice: *vocal music.*
**vocally** *adjective.*
[**Vocal** comes from the same Latin word as **voice**.]

**vocal cords** *plural noun*
Your **vocal cords** are in your throat. When you speak, air passes over the **vocal cords** and they vibrate, making sounds.

**vodka** *noun*
**Vodka** is an alcoholic drink made from rye.
[**Vodka** comes from Russian *vodka* 'little water'.]

**voice** *noun* **voices**
**1** Your **voice** is the sound that your mouth makes when you speak or sing: *a soft voice; a croaky voice.*
**2** Your **voice** is your ability to speak or sing.
**3** If you have a **voice**, you have the right to say what you think about something.
[**Voice** comes from Latin via French.]

**volcano** *noun* **volcanoes**
A **volcano** is a mountain with a hole at the top. When the **volcano** is active, molten rock, ash and gases spurt out, and you say that the **volcano** is erupting.
[**Volcano** comes via Italian from the Latin name of *Vulcan*, the Roman god of fire.]

**volleyball** *noun*
**Volleyball** is a sport in which two teams try to hit a large ball back and forth over a high net with their hands or arms, without letting it hit the ground.
[**Volleyball** comes from Latin *volare* 'to fly' and **ball**.]

**volt** *noun* **volts**
A **volt** is a unit that we use to measure the force of an electric current.
[The **volt** is named after Alessandro *Volta*, an Italian scientist who studied electricity.]

**volume** *noun* **volumes**
**1 Volume** is the amount of space taken up by something.
**2** A **volume** is a book, especially one book in a series.
**3** The **volume** is how loud the sound is on something like a television or cassette player: *Turn the volume down!*
[**Volume** comes via French from Latin *volumen* 'a roll', because the first books were written on rolls of parchment.]

**voluntary** *adjective*
If something is **voluntary**, you do not have to do it, but you can choose to do it.
[**Voluntary** comes from Latin via French.]

**volunteer** *noun* **volunteers**
A **volunteer** is a person who offers to do something.
[**Volunteer** comes from the same French word as **voluntary**.]

**volunteer** *verb* **volunteers**, **volunteering**, **volunteered**
To **volunteer** means to offer to do something.

**vomit** *verb* **vomits**, **vomiting**, **vomited**
When you **vomit**, liquid and undigested food comes up from your stomach and out through your mouth.
[**Vomit** comes from Latin via French.]

**vote** *verb* **votes, voting, voted**
**1** When people **vote** they say which thing they want out of a choice of two or more things: *Our class voted to visit the zoo.*
**2** If you **vote** for a person, you say that you would like that person to do a job.
[**Vote** comes from Latin *votum* 'a wish'.]

**vote** *noun* **votes**
If you have a **vote**, you can say which thing or person you would prefer.

**voucher** *noun* **vouchers**
A **voucher** is a piece of paper like a ticket. You can use it to pay for something.
[**Voucher** comes from Latin via French.]

**vowel** *noun* **vowels**

A **vowel** is one of the letters *a, e, i, o* or *u* and sometimes *y.*
[**Vowel** comes from Latin.]

**voyage** *noun* **voyages**
A **voyage** is a long journey across the sea or into space.
[**Voyage** comes from Latin via French.]

**vulnerable** *adjective* (th)
If you are **vulnerable**, it is easy for someone to hurt you or attack you.
[**Vulnerable** comes from Latin *vulnerare* 'to wound'.]

**vulture** *noun* **vultures**
A **vulture** is a large bird that eats dead animals.
[**Vulture** comes from Latin via French.]

# Dictionary Fun

**Etymology**
Which word comes from Latin *venenum*, which means poison?

**What do these idioms mean?**
1. To speak with one voice.
2. To vote with your feet.

**New words**
Clue: This is a screen that displays information from a computer.

**Riddle**
When I'm quiet I lie sleeping
When I'm angry I fire the air
I might erupt at any moment
But until then, just you beware!
What am I?

**Find out**
If a **vein** carries blood *to* the heart, what do we call the tube that carries blood *away* from the heart?

**Did you know?**
◆ Tradition holds that **vampires** can only be killed by burning them or by putting a stake through their hearts.
◆ The adder, which is a type of **viper**, is the only poisonous snake in the British Isles.

**Brainteaser**
Paul saw a girl in the street and said "I have no sisters or brothers but that girl's father is my father's son." Who was the girl?

a b c d e f g h i j k l m

# Ww

**waddle** *verb* **waddles, waddling, waddled** (th)
To **waddle** means to walk with short steps, swaying from side to side: *waddling like a duck*.
[**Waddle** probably comes from **wade**.]

**wade** *verb* **wades, wading, waded**
To **wade** means to walk through water.
[**Wade** comes from Old English.]

**waffle** *noun* **waffles**
A **waffle** is a thick, square pancake with a pattern of squares on it.
[**Waffle** comes from Dutch.]

**wag** *verb* **wags, wagging, wagged**
To **wag** something means to move it from side to side: *a dog wagging its tail*.
[**Wag** comes from Old English.]

**wage** *noun* **wages** (th)
A **wage** is money that you get regularly for a job that you do.
[**Wage** comes from an old French word.]

**wagon** *noun* **wagons**
1 A **wagon** is a cart with four wheels that is pulled by horses.
2 A **wagon** is a kind of railway truck or van. [**Wagon** comes from Dutch.]

**wail** *verb* **wails, wailing, wailed** (th)
To **wail** means to cry loudly.
[**Wail** comes from Old Norse.]

**waist** *noun* **waists**
Your **waist** is the part at the middle of your body: *He wore a belt round his waist*.
[**Waist** probably comes from Old English.]

**waistcoat** *noun* **waistcoats**
A **waistcoat** is a kind of short jacket with no sleeves that you wear over a shirt or blouse.
[A **waistcoat** was originally a coat that came to just below your waist, rather than a coat that reached below your knees.]

**wait** *verb* **waits, waiting, waited** (th)
1 If you **wait** somewhere, you stay there until something happens or someone arrives.
2 If you **wait**, you stop or pause for a while.
[**Wait** comes from an old French word.]

**waiter** *noun* **waiters**
A **waiter** is a man who brings food to the tables in a restaurant or hotel.
[**Waiter** comes from **wait**.]

**waitress** *noun* **waitresses**
A **waitress** is a woman who brings food to the tables in a restaurant or hotel.
[**Waitress** comes from **waiter**.]

**wake** *verb* **wakes, waking, woke, woken** (th)
1 To **wake** or **wake up** means to stop sleeping: *I woke early that day*.
2 To **wake** someone or **wake** someone **up** means to stop him/her sleeping: *Don't wake the baby!*
[**Wake** comes from Old English.]

**walk** *verb* **walks, walking, walked**
1 To **walk** means to move along on foot without running: *We walk to school*.
2 To **walk** an animal means to take it for a walk: *my turn to walk the dog*.
[**Walk** comes from Old English.]

**walk** *noun* **walks** (th)
1 A **walk** is a journey on foot: *went for a walk in the woods*.
2 Your **walk** is the way that you walk: *I recognised her by her strange walk*.

**wall** *noun* **walls**
A **wall** is a structure built up using bricks or stone, such as the side of a house.
[**Wall** comes from Old English.]

**wallaby** *noun* **wallabies**
A **wallaby** is a marsupial, smaller than a kangaroo, with large back feet and a long tail. **Wallabies** live in Australia.
[**Wallaby** comes from Dharuk, an Australian Aboriginal language.]

**wallet** *noun* **wallets**
A **wallet** is a small case for holding money and papers: *a leather wallet*.
[**Wallet** comes from an old French word.]

**wallow** *verb* **wallows, wallowing, wallowed**
To **wallow** means to roll in mud or water in a lazy way.
[**Wallow** comes from Old English.]

**wallpaper** *noun* **wallpapers**
**Wallpaper** is paper that you stick on a wall to decorate a room.

**walnut** *noun* **walnuts**
A **walnut** is a wrinkled nut that you can eat. [**Walnut** comes from Old English.]

**walrus** *noun* **walruses**
A **walrus** is a large sea animal with two long tusks. **Walruses** live in the Arctic. [**Walrus** comes from Dutch.]

**waltz** *noun* **waltzes**
A **waltz** is a kind of dance. The music for a **waltz** has three beats to the bar. [**Waltz** comes from German *walzen* 'to spin round'.]

**wan** *adjective* (th)
If you are **wan**, you look pale and tired or ill. [**Wan** comes from Old English.]

**wand** *noun* **wands**
A **wand** is a thin rod that a magician uses for doing magic. [**Wand** comes from Old Norse.]

**wander** *verb* **wanders, wandering, wandered** (th)
If you **wander**, you walk around slowly or without going in a particular direction. [**Wander** comes from Old English.]

**wane** *verb* **wanes, waning, waned** (th)
1 When the moon **wanes**, it seems to get smaller.
2 If your energy or enthusiasm for something **wanes**, you become less keen on it.
3 If your strength or power **wanes**, it becomes less. [**Wane** comes from Old English.]

**want** *verb* **wants, wanting, wanted** (th)
To **want** something means to feel that you would like to have it or need to have it. [**Want** comes from Old Norse.]

**war** *noun* **wars**
A **war** is fighting between two or more countries. [**War** comes from an old French word.]

**wardrobe** *noun* **wardrobes**
A wardrobe is a big cupboard for clothes. [**Wardrobe** comes from an old French word.]

**warehouse** *noun* **warehouses**
A **warehouse** is a large building used for storing things. [**Warehouse** comes from *ware* 'goods', which comes from Old English, and

house.]

**warily** *adverb*
If you do something **warily**, you do it in a careful way: *The mouse crept warily past the sleeping cat.* [**Warily** comes from **wary**.]

**warm** *adjective* **warmer, warmest** (th)
1 Someone or something that is **warm** is fairly hot.
2 **Warm** clothes are thick clothes that you wear when it is cold.
3 A **warm** welcome is a friendly welcome. **warmly** *adverb*.
[**Warm** comes from Old English.]

**warm** *verb* **warms, warming, warmed**
1 If you **warm** something, you make it warm or warmer: *Warm the baby's bottle.*
2 To **warm up** is to exercise gently so that your body is ready for sport or another activity.

**warm-blooded** *adjective*
If an animal is **warm-blooded**, its body temperature stays the same all the time.

**warn** *verb* **warns, warning, warned** (th)
To **warn** someone means to tell him/her about a danger or problem that is ahead. [**Warn** comes from Old English.]

**warning** *noun* **warnings** (th)
1 A **warning** is a sign that tells you about a danger.
2 If you give someone a **warning**, you tell him/her that something bad will happen if s/he does something or does not do something.

**warp** *verb* **warps, warping, warped** (th)
When a flat thing **warps**, it gets twisted or bent. [**Warp** comes from Old English.]

**warren** *noun* **warrens**
A **warren** is a set of tunnels under the ground where rabbits live. [**Warren** comes from an old French word.]

**warrior** *noun* **warriors**
A **warrior** is a fighter or a soldier. [**Warrior** comes from the same old French word as **war**.]

**wart** *noun* **warts**
A **wart** is a small, hard raised piece of skin on your body caused by a virus. [**Wart** comes from Old English.]

**wary** *adjective* **warier, wariest** (th)
To be **wary** means to be careful and to

look out for danger.
[**Wary** comes from Old English.]

**wash** *verb* **washes, washing, washed** (th)
**1** To **wash** something means to make it clean using water: *I washed my face; Let's wash the car.*
**2** To **wash up** is to clean the plates and cutlery after a meal.
**3** If something is **washed away**, it is carried away by water.
[**Wash** comes from Old English.]

**washer** *noun* **washers**
A **washer** is a ring of rubber, plastic or metal.
[No one knows where **washer** comes from.]

**washing machine** *noun* **washing machines**
A **washing machine** is a machine that washes and rinses clothes.

**wasp** *noun* **wasps**
A **wasp** is a striped insect that flies. **Wasps** can sting.
[**Wasp** comes from Old English.]

**waste** *noun* (th)
**1 Waste** is when something is wasted: *a waste of time.*
**2 Waste** is something that is thrown away because you do not need it or it is left over. [**Waste** comes from Latin.]

**waste** *verb* **wastes, wasting, wasted** (th)
To **waste** something means to not use it properly: *wasting time; wasting paper.*

**watch** *noun* **watches**
A **watch** is a small clock that you wear on your wrist.
[**Watch** comes from Old English.]

**watch** *verb* **watches, watching, watched** (th)
To **watch** something means to look at it: *Watch me!; watching television.*

**water** *noun*
**Water** is the clear liquid that falls as rain or flows in rivers to the sea.
[**Water** comes from Old English.]

**watercolour** *noun* **watercolours**
**1 Watercolours** are paints that are mixed with water, not oil.
**2** A **watercolour** is a painting done with watercolour paints.

**watercress** *noun*
**Watercress** is a plant with a sharp taste that you can put in salads. It grows in streams.

**waterfall** *noun* **waterfalls** (th)
A **waterfall** is a flow of water falling over a cliff or rocks.

**water lily** *noun* **water lilies**
A **water lily** is a plant that grows in ponds and lakes. It has large leaves that float on the water, and big flowers.

**waterlogged** *adjective*
If something is **waterlogged**, it is flooded or full of water.
[**Waterlogged** comes from **water** and **log**, because water would lie in the bottom of a ship like a log and weigh it down.]

**watermelon** *noun* **watermelons**
A **watermelon** is a large, smooth, green fruit. It is pink and juicy inside and has lots of black seeds.

**waterproof** *adjective*
Something that is **waterproof** does not let water in.

**water-skiing** *noun*
**Water-skiing** is a sport. You stand on skis and are pulled along on water by a boat.

**watt** *noun* **watts**
A **watt** is a unit that we use to measure electrical power.
[The **watt** is named after James *Watt*, a Scottish engineer who studied ways of producing and using energy.]

**wave** *noun* **waves** (th)
**1** A **wave** is a ridge of water that moves through the sea and curls over and breaks on the shore.
**2** A **wave** is a curling line or shape: *Her hair fell down her back in waves.*
**3** A **wave** is the wavelike movement of some forms of energy, such as light, sound or radio signals.
**4** A **wave** is the movement of your hand when you wave.
[**Wave** comes from Old English.]

**wave** *verb* **waves, waving, waved** (th)
**1** To **wave** means to move your hand from side to side, especially to say hello or goodbye to someone who is too far away to hear you.
**2** To **wave** means to move up and down

or from side to side: *flags waving in the wind.*

**wavy** *adjective* **wavier, waviest**
1 If your hair is **wavy**, it grows in long curls.
2 A **wavy** line curves up and down.

**wax¹** *noun*
Wax comes from fat or oil. We use **wax** to make candles and polish.
[**Wax¹**, comes from Old English *waex*.]

**wax¹** *verb* **waxes, waxing, waxed**
If you **wax** a table, you polish it.

**wax²** *verb* **waxes, waxing, waxed**
1 When the moon **waxes**, it seems to get bigger.
2 To **wax** means to get stronger or more important. **Wax** is a formal word.
[**Wax²** comes from Old English *weaxan*.]

**way** *noun* **ways** (th)
1 A **way** is a direction: *He looked the other way; East is that way.*
2 A **way** is a route or pathway: *found a new way home.*
3 A **way** is a method of doing something: *a good way of cooking potatoes.*
4 If something is **in your way**, you cannot get past or see past it.
[**Way** comes from Old English.]

**we** *pronoun*
You use **we** to talk about two or more people, including you, when both or all of you are the subject of a verb: *Tom and I had lunch and then we went out.*
[**We** comes from Old English.]

**weak** *adjective* **weaker, weakest** (th)
1 A **weak** ruler or a **weak** country does not have much power.
2 A **weak** drink does not have much flavour: *weak tea.*
3 A **weak** person cannot lift or carry heavy things: *He was weak after his illness.*
4 A **weak** object will break easily.
**weakly** *adverb.* **weakness** *noun.*

**weaken** *verb* **weakens, weakening, weakened** (th)
To **weaken** means to get weaker or to make something weaker.
[**Weaken** comes from **weak**.]

**wealth** *noun*
Wealth is a lot of money or valuable things. [**Wealth** comes from Old English.]

**wealthy** *adjective* **wealthier, wealthiest** (th)
If you are **wealthy**, you are rich.

**weapon** *noun* **weapons**
A **weapon** is something that can be used to hurt someone in a fight.
[**Weapon** comes from Old English.]

**wear** *verb* **wears, wearing, wore, worn** (th)
1 To **wear** clothes means to be dressed in them.
2 If something **wears out**, it becomes thin or in bad condition because it has been used a lot.
3 If something **wears** you **out**, it makes you very tired.
4 If something **wears away**, it is slowly rubbed away.
5 If something **wears off**, you gradually stop feeling it or noticing it.
[**Wear** comes from Old English.]

**weary** *adjective* **wearier, weariest** (th)
Someone who is very tired is **weary**.
[**Weary** comes from Old English.]

**weasel** *noun* **weasels**
A **weasel** is a small animal with short legs, a long, thin body, and reddish-brown fur. **Weasels** catch and eat other small animals.
[**Weasel** comes from Old English.]

**weather** *noun*
Rain, snow, sunshine and wind are kinds of **weather**.
[**Weather** comes from Old English.]

**weave** *verb* **weaves, weaving, wove, woven**
To **weave** means to make cloth by twisting threads under and over one another.
[**Weave** comes from Old English.]

**web** *noun* **webs**
A **web** is a net of thin, sticky threads spun by a spider.
[**Web** comes from Old English *webb* 'woven cloth'.]

**webbed** *adjective*
Webbed feet have skin connecting the toes, like a duck's feet.
[**Webbed** comes from **web**.]

**wedding** noun **weddings**
A **wedding** is the ceremony when two people get married.
[**Wedding** comes from Old English.]

**wedge** noun **wedges**
A **wedge** is a piece of something that has a triangular shape: *a wedge of cheese; a rubber wedge to keep the door open.*
[**Wedge** comes from Old English.]

**wedge** verb **wedges, wedging, wedged** (th)
To **wedge** something is to make it stay there by pushing it hard or fixing it tightly.

**weed** noun **weeds**
A **weed** is a wild plant that grows in a place where it is not wanted.
[**Weed** comes from Old English.]

**weed** verb **weeds, weeding, weeded**
If you **weed** a garden, you pull up the weeds that are growing in it.

**week** noun **weeks**
A **week** is seven days, especially the seven days from Monday to Sunday.
[**Week** comes from Old English.]

**weekday** noun **weekdays**
A **weekday** is one of the days of the week when you go to school and many people work. The **weekdays** are Monday, Tuesday, Wednesday, Thursday and Friday.

**weekend** noun **weekends**
A **weekend** is Saturday and Sunday.

**weekly** adjective
1 happening once a week: *I do the weekly shopping on Tuesdays.*
2 being published once a week: *a weekly comic.*

**weekly** adverb
once a week: *The bus comes weekly.*

**weep** verb **weeps, weeping, wept** (th)
When you **weep**, tears fall from your eyes because you are sad.
[**Weep** comes from Old English.]

**weigh** verb **weighs, weighing, weighed**
To **weigh** something means to find out how heavy it is by using scales.
[**Weigh** comes from Old English.]

**weight** noun **weights**
1 The **weight** of something is how heavy it is.
2 A **weight** is a piece of metal that you put on the scales to balance something that you are weighing.
3 A **weight** is something heavy.
[**Weight** comes from Old English.]

**weir** noun **weirs**
A **weir** is a wall or barrier built across a river to control the height of the water or to make it flow in a certain way.
[**Weir** comes from Old English.]

**weird** adjective **weirder, weirdest** (th)
Something that is **weird** is strange or mysterious.
**weirdly** adverb. **weirdness** noun.
[**Weird** comes from Old English.]

**welcome** verb **welcomes, welcoming, welcomed**
To **welcome** someone means to show that you are pleased to see him/her.
[**Welcome** comes from **well²** and **come**.]

**weld** verb **welds, welding, welded**
To **weld** metal means to heat it so that you can join two pieces together.
[**Weld** comes from Old English.]

**well¹** noun **wells**
A **well** is a deep hole dug to get water or oil out of the ground.
[**Well¹** comes from Old English *wella*.]

**well²** adjective **better, best** (th)
Someone who is healthy is **well**.
[**Well²** comes from Old English *wel*.]

**well²** adverb **better, best**
Someone who does something in a good way does it **well**.

**went** verb
**Went** is the past tense of **go**.

**wept** verb
**Wept** is the past tense and past participle of **weep**.

**werewolf** noun **werewolves**
A **werewolf** is a person who turns into a wolf. **Werewolves** are found only in horror stories.
[**Werewolf** comes from Old English *wer* 'a man' and **wolf**.]

**west** noun
**West** is one of the points of the compass,

and is the direction in which the sun sets.
[**West** comes from Old English.]

**westerly** *adjective*
**1** to the west or towards the west: *The road ran in a westerly direction.*
**2** A **westerly** wind blows from the west.

**western** *adjective*
in the west or from the west: *the western horizon; western technology.*

**wet** *adjective* **wetter, wettest** (th)
**1** Something that is **wet** is covered or soaked in water or any liquid.
**2** When it rains, you say that it is **wet**: *a wet day; the wettest summer for ten years.*
[**Wet** comes from Old English.]

**whale** *noun* **whales**
A **whale** is a very large mammal that lives in the sea.
[**Whale** comes from Old English.]

**what** *pronoun*
**1** **What** can be used to ask which kind, or how much: *What are you doing?; What do I owe you?*
**2** the thing or things that: *Show me what you have done.*
[**What** comes from Old English.]

**what** *adjective*
**1** **What** can mean whatever: *Say what you like.*
**2** **What** can be used when you emphasise something or to express surprise about something: *What a horrible experience!; What a waste of time!*
**3** **What** can be used to ask which thing or things: *What books shall I choose?*

**whatever** *pronoun*
anything or everything that: *Take whatever you want.*

**wheat** *noun*
**Wheat** is a cereal grown on farms. Flour is made from **wheat**.
[**Wheat** comes from Old English.]

**wheel** *noun* **wheels**
A **wheel** is a round object that can turn round and round on an axle, and can be used to guide a vehicle or to make it move: *a steering wheel; a truck with six wheels.* [**Wheel** comes from Old English.]

**wheel** *verb* **wheels, wheeling, wheeled**
To **wheel** something that has wheels

means to push it along.

**wheelbarrow** *noun* **wheelbarrows**
A **wheelbarrow** is a small cart with one wheel which is pushed along.

**wheelchair** *noun* **wheelchairs**
A **wheelchair** is a chair on wheels used by people who cannot walk properly.

**wheeze** *verb* **wheezes, wheezing, wheezed**
To **wheeze** means to breathe noisily or with difficulty because you cannot get enough air into your lungs.
[**Wheeze** probably comes from Old Norse.]

**when** *adverb*
**When** is used to ask about the time of something: *When does the plane arrive?*
[**When** comes from Old English.]

**when** *conjunction*
**1** **When** can be used to explain at what time something happened: *She left school when she was 18 years old.*
**2** **When** can mean as soon as something happens: *Come when I call you.*
**3** **When** can mean whenever: *I sing when I'm happy.*

**whenever** *conjunction*
**1** at any time: *We can go whenever we like.*
**2** every time: *Whenever we plan a picnic, it always rains.*

**where** *adverb*
at, in or to what place?: *Where is she?; Where does this road go?*
[**Where** comes from Old English.]

**where** *conjunction*
**Where** can mean wherever: *You can sit where you like.*

**where** *adjective*
**Where** is used to give information about a place: *This is the room where we have Art; The house where I live is small.*

**wherever** *conjunction*
**1** in, at or to any place: *We spend our holidays wherever we can afford to.*
**2** in, at or to every place: *They cause trouble wherever they go.*

**whether** *conjunction*
**1** You use **whether** to talk about if something will happen or be done, or not: *I don't know whether she'll come or not; He*

a b c d e f g h i j k l m

*asked whether he could borrow the car.*
**2** You use **whether** to say that something will happen or will be done in any of the circumstances you mention: *I'll go whether he wants to or not; We'll go there one day, whether it's next week, next month or next year.* [**Whether** comes from Old English.]

## which *adjective*
You use **which** to ask someone to name, or to show you, one particular person or thing, or a few particular people or things, out of a larger number.
*Which chair is yours? Which boys play cricket?*
[**Which** comes from Old English.]

## which *pronoun*
**1 Which** can be used to talk about a choice of things or one thing out of a limited number: *Which is your street?*
**2 Which** can be used to give more information about a person or thing already mentioned: *The cat, which was a tabby, ran up the tree.*

## while *conjunction*
**1** during this or that time: *While you're in the supermarket, could you get me some apples?*
**2** as long as: *While there's life, there's hope.*
**3** although: *My brother's got blue eyes, while mine are brown; While the film is a bit long, it's not boring.*
[**While** comes from Old English.]

## whine *noun* whines
A **whine** is a long, sad cry.
[**Whine** comes from Old English.]

## whine *verb* whines, whining, whined (th)
**1** To **whine** is to make a long, sad cry.
**2** To **whine** is to complain or moan about something in a silly or annoying way.

## whinge *verb* whinges, whinging, whinged (th)
To **whinge** means to complain or to moan about something that is not very important.
[**Whinge** comes from Old English.]

## whip *noun* whips
A **whip** is a piece of rope or a strip of leather joined to a handle. **Whips** are used to hit people or animals.
[**Whip** comes from an old German or Dutch word.]

## whip *verb* whips, whipping, whipped (th)
**1** To **whip** people or animals means to hit them with a whip.
**2** To **whip** cream means to beat it until it is thick.

## whirlwind *noun* whirlwinds
A **whirlwind** is a strong wind that blows in a circle or spiral.
[**Whirlwind** comes from *whirl* 'to spin round and round', which comes from Old Norse, and **wind**[1].]

## whisk *noun* whisks
A **whisk** is a tool that you use to stir sauces or to beat eggs or cream.
[**Whisk** comes from Old Norse.]

## whisk *verb* whisks, whisking, whisked
**1** If you **whisk** food, you stir it quickly or beat it.
**2** If you **whisk** something **away**, you take it away quickly.

## whisker *noun* whiskers
**1** A **whisker** is a strong hair that grows around an animal's nose or eyes.
**2** If a man has **whiskers**, he has a moustache or a beard.
[**Whisker** comes from **whisk**, and originally meant a bundle of feathers or twigs used for whisking.]

## whisky *noun* Also whiskey
**Whisky** is a strong alcoholic drink made from barley or rye.
[**Whisky** comes from Gaelic.]

## whisper *verb* whispers, whispering, whispered (th)
To **whisper** means to speak very quietly.
[**Whisper** comes from Old English.]

## whistle *verb* whistles, whistling, whistled
To **whistle** means to make a piercing sound by blowing air through your lips.
[**Whistle** comes from Old English.]

## whistle *noun* whistles
A **whistle** is a small instrument that makes a piercing sound when you blow it.

## white *noun*
**White** is the colour of snow.
[**White** comes from Old English.]

## white *adjective* whiter, whitest
**1** of the colour of snow: *a white swan.*

2 **White** coffee is coffee with milk in it.

**who** *pronoun*
1 **Who** is used to ask which person or people: *Who did you go with?*
2 **Who** can be used to give more information about the person or people already mentioned: *The woman who came today was my aunt.*
[**Who** comes from Old English.]

**whole** *noun*
A **whole** is a complete thing.
[**Whole** comes from Old English.]

**whole** *adjective* (th)
Something that is **whole** is complete or unbroken.

**whom** *pronoun*
**Whom** is sometimes used instead of who, when it is the object of a sentence: *the man whom we met yesterday.*
[**Whom** comes from the same Old English word as **who**.]

**whose** *adjective*
**Whose** is used to ask who something or someone belongs to: *Whose shoes are these?*
[**Whose** comes from Old English.]

**why** *adverb*
**Why** is used to ask the reason for something: *Why are you sad?* [**Why** comes from Old English.]

**wick** *noun* **wicks**
The **wick** of a candle is the strip that goes through it and sticks out at the top, and is burnt to give light.
[**Wick** comes from Old English.]

**wicked** *adjective* (th)
Someone who is **wicked** is very bad or cruel. **wickedly** *adverb*. **wickedness** *noun*.
[**Wicked** comes from Old English.]

**wide** *adjective* **wider, widest** (th)
1 Something that is **wide** measures a long way from one side to the other.
2 A **wide** range of things is a good selection or a large number of different things. [**Wide** comes from Old English.]

**wide** *adverb*
If you open something **wide**, you open it a long way. **widely** *adverb*.

**widow** *noun* **widows**
A **widow** is a woman whose husband has died. [**Widow** comes from Old English.]

**widower** *noun* **widowers**
A **widower** is a man whose wife has died.
[**Widower** comes from **widow**.]

**width** *noun* **widths**
The **width** of something is the distance from one side of it to the opposite side.
[**Width** comes from **wide**.]

**wield** *verb* **wields, wielding, wielded** (th)
To **wield** a weapon means to use it, or to hold it as if you are ready to use it.
[**Wield** comes from Old English.]

**wife** *noun* **wives**
A man's **wife** is the woman he is married to. [**Wife** comes from Old English.]

**wig** *noun* **wigs**
A **wig** is false hair that you can wear instead of your own hair.
[**Wig** is short for *periwig*, a kind of wig worn in the 18th century, which comes from French *perruque* 'a head of natural hair'.]

**wiggle** *verb* **wiggles, wiggling, wiggled**
To **wiggle** something means to move it backwards and forwards or from side to side.
[**Wiggle** comes from an old German or Dutch word.]

**wild** *adjective* **wilder, wildest** (th)
1 **Wild** plants and animals grow naturally and are not looked after: *wild flowers*.
2 Someone or something that is **wild** is very excited or out of control: *The crowd went wild when I scored a goal.* **wildly** *adverb*.
[**Wild** comes from Old English.]

**wildlife** *noun*
**Wildlife** is all wild animals, insects, and plants.

**will**[1] *verb* **would**
**Will** is used with other verbs to say or ask what is going to happen in the future: *I will try to keep my room tidy; Will you come tomorrow?*
[**Will**[1] comes from Old English *wyllan*.]

**will**[2] *noun* **wills**
1 A **will** is a document which explains what someone wants to happen to his/her possessions when s/he dies: *My grandfather left me a silver watch in his will.*
2 If you have the **will** to do something, you want to do it and have the determination to do it.

[**Will²** comes from Old English *willa*.]

**willing** *adjective*
Someone who is **willing** is ready and pleased to help.
[**Willing** comes from **will¹**.]

**willow** *noun* **willows**
A **willow** is a kind of tree with thin branches that bend over.
[**Willow** comes from Old English.]

**wilt** *verb* **wilts, wilting, wilted**
To **wilt** means to droop or become floppy.
[**Wilt** may come from an old German word.]

**win** *verb* **wins, winning, won** (th)
**1** To **win** means to come first or beat someone in a game, competition, fight or argument.
**2** To **win** means to get a prize.
[**Win** comes from Old English.]

**wind¹** *noun* **winds** (th)
**Wind** is a movement of air.
[**Wind¹** comes from Old English *wind*.]

**wind²** *verb* **winds, winding, wound**
**1** To **wind** a key or a handle means to turn it round and round.
**2** To **wind** something round means to twist it or bend it round.
[**Wind²** comes from Old English *windan*.]

**wind instrument** *noun* **wind instruments**
A **wind instrument** is a musical instrument that you blow. A flute is a **wind instrument**.

**windmill** *noun* **windmills**
A **windmill** is a mill with large sails turned by the wind, which provides the power to work the machinery to grind corn or to pump water.

**window** *noun* **windows**
A **window** is an opening in a wall filled with glass to let in the light.
[**Window** comes from Old Norse.]

**wine** *noun* **wines**
**Wine** is an alcoholic drink made from grapes.
[**Wine** comes via Old English from the same Latin word as **vine**.]

**wing** *noun* **wings**
**1** A **wing** is a part of a bird or an insect that it uses to fly.

**2** A **wing** is a part at the side of an aircraft that helps it to fly.
**3** A **wing** is a part of a large building: *They're building a new wing onto the hospital.* [**Wing** comes from Old Norse.]

**wink** *verb* **winks, winking, winked**
To **wink** means to close and open one eye.
[**Wink** comes from Old English.]

**winner** *noun* **winners** (th)
A **winner** is someone who wins a game, competition, fight or argument.

**wipe** *verb* **wipes, wiping, wiped**
To **wipe** means to clean or dry something by rubbing it with a cloth.
[**Wipe** comes from Old English.]

**wire** *noun* **wires**
A **wire** is a long, thin thread of metal that bends easily.
[**Wire** comes from Old English.]

**wisdom** *noun* (th)
**Wisdom** is having a lot of understanding and knowledge.
[**Wisdom** comes from the same Old English word as **wise**.]

**wisdom tooth** *noun* **wisdom teeth**
A **wisdom tooth** is one of four teeth that grow after all the others at the back of the mouth.
[**Wisdom teeth** are so called because they grow when you are grown up and you are supposed to be wiser than when your other teeth grew.]

**wise** *adjective* **wiser, wisest** (th)
Someone who is **wise** knows a lot and can understand things and use what s/he knows sensibly. **wisely** *adverb*.
[**Wise** comes from Old English.]

**wish** *noun* **wishes** (th)
**1** A **wish** is something you very much want or hope for.
**2** A **wish** is a friendly greeting: *with best wishes on your birthday.*
[**Wish** comes from Old English.]

**wish** *verb* **wishes, wishing, wished** (th)
**1** To **wish** means to want and hope for something very much.
**2** To **wish** means to express a hope for another person: *I wish you luck!*

**wit** *noun*
**Wit** is being able to say clever and funny

things. [**Wit** comes from Old English.]

**witch** *noun* **witches**
A **witch** is a woman who is supposed to have magical powers.
[**Witch** comes from Old English.]

**withdraw** *verb* **withdraws, withdrawing, withdrew, withdrawn** (th)
**1** To **withdraw** means to remove or take something away: *withdraw some money from the bank.*
**2** To **withdraw** means to leave something that you were taking part in: *She had to withdraw from the competition because of an injury.*
[**Withdraw** comes from Old English *with* 'away or back' and **draw**.]

**wither** *verb* **withers, withering, withered** (th)
To **wither** means to become dry through lack of water.
[**Wither** comes from **weather**.]

**within** *preposition*
**Within** means inside: *Dogs are not permitted within the grounds.*
[**Within** comes from Old English.]

**without** *preposition* (th)
If you are **without** something, you do not have it: *You can't live without water; I couldn't have done it without you; He faced the future without fear.*
[**Without** comes from Old English.]

**witness** *noun* **witnesses**
**1** A **witness** is someone who gives evidence and answers questions in a court of law.
**2** A **witness** is someone who saw something happen.
[**Witness** comes from the same Old English word as **wit**.]

**witness** *verb* **witnesses, witnessing, witnessed**
**1** If you **witness** something, you see it happen.
**2** If you **witness** a document or someone's signature, you sign your name to say that it is genuine.

**witty** *adjective* **wittier, wittiest** (th)
Someone who is **witty** says clever and funny things. [**Witty** comes from **wit**.]

**wives** *noun*
**Wives** is the plural of **wife**.

**wizard** *noun* **wizards**
A **wizard** is a man who is supposed to have magical powers.
[**Wizard** comes from **wise**.]

**wobble** *verb* **wobbles, wobbling, wobbled** (th)
To **wobble** means to stand or move unsteadily or to shake from side to side.
[No one knows where **wobble** comes from.]

**woe** *noun* (th)
**Woe** is a deep feeling of sadness.
[**Woe** comes from Old English.]

**wok** *noun* **woks**
A **wok** is a deep round pan used in Chinese cooking.
[**Wok** comes from Chinese.]

**woke** *verb*
**Woke** is the past tense of **wake**.

**woken** *verb*
**Woken** is the past participle of **wake**.

**wolf** *noun* **wolves**
A **wolf** is a wild animal like a large dog.
[**Wolf** comes from Old English.]

**woman** *noun* **women**
A **woman** is a female human being who is fully grown.
[**Woman** comes from Old English.]

**womb** *noun* **wombs**
A **womb** is the part of a woman's body where a baby develops before it is born.
[**Womb** comes from Old English.]

**won** *verb*
**Won** is the past tense and past participle of **win**.

**wonder** *noun* (th)
**Wonder** is a feeling of surprise or amazement.
[**Wonder** comes from Old English.]

**wonder** *verb* **wonders, wondering, wondered**
**1** To **wonder** means to think or say that you would like to know something: *He wondered whether he would ever see her again.*
**2** To **wonder** is to be surprised or amazed.

**wonderful** *adjective* (th)
Something that is **wonderful** is really good or gives you great pleasure.

**wood** *noun* **woods**
1 A **wood** is a large area covered with trees.
2 **Wood** is the trunk and branches of trees used to make things or burn on fires. [**Wood** comes from Old English.]

**wooden** *adjective*
Something that is made of wood is **wooden**.

**woodpecker** *noun* **woodpeckers**
A **woodpecker** is a bird that eats insects, which it finds by pecking tree trunks with its beak.

**woodwind** *adjective*
A **woodwind** instrument is a musical instrument that you blow into, such as a clarinet, oboe or flute. Most **woodwind** instruments are, or used to be, made of wood.

**woodwork** *noun*
1 **Woodwork** is the craft of making things out of wood.
2 The **woodwork** of a structure or building is the parts of it that are made of wood.

**wool** *noun*
**Wool** is the soft hair on sheep which is spun into threads and used for knitting or making cloth. [**Wool** comes from Old English.]

**woollen** *adjective*
Something that is made of wool is **woollen**.

**word** *noun* **words**
A **word** is a group of letters or sounds that means something when it is written or said. [**Word** comes from Old English.]

**word processing** *noun* **word processing**
**Word processing** is using a computer to write and store documents.

**wore** *verb*
**Wore** is the past tense of **wear**.

**work** *noun*
1 **Work** is a job or something that has to be done.
2 Someone's **work** is something that s/he has produced or created: *a work of art.* [**Work** comes from Old English.]

**work** *verb* **works, working, worked** (th)

1 To **work** means to do a job.
2 To **work** means to operate or function: *This video recorder doesn't work.*
3 To **work out** a problem or puzzle means to solve it.

**worker** *noun* **workers**
A **worker** is someone who works.

**world** *noun* **worlds**
1 The **world** is the earth and the people who live in it.
2 A **world** is an area of work or activity and the people involved in it: *the world of music.* [**World** comes from Old English.]

**World Wide Web** *noun*
The **World Wide Web** is a computer library. People who are connected to the Internet can gain information from it and can provide information through it for others.

**worm** *noun* **worms**
A **worm** is a long thin creature with no legs that lives in the soil. [**Worm** comes from Old English.]

**worn** *verb*
**Worn** is the past participle of **wear**.

**worn** *adjective* (th)
1 If something is **worn** or **worn out**, it has been damaged by being used a lot or for a long time.
2 If someone is **worn out**, s/he is very tired.

**worried** *adjective* (th)
If you are **worried**, you are upset because you are thinking about a problem or anxious about something.

**worry** *verb* **worries, worrying, worried** (th)
To **worry** means to be upset or anxious about something. [**Worry** comes from Old English.]

**worse** *adjective*
Something that is less good than something else is **worse** than that thing. **Worse** is the comparative of **bad**. [**Worse** comes from Old English.]

**worship** *verb* **worships, worshipping, worshipped**
1 To **worship** means to say prayers or perform rituals to show your love and respect for God or a god.

**2** To **worship** someone means to love and admire that person very much.
[**Worship** comes from the same Old English word as **worth**.]

**worst** *adjective*
Something that is less good than any similar things is the **worst**. **Worst** is the superlative of **bad**.
[**Worst** comes from Old English.]

**worth** *adjective*
Something that has a certain value is **worth** that amount: *How much is your necklace worth?*
[**Worth** comes from Old English.]

**worthwhile** *adjective* (th)
Something that is **worthwhile** deserves the time or attention you give it.
[**Worthwhile** comes from **worth** and **while** in the sense 'a period of time'.]

**would** *verb*
**1** **Would** is the past tense of **will**.
**2** You use **would** to ask something politely: *Would you like a drink?*
**3** You use **would** to say that someone will do something or something will happen only if someone else does something or something else happens: *He would come if you asked him.*
**4** You use **would** when someone has said that something was going to happen or that s/he was going to do something: *He said he would be late; She said she would see him tomorrow.*

**wound¹** *noun* **wounds**
A **wound** is an injury to the body.
[**Wound¹** comes from Old English.]

**wound¹** *verb* **wounds, wounding, wounded**
To **wound** someone is to injure him/her.

**wound²** *verb*
**Wound²** is the past tense and past participle of **wind**.

**wove** *verb*
**Wove** is the past tense of **weave**.

**woven** *verb*
**Woven** is the past participle of **weave**.

**wrap** *verb* **wraps, wrapping, wrapped**
To **wrap** means to put a covering of clothes or paper round someone or something.
[No one knows where **wrap** comes from.]

**wrath** *noun*
**Wrath** is very strong anger.
[**Wrath** comes from Old English.]

**wreath** *noun* **wreaths**
A **wreath** is a ring of flowers and leaves. **Wreaths** are often put on a grave, or hung on a door at Christmas.
[**Wreath** comes from Old English.]

**wreck** *noun* **wrecks**
A **wreck** is a very badly damaged or ruined ship or vehicle.
[**Wreck** comes from Old Norse via French.]

**wreck** *verb* **wrecks, wrecking, wrecked** (th)
To **wreck** something means to damage it so badly that it is no longer of any use.

**wren** *noun* **wrens**
A **wren** is a tiny brown bird.
[**Wren** comes from Old English.]

**wrench** *noun* **wrenches**
**1** A **wrench** is a forceful pull or twist.
**2** A **wrench** is a tool for holding and turning nuts or bolts.
[**Wrench** comes from Old English.]

**wrench** *verb* **wrenches, wrenching, wrenched** (th)
To **wrench** something means to pull or twist it with a lot of force.

**wrestle** *verb* **wrestles, wrestling, wrestled**
To **wrestle** means to fight with someone by trying to throw him/her to the ground.
[**Wrestle** comes from Old English.]

**wriggle** *verb* **wriggles, wriggling, wriggled** (th)
To **wriggle** means to move the body by twisting and turning.
[**Wriggle** comes from an old German word.]

**wring** *verb* **wrings, wringing, wrung**
To **wring** or **wring out** wet cloth means to get the water out of it by twisting and squeezing it with both hands.
[**Wring** comes from Old English.]

**wrinkle** *noun* **wrinkles**
**1** A **wrinkle** is a line that forms on the skin when people become old.
**2** A **wrinkle** is a line or fold in cloth or paper.

[No one knows where **wrinkle** comes from.]

**wrist** *noun* **wrists**
Your **wrist** is the part of your body where the arm and hand join.
[**Wrist** comes from Old English.]

**write** *verb* **writes**, **writing**, **wrote**, **written**
To **write** means to put words and letters on paper so they can be read.
[**Write** comes from Old English.]

**write-off** *noun* **write-offs**
A **write-off** is a vehicle that has been so badly damaged in a crash that it cannot be repaired.
[**Write-off** originally meant a note written in a company's books to say that something that they owned was no longer worth anything and should be taken off the records.]

**writer** *noun* **writers**
A **writer** is someone who writes, especially someone whose job is writing.

**writing** *noun*
**Writing** is something that has been written.

**written** *verb*
Written is the past participle of write.

**wrong** *adjective* (th)
1 Something that is **wrong** is not correct or true.
2 Something that is **wrong** is unfair or not the proper thing to do.
[**Wrong** probably comes from Old Norse.]

**wrote** *verb*
Wrote is the past tense of **write**.

**wrung** *verb*
Wrung is the past tense and past participle of **wring**.

---

# Dictionary Fun

**What do these idioms mean?**
1. A wet blanket
2. To wash your hands of a matter
3. A wild-goose chase

**Complete the proverbs**
1. All's well that ends w_____.
2. Where there's a w_____ there's a way.
3. It's an ill w_____ that blows nobody any good.

**New words**
Clue: It was developed by a scientist in 1989 to allow information-sharing between computers.

**Work it out**
What do these words have in common: evil, doom, parts, knits?

**Riddle**
If you put a white hat into the Black Sea, what will it become?

**Similes**
As w_____ as an owl.

**Find out**
Find the poem that begins, 'Monday's child is fair of face'. What 'w' word is Wednesday's child full of?

**Did you know?**
◆ **Wisdom teeth** are so called because they don't usually appear until after the age of 20.

# Xx

### x-ray *noun* x-rays
An **x-ray** is a photograph that shows the inside of someone or something.
[An **x-ray** is made using a kind of light ray which is also called an **x-ray**, because when they were first discovered no one really knew what they were, and *x* is often used in algebra to stand for something that you do not know.]

### xylophone *noun* xylophones
A **xylophone** is a musical instrument made from wooden or metal bars that are hit with hammers.
[**Xylophone** comes from Greek *xylon* 'wood' and *phone* 'sound'.]

# Yy

### yacht *noun* yachts
A **yacht** is a small boat with sails.
[**Yacht** comes from Dutch *jaghtschip* 'fast pirate ship'.]

### yak *noun* yaks
A **yak** is a large ox with long hair from Central Asia.
[**Yak** comes from Tibetan.]

### yank *verb* yanks, yanking, yanked (th)
To **yank** something means to pull it suddenly and very hard.
[No one knows where **yank** comes from.]

### yard¹ *noun* yards
A **yard** is an area of ground with a hard surface surrounded by walls or buildings.
[**Yard¹** comes from Old English *geard*.]

### yard² *noun* yards
A **yard** is a measurement in the imperial system of length, equal to about 91 centimetres.
[**Yard²** comes from Old English *gerd*.]

### yarn *noun* yarns (th)
1 **Yarn** is thread.
2 A **yarn** is a long story.
[**Yarn** comes from Old English.]

### yawn *verb* yawns, yawning, yawned
To **yawn** means to open your mouth and take a breath when you are tired or bored.
[**Yawn** comes from Old English.]

### year *noun* years
A **year** is a measure of time equal to 12 months or 365 days.
[**Year** comes from Old English.]

### yearn *verb* yearns, yearning, yearned (th)
To **yearn** means to have a great wish or longing for something.
[**Yearn** comes from Old English.]

### yeast *noun*
**Yeast** is a fungus that is used to make bread rise and to make beer and wine.
[**Yeast** comes from Old English.]

### yell *verb* yells, yelling, yelled (th)
To **yell** means to shout loudly.
[**Yell** comes from Old English.]

### yellow *noun*
**Yellow** is the colour of lemons.
[**Yellow** comes from Old English.]

### yellow *adjective*
of the colour of lemons: *yellow buttercups*.

### yelp *verb* yelps, yelping, yelped (th)
To **yelp** means to make a quick shrill cry.
[**Yelp** comes from Old English.]

### yes *adverb*
You use **yes** to show that you agree with something or approve of something.
[**Yes** comes from Old English.]

### yesterday *noun*
**Yesterday** is the day before today.
[**Yesterday** comes from Old English.]

### yesterday *adverb*
on or during the day before today: *The exams finished yesterday.*

### yoga *noun*
**Yoga** is a series of physical movements and exercise from India that help you to become fit and relaxed.
[**Yoga** comes from Sanskrit (a very old Indian language).]

### yoghurt *noun* yoghurts *Also* yogurt
**Yoghurt** is a kind of food made from sour milk. [**Yoghurt** comes from Turkish.]

### yolk *noun* yolks
A **yolk** is the yellow part of an egg.
[**Yolk** comes from the same Old English word as **yellow**.]

### Yom Kippur *noun*
**Yom Kippur** is a Jewish holy day when

people pray to be forgiven for what they have done wrong. They do not eat for 25 hours.
[**Yom Kippur** comes from Hebrew (the language spoken in Israel).]

**you** *pronoun*
**1 You** is the person or people being written or spoken to: *You can go tomorrow; Have you heard the news?*
**2** You use **you** to talk about any person: *You never know what might happen.*
[**You** comes from Old English.]

**young** *adjective* (th)
Someone or something that is **young** has not been living for very long and is not old. [**Young** comes from Old English.]

**your** *pronoun*
Something that belongs to you is **your** thing. [**Your** comes from Old English.]

**yourself** *pronoun* **yourselves**
**1** You use **yourself** to refer to the object of a verb in which the subject is you, when the subject and the object are the same person: *Have you locked yourself out?; It's always a surprise when you see yourself on a video.*
**2** If you do something **yourself** or **by yourself**, you do it alone or with no help from anyone.

**youth** *noun* **youths** (th)
**1 Youth** is the period of your life when you are young.
**2** A **youth** is a teenager.
[**Youth** comes from Old English.]

**yo-yo** *noun* **yo-yos**
A **yo-yo** is a toy made from a string wound round a groove in a pair of discs. You can make the **yo-yo** go up and down the string.
[No one knows where the word **yo-yo** comes from.]

# Zz

**zebra** *noun* **zebras**
A **zebra** is an animal like a horse with black and white stripes. **Zebras** live in Africa.
[**Zebra** comes from Italian, Spanish or Portuguese.]

**zebra crossing** *noun* **zebra crossings**
A **zebra crossing** is a place on the road marked by black and white stripes where people can cross.

**zero** *noun* **zeros**
**Zero** means the number nought and is written '0'. [**Zero** comes from Arabic.]

**zest** *noun* (th)
**1** The outside skin of a citrus fruit like an orange or lemon is the **zest**.
**2 Zest** is enthusiasm and enjoyment: *a zest for life.* [**Zest** comes from French.]

**zigzag** *noun* **zigzags**
A **zigzag** is a line that bends sharply from side to side.
[**Zigzag** comes from German via French.]

**zigzag** *verb* **zigzags, zigzagging, zigzagged**
To **zigzag** means to keep bending or moving from side to side: *The path zigzags among the trees.*

**zinc** *noun*
**Zinc** is a bluish-white metal that is often mixed with other metals or used to coat other metals so they will not rust.
[**Zinc** comes from German.]

**zip** *verb* **zips, zipping, zipped**
**1** To **zip** something or **zip** something **up** means to close it or fasten it with a zip.
**2** To **zip** means to move quickly, especially with a sharp sound: *Bullets zipped through the air.*
[The word **zip** is an imitation of the sound of something moving very quickly.]

**zip** *noun* **zips** *Also* **zipper**
A **zip** is a metal or plastic fastening with small teeth that joins two edges of material together.

**zodiac** *noun*
**1** The **zodiac** is an imaginary band that the sun and planets travel through across the sky. It is divided into twelve parts and each part is named after a constellation.
**2** The signs of the **zodiac** are the names of the twelve divisions of the stars that are used in astrology.
[**Zodiac** comes from Greek.]

**zone** *noun* **zones** (th)
A **zone** is an area with a particular purpose: *a pedestrian zone.*

[**Zone** comes via French or Latin from Greek *zone* 'a belt'.]

**zoo** *noun* **zoos**
A **zoo** is a place where different wild animals are kept to protect them and so that people can go and look at them. [**Zoo** is short for **zoological garden**; **zoological** comes from **zoology**.]

**zoology** *noun*
**Zoology** is the scientific study of animals. [**Zoology** comes from Greek *zoion* 'animal'.]

**zoom** *verb* **zooms, zooming, zoomed** (th)
To **zoom** means to travel or move very fast. [The word **zoom** is an imitation of the sound of something moving very fast.]

---

## Dictionary Fun

**Etymology**
Which 'y' word comes from early Dutch *jaghtschip*, which means 'fast pirate-ship'?

**Work it out**
I am two days before tomorrow. What am I?

**Find out**
1. What do these **years** have in common: 1976, 1996, 2004?
2. What is your sign of the **zodiac**? What is the symbol that represents that sign?

**Did you know?**
◆ **X-rays** are so named because the person that discovered them in 1895 did not know what sort of rays they were.

◆ Some people believe that their sign of the **zodiac** indicates what kind of personality they have.
◆ **Zinc** is a chemical element. There are over 100 chemical elements, which are organised according to their type in the periodic table of elements.

**Brainteaser**
One morning a night-guard told his manager, Mr Harmon, that he had dreamt the night before that Mrs Harmon would be in an accident. Mr Harmon went home and found his wife had fallen down the stairs. He rang for an ambulance. The next day, however, he sacked the night-guard. Why?

a b c d e f g h i j k l m

# Dictionary Fun answers

## Aa

### Etymology
1. atom
2. affair

### What do these idioms mean?
1. To keep something/someone from getting too close
2. To cost a lot of money
3. To welcome something/someone happily

### Complete the proverbs
1. *Actions* speak louder than words.
2. An *apple* a day keeps the doctor away.

### Riddle
A house can't jump!

### Work it out
Australia

## Bb

Complete the proverbs
1. *Beauty* is only skin deep.
2. *Birds* of a feather flock together.

### What do these idioms mean?
1. Alert
2. To discuss a subject without coming to the point
3. To be obsessed about something

### Homographs
bow

### Complete the similes
1. As busy as a *bee*.

2. As blind as a *bat*.

### Etymology
1. bonsai
2. They both have the prefix *bi-*, which means two. A bicycle has two wheels and someone who is bilingual speaks two languages.

### Work it out
buzz

## Cc

### Complete the proverbs
1. Cut your *coat* according to your cloth.
2. Don't *count* your *chickens* before they're hatched.
3. Every *cloud* has a silver lining.
4. Too many *cooks* spoil the broth.

### What do these idioms mean?
1. To sell quickly
2. To take the blame
3. To do something the wrong way round

### Etymology
1. café
2. They both have the prefix 'centi', which means one hundred or one-hundredth. A centipede has one hundred legs and a centimetre is a hundredth of a metre.
3. cemetery

### Riddle
coffin

## Dd

**What do these idioms mean?**
1. To be fast asleep
2. To deteriorate
3. To be unhappy

**Etymology**
1. They both have the prefix *dec-*, which means ten. A decade has ten years and in the decimal system, you count in units of ten.
2. defiant
3. dose

**Complete the proverbs**
1. Better the *devil* you know than the *devil* you don't.
2. Who *dares* wins.

**Riddle**
When it's ajar!

**Brainteaser**
The surgeon was the boy's mother.

## Ee

**Work it out**
The letter 'e' is not in it.

**What do these idioms mean?**
1. To look foolish
2. To admit that you were wrong
3. To live within your means

**Complete the proverbs**
1. *Empty* vessels make the most noise.
2. Don't put all your *eggs* in one basket.
3. The *early* bird catches the worm.

## Ff

**Complete the proverbs**
1. *Fire* is a good servant but a bad master.
2. A *fool* and his money are soon parted.
3. A *friend* in need is a friend indeed.

**What do these idioms mean?**
1. To face up to the blame
2. To achieve something
3. To stay neutral in an argument

**Etymology**
1. fascinate
2. false

**Work it out**
1. fables
2. fairy

**Think about it**
fish-eating cats = cats that eat fish
fish eating cats = a fish (or some fish) in the act of eating cats

## Gg

**Complete the proverbs**
1. Nothing ventured, nothing *gained*.
2. People who live in *glass* houses shouldn't throw stones.

**Complete the idioms**
1. Against the *grain*
2. To get in on the *ground* floor
3. To stick to your *guns*

**Etymology**
1. gala
2. grease

**Complete the simile**
As green as *grass*.

# Hh

**Complete the proverbs**
1. Make *hay* while the sun shines.
2. More *haste,* less speed.
3. *Half* a loaf is better than no bread.

**Complete the simile**
As old as the *hills*.

**What do these idioms mean?**
1. To be exactly correct
2. To show your emotions
3. To be busy

**Work it out**
hawk, heron

**Riddle**
A hole.

# Ii

**Work it out**
icon, coin

**Etymology**
Both **implicate** and **import** come from Latin words that included the prefix *im-*, meaning 'in'. **Impractical** comes from English *im-*, meaning 'not' and **practical**.

**Complete the simile**
As cold as *ice*.

**Brainteaser**
All of them!

# Jj
**Etymology**
India

**Work it out**
They played other people.

# Kk
**What do these idioms mean?**
1. Stay calm
2. Something that sets you back
3. In an amazing or particularly attractive outfit

**Etymology**
kennel

**Riddles**
1. A kitten
2. A knight (in both senses, a move refers to a knight moving on a chess board)

**Work it out**
1. They each have a silent 'k' at the beginning.
2. kangaroo, koala

**Brainteaser**
Barbara. Melissa would say "My sister says she's Melissa," because she lies; therefore it was Barbara who spoke.

## Ll

**Etymology**
1. laser
2. logic

**What do these idioms mean?**
1. To mislead someone
2. To take a course of action without knowing what will happen
3. To be unable to support an argument

**Complete the proverbs**
1. He who *laughs* last *laughs* longest.
2. Look before you *leap*.
3. A *leopard* does not change its spots.

**Complete the simile**
As gentle as a *lamb*.

## Mm

**What do these idioms mean?**
1. To treat something too fussily
2. To submit to something horrible
3. To survive on the income you have
4. To tell someone off

**Complete the proverbs**
1. While the cat's away the *mice* will play.
2. A *miss* is as good as a mile.

**Complete the similes**
1. As stubborn as a *mule*.
2. As poor as a church *mouse*.

**Work it out**
mammal

## Nn

**Etymology**
navigate

**What do these idioms mean?**
1. To be very deeply involved in something
2. Something that is very difficult to find

**Complete the proverbs**
1. No *news* is good news.
2. *Necessity* is the mother of invention.

**Think about it**
noon

**Riddle**
A newspaper

## Oo

**Etymology**
1. orangutan
2. origami

**What do these idioms mean?**
1. To not receive as much money as expected
2. Amazing
3. To be old

**Riddle**
An oak

**Complete the simile**
As *old* as the hills.

**Complete the proverb**
*Once* bitten, twice shy.

**Brainteaser**
An hour and a half

# Pp
**Complete the idioms**
1. To put someone through their *paces*
2. To *paint* the town red

**Complete the proverbs**
1. *Prevention* is better than cure.
2. He who *pays* the *piper* calls the tune.

**Complete the similes**
1. As bright as a new *pin*.
2. As *proud* as a peacock.

**Work it out**
palindrome

**Brainteaser**
The woman was flying to a place that was one hour behind in time.

# Qq
**Etymology**
quest, query, question

**Riddle**
Quicksand

**Think about it**
The 'q' is always followed by a 'u'.

**Brainteaser**
The word should start with 'on', for example, *once*. Each word begins with the last two letters of the previous word.

# Rr
**Etymology**
radar

**What do these idioms mean?**
1. To see the hidden meaning in something
2. To not give something or someone any freedom
3. Completely healthy

**New words**
1. RAM
2. rat race

**Complete the proverbs**
1. A *rolling* stone gathers no moss.
2. *Rome* was not built in a day.

**Riddle**
A river

# Ss
**Complete the idioms**
1. A *storm* in a teacup
2. The *salt* of the earth
3. *Save* your breath

**Complete the proverbs**
1. A *stitch* in time saves nine.
2. *Still* waters run deep.
3. Let *sleeping* dogs lie.

**New words**
satellite television

**Complete the similes**
1. As *slippery* as an eel.
2. As *sweet* as honey.
3. As white as *snow*.

## Tt

**What do these idioms mean?**
1. To start afresh
2. To completely surprise you
3. To talk constantly

**Complete the proverbs**
1. Time and *tide* wait for no man.
2. A liar is not believed when he speaks the *truth*.

**Riddle**
A table

**Find out**
1. tiger ('The Tyger')
2. toad (from *The Wind in the Willows*)

## Uu

**Etymology**
ultimate

**What does this idiom mean?**
Something is very close by

**New words**
User-friendly

**Work it out**
*Uni-* means one. A unicorn has one horn, a uniform is one outfit that everyone in a group wears.

**Find out**
university

**Brainteaser**
They were a grandma with her daughter and her granddaughter. (One women was both a mother and a daughter.)

## Vv

**Etymology**
venom

**What do these idioms mean?**
1. To all agree on something
2. To show how you feel by being present or absent

**New words**
VDU

**Riddle**
A volcano

**Find out**
An artery

**Brainteaser**
His daughter

## Ww

**What do these idioms mean?**
1. A person who stops others from enjoying themselves
2. To have no more to do with something
3. A quest for something that fails

**Complete the proverbs**
1. All's well that ends *well*.
2. Where there's a *will* there's a way.
3. It's an ill *wind* that blows nobody any good.

**New words**
World Wide Web

**Work it out**
They each spell another word when read backwards.

**Riddle**
wet!

**Simile**
As *wise* as an owl.

**Find out**
woe (woe is an old-fashioned word that means sorrow)

# Xx Yy Zz
**Etymology**
yacht

**Work it out**
yesterday

**Find out**
1. They are all leap years.

**Brainteaser**
If he was a night-guard he should not have been asleep the night before. He must have been asleep to dream about Mrs Harmon.

# Prefixes and suffixes

A *prefix* is letters added to the beginning of a word to change or add to its meaning. A *suffix* is letters added to the end of a word to make a new word that is related. Some of the more common prefixes and suffixes are listed below with their meanings. Most of these prefixes and suffixes come from other languages, and many words that have a prefix or a suffix already had it when they came into English. For example, if you look up the etymology of 'convenient' you will find that it comes from Latin *convenire* 'to go together', which was formed from the Latin prefix *con-* 'together' and *venire* 'to go'.

If you know the meaning of a prefix or suffix it may help you to work out the meaning of a word you do not know. Be careful – not all words that have these letters at the beginning or end have been formed using these prefixes and suffixes. For example, if you look up the etymology of 'biology', you will see that it does not begin with the prefix *bi-*.

| Prefix | Meaning | Example |
|---|---|---|
| aero- | related to air or aircraft | aerosol |
| anti- | against | antibiotic |
| aqua- | water | aquatic |
| auto- | self | autobiography |
| bi- | two | bicycle |
| co-, com-, con- | with, together | cooperate, co-driver connect |
| de- | **1** down **2** take away | **1** descent **2** decapitate |
| dis- | **1** not **2** remove | **1** disagree **2** discover |
| en-, em- (*before words beginning with b or p*) | in, inside, put into or on | endanger embalm |
| ex- | **1** out **2** formerly | **1** exhale **2** ex-wife |
| hydr- (*before a vowel*), hydro- | to do with water | hydrogen |
| in-, il- (*before l*), im- (*before b, m or p*), ir- (*before r*) | **1** not **2** without **3** in, on, onto | **1** inaudible, illegal, imperfect **2** inability **3** import |
| micro- | small | microchip |
| mis- | badly, wrongly | misbehave |

| Prefix | Meaning | Example |
| --- | --- | --- |
| non- | not | nonsense |
| octa-, octo-, oct- (*before a vowel*) | eight | octopus |
| omni- | all | omnivore |
| photo- | light | photograph |
| pre- | before | prejudice |
| pro- | 1 for, in favour of<br>2 forwards, onwards<br>3 acting as a substitute | 1 pro-life<br>2 progress<br>3 pronoun |
| re- | 1 again, back<br>2 in return<br>3 against<br>4 off, away | 1 renew<br>2 react<br>3 rebel<br>4 remove |
| sub-, sus- (*before c, p or t*) | below, under | submerge |
| tele- | at a distance | telephone |
| trans- | 1 across<br>2 into another state | 1 transplant<br>2 transform |
| tri- | three | triangle |
| un- | 1 not<br>2 reversing the action of a verb | unable<br>uncover |

| Suffix | Meaning | Example |
| --- | --- | --- |
| -able, -ible | 1 that may or must be<br>2 that is relevant | 1 forgivable, usable, edible<br>2 fashionable |
| -al | relating to | neutral, trivial |
| -ance, -ence | a quality or state | arrogance, impudence |
| -ant, -ent | person who does | assistant, president |
| -ary | connected with | primary |
| -ate | 1 forms nouns showing status or function<br>2 forms adjectives | 1 magnate<br><br>2 affectionate |
| er | forming comparative of adjectives | hotter, faster |
| -er, -or | what a person, animal or thing does | actor, computer |
| -ess | female | actress, lioness |
| -est | forming superlative of adjectives | hottest, fastest |
| -ette | 1 small<br>2 female | 1 cigarette<br>2 usherette |

| Suffix | Meaning | Example |
|---|---|---|
| -ful | full of | beautiful |
| -ic, -ical | to do with | aromatic, historical |
| -ing | forming adjectives and nouns to show the action of a verb | loving, asking |
| -ise, -ize | make or do | advertise, sympathise |
| -ish | 1 having the characteristics of<br>2 of the nationality | 1 reddish<br><br>2 British |
| -ive | having the nature of | supportive, talkative |
| -less | without | useless |
| -like | similar to | doglike |
| -logy, -ology | a subject of study | biology |
| -ly | 1 having the qualities of<br>2 recurring at intervals<br>3 used to form adverbs from adjectives | manly<br>daily<br>quietly |
| -ment | action or result | judgement, merriment |
| -ness | state or quality | kindness |
| -phobe | fear or dislike | technophobe (someone who dislikes/fears technology) |
| -proof | not affected by | waterproof |
| -scope | an instrument for looking through or observing | telescope |
| -ship | 1 quality or condition<br>2 position or skill | 1 hardship<br>2 leadership |
| -ward, -wards | in a direction | towards |
| -worthy | suitable for | newsworthy |

# Words we use a lot

This list contains 267 words that you will use a lot in your writing. If you learn how to spell these words you'll find writing much easier!

**A**
about
above
across
after
again
all
almost
along
also
always
am
an
and
animals
another
any
are
around
as
asked
at
away

**B**
baby
back
ball
balloon
be
because
bed
been
before
began
being
below
better

between
big
birthday
both
boy
brother
brought
but
by

**C**
call
called
came
can
can't
cat
change
children
clothes
come
coming
could

**D**
day
did
didn't
different
dig
do
does
dog
don't
door
down
during

**E**
earth
every
eyes

**F**
father
follow
following
found
friends

**G**
garden
get
girl
go
goes
going
gone
good
got
great

**H**
had
half
happy
has
have
he
head
heard
help
her
here
high
him

his
home
house
how

**I**
I
if
I'm
important
in
inside
is
it

**J**
jump
jumped
just

**K**
knew
know

**L**
lady
last
laugh
leave
light
like
little
live
lived
look
love

**M**
made
make
man
many
may
me
might
money
morning
mother
much
mum
must
my

**N**
name
near
never
new
night
no
not
now
number

**O**
of
off
often
old
on
once
one
only
opened
or
other
our
out
outside
over
own

**P**
paper
people
place
play
pull
push
put

**R**
ran
right
round

**S**
said
saw
school
second
see
seen
she
should
show
sister
small
so
some
something
sometimes
sound
started
still
stopped
such
suddenly
sure
swimming

**T**
take
than
that
the
their

them
then
there
these
they
think
this
those
thought
through
time
to
today
together
told
too
took
tree
tries
turn
turned
two

**U**
under
until
up
upon
us
used

**V**
very

**W**
walk
walked
walking
want
was
watch
water
way
we
went

were
what
when
where
while
who
whole
why
will
window
with
without
woke
woken
word
work
world
would
write

**Y**
year
yes
you
young
your

# Collective nouns (animals)

A *collective noun* refers to a group of individuals but is grammatically singular (i.e. you say *a* swarm of bees *is* ...).

Which collective noun is the most common?

a **hive** of **bees** living together

a **swarm** of **bees** flying

a **flock** of **birds**

a **herd** of **buffalo**

a **herd** of **cattle**

a **brood** or **clutch** of newly hatched **chicks**

a **litter** of **cubs**

a **herd** of **deer**

a **pack** of **dogs**

a **flight** of **doves**

a **herd** of **elephants**

a **shoal** of **fish**

a **cloud** or **swarm** of **flies**

a **gaggle** of **geese**

a **herd** of **giraffes**

a **herd** of **goats**

a **team** of working **horses**

a **herd** of wild **horses**

a **pack** of **hounds**

a **swarm** of **insects**

a **litter** of **kittens**

a **pride** of **lions**

a **troop** of **monkeys**

a **rookery** or **colony** of nesting **penguins**

a **herd** of **pigs**

a **litter** of **pups**

a **string** of **racehorses**

a **flock** of **sheep**

a **flight** of **swallows**

a **school** or **pod** of **whales**

a **pack** of **wolves**

# Countries of the world

This is a short list of some of the countries of the world. If you want to find a country not in the list try looking in an atlas.

| Country | Person | Currency |
| --- | --- | --- |
| America (see United States of America) | | |
| Argentina | Argentinean | Argentine Peso |
| Australia | Australian | Australian Dollar |
| Austria | Austrian | Schilling/Euro |
| Belgium | Belgian | Belgian Franc/Euro |
| Bolivia | Bolivian | Boliviano |
| Brazil | Brazilian | Cruzeiro |
| Britain | British or Briton | Pound Sterling |
| Bulgaria | Bulgarian | Lev |
| Canada | Canadian | Canadian Dollar |
| Chile | Chilean | Chilean Peso |
| Cuba | Cuban | Cuban Peso |
| Czech Republic | Czech | Koruna |
| Denmark | Dane | Danish Krone |
| Ecuador | Ecuadorean | Sucre |
| Egypt | Egyptian | Egyptian Pound |
| Ethiopia | Ethiopian | Birr |
| Finland | Finn | Markka/Euro |
| France | Frenchman, Frenchwoman | French Franc/Euro |
| Germany | German | Deutschmark/Euro |
| Greece | Greek | Drachma |
| Hungary | Hungarian | Forint |
| Iceland | Icelander | Iceland Krona |
| India | Indian | Indian Rupee |
| Indonesia | Indonesian | Rupiah |

| Country | Person | Currency |
|---------|--------|----------|
| Iran | Iranian | Rial |
| Iraq | Iraqi | Iraqi Dinar |
| Ireland, Republic of | Irishman, Irishwoman | Irish Punt/Euro |
| Israel | Israeli | Israeli Shekel |
| Italy | Italian | Lira/Euro |
| Japan | Japanese | Yen |
| Kenya | Kenyan | Kenya Shilling |
| Kuwait | Kuwaiti | Kuwaiti Dinar |
| Libya | Libyan | Libyan Dinar |
| Lithuania | Lithuanian | Litas |
| Luxembourg | Luxembourger | Luxembourg Franc/Euro |
| Malaysia | Malaysian | Malaysian Ringgit |
| Malta | Maltese | Maltese Pound |
| Mexico | Mexican | Mexican Peso |
| Morocco | Moroccan | Dirham |
| Netherlands, The | Dutchman, Dutchwoman, or Netherlander | Netherland Guilder/Euro |
| New Zealand | New Zealander | New Zealand Dollar |
| Nigeria | Nigerian | Naira |
| Norway | Norwegian | Norwegian Krone |
| Pakistan | Pakistani | Pakistan Rupee |
| Paraguay | Paraguayan | Guarani |
| Peru | Peruvian | Nuevo Sol |
| Poland | Pole | Zloty |
| Portugal | Portuguese | Portuguese Escudo/Euro |
| Romania | Romanian | Leu |
| Rwanda | Rwandan | Rwanda Franc |
| Saudi Arabia | Saudi Arabian or Saudi | Riyal |
| Singapore | Singaporean | Singapore Dollar |

| Country | Person | Currency |
|---|---|---|
| South Africa | South African | Rand |
| Spain | Spaniard | Spanish Peseta/Euro |
| Sri Lanka | Sri Lankan | Sri Lanka Rupee |
| Sweden | Swede | Swedish Krona |
| Switzerland | Swiss | Swiss Franc |
| Thailand | Thai | Baht |
| Turkey | Turk | Turkish Lira |
| United States of America | American | US Dollar |
| Venezuela | Venezuelan | Bolivar |
| Vietnam | Vietnamese | Dong |

# Calendar

The calendar used today throughout most of the Western world and in parts of Asia is called the Gregorian calendar. It was introduced in 1582 by Pope Gregory XIII (the thirteenth), altering the previous Julian (Roman) calendar. You will see that many of the names of the months of the year come from Roman names.

## Days of the Week

| Day | Old English Origin (given in italic) |
| --- | --- |
| Monday | *Monandaeg* 'day of the moon'; translation of Latin *dies lunae* |
| Tuesday | *Tiwesdaeg*, from *Tiw*, the Scandinavian god of war |
| Wednesday | *Wodnesdaeg*, named after the Scandinavian god Woden or Odin |
| Thursday | *Thunresdaeg*, 'day of thunder' from Thor, the Norse god of thunder. |
| Friday | *Frigedaeg*, named after the Scandinavian goddess Frigga |
| Saturday | *Saeternesdaeg*, 'day of Saturn'; translation of Latin *dies Saturni* |
| Sunday | *Sunnandaeg* 'day of the sun'; translation of Latin *dies solis* |

## Months of the Year

| Month | Latin Origin (given in italic) |
| --- | --- |
| January | *Januarius*, named after Janus, the Roman god of beginnings |
| February | *Februarius*, from *februa*, a feast that used to be held in this month |
| March | *Martius*, named after Mars, the god of war |
| April | *Aprilis* from *aprire* 'to open', probably because this is the month when buds open |
| May | *Maius*, month of the goddess Maia |
| June | *Junius*, named after Juno, a Roman goddess |
| July | *Julius*, named after Julius Caesar, a Roman leader |
| August | *Augustus*, named after Augustus Caesar, the first Roman emperor |
| September | *Septum* 'seven' (originally September was the seventh month of the Roman calendar) |
| October | *Octo* 'eight' (originally October was the eighth month of the Roman calendar) |
| November | *Novem* 'nine' (originally November was the ninth month of the Roman calendar) |
| December | *Decem* 'ten' (originally December was the tenth month of the Roman calendar) |

# Numbers

| cardinal | | ordinal | | cardinal | | ordinal | |
|---|---|---|---|---|---|---|---|
| 1 | one | 1st | first | 16 | sixteen | 16th | sixteenth |
| 2 | two | 2nd | second | 17 | seventeen | 17th | seventeenth |
| 3 | three | 3rd | third | 18 | eighteen | 18th | eighteenth |
| 4 | four | 4th | fourth | 19 | nineteen | 19th | nineteenth |
| 5 | five | 5th | fifth | 20 | twenty | 20th | twentieth |
| 6 | six | 6th | sixth | 21 | twenty-one | 21st | twenty-first |
| 7 | seven | 7th | seventh | 30 | thirty | 30th | thirtieth |
| 8 | eight | 8th | eighth | 40 | forty | 40th | fortieth |
| 9 | nine | 9th | ninth | 50 | fifty | 50th | fiftieth |
| 10 | ten | 10th | tenth | 60 | sixty | 60th | sixtieth |
| 11 | eleven | 11th | eleventh | 70 | seventy | 70th | seventieth |
| 12 | twelve | 12th | twelfth | 80 | eighty | 80th | eightieth |
| 13 | thirteen | 13th | thirteenth | 90 | ninety | 90th | ninetieth |
| 14 | fourteen | 14th | fourteenth | 100 | one hundred | 100th | hundredth |
| 15 | fifteen | 15th | fifteenth | | | | |

| | | | |
|---|---|---|---|
| **101** | one hundred and one | **101st** | hundred and first |
| **1000** | one thousand | **1000th** | thousandth |
| **1 000 000** | one million | **1 000 000th** | millionth |

# Planets of the solar system

The solar system is the only planetary system that we know exists, although there could be others. The planets are listed from the closest to the sun (Mercury) to the furthest (Pluto).

| Planet | Etymology |
|---|---|
| Mercury | Latin *Mercurius*, the name of the messenger of the gods and the god of traders |
| Venus | Latin *Venus*, the name of the goddess of love |
| Earth | Old English *eorthe* |
| Mars | Latin *Mars*, the name of the Roman god of war |
| Jupiter | Latin *Jupiter*, the king of the gods |
| Saturn | Latin *Saturnus*, the name of the Roman god of agriculture |
| Uranus | Greek *Ouranos* 'heaven, Uranus', who was the most ancient of the Greek gods and the first ruler of the universe |
| Neptune | Latin *Neptunus*, the name of the Roman god of water and the sea |
| Pluto | Greek *Plouton*, the name of the god of the underworld |

## What is a thesaurus?

How many words do you think you know? A hundred?
A thousand? Well, get to know how to use your
thesaurus and you will learn hundreds of new words.

Many ideas, feelings and actions can be described in
more than one way. A thesaurus helps you to find
different words or phrases to talk or write about the
same thing, so that your writing and stories will contain
more interesting and exciting language.

## How to use your thesaurus

Just like in a dictionary, the words in this thesaurus are
arranged in alphabetical order. After the main word you
are looking up, you will find alternative words that
have a similar meaning.

**gale** *noun*
*Alternative words:* hurricane, tempest, tornado, typhoon

These alternative words are called **synonyms**.

If a word has more than one meaning, the thesaurus will
help you to find the one you are looking for. Each
meaning has a number, and there is an explanation or an
example next to the number so that you can see clearly
which meaning is which.

**illusion** *noun*
**1** a false idea
*Alternative words:* deception, false impression, delusion
**2** something that is not real
*Alternative words:* fantasy, hallucination, mirage, figment of the
imagination

**reproduce** *verb*
**1** You can reproduce a photo thousands of times.
*Alternative words:* to copy, to duplicate, to replicate
**2** All animals and plants reproduce.
*Alternative words:* to breed, to multiply, to procreate

# THESAURUS

## Contents

**Flip the thesaurus over to use the dictionary.**

**kill** *verb*
　1 to kill a person
　*Alternative words:* to murder, to assassinate, to take someone's life
　2 to kill an animal
　*Alternative words:* to slaughter, to destroy, to put down, to put to sleep

Words with the same spelling but different meanings have different numbers. These are the same as the numbers in the dictionary.

**row¹** *noun*
　a row of houses
　*Alternative words:* line, column, file

**row²** *noun*
　1 a lot of noise
　*Alternative words:* racket, din, commotion
　2 an argument
　*Alternative words:* quarrel, dispute, squabble

The thesaurus also shows whether an alternative word or phrase is formal (used more in written language), informal (used when speaking or writing to people you know), old-fashioned or used mainly in stories.

**chief** *noun*
　*Alternative words:* leader, captain, head, boss (informal)

**fade** *verb*
　3 to fade from sight
　*Alternative words:* to disappear, to vanish, to melt away (used mainly in stories), to evaporate (used mainly in stories)

**Opposite words**

If a word has an opposite, this is given after the alternative words. The opposite word is called an **antonym**.

**panic** *verb*
　*Alternative words:* to be terrified, to lose your nerve, to go to pieces, to become hysterical
　*The opposite is* **stay calm**

If the word has more than one meaning, the antonym is given at the end of the meaning you are looking at.

**hard** *adjective*
　**1** not soft
　*Alternative words:* firm, solid, stiff
　*The opposite is* **soft**
　**2** not easy
　*Alternative words:* difficult, complicated, thorny
　*The opposite is* **easy**
　**3** not pleasant
　*Alternative words:* cruel, difficult, severe
　*The opposite is* **pleasant**

How many sentences can you think of using the word *nice*? Now think of some other words you could use instead of *nice* and rewrite the sentences. Use your thesaurus to help you.

Not all the synonyms and antonyms are in the dictionary. You will need an adult thesaurus if you want to look all of them up.

# Aa

**abandon** *verb*
1 to abandon a person
*Alternative words:* to leave, to desert, to leave behind
2 to abandon a place
*Alternative words:* to leave, to go away from

**able** *adjective*
*Alternative words:* capable, competent, expert, skilful, talented

**abnormal** *adjective*
*Alternative words:* strange, unusual, odd, uncommon
*The opposite is normal*

**about** *preposition*
*Alternative words:* regarding, concerning, referring to

**about** *adverb*
1 about ten people
*Alternative words:* roughly, approximately, more or less, nearly
2 I'm about to leave.
*Alternative words:* ready, going to, on the point of

**above** *adverb*
*Alternative words:* on top, high up, overhead
*The opposite is below*

**above** *preposition*
*Alternative words:* over, higher than, on top of
*The opposite is under*

**abrupt** *adjective*
1 She was very abrupt.
*Alternative words:* rude, unfriendly, impatient
*The opposite is polite*
2 came to an abrupt stop
*Alternative words:* sudden, unexpected, quick
*The opposite is gradual*

**absent** *adjective*
*Alternative words:* away, missing, not here, not present
*The opposite is present*

**abundant** *adjective*
*Alternative words:* plentiful, ample,
more than you need
*The opposite is scarce*

**abuse** *noun*
1 drug abuse
*Alternative words:* misuse
2 shouting abuse
*Alternative words:* insults, rude words, swearwords

**abuse** *verb*
*Alternative words:* to harm, to hurt, to treat badly, to treat wrongly, to insult

**accept** *verb*
*Alternative words:* to take, to receive, to get

**accident** *noun*
1 a car accident
*Alternative words:* crash, collision, disaster
2 by accident
*Alternative words:* chance, fluke, luck

**accomplish** *verb*
*Alternative words:* to manage, to do, to achieve, to carry out

**accurate** *adjective*
*Alternative words:* exact, correct, right, precise, true
*The opposite is inaccurate*

**achieve** *verb*
*Alternative words:* to do, to fulfil, to accomplish

**acquire** *verb*
*Alternative words:* to get, to obtain, to buy

**act** *noun*
1 something that you do
*Alternative words:* action, deed
2 a comedy act
*Alternative words:* sketch, show, performance, routine
3 an act of parliament
*Alternative words:* law, bill, decree

**act** *verb*
1 to act in a play
*Alternative words:* to perform, to play a part, to have a role
2 We must act quickly!
*Alternative words:* to do something, to move, to react, to take action
3 Why are you acting like that?
*Alternative words:* to behave, to be

**acute** *adjective*
**1** an acute sense
*Alternative words:* sharp, keen, perceptive
**2** an acute pain
*Alternative words:* intense, sharp, stabbing, shooting, excruciating
*The opposite is* **dull**

**adapt** *verb*
**1** We can adapt it.
*Alternative words:* to change, to alter, to modify
**2** I had to adapt.
*Alternative words:* to adjust, to change, to acclimatise

**add** *verb*
**1** Add 3 and 4.
*Alternative words:* to add up, to tot up, to work out
*The opposite is* **to subtract**
**2** He added the CD to his collection.
*Alternative words:* to include, to put in

**adequate** *adjective*
**1** an adequate amount
*Alternative words:* enough, sufficient, reasonable
**2** adequate work
*Alternative words:* satisfactory, good enough, acceptable, average
*The opposite is* **inadequate**

**adjacent** *adjective*
*Alternative words:* touching, attached, alongside, bordering

**adjust** *verb*
**1** to adjust a saddle
*Alternative words:* to alter, to change, to fix, to move
**2** to adjust to a new situation
*Alternative words:* to get used to, to adapt, to become accustomed to

**admire** *verb*
**1** to admire a person
*Alternative words:* to look up to, to respect, to think highly of
*The opposite is* **to look down on**
**2** to admire a building
*Alternative words:* to like, to take pleasure in, to appreciate, to marvel at

**admit** *verb*
**1** to admit that you did something
*Alternative words:* to own up, to confess
**2** to admit someone into a place
*Alternative words:* to let in, to allow to enter

**adult** *adjective*
*Alternative words:* fully grown, grown-up, mature

**advance** *noun*
**1** advances in medicine
*Alternative words:* progress, developments, headway
**2** in advance
*Alternative words:* earlier, previously, beforehand

**advance** *verb*
*Alternative words:* to go forward, to proceed, to move onward
*The opposite is* **to retreat**

**adventurous** *adjective*
*Alternative words:* daring, bold, intrepid
*The opposite is* **cautious**

**advertise** *verb*
*Alternative words:* to promote, to publicise, to give publicity to, to plug (informal)

**advice** *noun*
*Alternative words:* help, guidance, counselling, suggestions, recommendations, opinions

**advise** *verb*
*Alternative words:* to suggest, to recommend, to warn

**affair** *noun*
**1** a strange affair
*Alternative words:* episode, event, happening, incident, question, business
**2** a grand affair
*Alternative words:* occasion, party, gathering

**affect** *verb*
*Alternative words:* to have an effect on, to have an influence on, to have an impact on, to change

**affection** *noun*
*Alternative words:* love, fondness, tenderness, liking

**affectionate** *adjective*
*Alternative words:* kind, loving, warm-hearted, friendly
*The opposite is* **cold**

**afraid** *adjective*
**1** afraid of snakes
*Alternative words:* scared, frightened, terrified, anxious
*The opposite is* **fearless**
**2** afraid I can't come
*Alternative words:* sorry, regretful

**after** *adverb*
left a few minutes after
*Alternative words:* afterwards, later, subsequently
*The opposite is* **earlier**

**after** *preposition*
**1** after lunch
*Alternative words:* following, at the end of, later than
*The opposite is* **before**
**2** K is after J
*Alternative words:* next to, following
*The opposite is* **before**
**3** running after the dog
*Alternative words:* in pursuit of, behind
*The opposite is* **in front of**

**aggressive** *adjective*
*Alternative words:* quarrelsome, hostile, argumentative

**agile** *adjective*
*Alternative words:* nimble, supple, active, sprightly
*The opposite is* **clumsy**

**agony** *noun*
*Alternative words:* pain, suffering, distress, misery

**agree** *verb*
**1** We all agree.
*Alternative words:* to think alike, to see eye to eye
*The opposite is* **to disagree**
**2** to agree to something
*Alternative words:* to consent, to say yes
*The opposite is* **to refuse**

**agreement** *noun*
*Alternative words:* arrangement, bargain, deal, pact

**aim** *verb*
**1** to aim a weapon
*Alternative words:* to point, to focus, to position
**2** to aim to be a pop star
*Alternative words:* to intend, to plan, to try, to want

**aim** *noun*
*Alternative words:* plan, ambition, wish, desire, goal

**alarm** *noun*
**1** The alarm rang.
*Alternative words:* siren, bell, warning signal
**2** filled with alarm
*Alternative words:* fear, anxiety, terror, panic

**alert** *adjective*
*Alternative words:* observant, watchful, wide awake, on your guard

**alike** *adjective*
dressed the twins alike
*Alternative words:* the same, identically

**alike** *adverb*
treat them both alike
*Alternative words:* the same, equally

**alive** *adjective*
**1** The bird was still alive.
*Alternative words:* living, breathing
*The opposite is* **dead**
**2** felt more alive
*Alternative words:* full of life, energetic, lively, awake

**allow** *verb*
**1** We don't allow fighting.
*Alternative words:* to permit, to put up with (informal), to tolerate
**2** allow her to stay
*Alternative words:* to let, to permit, to give permission
**3** allow more time
*Alternative words:* to plan for, to put aside, to spare

**almost** *adverb*
*Alternative words:* nearly, not quite, just about, practically

**alone** *adjective, adverb*
**1** felt alone
*Alternative words:* lonely, abandoned, deserted
**2** sang it alone
*Alternative words:* on your own, by yourself, unaccompanied
**3** a tree standing alone
*Alternative words:* by itself, on its own, separate

**aloof** *adjective*
*Alternative words:* unfriendly, cold,

distant
*The opposite is* **warm**

**also** *adverb*
*Alternative words:* as well, too, besides, in addition

**alter** *verb*
**1** to alter something
*Alternative words:* to change, to transform, to modify
**2** to alter appearance
*Alternative words:* to change, to look different, to become different

**altogether** *adverb*
**1** 300 people altogether
*Alternative words:* in total, all told, in all
**2** It stopped altogether.
*Alternative words:* completely, totally, entirely
**3** Altogether, it was a good day.
*Alternative words:* on the whole, in general, by and large

**always** *adverb*
*Alternative words:* constantly, all the time, continually, incessantly, forever
*The opposite is* **never**

**amaze** *verb*
*Alternative words:* to astound, to surprise, to astonish

**amazing** *adjective*
*Alternative words:* astonishing, startling, surprising

**ambition** *noun*
*Alternative words:* dream, desire, goal, hope

**ambitious** *adjective*
*Alternative words:* enterprising, purposeful, eager, hopeful
*The opposite is* **unambitious**

**amiable** *adjective*
*Alternative words:* friendly, good-natured, likeable, charming
*The opposite is* **unfriendly**

**ample** *adjective*
*Alternative words:* abundant, plenty, copious, more than enough, lavish

**amuse** *verb*
This will amuse you
*Alternative words:* to make you laugh, to cheer you up, to entertain, to delight

**ancestor** *noun*
*Alternative words:* forebear, predecessor

**anger** *noun*
*Alternative words:* annoyance, fury, exasperation, resentment

**angry** *adjective*
**1** fairly angry
*Alternative words:* cross, annoyed, irritated
**2** very angry
*Alternative words:* furious, enraged, incensed, livid
*The opposite is* **calm**

**anguish** *noun*
*Alternative words:* distress, heartache, agony, sorrow, grief

**annoy** *verb*
*Alternative words:* to irritate, to bother, to provoke, to get on someone's nerves

**answer** *noun*
**1** answer to a question
*Alternative words:* reply, response, acknowledgement
**2** answer to a puzzle
*Alternative words:* solution, explanation

**answer** *verb*
**1** to give an answer
*Alternative words:* to reply, to respond, to say
**2** to answer the telephone
*Alternative words:* to pick up

**anxiety** *noun*
*Alternative words:* worry, nervousness, apprehension, foreboding

**anxious** *adjective*
*Alternative words:* worried, uneasy, nervous, tense

**apathy** *noun*
*Alternative words:* indifference, lack of interest, unresponsiveness
*The opposite is* **interest**

**appal** *verb*
*Alternative words:* to horrify, to shock, to dismay, to alarm

**appalling** *adjective*
*Alternative words:* awful, horrible, shocking, dreadful

**appear** *verb*
**1** A ship appeared.

*Alternative words:* to come into sight, to come into view, to materialise
*The opposite is* **to disappear**
**2** I don't think she'll appear.
*Alternative words:* to come, to turn up, to show up (informal), to show your face (informal)
**3** He appears happy.
*Alternative words:* to seem, to look, to give the impression of being

**appointment** *noun*
*Alternative words:* meeting, date, engagement

**apprehensive** *adjective*
*Alternative words:* worried, nervous, anxious, doubtful
*The opposite is* **confident**

**approach** *verb*
*Alternative words:* to come near, to go near, to move towards

**appropriate** *adjective*
*Alternative words:* suitable, right, proper
*The opposite is* **inappropriate**

**approve** *verb*
**1** to approve of a person or thing
*Alternative words:* to admire, to like, to have a good opinion of
*The opposite is* **to disapprove**
**2** to approve a plan
*Alternative words:* to agree to, to allow, to authorise, to permit

**approximate** *adjective*
*Alternative words:* rough, close, almost exact
*The opposite is* **precise**

**arduous** *adjective*
*Alternative words:* difficult, gruelling, laborious, tiring
*The opposite is* **easy**

**area** *noun*
**1** part of a town
*Alternative words:* district, neighbourhood
**2** area of a shape
*Alternative words:* size, measurements, dimensions
**3** marked out into areas
*Alternative words:* section, part, space

**arena** *noun*
*Alternative words:* ground, stadium, ring, stage

**argue** *verb*
*Alternative words:* to fight, to quarrel, to disagree, to squabble

**aroma** *noun*
*Alternative words:* smell, scent, fragrance

**arrange** *verb*
**1** to arrange objects
*Alternative words:* to put in order, to tidy, to sort out, to line up
**2** to arrange a party
*Alternative words:* to plan, to organise, to prepare

**arrangement** *noun*
**1** an arrangement to do something
*Alternative words:* plan, agreement, deal
**2** the arrangements for the holiday
*Alternative words:* plans, preparations, schedule
**3** an arrangement of objects
*Alternative words:* design, positioning, grouping

**arrest** *verb*
*Alternative words:* to capture, to catch, to take prisoner
*The opposite is* **to release**

**arrive** *verb*
*Alternative words:* to come, to turn up, to appear, to get there, to get here
*The opposite is* **to leave**

**arrogant** *adjective*
*Alternative words:* conceited, proud, boastful
*The opposite is* **modest**

**article** *noun*
**1** a thing
*Alternative words:* thing, item, object
**2** an article in a newspaper
*Alternative words:* piece, essay, report

**artificial** *adjective*
*Alternative words:* manufactured, synthetic, imitation

**ascend** *verb*
*Alternative words:* to climb, to go up, to mount
*The opposite is* **to descend**

**ashamed** *adjective*
**1** ashamed of what you have done
*Alternative words:* sorry, remorseful, repentant

*The opposite is **unrepentant***
**2** ashamed of her poverty
*Alternative words:* embarrassed, humiliated

**ask** *verb*
**1** to ask someone about something
*Alternative words:* to inquire, to question, to interrogate
**2** to ask someone to a party
*Alternative word:* to invite
**3** to ask for something
*Alternative words:* to beg, to demand, to implore, to plead

**assemble** *verb*
**1** to assemble in the hall
*Alternative words:* to meet, to come together, to gather
**2** to assemble a bookcase
*Alternative words:* to put together, to build, to fit together, to erect

**assess** *verb*
*Alternative words:* to judge, to evaluate, to rate

**assist** *verb*
**1** to assist someone
*Alternative words:* to help, to aid, to help out, to lend a hand (informal)
**2** to be someone's assistant
*Alternative words:* to support, to help, to work under

**associate** *verb*
**1** to associate with someone
*Alternative words:* to mix, to spend time with, to hang around with (informal)
**2** to associate two things
*Alternative words:* to think of together, to link, to connect

**assure** *verb*
*Alternative words:* to promise, to reassure, to guarantee, to declare

**attack** *noun*
*Alternative words:* assault, charge, raid, strike, onslaught

**attack** *verb*
**1** to attack a person
*Alternative words:* to assault, to set upon
*The opposite is **to defend***
**2** to attack a town
*Alternative words:* to storm, to invade, to lay siege to, to besiege
*The opposite is **to defend***

**attempt** *verb*
*Alternative words:* to try, to have a go (informal), to aim

**attitude** *noun*
*Alternative words:* opinion, point of view, reaction, thoughts

**authentic** *adjective*
*Alternative words:* genuine, real, original
*The opposite is **fake***

**aversion** *noun*
*Alternative words:* dislike, hatred, horror

**avoid** *verb*
**1** I think she's avoiding me.
*Alternative words:* to hide from, to keep away from, to steer clear of, to miss
**2** I couldn't avoid it.
*Alternative words:* to prevent, to stop, to avert

**awful** *adjective*
**1** saw something awful
*Alternative words:* nasty, horrible, ghastly, hideous
**2** an awful accident
*Alternative words:* terrible, appalling, dreadful
**3** some awful news
*Alternative words:* shocking, horrifying, alarming

**awkward** *adjective*
**1** an awkward person
*Alternative words:* clumsy, stiff, uncoordinated
*The opposite is **nimble***
**2** Don't be so awkward!
*Alternative words:* difficult, fussy, annoying, unhelpful
*The opposite is **easy to please***
**3** an awkward bundle
*Alternative words:* unwieldy, cumbersome, unmanageable
*The opposite is **convenient***
**4** an awkward angle
*Alternative words:* tricky, delicate, fiddly

# Bb

**babble** *verb*
1 a babbling stream
*Alternative words:* to murmur, to gurgle
2 a babbling baby
*Alternative words:* to gurgle, to burble, to chatter
3 Stop babbling!
*Alternative words:* to jabber, to gabble, to prattle

**bad** *adjective*
1 a bad illness
*Alternative words:* serious, severe, critical
*The opposite is* **minor**
2 a bad mistake
*Alternative words:* serious, disastrous, terrible
*The opposite is* **small**
3 bad food
*Alternative words:* rotten, off, mouldy, contaminated
*The opposite is* **fresh**
4 did a bad thing
*Alternative words:* naughty, dangerous, wicked, wrong
*The opposite is* **good**
5 bad weather
*Alternative words:* unpleasant, gloomy, miserable, rainy, cold, stormy
*The opposite is* **good**
6 a bad person
*Alternative words:* dishonest, sinful, naughty, wicked
*The opposite is* **good**
7 bad work
*Alternative words:* unsatisfactory, poor, incomplete, unacceptable
*The opposite is* **good**
8 bad for you
*Alternative words:* unhealthy, damaging, dangerous, harmful
*The opposite is* **good**

**baggage** *noun*
*Alternative words:* luggage, bags, suitcases, cases

**ban** *verb*
*Alternative words:* to forbid, to prohibit
*The opposite is* **to allow**

**band**¹ *noun*
band of material
*Alternative words:* belt, ribbon, cord, strap

**band**² *noun*
band of musicians
*Alternative words:* group, orchestra, ensemble

**bandit** *noun*
*Alternative words:* robber, brigand, outlaw

**banish** *verb*
*Alternative words:* to exile, to cast out, to expel, to throw out

**barbaric** *adjective*
*Alternative words:* savage, brutal, cruel

**bare** *adjective*
1 a bare person
*Alternative words:* naked, nude, undressed
2 a bare room
*Alternative words:* empty, unfurnished

**bare** *verb*
*Alternative words:* to show, to reveal, to expose

**barely** *adverb*
*Alternative words:* hardly, scarcely, only just

**bargain** *noun*
1 got a bargain
*Alternative words:* good deal, discount, reduction
2 made a bargain
*Alternative words:* pact, deal, agreement, contract

**barrier** *noun*
*Alternative words:* barricade, wall, fence, railing

**base** *noun*
1 base of a tree
*Alternative words:* bottom, foot
2 base of a statue
*Alternative words:* stand, pedestal, plinth
3 went back to their base
*Alternative words:* headquarters, camp, centre

**bashful** *adjective*
*Alternative words:* shy, timid, self-conscious, easily embarrassed
*The opposite is* **bold**

**basic** *adjective*
*Alternative words:* fundamental, key, essential

**bathe** *verb*
1 bathe in the sea
*Alternative words:* to swim, to go for a swim
2 bathe your cut
*Alternative words:* to wash, to clean

**batter** *verb*
*Alternative words:* to beat, to hit, to assault, to bash (informal)

**battle** *noun*
1 armies fighting
*Alternative words:* war, fight, attack
2 fight against something
*Alternative words:* fight, campaign, crusade, struggle

**beach** *noun*
*Alternative words:* seaside, seashore, coast, sands

**beam** *noun*
1 a beam of light
*Alternative words:* ray, shaft, streak, stream
2 a beam on her face
*Alternative words:* grin, smile
3 beam of wood or metal
*Alternative words:* plank, rafter, girder, joist

**bear**[2] *verb*
1 can't bear it
*Alternative words:* to stand, to put up with, to tolerate
2 to bear fruit
*Alternative words:* to produce, to yield, to give
3 to bear children
*Alternative words:* to have, to give birth to

**beat** *verb*
1 to beat a donkey
*Alternative words:* to hit, to wallop, to smack, to strike
2 to beat a drum
*Alternative words:* to bang, to strike, to hit, to pound
3 to beat a mixture
*Alternative words:* to stir, to whisk, to mix, to whip
4 to beat someone in a race

*Alternative words:* to defeat, to outdo, to outrun

**beautiful** *adjective*
1 a beautiful child
*Alternative words:* good-looking, pretty, attractive, handsome
2 a beautiful dress
*Alternative words:* gorgeous, lovely, pretty
3 a beautiful view
*Alternative words:* delightful, pleasant, magnificent, wonderful

**beauty** *noun*
*Alternative words:* loveliness, prettiness, attractiveness
*The opposite is* **ugliness**

**become** *verb*
1 She became tired.
*Alternative words:* to begin to be, to grow, to start to be
2 He became a friend.
*Alternative words:* to turn out to be, to turn into, to come to be

**bed** *noun*
1 asleep in a bed
*Alternative words:* cot, bunk bed, single bed, double bed, four-poster bed
2 a bed of flowers
*Alternative words:* patch, plot, border
3 the bed of the ocean
*Alternative words:* floor, bottom

**before** *preposition*
1 at an earlier time
*Alternative words:* earlier than, sooner than, prior to, in advance of
*The opposite is* **after**
2 in front of
*Alternative words:* ahead of, in front of
*The opposite is* **behind**

**before** *adverb*
*Alternative words:* previously, in the past, at an earlier time

**beg** *verb*
1 to beg for help
*Alternative words:* to ask, to plead, to request
2 to beg in the streets
*Alternative words:* to ask for money, to ask for charity, to scrounge

**begin** *verb*
*Alternative words:* to start, to

commence, to get going, to kick off (informal)
*The opposite is* **to end**

**beginner** *noun*
*Alternative words:* learner, student, trainee, apprentice

**belief** *noun*
*Alternative words:* opinion, view, feeling, conviction

**believe** *verb*
**1** to believe someone
*Alternative words:* to trust, to be convinced by, to be persuaded by
*The opposite is* **doubt**
**2** to believe in God
*Alternative words:* to have faith in, to be sure of, to be convinced about
**3** to believe it's going to rain
*Alternative words:* to think, to reckon, to suppose

**belong** *verb*
**1** to belong to someone
*Alternative words:* to be owned by, to be the property of
**2** to belong to a club
*Alternative words:* to be a member of, to be included in
**3** Shoes belong in the cupboard.
*Alternative words:* to go, to have a place, to fit

**belongings** *plural noun*
*Alternative words:* things, possessions, property, stuff, (informal)

**bend** *noun*
*Alternative words:* corner, curve, angle, turn

**bend** *verb*
**1** to bend something
*Alternative words:* to twist, to curve, to warp, to make crooked
**2** to bend in a particular direction
*Alternative words:* to curve, to curl, to veer, to turn, to twist
**3** to bend down
*Alternative words:* to stoop, to lean, to crouch

**berserk** *adjective*
*Alternative words:* crazy, wild, insane

**best** *adjective*
*Alternative words:* finest, highest, top, leading

*The opposite is* **worst**

**betray** *verb*
**1** to betray a person
*Alternative words:* to be disloyal to, to be unfaithful to, to double-cross
**2** to betray a secret
*Alternative words:* to give away, to reveal, to let slip

**better** *adjective*
**1** better than something else
*Alternative words:* superior, of higher quality, preferable
*The opposite is* **worse**
**2** a better thing to do
*Alternative words:* more suitable, more appropriate, more desirable
*The opposite is* **worse**
**3** feeling better
*Alternative words:* healthier, fitter, stronger
*The opposite is* **worse**
**4** better off
*Alternative words:* richer, wealthier, more prosperous, luckier
*The opposite is* **worse off**

**beware** *verb*
*Alternative words:* to be careful, to watch out, to be on your guard

**big** *adjective*
**1** a big thing
*Alternative words:* huge, large, enormous, gigantic, vast
*The opposite is* **small**
**2** a big person
*Alternative words:* tall, fat, heavy, stout
*The opposite is* **small**
**3** a big day
*Alternative words:* important, historic, momentous, significant

**bind** *verb*
*Alternative words:* to tie, to secure, to truss

**bit¹** *noun*
**1** bit of cloth
*Alternative words:* piece, fragment, scrap
**2** bit of cheese
*Alternative words:* crumb, sliver, morsel
**3** bit of garlic in the soup
*Alternative words:* hint, speck, trace

**bite** *verb*
**1** biting food

*Alternative words:* to gnaw, to chew, to nibble
2 a dog biting someone
*Alternative words:* to nip, to wound, to sink your teeth into, to snap at
3 A mosquito bit me.
*Alternative words:* to sting, to prick

**bitter** *adjective*
1 a bitter taste
*Alternative words:* sharp, sour, tart
*The opposite is* **sweet**
2 a bitter wind
*Alternative words:* freezing, severe, fierce
*The opposite is* **gentle**
3 feeling bitter about something
*Alternative words:* aggrieved, resentful, indignant

**blank** *adjective*
1 a blank page
*Alternative words:* clean, empty, unmarked
2 a face looking blank
*Alternative words:* impassive, lifeless, expressionless

**block** *noun*
*Alternative words:* slab, chunk, cube, hunk

**block** *verb*
*Alternative words:* to obstruct, to stop, to impede, to hinder

**bloodthirsty** *adjective*
*Alternative words:* brutal, cruel, savage, vicious

**blur** *verb*
*Alternative words:* to obscure, to make hazy, to smudge

**blurt** *verb*
*Alternative words:* to cry out, to call out, to exclaim

**boast** *verb*
*Alternative words:* to show off, to exaggerate, to blow your own trumpet

**bog** *noun*
*Alternative words:* marsh, swamp, quagmire

**bogus** *adjective*
*Alternative words:* fake, false, counterfeit, phoney

**boisterous** *adjective*
*Alternative words:* rough, unruly, lively

**bold** *adjective*
1 a bold person
*Alternative words:* courageous, daring, brave
*The opposite is* **timid**
2 bold colours
*Alternative words:* eye-catching, strong, vivid, striking
*The opposite is* **pale**

**bond** *noun*
*Alternative words:* link, connection, tie

**book** *verb*
*Alternative words:* to reserve, to order, to arrange

**boost** *verb*
*Alternative words:* to improve, to add to, to increase

**border** *noun*
1 the border between countries
*Alternative words:* boundary, frontier, line
2 the border on a poster
*Alternative words:* edge, margin

**bother** *verb*
1 something bothers you
*Alternative words:* to annoy, to disturb, to upset
2 to bother to do something
*Alternative words:* to go to the trouble, to make the effort, to take the time

**bottom** *noun*
1 an animal's bottom
*Alternative words:* rear, hindquarters, posterior, buttocks
2 the bottom of a mountain
*Alternative words:* foot, base, lowest part
*The opposite is* **top**
3 the bottom of a plate
*Alternative words:* underside, underneath, base

**bounce** *verb*
1 to bounce off the wall
*Alternative words:* to rebound, to come back, to ricochet
2 bounce on the bed
*Alternative words:* to jump, to jump up and down, to bound

**bound¹** *verb*
*Alternative words:* to leap, to jump, to spring

**boundary** *noun*
*Alternative words:* border, verge, frontier, dividing line

**bout** *noun*
1 a bout in boxing
*Alternative words:* contest, round, match
2 a bout of illness
*Alternative words:* period, spell, attack

**box¹** *noun*
*Alternative words:* crate, chest, carton

**boy** *noun*
*Alternative words:* lad, youngster, youth

**brag** *verb*
*Alternative words:* to boast, to swagger, to show off

**brain** *noun*
Use your brain!
*Alternative words:* head, brains, intelligence, brainpower

**branch** *noun*
1 tree branch
*Alternative words:* limb, bough, shoot
2 a branch of a company
*Alternative words:* division, section, part

**brave** *adjective*
*Alternative words:* courageous, intrepid, fearless, plucky
*The opposite is* **cowardly**

**brawl** *noun*
*Alternative words:* fight, scuffle, clash

**break** *verb*
1 The plate broke.
*Alternative words:* to smash, to shatter, to crack
2 The bag broke.
*Alternative words:* to tear, to burst, to come apart, to split
3 The branch broke.
*Alternative words:* to snap, to splinter, to split
4 to break the rules
*Alternative words:* to disobey, to ignore, to defy
5 to break down
*Alternative words:* to stop working, to stop moving, to be damaged, to collapse

**breakthrough** *noun*
*Alternative words:* discovery, find, advance, step forward

**breed** *noun*
*Alternative words:* kind, sort, class, species

**brief** *adjective*
1 a brief visit
*Alternative words:* short, hasty, fleeting
2 a brief description
*Alternative words:* short, concise, to the point
*The opposite is* **lengthy**

**bright** *adjective*
1 bright sunlight
*Alternative words:* blazing, blinding, dazzling
*The opposite is* **dim**
2 bright coins
*Alternative words:* glittering, glinting, shining
*The opposite is* **dull**
3 a bright child
*Alternative words:* intelligent, quick, clever
*The opposite is* **unintelligent**
4 woke up feeling bright
*Alternative words:* cheerful, happy, light-hearted
*The opposite is* **miserable**

**brilliant** *adjective*
1 brilliant jewels
*Alternative words:* sparkling, shining, glittering
*The opposite is* **dull**
2 brilliant at drawing
*Alternative words:* talented, gifted, expert, skilful
*The opposite is* **no good at**
3 a brilliant story
*Alternative words:* excellent, outstanding, superb

**broad** *adjective*
*Alternative words:* wide, large, vast
*The opposite is* **narrow**

**broadminded** *adjective*
*Alternative words:* open-minded, tolerant, flexible
*The opposite is* **narrow-minded**

**brood** *verb*
to brood about a problem

*Alternative words:* to worry, to ponder, to think, to agonise

**brook** *noun*
*Alternative words:* stream, burn, beck

**brute** *noun*
*Alternative words:* beast, savage, monster

**bubble** *verb*
*Alternative words:* to fizz, to froth, to foam, to boil

**buckle** *verb*
1 to buckle your shoes
*Alternative words:* to fasten, to do up, to clasp
2 to buckle in the heat
*Alternative words:* to bend, to crumple, to warp, to twist

**build** *verb*
*Alternative words:* to construct, to make, to erect, to assemble

**bulky** *adjective*
*Alternative words:* cumbersome, awkward, unwieldy

**bully** *verb*
*Alternative words:* to persecute, to torment, to push around (informal)

**bunch** *noun*
a bunch of flowers
*Alternative words:* bouquet, posy

**bundle** *noun*
*Alternative words:* parcel, roll, bale

**burden** *noun*
1 something heavy
*Alternative words:* load, weight
2 something worrying you
*Alternative words:* responsibility, worry, care, anxiety

**burly** *adjective*
*Alternative words:* muscular, strong, brawny, hulking
*The opposite is* **puny**

**burn** *verb*
1 Don't burn the toast!
*Alternative words:* to scorch, to char, to singe, to set on fire
2 The spicy meal made my lips burn.
*Alternative words:* to hurt, to sting, to tingle

3 to burn in a fire
*Alternative words:* to be on fire, to be alight, to be ablaze, to go up in smoke
4 The coal wouldn't burn.
*Alternative words:* ignite, light, catch fire, blaze

**business** *noun*
1 works in the hotel business
*Alternative words:* trade, occupation, profession
2 runs a successful business
*Alternative words:* company, shop, firm, organisation
3 doing business
*Alternative words:* trade, buying and selling, dealings
4 It's my business.
*Alternative words:* affair, concern, responsibility

**busy** *adjective*
1 a busy person
*Alternative words:* active, occupied, hard at work
*The opposite is* **idle**
2 a busy place
*Alternative words:* full, bustling, hectic
*The opposite is* **quiet**

# Cc

**cabin** *noun*
**1** a log cabin
*Alternative words:* house, hut, chalet, shack
**2** a cabin on a ship
*Alternative words:* room, berth, compartment

**cacophony** *noun*
*Alternative words:* caterwauling, grating, racket, din

**cake** *noun*
**1** a cake that you eat
*Alternative words:* gateau, bun, pastry
**2** a cake of soap
*Alternative words:* bar, block, slab

**calamity** *noun*
*Alternative words:* disaster, catastrophe, tragedy

**calculate** *verb*
*Alternative words:* to work out, to estimate, to figure out

**call** *verb*
**1** to call someone
*Alternative words:* to shout to, to call out to, to summon
**2** to call something out
*Alternative words:* to cry out, to say, to shout out
**3** to call someone something
*Alternative words:* to name, to christen, to dub
**4** to call someone on the telephone
*Alternative words:* to ring, to ring up, to phone, to telephone, to dial

**callous** *adjective*
*Alternative words:* cold, uncaring, unfeeling, heartless
*The opposite is* **compassionate**

**calm** *adjective*
**1** calm sea
*Alternative words:* still, smooth, not moving
*The opposite is* **stormy**
**2** calm surroundings
*Alternative words:* peaceful, restful, tranquil
*The opposite is* **noisy**
**3** feeling calm

*Alternative words:* relaxed, composed, cool

**cancel** *verb*
*Alternative words:* to call off, to abolish, to stop

**capable** *adjective*
**1** capable of doing something
*Alternative words:* able, competent
*The opposite is* **incapable**
**2** a capable swimmer
*Alternative words:* good, skilful, proficient, experienced
*The opposite is* **poor**

**caper**[2] *verb*
*Alternative words:* to dance, to frolic, to gambol

**captive** *noun*
*Alternative words:* prisoner, hostage, slave

**captive** *adjective*
*Alternative words:* locked up, imprisoned, confined
*The opposite is* **free**

**capture** *verb*
*Alternative words:* to seize, to take prisoner, to catch

**care** *noun*
**1** do something with care
*Alternative words:* attention, carefulness, consideration, thought
**2** to take care
*Alternative words:* to be careful, to be cautious, to beware, to watch your step
**3** to take care of someone
*Alternative words:* to care for, to tend, to look after, to nurse

**care** *verb*
**1** to care about something
*Alternative words:* to be concerned, to be interested, to bother, to mind
**2** to care for someone
*Alternative words:* to be fond of, to love, to like
**3** to care for an injured animal
*Alternative words:* to look after, to tend, to nurse, to take care of

**careful** *adjective*
**1** careful working
*Alternative words:* accurate, thoughtful, conscientious, painstaking
*The opposite is* **careless**

**2** careful crossing a road
*Alternative words:* alert, wary, vigilant
*The opposite is* **careless**

**careless** *adjective*
**1** careless working
*Alternative words:* inaccurate, hasty,
slapdash
*The opposite is* **careful**
**2** careless crossing a road
*Alternative words:* absent-minded,
inattentive, unthinking
*The opposite is* **careful**

**caress** *verb*
*Alternative words:* to stroke, to fondle,
to nuzzle, to cuddle

**carry** *verb*
**1** to carry something
*Alternative words:* to lift, to take,
to bring, to transport
**2** to carry on doing something
*Alternative words:* to continue, to go on,
to keep, to persist
**3** to carry out a plan
*Alternative words:* to fulfil, to achieve,
to carry through

**carve** *verb*
**1** to carve meat
*Alternative words:* to cut, to slice, to cut
up
**2** to carve wood
*Alternative words:* to sculpt, to whittle,
to hew
**3** letters carved in stone
*Alternative words:* to engrave, to incise,
to cut

**castle** *noun*
*Alternative words:* fortress, palace,
tower, keep

**casual** *adjective*
**1** casual clothes
*Alternative words:* comfortable, leisure,
informal
*The opposite is* **smart**
**2** acting in a casual way
*Alternative words:* relaxed, calm,
unconcerned
**3** a casual meeting
*Alternative words:* chance, accidental,
unforeseen
*The opposite is* **planned**

**catalogue** *noun*
*Alternative words:* list, directory, index,
brochure, guide

**catastrophe** *noun*
*Alternative words:* disaster, tragedy,
calamity

**catch** *verb*
**1** to catch a thief
*Alternative words:* to seize, to arrest,
to capture
**2** to catch a rabbit
*Alternative words:* to trap, to snare
**3** to catch a ball
*Alternative words:* to grasp, to clutch,
to hold
**4** to catch an illness
*Alternative words:* to get, to develop,
to come down with (informal)
**5** to catch someone in the act
*Alternative words:* to discover, to
surprise, to detect
**6** to catch a bus
*Alternative words:* to get on, to be in
time for, to board

**category** *noun*
*Alternative words:* group, classification,
sort, kind, type

**cause** *noun*
**1** the cause of something
*Alternative words:* reason, origin,
beginning
**2** fighting for a cause
*Alternative words:* principle, belief, ideal

**cause** *verb*
*Alternative words:* to bring about,
to lead to, to result in

**cautious** *adjective*
*Alternative words:* careful, wary,
tentative
*The opposite is* **reckless**

**celebrate** *verb*
**1** Let's celebrate!
*Alternative words:* to enjoy yourself,
to rejoice, to party (informal)
**2** to celebrate an anniversary
*Alternative words:* to commemorate,
to honour, to mark

**central** *adjective*
**1** central on the page
*Alternative words:* centred, in the
middle, in the centre
**2** a central character
*Alternative words:* important, main, key

**centre** noun
*Alternative words:* middle, heart, midpoint

**certain** adjective
1 Are you certain?
*Alternative words:* sure, positive, convinced
*The opposite is **uncertain***
2 certain things
*Alternative words:* some, particular, specific

**challenge** verb
*Alternative words:* to dare, to defy, to tackle

**challenging** adjective
*Alternative words:* testing, stimulating, taxing

**chance** noun
1 a chance to do it
*Alternative words:* opportunity, occasion, possibility
2 a chance that it will happen
*Alternative words:* possibility, prospect, likelihood
3 happening by chance
*Alternative words:* accident, luck, coincidence, fortune

**change** noun
1 make some changes
*Alternative words:* alteration, innovation, modification, difference
2 enjoyed the change
*Alternative words:* variety, novelty, variation
3 change in your pocket
*Alternative words:* coins, cash

**change** verb
1 to become different
*Alternative words:* to alter, to adapt, to vary, to look different, to be different
2 to make something different
*Alternative words:* to alter, to adapt, to revise, to modify, to transform

**chaos** noun
*Alternative words:* confusion, pandemonium, upheaval

**character** noun
1 a character in a story
*Alternative words:* person, part, role
2 someone's character
*Alternative words:* nature, personality, temperament

**charge** verb
1 to charge a price
*Alternative words:* to ask, to fix, to expect
2 to charge at someone
*Alternative words:* to attack, to assault, to rush
3 to charge a building
*Alternative words:* to storm, to attack, to open fire on

**charm** noun
*Alternative words:* amulet, talisman, good-luck charm

**charming** adjective
1 a charming person
*Alternative words:* likeable, agreeable, pleasant
2 a charming thing
*Alternative words:* lovely, irresistible, appealing
3 a charming place
*Alternative words:* pleasant, enchanting, delightful

**chase** verb
*Alternative words:* to run after, to pursue, to follow, to hunt

**chat** verb
*Alternative words:* to natter, to gossip, to talk

**chatter** verb
1 people chattering
*Alternative words:* to chat, to jabber, to prattle
2 teeth chattering
*Alternative words:* to knock, to rattle, to click

**cheap** adjective
*Alternative words:* inexpensive, cut-price, reasonable, reduced
*The opposite is **expensive***

**cheat** verb
*Alternative words:* to act unfairly, to deceive, to trick

**check** verb
1 to check the oil in the car
*Alternative words:* to look at, to inspect, to test, to examine
2 to check that you have done something
*Alternative words:* to make sure,

to verify, to confirm
**3** to check someone's progress
*Alternative words:* to stop, to impede, to halt

**cheeky** *adjective*
*Alternative words:* impudent, impertinent, insolent, rude

**cheerful** *adjective*
*Alternative words:* happy, light-hearted, in good spirits
*The opposite is* **depressed**

**chew** *verb*
*Alternative words:* to gnaw, to grind, to munch, to bite

**chief** *noun*
*Alternative words:* leader, captain, head, boss (informal)

**chief** *adjective*
*Alternative words:* main, primary, principal, essential

**child** *noun*
*Alternative words:* infant, toddler, youngster, kid (informal)

**childish** *adjective*
*Alternative words:* immature, silly, foolish, infantile
*The opposite is* **mature**

**choose** *verb*
*Alternative words:* to pick, to select, to opt for

**chop** *verb*
**1** to chop down a tree
*Alternative words:* to cut down, to fell, to hack down
**2** to chop wood
*Alternative words:* to cut up, to hew

**circuit** *noun*
*Alternative words:* track, loop, route

**claim** *verb*
**1** to claim what is yours
*Alternative words:* to demand, to ask for, to call for
**2** to claim that you are right
*Alternative words:* to state, to insist, to maintain

**clamber** *verb*
*Alternative words:* to climb, to scramble, to scrabble

**class** *noun*
**1** your class at school
*Alternative words:* form, set, group
**2** a class of animals, plants or objects
*Alternative words:* category, kind, grouping, species, group, set, sort, type
**3** a class in society
*Alternative words:* rank, level, group

**classic** *adjective*
**1** a classic example
*Alternative words:* typical, model, standard
**2** a classic novel
*Alternative words:* long-lasting, enduring

**classify** *verb*
*Alternative words:* to sort, to categorise, to arrange

**clean** *verb*
*Alternative words:* to wash, to scrub, to scour

**clean** *adjective*
**1** a clean shirt
*Alternative words:* washed, laundered, immaculate, fresh
*The opposite is* **dirty**
**2** a clean face
*Alternative words:* washed, scrubbed
*The opposite is* **dirty**
**3** clean water
*Alternative words:* pure, clear, unpolluted
*The opposite is* **dirty**

**clear** *verb*
**1** to clear things away
*Alternative words:* to tidy, to remove, to take away
**2** to clear a gate
*Alternative words:* to leap over, to jump over, to vault
**3** to clear someone of a crime
*Alternative words:* to acquit, to absolve, to pardon

**clear** *adjective*
**1** make something clear
*Alternative words:* obvious, apparent, plain, unmistakable
**2** clear voices
*Alternative words:* distinct, audible, recognisable
*The opposite is* **indistinct**
**3** clear glass

*Alternative words:* transparent, see-through
*The opposite is* **opaque**
**4** a clear road ahead
*Alternative words:* open, empty, unobstructed
*The opposite is* **blocked**

**clever** *adjective*
**1** a clever person
*Alternative words:* quick-witted, intelligent, educated, brainy (informal)
**2** a clever plan
*Alternative words:* cunning, inventive, sensible, wise

**cliff** *noun*
*Alternative words:* precipice, rock-face, crag

**close** *adjective*
**1** close to something
*Alternative words:* near, adjacent, neighbouring
**2** close in time
*Alternative words:* approaching, coming up to, looming
**3** close friends
*Alternative words:* intimate, dear, inseparable
**4** a close look
*Alternative words:* careful, thorough, detailed
**5** a close contest
*Alternative words:* evenly matched, neck-and-neck, hard-fought

**cloth** *noun*
**1** thick cloth
*Alternative words:* material, fabric, textile
**2** a wet cloth
*Alternative words:* rag, sponge, flannel

**club** *noun*
**1** a chess club
*Alternative words:* group, association, society
**2** a club for hitting with
*Alternative words:* stick, cudgel, truncheon

**clumsy** *adjective*
*Alternative words:* awkward, ungainly, uncoordinated, accident-prone, gawky

**clutch** *verb*
*Alternative words:* to grasp, to grab, to grip, to snatch

**coast** *noun*
*Alternative words:* coastline, beach, shore, seaside

**coax** *verb*
*Alternative words:* to entice, to cajole, to persuade

**cold** *adjective*
**1** cold outside
*Alternative words:* freezing, wintry, icy, frosty, bitter
*The opposite is* **hot**
**2** a cold drink
*Alternative words:* cool, refreshing, chilled, iced
*The opposite is* **hot**

**collapse** *verb*
**1** to collapse in the playground
*Alternative words:* to faint, to pass out, to fall
**2** to collapse under the weight
*Alternative words:* to crumple, to give way, to cave in

**collect** *verb*
**1** to collect your things
*Alternative words:* to gather, to put together, to accumulate, to assemble
**2** to collect someone from the station
*Alternative words:* to meet, to pick up, to fetch, to go and get

**collection** *noun*
**1** a collection of old newspapers
*Alternative words:* pile, heap, store, stack
**2** a collection of stories
*Alternative words:* anthology, compilation, treasury
**3** a collection of stamps
*Alternative words:* set, assortment

**collide** *verb*
*Alternative words:* to bump, to hit, to crash

**colour** *noun*
*Alternative words:* shade, hue, tone

**column** *noun*
**1** a stone column
*Alternative words:* pillar, support, post, obelisk
**2** a column of ants
*Alternative words:* line, string, procession, file
**3** a column in a newspaper

21

*Alternative words:* article, piece, item

**combine** *verb*
*Alternative words:* to mix, to blend,
to join, to unite

**come** *verb*
1 to come on Thursday
*Alternative words:* to arrive, to get there,
to turn up (informal)
2 tried to get the dog to come
*Alternative words:* to approach, to come
near, to move nearer

**comfort** *verb*
*Alternative words:* to console,
to reassure, to soothe

**comfortable** *adjective*
1 a comfortable bed
*Alternative words:* soft, cosy, snug
*The opposite is* **uncomfortable**
2 felt comfortable
*Alternative words:* relaxed, at ease,
contented
*The opposite is* **uncomfortable**

**comic** *adjective*
*Alternative words:* funny, humorous,
amusing

**command** *verb*
1 to command someone to leave
*Alternative words:* to order, to tell,
to instruct
2 to command a ship
*Alternative words:* to be in charge of,
to control, to be in command of

**compete** *verb*
*Alternative words:* to challenge, to take
part, to enter

**competitor** *noun*
*Alternative words:* contestant,
challenger, rival, opponent

**complain** *verb*
*Alternative words:* to grumble, to moan,
to find fault, to whinge (informal)

**complete** *verb*
1 to complete a task
*Alternative words:* to finish, to do,
to accomplish
2 to complete the effect
*Alternative words:* to round off, to make
perfect, to add the finishing touches to

**complete** *adjective*
1 a complete set

*Alternative words:* full, whole, entire
*The opposite is* **incomplete**
2 Is your work complete?
*Alternative words:* finished,
accomplished, completed
3 a complete change
*Alternative words:* total, utter, absolute,
thorough

**complicated** *adjective*
1 a complicated plot
*Alternative words:* intricate, complex,
involved
*The opposite is* **simple**
2 a complicated problem
*Alternative words:* difficult, puzzling,
problematic
*The opposite is* **simple**

**condemn** *verb*
*Alternative words:* to denounce,
to disapprove, to criticise

**confess** *verb*
*Alternative words:* to admit, to own up,
to plead guilty

**confine** *verb*
*Alternative words:* to keep in, to shut
up, to coop up

**confuse** *verb*
1 to confuse someone
*Alternative words:* to muddle,
to bewilder, to mystify, to perplex
2 to confuse two things
*Alternative words:* to mix up, to mistake

**connect** *verb*
1 a road connecting the towns
*Alternative words:* to join, to link,
to bridge
2 to connect one part to another
*Alternative words:* to fasten, to attach,
to couple
3 to connect things in your mind
*Alternative words:* to associate, to relate,
to link

**conquer** *verb*
*Alternative words:* to defeat, to
overthrow, to beat, to vanquish

**consequence** *noun*
*Alternative words:* result, outcome,
effect

**consider** *verb*
*Alternative words:* to think about,
to mull over, to weigh up

**construct** *verb*
*Alternative words:* to build, to make, to put together

**consult** *verb*
**1** to consult the doctor
*Alternative words:* to talk to, to get advice from, to ask
**2** to consult a dictionary
*Alternative words:* to look at, to refer to, to study

**contact** *verb*
*Alternative words:* to get in touch with, to communicate with, to write to, to speak to

**contain** *verb*
*Alternative words:* to hold, to have room for, to include

**contaminate** *verb*
*Alternative words:* to pollute, to infect, to spoil

**contempt** *noun*
*Alternative words:* disrespect, scorn, loathing

**continue** *verb*
**1** The rain continued.
*Alternative words:* to last, to persist, to keep on
*The opposite is* **to stop**
**2** Continue with your work.
*Alternative words:* to go on, to carry on, to persevere
*The opposite is* **to stop**

**contribution** *noun*
*Alternative words:* donation, offering, gift

**convenient** *adjective*
**1** a convenient shop
*Alternative words:* handy, nearby, useful
**2** a convenient moment
*Alternative words:* suitable, opportune, well-timed
*The opposite is* **inconvenient**
**3** a convenient gadget
*Alternative words:* helpful, labour-saving, handy, useful
*The opposite is* **useless**

**conversation** *noun*
*Alternative words:* chat, talk, discussion

**convince** *verb*
*Alternative words:* to persuade, to satisfy, to win over

**cook** *verb*
**1** to cook dinner
*Alternative words:* to prepare, to make, to get ready
**2** to cook food
*Alternative words:* to bake, to roast, to fry, to boil, to steam, to grill

**cool** *adjective*
**1** cool water
*Alternative words:* refreshing, chilled, cold
*The opposite is* **warm**
**2** Keep cool!
*Alternative words:* calm, composed, level-headed
*The opposite is* **excited**

**cooperate** *verb*
*Alternative words:* to work together, to help each other, to collaborate, to join forces

**cooperation** *noun*
*Alternative words:* teamwork, combined effort, unity

**copy** *verb*
**1** to copy a poem
*Alternative words:* to write out, to reproduce, to photocopy
**2** to copy someone's actions
*Alternative words:* to mimic, to imitate, to repeat

**correct** *adjective*
**1** The sums were correct.
*Alternative words:* right, accurate
*The opposite is* **incorrect**
**2** the correct time
*Alternative words:* right, accurate, exact, precise
**3** the correct thing to do
*Alternative words:* right, proper, appropriate, acceptable, polite
*The opposite is* **wrong**

**correct** *verb*
*Alternative words:* to put right, to amend, to rectify

**count** *verb*
**1** to count objects
*Alternative words:* to add up, to calculate, to tot up
**2** Your vote will count
*Alternative words:* to matter, to be

23

important, to mean something

**couple** *noun*
**1** a couple of days
*Alternative words:* two, a few, two or three
**2** a couple of things or people
*Alternative words:* pair, duo, twosome
**3** a happy couple
*Alternative words:* husband and wife

**cover** *noun*
**1** a cover to protect something
*Alternative words:* case, covering, canopy, wrapper
**2** covers on a bed
*Alternative words:* bedclothes, bedspread, blanket, duvet, sheet

**cover** *verb*
**1** to cover a baby
*Alternative words:* to wrap, to clothe
**2** to cover a cake with icing
*Alternative words:* to coat, to spread, to plaster
**3** to cover a distance
*Alternative words:* to travel, to go, to traverse
**4** a book covering several subjects
*Alternative words:* to include, to contain, to deal with, to comprise

**crack** *noun*
**1** a crack in a plate
*Alternative words:* chip, break
**2** looking through a crack
*Alternative words:* gap, space, slit, chink
**3** a crack of thunder
*Alternative words:* crash, clap, burst, bang

**crafty** *adjective*
*Alternative words:* cunning, clever, sly

**craze** *noun*
*Alternative words:* fad, fashion, enthusiasm, obsession

**crazy** *adjective*
**1** a crazy thing to do
*Alternative words:* mad, foolish, silly, idiotic
*The opposite is* **sensible**
**2** crazy ideas
*Alternative words:* eccentric, unusual, bizarre
**3** crazy about something or someone
*Alternative words:* mad about, keen on, infatuated with

*The opposite is* **indifferent**

**create** *verb*
*Alternative words:* to make, to design, to invent

**creation** *noun*
**1** the creation of life
*Alternative words:* making, starting, producing
**2** my own creation
*Alternative words:* idea, invention, handiwork, brainchild
**3** the fiercest giant in creation
*Alternative words:* the world, the universe, nature

**creator** *noun*
*Alternative words:* maker, designer, inventor, originator

**credible** *adjective*
*Alternative words:* believable, plausible, likely, reasonable
*The opposite is* **implausible**

**criminal** *noun*
*Alternative words:* law-breaker, offender, wrong-doer, crook (informal)

**cripple** *verb*
**1** to cripple someone
*Alternative words:* to injure, to maim, to paralyse
**2** to cripple something
*Alternative words:* to damage, to put out of action, to bring to a standstill

**crisis** *noun*
*Alternative words:* dilemma, emergency

**critical** *adjective*
**1** critical of other people
*Alternative words:* disapproving, fault-finding, scathing
**2** a critical situation
*Alternative words:* crucial, decisive, important, momentous
**3** in a critical condition in hospital
*Alternative words:* serious, dangerous, risky, touch-and-go

**criticise** *verb*
**1** to criticise things or people
*Alternative words:* to complain, to nag, to find fault
*The opposite is* **to praise**
**2** to criticise a book
*Alternative words:* to review, to give an opinion, to comment

**crooked** *adjective*
**1** crooked teeth
*Alternative words:* misshapen, irregular, twisted, bent
*The opposite is* **straight**
**2** a crooked path
*Alternative words:* curving, winding, zigzag
*The opposite is* **straight**
**3** a crooked picture
*Alternative words:* lopsided, slanting, tilted, asymmetrical
*The opposite is* **straight**
**4** a crooked scheme
*Alternative words:* dishonest, illegal, deceitful
*The opposite is* **honest**

**crouch** *verb*
*Alternative words:* to stoop, to bend down, to squat

**crowd** *noun*
*Alternative words:* mob, throng, horde, group

**cruel** *adjective*
**1** a cruel person
*Alternative words:* harsh, vicious, ruthless, unkind
*The opposite is* **kind**
**2** a cruel thing to say
*Alternative words:* spiteful, unkind, heartless, mean
*The opposite is* **kind**

**crush** *verb*
**1** to crush grapes
*Alternative words:* to squash, to squeeze, to press
**2** to crush a sugar lump
*Alternative words:* to crumble, to pound, to smash
**3** to crush an army
*Alternative words:* to overcome, to conquer, to put down

**cry** *verb*
**1** to cry
*Alternative words:* to weep, to sob, to shed tears
**2** to cry out
*Alternative words:* to shout, to exclaim, to shriek, to yell

**cure** *verb*
*Alternative words:* to heal, to make well, to treat

**cure** *noun*
*Alternative words:* treatment, remedy, therapy

**curious** *adjective*
**1** curious about someone
*Alternative words:* interested, inquisitive, nosy (informal)
**2** a curious sight
*Alternative words:* strange, unusual, odd

**curve** *noun*
*Alternative words:* bend, arc, arch

**custom** *noun*
*Alternative words:* habit, tradition, ritual, way

**cut** *verb*
**1** to cut hair
*Alternative words:* to trim, to snip, to clip
**2** to cut food
*Alternative words:* to cut up, to chop up, to carve
**3** to cut your leg
*Alternative words:* to nick, to wound, to gash, to slash

# Dd

**damage** *noun*
1 damage to your body or health
*Alternative words:* harm, injury
2 damage to something
*Alternative words:* harm, destruction, devastation

**damage** *verb*
1 to damage something
*Alternative words:* to break, to spoil, to wreck
*The opposite is* **to repair**
2 to damage your body or health
*Alternative words:* to harm, to hurt, to injure, to wound, to maim, to mutilate

**danger** *noun*
1 something that is not safe
*Alternative words:* risk, hazard, peril
2 someone or something that could hurt you
*Alternative words:* risk, threat, menace
3 to be in danger
*Alternative words:* in trouble, in distress, at risk

**dangerous** *adjective*
1 a dangerous act
*Alternative words:* risky, perilous, hazardous
*The opposite is* **safe**
2 a dangerous substance
*Alternative words:* harmful, poisonous, toxic, deadly, lethal
*The opposite is* **harmless**
3 a dangerous person
*Alternative words:* violent, desperate
*The opposite is* **harmless**

**dark** *adjective*
1 a dark night
*Alternative words:* black, pitch-black, starless
*The opposite is* **light**
2 a dark place
*Alternative words:* gloomy, shady
*The opposite is* **bright**

**dawn** *noun*
1 early in the morning
*Alternative words:* daybreak, sunrise, first light
*The opposite is* **dusk**
2 the beginning of something new
*Alternative words:* start, beginning, birth
*The opposite is* **end**

**dead** *adjective*
1 a dead person
*Alternative words:* deceased, at rest, departed
*The opposite is* **alive**
2 a dead place
*Alternative words:* quiet, empty, deserted
*The opposite is* **busy**

**deadly** *adjective*
1 a deadly disease or injury
*Alternative words:* terminal, fatal, mortal
2 a deadly poison
*Alternative words:* toxic, lethal, killer (informal)
*The opposite is* **harmless**

**deal** *noun*
*Alternative words:* agreement, arrangement, contract

**deal** *verb*
1 to deal with something or someone
*Alternative words:* manage, handle, attend to
2 to deal with someone in business
*Alternative words:* to do business, to trade, to buy and sell (informal)

**dear** *adjective*
1 costing a lot of money
*Alternative words:* expensive, costly
*The opposite is* **cheap**
2 a dear friend
*Alternative words:* loved, beloved, close, intimate

**debate** *verb*
*Alternative words:* to exchange views, to discuss, to thrash out (informal)

**decay** *verb*
*Alternative words:* to go bad, to rot, to decompose, to putrefy

**deceive** *verb*
*Alternative words:* to trick, to cheat, to mislead, to double-cross, to con (informal)

**decide** *verb*
*Alternative words:* to conclude, to come to a conclusion, to make up your mind

**decided** *adjective*
*Alternative words:* certain, definite,

settled
*The opposite is* **undecided**

**decisive** *adjective*
1 a decisive person
*Alternative words:* firm, strong-minded, resolute
*The opposite is* **indecisive**
2 a decisive event
*Alternative words:* conclusive, crucial, final
*The opposite is* **inconclusive**

**decline** *verb*
1 to become less
*Alternative words:* to decrease, to dwindle, to diminish
*The opposite is* **to increase**
2 to become worse
*Alternative words:* to get worse, to get weaker, to deteriorate
*The opposite is* **to improve**
3 to say no
*Alternative words:* to refuse, to turn down, to send your regrets (formal)
*The opposite is* **to accept**

**decorate** *verb*
1 a hat decorated with flowers
*Alternative words:* to adorn, to ornament
2 Dad decorated my bedroom.
*Alternative words:* to wallpaper, to paper, to paint, to do up (informal)

**decrease** *verb*
1 to decrease the amount
*Alternative words:* to cut, to cut down, to reduce
*The opposite is* **to increase**
2 the number decreased
*Alternative words:* to get smaller, to go down, to lessen
*The opposite is* **to increase**

**decrease** *noun*
*Alternative words:* drop, reduction, decline
*The opposite is* **increase**

**decrepit** *adjective*
1 a decrepit person
*Alternative words:* old and infirm
2 a decrepit thing
*Alternative words:* dilapidated, broken-down

**dedicate** *verb*
1 to dedicate time

*Alternative words:* to devote, to commit, to give over
2 to dedicate a book
*Alternative words:* to inscribe, to address

**deface** *verb*
*Alternative words:* to spoil, to vandalise, to trash (informal)

**defeat** *verb*
*Alternative words:* to beat, to conquer, to thrash (informal)

**defective** *adjective*
*Alternative words:* faulty, imperfect, out of order
*The opposite is* **perfect**

**defer** *verb*
*Alternative words:* to put off, to postpone, to delay
*The opposite is* **to bring forward**

**dejected** *adjective*
*Alternative words:* downhearted, depressed, in low spirits, dispirited
*The opposite is* **optimistic**

**delay** *verb*
1 to do later
*Alternative words:* to put off, to postpone, to defer
2 to make late
*Alternative words:* to hold up, to set back, to slow down

**deliberate** *adjective*
*Alternative words:* on purpose, intentional, planned
*The opposite is* **accidental**

**deliberate** *verb*
*Alternative words:* to think over, to mull over, to reflect on

**delicate** *adjective*
1 carefully made
*Alternative words:* fine, elegant, exquisite
*The opposite is* **rough**
2 easily broken
*Alternative words:* fragile, breakable, brittle
*The opposite is* **sturdy**

**delicious** *adjective*
*Alternative words:* appetising, delectable, mouth-watering

**delight** *noun*
*Alternative words:* joy, happiness, bliss
*The opposite is* **despair**

**delusion** *noun*
*Alternative words:* false impression, illusion, misbelief, misconception

**demand** *verb*
*Alternative words:* to order, to claim, to insist on, to request

**demolish** *verb*
to demolish a building
*Alternative words:* to destroy, to knock down, to raze

**demonstrate** *verb*
**1** to demonstrate a machine
*Alternative words:* to show how, to explain, to illustrate
**2** to demonstrate against something
*Alternative words:* to protest, to picket, to rally, to march

**descend** *verb*
*Alternative words:* to go down, to sink, to drop
*The opposite is* **to ascend**

**desert** *verb*
*Alternative words:* to abandon, to walk out on, to leave in the lurch (informal)

**deserve** *verb*
*Alternative words:* to earn, to merit, to be entitled to

**destroy** *verb*
to destroy a thing or place
*Alternative words:* to wreck, to demolish, to devastate

**deteriorate** *verb*
*Alternative words:* to get worse, to go downhill (informal), to decline, to degenerate
*The opposite is* **to improve**

**devour** *verb*
*Alternative words:* to wolf down, to gobble up

**different** *adjective*
*Alternative words:* unlike, dissimilar, contrasting
*The opposite is* **the same**

**difficult** *adjective*
*Alternative words:* hard, complicated, tricky
*The opposite is* **easy**

**difficulty** *noun*
*Alternative words:* trouble, problem, complication, obstacle

**dingy** *adjective*
*Alternative words:* shabby, dark, dull, gloomy, dreary

**diplomatic** *adjective*
*Alternative words:* tactful, polite, subtle
*The opposite is* **blunt**

**dire** *adjective*
*Alternative words:* terrible, awful, dreadful, atrocious
*The opposite is* **wonderful**

**dirt** *noun*
**1** a substance that makes things dirty
*Alternative words:* muck, filth, grime, gunge (informal)
**2** earth
*Alternative words:* soil, loam

**dirty** *adjective*
not clean
*Alternative words:* filthy, grimy, grubby, soiled
*The opposite is* **clean**

**disaster** *noun*
*Alternative words:* catastrophe, calamity, tragedy

**discover** *verb*
**1** to discover information
*Alternative words:* to find out, to ascertain
**2** to discover something lost or unknown
*Alternative words:* to find, to come across, to bring to light, to uncover
**3** to discover a new thing
*Alternative words:* to invent, to originate

**discuss** *verb*
*Alternative words:* to talk over, to debate, to consult with, to thrash out (informal)

**dishonest** *adjective*
*Alternative words:* deceitful, untruthful, crooked (informal)
*The opposite is* **honest**

**dislike** *verb*
*Alternative words:* to detest, to hate, to loathe, to despise
*The opposite is* **to like**

**disobey** *verb*
*Alternative words:* to violate, to flout, to overstep the mark, to defy

*The opposite is* **to obey**

**display** *verb*
*Alternative words:* to show, to exhibit,
to put on view

**distress** *noun*
**1** a feeling of distress
*Alternative words:* misery, torment,
anguish
**2** a ship in distress
*Alternative words:* in trouble, in danger,
in peril

**disturb** *verb*
**1** to disturb a busy person
*Alternative words:* to bother,
to interrupt, to butt in
**2** to worry someone
*Alternative words:* to upset, to perturb
**3** to disturb something
*Alternative words:* to mess up, to fiddle
with (informal), to interfere with

**dive** *verb*
*Alternative words:* to plunge, to plummet

**divide** *verb*
**1** to divide something into smaller
parts
*Alternative words:* to break up,
to separate, to subdivide
**2** to divide something between people
*Alternative words:* to share out,
to distribute

**dominate** *verb*
*Alternative words:* to control, to rule,
to command

**donate** *verb*
*Alternative words:* to give, to contribute,
to bestow, to bequeath

**donation** *noun*
*Alternative words:* gift, contribution,
pledge

**doom** *noun*
*Alternative words:* fate, ruin, downfall

**doomed** *adjective*
**1** doomed to fail
*Alternative words:* cursed, jinxed
**2** doomed to something
*Alternative words:* fated, destined

**doubt** *verb*
*Alternative words:* to question,
to mistrust, to feel unsure

**doubtful** *adjective*
**1** something that is doubtful
*Alternative words:* uncertain, unlikely,
questionable, dubious
**2** to feel doubtful
*Alternative words:* uncertain, dubious,
sceptical
*The opposite is* **certain**

**doubtless** *adverb*
*Alternative words:* certainly, definitely,
most likely

**downhearted** *adjective*
*Alternative words:* sad, in low spirits,
dejected
*The opposite is* **optimistic**

**drag** *verb*
*Alternative words:* to pull, to haul, to tow

**dramatic** *adjective*
**1** a dramatic event
*Alternative words:* breathtaking,
electrifying, sensational, spectacular
**2** a dramatic change
*Alternative words:* sudden, rapid,
complete, radical

**drastic** *adjective*
*Alternative words:* extreme, radical
*The opposite is* **moderate**

**drawback** *noun*
*Alternative words:* problem,
disadvantage, hitch
*The opposite is* **advantage**

**dread** *noun*
*Alternative words:* fear, terror, horror

**dread** *verb*
*Alternative words:* to fear, to be afraid of

**dreadful** *adjective*
*Alternative words:* awful, terrible,
appalling

**dream** *noun*
*Alternative words:* vision, illusion,
fantasy

**dreary** *adjective*
*Alternative words:* boring, dull, depressing

**drench** *verb*
*Alternative words:* to soak, to drown,
to saturate

**drink** *noun*
**1** alcohol

*Alternative words:* liquor, spirits, booze (informal)

**2** a non-alcoholic drink
*Alternative words:* beverage, soft drink, mineral

**3** a drink of something
*Alternative words:* sip, gulp, swig (informal)

**drink** *verb*
**1** to drink any liquid
*Alternative words:* to sip, to gulp, to guzzle (informal), to swig (informal)

**2** to drink a lot of alcohol
*Alternative words:* to booze (informal), to hit the bottle (informal)

**drip** *verb*
*Alternative words:* to splash, to trickle, to dribble, to plop

**drop** *noun*
**1** a drop of something to drink
*Alternative words:* sip, dash, splash

**2** a drop of liquid
*Alternative words:* droplet, bead, dribble, trickle

**drop** *verb*
**1** to let something drop
*Alternative words:* to let fall, to let go, to lower
*The opposite is **to raise***

**2** something that drops
*Alternative words:* to fall, to dive, to descend, to plummet
*The opposite is **to rise***

**3** to drop in price or value
*Alternative words:* to fall, to dip, to slump
*The opposite is **to increase***

**drowsy** *adjective*
*Alternative words:* sleepy, half-asleep, tired
*The opposite is **wide awake***

**drunk** *adjective*
**1** slightly drunk
*Alternative words:* merry, sloshed (informal)

**2** very drunk
*Alternative words:* inebriated, plastered (informal), paralytic (informal)
*The opposite is **sober***

**dry** *adjective*
a dry area
*Alternative words:* arid, barren

*The opposite is **humid***

**due** *adjective*
*Alternative words:* expected, anticipated, scheduled

**dull** *adjective*
**1** not interesting
*Alternative words:* boring, mind-numbing, dreary, tedious
*The opposite is **interesting***

**2** a dull colour
*Alternative words:* faded, drab, washed out
*The opposite is **bright***

**3** a dull day
*Alternative words:* cloudy, overcast, gloomy, dismal
*The opposite is **sunny***

**4** a dull blade
*Alternative word:* blunt
*The opposite is **sharp***

**dusk** *noun*
*Alternative words:* twilight, nightfall, sunset
*The opposite is **dawn***

**dwelling** *noun*
*Alternative words:* home, house, abode (formal)

**dwindle** *verb*
**1** to become less
*Alternative words:* to decline, to shrink, to decrease, to diminish
*The opposite is **to increase***

**2** to become weaker
*Alternative words:* to fade, to weaken
*The opposite is **to get stronger***

# Ee

**eager** *adjective*
*Alternative words:* keen, enthusiastic, raring to go (informal)

**early** *adverb*
*Alternative words:* ahead of time, in advance, prematurely
*The opposite is* **late**

**earn** *verb*
**1** to earn money
*Alternative words:* to make, to bring in, to work for
**2** to earn praise
*Alternative words:* to deserve, to merit, to warrant

**easily** *adverb*
*Alternative words:* without trouble, without difficulty, effortlessly, without a hitch (informal)
*The opposite is* **with difficulty**

**easy** *adjective*
**1** not difficult
*Alternative words:* straightforward, simple, not difficult, not complicated, child's play
*The opposite is* **hard** or **difficult**
**2** an easy life
*Alternative words:* carefree, comfortable, cushy (informal)
*The opposite is* **hard**

**ebb** *verb*
**1** the tide or water ebbs
*Alternative words:* to go out, to flow back, to retreat, to recede
**2** to get weaker and weaker
*Alternative words:* to fade, to decline, to wane

**eccentric** *adjective*
*Alternative words:* odd, unconventional, weird
*The opposite is* **normal**

**economise** *verb*
*Alternative words:* to save, to cut back, to tighten your belt (informal)

**edge** *noun*
**1** the edge of an area
*Alternative words:* side, border, margin, perimeter, limits
**2** the edge of a container

*Alternative words:* rim, brim, lip
**3** the edge of a cliff
*Alternative words:* brink, verge, ridge

**edgy** *adjective*
*Alternative words:* tense, anxious, nervous, uptight (informal)
*The opposite is* **calm**

**educate** *verb*
*Alternative words:* to teach, to train, to instruct

**education** *noun*
*Alternative words:* schooling, teaching, training, instruction

**educational** *adjective*
*Alternative words:* informative, instructive, enlightening

**eerie** *adjective*
*Alternative words:* creepy, scary, spooky

**effect** *noun*
*Alternative words:* result, outcome, consequence

**effective** *adjective*
**1** an effective person
*Alternative words:* able, capable, efficient, competent
*The opposite is* **ineffective**
**2** an effective thing
*Alternative words:* effectual, efficacious, working well
*The opposite is* **ineffective**

**effort** *noun*
**1** He put in a lot of effort.
*Alternative words:* energy, hard work, exertion, diligence
**2** It's such an effort!
*Alternative words:* chore, grind, struggle, strain
**3** to make an effort
*Alternative words:* to try, to attempt, to have a go, to endeavour

**elated** *adjective*
*Alternative words:* overjoyed, ecstatic, euphoric, over the moon (informal)
*The opposite is* **depressed**

**element** *noun*
**1** an element of a thing or substance
*Alternative words:* part, component, constituent
**2** an element of a subject
*Alternative words:* basic fact, point,

factor, detail

**elementary** adjective
*Alternative words:* simple, easy, straightforward, uncomplicated
*The opposite is* **complicated**

**eligible** adjective
**1** a person eligible for something
*Alternative words:* qualified, suitable
*The opposite is* **ineligible**
**2** an eligible bachelor
*Alternative words:* marriageable, desirable

**eliminate** verb
**1** to eliminate something or someone
*Alternative words:* to eradicate, to destroy, to get rid of, to kill
**2** to eliminate someone
*Alternative words:* to exclude, to cut out, to reject

**embark** verb
**1** to embark on a ship
*Alternative words:* to board, to go on board, to go aboard
*The opposite is* **to disembark**
**2** to embark on something new
*Alternative words:* to begin, to start, to commence
*The opposite is* **to finish**

**embarrassed** adjective
*Alternative words:* ashamed, humiliated, mortified

**emergency** noun
*Alternative words:* crisis, danger, a matter of life and death

**emit** verb
*Alternative words:* to give out, to give off, to radiate

**emotional** adjective
*Alternative words:* moved, upset, touched
*The opposite is* **unemotional**

**emphasise** verb
*Alternative words:* to underline, to stress, to highlight

**end** noun
**1** the end of term
*Alternative words:* finish, conclusion, completion
*The opposite is* **beginning**
**2** the end of the table

*Alternative words:* tip, edge, extremity, furthest point

**end** verb
*Alternative words:* to finish, to stop, to terminate
*The opposite is* **to start**

**endanger** verb
*Alternative words:* to risk, to put at risk, to imperil, to jeopardise
*The opposite is* **to protect**

**endeavour** verb
*Alternative words:* to try, to attempt, to have a go at (informal)

**endure** verb
*Alternative words:* to put up with, to bear, to cope with

**enemy** noun
*Alternative words:* foe, rival, opponent
*The opposite is* **ally**

**energetic** adjective
*Alternative words:* lively, tireless, dynamic, unflagging
*The opposite is* **lethargic**

**energy** noun
**1** physical strength and power
*Alternative words:* vigour, vitality, get-up-and-go (informal)
**2** energy to make things move
*Alternative words:* power, force

**engrossed** adjective
*Alternative words:* absorbed, caught up in, immersed in, lost in

**enigma** noun
*Alternative words:* mystery, puzzle, riddle

**enjoy** verb
*Alternative words:* to like, to love, to take pleasure in

**enormous** adjective
**1** an enormous thing
*Alternative words:* massive, gigantic, colossal
**2** an enormous area
*Alternative words:* vast, immense, huge
**3** an enormous amount
*Alternative words:* huge, excessive, astronomic, tremendous
*The opposite is* **tiny**

**enough** *adjective*
*Alternative words:* the right amount, sufficient, plenty, ample
*The opposite is* **insufficient**

**enquire** *verb*
*Alternative words:* to ask, to request information, to make enquiries, to investigate

**ensure** *verb*
*Alternative words:* to make sure, to make certain, to guarantee

**enter** *verb*
**1** to enter a place
*Alternative words:* to come in, to go in, to come into, to go into
*The opposite is* **to exit**
**2** to enter a competition
*Alternative words:* to take part in, to participate in, to have a go (informal)

**entertain** *verb*
**1** to keep people happy and interested
*Alternative words:* to amuse, to occupy, to divert
**2** to invite friends to your home
*Alternative words:* to have company, to have guests, to be the host

**entertainment** *noun*
*Alternative words:* fun, amusement, distraction

**entire** *adjective*
*Alternative words:* complete, whole, total
*The opposite is* **partial**

**entrance** *noun*
*Alternative words:* entry, way in, point of admission
*The opposite is* **exit**

**entrance** *verb*
*Alternative words:* to enchant, to captivate, to fascinate, to mesmerise

**envelop** *verb*
*Alternative words:* to surround, to enclose, to swathe

**episode** *noun*
*Alternative words:* part, instalment, chapter

**equal** *adjective*
*Alternative words:* the same, identical, equivalent

*The opposite is* **unequal**

**equip** *verb*
**1** to equip a person
*Alternative words:* to provide, to supply, to kit out
**2** to equip a place
*Alternative words:* to fit out, to furnish

**equipment** *noun*
*Alternative words:* tools, apparatus, kit, gear (informal)

**error** *noun*
*Alternative words:* mistake, slip, blunder

**escape** *verb*
*Alternative words:* to get away, to run away, to make a getaway, to make your escape

**estimate** *verb*
*Alternative words:* to reckon, to calculate roughly, to guess

**eternal** *adjective*
*Alternative words:* everlasting, never-ending, immortal

**event** *noun*
**1** something that happens
*Alternative words:* incident, happening, occasion
**2** a special event
*Alternative words:* celebration, special occasion, function
**3** a sports event
*Alternative words:* contest, competition, tournament

**eventually** *adverb*
*Alternative words:* finally, at last, in the end, ultimately, in the long run

**ever** *adverb*
**1** for ever
*Alternative words:* always, for all time, eternally
**2** at any time
*Alternative words:* in your life, on any occasion, at any time

**evident** *adjective*
*Alternative words:* clear, obvious, apparent

**evil** *adjective*
*Alternative words:* wicked, bad, sinful
*The opposite is* **good**

**exactly** adverb
*Alternative words:* precisely, accurately

**examine** verb
**1** to look carefully
*Alternative words:* to inspect, to scrutinise, to check
**2** to test someone's skill
*Alternative words:* to test, to put someone through his/her paces, to quiz
**3** to examine a patient
*Alternative words:* to check over, to have a look at, to give the once-over (informal)

**example** noun
**1** an example of something
*Alternative words:* instance, illustration, specimen
**2** a good example to others
*Alternative words:* model, ideal, role model, paragon

**excellent** adjective
*Alternative words:* great, outstanding, superb, brilliant
*The opposite is* **appalling**

**except** preposition
*Alternative words:* but, excluding, other than, bar

**excite** verb
*Alternative words:* to thrill, to exhilarate, to inspire

**excuse** verb
**1** to forgive
*Alternative words:* to forgive, to pardon
**2** to give permission not to do something
*Alternative words:* to let off, to exempt

**exercise** verb
*Alternative words:* to work out, to get fit, to train

**exhaust** verb
**1** to tire someone
*Alternative words:* to wear out, to tire out, to drain, to do in (informal)
*The opposite is* **to refresh**
**2** to use up
*Alternative words:* to use up, to finish, to empty
*The opposite is* **to replenish**

**exhausted** adjective
*Alternative words:* worn out, tired out,

ready to drop (informal)

**exotic** adjective
*Alternative words:* unusual, different, curious, foreign
*The opposite is* **mundane**

**expand** verb
*Alternative words:* to enlarge, to increase, to swell
*The opposite is* **contract**

**expect** verb
expect something to happen
*Alternative words:* to think, to imagine, to presume

**expensive** adjective
*Alternative words:* dear, costly
*The opposite is* **inexpensive**

**explain** verb
**1** to make something easy to understand
*Alternative words:* to make clear, to clarify, to spell out (informal)
**2** to give a reason for something
*Alternative words:* to justify, to account for, to give a reason for

**explanation** noun
**1** an explanation that helps you understand something
*Alternative words:* clarification, elucidation
**2** an explanation of why something happened
*Alternative words:* reason, excuse, justification

**explode** verb
*Alternative words:* to blow up, to go off, to go bang, to detonate

**express** verb
**1** to express with words
*Alternative words:* to say, to tell, to declare
**2** to express without words
*Alternative words:* to show, to convey, to display

**extra** adjective
*Alternative words:* added, additional, more
*The opposite is* **less**

**extra** adverb
*Alternative words:* even more, especially, extremely, particularly

# Ff

**fabric** *noun*
*Alternative words:* material, cloth, textile

**face** *verb*
1 to face a direction
*Alternative words:* to point towards,
to look onto, to look at
2 to face a problem
*Alternative words:* to confront, to tackle

**fact** *noun*
*Alternative words:* reality, truth, certainty

**factory** *noun*
*Alternative words:* plant, firm, works,
mill

**fade** *verb*
1 The colour faded
*Alternative words:* to bleach, to wash out,
to discolour
2 The light faded.
*Alternative words:* to dim, to fail,
to recede
3 to fade from sight
*Alternative words:* to disappear,
to vanish, to melt away (used mainly in
stories), to evaporate (used mainly in
stories)
4 to fade through illness
*Alternative words:* to weaken,
to deteriorate, to decline

**fail** *verb*
1 to fail to do something important
*Alternative words:* to overlook, to omit,
to neglect
2 to be unable to do something
*Alternative words:* to be unsuccessful,
to be in vain
3 to fail an exam
*Alternative words:* to be unsuccessful,
not to pass, not to make the grade

**failing** *noun*
*Alternative words:* fault, shortcoming,
defect, weakness
*The opposite is* **strength**

**faint** *adjective*
1 to feel faint
*Alternative words:* dizzy, light-headed,
unsteady, woozy (informal)
2 difficult to see, hear or smell
*Alternative words:* weak, indistinct,
unclear
*The opposite is* **distinct**

**fair** *adjective*
1 fair hair and skin
*Alternative words:* light, pale, blond
*The opposite is* **dark**
2 a fair price
*Alternative words:* reasonable,
satisfactory, acceptable, adequate
*The opposite is* **unreasonable**
3 fair treatment
*Alternative words:* just, honest,
reasonable
*The opposite is* **unfair**

**faith** *noun*
1 to have faith in someone or
something
*Alternative words:* trust, confidence,
belief
2 a religious faith
*Alternative words:* religion, belief

**faithful** *adjective*
*Alternative words:* loyal, reliable, trusty
*The opposite is* **unfaithful**

**fake** *adjective*
*Alternative words:* imitation, counterfeit,
artificial
*The opposite is* **genuine**

**fake** *verb*
1 to fake an illness
*Alternative words:* to pretend, to put on,
to feign
2 to fake an object
*Alternative words:* to copy, to counterfeit,
to forge

**fall** *verb*
1 to fall to the ground
*Alternative words:* to tumble, to sprawl,
to topple, to go head over heels
(informal)
2 to fall to a lower place from a higher
place
*Alternative words:* to go down, to drop,
to descend

**fallacy** *noun*
*Alternative words:* delusion,
misapprehension, untruth

**false** *adjective*
*Alternative words:* wrong, incorrect, not
right, untrue
*The opposite is* **true**

**family** *noun*
*Alternative words:* relatives, relations, next of kin, flesh and blood (informal)

**famished** *adjective*
*Alternative words:* starving, ravenous

**famous** *adjective*
*Alternative words:* well-known, celebrated, legendary

**fan** *noun*
a football fanatic
*Alternative words:* enthusiast, devotee, addict

**fanatic** *noun*
a religious fanatic
*Alternative words:* extremist, fundamentalist, radical

**fancy** *verb*
**1** to fancy something
*Alternative words:* to want, to crave, to desire, to have a yen for
**2** to fancy someone
*Alternative words:* to be attracted to, to desire

**fantastic** *adjective*
*Alternative words:* marvellous, great, wonderful, tremendous, amazing

**far** *adjective, adverb*
*Alternative words:* long way, a great distance, distant

**fascinate** *verb*
*Alternative words:* to captivate, to mesmerise

**fashion** *noun*
**1** clothes that are in fashion
*Alternative words:* style, vogue
**2** She greeted us in a friendly fashion.
*Alternative words:* way, manner, mode
**3** Rollerblading is the lastest fashion.
*Alternative words:* fad, craze, mania, the latest thing (informal)

**fashionable** *adjective*
*Alternative words:* in fashion, stylish, smart, up to the minute, trendy (informal)

**fast²** *adjective*
*Alternative words:* quick, speedy, rapid
*The opposite is **slow***

**fast²** *adverb*
*Alternative words:* quickly, speedily, rapidly
*The opposite is **slowly***

**fasten** *verb*
*Alternative words:* to stick, to affix, to bond, to tie, to attach, to secure

**fat** *adjective*
**1** a fat person
*Alternative words:* plump, chubby, podgy, overweight, obese
*The opposite is **thin***
**2** a fat thing
*Alternative words:* thick, broad, sizeable

**fatal** *adjective*
**1** a fatal illness or injury
*Alternative words:* terminal, deadly, mortal
**2** a fatal action
*Alternative words:* disastrous, catastrophic, lethal
*The opposite is **harmless***

**fate** *noun*
**1** a force that controls the future
*Alternative words:* destiny, providence
**2** the things that will happen to you
*Alternative words:* future, lot, destiny, doom

**fatigue** *noun*
*Alternative words:* tiredness, exhaustion, weariness

**fault** *noun*
**1** a fault in someone's character
*Alternative words:* failing, shortcoming, weakness, flaw
**2** a fault in something
*Alternative words:* defect, error, flaw

**faulty** *adjective*
*Alternative words:* damaged, defective, imperfect, malfunctioning

**favourite** *adjective*
*Alternative words:* best-liked, most-liked, favoured, selected, preferred, chosen

**fear** *noun*
*Alternative words:* terror, dread, panic, fright

**fear** *verb*
*Alternative words:* to be afraid of, to be frightened of, to dread, to have a horror of

**feast** *noun*
*Alternative words:* banquet, dinner, slap-

up meal (informal)

**feat** *noun*
*Alternative words:* achievement, accomplishment, exploit

**feeble** *adjective*
**1** a feeble person
*Alternative words:* weak, frail, puny
*The opposite is* **strong**
**2** a feeble sound
*Alternative words:* weak, faint, muted
*The opposite is* **loud**
**3** a feeble excuse
*Alternative words:* weak, flimsy, insubstantial
*The opposite is* **plausible**

**feed** *verb*
**1** to feed someone or something
*Alternative words:* to give food to, to nourish, to cater for
**2** to eat
*Alternative words:* to eat, to snack, to graze

**feel** *verb*
**1** to sense something
*Alternative words:* to sense, to perceive, to have a hunch
**2** to touch
*Alternative words:* to touch, to handle, to finger

**feeling** *noun*
**1** something that your body is aware of
*Alternative words:* sensation, sense
**2** to have a feeling about something
*Alternative words:* idea, suspicion, hunch
**3** to hurt someone's feelings
*Alternative words:* emotions, sensitivity

**feign** *verb*
*Alternative words:* to pretend, to put on, to fake, to play-act

**ferocious** *adjective*
a ferocious animal
*Alternative words:* fierce, vicious, savage

**festival** *noun*
*Alternative words:* fiesta, carnival, gala, fête, celebration

**fetch** *verb*
*Alternative words:* to get, to bring back, to retrieve

**feud** *noun*
*Alternative words:* dispute, hatred,

conflict, rivalry, argument

**few** *adjective, noun*
*Alternative words:* hardly any, not many
*The opposite is* **many**

**fiasco** *noun*
*Alternative words:* disaster, catastrophe, failure, wash-out (informal)
*The opposite is* **success**

**fiction** *noun*
**1** fiction in books
*Alternative words:* story, tale, fable, make-believe
*The opposite is* **fact**
**2** something that is not true
*Alternative words:* lie, myth, fantasy, untruth
*The opposite is* **truth**

**fiddle** *verb*
**1** to fiddle with something
*Alternative words:* to tinker, to tweak, to meddle, to interfere
**2** to fiddle about
*Alternative words:* to potter around, to mess about
**3** to fiddle money
*Alternative words:* to swindle, to diddle, to cheat, to embezzle, to cook the books (informal)

**fidget** *verb*
*Alternative words:* to wriggle, to fuss, to squirm, to twitch

**field** *noun*
*Alternative words:* land, meadow, common, pasture, grassland

**fiend** *noun*
**1** an evil spirit
*Alternative words:* ghoul, demon, vampire
**2** a cruel person
*Alternative words:* beast, monster, brute

**fierce** *adjective*
**1** a fierce animal
*Alternative words:* savage, vicious, wild
*The opposite is* **tame**
**2** a fierce person
*Alternative words:* hostile, surly, aggressive
*The opposite is* **friendly**
**3** fierce fighting
*Alternative words:* ferocious, vicious, violent

**fight** *noun*
**1** a fight with words
*Alternative words:* row, argument, quarrel
**2** a fight with punches
*Alternative words:* scrap, scuffle, punch-up (informal), battle
**3** to have a lot of fight in you
*Alternative words:* spirit, pluck, mettle, the will to resist

**fight** *verb*
**1** to fight with words
*Alternative words:* to row, to argue, to quarrel
**2** to fight with punches
*Alternative words:* to come to blows, to scrap, to beat each other up, to exchange blows
**3** to fight a battle or war
*Alternative words:* to go into battle, to do battle, to go to war, to see action

**filthy** *adjective*
**1** very dirty
*Alternative words:* dirty, grimy, mucky, foul
*The opposite is* **clean**
**2** filthy jokes and language
*Alternative words:* dirty, smutty, obscene
*The opposite is* **polite**

**final** *adjective*
coming at the end
*Alternative words:* last, closing, concluding, ultimate
*The opposite is* **opening**

**finally** *adverb*
*Alternative words:* eventually, at last, in the end
*The opposite is* **initially**

**find** *verb*
**1** to find what you are looking for
*Alternative words:* to discover, to come across, to locate
*The opposite is* **to lose**
**2** to find something interesting, terrifying, etc.
*Alternative words:* to regard as, to consider, to think

**fine** *adjective*
**1** to feel fine
*Alternative words:* well, fit, all right
*The opposite is* **unwell**
**2** fine weather

*Alternative words:* dry, bright, sunny
*The opposite is* **dull**
**3** fine cloth
*Alternative words:* thin, flimsy, lightweight, gauzy
*The opposite is* **thick**
**4** fine china
*Alternative words:* fragile, delicate, dainty
**5** fine food
*Alternative words:* expensive, choice, good quality

**finish** *noun*
the end or last part
*Alternative words:* end, close, completion
*The opposite is* **start**

**finish** *verb*
**1** to finish something
*Alternative words:* to end, to complete, to conclude
**2** to stop doing something
*Alternative words:* to stop, to leave off, to cease
*The opposite is* **to begin** or **to start**

**firm** *adjective*
**1** a firm mattress
*Alternative words:* hard, rigid
*The opposite is* **soft**
**2** fixed in a firm way
*Alternative words:* secure, strong, rock-solid
*The opposite is* **unstable**
**3** a firm person
*Alternative words:* strict, assertive, unbending, severe
*The opposite is* **lenient**

**fit²** *verb*
**1** to fit a carpet
*Alternative words:* to lay, to put down
**2** to fit one thing onto another
*Alternative words:* to attach

**fit²** *adjective*
**1** a fit person
*Alternative words:* healthy, well, robust, in good shape (informal)
*The opposite is* **unfit**
**2** food that is fit for babies
*Alternative words:* suitable, appropriate
*The opposite is* **unsuitable**

**fix** *verb*
**1** to fix something that is broken
*Alternative words:* to mend, to repair,

to patch up, to see to (informal)
**2** to fix something to something else
*Alternative words:* to join, to attach, to stick, to fasten

**flag** *noun*
*Alternative words:* banner, standard, pennant

**flap** *verb*
**1** The bird flapped its wings.
*Alternative word:* to beat
**2** to flap in the wind
*Alternative words:* to flutter, to wave, to swing
**3** to behave in a nervous way
*Alternative words:* to panic, to be flustered, to get into a state, to be in a tizzy (informal)

**flash** *verb*
**1** to flash gently
*Alternative words:* to glitter, to glint, to glimmer, to sparkle
**2** to flash very brightly
*Alternative words:* to blaze, to flare, to gleam
**3** to move very quickly
*Alternative words:* to race, to speed, to fly, to shoot
*The opposite is* **to crawl**

**flat** *adjective*
*Alternative words:* level, even, smooth, horizontal

**flexible** *adjective*
**1** easy to bend
*Alternative words:* elastic, supple, stretchy, springy
**2** a flexible person
*Alternative words:* adaptable, malleable, compliant

**flounder** *verb*
**1** to flounder through mud
*Alternative words:* to stumble, to thrash, to blunder
**2** to flounder with work
*Alternative words:* to struggle, to be out of your depth
*The opposite is* **to cope**
**3** the business floundered
*Alternative words:* to fail, to falter, to go under

**flout** *verb*
*Alternative words:* to defy, to disobey, to ignore

*The opposite is* **to obey**

**flow** *verb*
**1** to flow quickly
*Alternative words:* to pour, to stream, to gush, to surge
**2** to flow slowly
*Alternative words:* to trickle, to seep, to meander

**flower** *noun*
part of a plant
*Alternative words:* blossom, bloom, bud

**fluctuate** *verb*
*Alternative words:* to change, to vary, to rise and fall

**fly** *verb*
**1** to fly through the air
*Alternative words:* to flutter, to soar, to flit
**2** to move quickly
*Alternative words:* to rush, to race, to speed

**focus** *noun*
**1** focus of someone's interest
*Alternative words:* centre, focal point, core, target
**2** the picture is in focus
*Alternative words:* clear, well-defined, distinct

**fold** *verb*
**1** to fold paper
*Alternative words:* to bend, to double over, to crease
**2** a business that folds
*Alternative words:* to shut down, to fail, to close, to collapse, to go under, to go bust (informal)

**follow** *verb*
**1** to come after something
*Alternative words:* to come after, to come next, to succeed
*The opposite is* **to precede**
**2** to follow someone
*Alternative words:* to trail, to track, to pursue
**3** to follow orders
*Alternative words:* to obey, to comply with, to abide by, to adhere to
*The opposite is* **to disobey**
**4** to follow what someone says
*Alternative words:* to understand, to see, to grasp, to comprehend

**folly** *noun*
*Alternative words:* silliness, foolishness, stupidity

**fool** *verb*
*Alternative words:* to trick, to mislead, to hoodwink

**foolish** *adjective*
*Alternative words:* silly, stupid, idiotic

**forbid** *verb*
*Alternative words:* to ban, to outlaw, to prohibit
*The opposite is* **to allow**

**forbidding** *adjective*
**1** a forbidding person
*Alternative words:* frightening, hostile, unfriendly
**2** a forbidding place
*Alternative words:* sinister, ominous, menacing
*The opposite is* **welcoming**

**force** *noun*
*Alternative words:* strength, power, energy

**force** *verb*
**1** to force someone to do something
*Alternative words:* to make, to compel, to pressurise, to twist someone's arm (informal),
**2** to force your way through a crowd
*Alternative words:* to push, to shove, to thrust
**3** to force something open
*Alternative words:* to break open, to wrench, to prise

**forecast** *noun*
*Alternative words:* prediction, outlook, prophecy

**foreign** *adjective*
**1** a foreign person
*Alternative words:* alien, from overseas
**2** a foreign thing
*Alternative words:* exotic, imported
*The opposite is* **native**

**foreigner** *noun*
*Alternative words:* immigrant, non-national, alien
*The opposite is a* **native**

**forever** *adverb*
*Alternative words:* constantly, continually, endlessly

**forge** *verb*
*Alternative words:* to counterfeit, to fake, to falsify

**forgetful** *adjective*
*Alternative words:* absent-minded, scatty

**forgive** *verb*
*Alternative words:* to excuse, to pardon

**forlorn** *adjective*
*Alternative words:* lonely, abandoned, bereft

**form** *noun*
**1** a type of something
*Alternative words:* type, kind, sort, variety
**2** the shape of something
*Alternative words:* shape, design, appearance

**form** *verb*
*Alternative words:* to make, to create, to construct, to fashion

**format** *noun*
format of the magazine
*Alternative words:* appearance, look, design, plan

**fortunately** *adverb*
*Alternative words:* happily, luckily, by a stroke of good luck
*The opposite is* **unfortunately**

**foul** *adjective*
*Alternative words:* horrible, disgusting, repulsive

**foul** *verb*
*Alternative words:* to pollute, to contaminate, to dirty

**fragile** *adjective*
**1** to feel fragile
*Alternative words:* weak, feeble, frail
**2** fragile china
*Alternative words:* breakable, brittle, delicate
*The opposite is* **strong**

**fragment** *noun*
*Alternative words:* speck, shred, piece

**frame** *noun*
**1** a picture frame
*Alternative words:* border, outline
**2** a person's frame
*Alternative words:* build, physique

**free** *adjective*
**1** not costing anything
*Alternative words:* complimentary, without charge, gratis, on the house (informal)
**2** a free person
*Alternative words:* independent, footloose, liberated
**3** a free animal
*Alternative words:* wild, undomesticated, at liberty, uncaged
*The opposite is* **captive**

**free** *verb*
*Alternative words:* to let go, to let out, to release
*The opposite is* **imprison**

**freedom** *noun*
*Alternative words:* liberty, independence, autonomy

**frequently** *adverb*
*Alternative words:* often, repeatedly, over and over again, commonly
*The opposite is* **infrequently**

**fresh** *adjective*
**1** fresh ideas
*Alternative words:* new, modern, up-to-date, innovative
*The opposite is* **outdated**
**2** fresh sheets
*Alternative words:* new, clean
*The opposite is* **old**
**3** a fresh breeze
*Alternative words:* cool, refreshing, invigorating
*The opposite is* **warm**

**friend** *noun*
*Alternative words:* pal, chum, mate (informal), buddy (informal), ally
*The opposite is* **enemy**

**fright** *noun*
*Alternative words:* scare, shock, panic

**frighten** *verb*
*Alternative words:* to scare, to terrify, to put the wind up someone (informal)

**frolic** *verb*
*Alternative words:* to romp, to gambol, to cavort

**full** *adjective*
**1** with no spare space
*Alternative words:* chock-full, crammed, chock-a-block (informal), brimming
*The opposite is* **empty**
**2** a full report
*Alternative words:* in-depth, complete, thorough
*The opposite is* **superficial**

**funny** *adjective*
**1** a funny story
*Alternative words:* humorous, amusing, comic, comical
**2** a funny smell
*Alternative words:* strange, odd, peculiar, weird

**further** *adjective*
*Alternative words:* more, extra, additional

**fury** *noun*
*Alternative words:* anger, rage, wrath

# Gg

**gain** *verb*
1 to get something
*Alternative words:* to achieve, to acquire, to win
*The opposite is* **to lose**
2 to gain on someone
*Alternative words:* to go faster, to catch up with, to overtake

**gale** *noun*
*Alternative words:* hurricane, tempest, tornado, typhoon

**gambol** *verb*
*Alternative words:* to skip, to frolic, to caper (old-fashioned)

**game** *noun*
a sport
*Alternative words:* match, competition, contest, tournament

**gap** *noun*
1 an empty space
*Alternative words:* break, crack, chink, opening
2 time between things
*Alternative words:* break, interruption, interlude, intermission

**gape** *verb*
1 to look in surprise
*Alternative words:* to stare, to ogle
2 a gaping hole
*Alternative words:* to be wide open, to hang open, to yawn

**garbage** *noun*
*Alternative words*: rubbish, waste, junk, litter

**garish** *adjective*
*Alternative words:* loud, gaudy, flashy

**gather** *verb*
1 to bring together
*Alternative words:* to collect, to accumulate, to amass
2 to form a group
*Alternative words:* to assemble, to congregate, to flock
*The opposite is* **to scatter**

**gaudy** *adjective*
*Alternative words:* loud, glaring, garish

**gaunt** *adjective*
*Alternative words:* wasted, haggard, emaciated, scrawny

**gaze** *verb*
*Alternative words:* to look at, to stare, to watch

**general** *adjective*
1 relating to everything and everyone
*Alternative words:* common, universal, popular
2 connected with many different things
*Alternative words:* broad, ordinary, unspecific
*The opposite is* **specific**

**generous** *adjective*
1 willing to share
*Alternative words:* kind, hospitable, unselfish
2 more than expected
*Alternative words:* ample, plentiful, lavish
*The opposite is* **mean**

**gentle** *adjective*
*Alternative words:* kind, soft, tender
*The opposite is* **harsh**

**genuine** *adjective*
*Alternative words:* real, authentic, original
*The opposite is* **fake**

**get** *verb*
1 to be given
*Alternative words:* to receive, to acquire, to obtain
2 to have got something
*Alternative words:* to have, to own, to possess
3 to get hungry
*Alternative words:* to become, to grow, to turn
4 to get to a place
*Alternative words:* to arrive, to reach, to come

**ghastly** *adjective*
*Alternative words*: horrible, hideous, gruesome

**ghost** *noun*
*Alternative words:* spirit, phantom, spook (informal)

**gift** *noun*
1 something you give
*Alternative words:* present, donation,

offering
**2** a natural ability
*Alternative words:* talent, aptitude, flair

**gigantic** *adjective*
*Alternative words:* huge, enormous,
immense, vast
*The opposite is* **tiny**

**give** *verb*
**1** to give something
*Alternative words:* to donate, to present,
to supply
**2** to give in
*Alternative words:* to admit defeat,
to surrender, to resign
**3** to give something up
*Alternative words:* to stop, to quit,
to abandon

**glad** *adjective*
*Alternative words:* pleased, happy,
cheerful
*The opposite is* **sad**

**glamorous** *adjective*
*Alternative words:* attractive, elegant,
exciting

**glare** *verb*
**1** The light glared.
*Alternative words:* to shine, to dazzle,
to blaze
**2** to glare at someone
*Alternative words:* to look angrily,
to glower, to stare, to give someone a
dirty look (informal)

**gleam** *verb*
*Alternative words:* to shine, to sparkle,
to glow, to glimmer

**glide** *verb*
*Alternative words:* to float, to sail,
to skate

**glory** *noun*
*Alternative words:* honour, triumph,
admiration

**glow** *verb*
*Alternative words:* to burn, to gleam,
to smoulder

**gnarled** *adjective*
*Alternative words:* knotted, twisted,
weather-beaten, bumpy

**gnaw** *verb*
*Alternative words:* to chew, to bite,
to nibble, to munch

**go** *verb*
**1** I'm going.
*Alternative words:* to travel, to move,
to leave, to depart
*The opposite is* **to stay**
**2** The car doesn't go.
*Alternative words:* to work, to operate,
to function
*The opposite is* **to stop**
**3** His face went red.
*Alternative words:* to become, to get,
to turn, to change

**good** *adjective*
**1** a good book
*Alternative words:* enjoyable, fine,
excellent, great (informal)
**2** a good child
*Alternative words:* well-behaved, polite,
obedient
**3** a good person
*Alternative words:* kind, benevolent,
charitable
*The opposite is* **bad**

**gorge** *noun*
*Alternative words:* canyon, ravine, chasm

**govern** *verb*
**1** to govern a country
*Alternative words:* to rule, to be in
power, to reign
**2** to govern something
*Alternative words:* to control, to rule,
to direct

**grab** *verb*
*Alternative words:* to take hold of,
to snatch, to clutch, to seize

**gradual** *adjective*
*Alternative words:* regular, steady,
unhurried, step-by-step
*The opposite is* **sudden**

**grand** *adjective*
*Alternative words:* great, impressive,
splendid, important

**grant** *verb*
*Alternative words:* to permit, to allow,
to consent to

**grateful** *adjective*
*Alternative words:* thankful, appreciative
*The opposite is* **ungrateful**

**grave** *adjective*
**1** looking or sounding grave

*Alternative words:* serious, solemn, grim
*The opposite is* **cheerful**
**2** a grave situation
*Alternative words:* serious, dangerous, critical
*The opposite is* **unimportant**

**great** *adjective*
**1** a great story
*Alternative words:* brilliant, fantastic, wonderful
**2** a great man
*Alternative words:* important, famous, distinguished
**3** a great ocean
*Alternative words:* enormous, immense, vast

**grief** *noun*
*Alternative words:* sadness, sorrow, bereavement
*The opposite is* **joy**

**grieve** *verb*
*Alternative words:* to mourn, to wail, to lament
*The opposite is* **to rejoice**

**grind** *verb*
*Alternative words:* to crush, to mill, to pulverise

**grip** *verb*
*Alternative words:* to hold tightly, to clasp, to grasp

**ground¹** *noun*
**1** the ground you walk on
*Alternative words:* earth, soil, land
**2** a sports ground
*Alternative words:* field, pitch, arena
**3** the grounds of a house
*Alternative words:* gardens, estate, surroundings

**group** *noun*
**1** a group of people
*Alternative words:* crowd, circle, gang, gathering, organisation
**2** a group of things
*Alternative words:* collection, set, bunch, clump

**grow** *verb*
**1** to grow in size
*Alternative words:* to expand, to develop, to increase
**2** to grow plants
*Alternative words:* to cultivate, to raise, to nurture, to farm

**grown-up** *noun*
*Alternative words:* adult, man, woman

**gruelling** *adjective*
*Alternative words:* exhausting, backbreaking, arduous
*The opposite is* **very easy**

**gruesome** *adjective*
*Alternative words:* shocking, hideous, repulsive

**guarantee** *verb*
*Alternative words:* to promise, to assure, to warrant

**guard** *verb*
*Alternative words:* to watch over, to protect, to safeguard

**guess** *verb*
*Alternative words:* to estimate, to reckon, to surmise
*The opposite is* **to be certain**

**guilt** *noun*
*Alternative words:* bad conscience, remorse, responsibility
*The opposite is* **innocence**

**guilty** *adjective*
*Alternative words:* at fault, to blame, responsible
*The opposite is* **innocent**

**gush** *verb*
*Alternative words:* to pour, to flood, to spurt, to cascade

# Hh

**habit** *noun*
*Alternative words:* custom, practice, tendency

**haggle** *verb*
*Alternative words:* to bargain, to negotiate, to argue

**handicap** *noun*
**1** a thing that makes something more difficult
*Alternative words:* disadvantage, obstacle, stumbling block
**2** in sport
*Alternative words:* penalty
*The opposite is* **advantage**

**handle** *verb*
*Alternative words:* to touch, to feel, to pick up

**happen** *verb*
*Alternative words:* to take place, to come about, to occur

**happy** *adjective*
*Alternative words:* pleased, cheerful, contented
*The opposite is* **unhappy**

**harass** *verb*
*Alternative words:* to annoy, to pester, to badger

**harbour** *noun*
*Alternative words:* port, shelter, destination, haven

**hard** *adjective*
**1** not soft
*Alternative words:* firm, solid, stiff
*The opposite is* **soft**
**2** not easy
*Alternative words:* difficult, complicated, thorny
*The opposite is* **easy**
**3** not pleasant
*Alternative words:* cruel, difficult, severe
*The opposite is* **pleasant**

**hardy** *adjective*
*Alternative words:* healthy, sturdy, vigorous, robust

**harm** *verb*
*Alternative words:* to hurt, to damage, to injure

**harmony** *noun*
**1** harmony in music
*Alternative words:* melodiousness, tunefulness
**2** harmony between people
*Alternative words:* agreement, peace, concord
*The opposite is* **discord**

**harness** *verb*
**1** to put a harness on a horse
*Alternative words:* to saddle, to hitch up, to attach
**2** to use something
*Alternative words:* to control, to exploit, to utilise

**harsh** *adjective*
**1** a harsh person
*Alternative words:* strict, cruel, unforgiving
*The opposite is* **kind**
**2** a harsh climate
*Alternative words:* unpleasant, bitter, bleak
*The opposite is* **mild**
**3** a harsh thing
*Alternative words:* rough, coarse, harmful
*The opposite is* **soft**

**harvest** *verb*
*Alternative words:* to gather, to pick, to reap

**hate** *verb*
*Alternative words:* to detest, to abhor, to loathe
*The opposite is* **love**

**have** *verb*
**1** They have a big house.
*Alternative words:* to own, to possess
**2** The building has ten floors.
*Alternative words:* to contain, to hold, to comprise
**3** to have to do something
*Alternative words:* must, to be responsible for, to be obliged

**head** *noun*
**1** person in charge
*Alternative words:* boss, captain, leader
**2** the head of something
*Alternative words:* top, tip

**health** *noun*
*Alternative words:* fitness, well-being, robustness

*The opposite is* **sickness**

**healthy** *adjective*
*Alternative words:* fit, well, robust
*The opposite is* **ill**

**heap** *noun*
*Alternative words:* pile, mass, stack

**hear** *verb*
*Alternative words:* to listen to, to catch,
to hark (old-fashioned)

**heartless** *adjective*
*Alternative words:* callous, brutal,
cold-hearted
*The opposite is* **compassionate**

**heavy** *adjective*
*Alternative words:* weighty, hefty, bulky
*The opposite is* **light**

**help** *verb*
*Alternative words:* to assist, to aid,
to give a hand
*The opposite is* **to hinder**

**helpful** *adjective*
*Alternative words:* willing, supportive
*The opposite is* **unhelpful**

**helping** *noun*
*Alternative words:* serving, portion,
dollop (informal)

**helpless** *adjective*
*Alternative words:* weak, vulnerable,
defenceless, incapable

**heritage** *noun*
*Alternative words:* inheritance, legacy,
tradition

**heroic** *adjective*
*Alternative words:* brave, courageous,
valiant
*The opposite is* **cowardly**

**heroism** *noun*
*Alternative words:* bravery,
courageousness, valour

**hesitate** *verb*
*Alternative words:* to delay, to pause,
to dither

**hesitation** *noun*
*Alternative words:* delay, indecision,
uncertainty

**hide¹** *verb*
**1** to hide in a place

*Alternative words:* to go into hiding,
to lie low, to take cover
**2** to hide a person or thing
*Alternative words:* to conceal, to shelter,
to stash (informal)
**3** to hide feelings
*Alternative words:* to keep secret, to keep
them to yourself, to disguise
*The opposite is* **reveal**

**high** *adjective*
**1** a high mountain
*Alternative words:* tall, a long way up,
towering
**2** a high temperature
*Alternative words:* extreme, excessive
**3** a high musical note
*Alternative words:* high-pitched, shrill,
soaring
*The opposite is* **low**

**highlight** *noun*
*Alternative words:* climax, focus, high
point
*The opposite is* **low point**

**highlight** *verb*
*Alternative words:* to underline,
to emphasise, to accentuate
*The opposite is* **to play down**

**hijack** *verb*
*Alternative words:* to take over, to seize

**hike** *noun*
*Alternative words:* walk, trek, ramble,
tramp

**hinder** *verb*
*Alternative words:* to delay, to hamper,
to obstruct

**hint** *noun*
**1** Give me a hint.
*Alternative words:* clue, idea, inkling
**2** a helpful hint
*Alternative words:* suggestion, pointer,
tip
**3** a small amount
*Alternative words:* dash, speck, trace

**hit** *verb*
**1** to hit someone
*Alternative words:* to beat, to clout,
to smack
**2** to hit something
*Alternative words:* to bang, to strike,
to whack

**hoard** *noun*
*Alternative words*: stockpile, reserve, cache, stash (informal)

**hoard** *verb*
*Alternative words:* to collect, to store, to save, to put by, to stockpile, to accumulate

**hoax** *noun*
*Alternative words:* trick, prank, practical joke

**hoist** *verb*
*Alternative words:* to raise, to lift, to elevate

**hold¹** *verb*
**1** She held my hand.
*Alternative words:* to grip, to grasp, to clasp
**2** This bottle holds a litre.
*Alternative words:* to take, to contain, to have room for, to accommodate
**3** We're holding a party.
*Alternative words:* to have, to organise, to run

**hold¹** *noun*
*Alternative words:* grip, grasp, clasp

**hole** *noun*
**1** a hole in the surface of something
*Alternative words:* hollow, dip, dent, tear
**2** an opening in something
*Alternative words:* gap, puncture, aperture (formal)

**hollow** *noun*
*Alternative words:* empty space, hole, cavity

**hollow** *adjective*
not solid
*Alternative words:* empty, cavernous, void

**holy** *adjective*
**1** a holy thing
*Alternative words:* blessed, sacred, sacrosanct
**2** a holy person
*Alternative words:* devout, pious, divine, saintly

**home** *noun*
**1** where you live
*Alternative words:* house, dwelling, residence, abode (formal)
**2** where you belong

*Alternative words:* territory, home ground, habitat

**honest** *adjective*
*Alternative words:* truthful, trustworthy, sincere, above board
*The opposite is **dishonest***

**hooligan** *noun*
*Alternative words:* troublemaker, vandal, ruffian

**hope** *noun*
**1** hope for the future
*Alternative words:* faith, confidence, optimism
*The opposite is **despair***
**2** a hope for something good to happen
*Alternative words:* wish, dream, ambition

**hopeful** *adjective*
*Alternative words:* confident, optimistic, cheerful
*The opposite is **despairing***

**hopeless** *adjective*
**1** a hopeless situation
*Alternative words:* impossible, futile, pointless
*The opposite is **promising***
**2** having no hope
*Alternative words:* despondent, pessimistic, forlorn
*The opposite is **confident***

**horrible** *adjective*
*Alternative words:* ghastly, revolting, awful
*The opposite is **delightful***

**horrid** *adjective*
*Alternative words:* nasty, unpleasant
*The opposite is **pleasant***

**horrific** *adjective*
*Alternative words:* dreadful, shocking, terrifying

**horrified** *adjective*
*Alternative words:* shocked, disgusted, appalled

**horrifying** *adjective*
*Alternative words:* shocking, disgusting, alarming

**horror** *noun*
**1** a feeling of fear
*Alternative words:* fear, dread, terror
**2** a feeling of disgust

*Alternative words:* disgust, revulsion
**3** a horror of something
*Alternative words:* hatred, abhorrence, terror

**hospitable** *adjective*
*Alternative words:* generous, welcoming, friendly
*The opposite is* **inhospitable**

**host²** *noun*
a large number
*Alternative words:* array, swarm, multitude

**hostile** *adjective*
*Alternative words:* unfriendly, antagonistic, belligerent
*The opposite is* **friendly**

**hot** *adjective*
**1** a hot day
*Alternative words:* scorching, boiling, sweltering
*The opposite is* **cold**
**2** a hot taste
*Alternative words:* spicy, piquant, peppery
*The opposite is* **mild**

**house** *noun*
*Alternative words:* home, dwelling, residence, abode (formal)

**hovel** *noun*
*Alternative words:* shack, slum, den

**hover** *verb*
**1** to hover in the air
*Alternative words:* to hang, to flutter, to float
**2** to wait
*Alternative words:* to linger, to drift, to hang about

**hug** *verb*
*Alternative words:* to cuddle, to embrace, to squeeze

**huge** *adjective*
*Alternative words:* enormous, gigantic, vast, massive
*The opposite is* **tiny**

**humble** *adjective*
*Alternative words:* modest, self-effacing, unassuming

**humid** *adjective*
*Alternative words:* damp, muggy, steamy
*The opposite is* **fresh**

**humiliate** *verb*
*Alternative words:* to embarrass, to degrade, to shame

**humorous** *adjective*
*Alternative words:* funny, amusing, comical, entertaining

**humour** *noun*
*Alternative words:* comedy, amusement, wit

**hungry** *adjective*
**1** a little hungry
*Alternative word:* peckish
**2** very hungry
*Alternative words:* starving, ravenous, famished

**hunt** *verb*
**1** to hunt animals
*Alternative words:* to chase, to pursue, to go hunting
**2** to look for something
*Alternative words:* to try to find, to search, to seek

**hurry** *verb*
*Alternative words:* to rush, to dash, to fly
*The opposite is* **to dawdle**

**hurt** *verb*
**1** to make someone feel pain
*Alternative words:* to injure, to harm, to wound
**2** to make someone feel sad
*Alternative words:* to upset, to distress, to sadden
**3** to feel pain
*Alternative words:* to ache, to be sore, to throb, to sting

**hut** *noun*
*Alternative words:* shelter, cabin, shed

# Ii

**idea** *noun*
**1** a good idea
*Alternative words:* thought, concept, plan
**2** your idea of something
*Alternative words:* thought, belief,
opinion, view

**ideal** *noun*
*Alternative words:* principle, value,
moral standard

**ideal** *adjective*
*Alternative words:* perfect, tailor-made,
just the thing (informal)

**identical** *adjective*
*Alternative words:* alike,
indistinguishable, matching
*The opposite is **different***

**idle** *adjective*
**1** not being used
*Alternative words:* inactive, not working,
stationary
*The opposite is **active***
**2** not wanting to work
*Alternative words:* lazy, shiftless,
indolent
*The opposite is **hard-working***

**ignite** *verb*
*Alternative words:* to burn, to catch fire,
to burst into flames
*The opposite is **to extinguish***

**ignorant** *adjective*
**1** not knowing about something
*Alternative words:* unaware,
inexperienced, green
*The opposite is **knowledgeable***
**2** not having an education
*Alternative words:* uneducated, illiterate
*The opposite is **learned***

**ill** *adjective*
**1** ill health
*Alternative words:* sick, poorly, unwell,
not well
*The opposite is **well***
**2** ill effects
*Alternative words:* bad, damaging,
harmful
*The opposite is **favourable***

**illegal** *adjective*
*Alternative words:* against the law,
prohibited, criminal
*The opposite is **legal***

**illegible** *adjective*
*Alternative words:* unreadable,
indecipherable, hard to make out
*The opposite is **legible***

**illicit** *adjective*
*Alternative words:* illegitimate,
prohibited, unlawful
*The opposite is **lawful***

**illness** *noun*
**1** an illness
*Alternative words:* disease, ailment,
complaint
**2** being ill
*Alternative words:* poor health, sickness

**illuminate** *verb*
**1** to use lights
*Alternative words:* to light, to light up,
to brighten
*The opposite is **to darken***
**2** to make something clear
*Alternative words:* to explain, to make
clear, to clarify, to elucidate
*The opposite is **to obscure***

**illusion** *noun*
**1** a false idea
*Alternative words:* deception, false
impression, delusion
**2** something that is not real
*Alternative words:* fantasy, hallucination,
mirage, figment of the imagination

**imaginary** *adjective*
*Alternative words:* fictitious, made-up,
unreal, make-believe
*The opposite is **real***

**imagine** *verb*
**1** to have an idea in your mind
*Alternative words:* to envisage,
to picture, to visualise
**2** to think something exists
*Alternative words:* to suppose, to dream,
to guess

**imitate** *verb*
**1** to imitate something
*Alternative words:* to copy, to counterfeit,
to reproduce
**2** to imitate someone
*Alternative words:* to mimic,

to impersonate, to ape

**immaculate** *adjective*
**1** very clean
*Alternative words:* spotless, spick-and-span, squeaky-clean (informal)
*The opposite is **filthy***
**2** perfect
*Alternative words:* impeccable, pure, faultless
*The opposite is **impure***

**immaterial** *adjective*
*Alternative words:* unimportant, insignificant, irrelevant
*The opposite is **relevant***

**immature** *adjective*
*Alternative words:* young, childish, juvenile
*The opposite is **mature***

**immediately** *adverb*
*Alternative words:* at once, straightaway, without delay, forthwith (formal)
*The opposite is **later***

**immense** *adjective*
*Alternative words:* colossal, huge, mammoth
*The opposite is **minute***

**immerse** *verb*
**1** to immerse yourself in something
*Alternative words:* to engross, to occupy
**2** to immerse something in a liquid
*Alternative words:* to submerge, to dunk, to plunge

**imminent** *adjective*
*Alternative words:* impending, fast-approaching, at any moment
*The opposite is **distant***

**immobile** *adjective*
*Alternative words:* stationary, motionless, frozen
*The opposite is **mobile***

**immobilise** *verb*
*Alternative words:* to stop, to halt, to bring to a standstill

**immovable** *adjective*
*Alternative words:* fixed, stable, immutable, jammed
*The opposite is **movable***

**impatient** *adjective*
**1** impatient to do something
*Alternative words:* eager, keen, restive
**2** an impatient person
*Alternative words:* quick-tempered, hasty, irritable
*The opposite is **patient***

**impeccable** *adjective*
*Alternative words:* perfect, stainless, immaculate

**impediment** *noun*
*Alternative words:* problem, defect, obstacle
*The opposite is **advantage***

**impenetrable** *adjective*
**1** impossible to enter
*Alternative words:* dense, impermeable, solid, impassable
*The opposite is **accessible***
**2** impossible to understand
*Alternative words:* baffling, incomprehensible, unintelligible
*The opposite is **clear***

**imperfect** *adjective*
*Alternative words:* defective, faulty, impaired
*The opposite is **perfect***

**impertinent** *adjective*
*Alternative words:* cheeky, insolent, rude
*The opposite is **respectful***

**implement** *noun*
*Alternative words:* tool, instrument, utensil

**imply** *verb*
*Alternative words:* to suggest, to hint, to intimate

**important** *adjective*
**1** something important
*Alternative words:* significant, meaningful, serious
**2** an important person
*Alternative words:* eminent, powerful, leading
*The opposite is **unimportant***

**impractical** *adjective*
**1** not sensible or useful
*Alternative words:* impossible, unrealistic, unworkable
**2** an impractical person
*Alternative words:* unrealistic, incompetent

**imprecise** *adjective*
*Alternative words:* vague, inexact, ambiguous
*The opposite is **precise***

**impression** *noun*
**1** a feeling
*Alternative words:* idea, sense, notion
**2** an imitation
*Alternative words:* impersonation, take-off (informal)
**3** a mark
*Alternative words:* imprint, indentation, stamp

**impressive** *adjective*
*Alternative words:* striking, powerful, admirable
*The opposite is **unimpressive***

**imprison** *verb*
*Alternative words:* to detain, to incarcerate, to lock away
*The opposite is **to set free***

**imprisonment** *noun*
*Alternative words:* custody, detention, incarceration
*The opposite is **freedom***

**improve** *verb*
*Alternative words:* to get better, to make progress, to advance
*The opposite is **to worsen***

**improvement** *noun*
*Alternative words:* a change for the better, advancement, development

**impudent** *adjective*
*Alternative words:* cheeky, impertinent, rude
*The opposite is **respectful***

**impure** *adjective*
*Alternative words:* contaminated, polluted, adulterated
*The opposite is **pure***

**inability** *noun*
*Alternative words:* inadequacy, incompetence, powerlessness
*The opposite is **ability***

**inaccurate** *adjective*
*Alternative words:* careless, inexact, imprecise, wide of the mark
*The opposite is **accurate***

**inadequate** *adjective*
**1** an inadequate thing
*Alternative words:* imperfect, deficient, not up to scratch (informal)
**2** an inadequate person
*Alternative words:* incompetent, incapable
*The opposite is **adequate***

**incense** *verb*
*Alternative words:* to enrage, to infuriate, to make your blood boil

**incessant** *adjective*
*Alternative words:* ceaseless, never-ending, interminable

**incident** *noun*
*Alternative words:* event, occurrence, happening

**incite** *verb*
*Alternative words:* to encourage, to drive, to urge, to stir up
*The opposite is **to deter***

**incline** *verb*
**1** to be inclined to do something
*Alternative words:* to tend to, to want to, to be disposed to
**2** to slope
*Alternative words:* to lean, to tilt, to slant

**include** *verb*
*Alternative words:* to count, to involve, to allow for
*The opposite is **to exclude***

**incompetent** *adjective*
*Alternative words:* inept, unskilful, bungling
*The opposite is **competent***

**incomprehensible** *adjective*
*Alternative words:* unintelligible, baffling, above your head
*The opposite is **comprehensible***

**inconceivable** *adjective*
*Alternative words:* unbelievable, unimaginable, mind-boggling (informal)
*The opposite is **believable***

**inconvenient** *adjective*
*Alternative words:* awkward, unsuitable, troublesome
*The opposite is **convenient***

**increase** verb
*Alternative words*: to grow, to expand, to multiply
*The opposite is* **to decrease**

**indecisive** adjective
**1** an indecisive person
*Alternative words*: uncertain, hesitant, in two minds
*The opposite is* **decisive**
**2** an indecisive result
*Alternative words*: uncertain, inconclusive, unclear
*The opposite is* **decisive**

**indicate** verb
**1** The test indicates that nothing is wrong.
*Alternative words*: to show, to suggest, to point out
**2** The driver indicated left.
*Alternative word*: to signal

**indifference** noun
*Alternative words*: lack of interest, apathy, detachment
*The opposite is* **interest**

**indifferent** adjective
*Alternative words*: uninterested, apathetic, unconcerned
*The opposite is* **interested**

**indignant** adjective
*Alternative words*: angry, irate, offended, in a huff

**indispensable** adjective
*Alternative words*: essential, necessary, crucial

**indoctrinate** verb
*Alternative words*: to drill, to brainwash, to train

**induce** verb
**1** to make something happen
*Alternative words*: to encourage, to promote, to instigate
**2** to make someone do something
*Alternative words*: to persuade, to influence, to convince
*The opposite is* **to deter**

**indulge** verb
*Alternative words*: to spoil, to give in to, to treat

**industrious** adjective
*Alternative words*: hard-working,
energetic, diligent
*The opposite is* **idle**

**inefficient** adjective
*Alternative words*: disorganised, wasteful, incompetent
*The opposite is* **efficient**

**inertia** noun
a feeling of inertia
*Alternative words*: apathy, lethargy, stupor
*The opposite is* **vigour**

**inevitable** adjective
*Alternative words*: unavoidable, inescapable, destined

**inexpensive** adjective
*Alternative words*: cheap, low-cost, reasonable
*The opposite is* **expensive**

**infallible** adjective
**1** an infallible thing
*Alternative words*: reliable, foolproof, unbeatable
*The opposite is* **unreliable**
**2** an infallible person
*Alternative words*: perfect, faultless, impeccable
*The opposite is* **fallible**

**infamous** adjective
*Alternative words*: notorious, disreputable, scandalous
*The opposite is* **esteemed**

**information** noun
*Alternative words*: facts, knowledge, data

**inhabitant** noun
*Alternative words*: citizen, native, resident

**injure** verb
*Alternative words*: to hurt, to harm, to wound, to maim

**innocent** adjective
**1** not guilty
*Alternative words*: blameless, honest, guiltless
*The opposite is* **guilty**
**2** not aware of bad things
*Alternative words*: pure, ignorant, naive

**insensitive** adjective
*Alternative words*: callous, unfeeling, thick-skinned
*The opposite is* **sensitive**

**instead** *adverb*
*Alternative words:* alternatively, preferably

**instruction** *noun*
**1** driving instruction
*Alternative words:* training, tuition, coaching
**2** follow the instructions
*Alternative words:* directions, guidance, rules

**insufficient** *adjective*
*Alternative words:* short, lacking, inadequate
*The opposite is* **sufficient**

**insult** *verb*
*Alternative words:* to abuse, to offend, to call names

**intelligent** *adjective*
*Alternative words:* clever, bright, brainy
*The opposite is* **unintelligent**

**intend** *verb*
*Alternative words:* to plan, to aim, to propose, to have in mind

**intense** *adjective*
**1** an intense feeling
*Alternative words:* strong, acute, extreme
*The opposite is* **mild**
**2** an intense person
*Alternative words:* ardent, fervent, impassioned
*The opposite is* **indifferent**

**intent** *adjective*
*Alternative words:* determined to, resolved to
*The opposite is* **undecided**

**intentional** *adjective*
*Alternative words:* deliberate, on purpose, premeditated
*The opposite is* **accidental**

**interfere** *verb*
*Alternative words:* to meddle, to poke your nose in, to intervene

**interrupt** *verb*
*Alternative words:* to break in, to cut short, to butt in, to intervene

**invent** *verb*
**1** to invent a machine
*Alternative words:* to design, to create, to devise

**2** to invent an excuse
*Alternative words:* to make up, to dream up, to concoct

**investigate** *verb*
*Alternative words:* to explore, to look into, to make enquiries

**irregular** *adjective*
**1** not even
*Alternative words:* uneven, asymmetrical, odd
**2** not happening regularly
*Alternative words:* occasional, haphazard, intermittent
**3** not following rules
*Alternative words:* unusual, abnormal, anomalous
*The opposite is* **regular**

**irresponsible** *adjective*
*Alternative words:* reckless, unreliable, careless
*The opposite is* **responsible**

**isolate** *verb*
*Alternative words:* to cut off, to separate, to quarantine

**itinerary** *noun*
*Alternative words:* route, timetable, schedule

# Jj

**jab** *verb*
*Alternative words:* to poke, to prod, to stab

**jagged** *adjective*
*Alternative words:* rough, ragged, spiked
*The opposite is* **smooth**

**jeer** *verb*
*Alternative words:* to mock, to ridicule, to jibe

**jeopardy** *noun*
*Alternative words:* danger, risk, peril
*The opposite is* **safety**

**jerk** *verb*
*Alternative words:* to jolt, to lurch, to yank

**jetty** *noun*
*Alternative words:* quay, wharf, pier

**jingle** *verb*
*Alternative words:* to jangle, to tinkle, to clink

**job** *noun*
**1** someone's job
*Alternative words:* occupation, profession, trade
**2** piece of work
*Alternative words:* task, chore, errand

**joint** *adjective*
*Alternative words:* shared, mutual, collective
*The opposite is* **sole**

**jolt** *verb*
**1** to move suddenly
*Alternative words:* to jerk, to jostle, to knock
**2** to surprise
*Alternative words:* to startle, to shock, to disturb

**jostle** *verb*
*Alternative words:* to jog, to bump, to shove

**journalist** *noun*
*Alternative words:* reporter, correspondent, commentator

**journey** *noun*
*Alternative words:* trip, expedition, voyage

**joy** *noun*
**1** great happiness
*Alternative words:* bliss, elation, ecstasy
*The opposite is* **misery**
**2** a thing that makes you happy
*Alternative words:* delight, treasure, gem

**jubilant** *adjective*
*Alternative words:* thrilled, triumphant, overjoyed

**judge** *verb*
**1** to judge in a court of law
*Alternative words:* to rule, to pass sentence, to decree
**2** to judge in a competition or argument
*Alternative words:* to decide, to referee, to adjudicate (formal)

**judgement** *noun*
**1** in a court of law
*Alternative words:* sentence, ruling, verdict
**2** in a competition
*Alternative words:* decision, ruling
**3** the ability to decide
*Alternative words:* common sense, understanding, acumen
**4** an opinion
*Alternative words:* belief, conviction, diagnosis

**jump** *verb*
*Alternative words:* to leap, to bound, to spring

**junk**[1] *noun*
*Alternative words:* rubbish, clutter, scrap, garbage

**just** *adjective*
*Alternative words:* fair, unbiased, right
*The opposite is* **unjust**

**just** *adverb*
**1** It's just what I want.
*Alternative words:* exactly, precisely, completely
**2** He's just arrived.
*Alternative words:* recently, lately, only now
**3** There's just one more day of school.
*Alternative words:* only, merely, simply

**justice** *noun*
*Alternative words:* law, fairness, right
*The opposite is* **injustice**

**justify** *verb*
*Alternative words:* to explain, to defend

# Kk

**keep** *verb*
**1** to keep something
*Alternative words:* to hold on to, to save, to retain
*The opposite is* **to give away**
**2** to keep doing something
*Alternative words:* to continue, to persist, to carry on
*The opposite is* **to stop**
**3** to make something stay the same
*Alternative words:* to maintain, to conserve, to preserve

**keg** *noun*
*Alternative words:* cask, barrel

**kidnap** *verb*
*Alternative words:* to abduct, to seize, to capture, to snatch (informal)

**kill** *verb*
**1** to kill a person
*Alternative words:* to murder, to assassinate, to take someone's life
**2** to kill an animal
*Alternative words:* to slaughter, to destroy, to put down, to put to sleep

**kind** *noun*
*Alternative words:* type, sort, variety, form

**kind** *adjective*
*Alternative words:* gentle, thoughtful, considerate, generous
*The opposite is* **unkind**

**kindness** *noun*
*Alternative words:* gentleness, generosity, consideration
*The opposite is* **cruelty**

**king** *noun*
*Alternative words:* majesty, sovereign, monarch, ruler

**kingdom** *noun*
*Alternative words:* realm, principality, monarchy, empire

**kit** *noun*
tool kit
*Alternative words:* gear, equipment, supplies, tools, utensils

**knack** *noun*
*Alternative words:* talent, gift, skill, ability, flair

**knead** *verb*
*Alternative words:* to stretch, to punch, to massage, to mould, to work

**knick-knack** *noun*
*Alternative words:* trinket, souvenir, ornament

**knobbly** *adjective*
*Alternative words:* bumpy, gnarled, bony

**knock** *verb*
*Alternative words:* to strike, to hit, to rap, to thump, to bang

**know** *verb*
**1** to know something
*Alternative words:* to understand, to be knowledgeable about, to realise
*The opposite is* **to be ignorant of**
**2** to know someone
*Alternative words:* to be acquainted with, to recognise, to be familiar with

**knowledge** *noun*
*Alternative words:* education, learning, expertise, know-how
*The opposite is* **ignorance**

# Ll

**label** *noun*
  *Alternative words:* tag, ticket, sticker

**labour** *noun*
  **1** hard work
  *Alternative words:* work, effort, toil
  **2** having a baby
  *Alternative words:* childbirth, contractions

**lack** *noun*
  *Alternative words:* shortage, scarcity, need, absence

**lair** *noun*
  *Alternative words:* hole, burrow, den

**land** *noun*
  **1** on land
  *Alternative words:* dry land, solid ground, earth
  **2** another land
  *Alternative words:* country, nation, realm

**land** *verb*
  **1** aircraft landing
  *Alternative words:* to touch down, to come in to land, to alight
  *The opposite is* **to take off**
  **2** birds landing
  *Alternative words:* to come to rest, to alight
  *The opposite is* **to take flight**
  **3** ships landing
  *Alternative words:* to dock, to berth, to reach the shore
  *The opposite is* **to set sail**
  **4** coming off a ship
  *Alternative words:* to disembark, to come ashore, to go ashore
  The opposite is **to board**

**large** *adjective*
  **1** a large room
  *Alternative words:* big, spacious, roomy
  *The opposite is* **small**
  **2** a large building
  *Alternative words:* enormous, huge, tall
  *The opposite is* **small**
  **3** a large person
  *Alternative words:* big, heavy, fat
  *The opposite is* **small**
  **4** a large portion of food
  *Alternative words:* big, ample, generous, substantial
  *The opposite is* **small**

**lash** *noun*
  **1** something that you hit with
  *Alternative words:* whip, horsewhip, cat-o'-nine-tails
  **2** a lash of the whip
  *Alternative words:* stroke, blow, swipe (informal)

**lash** *verb*
  **1** rain lashing against a window
  *Alternative words:* to beat, to hammer, to drum
  **2** to hit with a whip
  *Alternative words:* to whip, to thrash, to flog
  **3** to tie with rope
  *Alternative words:* to fasten, to tie, to tether

**last** *noun*
  *Alternative words:* end, finish, conclusion

**last** *verb*
  *Alternative words:* to continue, to carry on, to go on, to persist

**late** *adjective*
  **1** The train was late
  *Alternative words:* delayed, overdue, unpunctual, behind schedule
  *The opposite is* **on time**
  **2** made some late changes
  *Alternative words:* belated, last-minute
  The opposite is **early**
  **3** my late father
  *Alternative words:* deceased, dead

**lately** *adverb*
  *Alternative words:* recently, of late, in the past few days

**laugh** *verb*
  **1** Did you laugh at the clown?
  *Alternative words:* to roar with laughter, to split your sides, to burst out laughing, to chuckle, to guffaw
  **2** a little laugh
  *Alternative words:* to giggle, to snigger, to titter

**law** *noun*
  **1** obey a law
  *Alternative words:* rule, commandment, regulation, decree, order
  **2** a law in science
  *Alternative words:* principle, formula, rule

**lay¹** *verb*
**1** to lay the baby in its cot
*Alternative words:* to put, to put down, to place, to leave
**2** to lay an egg
*Alternative words:* to produce, to deposit

**layer** *noun*
*Alternative words:* coating, thickness, covering, stratum

**lazy** *adjective*
*Alternative words:* idle, indolent, inactive
*The opposite is* **hard-working**

**lead²** *verb*
**1** to lead the procession
*Alternative words:* to be at the front, to be first, to guide
**2** The waitress led us to a table.
*Alternative words:* to show, to escort, to guide, to usher
**3** to lead people
*Alternative words:* to be in charge, to rule, to manage

**leader** *noun*
*Alternative words:* chief, head, captain, manager, boss (informal)

**lean¹** *verb*
**1** to lean to one side
*Alternative words:* to slope, to slant, to tilt, to be at an angle
**2** to lean your bike on the wall
*Alternative words:* to rest, to prop, to support
**3** to lean against someone
*Alternative words:* to be supported, to be propped

**lean²** *adjective*
**1** a lean animal
*Alternative words:* thin, bony, gaunt, scrawny, slim
*The opposite is* **fat**
**2** lean meat
*Alternative words:* unfatty, low-fat
*The opposite is* **fatty**

**leap** *verb*
*Alternative words:* to jump, to spring, to bound

**learn** *verb*
*Alternative words:* to study, to master, to pick up, to acquire, to understand, to become good at, to become skilled at

**leave** *verb*
**1** to leave at nine
*Alternative words:* to go, to set off, to take your leave
**2** caught her trying to leave
*Alternative words:* to escape, to run away, to abscond
**3** Leave the room quietly!
*Alternative words:* to go out, to exit

**lecture** *noun*
*Alternative words:* talk, speech, lesson, sermon

**legal** *adjective*
*Alternative words:* lawful, legitimate, allowed, permitted
*The opposite is* **illegal**

**legible** *adjective*
*Alternative words:* clear, easy to read
*The opposite is* **illegible**

**lend** *verb*
*Alternative words:* to loan, to let someone use

**length** *noun*
**1** the length of the garden
*Alternative words:* extent, distance, measurement
**2** the length of the movie
*Alternative words:* time, duration

**lengthen** *verb*
**1** to lengthen curtains
*Alternative words:* to make longer, to let down
**2** to lengthen a story
*Alternative words:* to prolong, to make longer, to draw out, to spin out
*The opposite is* **to shorten**

**lenient** *adjective*
*Alternative words:* forgiving, merciful, easygoing, indulgent
*The opposite is* **strict**

**lesson** *noun*
**1** a science lesson
*Alternative words:* class, lecture, period
**2** a story with a lesson
*Alternative words:* moral, message, point

**let** *verb*
*Alternative words:* to allow, to permit, to agree, to give permission

**lethal** *adjective*
*Alternative words:* deadly, poisonous,

toxic, fatal
*The opposite is* **harmless**

**level** *adjective*
**1** a level table
*Alternative words:* flat, smooth, horizontal, even
*The opposite is* **uneven**
**2** a level score
*Alternative words:* equal, tied, balanced, neck and neck
*The opposite is* **unequal**

**liable** *adjective*
*Alternative words:* responsible, accountable, at fault

**liberate** *verb*
*Alternative words:* to set free, to let out, to release, to emancipate

**liberty** *noun*
*Alternative words:* freedom, independence, emancipation

**licence** *noun*
*Alternative words:* certificate, permit, warrant, document

**license** *verb*
*Alternative words:* to permit, to authorise, to entitle, to give permission

**lie¹** *verb*
to lie down
*Alternative words:* to recline, to rest, to stretch out

**lie²** *verb*
to tell a lie
*Alternative words:* to fib, to make up a story
*The opposite is* **to tell the truth**

**lift** *verb*
*Alternative words:* to raise, to lift up, to hoist, to pick up

**light¹** *noun*
**1** surrounded by light
*Alternative words:* brightness, illumination, radiance
**2** something that gives light
*Alternative words:* lamp, torch, lantern, candle

**light¹** *adjective*
**1** light colours
*Alternative words:* pale, pastel, fair
**2** a light room

*Alternative words:* bright, sunny, well-lit
*The opposite is* **dark**

**light¹** *verb*
**1** light a fire
*Alternative words:* to kindle, to set a match to, to set fire to, to ignite
**2** light a room
*Alternative words:* to illuminate, to make bright, to floodlight

**like¹** *verb*
**1** to like something
*Alternative words:* to enjoy, to be keen on, to love
*The opposite is* **to dislike**
**2** to like someone
*Alternative words:* to be fond of, to be attracted to, to get on well with, to love
*The opposite is* **to dislike**
**3** whatever you like
*Alternative words:* to want, to desire, to prefer, to wish

**like²** *preposition*
*Alternative words:* similar to, identical to, the same as

**likely** *adjective*
*Alternative words:* probable, to be expected, possible
*The opposite is* **unlikely**

**limit** *noun*
**1** the limits of the city
*Alternative words:* boundary, perimeter, edge
**2** a speed limit
*Alternative words:* restriction, limitation, maximum

**limp** *verb*
*Alternative words:* to hobble, to shuffle, to shamble

**limp** *adjective*
*Alternative words:* floppy, drooping, soft

**line¹** *noun*
**1** a line on a page
*Alternative words:* dash, rule, stroke
**2** a line on the ground
*Alternative words:* groove, channel, furrow, mark
**3** a line on a face
*Alternative words:* wrinkle, scar, mark
**4** a line of colour
*Alternative words:* stripe, band, strip
**5** a line of people

*Alternative words:* queue, row, procession
**6** The line broke.
*Alternative words:* string, thread, rope, wire, cord

**linger** *verb*
**1** a smell that lingers
*Alternative words:* to stay around, to last, to persist
**2** Don't linger!
*Alternative words:* to hang around, to take your time, to dawdle

**link** *noun*
**1** a link in a chain
*Alternative words:* ring, loop, connection
**2** a link between things or people
*Alternative words:* connection, relationship, association

**link** *verb*
*Alternative words:* to connect, to join, to tie

**list¹** *noun*
*Alternative words:* register, catalogue, record, inventory

**list²** *verb*
*Alternative words:* to lean, to tilt, to tip

**listen** *verb*
**1** Listen to me!
*Alternative words:* to pay attention, to be attentive, to take notice
**2** listening for a sound
*Alternative words:* to keep your ears open, to prick up your ears, to hark (old-fashioned)

**little** *adjective*
*Alternative words:* small, tiny, short
*The opposite is* **big**

**live¹** *verb*
**1** to be alive
*Alternative words:* to stay alive, to exist, to survive
**2** to live in a place
*Alternative words:* to dwell, to have your home, to reside (formal)

**live²** *adjective*
**1** live animals
*Alternative words:* living, breathing, alive
*The opposite is* **dead**
**2** a live programme
*Alternative words:* instant, not recorded
*The opposite is* **recorded**

**3** live electricity
*Alternative words:* connected, switched on, charged, active

**livelihood** *noun*
*Alternative words:* job, living, income, work

**load** *noun*
a load being carried
*Alternative words:* cargo, weight, freight, consignment

**loathe** *verb*
*Alternative words:* to hate, to detest, to despise, to abhor

**lob** *verb*
*Alternative words:* to throw, to toss, to hurl

**locate** *verb*
**1** I managed to locate her house.
*Alternative words:* to find, to track down, to discover, to identify
**2** shops located in the town centre
*Alternative words:* to situate, to position, to establish, to site

**lock¹** *noun*
a lock on the door
*Alternative words:* bolt, padlock, fastening, catch

**lock¹** *verb*
*Alternative words:* to bolt, to bar, to fasten, to secure

**lock²** *noun*
a lock of hair
*Alternative words:* strand, curl, tress, ringlet

**lonely** *adjective*
**1** feeling lonely
*Alternative words:* alone, on your own, friendless, abandoned
**2** a lonely island
*Alternative words:* secluded, remote, out-of-the way, isolated

**long²** *verb*
*Alternative words:* to yearn, to wish, to desire, to crave

**look** *verb*
**1** Don't look!
*Alternative words:* to peep, to peek, to watch, to spy
**2** to look at a picture
*Alternative words:* to view, to study,

59

to cast your eye over
**3** to look carefully
*Alternative words:* to examine, to check, to inspect, to scrutinise
**4** to look out of the window
*Alternative words:* to gaze, to glance, to peer, to stare
**5** You look tired.
*Alternative words:* to seem, to appear

**loose** *adjective*
**1** a loose shirt
*Alternative words:* baggy, large
*The opposite is* **tight**
**2** a loose tooth
*Alternative words:* wobbly, movable, insecure
*The opposite is* **firm**

**lose** *verb*
**1** to lose your pencil
*Alternative words:* to mislay, to drop, to be unable to find
*The opposite is* **to find**
**2** to lose a game
*Alternative words:* to be defeated, to be beaten, to be the loser
*The opposite is* **to win**
**3** to lose your place in a queue
*Alternative words:* to miss, to forfeit, to be deprived of

**lot** *noun*
**1** a lot or lots
*Alternative words:* many, plenty, a great quantity, a large amount, heaps (informal)
**2** the lot
*Alternative words:* all, everything, the whole amount, the whole thing

**loud** *adjective*
*Alternative words:* noisy, deafening, blaring, ear-piercing
*The opposite is* **quiet**

**love** *verb*
**1** She loved all the children.
*Alternative words:* to be fond of, to adore, to care for, to think the world of
*The opposite is* **to hate**
**2** I love ice cream.
*Alternative words:* to enjoy, to have a weakness for, to be partial to
*The opposite is* **to dislike** *or* **to hate**

**lovely** *adjective*
**1** having a lovely time
*Alternative words:* enjoyable, exciting, great, pleasant, delightful
*The opposite is* **horrible**
**2** a lovely dress
*Alternative words:* beautiful, exquisite, pretty
*The opposite is* **ugly**

**low** *adjective*
**1** a low plant
*Alternative words:* small, little, short, stunted
*The opposite is* **tall**
**2** low prices
*Alternative words:* cheap, reasonable, inexpensive, bargain
*The opposite is* **high**
**3** a low voice
*Alternative words:* deep, gruff, bass
*The opposite is* **high**

**loyal** *adjective*
*Alternative words:* trustworthy, faithful, reliable, dependable
*The opposite is* **disloyal**

**luck** *noun*
**1** It was pure luck!
*Alternative words:* chance, fortune, coincidence, fate, destiny
**2** to wish someone luck
*Alternative words:* good luck, good fortune, success, prosperity

**lucky** *adjective*
a lucky person
*Alternative words:* fortunate, blessed, charmed, favoured
*The opposite is* **unlucky**

# Mm

**mad** *adjective*
**1** mentally ill
*Alternative words:* insane, deranged, lunatic, crazy (informal)
*The opposite is* **sane**
**2** a mad idea
*Alternative words:* stupid, foolish, idiotic
*The opposite is* **sensible**
**3** That makes me mad!
*Alternative words:* furious, angry, livid (informal)
**4** mad about something
*Alternative words:* crazy, wild, enthusiastic

**magazine** *noun*
*Alternative words:* periodical, comic, journal

**maim** *verb*
*Alternative words:* to injure, to mutilate, to cripple

**main** *adjective*
**1** the main character
*Alternative words:* most important, central, major
**2** the main thing to remember
*Alternative words:* essential, crucial, most important

**major** *adjective*
*Alternative words:* leading, chief, main, important
*The opposite is* **minor**

**make** *verb*
**1** a factory making cars
*Alternative words:* to produce, to build, to assemble
**2** to make someone do something
*Alternative words:* to force, to compel, to pressurise
**3** 2 and 2 make 4
*Alternative words:* to add up to, to total

**malfunction** *verb*
*Alternative words:* to go wrong, to break down, to stop working

**man** *noun*
Who is that man?
*Alternative words:* gentleman, guy (informal)

**manage** *verb*
**1** to manage a football team
*Alternative words:* to be in charge of, to run, to control
**2** to manage to do something
*Alternative words:* to accomplish, to achieve, to succeed in

**manager** *noun*
a person in charge
*Alternative words:* director, supervisor, organiser, boss (informal)

**mangle** *verb*
*Alternative words:* to distort, to destroy, to mutilate, to spoil

**manipulate** *verb*
*Alternative words:* to influence, to exploit, to control

**manoeuvre** *verb*
*Alternative words:* to steer, to direct, to guide

**many** *adjective*
*Alternative words:* lots of, numerous, countless, innumerable

**march** *verb*
**1** soldiers marching
*Alternative words:* to parade, to file past
**2** to walk with determination
*Alternative words:* to strut, to stride

**mark** *noun*
**1** a dirty mark
*Alternative words:* stain, spot, blemish, smudge
**2** a low mark
*Alternative words:* score, result, total

**marsh** *noun*
*Alternative words:* bog, swamp, quagmire

**marvellous** *adjective*
*Alternative words:* wonderful, amazing, spectacular, extraordinary

**match²** *noun*
**1** Who won the match?
*Alternative words:* game, competition, tournament
**2** an exact match
*Alternative words:* copy, replica, duplicate
**3** He's a match for her when it comes to swimming.
*Alternative words:* equal, rival,

competitor

**match²** *verb*
1 Your shoes match.
*Alternative words:* to go together, to look the same, to be a set
2 His T-shirt matches his shorts.
*Alternative words:* to go with, to coordinate with, to complement
3 His stubbornness matches yours.
*Alternative words:* to equal, to rival, to compare with

**matter** *noun*
1 waste matter
*Alternative words:* stuff, material, substance
2 need to deal with the matter
*Alternative words:* situation, incident, affair
3 an important matter
*Alternative words:* subject, issue, question

**matter** *verb*
*Alternative words:* to count, to be important, to be significant, to make a difference

**meadow** *noun*
*Alternative words:* field, pasture, grassland

**mean¹** *verb*
1 What does the sign mean?
*Alternative words:* to indicate, to say, to symbolise, to tell you
2 The footprint means they have been here.
*Alternative words:* to show, to signify, to suggest
3 I didn't mean to do that!
*Alternative words:* to intend, to plan, to set out, to want
4 It means a lot to me.
*Alternative words:* to matter, to be important

**mean²** *adjective*
*Alternative words:* stingy, ungenerous, miserly, selfish
*The opposite is* **generous**

**meander** *verb*
*Alternative words:* to wind, to snake, to zigzag

**meaning** *noun*
1 the meaning of a message

*Alternative words:* explanation, sense, interpretation
2 It has no meaning.
*Alternative words:* point, purpose, aim, significance

**meaningful** *adjective*
1 tried to think of something meaningful to say
*Alternative words:* relevant, valid, worthwhile, important
*The opposite is* **trivial**
2 gave her a meaningful look
*Alternative words:* expressive, significant, eloquent
*The opposite is* **meaningless**

**meaningless** *adjective*
1 meaningless sounds
*Alternative words:* incomprehensible, unintelligible, indecipherable
*The opposite is* **meaningful**
2 a meaningless thing to do
*Alternative words:* pointless, worthless, futile, aimless
*The opposite is* **valuable**

**medicine** *noun*
*Alternative words:* medication, drug, remedy

**meet** *verb*
1 I first met him at school.
*Alternative words:* to come across, to get to know, to come into contact with, to encounter
2 where the two walls meet
*Alternative words:* to join, to touch, to come together
3 Let's all meet at the bus stop.
*Alternative words:* to get together, to gather, to assemble
4 Look who I met in town!
*Alternative words:* to bump into, to see, to encounter

**meeting** *noun*
*Alternative words:* gathering, assembly, congregation, get-together (informal)

**melt** *verb*
*Alternative words:* to thaw, to liquefy, to soften

**memorable** *adjective*
*Alternative words:* unforgettable, historic, momentous, noteworthy
*The opposite is* **unmemorable**

**mend** *verb*
*Alternative words:* to repair, to fix, to put back together

**merciful** *adjective*
*Alternative words:* forgiving, compassionate, tender-hearted
*The opposite is* **merciless**

**merciless** *adjective*
*Alternative words:* callous, cruel, ruthless
*The opposite is* **merciful**

**mercy** *noun*
*Alternative words:* forgiveness, compassion, pity

**merge** *verb*
**1** where the rivers merge
*Alternative words:* to join, to come together, to meet
*The opposite is* **to separate**
**2** Our two schools are going to merge.
*Alternative words:* to amalgamate, to combine, to unite
*The opposite is* **to separate**
**3** to merge into something else
*Alternative words:* to blend, to fuse, to mingle
*The opposite is* **to separate**

**merry** *adjective*
*Alternative words:* cheerful, jolly, happy
*The opposite is* **sad**

**mess** *noun*
*Alternative words:* jumble, clutter, muddle, dirtiness, filth, untidiness, chaos

**mess** *verb*
**1** to mess around
*Alternative words:* to play about, to fool about, to muck about (informal)
**2** to mess up a plan
*Alternative words:* to spoil, to ruin, to botch
**3** to mess up a room
*Alternative words:* to dirty, to clutter up, to litter

**messy** *adjective*
*Alternative words:* untidy, cluttered, disorganised
*The opposite is* **tidy**

**method** *noun*
*Alternative words:* way, procedure, technique, system

**methodical** *adjective*
*Alternative words:* neat, organised, systematic, logical
*The opposite is* **disorderly**

**middle** *noun*
*Alternative words:* centre, halfway point, midpoint

**mighty** *adjective*
**1** a mighty emperor
*Alternative words:* powerful, great, strong
*The opposite is* **weak**
**2** heard a mighty bang
*Alternative words:* enormous, huge, tremendous
*The opposite is* **small**

**mild** *adjective*
**1** She has a mild nature.
*Alternative words:* gentle, easy-going, calm
*The opposite is* **violent**
**2** a mild taste
*Alternative words:* bland, not spicy
*The opposite is* **strong**
**3** mild weather
*Alternative words:* calm, temperate, warm
*The opposite is* **severe**

**mimic** *verb*
*Alternative words:* to copy, to imitate, to impersonate

**mind** *verb*
**1** I don't mind when we go.
*Alternative words:* to care, to be concerned about, to worry about
**2** Do you mind if I watch television?
*Alternative words:* to object, to disapprove, to take offence
**3** minding the baby
*Alternative words:* to look after, to care for, to keep an eye on
**4** Mind the hole!
*Alternative words:* beware of, to watch out for, to look out for, to be careful of

**miniature** *adjective*
*Alternative words:* scaled-down, mini, small, tiny
*The opposite is* **enormous**

**minor** *adjective*
**1** a minor road
*Alternative words:* small, secondary

2 a minor character
*Alternative words:* unimportant, insignificant
*The opposite is* **major**

**minute** *adjective*
*Alternative words:* tiny, microscopic, teeny-weeny
*The opposite is* **huge**

**miraculous** *adjective*
*Alternative words:* amazing, unbelievable, inexplicable, wonderful

**misbehave** *verb*
*Alternative words:* to be naughty, to behave badly, to get up to mischief
*The opposite is* **to behave**

**miscellaneous** *adjective*
*Alternative words:* various, assorted, mixed

**mischief** *noun*
*Alternative words:* naughtiness, bad behaviour, trouble

**mischievous** *adjective*
*Alternative words:* naughty, playful, badly behaved, wayward

**miser** *noun*
*Alternative words:* skinflint, hoarder, Scrooge, cheap-skate (informal)

**miserable** *adjective*
*Alternative words:* sorrowful, broken-hearted, downcast, wretched
*The opposite is* **happy**

**misery** *noun*
*Alternative words:* sadness, sorrow, unhappiness, suffering
*The opposite is* **joy**

**miss** *verb*
1 to miss the bus
*Alternative words:* to be late for, to fail to catch
*The opposite is* **to catch**
2 to miss a television programme
*Alternative words:* to fail to see, to overlook
3 to miss a ball
*Alternative words:* to fail to catch, to let go, to drop, to fumble
*The opposite is* **to catch**
4 to miss your friends
*Alternative words:* to need, to long for, to want

5 to miss your stop
*Alternative words:* to pass, to omit, to skip

**missing** *adjective*
*Alternative words:* lost, mislaid, astray, nowhere to be found

**mist** *noun*
*Alternative words:* fog, haze, smog, vapour

**mistake** *noun*
*Alternative words:* error, blunder, misunderstanding, slip

**misty** *adjective*
*Alternative words:* cloudy, foggy, dim, hazy, murky

**mix** *verb*
*Alternative words:* to combine, to blend, to mingle, to put together

**moan** *verb*
1 to moan with pain
*Alternative words:* to groan, to whine, to whimper, to wail
2 to moan about something
*Alternative words:* to grumble, to complain, to whinge (informal)

**mob** *noun*
*Alternative words:* crowd, rabble, mass, throng

**mobile** *adjective*
*Alternative words:* unfixed, portable, moveable, non-stationary

**model** *noun*
1 a model of a house
*Alternative words:* replica, copy, dummy, representation
2 the latest model
*Alternative words:* design, style, type

**modern** *adjective*
*Alternative words:* new, up-to-date, current, fashionable
*The opposite is* **old-fashioned**

**modest** *adjective*
1 a modest person
*Alternative words:* unassuming, humble, reserved
2 a modest amount
*Alternative words:* limited, small, understated

**moist** *adjective*
*Alternative words:* damp, wet, clammy, humid
*The opposite is* **dry**

**moment** *noun*
*Alternative words:* instant, minute, second

**money** *noun*
*Alternative words:* coins, banknotes, change, cash, currency

**monument** *noun*
*Alternative words:* memorial, statue, obelisk, shrine

**mourn** *verb*
*Alternative words:* to grieve, to weep, to sorrow

**move** *verb*
**1** a beetle moving slowly
*Alternative words:* to walk, to go, to proceed
**2** Help me move the table.
*Alternative words:* to carry, to shift, to transport, to reposition
**3** We're moving next week.
*Alternative words:* to move away, to move house, to leave, to relocate
**4** Wind it up to make it move.
*Alternative words:* to start, to go

**much** *adverb*
*Alternative words:* a great deal, exceedingly, a lot (informal)

**mud** *noun*
*Alternative words:* dirt, clay, silt, sludge

**muddle** *verb*
*Alternative words:* to jumble, to confuse, to mix up, to tangle

**mumble** *verb*
*Alternative words:* to murmur, to mutter, to swallow your words

**mundane** *adjective*
*Alternative words:* ordinary, boring, everyday
*The opposite is* **exciting**

**murder** *verb*
*Alternative words:* to kill, to slaughter, to assassinate

**murmur** *verb*
*Alternative words:* to mumble, to whisper, to speak in an undertone

**mutilate** *verb*
*Alternative words:* to damage, to cut to pieces, to cut up, to dismember

**mutiny** *noun*
*Alternative words:* rebellion, uprising, revolt

**mutter** *verb*
*Alternative words:* to mumble, to talk under your breath, to talk to yourself

**mysterious** *adjective*
*Alternative words:* secret, strange, mystifying, baffling

# Nn

**naked** *adjective*
*Alternative words:* bare, nude, undressed
*The opposite is* **clothed**

**name** *verb*
*Alternative words:* to call, to entitle,
to label

**nap** *verb*
*Alternative words:* to rest, to doze, to lie
down

**narrate** *verb*
*Alternative words:* to tell, to relate,
to recount

**narrow** *adjective*
**1** a narrow path
*Alternative words:* not wide, not broad
*The opposite is* **wide**
**2** a narrow space
*Alternative words:* cramped, tight,
confined
*The opposite is* **wide**
**3** a narrow range of books
*Alternative words:* limited, restricted
*The opposite is* **wide**

**nasty** *adjective*
**1** a nasty smell
*Alternative words:* disgusting,
unpleasant, horrible, foul
*The opposite is* **pleasant**
**2** a nasty thing to do
*Alternative words:* mean, unkind,
spiteful
*The opposite is* **kind**
**3** a nasty accident
*Alternative words:* serious, bad, alarming

**natural** *adjective*
**1** a natural reaction
*Alternative words:* normal, common,
typical
*The opposite is* **abnormal**
**2** natural foods
*Alternative words:* pure, organic,
unrefined, whole

**nature** *noun*
**1** studying nature
*Alternative words:* natural history,
biology, the environment, the earth
**2** It's her nature.
*Alternative words:* character, personality,
temperament

**naughty** *adjective*
*Alternative words:* badly behaved,
disobedient, mischievous, wicked
*The opposite is* **good**

**navigate** *verb*
**1** to navigate a ship
*Alternative words:* to steer, to pilot,
to manoeuvre
**2** I need someone to navigate.
*Alternative words:* to find the way,
to map-read, to plot a route, to give
directions

**near** *adjective*
**1** His house is near.
*Alternative words:* close, nearby, not far
**2** Her birthday is near.
*Alternative words:* approaching, coming,
imminent

**nearly** *adverb*
*Alternative words:* almost, roughly,
practically, close to

**neat** *adjective*
**1** She always looks neat.
*Alternative words:* tidy, smart, well-
groomed
**2** Your desk is very neat.
*Alternative words:* tidy, well-organised,
uncluttered
*The opposite is* **untidy**

**necessary** *adjective*
*Alternative words:* essential, needed,
vital, compulsory
*The opposite is* **unnecessary**

**negotiate** *verb*
**1** We negotiated an arrangement.
*Alternative words:* to work out, to agree
on, to thrash out
**2** The two sides came together to
negotiate.
*Alternative words:* to talk, to bargain,
to deal

**nervous** *adjective*
*Alternative words:* anxious, worried,
fearful, tense
*The opposite is* **confident**

**neuter** *verb*
*Alternative words:* to castrate, to spay, to
doctor

**new** *adjective*
**1** new ideas
*Alternative words:* modern, up-to-date, recent
*The opposite is* **old**
**2** a new way of doing it
*Alternative words:* original, different, innovative
*The opposite is* **old**
**3** saving up for a new car
*Alternative words:* brand new, unused, in mint condition
*The opposite is* **old**

**next** *adjective*
**1** the next street
*Alternative words:* nearest, closest, neighbouring
**2** the next train
*Alternative words:* following, later, subsequent

**nice** *adjective*
**1** a nice person
*Alternative words:* friendly, kind, likeable, pleasant
**2** a nice meal
*Alternative words:* delicious, tasty, enjoyable
**3** a nice day
*Alternative words:* fine, warm, sunny
**4** nice handwriting
*Alternative words:* neat, fine, beautiful
**5** nice manners
*Alternative words:* polite, courteous, charming
**6** a nice outfit
*Alternative words:* pretty, smart, attractive

**noise** *noun*
**1** heard a noise
*Alternative words:* sound
**2** a lot of noise
*Alternative words:* racket, commotion, din

**noisy** *adjective*
**1** noisy instruments
*Alternative words:* loud, deafening, blaring
*The opposite is* **quiet**
**2** noisy children
*Alternative words:* rowdy, chattering, boisterous
*The opposite is* **quiet**

**nonsense** *noun*
*Alternative words:* rubbish, gibberish, drivel

**normal** *adjective*
**1** on a normal day
*Alternative words:* average, typical, usual, standard
*The opposite is* **special**
**2** It's normal to feel shy.
*Alternative words:* natural, common
*The opposite is* **abnormal**
**3** spending time doing normal things
*Alternative words:* routine, everyday, ordinary
*The opposite is* **unusual**

**nosy** *adjective*
*Alternative words:* inquisitive, prying, interfering

**notice** *verb*
*Alternative words:* to see, to detect, to spot

**nude** *adjective*
*Alternative words:* naked, bare, undressed, stark naked

**nuisance** *noun*
*Alternative words:* problem, inconvenience, bother

**numerous** *adjective*
*Alternative words:* countless, many, lots of (informal)

# Oo

**obey** *verb*
*Alternative words:* to agree, to submit, to conform, to yield

**object** *noun*
1 a strange object
*Alternative words:* thing, article, item
2 the object of this game
*Alternative words:* aim, purpose, point, goal

**object** *verb*
*Alternative words:* to disapprove, to have objections, to complain, to protest

**objective** *noun*
*Alternative words:* aim, target, goal

**objective** *adjective*
*Alternative words:* fair, unbiased, open-minded
*The opposite is* **subjective**

**obligation** *noun*
*Alternative words:* duty, responsibility, necessity

**oblige** *verb*
1 obliged to go home
*Alternative words:* to have to, to make, to force, to demand
2 to oblige a friend
*Alternative words:* to indulge, to help, to serve, to please

**obliterate** *verb*
*Alternative words:* to destroy, to wipe out, to eradicate

**oblivious** *adjective*
*Alternative words:* unaware, unconscious, insensitive, abstracted, absent-minded

**obnoxious** *adjective*
*Alternative words:* offensive, objectionable, revolting

**obscure** *adjective*
1 an obscure writer
*Alternative words:* little-known, unimportant, minor
*The opposite is* **well-known**
2 The clues were rather obscure.
*Alternative words:* mysterious, unclear, vague, confusing

*The opposite is* **obvious**

**observe** *verb*
*Alternative words:* to watch, to keep under observation, to keep watch on

**obsession** *noun*
*Alternative words:* preoccupation, fixation, bee in your bonnet (informal)

**obsolete** *adjective*
*Alternative words:* out-of-date, no longer in use, old-fashioned, archaic
*The opposite is* **current**

**obstacle** *noun*
*Alternative words:* barrier, obstruction, stumbling block

**obvious** *adjective*
1 It was obvious that she was upset.
*Alternative words:* clear, easy to see, evident, noticeable
2 a story with an obvious plot
*Alternative words:* recognisable, straightforward, undisguised

**occasion** *noun*
1 a big occasion
*Alternative words:* event, affair, happening
2 saw her on several occasions
*Alternative words:* time, instance, situation

**occasional** *adjective*
*Alternative words:* infrequent, irregular, rare, odd
*The opposite is* **frequent**

**occupation** *noun*
*Alternative words:* job, profession, work

**occupy** *verb*
1 occupying a corner of the room
*Alternative words:* to take up, to fill
2 occupying the ground floor
*Alternative words:* to use, to live in, to have
3 occupying themselves
*Alternative words:* to amuse, to entertain, to keep busy
4 occupying a country
*Alternative words:* to invade, to seize, to take over

**occur** *verb*
1 When did the accident occur?
*Alternative words:* to happen, to take place

**2** A thought occurred to me.
*Alternative words:* to come to mind, to spring to mind, to dawn on you

**odd** *adjective*
**1** wearing an odd hat
*Alternative words:* strange, peculiar, unusual, funny
**2** He has some odd ideas.
*Alternative words:* eccentric, bizarre, unconventional, weird
**3** odd socks
*Alternative words:* different, not matching

**odour** *noun*
*Alternative words:* smell, stink, scent

**offend** *verb*
to offend someone's feelings
*Alternative words:* to hurt, to insult, to upset

**offensive** *noun*
*Alternative words:* attack, onslaught, invasion

**offensive** *adjective*
**1** offensive language
*Alternative words:* rude, objectionable, abusive
**2** an offensive smell
*Alternative words:* disgusting, revolting, nasty

**often** *adverb*
*Alternative words:* frequently, usually, commonly, repeatedly, continually

**old** *adjective*
**1** He was old.
*Alternative words:* elderly, aged, getting on
*The opposite is* ***young***
**2** a house full of old things
*Alternative words:* antique, old-fashioned, out-of-date
*The opposite is* ***new***
**3** old clothes
*Alternative words:* worn-out, shabby, tattered
*The opposite is* ***new***

**old-fashioned** *adjective*
*Alternative words:* old, unfashionable, dated
*The opposite is* ***fashionable***

**ominous** *adjective*
*Alternative words:* sinister, threatening, menacing
*The opposite is* ***promising***

**once** *adverb*
**1** We had a dog once.
*Alternative words:* at one time, in the past, in the old days
**2** I only hit him once.
*Alternative words:* on one occasion, one single time
**3** Come here at once!
*Alternative words:* right away, immediately, right now
**4** Two buses arrived at once.
*Alternative words:* at the same time, together, simultaneously

**only** *adverb*
*Alternative words:* just, not more than, simply, merely

**ooze** *verb*
*Alternative words:* to leak, to trickle, to weep, to seep

**opaque** *adjective*
*Alternative words:* obscure, cloudy, dark, non-transparent, blurred, murky

**open** *adjective*
**1** The window was open.
*Alternative words:* not shut, not closed, wide open, ajar
*The opposite is* ***closed***
**2** We'll be open at nine.
*Alternative words:* ready for business, open to the public
*The opposite is* ***closed***
**3** Open countryside all around us
*Alternative words:* unfenced, undeveloped, exposed

**open** *verb*
**1** Open the door.
*Alternative words:* to unlock, to unbolt, to throw open
**2** Open your present.
*Alternative words:* to unwrap, to undo, to untie
**3** Put tape on it so that it doesn't open.
*Alternative words:* to come open, to come apart, to undo

**opening** *noun*
**1** crawled through the opening
*Alternative words:* gap, hole, crack

**2** We have an opening for a trainee.
*Alternative words:* opportunity, vacancy, job

**opinion** *noun*
*Alternative words:* point of view, belief, thought

**opponent** *noun*
**1** a strong opponent of foxhunting
*Alternative words:* opposer, enemy
*The opposite is* **supporter**
**2** I beat my opponent at chess.
*Alternative words:* competitor, rival, challenger

**oppose** *verb*
*Alternative words:* to defy, to withstand, to resist, to object

**opposite** *adjective*
in opposite directions
*Alternative words:* different, opposing

**opposite** *preposition*
the house opposite the mosque
*Alternative words:* facing, across from

**oppress** *verb*
*Alternative words:* to tyrannise, to persecute, to crush

**opt** *verb*
*Alternative words:* to choose, to pick, to plump for

**optimistic** *adjective*
*Alternative words:* positive, hopeful, confident

**orbit** *noun*
*Alternative words:* circuit, path, track

**order** *noun*
**1** That is an order!
*Alternative words:* command, instruction, decree
**2** The waiter will bring your order.
*Alternative words:* request, demand, requirement
**3** restoring order
*Alternative words:* tidiness, orderliness, harmony
**4** The machine is out of order.
*Alternative words:* broken, not working, broken-down

**order** *verb*
**1** The king ordered him to go.
*Alternative words:* to command,

to instruct, to bid
**2** Have you ordered your meal?
*Alternative words:* to ask for, to call for, to request
**3** We can order that book for you.
*Alternative words:* to reserve, to send off for
**4** You need to order your things better.
*Alternative words:* to arrange, to organise, to put in order

**ordinary** *adjective*
*Alternative words:* usual, normal, common, typical

**organisation** *noun*
*Alternative words:* company, firm, group, corporation

**organise** *verb*
**1** to organise the school fair
*Alternative words:* to plan, to be responsible for, to arrange, to run
**2** to organise people
*Alternative words:* to manage, to set to work, to lead, to guide

**origin** *noun*
**1** the origin of the dispute
*Alternative words:* cause, basis, roots
**2** proud of his origins
*Alternative words:* ancestry, heritage, family, background

**original** *adjective*
**1** the original owner of my house
*Alternative words:* first, earliest, initial
**2** an original work of art
*Alternative words:* genuine, authentic, not copied
**3** has several original ideas
*Alternative words:* new, imaginative, fresh, innovative

**originate** *verb*
*Alternative words:* to create, to bring about, to give birth to, to begin, to start, to establish, to invent

**ornate** *adjective*
*Alternative words:* elaborate, decorated, fussy
*The opposite is* **simple**

**out** *adverb*
*Alternative words:* not in, outside, out of doors
*The opposite is* **in**

**outburst** *noun*
*Alternative words:* fit of temper, attack, explosion, storm

**outcome** *noun*
*Alternative words:* result, consequence, upshot

**outfit** *noun*
*Alternative words:* clothes, costume, suit

**outlaw** *noun*
*Alternative words:* fugitive, bandit, outcast

**outline** *noun*
**1** Draw the outline first.
*Alternative words:* framework, contour, perimeter
**2** the outline of a story
*Alternative words:* framework, rough draft, layout, plan

**out-of-date** *adjective*
**1** no longer fashionable
*Alternative words:* old-fashioned, old, unfashionable
*The opposite is* **modern**
**2** no longer valid
*Alternative words:* invalid, expired, elapsed
*The opposite is* **valid**

**outset** *noun*
*Alternative words:* beginning, start, starting point

**outside** *adverb*
*Alternative words:* out of doors, out of the house, outdoors
*The opposite is* **inside**

**outskirts** *plural noun*
*Alternative words:* edge, suburbs, outlying areas

**outstanding** *adjective*
**1** outstanding results
*Alternative words:* excellent, exceptional, remarkable
**2** payment still outstanding
*Alternative words:* owing, due, unpaid

**ovation** *noun*
*Alternative words:* applause, cheers, clapping

**over** *adverb*
**1** had some left over
*Alternative words:* surplus, remaining, unused, left
**2** when the match was over
*Alternative words:* finished, at an end, concluded

**over** *preposition*
**1** flying over the clouds
*Alternative words:* above, higher than
*The opposite is* **below**
**2** wearing a shirt over his vest
*Alternative words:* on top of
*The opposite is* **under**
**3** over 300 people
*Alternative words:* more than, in excess of
*The opposite is* **under**

**overcast** *adjective*
*Alternative words:* cloudy, grey, dull
*The opposite is* **cloudless**

**overcrowded** *adjective*
*Alternative words:* congested, crowded, packed
*The opposite is* **deserted**

**own** *verb*
**1** to own a house
*Alternative words:* to have, to be the owner of, to possess
**2** to own up to something
*Alternative words:* to admit, to confess, to tell the truth about

# Pp

**pace** *noun*
  **1** Take three paces forward!
  *Alternative words:* step, stride, footstep
  **2** She walks at a fast pace.
  *Alternative words:* speed, rate

**pack** *noun*
  **1** a pack of dogs
  *Alternative words:* group, band
  **2** a pack of cards
  *Alternative words:* set, deck
  **3** an information pack
  *Alternative words:* set, kit, package

**pack** *verb*
  **1** I packed my bag.
  *Alternative words:* to fill, to load, to store
  *The opposite is* **to unpack**
  **2** The cinema was packed.
  *Alternative words:* to fill, to crowd,
  to cram
  *The opposite is* **to empty**

**pact** *noun*
  *Alternative words:* promise, agreement,
  treaty

**paddock** *noun*
  *Alternative words:* field, pasture, green

**page¹** *noun*
  a page of a book
  *Alternative words:* sheet, leaf, side

**pain** *noun*
  **1** an unpleasant feeling
  *Alternative words:* soreness, ache, cramp,
  twinge
  **2** severe pain
  *Alternative words:* agony, torment,
  suffering

**painful** *adjective*
  *Alternative words:* sore, aching, tender,
  stiff
  *The opposite is* **painless**

**pair** *noun*
  **1** two things
  *Alternative words:* couple, brace
  **2** two people
  *Alternative words:* couple, duo, twosome

**pale** *adjective*
  **1** a pale colour
  *Alternative words:* light, dim, faint

*The opposite is* **bright**
  **2** a pale face
  *Alternative words:* white, ashen, wan
  (old-fashioned)

**pamper** *verb*
  *Alternative words:* to spoil, to make a
  fuss of, to indulge

**panic** *noun*
  *Alternative words:* fear, fright, terror,
  hysteria

**panic** *verb*
  *Alternative words:* to be terrified, to lose
  your nerve, to go to pieces, to become
  hysterical
  *The opposite is* **to stay calm**

**parade** *noun*
  *Alternative words:* march, procession,
  pageant

**paraphernalia** *noun*
  *Alternative words:* things, gear, stuff
  (informal)

**paraphrase** *verb*
  *Alternative words:* to summarise,
  to reword, to say in your own words

**parcel** *noun*
  *Alternative words:* package, packet,
  carton

**parched** *adjective*
  **1** very thirsty
  *Alternative words:* dry, dehydrated,
  dying of thirst (informal)
  **2** needing water
  *Alternative words:* arid, scorched,
  withered

**pardon** *verb*
  *Alternative words:* to forgive, to excuse,
  to reprieve
  *The opposite is* **to punish**

**part** *noun*
  **1** some but not all
  *Alternative words:* share, slice, portion
  **2** a small piece
  *Alternative words:* bit, element, section,
  component
  **3** a part in a play
  *Alternative words:* role, character, lines

**part** *verb*
  **1** to divide into parts
  *Alternative words:* to separate, to divide,
  to split

*The opposite is* **to join**
2 They parted at the airport.
*Alternative words:* to separate, to say goodbye, to go different ways

**partial** *adjective*
*Alternative words:* incomplete, unfinished, limited
*The opposite is* **complete**

**particle** *noun*
*Alternative words:* grain, speck, atom

**partly** *adverb*
*Alternative words:* partially, to some extent, halfway
*The opposite is* **totally**

**partner** *noun*
1 someone who you do something with
*Alternative words:* team-mate, associate, colleague, collaborator
2 husband or wife
*Alternative words:* spouse, mate, companion

**party** *noun*
1 a birthday party
*Alternative words:* celebration, festivity, get-together
2 a group of people
*Alternative words:* band, company, team
3 an organisation
*Alternative words:* alliance, league, coalition

**pass¹** *noun*
1 a successful result
*Alternative words:* qualification, success
*The opposite is* **failure**
2 a document
*Alternative words:* permit, identity card, licence

**pass¹** *verb*
1 Everyone passed the test.
*Alternative words:* to succeed, to get through, to qualify
*The opposite is* **to fail**
2 Pass it to me.
*Alternative words:* to give, to hand, to deliver
3 The bus passed us.
*Alternative words:* to go past, to pass by, to overtake

**passage** *noun*
1 a hall
*Alternative words:* corridor, hallway,

lobby
2 a short piece of writing or music
*Alternative words:* section, extract, verse

**passer-by** *noun*
*Alternative words:* bystander, onlooker, witness

**passion** *noun*
1 a strong feeling
*Alternative words:* excitement, fervour, zeal
2 a great love
*Alternative words:* adoration, desire, ardour (formal)
*The opposite is* **indifference**

**passionate** *adjective*
*Alternative words:* enthusiastic, impassioned, ardent
*The opposite is* **half-hearted**

**past** *adjective*
*Alternative words:* former, previous, recent
*The opposite is* **future**

**past** *preposition*
*Alternative words:* after, beyond, farther than
*The opposite is* **before**

**pastime** *noun*
*Alternative words:* hobby, recreation, sport

**pasture** *noun*
*Alternative words:* grassland, meadow, grazing land

**pat** *verb*
1 to pat something
*Alternative words:* to tap, to dab
2 to pat the dog
*Alternative words:* to pet, to caress

**patch** *noun*
a patch of ground
*Alternative words:* plot, allotment, area

**path** *noun*
*Alternative words:* footpath, track, trail

**pathetic** *adjective*
1 a pathetic person
*Alternative words:* sad, helpless, pitiful
2 a pathetic excuse
*Alternative words:* weak, feeble, useless

**patrol** *verb*
*Alternative words:* to guard, to inspect,

to keep watch

**patronise** *verb*
*Alternative words:* to look down on, to talk down to, to treat like a child

**pattern** *noun*
**1** a pretty pattern
*Alternative words:* design, decoration, motif
**2** a sewing pattern
*Alternative words:* plan, template, stencil

**pay** *verb*
*Alternative words:* to settle, to meet the cost of, to fork out (informal)

**peace** *noun*
**1** peace between people or countries
*Alternative words:* harmony, friendship, goodwill, accord
**2** the end of war
*Alternative words:* ceasefire, truce, armistice
**3** not noisy or busy
*Alternative words:* quiet, tranquillity, serenity

**peak** *noun*
the highest point
*Alternative words:* top, crest, summit
*The opposite is* **bottom**

**peculiar** *adjective*
*Alternative words:* strange, odd, bizarre, weird
*The opposite is* **ordinary**

**pelt** *verb*
*Alternative words:* to throw, to hurl, to bombard

**pen¹** *noun*
*Alternative words:* ball-point pen, fountain pen, Biro (trade mark), quill (old-fashioned)

**pen²** *noun*
a pen for animals
*Alternative words:* enclosure, fold, sty, coop

**penalty** *noun*
penalty for breaking the law
*Alternative words:* punishment, fine, price you have to pay

**penetrate** *verb*
*Alternative words:* to enter, to pierce, to go through

**perceptive** *adjective*
*Alternative words:* astute, observant, intuitive
*The opposite is* **slow-witted**

**perfect** *adjective*
*Alternative words:* ideal, faultless, immaculate
*The opposite is* **imperfect**

**perform** *verb*
**1** to perform in front of an audience
*Alternative words:* to act, to play, to appear as
**2** to do something
*Alternative words:* to carry out, to accomplish, to complete

**perhaps** *adverb*
*Alternative words:* maybe, possibly, you never know
*The opposite is* **certainly**

**period** *noun*
**1** a period of time
*Alternative words:* term, season, era, span
**2** a woman's period
*Alternative words:* monthly cycle, menstruation (formal), time of the month (informal)

**permanent** *adjective*
*Alternative words:* lasting, constant, perpetual
*The opposite is* **temporary**

**permission** *noun*
*Alternative words:* consent, authorisation, the go-ahead (informal)

**permit** *verb*
*Alternative words:* to allow, to let, to consent
*The opposite is* **to refuse**

**personal** *adjective*
*Alternative words:* individual, private, own

**persuade** *verb*
*Alternative words:* to encourage, to talk into, to coax, to convince

**petrified** *adjective*
*Alternative words:* terrified, scared stiff, frightened

**phantom** *noun*
*Alternative words:* ghost, spirit, spook (informal)

**procession** noun
*Alternative words:* march, parade, cavalcade

**prod** verb
*Alternative words:* to poke, to nudge, to elbow

**progress** noun
1 scientific progress
*Alternative words:* improvement, advance, development
*The opposite is* **decline**
2 The match is in progress.
*Alternative words:* happening, taking place, under way

**project** noun
a plan
*Alternative words:* enterprise, venture, undertaking

**prominent** adjective
1 easy to see
*Alternative words:* obvious, conspicuous, pronounced
*The opposite is* **inconspicuous**
2 important
*Alternative words:* famous, eminent, renowned
*The opposite is* **unknown**

**promise** noun
1 She made a promise.
*Alternative words:* vow, pledge, word of honour
2 He shows promise as a tennis player.
*Alternative words:* ability, talent, potential

**promise** verb
*Alternative words:* to vow, to give your word, to swear

**proof** noun
*Alternative words:* evidence, confirmation, verification

**prop** verb
1 He propped the bike against the shed.
*Alternative words:* to lean on
2 The baby's head was propped up on a pillow.
*Alternative words:* to support, to hold up.

**proper** adjective
1 You should have a proper breakfast.
*Alternative words:* suitable, appropriate, fitting

*The opposite is* **unsuitable**
2 Is this the proper way to do it?
*Alternative words:* correct, right, accepted
*The opposite is* **wrong**

**properly** adverb
*Alternative words:* correctly, right, well, by the book
*The opposite is* **wrongly**

**property** noun
1 something you own
*Alternative words:* belongings, possession, asset
2 buildings or land
*Alternative words:* real estate, estate, holding

**prophecy** noun
*Alternative words:* prediction, forecast

**prophesy** verb
*Alternative words:* to predict, to forecast, to foretell

**propose** verb
1 to propose a plan
*Alternative words:* to suggest, to submit, to put forward
2 to propose marriage
*Alternative words:* to ask someone to marry you, to ask for someone's hand (old-fashioned), to pop the question (informal)

**prosperous** adjective
*Alternative words:* wealthy, rich, successful, thriving
*The opposite is* **poor**

**protect** verb
*Alternative words:* to safeguard, to screen, to shield, to guard, to look after, to watch over
*The opposite is* **to expose**

**protest** verb
*Alternative words:* to complain, to oppose, to demonstrate

**protest** noun
*Alternative words:* complaint, demonstration, outcry

**proud** adjective
1 feeling pride
*Alternative words:* pleased with, delighted with, honoured
*The opposite is* **humble**

**2** feeling too much pride in yourself
*Alternative words:* vain, conceited, arrogant
*The opposite is* **modest**

**prove** *verb*
*Alternative words:* to show, to confirm, to verify
*The opposite is* **to disprove**

**provide** *verb*
*Alternative words:* to give, to supply, to lay on (informal)

**provoke** *verb*
*Alternative words:* to annoy, to irritate, to needle, to wind someone up (informal)

**public** *noun*
*Alternative words:* people, society, community

**publicity** *noun*
*Alternative words:* advertising, promotion, propaganda

**publish** *verb*
*Alternative words:* to print, to bring out, to issue

**puff** *verb*
**1** to breathe quickly
*Alternative words:* to blow, to pant, to gasp
**2** to puff up or puff out
*Alternative words:* to expand, to swell, to inflate

**pull** *verb*
**1** to pull something up or out
*Alternative words:* to draw, to tug, to jerk
**2** to pull something behind you
*Alternative words:* to drag, to tow, to draw
*The opposite is* **to push**

**pulp** *noun*
*Alternative words:* paste, mash, mush

**punch** *verb*
*Alternative words:* to hit, to box, to clout, to thump

**punctual** *adjective*
*Alternative words:* on time, prompt, on the dot
*The opposite is* **unpunctual**

**punish** *verb*
*Alternative words:* to discipline, to penalise, to teach someone a lesson, to sentence
*The opposite is* **to reward**

**punishment** *noun*
*Alternative words:* discipline, penalty, retribution

**pure** *adjective*
**1** clean and not mixed with anything else
*Alternative words:* untainted, unadulterated, uncontaminated
*The opposite is* **impure**
**2** It's a pure coincidence.
*Alternative words:* total, absolute, sheer, outright

**purpose** *noun*
*Alternative words:* reason, aim, point

**push** *verb*
*Alternative words:* to press, to shove, to drive
*The opposite is* **to pull**

**put** *verb*
**1** to put something somewhere
*Alternative words:* to place, to lay, to set
**2** to put an animal down
*Alternative words:* to kill, to destroy, to put to sleep
**3** to put something off
*Alternative words:* to delay, to postpone, to defer
**4** to put someone off
*Alternative words:* to confuse, to distract, to perturb

**puzzle** *verb*
**1** We puzzled for hours over the problem.
*Alternative words:* to rack your brains, to ponder, to muse
**2** The mystery puzzled everyone.
*Alternative words:* to baffle, to bewilder, to perplex

**puzzled** *adjective*
*Alternative words:* bewildered, mystified, perplexed

# Qq

**quail²** *verb*
*Alternative words:* to flinch, to quake

**qualified** *adjective*
*Alternative words:* suitable, able, proficient, equipped

**quality** *noun*
**1** a good-quality shirt.
*Alternative words:* value, worth, grade
**2** He has the qualities of a good singer.
*Alternative words:* attribute, property, characteristic

**quantity** *noun*
*Alternative words:* amount, volume, extent

**quarrel** *verb*
*Alternative words:* to argue, to bicker, to squabble
*The opposite is* **to agree**

**quarrel** *noun*
*Alternative words:* argument, feud, squabble
*The opposite is* **agreement**

**queer** *adjective*
*Alternative words:* strange, odd, peculiar
*The opposite is* **normal**

**quench** *verb*
**1** quench your thirst
*Alternative words:* satisfy, sate, allay
**2** quench a fire
*Alternative words:* put out, extinguish, douse

**quest** *noun*
*Alternative words:* search, mission, crusade, pursuit

**question** *noun*
*Alternative words:* query, enquiry

**queue** *noun*
*Alternative words:* line, row, file, string

**quick** *adjective*
**1** quick movement
*Alternative words:* fast, rapid, speedy, swift
**2** quick thinking
*Alternative words:* bright, sharp, efficient
*The opposite is* **slow**

**quickly** *adverb*
*Alternative words:* fast, rapidly, speedily, swiftly

**quiet** *adjective*
**1** not noisy
*Alternative words:* hushed, soft, silent
*The opposite is* **loud**
**2** not busy
*Alternative words:* peaceful, calm, tranquil

**quite** *adverb*
**1** I'm not quite finished.
*Alternative words:* completely, totally, absolutely
**2** It was quite hot today.
*Alternative words:* fairly, rather, pretty (informal)

**quiver²** *verb*
*Alternative words:* to shiver, to shudder, to tremble

**quiz** *noun*
*Alternative words:* test, examination, exam (informal)

# Rr

**rabble** *noun*
*Alternative words:* crowd, mob, horde

**racket²** *noun*
1 a loud noise
*Alternative words:* din, hullabaloo, commotion
2 a dishonest way of making money
*Alternative words:* scheme, fraud, scam (informal)

**radiant** *adjective*
happy and healthy
*Alternative words:* beaming, glowing, rapturous

**radiate** *verb*
1 to radiate light
*Alternative words:* to send out, to shine, to emanate
2 to radiate from a place
*Alternative words:* to branch out, to spread out, to go out

**radical** *adjective*
1 a radical change
*Alternative words:* complete, extreme, sweeping
2 radical opinions
*Alternative words:* revolutionary, extreme, extremist
*The opposite is* **conservative**

**rage** *noun*
*Alternative words:* anger, fury, wrath

**raid** *noun*
*Alternative words:* attack, invasion, break-in

**rain** *verb*
*Alternative words:* to spit, to drizzle, to pour

**raise** *verb*
1 Everyone raised their glasses.
*Alternative words:* to lift, to elevate, to hoist
*The opposite is* **to lower**
2 The bus company has raised its prices.
*Alternative words:* to increase, to put up, to boost
*The opposite is* **to reduce**
3 My grandmother raised six children.

*Alternative words:* to bring up, to look after, to rear

**ram** *verb*
1 to push hard
*Alternative words:* to force, to drive, to thrust
2 to crash into
*Alternative words:* to collide with, to run into, to slam into

**ramble** *verb*
1 to go for a long walk
*Alternative words:* to hike, to roam, to wander
2 to talk aimlessly
*Alternative words:* to digress, to waffle, to lose the thread, to rabbit on (informal)

**rampage** *noun*
on the rampage
*Alternative words:* on the warpath, out of control, berserk

**random** *adjective*
1 with no fixed order
*Alternative words:* arbitrary, haphazard, hit or miss
*The opposite is* **deliberate**
2 a random choice
*Alternative words:* chance, haphazard, unsystematic
*The opposite is* **systematic**

**rapid** *adjective*
*Alternative words:* fast, swift, express
*The opposite is* **slow**

**rare¹** *adjective*
*Alternative words:* unusual, scarce, uncommon
*The opposite is* **common**

**ration** *noun*
*Alternative words:* share, quota, allowance

**rave** *verb*
1 to say that something is wonderful
*Alternative words:* to enthuse, to praise, to be wild about
2 to talk in a wild way
*Alternative words:* to be delirious, to babble, to rant

**ravenous** *adjective*
*Alternative words:* starving, famished

**reach** *verb*
1 We reached the campsite in the afternoon.
*Alternative words:* to get to, to come to, to arrive at
2 The temperature reached 35°C today.
*Alternative words:* to get to, to rise to, to climb to
3 I can't reach the top shelf.
*Alternative words:* to touch, to get hold of, to stretch to

**ready** *adjective*
*Alternative words:* prepared, all set, arranged

**real** *adjective*
1 Is Father Christmas real?
*Alternative words:* actual, true
The opposite is **imaginary**
2 Her real name is Winifred, but we call her Wendy.
*Alternative words:* true, actual, proper, bona fide (formal)
The opposite is **false**
3 These diamonds are real.
*Alternative words:* genuine, authentic, the real McCoy (informal)
The opposite is **artificial**

**realise** *verb*
1 I realise how busy you are.
*Alternative words:* to understand, to recognise, to appreciate
2 I didn't realise he had moved.
*Alternative words:* to know, to become aware of, to take in

**realistic** *adjective*
1 a realistic monster
*Alternative words:* lifelike, true to life, vivid
2 a realistic attitude
*Alternative words:* down-to-earth, sensible, rational
The opposite is **unrealistic**

**really** *adverb*
1 I'm really hungry.
*Alternative words:* very, ever so, decidedly
2 Is it really your birthday today?
*Alternative words:* truly, actually, genuinely

**rear²** *noun*
*Alternative words:* back, tail end, stern
The opposite is **front**

**reason** *noun*
1 a good reason
*Alternative words:* explanation, justification, cause
2 the ability to think sensibly
*Alternative words:* judgement, logic, rationality

**reason** *verb*
1 to think in a sensible way
*Alternative words:* to explain, to deduce, to work out
2 to reason with someone
*Alternative words:* to persuade, to talk into, to remonstrate (formal)

**reassure** *verb*
*Alternative words:* to comfort, to relieve, to put someone's mind at rest

**receive** *verb*
*Alternative words:* to get, to be given, to acquire

**reckless** *adjective*
*Alternative words:* careless, harebrained, daredevil
The opposite is **careful**

**reckon** *verb*
1 to count
*Alternative words:* to add up, to calculate, to total
2 to think
*Alternative words:* to believe, to suppose, to imagine

**recognise** *verb*
*Alternative words:* to know, to identify, to place

**recollect** *verb*
*Alternative words:* to remember, to recall, to call to mind

**recommend** *verb*
*Alternative words:* to suggest, to advise, to prescribe

**recover** *verb*
1 to recover from an illness
*Alternative words:* to get better, to convalesce, to recuperate
2 to recover something you have lost
*Alternative words:* to get back, to retrieve, to reclaim

**recreation** *noun*
*Alternative words:* relaxation, enjoyment, leisure activity

*The opposite is work*

**rectify** *verb*
*Alternative words:* to put right, to correct, to remedy

**recur** *verb*
*Alternative words:* to happen again, to reappear, to return

**reduce** *verb*
*Alternative words:* to lower, to cut, to lessen
*The opposite is to increase*

**reel** *verb*
1 to stagger
*Alternative words:* to stumble, to sway, to lurch
2 to feel dizzy
*Alternative words:* to spin, to swirl, to whirl

**refer** *verb*
1 He never refers to his life during the war.
*Alternative words:* to mention, to allude to, to make reference to
2 You may refer to a dictionary during the test.
*Alternative words:* to consult, to turn to, to look up
3 The doctor referred her to a specialist.
*Alternative words:* to send, to direct, to guide, to recommend

**refine** *verb*
*Alternative words:* to process, to purify, to distil

**reform** *verb*
*Alternative words:* to change, to improve, to reorganise

**reform** *noun*
*Alternative words:* change, improvement, reorganisation

**refrain** *verb*
*Alternative words:* to stop, to hold back, to do without, to desist (formal)

**refrigerate** *verb*
*Alternative words:* to chill, to keep cold, to freeze

**refuse** *noun*
*Alternative words:* waste, rubbish, litter, garbage

**refuse** *verb*
*Alternative words:* to turn down, to decline, to reject
*The opposite is to accept*

**regain** *verb*
*Alternative words:* to get back, to recapture, to repossess

**regard** *noun*
*Alternative words:* care, consideration, respect

**regret** *noun*
*Alternative words*: remorse, sorrow

**regret** *verb*
*Alternative words:* to be sorry, to wish you had, to feel remorse

**regular** *adjective*
1 a regular event
*Alternative words:* routine, customary, habitual
*The opposite is occasional*
2 regular breathing
*Alternative words:* even, rhythmic, constant
*The opposite is irregular*

**reinforce** *verb*
*Alternative words:* to strengthen, to support, to fortify

**reject** *verb*
*Alternative words:* to refuse, to discard, to cast aside, to turn down
*The opposite is to accept*

**rejoice** *verb*
*Alternative words:* to celebrate, to jump for joy, to revel

**relate** *verb*
1 to relate one thing to another
*Alternative words:* to connect, to link, to associate
2 to relate to someone's feelings
*Alternative words:* to understand, to sympathise
3 to relate a story
*Alternative words:* to tell, to describe, to narrate

**relation** *noun*
1 a relation between things
*Alternative words:* connection, link
2 a member of the family
*Alternative words:* relative, family member, kin

**relatively** *adverb*
*Alternative words:* comparatively, by comparison

**relax** *verb*
**1** to rest
*Alternative words:* to unwind, to take it easy, to chill out (informal)
**2** to become less stiff
*Alternative words:* to ease, to loosen
*The opposite is* **to stiffen**
**3** to make something less strict
*Alternative words:* to moderate, to ease

**relaxed** *adjective*
*Alternative words:* calm, at ease, laid-back (informal)

**release** *verb*
**1** He was released from prison.
*Alternative words:* to free, to set free, to liberate
**2** The CD will be released next week.
*Alternative words:* to distribute, to issue

**reliable** *adjective*
*Alternative words:* dependable, trustworthy, reputable
*The opposite is* **unreliable**

**remain** *verb*
**1** to remain after others have gone
*Alternative words:* to linger, to be left, to be still standing, to survive
**2** to remain the same
*Alternative words:* to continue, to stay, to persist

**remarkable** *adjective*
*Alternative words:* impressive, outstanding, unusual
*The opposite is* **unremarkable**

**remedy** *noun*
*Alternative words:* cure, antidote, treatment

**remorse** *noun*
*Alternative words:* guilt, regret, shame

**remote** *adjective*
*Alternative words:* distant, out-of-the-way, secluded

**remove** *verb*
*Alternative words:* to take away, to delete, to detach
*The opposite is* **to add**

**renowned** *adjective*
*Alternative words:* famous, distinguished, celebrated
*The opposite is* **little-known**

**repair** *verb*
*Alternative words:* to fix, to mend, to put right

**repay** *verb*
*Alternative words:* to pay back, to refund, to reimburse

**replace** *verb*
**1** Replace your books on the shelf after use.
*Alternative words:* to put back, to restore
**2** The new teacher will replace Mrs Jones.
*Alternative words:* to take over from, to take the place of, to succeed
**3** I must replace that broken light bulb.
*Alternative words:* to change, to substitute, to renew

**replica** *noun*
*Alternative words:* copy, imitation, reproduction
*The opposite is* **original**

**reply** *verb*
*Alternative words:* to answer, to respond to, to acknowledge

**represent** *verb*
**1** to represent other people
*Alternative words:* to act for, to do something on behalf of, to serve as
**2** to represent something
*Alternative words:* to stand for, to mean, to correspond to, to be a symbol of

**representative** *noun*
*Alternative words:* delegate, spokesperson, agent

**reproduce** *verb*
**1** You can reproduce a photo thousands of times.
*Alternative words:* to copy, to duplicate, to replicate
**2** All animals and plants reproduce.
*Alternative words:* to breed, to multiply, to procreate

**repugnant** *adjective*
*Alternative words:* disgusting, abhorrent, loathsome

**repulsive** *adjective*
*Alternative words:* revolting, offensive, vile

**reputable** *adjective*
*Alternative words:* trustworthy, reliable, well-thought-of, highly regarded
*The opposite is* **disreputable**

**research** *verb*
*Alternative words:* to investigate, to explore, to look into

**resemblance** *noun*
*Alternative words:* likeness, similarity

**resemble** *verb*
*Alternative words:* to look like, to take after, to remind you of

**resentful** *adjective*
*Alternative words:* hurt, indignant, aggrieved

**reserve** *verb*
1 to ask someone to keep something for you
*Alternative words:* to book, to arrange, to save
2 to save something for later
*Alternative words:* to put by, to set aside, to conserve

**resident** *noun*
*Alternative words:* inhabitant, occupant, tenant
*The opposite is* **visitor**

**resist** *verb*
1 to fight against something
*Alternative words:* to struggle against, to withstand, to repel
*The opposite is* **to surrender**
2 to resist temptation
*Alternative words:* to abstain, to refrain from
*The opposite is* **to indulge in**

**resistance** *noun*
resistance to an enemy
*Alternative words:* struggle, opposition, defiance

**respect** *verb*
1 He respects his parents.
*Alternative words:* to honour, to think highly of, to esteem
*The opposite is* **to ignore**
2 I respect your wishes.
*Alternative words:* to accept, to abide by, to comply with
*The opposite is* **to disregard**

**respond** *verb*
*Alternative words:* to reply, to react, to acknowledge

**response** *noun*
*Alternative words:* answer, reaction, acknowledgement

**responsibility** *noun*
1 something you have to do
*Alternative words:* duty, obligation, liability
2 to take responsibility for something
*Alternative words:* blame, fault

**responsible** *adjective*
1 She is a very responsible girl.
*Alternative words:* trustworthy, sensible, reliable
*The opposite is* **irresponsible**
2 The headteacher is responsible for the whole school.
*Alternative words:* in charge, liable, accountable
*The opposite is* **not responsible**

**rest**[1] *noun*
1 a rest from working
*Alternative words:* break, pause, breather
2 a short sleep
*Alternative words:* nap, snooze, doze

**restful** *adjective*
*Alternative words:* peaceful, calm, soothing
*The opposite is* **disturbing**

**restless** *adjective*
*Alternative words:* unsettled, fidgety, agitated
*The opposite is* **relaxed**

**restore** *verb*
1 to restore a painting
*Alternative words:* to renovate, to renew, to recondition
2 to restore something to its correct place
*Alternative words:* to bring back, to return, to reinstate

**restrict** *verb*
*Alternative words:* to limit, to ration, to regulate

**result** *noun*
1 the result of your hard work

*Alternative words:* consequence, outcome, upshot
**2** the result of the game
*Alternative words:* score, outcome

**resume** *verb*
*Alternative words:* to start again, to carry on, to continue, to pick up where you left off
*The opposite is* ***to stop***

**retain** *verb*
*Alternative words:* to keep, to save, to reserve
*The opposite is* ***to let go***

**retaliate** *verb*
*Alternative words:* to take revenge, to get your own back, to hit back

**return** *verb*
**1** to return somewhere
*Alternative words:* to go back, to come back, to reappear
**2** to return something to someone
*Alternative words:* to give back, to replace, to restore

**reveal** *verb*
**1** He took off the mask and revealed his face.
*Alternative words:* to show, to exhibit, to uncover, to expose
**2** The book reveals the truth.
*Alternative words:* to disclose, to divulge, to make public
*The opposite is* ***to hide***

**revenge** *noun*
*Alternative words:* retaliation, vengeance, an eye for an eye

**revolt** *noun*
*Alternative words:* rebellion, insurrection, mutiny

**revolting** *adjective*
*Alternative words:* disgusting, horrible, foul

**revolution** *noun*
*Alternative words:* rebellion, uprising, coup

**rewarding** *adjective*
*Alternative words:* satisfying, worthwhile, beneficial, fulfilling
*The opposite is* ***unrewarding***

**rich** *adjective*
**1** a rich person

*Alternative words:* wealthy, well-off, prosperous
*The opposite is* ***poor***
**2** rich food
*Alternative words:* heavy, fatty, creamy
*The opposite is* ***light***

**ridiculous** *adjective*
*Alternative words:* silly, foolish, absurd
*The opposite is* ***sensible***

**right** *adjective*
**1** the right answer
*Alternative words:* correct, true, accurate
*The opposite is* ***wrong***
**2** the right decision
*Alternative words:* fair, just, proper
*The opposite is* ***unfair***

**rise** *verb*
**1** The plane rose in the sky.
*Alternative words:* to go up, to climb, to ascend, to soar
*The opposite is* ***to fall***
**2** She never rises till noon.
*Alternative words:* to get up, to arise, to get out of bed, to surface (informal)
**3** She rose to greet us.
*Alternative words:* to stand up, to jump up, to get to your feet

**risky** *adjective*
*Alternative words:* dangerous, perilous, chancy (informal)
*The opposite is* ***safe***

**rival** *noun*
*Alternative words:* opponent, contender, adversary
*The opposite is* ***ally***

**roam** *verb*
*Alternative words:* to wander, to ramble, to meander

**rob** *verb*
*Alternative words:* to burgle, to steal from, to defraud, to rip off (informal)

**romantic** *adjective*
**1** a romantic story
*Alternative words:* sentimental, tender, soppy
*The opposite is* ***unromantic***
**2** a romantic idea
*Alternative words:* unrealistic, idealistic, impractical
*The opposite is* ***realistic***

**rot** *verb*
1 The fruit will rot.
*Alternative words:* to decay, to perish, to putrefy
2 The wood will rot.
*Alternative words:* to decompose, to disintegrate, to corrode, to crumble

**rotten** *adjective*
*Alternative words:* bad, decayed, decomposed, mouldy

**rough** *adjective*
1 not smooth
*Alternative words:* coarse, rugged, knobbly, bumpy
*The opposite is* **smooth**
2 not gentle
*Alternative words:* coarse, harsh, brusque
*The opposite is* **gentle**
3 not exact
*Alternative words:* estimated, approximate, vague
*The opposite is* **exact**

**round** *adjective*
*Alternative words:* circular, spherical, curved

**routine** *noun*
*Alternative words:* habit, order, procedure

**row**[1] *noun*
a row of houses
*Alternative words:* line, column, file

**row**[2] *noun*
1 a lot of noise
*Alternative words:* racket, din, commotion
2 an argument
*Alternative words:* quarrel, dispute, squabble

**rubbish** *noun*
1 Take the rubbish out.
*Alternative words:* waste, refuse, garbage
2 That's rubbish!
*Alternative words:* nonsense, drivel, gibberish, codswallop (informal)

**rude** *adjective*
*Alternative words:* impolite, offensive, bad-mannered, cheeky, insolent
*The opposite is* **polite**

**ruin** *verb*
*Alternative words:* to spoil, to wreck, to destroy

**run** *verb*
1 I ran for the bus.
*Alternative words:* to dash, to race, to sprint
2 The engine is running.
*Alternative words:* to work, to operate, to function, to go
3 He runs a small company.
*Alternative words:* to be in charge of, to control, to manage
4 Water is running down the wall.
*Alternative words:* to flow, to pour, to stream
5 The colours ran in the wash.
*Alternative words:* to spread, to mix

**rupture** *verb*
*Alternative words:* to burst, to split, to tear

**rush**[1] *verb*
*Alternative words:* to hurry, to fly, to dash
*The opposite is* **to dawdle**

**ruthless** *adjective*
*Alternative words:* cruel, hard-hearted, brutal
*The opposite is* **compassionate**

# Ss

**sack** *verb*
*Alternative words:* to dismiss, to lay off, to fire (informal), to make redundant

**sacred** *adjective*
*Alternative words:* holy, blessed, sacrosanct

**sad** *adjective*
*Alternative words:* unhappy, miserable, depressed, low, down in the dumps (informal)
*The opposite is* **happy**

**safe²** *adjective*
**1** safe to use
*Alternative words:* harmless, nontoxic, innocuous
*The opposite is* **dangerous**
**2** safe from harm
*Alternative words:* safe and sound, secure, out of danger
*The opposite is* **in danger**

**same** *adjective*
**1** the same as something else
*Alternative words:* equivalent, identical, alike
*The opposite is* **different**
**2** the same as it was
*Alternative words:* constant, unchanged, unchanging, unvarying
*The opposite is* **different**

**sample** *noun*
*Alternative words:* specimen, taste, example, selection

**sanctuary** *noun*
**1** a place where you feel safe
*Alternative words:* shelter, refuge, safe haven
**2** a holy place
*Alternative words:* house of worship, shrine, temple
**3** a place where wildlife is protected
*Alternative words:* reserve, reservation, conservation area, wildlife park

**sane** *adjective*
*Alternative words:* rational, balanced, in your right mind, of sound mind
*The opposite is* **mad**

**satisfaction** *noun*
*Alternative words:* fulfilment, achievement, happiness
*The opposite is* **dissatisfaction**

**satisfactory** *adjective*
*Alternative words:* good enough, adequate, passable
*The opposite is* **unsatisfactory**

**satisfy** *verb*
**1** to satisfy a customer
*Alternative words:* to please, to content, to make someone happy
**2** an explanation that satisfies you
*Alternative words:* to convince, to reassure, to put your mind at rest

**saturate** *verb*
*Alternative words:* to drench, to soak, to drown, to flood

**savage** *adjective*
**1** a savage animal
*Alternative words:* wild, fierce, ferocious
*The opposite is* **tame**
**2** a savage person
*Alternative words:* brutal, vicious, sadistic
*The opposite is* **gentle**

**savage** *verb*
*Alternative words:* to attack, to maul, to rip to shreds

**save** *verb*
**1** to save money
*Alternative words:* to economise, to be thrifty, to squirrel away (informal)
*The opposite is* **to spend**
**2** to save energy, space and time
*Alternative words:* to conserve, to preserve, to use efficiently
*The opposite is* **to waste**

**say** *verb*
*Alternative words:* to speak, to mention, to utter, to come out with

**scan** *verb*
**1** to read something quickly
*Alternative words:* to skim, to glance at, to flick through, to run your eye over
**2** to look at something carefully
*Alternative words:* to examine, to search, to scrutinise

**scarce** *adjective*
*Alternative words:* rare, in short supply, few and far between
*The opposite is* **plentiful**

**scare** *verb*
*Alternative words:* to frighten, to terrify, to petrify

**scatter** *verb*
**1** to scatter seeds
*Alternative words:* to sprinkle, to strew
**2** the crowd scattered
*Alternative words:* to break up, to disperse, to disband

**scene** *noun*
**1** a place where something has happened
*Alternative words:* place, setting, location
**2** a scene in a play or film
*Alternative words:* act, episode, part

**scent** *noun*
**1** a pleasant smell
*Alternative words:* perfume, fragrance, aroma
**2** liquid you put on your skin
*Alternative words:* perfume, fragrance, cologne
**3** an animal's scent
*Alternative words:* smell, odour, trail, track

**schedule** *noun*
*Alternative words:* timetable, programme, agenda

**scheme** *noun*
**1** a scheme to do something good
*Alternative words:* plan, programme, course of action, strategy
**2** a scheme to do something bad
*Alternative words:* plot, ruse, racket

**scoff** *verb*
to scoff food
*Alternative words:* to gobble, to guzzle, to bolt

**scorch** *verb*
*Alternative words:* to singe, to blacken, to char

**score** *verb*
*Alternative words:* to get, to achieve, to win a point, to chalk up (informal)

**scorn** *noun*
*Alternative words:* mockery, contempt, derision

**scramble** *verb*
*Alternative words:* to clamber, to scrabble

**scrap** *noun*
**1** a small piece of something
*Alternative words:* speck, shred, fragment
**2** the leftovers are scrap
*Alternative words:* rubbish, junk, waste

**scratch** *noun*
*Alternative words:* scrape, graze, mark

**scratch** *verb*
*Alternative words:* to scrape, to graze, to mark

**scream** *noun*
*Alternative words:* cry, shriek, screech

**scream** *verb*
*Alternative words:* to cry, to yell, to shriek

**screen** *verb*
**1** to hide something
*Alternative words:* to hide, to conceal, to shroud
**2** to examine someone
*Alternative words:* to scan, to examine
**3** to screen a television programme
*Alternative words:* to broadcast, to show, to transmit, to put on

**scruffy** *adjective*
*Alternative words:* untidy, shabby, down-at-heel, unkempt
*The opposite is **smart***

**search** *verb*
to search for something
*Alternative words:* to look for, to hunt for, to look high and low

**secluded** *adjective*
*Alternative words:* hidden, concealed, screened, out-of-the-way

**second-hand** *adjective*
*Alternative words:* used, nearly new, hand-me-down
*The opposite is **new***

**secure** *adjective*
**1** a secure place
*Alternative words:* safe, sheltered, protected, well-guarded
*The opposite is **vulnerable***
**2** Make sure that the gate is secure.
*Alternative words:* fastened, locked
**3** shelves that feel secure
*Alternative words:* firm, steady, stable, solid

*The opposite is shaky*
**4** feeling secure
*Alternative words:* safe, comfortable, confident, self-assured
*The opposite is insecure*
**5** a secure future
*Alternative words:* safe, fixed, established, reliable

**security** *noun*
**1** feeling safe
*Alternative words:* safety, freedom from harm, freedom from danger
**2** something that keeps you safe
*Alternative words:* safeguard, precaution, protection, safety measure

**sedate** *adjective*
*Alternative words:* calm, placid, staid

**see** *verb*
**1** to see with your eyes
*Alternative words:* to look, to notice, to observe, to witness
**2** to understand
*Alternative words:* to understand, to follow, to grasp

**seek** *verb*
**1** to seek something that is lost
*Alternative words:* to look for, to search for, to hunt for, to look high and low
**2** to seek permission or advice
*Alternative words:* to ask, to request, to beg for

**seem** *verb*
*Alternative words:* to look like, to sound like, to appear

**seldom** *adverb*
*Alternative words:* hardly ever, rarely, infrequently

**select** *verb*
*Alternative words:* to choose, to pick, to opt for

**self-conscious** *adjective*
*Alternative words:* ill at ease, awkward, bashful, shy
*The opposite is confident*

**sell** *verb*
**1** We're selling the house.
*Alternative words:* to put up for sale, to put on the market, to auction
**2** This shop sells sweets.
*Alternative words:* to deal in, to stock, to keep, to carry

*The opposite is to buy*

**sensation** *noun*
*Alternative words:* feeling, impression, sense

**sense** *verb*
*Alternative words:* to feel, to be aware of, to perceive

**senseless** *adjective*
*Alternative words:* meaningless, pointless, idiotic
*The opposite is meaningful*

**sensible** *adjective*
*Alternative words:* level-headed, rational, down-to-earth

**separate** *adjective*
**1** not shared
*Alternative words:* individual, single, independent
**2** not joined together
*Alternative words:* detached, unconnected, distinct, independent

**separate** *verb*
**1** to separate two or more things
*Alternative words:* to part, to sever, to divide, to keep apart
*The opposite is to put together*
**2** a husband and wife who separate
*Alternative words:* to break up, to split up, to go different ways, to part

**sequence** *noun*
**1** a sequence of events
*Alternative words:* series, chain, course
**2** arranged in a sequence
*Alternative words:* order, arrangement, set

**series** *noun*
*Alternative words:* course, string, chain, succession, sequence

**serious** *adjective*
**1** not funny
*Alternative words:* important, worrying, no laughing matter
**2** a serious illness
*Alternative words:* critical, severe, dangerous, grave
*The opposite is mild*
**3** a serious person
*Alternative words:* thoughtful, unsmiling, solemn, stern

**set** *noun*
**1** a set of things
*Alternative words:* group, batch, collection, assortment
**2** a set of people
*Alternative words:* group, circle, clique, gang, crowd

**set** *verb*
**1** to set a date
*Alternative words:* to fix, to arrange, to agree on
**2** to set the table
*Alternative words:* to lay, to arrange, to prepare
**3** to set homework
*Alternative words:* to give, to allot, to assign, to specify
**4** liquid that sets
*Alternative words:* to harden, to solidify, to congeal
*The opposite is* **to liquefy**
**5** the sun sets
*Alternative words:* to go down, to sink, to dip
*The opposite is* **rise**

**several** *adjective, pronoun*
*Alternative words:* a few, a handful, one or two, a number of

**severe** *adjective*
**1** severe weather
*Alternative words:* very bad, rough, bleak, appalling
**2** a severe illness
*Alternative words:* serious, critical, grave, dangerous
**3** a severe person
*Alternative words:* strict, stern, austere
*The opposite is* **mild**

**shake** *verb*
**1** to shake something up and down
*Alternative words:* to jiggle, to rock, to agitate
**2** to shake with fear or cold
*Alternative words:* to tremble, to shiver, to quiver, to vibrate
**3** something upsetting that shakes you
*Alternative words:* to distress, to disturb, to frighten, to upset

**shame** *noun*
**1** a bad feeling
*Alternative words:* embarrassment, humiliation, disgrace, guilt
**2** It's a shame!

*Alternative words:* a pity, bad luck, sad

**share** *noun*
an amount that someone gets
*Alternative words:* part, portion, quota, ration, cut (informal)

**share** *verb*
to share something out
*Alternative words:* to divide, to parcel out, to distribute

**sharp** *adjective*
**1** a sharp knife
*Alternative words:* jagged, razor-sharp, keen (mainly used in stories)
*The opposite is* **blunt**
**2** a sharp person
*Alternative words:* bright, clever, quick-thinking, astute
*The opposite is* **slow**
**3** a sharp taste
*Alternative words:* sour, vinegary, tart
*The opposite is* **sweet**
**4** a sharp pain
*Alternative words:* shooting, stabbing, piercing
*The opposite is* **dull**
**5** a sharp rise in prices
*Alternative words:* sudden, abrupt, steep
*The opposite is* **gradual**

**sheer** *adjective*
**1** sheer material
*Alternative words:* fine, see-through, transparent
*The opposite is* **opaque**
**2** a sheer cliff
*Alternative words:* steep, abrupt, sharp, precipitous

**shield** *verb*
*Alternative words:* to protect, to shelter, to safeguard

**shimmer** *verb*
*Alternative words:* to glint, to glitter, to sparkle

**shine** *verb*
*Alternative words:* to gleam, to glow, to glisten, to sparkle

**shiver** *verb*
*Alternative words:* to shake, to tremble, to quiver

**shock** *verb*
**1** to shock someone slightly
*Alternative words:* to unsettle, to shake,

to upset, to offend
**2** to shock someone seriously
*Alternative words:* to stun, to stagger, to sicken, to horrify

**short** *adjective*
**1** not long
*Alternative words:* brief, concise
**2** not tall
*Alternative words:* little, small, low, stunted
**3** not lasting long
*Alternative words:* brief, fleeting, momentary

**shortage** *noun*
*Alternative words:* lack, deficiency, scarcity

**shortly** *adverb*
*Alternative words:* soon, any minute now, before long, in a little while

**shout** *verb*
*Alternative words:* to raise your voice, to yell, to scream, to bellow
*The opposite is* **to whisper**

**shove** *verb*
*Alternative words:* to push, to elbow, to shoulder, to barge

**show** *verb*
**1** to let people see something
*Alternative words:* to put on show, to display, to exhibit
**2** to show something to someone
*Alternative words:* to point out, to indicate, to present
**3** to show someone how to do something
*Alternative words:* to explain, to demonstrate, to illustrate

**shrink** *verb*
**1** to become smaller
*Alternative words:* to contract, to diminish, to shrivel
**2** to shrink from something nasty
*Alternative words:* to shy away, to flinch, to cower

**shrivel** *verb*
*Alternative words:* to dry up, to shrink, to wrinkle
*The opposite is* **to puff up**

**shudder** *verb*
*Alternative words:* to shake, to quake, to quiver, to tremble

**shy** *adjective*
*Alternative words:* timid, bashful, self-conscious, introverted
*The opposite is* **outgoing**

**sick** *adjective*
**1** She's been sick with the flu.
*Alternative words:* ill, unwell, poorly, under the weather (informal)
*The opposite is* **well**
**2** I feel sick!
*Alternative words:* queasy, nauseous, green around the gills (informal)
**3** I'm sick of exams.
*Alternative words:* tired of, bored with, fed up with, have had enough of

**side** *noun*
**1** the side of the stadium
*Alternative words:* edge, perimeter, border, boundary
**2** a side in an argument
*Alternative words:* camp, faction
**3** a side in a game
*Alternative words:* team, squad

**sign** *noun*
**1** a symbol that means something
*Alternative words:* symbol, logo, emblem, mark
**2** a board that gives you information
*Alternative words:* board, notice, placard
**3** a movement that means something
*Alternative words:* gesture, signal, indication

**sign** *verb*
**1** to sign your name
*Alternative words:* to autograph, to initial
**2** to make a sign
*Alternative words:* to gesture, to signal, to indicate

**silence** *noun*
*Alternative words:* quiet, peace, hush
*The opposite is* **noise**

**silent** *adjective*
*Alternative words:* quiet, soundless, noiseless, hushed
*The opposite is* **noisy**

**silly** *adjective*
**1** a silly joke
*Alternative words:* funny, amusing, entertaining
**2** not sensible
*Alternative words:* daft, crazy, foolish,

ridiculous

**similar** *adjective*
*Alternative words:* like, alike, much the same
*The opposite is **different***

**simple** *adjective*
1 a simple sum
*Alternative words:* easy, straightforward, uncomplicated
*The opposite is **difficult***
2 a simple meal
*Alternative words:* plain, unfussy, undecorated
*The opposite is **elaborate***

**sincere** *adjective*
*Alternative words:* honest, truthful, genuine, frank
*The opposite is **false***

**singe** *verb*
*Alternative words:* to scorch, to blacken, to char

**sink** *verb*
1 to sink under water
*Alternative words:* to go under, to submerge, to submerse
2 to get lower
*Alternative words:* to go down, to descend, to dip, to lower
*The opposite is **to come up***

**situation** *noun*
1 the way something is
*Alternative words:* state of affairs, state, circumstance, predicament
2 the place where something is
*Alternative words:* place, position, spot, location

**size** *noun*
1 the size of something
*Alternative words:* measurement, dimensions, proportions
2 the large size of something
*Alternative words:* largeness, hugeness, vastness, magnitude
3 the size of the space something fills
*Alternative words:* bulk, extent, volume

**skilful** *adjective*
*Alternative words:* expert, clever, accomplished

**skill** *noun*
1 the skill to do something well
*Alternative words:* expertise, know-how,

knack, capability
2 natural skill
*Alternative words:* talent, flair, gift

**skim** *verb*
1 to skim over the surface
*Alternative words:* to glide, to sail
2 to skim read
*Alternative words:* to scan, to flick through, to glance over, to run your eye over

**skip**[1] *verb*
1 to skip along
*Alternative words:* to hop, to dance, to bound
2 to skip over a rope
*Alternative words:* to hop, to caper, to jump, to trip
3 to miss something or miss something out
*Alternative words:* to miss, to miss out, to leave out, to omit

**slack** *adjective*
1 a slack rope
*Alternative words:* loose, limp
*The opposite is **taut***
2 a slack person or job
*Alternative words:* careless, slapdash, lax
*The opposite is **careful***

**slant** *verb*
*Alternative words:* to slope, to lean, to tilt

**slapdash** *adjective*
*Alternative words:* sloppy, careless, lax, slack
*The opposite is **careful***

**slaughter** *verb*
1 to kill animals
*Alternative words:* to kill, to butcher
2 to kill people
*Alternative words:* to kill, to massacre, to butcher, to exterminate

**slay** *verb*
*Alternative words:* to kill, to murder, to slaughter, to exterminate

**sleep** *verb*
1 to sleep
*Alternative words:* to be asleep, to slumber, to snooze (informal)
*The opposite is **to wake***
2 to sleep for a short time
*Alternative words:* to doze, to nap,

to have a nap, to have forty winks

**slender** *adjective*
*Alternative words:* slim, thin, slight, svelte, willowy
*The opposite is* **fat**

**slice** *noun*
*Alternative words:* piece, sliver, wedge, chunk

**slice** *verb*
*Alternative words:* to cut up, to chop, to carve, to divide

**slide** *verb*
*Alternative words*: to glide, to slither, to slip, to skid

**slight** *adjective*
1 a slight problem
*Alternative words:* little, small, minor
*The opposite is* **major**
2 a slight person
*Alternative words:* small, slender, slim, petite
*The opposite is* **large**

**slim** *adjective*
*Alternative words:* slender, thin, svelte, petite
*The opposite is* **fat**

**sling** *verb*
to throw carelessly
*Alternative words:* to fling, to toss, to lob (informal), to chuck (informal)

**slip** *verb*
*Alternative words:* to slide, to slither, to skid

**slit** *noun*
*Alternative words:* slash, split, tear

**slope** *noun*
*Alternative words:* slant, gradient, incline, tilt

**slope** *verb*
*Alternative words:* to slant, to tilt, to lean, to incline

**sly** *adjective*
*Alternative words:* cunning, crafty, devious, sneaky

**small** *adjective*
1 a small person
*Alternative words:* short, petite, slight, diminutive, puny
*The opposite is* **large**

2 a small thing
*Alternative words:* little, mini, miniature
*The opposite is* **big**
3 a small matter
*Alternative words:* unimportant, trivial, insignificant, minor
*The opposite is* **major**
4 very small
*Alternative words:* tiny, minute, teeny-weeny
*The opposite is* **huge**

**smart** *adjective*
1 to look smart
*Alternative words:* neat, well turned-out, well-dressed
*The opposite is* **scruffy**
2 intelligent
*Alternative words:* clever, bright
*The opposite is* **stupid**

**smash** *verb*
*Alternative words:* to shatter, to splinter, to break

**smear** *verb*
*Alternative words:* to spread, to smudge, to daub

**smell** *noun*
1 a pleasant smell
*Alternative words:* scent, fragrance, aroma, perfume
2 a bad smell
*Alternative words:* stink, stench, pong (informal)
3 any kind of smell
*Alternative words:* aroma, odour, whiff

**smell** *verb*
1 to smell something
*Alternative words:* to sniff, to scent, to get a whiff of
2 something smells
*Alternative words:* to have a (good or bad) smell, to reek, to stink, to pong (informal)

**smother** *verb*
1 to stop someone from breathing
*Alternative words:* to suffocate, to asphyxiate
2 to cover something completely
*Alternative words:* to cover, to envelop, to heap
3 to protect someone too much
*Alternative words:* to mollycoddle, to cosset, to stifle,

**smudge** *noun*
*Alternative words:* dirty mark, smear, blotch

**smudge** *verb*
*Alternative words:* to smear, to blur, to mark

**smug** *adjective*
*Alternative words:* self-satisfied, superior, complacent, holier-than-thou

**snack** *noun*
*Alternative words:* a bite, a bite to eat, a light meal, nibbles

**snap** *verb*
**1** to break
*Alternative words:* to break in two, to crack, to fracture
**2** to bite suddenly
*Alternative words:* to bite, to nip
**3** to snap at someone
*Alternative words:* to speak sharply, to bite someone's head off, to bark at someone, to lash out at

**snatch** *verb*
**1** to take something suddenly
*Alternative words:* to grab, to seize, to wrench out of someone's hands
**2** to snatch a person
*Alternative words:* to kidnap, to abduct

**sneak** *verb*
*Alternative words:* to sidle, to slink, to creep

**snoop** *verb*
*Alternative words:* to pry, to spy, to poke your nose in, to nose around

**snug** *adjective*
*Alternative words:* cosy, comfortable, warm

**soak** *verb*
**1** to soak
*Alternative words:* to drench, to drown, to saturate, to steep
**2** to soak up
*Alternative words:* to absorb, to take up

**soar** *verb*
**1** a bird that soars
*Alternative words:* to fly, to rise, to climb
**2** prices that soar
*Alternative words:* to rise, to shoot up, to skyrocket

**sociable** *adjective*
*Alternative words:* friendly, outgoing, social
*The opposite is* **unsociable**

**society** *noun*
**1** people who live in a place
*Alternative words:* civilisation, the general public, the community
**2** the art society
*Alternative words:* club, group, association, circle

**soft** *adjective*
**1** a soft bed
*Alternative words:* squashy, cushioned
*The opposite is* **hard**
**2** soft ground
*Alternative words:* swampy, boggy
*The opposite is* **firm**
**3** soft skin
*Alternative words:* smooth, velvety, silky
*The opposite is* **rough**
**4** a soft breeze
*Alternative words:* gentle, light, mild, balmy
**5** a soft sound
*Alternative words:* quiet, faint, low, hushed
*The opposite is* **loud**

**soggy** *adjective*
**1** very moist
*Alternative words:* wet, mushy, sodden
**2** full of water
*Alternative words:* soaking wet, sopping, saturated
*The opposite is* **dry**

**solemn** *adjective*
*Alternative words:* serious, grave, sombre

**solid** *adjective*
hard and firm
*Alternative words:* set, hardened, congealed

**solidify** *verb*
*Alternative words:* to set, to harden, to congeal
*The opposite is* **to liquefy**

**solitary** *adjective*
**1** a solitary person
*Alternative words:* unsociable, reclusive
*The opposite is* **sociable**
**2** just one of something
*Alternative words:* single, lone, sole, isolated

**staff** *noun*
1 the staff of a company
*Alternative words:* workforce, employees, personnel
2 a wooden staff
*Alternative words:* stick, rod

**stage** *noun*
1 a stage in a theatre
*Alternative words:* platform, dais
2 a stage in your life
*Alternative words:* period, phase, point

**stain** *noun*
*Alternative words:* dirty mark, blot, blemish

**stalk²** *verb*
*Alternative words:* to shadow, to tail, to track, to pursue

**stare** *verb*
*Alternative words:* to gaze, to gape, to goggle

**start** *verb*
1 to start to do something
*Alternative words:* to begin, to commence, to get going
2 to make something begin
*Alternative words:* to set in motion, to get going, to trigger, to activate

**startle** *verb*
*Alternative words:* to shock, to scare, to make someone jump

**state** *verb*
*Alternative words:* to declare, to assert, to say

**stay** *verb*
1 to stay somewhere for a long time
*Alternative words:* to settle, to stay put, to remain, to put down roots
2 to stay somewhere for a shorter time
*Alternative words:* to stop, to remain, to linger, to hang around (informal)
3 to stay in a hotel
*Alternative words:* to board, to lodge

**steady** *adjective*
1 not moving or shaking
*Alternative words:* firm, stable, solid
*The opposite is* **unsteady**
2 a steady rise in prices
*Alternative words:* regular, constant, uniform

**steal** *verb*
*Alternative words:* to thieve, to filch, to pinch, to nick (informal)

**steep** *adjective*
*Alternative words:* sharp, sheer, precipitous
*The opposite is* **gradual**

**step** *verb*
*Alternative words:* to walk, to tread, to pace

**stern²** *adjective*
*Alternative words:* firm, strict, harsh, no-nonsense
*The opposite is* **easy-going**

**stiff** *adjective*
*Alternative words:* hard, rigid, inflexible
*The opposite is* **flexible**

**still** *adjective*
not moving
*Alternative words:* stationary, motionless, stock-still
*The opposite is* **moving**

**stop** *verb*
1 to stop smoking
*Alternative words:* to give up, to quit, to pack in
*The opposite is* **to start**
2 to stop working
*Alternative words:* to finish, to cease, to call it a day, to pack up
*The opposite is* **to start**
3 to stop something happening
*Alternative words:* to hinder, to prevent, to ban, to prohibit
4 the machine stopped
*Alternative words:* to come to a halt, to come to a standstill, to shut down
*The opposite is* **to start**
5 the music stopped
*Alternative words:* to end, to finish, to cease, to come to an end
*The opposite is* **to begin**
6 to stop somewhere for a while
*Alternative words:* to remain, to stay, to hang around (informal), to stick around (informal)

**store** *verb*
*Alternative words:* to put away, to save, to put in storage

**storm** *noun*
1 a windy storm

*Alternative words:* gale, hurricane, whirlwind
**2** a wet and windy storm
*Alternative words:* blizzard, squall, tempest (mainly used in stories)

**story** *noun*
**1** the story of an imaginary event
*Alternative words:* tale, fairy tale, fable, legend
**2** the story of a real event
*Alternative words:* account, history, record, report

**straightaway** *adverb*
*Alternative words:* now, at once, right away, immediately
*The opposite is* **later**

**strange** *adjective*
**1** a strange thing or person
*Alternative words:* funny, weird, odd
**2** a strange place
*Alternative words:* new, unfamiliar, alien

**strength** *noun*
**1** physical strength
*Alternative words:* muscle, power, stamina
**2** a good quality
*Alternative words:* advantage, strong point, asset
*The opposite is* **weakness**

**strenuous** *adjective*
*Alternative words:* hard, tough, exhausting

**stress** *noun*
*Alternative words:* worry, pressure, anxiety, strain

**stretch** *noun*
**1** a stretch of time
*Alternative words:* time, spell, period
**2** a stretch of water or land
*Alternative words:* area, expanse, tract

**strict** *adjective*
*Alternative words:* stern, no-nonsense, firm, severe

**strike** *verb*
**1** to strike someone with your fist
*Alternative words:* to punch, to thump, to hit, to wallop
**2** to strike from your job
*Alternative words:* to walk out, to down tools, to take industrial action
**3** a clock that strikes

*Alternative words:* to chime, to peal

**stroke²** *verb*
*Alternative words:* to pat, to fondle, to caress

**stroll** *noun*
*Alternative words:* walk, amble, saunter

**strong** *adjective*
**1** a strong person
*Alternative words:* muscular, burly, brawny, beefy (informal)
*The opposite is* **weak**
**2** strong material
*Alternative words:* tough, durable, hard-wearing
*The opposite is* **delicate**
**3** a strong taste
*Alternative words:* hot, spicy, highly-seasoned
*The opposite is* **mild**
**4** a strong drink
*Alternative words:* alcoholic, potent
*The opposite is* **weak**

**structure** *noun*
**1** something that has been built
*Alternative words:* building, construction, edifice
**2** the way something is connected
*Alternative words:* arrangement, make up, organisation, configuration

**struggle** *noun*
**1** a struggle to achieve something
*Alternative words:* effort, long haul, grind
**2** a struggle between people
*Alternative words:* scuffle, tussle, skirmish

**struggle** *verb*
**1** to struggle to achieve something
*Alternative words:* to work very hard, to make a real effort, to strive
**2** to struggle with a burglar
*Alternative words:* to fight, to grapple with, to wrestle

**stubborn** *adjective*
*Alternative words:* headstrong, obstinate, pig-headed

**study** *verb*
**1** to study for an exam
*Alternative words:* to read up on, to swot (informal), to revise
**2** to look at something carefully

*Alternative words:* to examine, to inspect, to scrutinise, to go over

**stuff** *noun*
**1** the stuff that something is made of
*Alternative words:* material, substance, ingredients
**2** your school stuff
*Alternative words:* things, gear, bits and pieces, equipment

**stuff** *verb*
*Alternative words:* to cram, to jam, to pack

**stuffy** *adjective*
*Alternative words:* close, airless, stifling
*The opposite is* **airy**

**stupid** *adjective*
**1** not very intelligent
*Alternative words:* simple, dim, slow, dense
*The opposite is* **intelligent**
**2** foolish
*Alternative words:* silly, crazy, idiotic
*The opposite is* **sensible**

**sturdy** *adjective*
*Alternative words:* strong, stable, solid, firm
*The opposite is* **flimsy**

**submerge** *verb*
**1** to submerge something in water
*Alternative words:* to submerse, to immerse, to plunge, to dunk
**2** the rain submerged the road
*Alternative words:* to flood, to drown, to engulf

**substitute** *noun*
*Alternative words:* stand-in, replacement, fill-in

**sudden** *adjective*
**1** happening quickly
*Alternative words:* hurried, rapid, hasty
*The opposite is* **gradual**
**2** unexpected
*Alternative words:* unforeseen
*The opposite is* **expected**
**3** unplanned
*Alternative words:* impulsive, spur-of-the-moment
*The opposite is* **planned**

**suddenly** *adverb*
*Alternative words:* unexpectedly, without warning, out of the blue

**suffer** *verb*
*Alternative words:* to grieve, to be miserable, to ache

**suitable** *adjective*
**1** someone who is suitable for a job
*Alternative words:* eligible, qualified, right
**2** clothes suitable for a party
*Alternative words:* appropriate, fitting, right
*The opposite is* **unsuitable**

**summit** *noun*
*Alternative words:* top, peak, crest

**summon** *verb*
*Alternative words:* to send for, to call for

**superb** *adjective*
*Alternative words:* wonderful, marvellous, excellent
*The opposite is* **awful**

**superior** *adjective*
**1** a superior thing
*Alternative words:* superb, first-class, top-quality
*The opposite is* **inferior**
**2** a superior person
*Alternative words:* aloof, snobbish, stuck-up, high-and-mighty

**supervise** *verb*
*Alternative words:* to manage, to control, to oversee

**supple** *adjective*
*Alternative words:* lithe, flexible, elastic, pliable

**supply** *noun*
*Alternative words:* stock, store, source

**supply** *verb*
*Alternative words:* to give, to provide, to make available

**support** *noun*
**1** He gave her his support.
*Alternative words:* backing, encouragement, help
**2** a support that holds something up
*Alternative words:* prop, reinforcement, bolster

**support** *verb*
**1** to hold something up
*Alternative words:* to prop up, to bolster, to hold up

**2** She supports his idea.
*Alternative words:* to back, to go along with, to encourage, to get behind someone, to agree with

**suppose** *verb*
to suppose that something is true
*Alternative words:* to assume, to imagine, to guess, to think, to presume

**sure** *adjective*
**1** to be sure about something
*Alternative words:* certain, positive, definite, convinced
*The opposite is* **unsure**
**2** sure to happen
*Alternative words:* bound, guaranteed, certain
*The opposite is* **uncertain**

**surprise** *noun*
**1** something that was not expected
*Alternative words:* shock, a bolt from the blue, bombshell
**2** a feeling of surprise
*Alternative words:* amazement, astonishment, bewilderment

**surprise** *verb*
*Alternative words:* to shock, to astonish, to amaze

**surrender** *verb*
*Alternative words:* to give in, to give up, to submit

**surround** *verb*
*Alternative words:* to circle, to ring, to enclose

**survive** *verb*
**1** to survive after something dangerous
*Alternative words:* to live, to stay alive, to hold out, to pull through
**2** to survive for a long time
*Alternative words:* to exist, to live on, to last

**suspend** *verb*
**1** to suspend something from the ceiling
*Alternative words:* to hang, to dangle
**2** to suspend someone from school
*Alternative words:* to exclude, to bar, to throw out
**3** to stop something for a short time
*Alternative words:* to stop, to interrupt, to postpone

**suspense** *noun*
*Alternative words:* worry, anxiety, expectation

**swallow²** *verb*
*Alternative words:* to down, to gulp, to wash down

**swamp** *noun*
*Alternative words:* bog, marsh, mire

**swap** *verb*
*Alternative words:* to exchange, to trade, to switch

**sway** *verb*
**1** to move back and forth
*Alternative words:* to wave, to swing, to rock
**2** to sway someone's opinion
*Alternative words:* to influence, to persuade, to affect, to bias

**swell** *verb*
*Alternative words:* to expand, to bulge, to enlarge, to become bloated

**swift** *adjective*
*Alternative words:* fast, quick, rapid
*The opposite is* **slow**

**swindle** *verb*
*Alternative words:* to cheat, to trick, to con (informal), to defraud (formal)

**swing** *verb*
*Alternative words:* to rock, to sway, to oscillate (formal)

**swirl** *verb*
*Alternative words:* to whirl, to spin, to gyrate (formal)

**sympathetic** *adjective*
*Alternative words:* understanding, caring, kind
*The opposite is* **unsympathetic**

**sympathy** *noun*
*Alternative words:* understanding, feeling, pity

# Tt

**tackle** *verb*
1 to tackle a football player
*Alternative words:* to challenge, to block, to intercept
2 to tackle a hard job
*Alternative words:* to attempt, to begin, to have a go at

**tact** *noun*
*Alternative words:* thoughtfulness, understanding, sensitivity

**tactful** *adjective*
*Alternative words:* considerate, polite
*The opposite is* **blunt**

**tailor** *verb*
*Alternative words:* adapt, modify, adjust

**tainted** *adjective*
*Alternative words:* spoilt, damaged, contaminated

**take** *verb*
1 to take suitcases to the car
*Alternative words:* to carry, to convey, to haul, to lug (informal)
2 to take the parcel
*Alternative words:* to hold, to get hold of, to carry, to hang on to (informal)
3 to steal something
*Alternative words:* to steal, to pilfer, to nick (informal), to swipe (informal)
4 to take something away
*Alternative words:* to move, to remove, to walk off with

**talk** *verb*
*Alternative words:* to speak, to chat

**talk** *noun*
1 a talk to an audience
*Alternative words:* lecture, speech, address
2 a talk between groups or countries
*Alternative words:* discussion, negotiation, dialogue

**tame** *adjective*
1 a tame animal
*Alternative words:* domesticated, used to human contact, docile
*The opposite is* **wild**
2 not very exciting
*Alternative words:* boring, unexciting, ordinary

*The opposite is* **exciting**

**tamper** *verb*
*Alternative words:* to damage, to tinker with, to interfere with, to fiddle with

**tap²** *noun*
a gentle touch or hit
*Alternative words:* rap, knock, pat

**tap²** *verb*
*Alternative words:* to rap, to knock, to hit gently

**task** *noun*
*Alternative words:* job, chore, duty

**taste** *noun*
1 the taste of food
*Alternative words:* flavour, tang
2 someone with good taste
*Alternative words:* judgement, discrimination, discernment, style

**taunt** *verb*
*Alternative words:* to tease, to mock, to torment

**teach** *verb*
1 to teach someone
*Alternative words:* to educate, to train, to coach, to instruct
2 to teach something
*Alternative words:* to give lessons in, to instil, to show how to

**team** *noun*
*Alternative words:* group, side, squad

**tear²** *verb*
*Alternative words:* to rip, to shred, to pull apart

**tease** *verb*
1 to tease gently
*Alternative words:* to rib, to wind up
2 to tease spitefully
*Alternative words:* to taunt, to torment, to mock

**tell** *verb*
1 to tell someone something
*Alternative words:* to inform, to advise, to notify
2 to tell someone to do something
*Alternative words:* to order, to instruct, to direct
3 to tell what something is
*Alternative words:* to know, to say, to make out, to work out

**temper** *noun*
Alternative words: anger, rage, bad mood, tantrum

**temperament** *noun*
Alternative words: nature, character, frame of mind

**temperate** *adjective*
Alternative words: moderate, mild, equable
The opposite is **extreme**

**temporary** *adjective*
Alternative words: short-lived, short-term, fleeting
The opposite is **permanent**

**tempt** *verb*
Alternative words: to appeal to, to attract, to entice

**tender** *adjective*
1 a tender part of your body
Alternative words: sore, painful, sensitive
2 a tender person
Alternative words: kind, loving, warm
The opposite is **cold**

**tense²** *adjective*
1 a tense person
Alternative words: on edge, anxious, uptight (informal)
The opposite is **relaxed**
2 tense muscles
Alternative words: stiff, rigid, taut
The opposite is **relaxed**

**tension** *noun*
1 a feeling of tension
Alternative words: stress, worry, anxiety
2 the tension of a rope
Alternative words: tightness, tautness

**terrible** *adjective*
Alternative words: very bad, awful, dreadful, fearsome

**terrific** *adjective*
1 a terrific film
Alternative words: excellent, brilliant, fabulous
The opposite is **awful**
2 a terrific noise
Alternative words: great, enormous, tremendous

**terrify** *verb*
Alternative words: to scare to death, to petrify, to frighten the life out of

**territory** *noun*
Alternative words: area, patch, region

**terror** *noun*
Alternative words: great fear, dread, panic, horror

**test** *noun*
1 a test at school
Alternative words: exam, examination, assessment
2 a test in a laboratory
Alternative words: experiment, trial, analysis
3 a medical test
Alternative words: check, examination, investigation, assessment

**test** *verb*
1 to test a person
Alternative words: to examine, to assess, to evaluate
2 to test something
Alternative words: to analyse, to investigate, to try out, to evaluate

**thankful** *adjective*
Alternative words: grateful, appreciative, pleased

**theft** *noun*
Alternative words: stealing, robbery, pilfering, thieving

**thick** *adjective*
1 a thick piece of wood
Alternative words: broad, wide, fat
2 dense or closely packed together
Alternative words: dense, concentrated, condensed, solid

**thief** *noun*
Alternative words: robber, burglar, pick-pocket, shoplifter

**thin** *adjective*
1 a thin person
Alternative words: slim, slender, skinny, bony, scrawny
The opposite is **fat**
2 thin soup
Alternative words: weak, watery
The opposite is **thick**

**think** *verb*
1 to think something is true
Alternative words: to believe, to consider, to suppose
2 to form an idea in your mind
Alternative words: to have an idea,

to dream up, to imagine, to picture
**3** to think about something
*Alternative words:* to consider, to rack your brains, to ponder, to meditate

**thirsty** *adjective*
*Alternative words:* dry, parched, dying of thirst

**thought** *noun*
*Alternative words:* idea, belief, opinion

**threaten** *verb*
*Alternative words:* to bully, to menace, to intimidate

**throw** *verb*
**1** to throw a stone
*Alternative words:* to toss, to hurl, to fling
**2** to throw something away
*Alternative words:* to throw out, to discard, to reject, to bin (informal)

**thrust** *verb*
*Alternative words:* to shove, to ram, to force

**thump** *verb*
**1** to thump someone or something
*Alternative words:* to wallop, to whack, to punch
**2** when your heart thumps
*Alternative words:* to thud, to pound, to hammer

**tidy** *adjective*
*Alternative words:* neat, orderly
*The opposite is* **untidy**

**tight** *adjective*
**1** tight clothes
*Alternative words:* too small, close-fitting, figure-hugging, constricting
*The opposite is* **loose**
**2** firm and hard to move
*Alternative words:* firm, secure, fixed
*The opposite is* **loose**
**3** a tight rope
*Alternative words:* stretched, tense, taut
*The opposite is* **slack**

**tilt** *verb*
*Alternative words:* to slant, to slope, to lean

**timid** *adjective*
*Alternative words:* shy, nervous, afraid

**tingle** *verb*
*Alternative words:* to tickle, to prickle

**tinkle** *verb*
*Alternative words:* to chink, to clink, to jingle

**tire** *verb*
**1** to become tired
*Alternative words:* to weaken, to droop, to flag
**2** to make someone tired
*Alternative words:* to wear out, to take it out of someone, to exhaust

**tired** *adjective*
**1** to be tired after exercise
*Alternative words:* weary, worn out, exhausted
**2** to be tired of something
*Alternative words:* to be bored with, to be fed up with, to be sick of

**tiresome** *adjective*
*Alternative words:* irritating, annoying, trying, boring, dull, annoying

**tolerate** *verb*
**1** to tolerate pain
*Alternative words:* to stand, to bear, to put up with
**2** to tolerate things you don't agree with
*Alternative words:* to accept, to respect

**tool** *noun*
*Alternative words:* device, instrument, utensil

**top¹** *noun*
**1** the highest part of something
*Alternative words:* peak, summit, crest
*The opposite is* **bottom**
**2** the top of a container
*Alternative words:* lid, cover, cap

**top¹** *adjective*
*Alternative words:* highest, upper, uppermost
*The opposite is* **lowest**

**topsy-turvy** *adjective*
*Alternative words:* upside-down, mixed up, messy

**torrent** *noun*
*Alternative words:* gush, rush, cascade

**toss** *verb*
*Alternative words:* to throw, to fling, to chuck (informal)

**totter** *verb*
*Alternative words:* to walk unsteadily,

to stagger, to stumble

**touch** *verb*
1 to touch with your hand
*Alternative words:* to feel, to handle,
to finger, to brush, to caress
2 one thing touching another
*Alternative words:* to be in contact with,
to border, to adjoin

**tough** *adjective*
1 a tough thing or person
*Alternative words:* strong, sturdy,
rugged, robust
*The opposite is* **weak**
2 tough meat
*Alternative words:* chewy, stringy, gristly
*The opposite is* **tender**
3 something that is difficult
*Alternative words:* hard, difficult
*The opposite is* **easy**

**tow** *verb*
*Alternative words:* to pull along, to drag,
to haul

**trace** *noun*
1 a very small amount
*Alternative words:* bit, drop, hint
2 a mark that shows where something
has been
*Alternative words:* mark, indication

**trace** *verb*
1 to trace a missing person
*Alternative words:* to track down, to find,
to discover
2 to trace a shape
*Alternative words:* to draw round,
to outline, to copy

**track** *noun*
1 the track leading to the farm
*Alternative words:* path, pathway, green
lane, trail
2 The bear's track leads to its den.
*Alternative words:* trail, trace, prints,
footprints

**track** *verb*
*Alternative words:* to follow, to trail,
to stalk, to follow the trail of

**tragedy** *noun*
a sad event
*Alternative words:* catastrophe, disaster,
calamity, blow

**tragic** *adjective*
*Alternative words:* awful, terrible, very

sad, heartbreaking

**train** *verb*
1 to train people or animals
*Alternative words:* teach, instruct, coach
2 an athlete who trains
*Alternative words:* to work out,
to practise, to prepare

**trance** *noun*
*Alternative words:* daze, stupor

**transfer** *verb*
1 to transfer something from one place
to another
*Alternative words:* to move, to shift,
to transport
2 to transfer something to someone else
*Alternative words:* to give, to pass on,
to hand over

**transform** *verb*
*Alternative words:* to alter, to change,
to convert

**trap** *noun*
1 a trap for an animal
*Alternative words:* snare, net
2 a plan to trick or capture someone
*Alternative words:* trick, ruse, decoy

**travel** *verb*
1 to travel a long distance
*Alternative words:* to journey, to tour,
to voyage
2 to travel shorter distances
*Alternative words:* to go, to get to,
to commute

**traveller** *noun*
1 someone who visits places
*Alternative words:* tourist, tripper,
explorer, globetrotter
2 someone who always moves around
*Alternative words:* nomad, gypsy,
migrant, wanderer

**treasure** *noun*
1 a chest of treasure
*Alternative words:* gold, jewels, money,
riches
2 person or thing very precious
*Alternative words:* pride and joy, jewel in
the crown, darling

**treat** *verb*
1 to treat someone who is ill
*Alternative words:* to care for, to attend
to, to nurse
2 to treat someone well

*Alternative words:* to act towards,
to behave towards, to deal with
**3** to treat someone to a meal
*Alternative words:* to buy, to pay for,
to foot the bill

**tremble** *verb*
*Alternative words:* to quiver, to shake,
to quake

**tremendous** *adjective*
**1** a tremendous noise
*Alternative words:* enormous, great,
terrific
**2** a tremendous concert
*Alternative words:* excellent, wonderful,
marvellous, brilliant

**trench** *noun*
*Alternative words:* ditch, channel, moat

**trick** *verb*
*Alternative words:* to deceive, to mislead,
to have someone on, to cheat,
to swindle, to con (informal)

**trickle** *verb*
*Alternative words:* to dribble, to drip
*The opposite is* **to gush**

**tricky** *adjective*
*Alternative words:* fiddly, awkward,
difficult

**trim** *verb*
**1** to trim hair
*Alternative words:* to cut, to snip, to clip,
to even up, to tidy
**2** to trim a hat
*Alternative words:* to decorate, to adorn,
to ornament

**trip** *noun*
*Alternative words:* outing, excursion,
journey

**trivial** *adjective*
*Alternative words:* unimportant,
insignificant, meaningless
*The opposite is* **important**

**trouble** *noun*
*Alternative words:* bother, difficulty,
hassle, adversity

**trouble** *verb*
*Alternative words:* to worry, to bother,
to disturb

**truce** *noun*
*Alternative words:* ceasefire, letup,
suspension of hostilities

**true** *adjective*
*Alternative words:* real, correct, genuine

**trust** *verb*
*Alternative words:* to rely on, to bank on,
to count on, to depend on, to believe in

**trustworthy** *adjective*
*Alternative words:* dependable, reliable,
honest, responsible
*The opposite is* **untrustworthy**

**try** *verb*
**1** to try to do something
*Alternative words:* to attempt,
to endeavour, to have a go
**2** to try something new
*Alternative words:* to taste, to test,
to sample

**tug** *verb*
*Alternative words:* to pull, to yank,
to wrench, to jerk

**turn** *verb*
**1** to turn something round in a circle
*Alternative words:* to swivel, to twist,
to rotate
**2** to change direction
*Alternative words:* to change direction,
to change course, to go around
**3** to turn into something else
*Alternative words:* to become, to go,
to change

**twinkle** *verb*
*Alternative words:* to shine, to sparkle,
to glint

**twirl** *verb*
*Alternative words:* to turn round and
round, to spin, to revolve

**twist** *verb*
**1** to turn round
*Alternative words:* to turn, to bend,
to swivel
**2** to twist one thing round another
*Alternative words:* to wind, to curl

**type** *noun*
*Alternative words:* kind, sort, variety

**typhoon** *noun*
*Alternative words:* hurricane, violent
tropical storm, tempest

**typical** *adjective*
*Alternative words:* normal, usual,
average

*Alternative words:* moody, unbalanced, unpredictable, temperamental
*The opposite is* **stable**
3 The situation is unstable.
*Alternative words:* unsettled, volatile
*The opposite is* **stable**

**unsuitable** *adjective*
*Alternative words:* inappropriate, unacceptable, unseemly
*The opposite is* **suitable**

**unsure** *adjective*
*Alternative words:* doubtful, hesitant, unconvinced, uncertain
*The opposite is* **sure**

**unsympathetic** *adjective*
*Alternative words:* insensitive, unkind, uncaring
*The opposite is* **sympathetic**

**untidy** *adjective*
1 an untidy house
*Alternative words:* messy, chaotic, cluttered, higgledy-piggledy (informal)
*The opposite is* **tidy**
2 untidy work
*Alternative words:* messy, sloppy, careless, disorganised
*The opposite is* **neat**
3 She always looks untidy.
*Alternative words:* dishevelled, unkempt, bedraggled
*The opposite is* **neat**

**untie** *verb*
*Alternative words:* to undo, to loosen, to unfasten
*The opposite is* **to tie**

**unusual** *adjective*
*Alternative words:* rare, uncommon, out of the ordinary
*The opposite is* **commonplace**

**unwieldy** *adjective*
*Alternative words:* bulky, awkward, cumbersome, unmanageable

**unwilling** *adjective*
*Alternative words:* reluctant, unenthusiastic
*The opposite is* **willing**

**unwind** *verb*
1 to unwind the hose
*Alternative words:* to unroll, to uncoil, to unravel, to undo

2 to unwind after work
*Alternative words:* to relax, to wind down, to calm down

**upright** *adjective*
1 standing upright
*Alternative words:* straight, vertical, erect
2 an upright person
*Alternative words:* honest, virtuous, respectable, decent

**uproar** *noun*
*Alternative words:* confusion, commotion, pandemonium

**upset** *verb*
1 The news upset me.
*Alternative words:* to alarm, to bother, to worry
2 I upset the jar.
*Alternative words:* to knock over, to spill, to tip over

**use** *verb*
1 to use a ladder
*Alternative words:* to make use of, to utilise, to avail yourself of
2 to use a machine
*Alternative words:* to operate, to work
3 to use your skill
*Alternative words:* to exercise, to apply, to put to use
4 to use something up
*Alternative words:* to finish, to get through, to consume

**usual** *adjective*
*Alternative words:* normal, customary, expected, habitual
*The opposite is* **unusual**

**usually** *adverb*
*Alternative words:* normally, generally, on the whole

# Vv

**vacant** *adjective*
*Alternative words:* empty, unoccupied, free
*The opposite is* **occupied**

**vague** *adjective*
**1** a vague idea of what to do
*Alternative words:* rough, dim, hazy
**2** a vague shape in the distance
*Alternative words:* indistinct, unclear, shadowy

**value** *noun*
**1** the value of the jewels
*Alternative words:* worth, cost, price
**2** His friendship is of great value to me.
*Alternative words:* importance, benefit, usefulness, merit
**3** someone's values
*Alternative words:* principles, morals, standards

**variety** *noun*
**1** We stock a variety of products.
*Alternative words:* range, selection, array, assortment
**2** a new variety of tomato
*Alternative words:* kind, strain, breed

**various** *adjective*
*Alternative words:* varying, different, assorted, several

**vast** *adjective*
*Alternative words:* immense, wide, extensive

**vertical** *adjective*
*Alternative words:* upright, perpendicular, on end
*The opposite is* **horizontal**

**vibrant** *adjective*
**1** decorated with vibrant colours
*Alternative words:* bright, vivid, bold
*The opposite is* **dull**
**2** He has a vibrant personality.
*Alternative words:* lively, dynamic, sparkling
*The opposite is* **dull**

**vibrate** *verb*
*Alternative words:* to pulsate, to resonate, to tremble, to throb

**view** *noun*
**1** a beautiful view from the window
*Alternative words:* vista, panorama, scene

**2** What was your view of the matter?
*Alternative words:* opinion, feeling, point of view

**vigorous** *adjective*
*Alternative words:* energetic, strong, healthy

**vile** *adjective*
*Alternative words:* nasty, foul, disgusting

**villain** *noun*
*Alternative words:* criminal, rogue

**violence** *noun*
*Alternative words:* brute force, roughness, savagery

**violent** *adjective*
**1** violent criminals
*Alternative words:* brutal, vicious, savage
*The opposite is* **gentle**
**2** violent weather
*Alternative words:* raging, wild, blustery
*The opposite is* **calm**

**visible** *adjective*
*Alternative words:* perceptible, noticeable, evident

**visit** *verb*
**1** visiting Germany
*Alternative words:* to tour, to go to see, to stay in, to travel round
**2** visiting his sister
*Alternative words:* to call in on, to pay a visit to, to go to see, to drop in on (informal)

**visit** *noun*
*Alternative words:* stay, call, stop

**vital** *adjective*
*Alternative words:* essential, indispensable, necessary
*The opposite is* **unimportant**

**vivid** *adjective*
**1** a vivid red
*Alternative words:* rich, strong, bright, intense
*The opposite is* **pale**
**2** a vivid memory
*Alternative words:* clear, strong, sharp
*The opposite is* **faint**
**3** a vivid account
*Alternative words:* dramatic, powerful, graphic

**vulnerable** *adjective*
*Alternative words:* defenceless, open to attack, unprotected
*The opposite is* **secure**

# Ww

**waddle** *verb*
*Alternative words:* to shuffle, to totter, to toddle

**wage** *noun*
*Alternative words:* salary, fee, pay, remuneration

**wail** *verb*
*Alternative words:* to cry, to sob, to moan

**wait** *verb*
**1** to wait somewhere
*Alternative words:* to stay, to linger, to rest
**2** to wait until something happens
*Alternative words:* to be patient, to bide your time, to sit tight (informal)

**wake** *verb*
*Alternative words:* to wake up, to stir, to awaken

**walk** *noun*
**1** a gentle walk
*Alternative words:* ramble, stroll, saunter
**2** a long walk
*Alternative words:* hike, trek, march
**3** a way of walking
*Alternative words:* gait, stride, carriage

**wan** *adjective*
*Alternative words:* pale, ashen, white

**wander** *verb*
*Alternative words:* to roam, to ramble, to rove, to stray

**wane** *verb*
**1** the moon waning
*Alternative words:* to get smaller, to decrease
*The opposite is* **to wax**
**2** your strength waning
*Alternative words:* to dwindle, to decrease, to ebb
*The opposite is* **to increase**

**want** *verb*
*Alternative words:* to desire, to need, to wish for, to long for

**warm** *adjective*
**1** warm food
*Alternative words:* heated, lukewarm, moderately hot
**2** a warm welcome
*Alternative words:* friendly, cordial, hospitable
*The opposite is* **cool**
**3** warm clothes
*Alternative words:* thick, woolly, snug
*The opposite is* **thin**

**warn** *verb*
**1** I warned the children about the river.
*Alternative words:* to make aware, to give a warning to, to alert
**2** I warn you not to go there.
*Alternative words:* to advise, to urge
**3** I warned her that the shop was closing.
*Alternative words:* to tell, to inform, to notify

**warning** *noun*
**1** Read the warning.
*Alternative words:* notice, information, sign
**2** She ignored my warning.
*Alternative words:* advice, threat, tip-off

**warp** *verb*
*Alternative words:* to bend, to become twisted, to become distorted

**wary** *adjective*
*Alternative words:* cautious, careful, on your guard

**wash** *verb*
**1** to wash your hands
*Alternative words:* to clean, to scrub, to rinse
**2** to wash your hair
*Alternative words:* to shampoo
**3** to wash clothes
*Alternative words:* to launder, to clean
**4** The sea washes away the sand.
*Alternative words:* to carry away, to sweep away

**waste** *noun*
**1** a waste of time
*Alternative words:* misuse, squandering, loss
**2** doesn't like waste
*Alternative words:* extravagance, wastefulness
**3** throw away the waste
*Alternative words:* rubbish, refuse, garbage

**waste** *verb*
*Alternative words:* to squander, to misuse, to fritter away

**watch** *verb*
**1** to watch what is happening
*Alternative words:* to look at, to observe, to see, to keep an eye on
**2** to watch closely
*Alternative words:* to inspect, to scrutinise, to examine
**3** Watch the traffic!
*Alternative words:* to look out for, to pay attention to, to be aware of
**4** to watch television
*Alternative words:* to look at, to view

**waterfall** *noun*
*Alternative words:* cascade, falls

**wave** *noun*
**1** paddling in the waves
*Alternative words:* breaker, ripple, roller
**2** a wave in your hair
*Alternative words:* kink, curl
**3** sound waves
*Alternative words:* oscillation, vibration
**4** gave me a wave
*Alternative words:* gesture, hand signal, gesticulation

**wave** *verb*
**1** I saw him wave.
*Alternative words:* to gesticulate, to beckon, to signal
**2** She waved her sword.
*Alternative words:* to flourish, to brandish, to wield
**3** The flags were waving.
*Alternative words:* to flap, to flutter, to move to and fro

**way** *noun*
**1** the way home
*Alternative words:* route, road, direction
**2** a way of doing something
*Alternative words:* method, technique, system

**weak** *adjective*
**1** a weak king
*Alternative words:* powerless, spineless, ineffectual, soft
*The opposite is* **powerful**
**2** a weak drink
*Alternative words:* watery, diluted, thin, tasteless

*The opposite is* **strong**
**3** feeling weak
*Alternative words:* frail, fragile, feeble
*The opposite is* **strong**
**4** a weak bridge
*Alternative words:* flimsy, rickety, tumbledown
*The opposite is* **solid**

**weaken** *verb*
**1** tried to weaken her power
*Alternative words:* to reduce, to undermine, to sap
**2** The wind began to weaken.
*Alternative words:* to let up, to diminish, to abate

**wealthy** *adjective*
*Alternative words:* rich, prosperous, well off
*The opposite is* **poor**

**wear** *verb*
**1** wear a jumper
*Alternative words:* to be dressed in, to be clothed in, to have on
**2** wear a hat
*Alternative words:* to have on, to put on, to sport
**3** a carpet wearing out
*Alternative words:* to wear thin, to become worn, to fray, to become threadbare
**4** It wore him out.
*Alternative words:* to exhaust, to tire, to make weary
**5** wear away the cliffs
*Alternative words:* to rub away, to wash away, to erode
**6** a feeling wearing off
*Alternative words:* to fade, to subside

**weary** *adjective*
*Alternative words:* tired, exhausted, worn out

**wedge** *verb*
*Alternative words:* to jam, to squeeze, to force

**weep** *verb*
*Alternative words:* to cry, to shed tears, to sob

**weird** *adjective*
*Alternative words:* mysterious, strange, eerie, mystifying

**well²** *adjective*
*Alternative words:* healthy, fit, strong

**wet** *adjective*
**1** wet grass
*Alternative words:* damp, waterlogged, soaked
**2** a wet towel
*Alternative words:* saturated, sopping, wringing wet
**3** wet weather
*Alternative words:* rainy, damp, drizzling
*The opposite is* **dry**

**whine** *verb*
**1** The baby began to whine.
*Alternative words:* to whimper, to wail, to cry
**2** She's always whining.
*Alternative words:* to moan, to complain, to whinge

**whinge** *verb*
*Alternative words:* to complain, to grumble, to moan

**whip** *verb*
**1** to whip an animal
*Alternative words:* to beat, to thrash, to flog
**2** to whip cream
*Alternative words:* to beat, to whisk

**whisper** *verb*
*Alternative words:* to murmur, to mutter, to mumble

**whole** *adjective*
*Alternative words:* complete, entire, unbroken

**wicked** *adjective*
*Alternative words:* cruel, villainous, evil
*The opposite is* **good**

**wide** *adjective*
**1** a wide garden
*Alternative words:* broad, spacious, large
**2** a wide range of things
*Alternative words:* extensive, large, comprehensive
*The opposite is* **narrow**

**wield** *verb*
*Alternative words:* to brandish, to wave, to flourish

**wild** *adjective*
**1** wild flowers
*Alternative words:* natural, uncultivated, native
**2** wild animals
*Alternative words:* untamed, undomesticated, ferocious, fierce
*The opposite is* **tame**
**3** wild children
*Alternative words:* unruly, out of control, excited

**win** *verb*
**1** to win a game
*Alternative words:* to come first, to carry the day
**2** to win a fight
*Alternative words:* to overcome, to conquer, to triumph
**3** to win a prize
*Alternative words:* to receive, to net, to bag

**wind¹** *noun*
*Alternative words:* breeze, draught, current of air, gust

**winner** *noun*
*Alternative words:* champion, victor, conqueror

**wisdom** *noun*
*Alternative words:* knowledge, sense, intelligence, insight, understanding

**wise** *adjective*
*Alternative words:* learned, clever, knowledgeable, erudite

**wish** *noun*
**1** his greatest wish
*Alternative words:* desire, request, fancy
**2** birthday wishes
*Alternative words:* greeting, salutation

**wish** *verb*
**1** to wish for something
*Alternative words:* to hope, to set your heart on, to long, to yearn
**2** I wish you good day.
*Alternative words:* to bid, to hope someone has

**withdraw** *verb*
**1** to withdraw money from the bank

*Alternative words:* to take out, to remove, to take back
**2** to withdraw from a competition
*Alternative words:* to drop out, to pull out, to retire

**wither** *verb*
*Alternative words:* to dry up, to shrivel, to die

**without** *preposition*
**1** without something or someone
*Alternative words:* not including, excluding, in the absence of
**2** without something you need
*Alternative words:* in need of, lacking, short of, wanting

**witty** *adjective*
*Alternative words:* amusing, humorous, clever

**wobble** *verb*
**1** a chair wobbling
*Alternative words:* to teeter, to move, to rock, to sway
**2** a person wobbling
*Alternative words:* to totter, to stagger

**woe** *noun*
*Alternative words:* grief, misery, sadness

**wonder** *noun*
*Alternative words:* amazement, awe, astonishment

**wonderful** *adjective*
*Alternative words:* outstanding, marvellous, fantastic, amazing

**work** *verb*
**1** Where do you work?
*Alternative words:* to be employed, to have a job, to earn your living
**2** The plan didn't work.
*Alternative words:* to succeed, to be successful, to work out
**3** It works by electricity.
*Alternative words:* to go, to function, to operate
**4** I'm working something out.
*Alternative words:* to figure out, to solve, to calculate
**5** He works hard.
*Alternative words:* to toil, to labour

**worn** *adjective*
**1** a worn old carpet
*Alternative words:* threadbare, tattered, shabby, frayed
**2** feel worn out
*Alternative words:* tired out, exhausted, drained

**worried** *adjective*
*Alternative words:* anxious, troubled, apprehensive

**worry** *verb*
**1** sitting and worrying
*Alternative words:* to fret, to brood, to be anxious
**2** It worries me.
*Alternative words:* to bother, to upset, to distress

**worthwhile** *adjective*
*Alternative words:* useful, valuable, beneficial

**wreck** *verb*
*Alternative words:* to destroy, to ruin, to demolish

**wrench** *verb*
*Alternative words:* to twist, to pull, to yank

**wriggle** *verb*
*Alternative words:* to squirm, to writhe, to twist

**wrong** *adjective*
**1** Your answer was wrong.
*Alternative words:* incorrect, inaccurate, wide of the mark
*The opposite is* **correct**
**2** It's wrong to treat animals badly.
*Alternative words:* bad, wicked, unfair, illegal
*The opposite is* **right**
**3** the wrong clothes to wear at a funeral
*Alternative words:* unsuitable, unacceptable, inappropriate
*The opposite is* **right**

# Yy

**yank** *verb*
   *Alternative words:* to jerk, to tug, to pull

**yarn** *noun*
   **1** knit with yarn
   *Alternative words:* thread, fibre
   **2** tell a yarn
   *Alternative words:* tale, story, narrative

**yearn** *verb*
   *Alternative words:* to long, to pine,
   to crave

**yell** *verb*
   *Alternative words:* to shout, to cry out,
   to bellow

**yelp** *verb*
   *Alternative words:* to whoop, to shout

**young** *adjective*
   *Alternative words:* childlike, adolescent,
   immature
   *The opposite is* **old**

**youth** *noun*
   **1** in my youth
   *Alternative words:* childhood, young
   days, boyhood, girlhood
   **2** a group of youths
   *Alternative words:* teenager, adolescent,
   youngster

# Zz

**zest** *noun*
   **1** the zest of a lemon
   *Alternative words:* skin, rind, peel
   **2** zest for life
   *Alternative words:* enthusiasm, zeal,
   eagerness

**zone** *noun*
   *Alternative words:* area, sector, section,
   belt

**zoom** *verb*
   *Alternative words:* to fly, to dash,
   to shoot, to whiz (informal)